OPEN BORDERS

THE SCIENCE AND ETHICS OF IMMIGRATION

WRITTEN BY
BRYAN CAPLAN

ARTWORK BY
ZACH WEINERSMITH

COLOR BY
MARY CAGLE

:01
First Second
NEW YORK

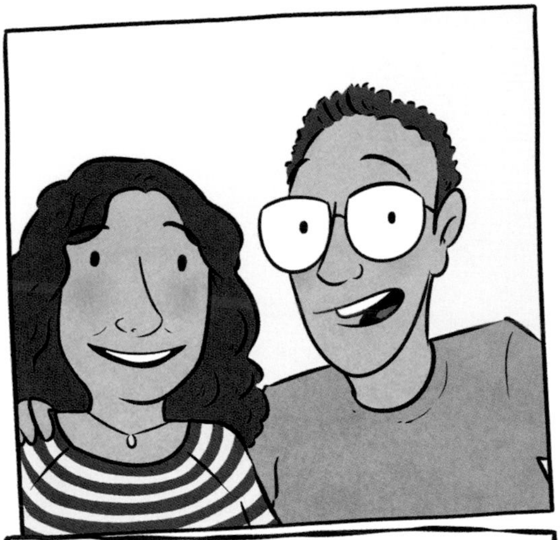

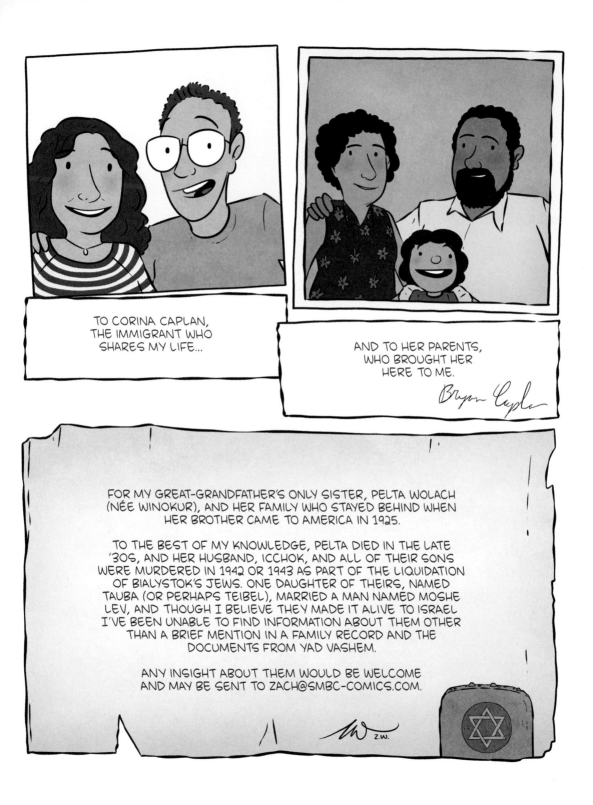

TO CORINA CAPLAN,
THE IMMIGRANT WHO
SHARES MY LIFE...

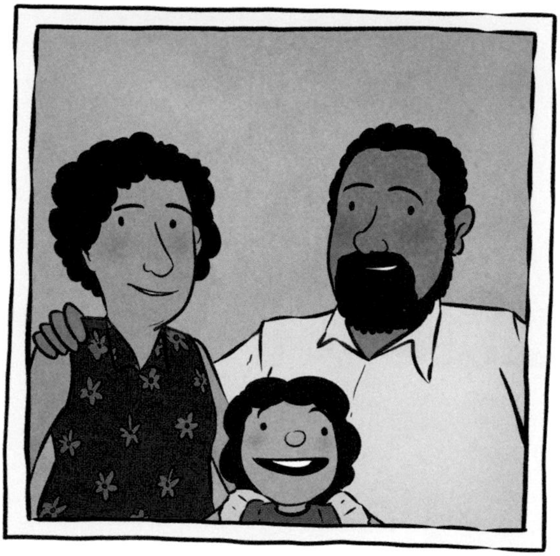

AND TO HER PARENTS,
WHO BROUGHT HER
HERE TO ME.

Bryan Caplan

FOR MY GREAT-GRANDFATHER'S ONLY SISTER, PELTA WOLACH (NÉE WINOKUR), AND HER FAMILY WHO STAYED BEHIND WHEN HER BROTHER CAME TO AMERICA IN 1925.

TO THE BEST OF MY KNOWLEDGE, PELTA DIED IN THE LATE '30S, AND HER HUSBAND, ICCHOK, AND ALL OF THEIR SONS WERE MURDERED IN 1942 OR 1943 AS PART OF THE LIQUIDATION OF BIALYSTOK'S JEWS. ONE DAUGHTER OF THEIRS, NAMED TAUBA (OR PERHAPS TEIBEL), MARRIED A MAN NAMED MOSHE LEV, AND THOUGH I BELIEVE THEY MADE IT ALIVE TO ISRAEL I'VE BEEN UNABLE TO FIND INFORMATION ABOUT THEM OTHER THAN A BRIEF MENTION IN A FAMILY RECORD AND THE DOCUMENTS FROM YAD VASHEM.

ANY INSIGHT ABOUT THEM WOULD BE WELCOME AND MAY BE SENT TO ZACH@SMBC-COMICS.COM.

Z.W.

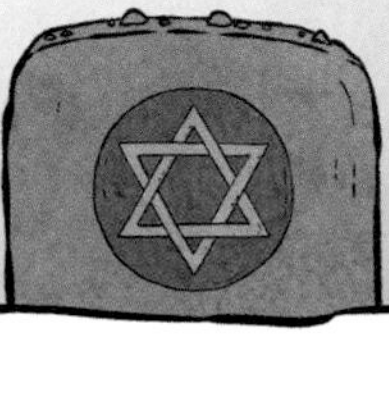

CONTENTS

CHAPTER 1

GLOBAL APARTHEID

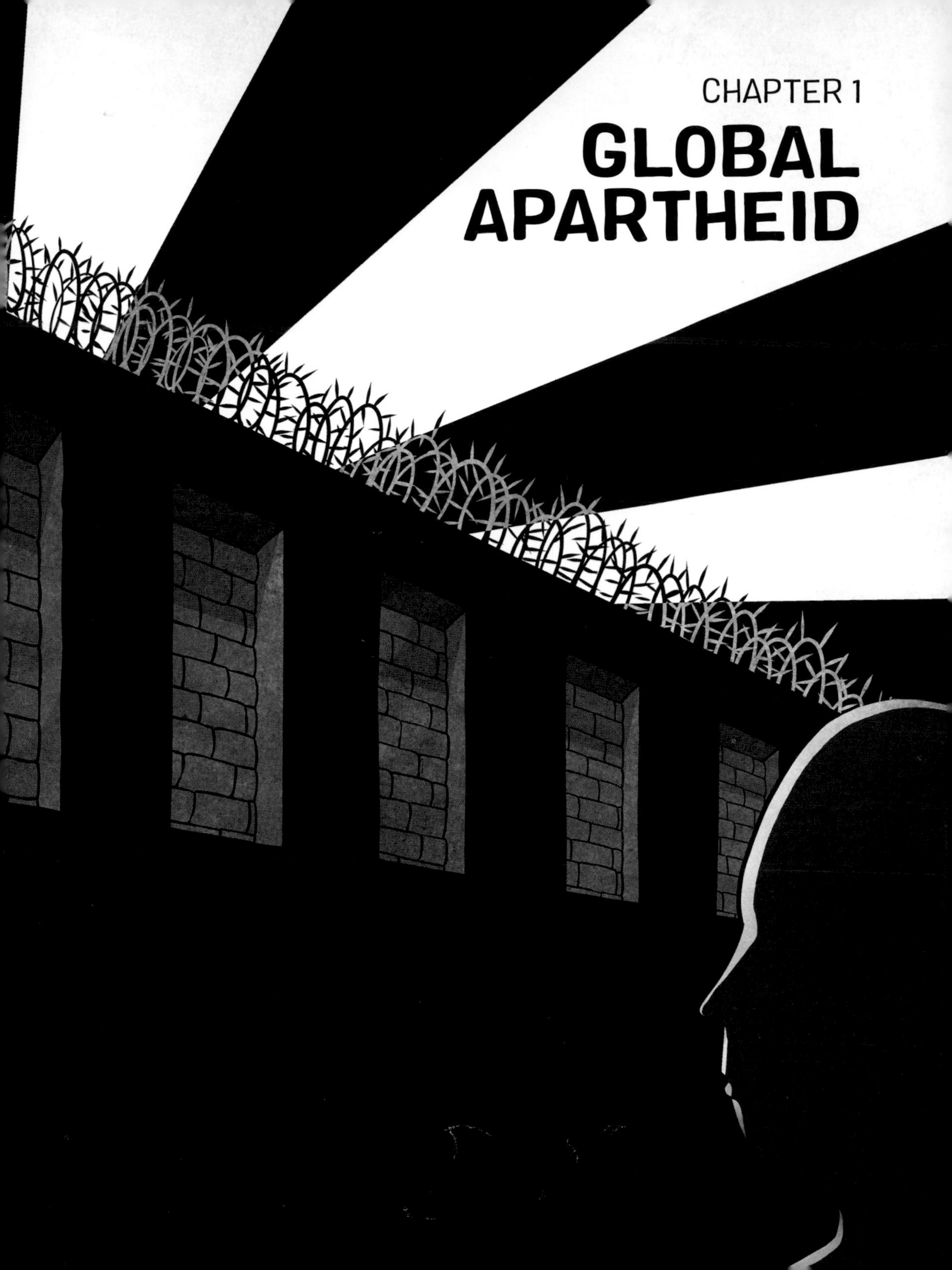

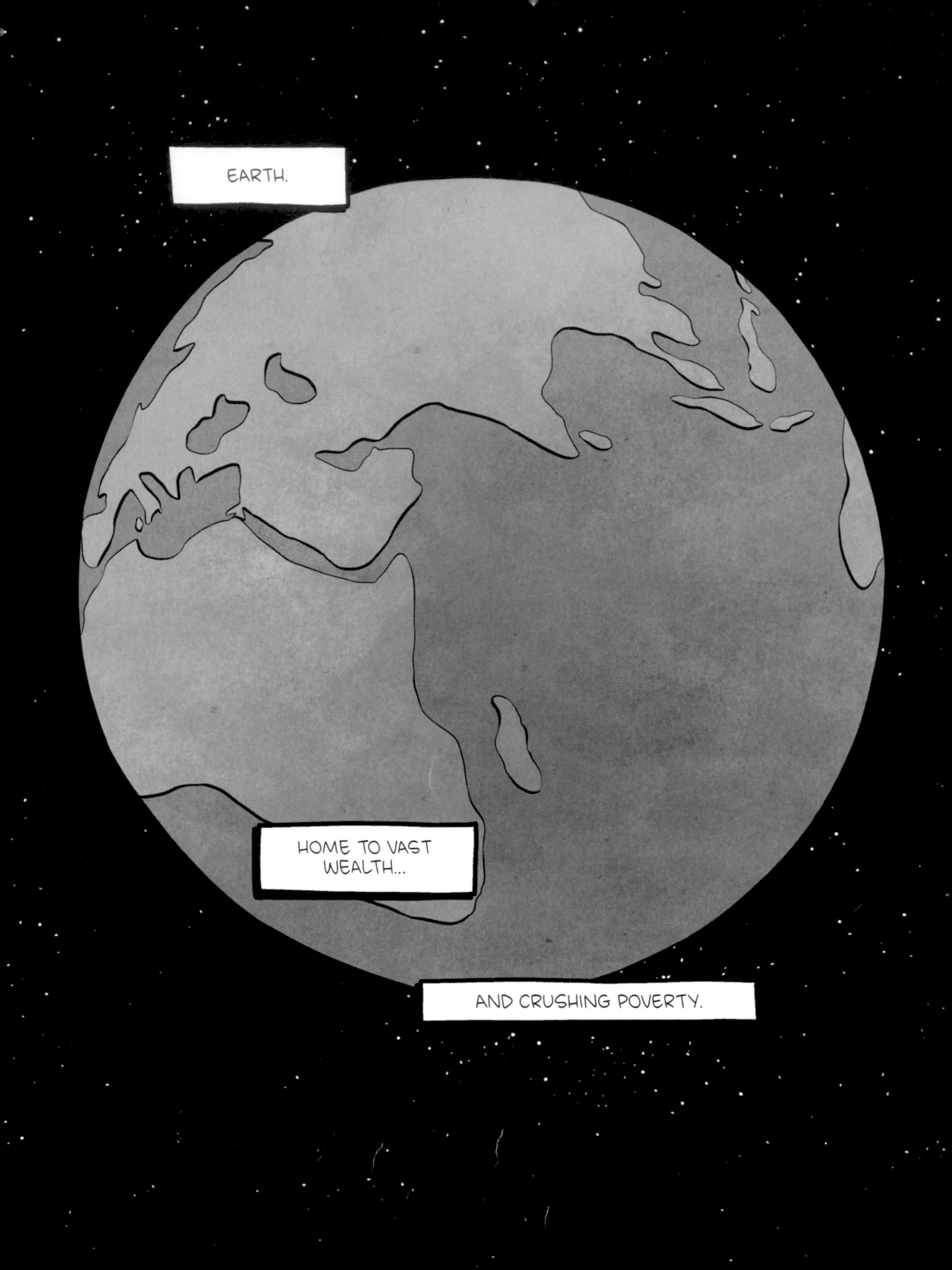
EARTH.
HOME TO VAST WEALTH...
AND CRUSHING POVERTY.

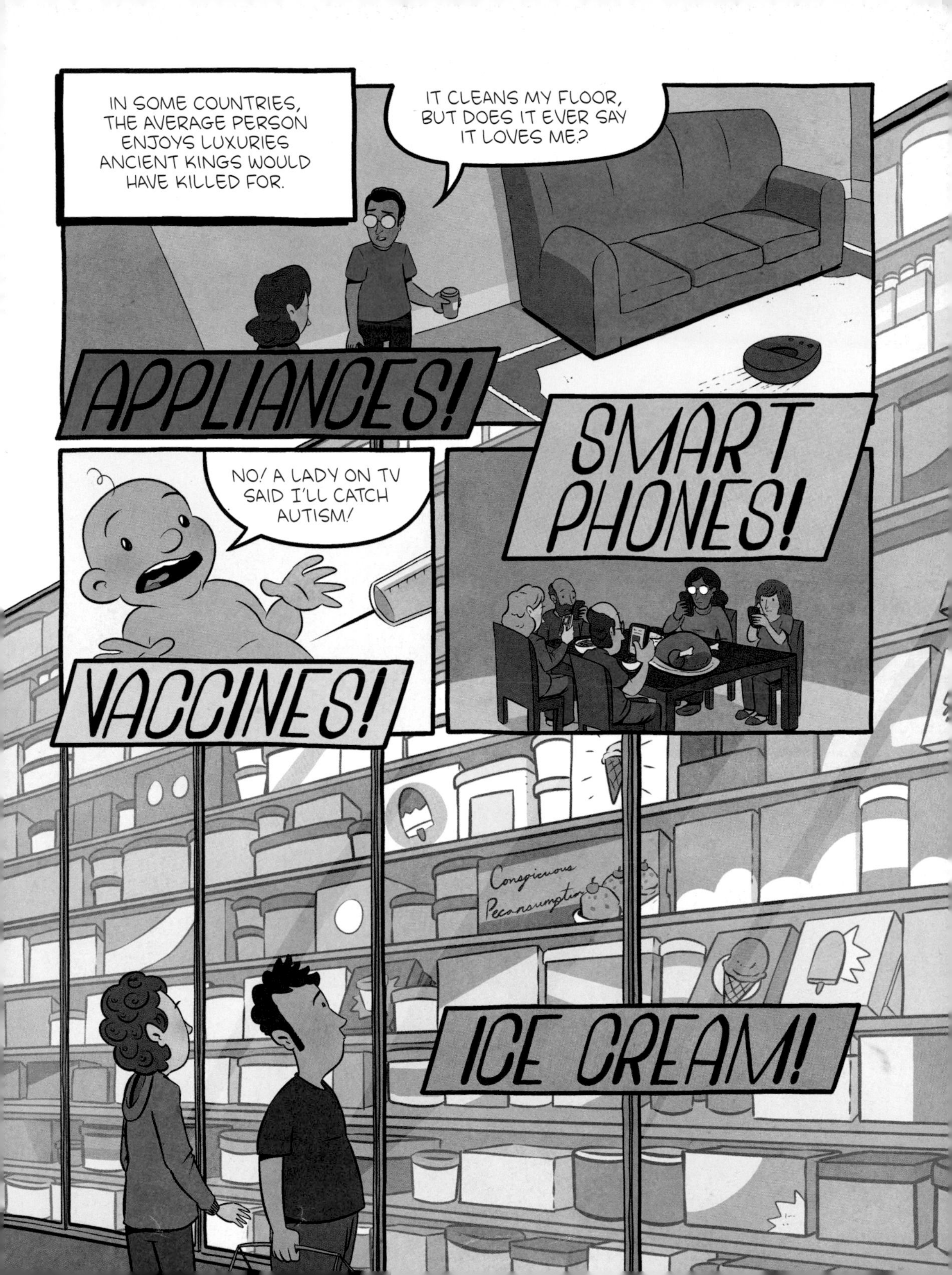
IN SOME COUNTRIES, THE AVERAGE PERSON ENJOYS LUXURIES ANCIENT KINGS WOULD HAVE KILLED FOR.
IT CLEANS MY FLOOR, BUT DOES IT EVER SAY IT LOVES ME?
APPLIANCES!
SMART PHONES!
NO! A LADY ON TV SAID I'LL CATCH AUTISM!
VACCINES!
Conspicuous Pecansumption
ICE CREAM!

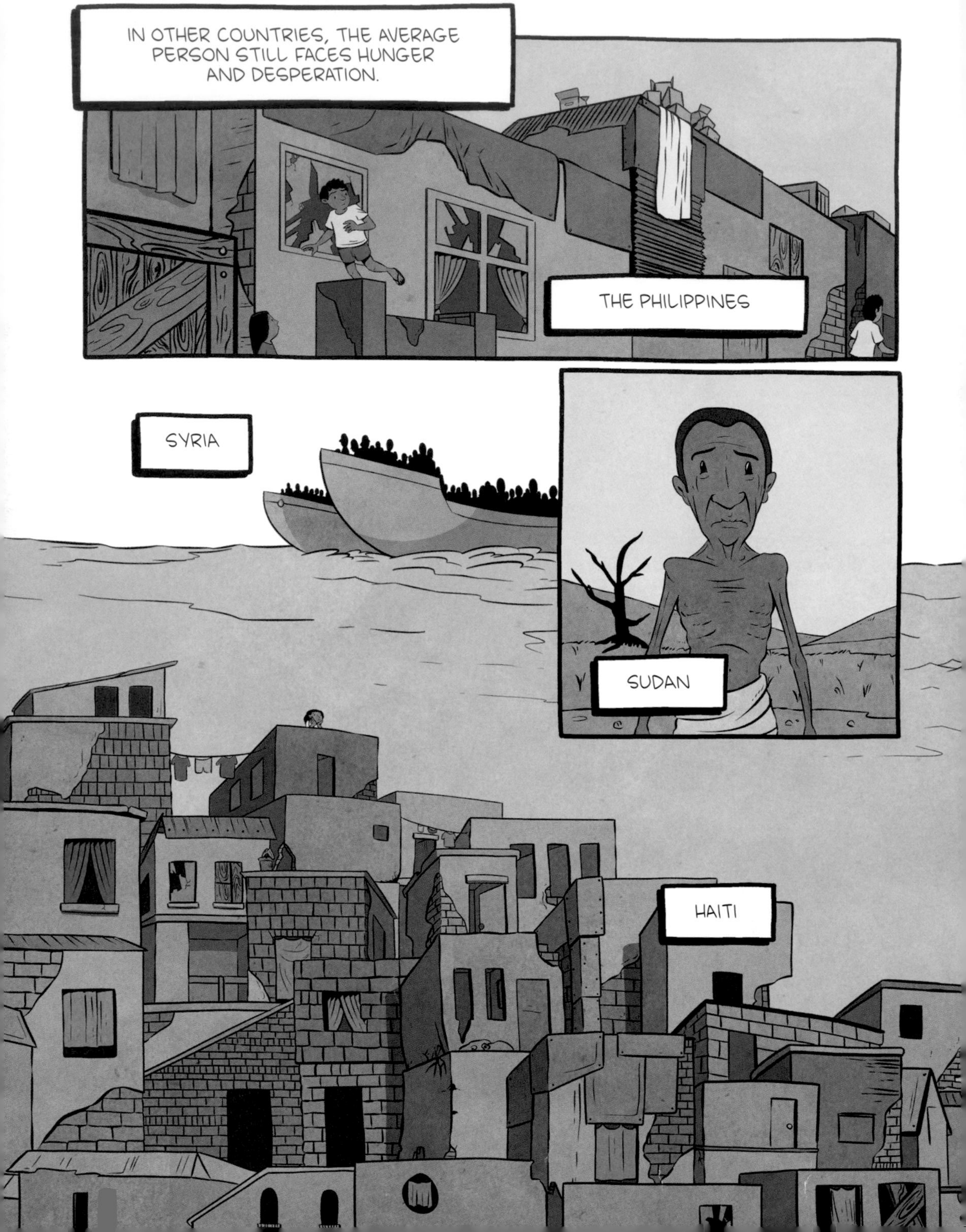
IN OTHER COUNTRIES, THE AVERAGE PERSON STILL FACES HUNGER AND DESPERATION.
THE PHILIPPINES
SYRIA
SUDAN
HAITI

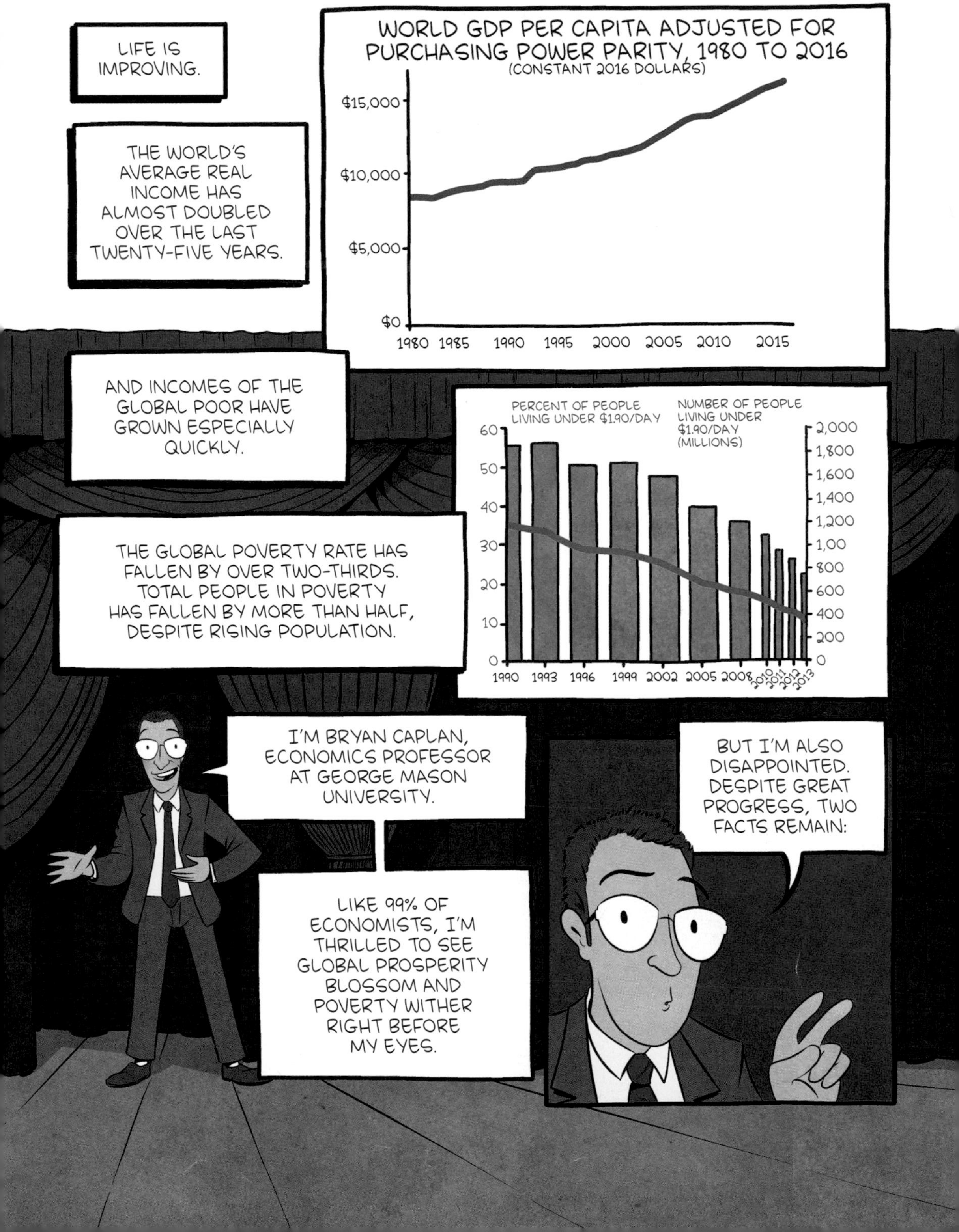
LIFE IS IMPROVING.
WORLD GDP PER CAPITA ADJUSTED FOR PURCHASING POWER PARITY, 1980 TO 2016
(CONSTANT 2016 DOLLARS)
$15,000
$10,000
$5,000
$0
1980 1985 1990 1995 2000 2005 2010 2015
THE WORLD'S AVERAGE REAL INCOME HAS ALMOST DOUBLED OVER THE LAST TWENTY-FIVE YEARS.
AND INCOMES OF THE GLOBAL POOR HAVE GROWN ESPECIALLY QUICKLY.
PERCENT OF PEOPLE LIVING UNDER $1.90/DAY
NUMBER OF PEOPLE LIVING UNDER $1.90/DAY (MILLIONS)
60 50 40 30 20 10 0
2,000 1,800 1,600 1,400 1,200 1,00 800 600 400 200 0
1990 1993 1996 1999 2002 2005 2008 2010 2011 2012 2013
THE GLOBAL POVERTY RATE HAS FALLEN BY OVER TWO-THIRDS. TOTAL PEOPLE IN POVERTY HAS FALLEN BY MORE THAN HALF, DESPITE RISING POPULATION.
I'M BRYAN CAPLAN, ECONOMICS PROFESSOR AT GEORGE MASON UNIVERSITY.
LIKE 99% OF ECONOMISTS, I'M THRILLED TO SEE GLOBAL PROSPERITY BLOSSOM AND POVERTY WITHER RIGHT BEFORE MY EYES.
BUT I'M ALSO DISAPPOINTED. DESPITE GREAT PROGRESS, TWO FACTS REMAIN:

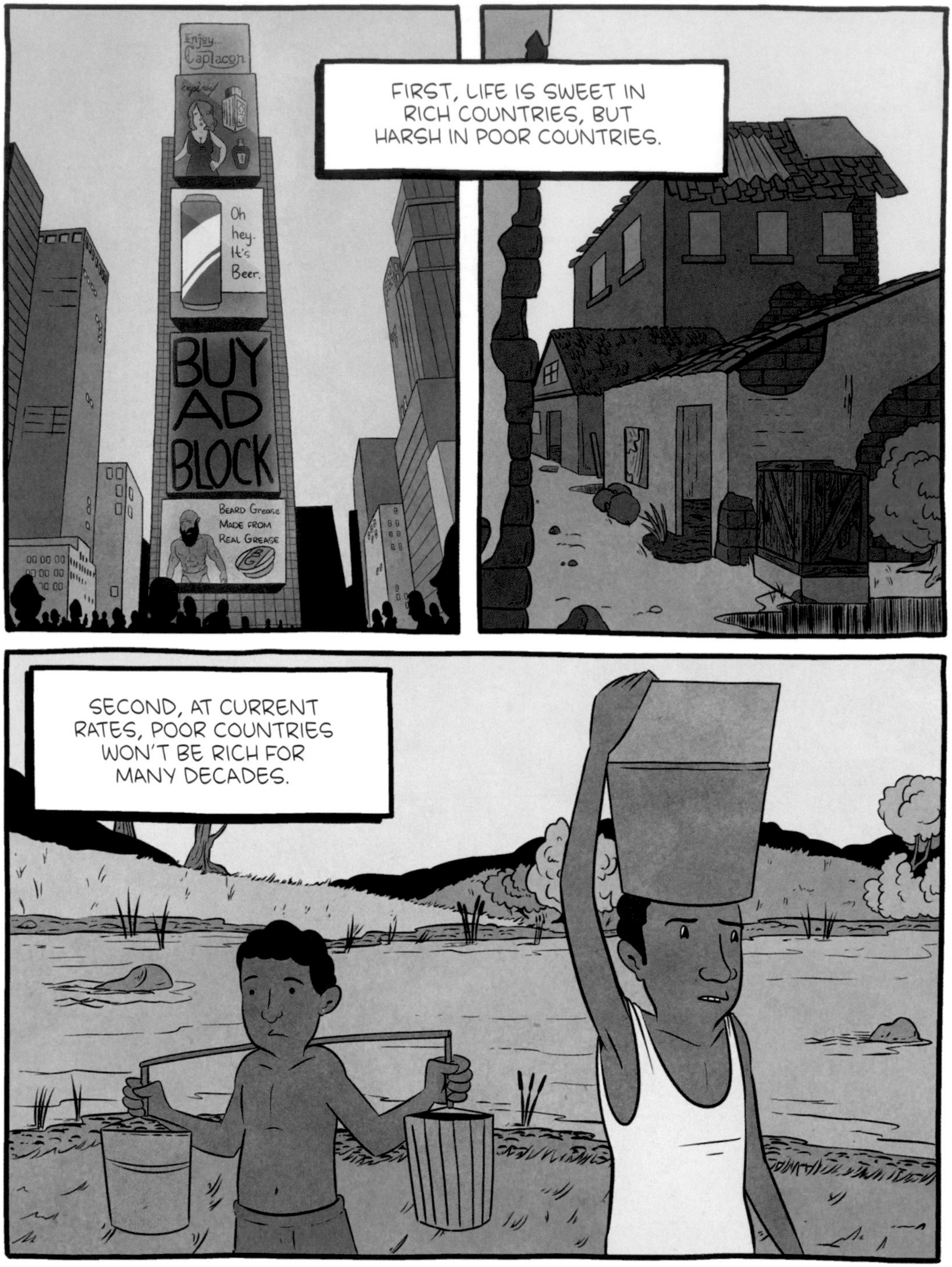
Enjoy... Caplacon
Oh hey. It's Beer.
BUY AD BLOCK
Beard Grease Made from Real Grease
FIRST, LIFE IS SWEET IN RICH COUNTRIES, BUT HARSH IN POOR COUNTRIES.
SECOND, AT CURRENT RATES, POOR COUNTRIES WON'T BE RICH FOR MANY DECADES.

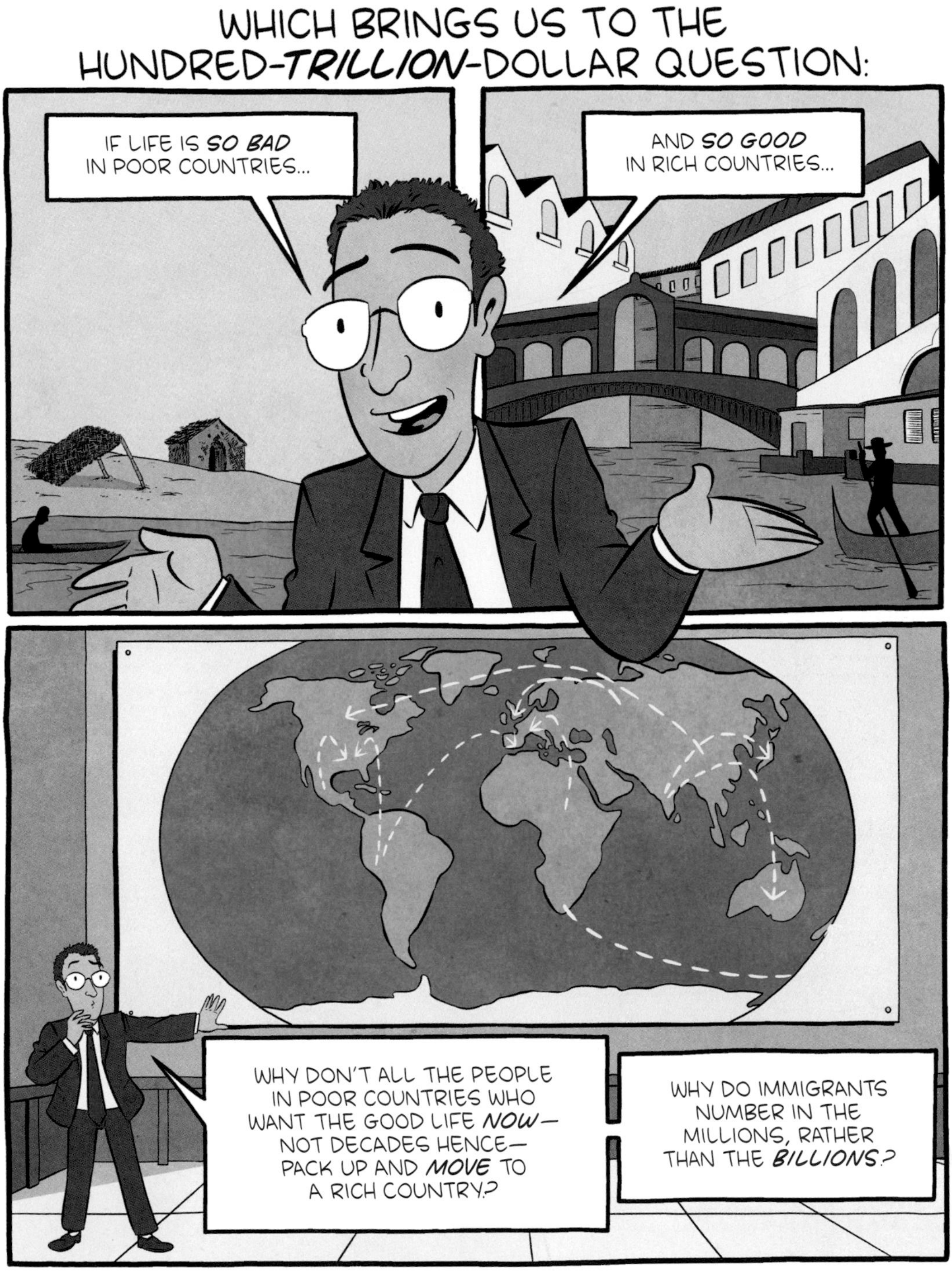
WHICH BRINGS US TO THE HUNDRED-*TRILLION*-DOLLAR QUESTION:
IF LIFE IS ***SO BAD*** IN POOR COUNTRIES...
AND ***SO GOOD*** IN RICH COUNTRIES...
WHY DON'T ALL THE PEOPLE IN POOR COUNTRIES WHO WANT THE GOOD LIFE *NOW*—NOT DECADES HENCE—PACK UP AND *MOVE* TO A RICH COUNTRY?
WHY DO IMMIGRANTS NUMBER IN THE MILLIONS, RATHER THAN THE ***BILLIONS***?

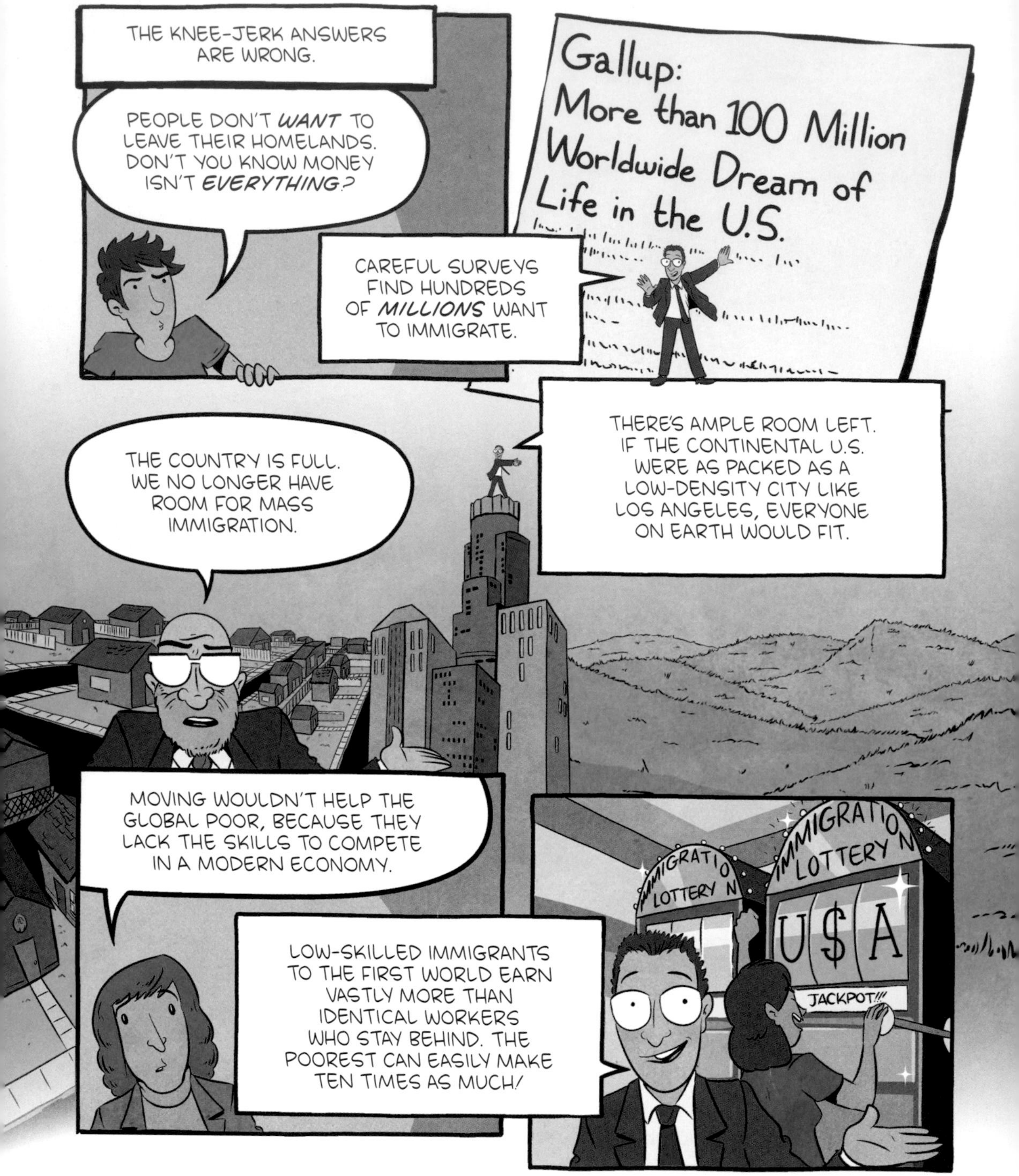
THE KNEE-JERK ANSWERS ARE WRONG.
PEOPLE DON'T *WANT* TO LEAVE THEIR HOMELANDS. DON'T YOU KNOW MONEY ISN'T *EVERYTHING*?
Gallup: More than 100 Million Worldwide Dream of Life in the U.S.
CAREFUL SURVEYS FIND HUNDREDS OF *MILLIONS* WANT TO IMMIGRATE.
THE COUNTRY IS FULL. WE NO LONGER HAVE ROOM FOR MASS IMMIGRATION.
THERE'S AMPLE ROOM LEFT. IF THE CONTINENTAL U.S. WERE AS PACKED AS A LOW-DENSITY CITY LIKE LOS ANGELES, EVERYONE ON EARTH WOULD FIT.
MOVING WOULDN'T HELP THE GLOBAL POOR, BECAUSE THEY LACK THE SKILLS TO COMPETE IN A MODERN ECONOMY.
LOW-SKILLED IMMIGRANTS TO THE FIRST WORLD EARN VASTLY MORE THAN IDENTICAL WORKERS WHO STAY BEHIND. THE POOREST CAN EASILY MAKE TEN TIMES AS MUCH!
IMMIGRATION LOTTERY
IMMIGRATION LOTTERY
U$A
JACKPOT!!!

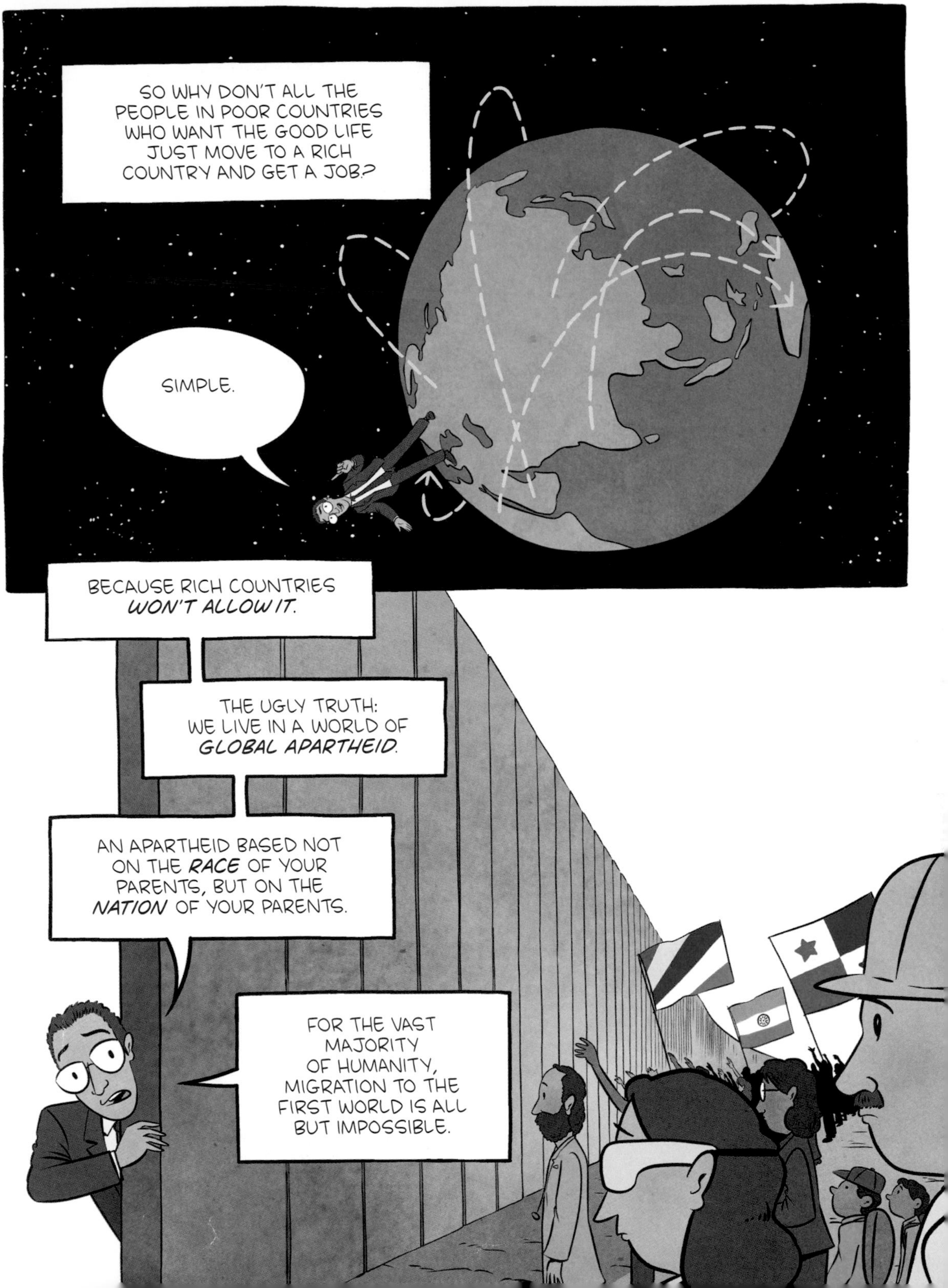
SO WHY DON'T ALL THE PEOPLE IN POOR COUNTRIES WHO WANT THE GOOD LIFE JUST MOVE TO A RICH COUNTRY AND GET A JOB?
SIMPLE.
BECAUSE RICH COUNTRIES *WON'T ALLOW IT.*
THE UGLY TRUTH: WE LIVE IN A WORLD OF *GLOBAL APARTHEID.*
AN APARTHEID BASED NOT ON THE *RACE* OF YOUR PARENTS, BUT ON THE *NATION* OF YOUR PARENTS.
FOR THE VAST MAJORITY OF HUMANITY, MIGRATION TO THE FIRST WORLD IS ALL BUT IMPOSSIBLE.

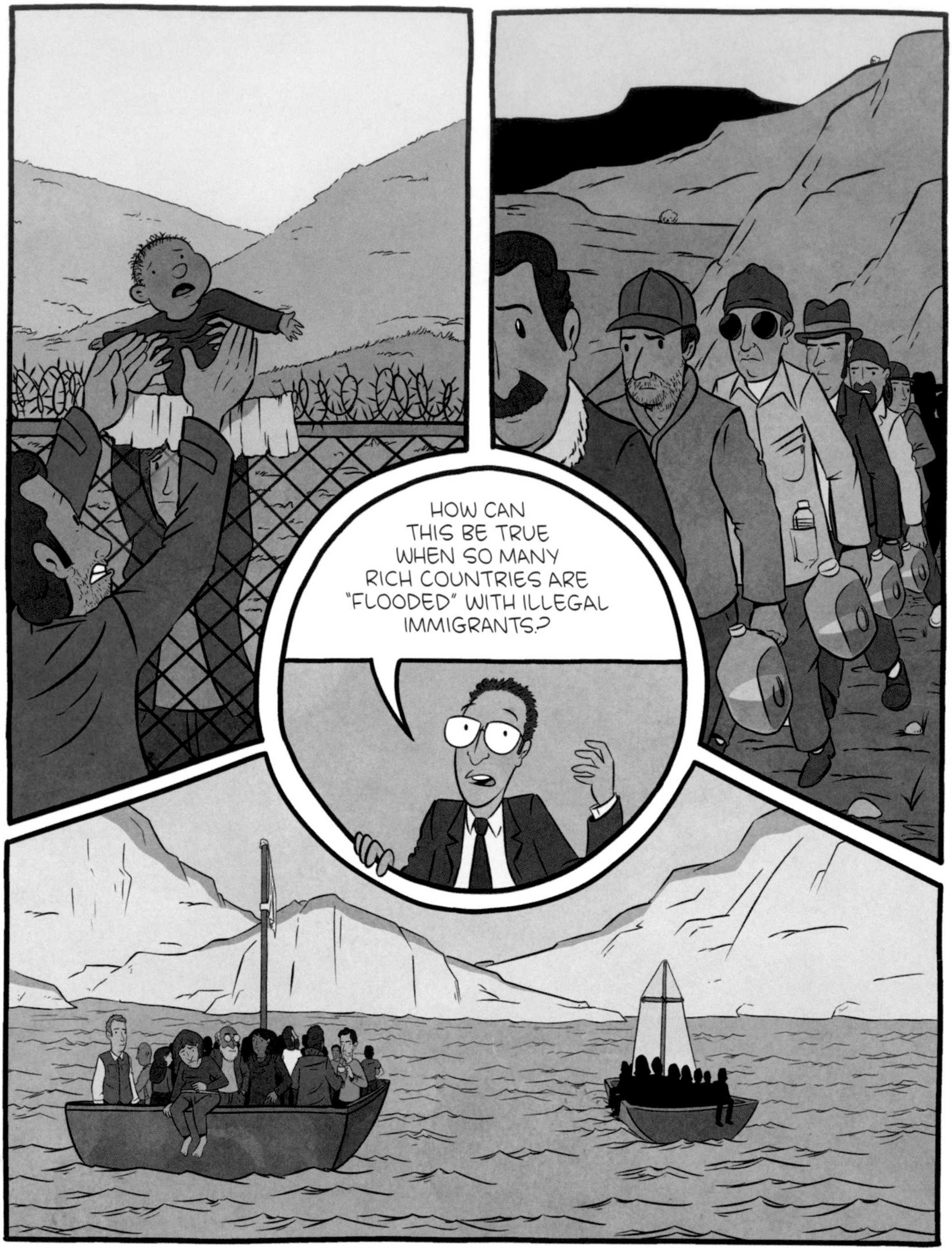
HOW CAN THIS BE TRUE WHEN SO MANY RICH COUNTRIES ARE "FLOODED" WITH ILLEGAL IMMIGRANTS?

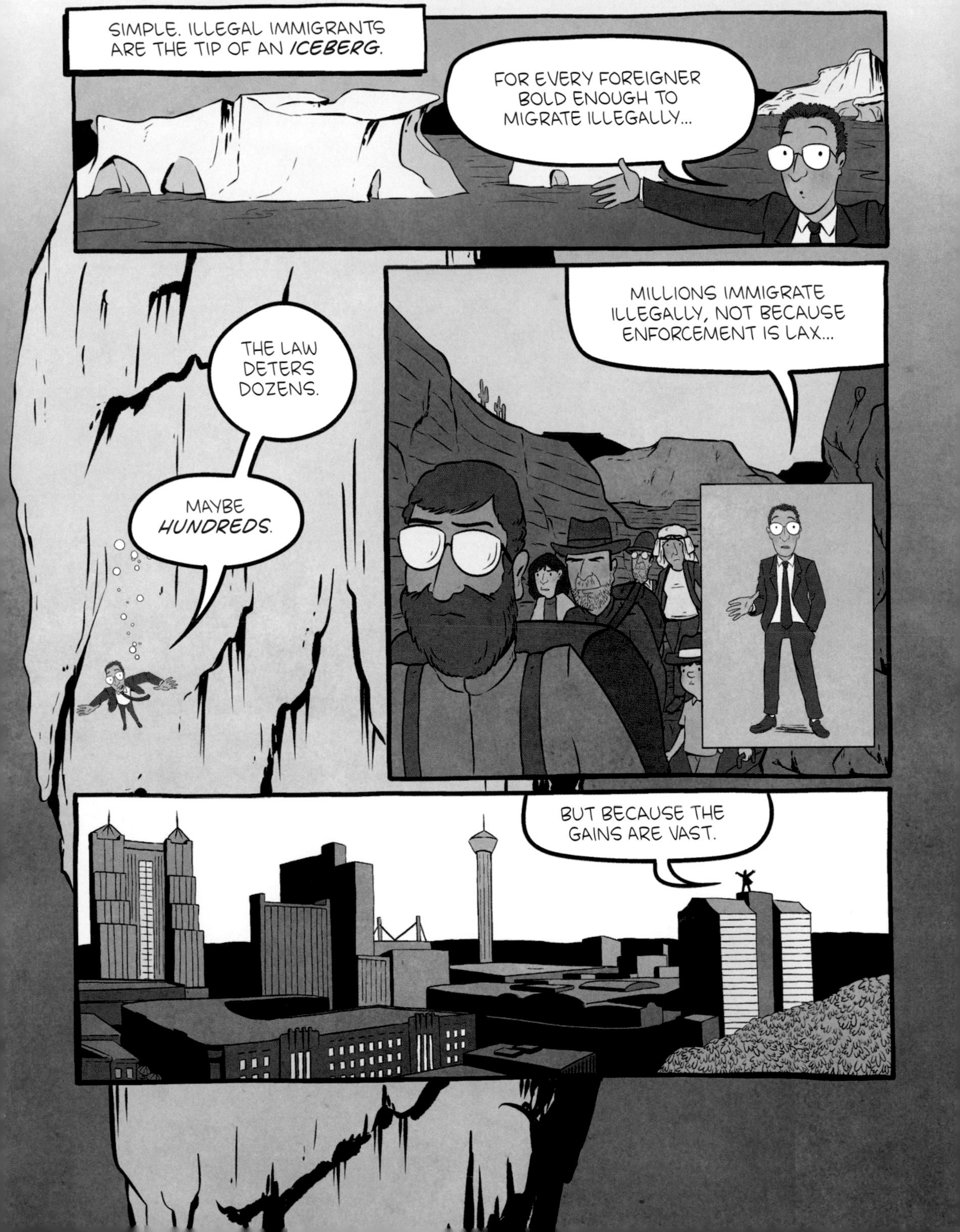
SIMPLE. ILLEGAL IMMIGRANTS ARE THE TIP OF AN *ICEBERG*.
FOR EVERY FOREIGNER BOLD ENOUGH TO MIGRATE ILLEGALLY...
THE LAW DETERS DOZENS.
MAYBE *HUNDREDS*.
MILLIONS IMMIGRATE ILLEGALLY, NOT BECAUSE ENFORCEMENT IS LAX...
BUT BECAUSE THE GAINS ARE VAST.

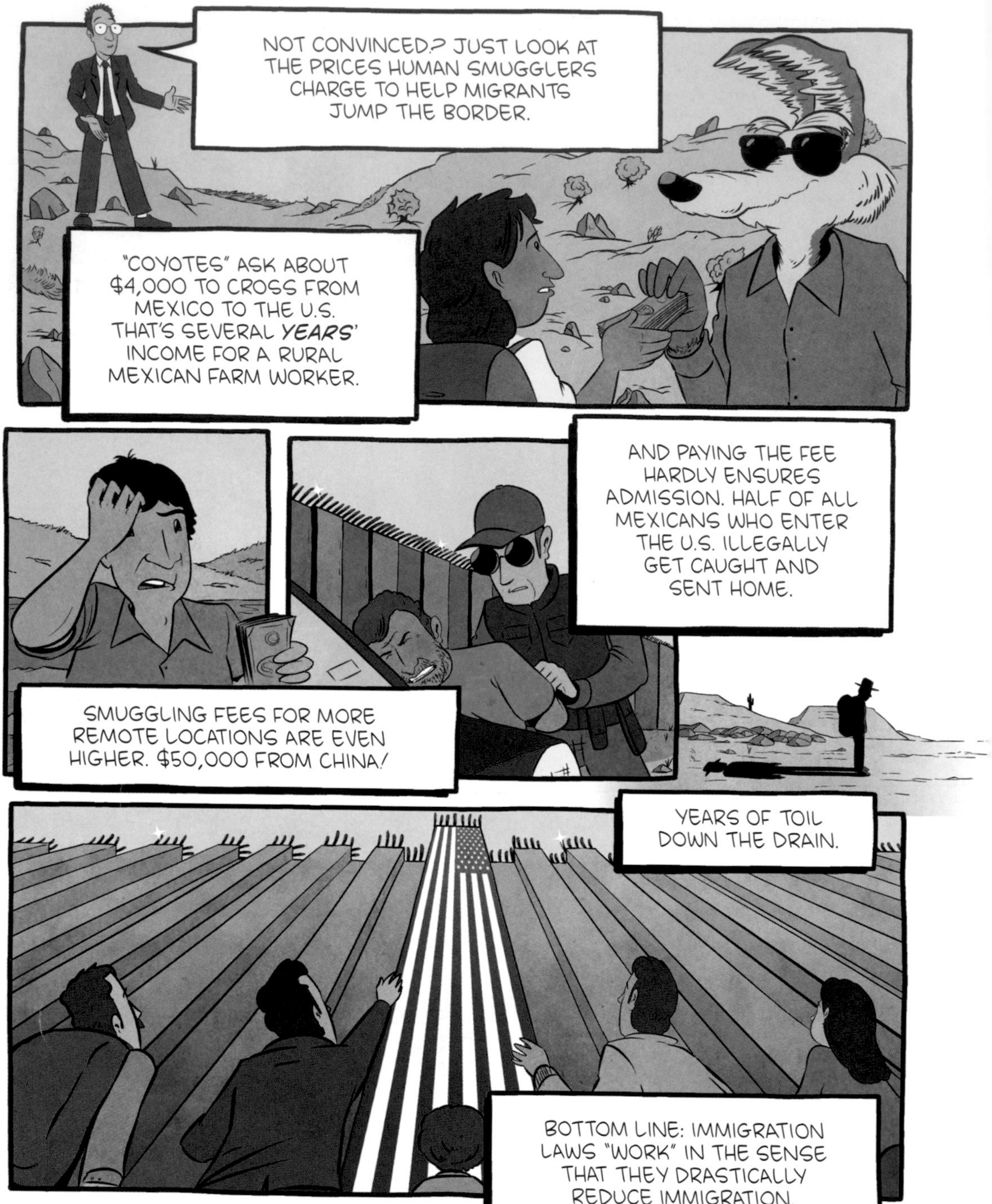
NOT CONVINCED? JUST LOOK AT THE PRICES HUMAN SMUGGLERS CHARGE TO HELP MIGRANTS JUMP THE BORDER.
"COYOTES" ASK ABOUT $4,000 TO CROSS FROM MEXICO TO THE U.S. THAT'S SEVERAL *YEARS'* INCOME FOR A RURAL MEXICAN FARM WORKER.
SMUGGLING FEES FOR MORE REMOTE LOCATIONS ARE EVEN HIGHER. $50,000 FROM CHINA!
AND PAYING THE FEE HARDLY ENSURES ADMISSION. HALF OF ALL MEXICANS WHO ENTER THE U.S. ILLEGALLY GET CAUGHT AND SENT HOME.
YEARS OF TOIL DOWN THE DRAIN.
BOTTOM LINE: IMMIGRATION LAWS "WORK" IN THE SENSE THAT THEY DRASTICALLY REDUCE IMMIGRATION.

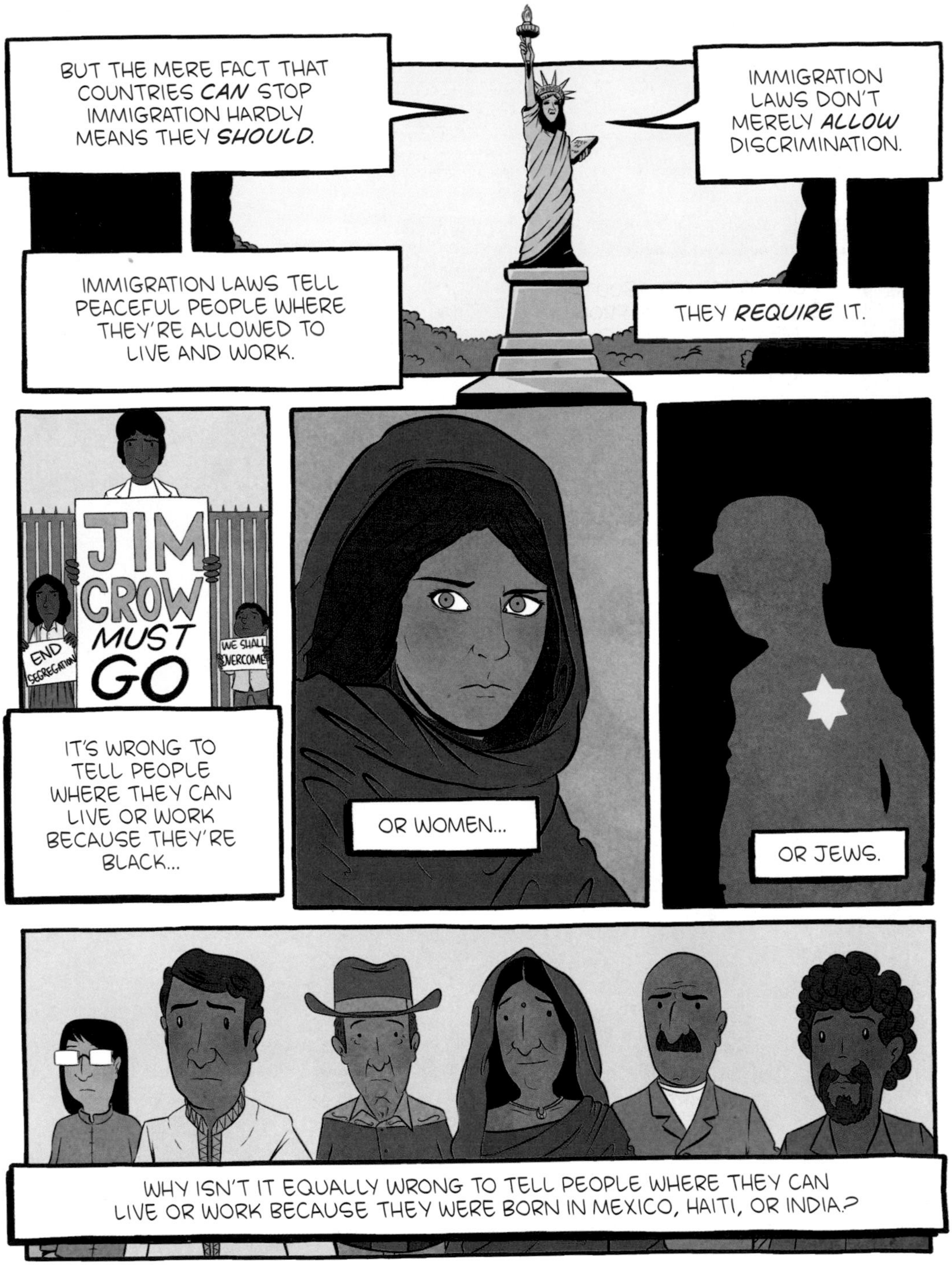
BUT THE MERE FACT THAT COUNTRIES *CAN* STOP IMMIGRATION HARDLY MEANS THEY *SHOULD*.
IMMIGRATION LAWS DON'T MERELY *ALLOW* DISCRIMINATION.
IMMIGRATION LAWS TELL PEACEFUL PEOPLE WHERE THEY'RE ALLOWED TO LIVE AND WORK.
THEY *REQUIRE* IT.
JIM CROW MUST GO
END SEGREGATION
WE SHALL OVERCOME
IT'S WRONG TO TELL PEOPLE WHERE THEY CAN LIVE OR WORK BECAUSE THEY'RE BLACK...
OR WOMEN...
OR JEWS.
WHY ISN'T IT EQUALLY WRONG TO TELL PEOPLE WHERE THEY CAN LIVE OR WORK BECAUSE THEY WERE BORN IN MEXICO, HAITI, OR INDIA?

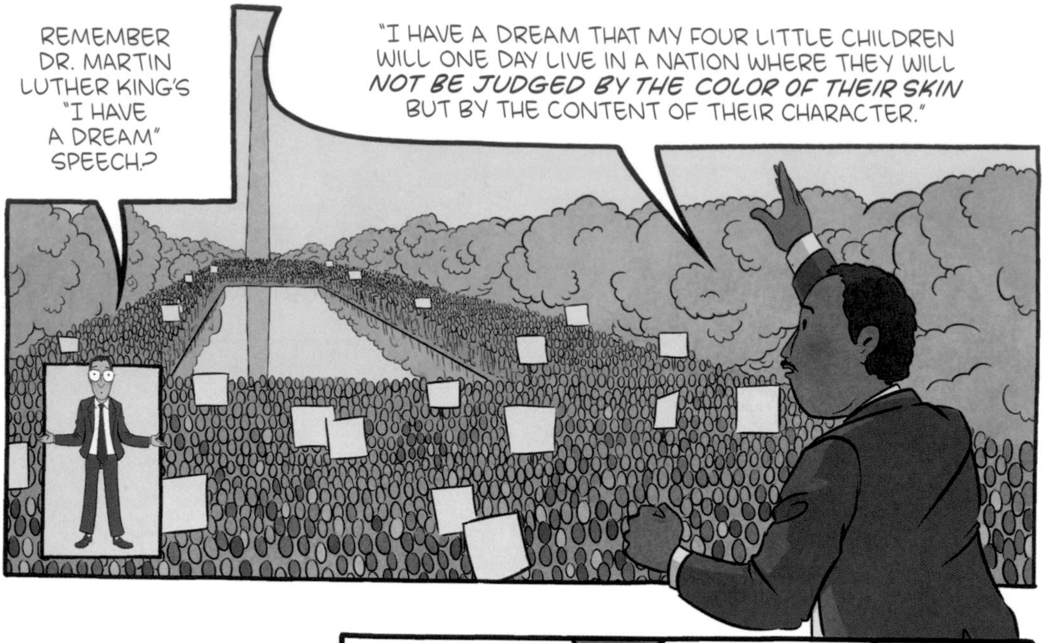
REMEMBER DR. MARTIN LUTHER KING'S "I HAVE A DREAM" SPEECH?
"I HAVE A DREAM THAT MY FOUR LITTLE CHILDREN WILL ONE DAY LIVE IN A NATION WHERE THEY WILL ***NOT BE JUDGED BY THE COLOR OF THEIR SKIN*** BUT BY THE CONTENT OF THEIR CHARACTER."

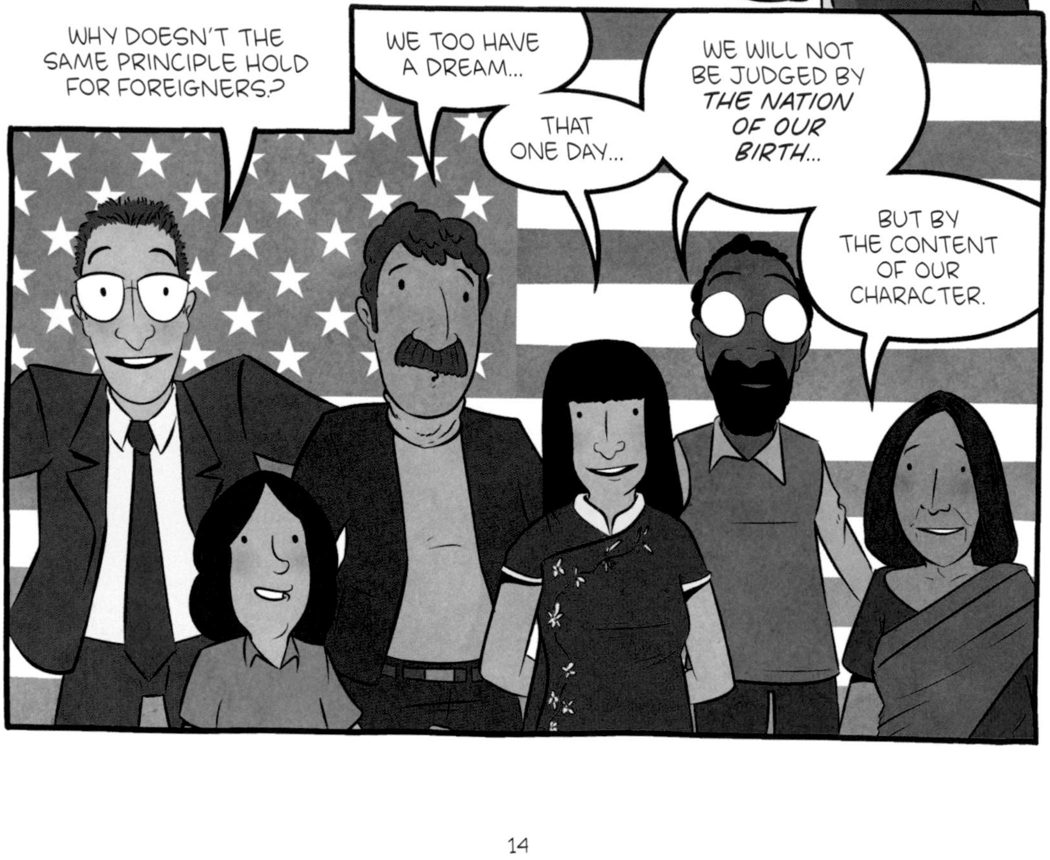
WHY DOESN'T THE SAME PRINCIPLE HOLD FOR FOREIGNERS?
WE TOO HAVE A DREAM...
THAT ONE DAY...
WE WILL NOT BE JUDGED BY ***THE NATION OF OUR BIRTH***...
BUT BY THE CONTENT OF OUR CHARACTER.

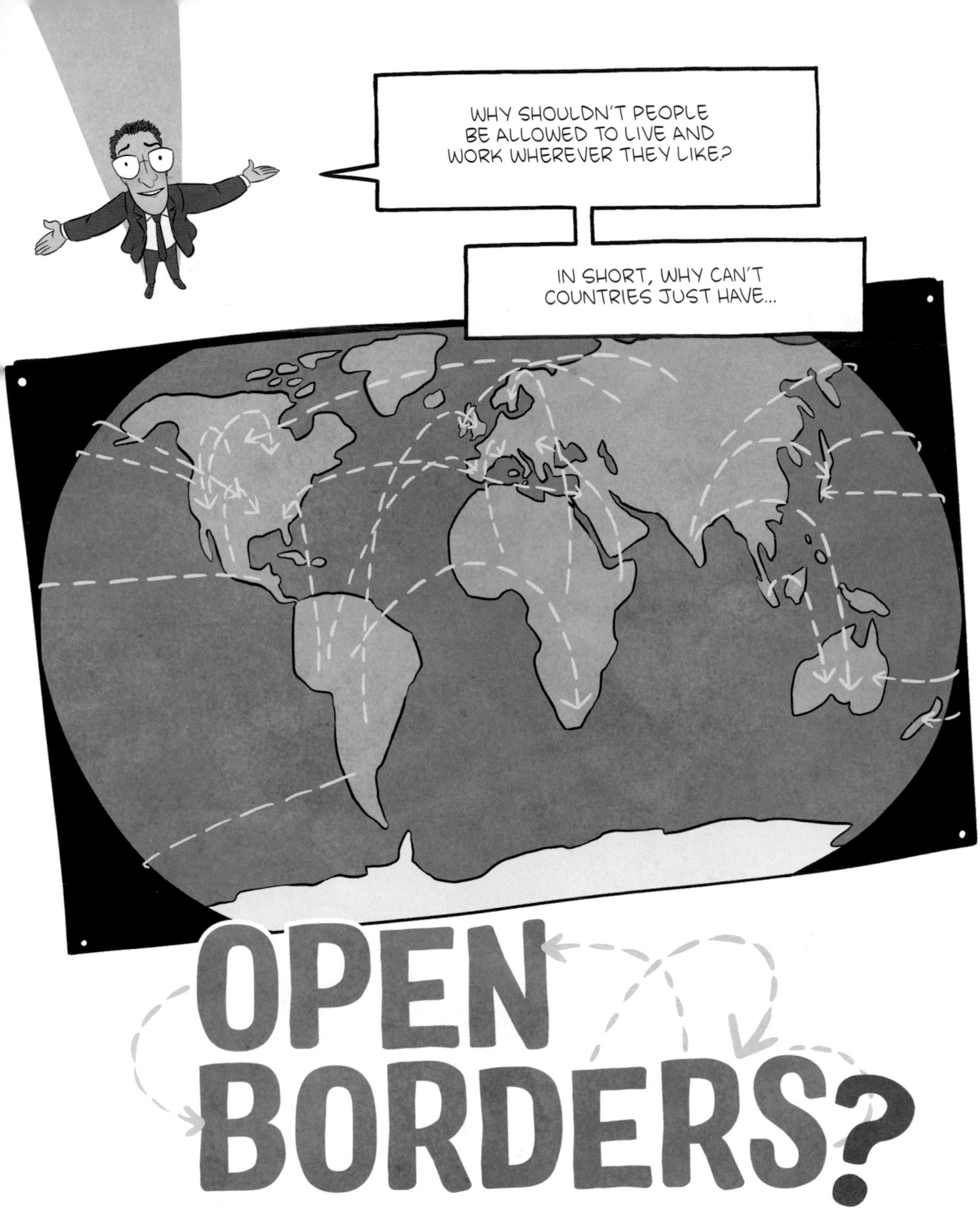
WHY SHOULDN'T PEOPLE BE ALLOWED TO LIVE AND WORK WHEREVER THEY LIKE?
IN SHORT, WHY CAN'T COUNTRIES JUST HAVE...
OPEN BORDERS?

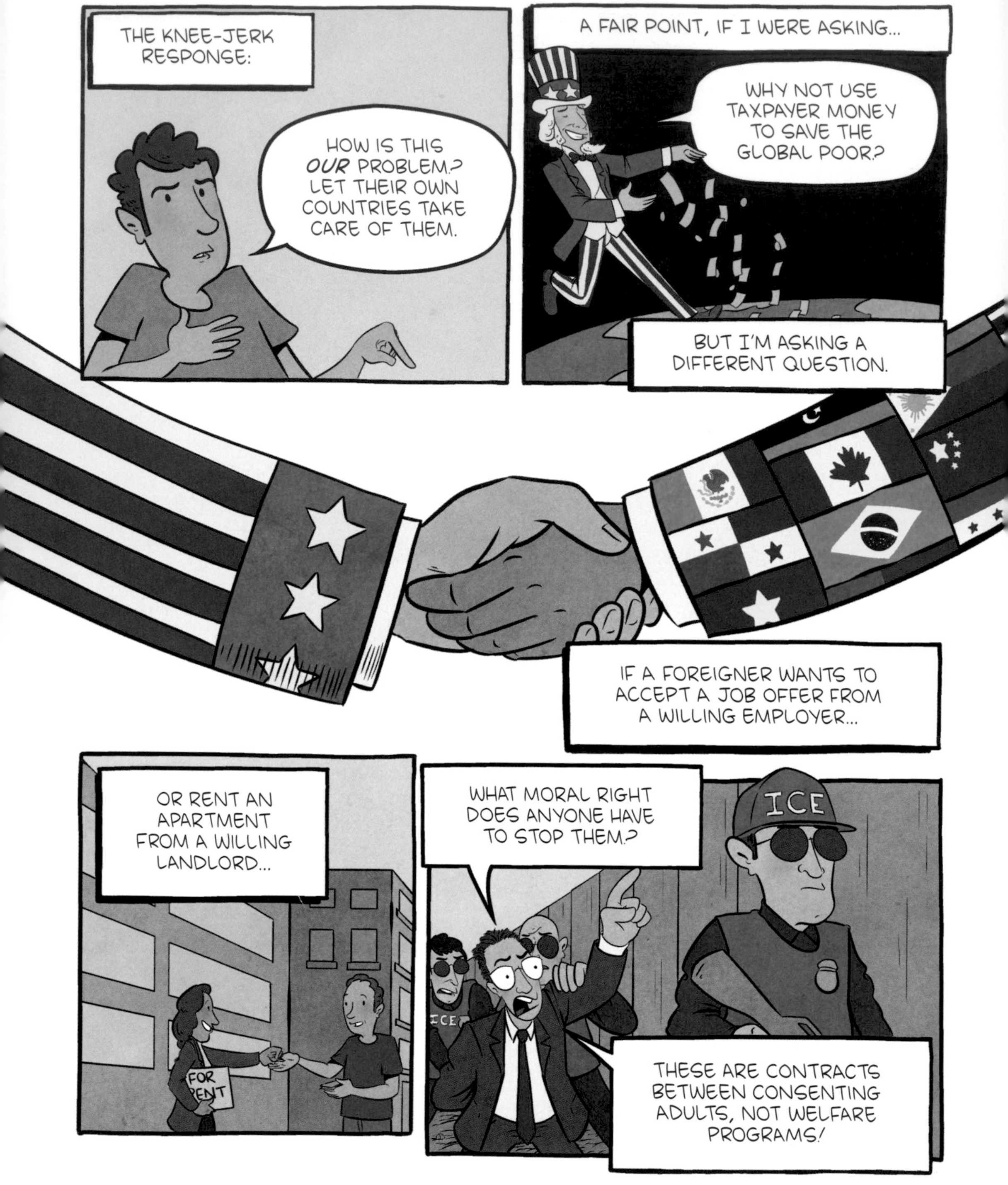
THE KNEE-JERK RESPONSE:
HOW IS THIS *OUR* PROBLEM? LET THEIR OWN COUNTRIES TAKE CARE OF THEM.
A FAIR POINT, IF I WERE ASKING...
WHY NOT USE TAXPAYER MONEY TO SAVE THE GLOBAL POOR?
BUT I'M ASKING A DIFFERENT QUESTION.
IF A FOREIGNER WANTS TO ACCEPT A JOB OFFER FROM A WILLING EMPLOYER...
OR RENT AN APARTMENT FROM A WILLING LANDLORD...
FOR RENT
WHAT MORAL RIGHT DOES ANYONE HAVE TO STOP THEM?
ICE
THESE ARE CONTRACTS BETWEEN CONSENTING ADULTS, NOT WELFARE PROGRAMS!

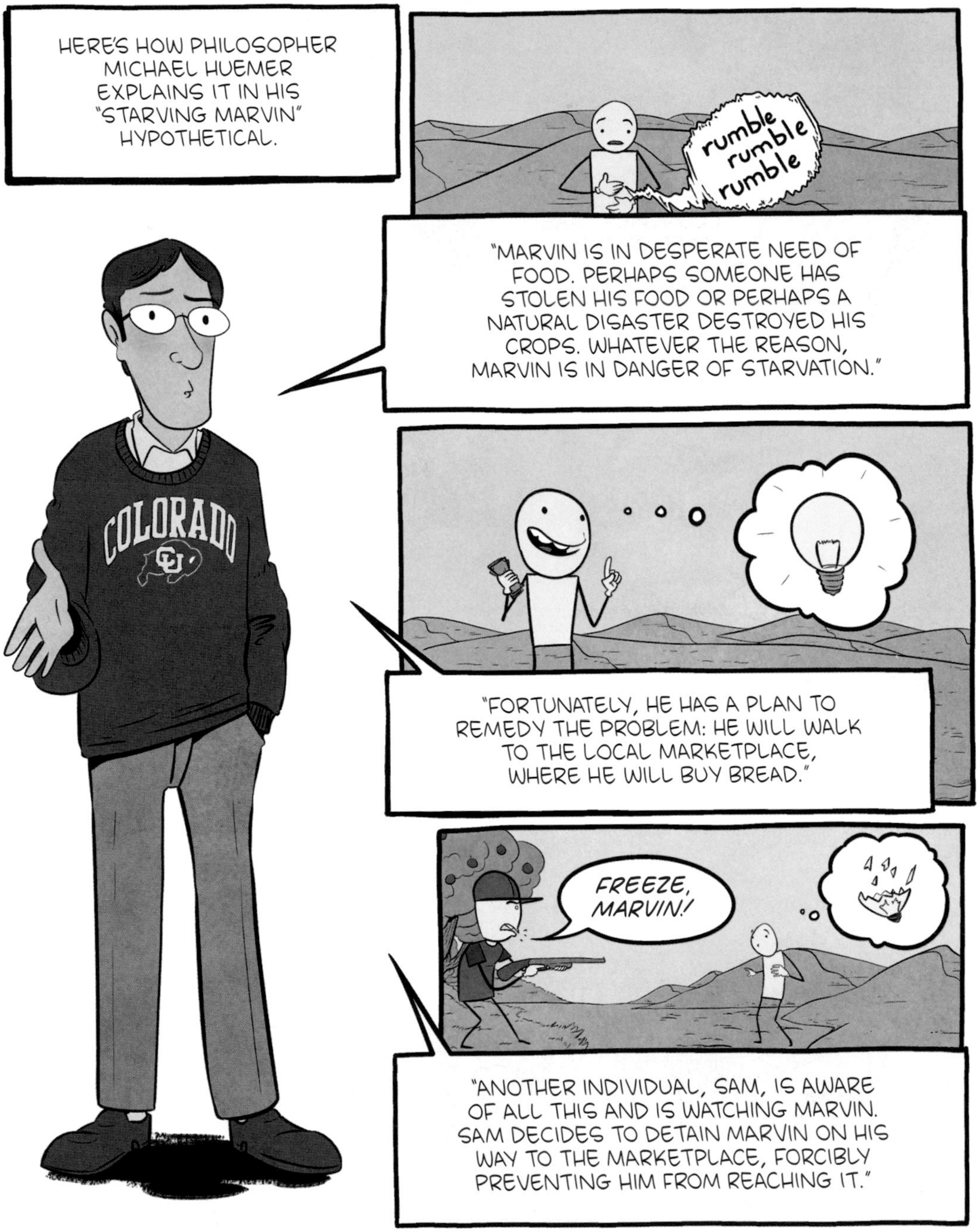
HERE'S HOW PHILOSOPHER MICHAEL HUEMER EXPLAINS IT IN HIS "STARVING MARVIN" HYPOTHETICAL.
rumble rumble rumble
"MARVIN IS IN DESPERATE NEED OF FOOD. PERHAPS SOMEONE HAS STOLEN HIS FOOD OR PERHAPS A NATURAL DISASTER DESTROYED HIS CROPS. WHATEVER THE REASON, MARVIN IS IN DANGER OF STARVATION."
COLORADO
"FORTUNATELY, HE HAS A PLAN TO REMEDY THE PROBLEM: HE WILL WALK TO THE LOCAL MARKETPLACE, WHERE HE WILL BUY BREAD."
FREEZE, MARVIN!
"ANOTHER INDIVIDUAL, SAM, IS AWARE OF ALL THIS AND IS WATCHING MARVIN. SAM DECIDES TO DETAIN MARVIN ON HIS WAY TO THE MARKETPLACE, FORCIBLY PREVENTING HIM FROM REACHING IT."

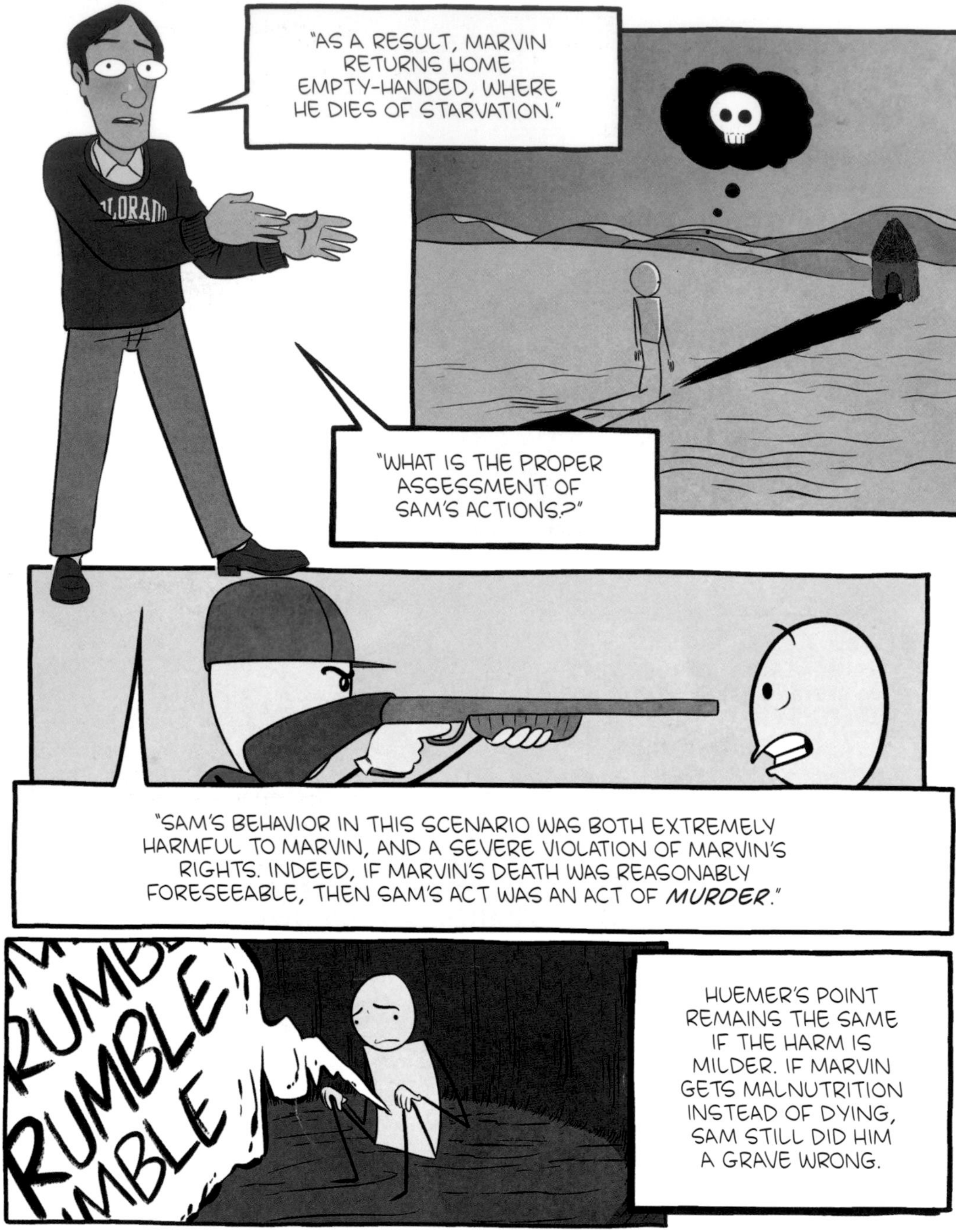
"AS A RESULT, MARVIN RETURNS HOME EMPTY-HANDED, WHERE HE DIES OF STARVATION."
"WHAT IS THE PROPER ASSESSMENT OF SAM'S ACTIONS?"
"SAM'S BEHAVIOR IN THIS SCENARIO WAS BOTH EXTREMELY HARMFUL TO MARVIN, AND A SEVERE VIOLATION OF MARVIN'S RIGHTS. INDEED, IF MARVIN'S DEATH WAS REASONABLY FORESEEABLE, THEN SAM'S ACT WAS AN ACT OF *MURDER*."
RUMBLE RUMBLE
HUEMER'S POINT REMAINS THE SAME IF THE HARM IS MILDER. IF MARVIN GETS MALNUTRITION INSTEAD OF DYING, SAM STILL DID HIM A GRAVE WRONG.

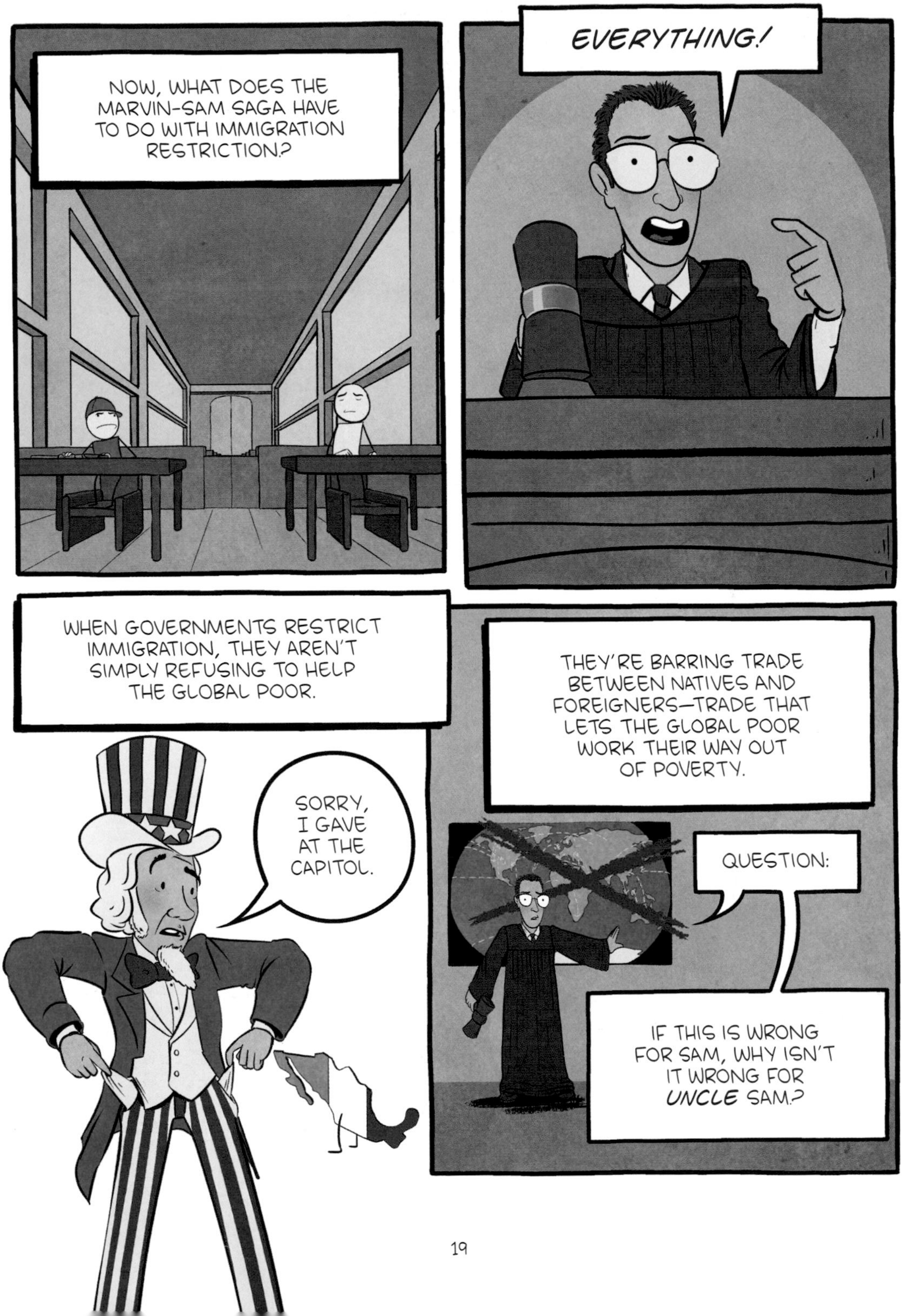
NOW, WHAT DOES THE MARVIN-SAM SAGA HAVE TO DO WITH IMMIGRATION RESTRICTION?
EVERYTHING!
WHEN GOVERNMENTS RESTRICT IMMIGRATION, THEY AREN'T SIMPLY REFUSING TO HELP THE GLOBAL POOR.
SORRY, I GAVE AT THE CAPITOL.
THEY'RE BARRING TRADE BETWEEN NATIVES AND FOREIGNERS—TRADE THAT LETS THE GLOBAL POOR WORK THEIR WAY OUT OF POVERTY.
QUESTION:
IF THIS IS WRONG FOR SAM, WHY ISN'T IT WRONG FOR *UNCLE* SAM?

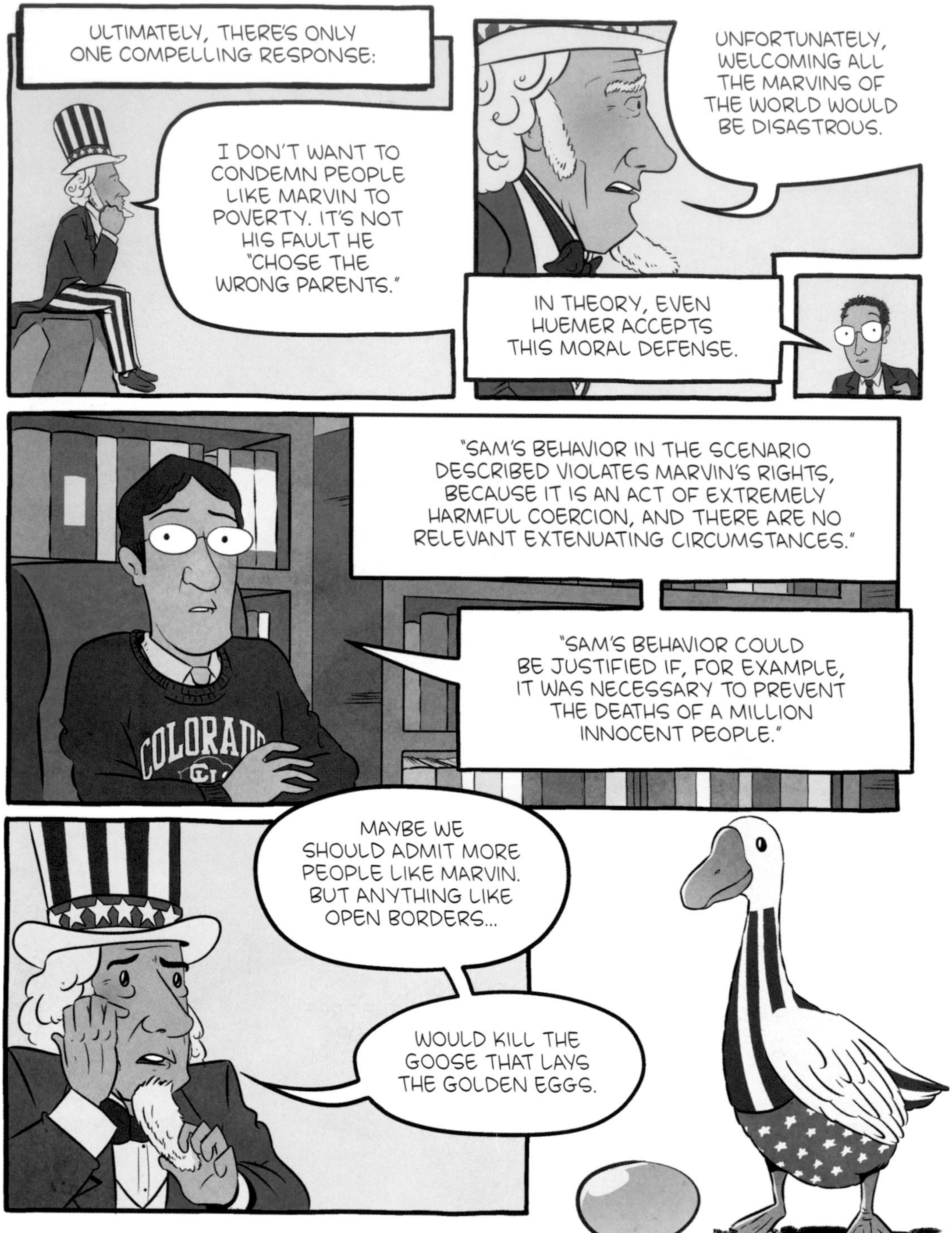
ULTIMATELY, THERE'S ONLY ONE COMPELLING RESPONSE:
I DON'T WANT TO CONDEMN PEOPLE LIKE MARVIN TO POVERTY. IT'S NOT HIS FAULT HE "CHOSE THE WRONG PARENTS."
UNFORTUNATELY, WELCOMING ALL THE MARVINS OF THE WORLD WOULD BE DISASTROUS.
IN THEORY, EVEN HUEMER ACCEPTS THIS MORAL DEFENSE.
"SAM'S BEHAVIOR IN THE SCENARIO DESCRIBED VIOLATES MARVIN'S RIGHTS, BECAUSE IT IS AN ACT OF EXTREMELY HARMFUL COERCION, AND THERE ARE NO RELEVANT EXTENUATING CIRCUMSTANCES."
"SAM'S BEHAVIOR COULD BE JUSTIFIED IF, FOR EXAMPLE, IT WAS NECESSARY TO PREVENT THE DEATHS OF A MILLION INNOCENT PEOPLE."
MAYBE WE SHOULD ADMIT MORE PEOPLE LIKE MARVIN. BUT ANYTHING LIKE OPEN BORDERS...
WOULD KILL THE GOOSE THAT LAYS THE GOLDEN EGGS.

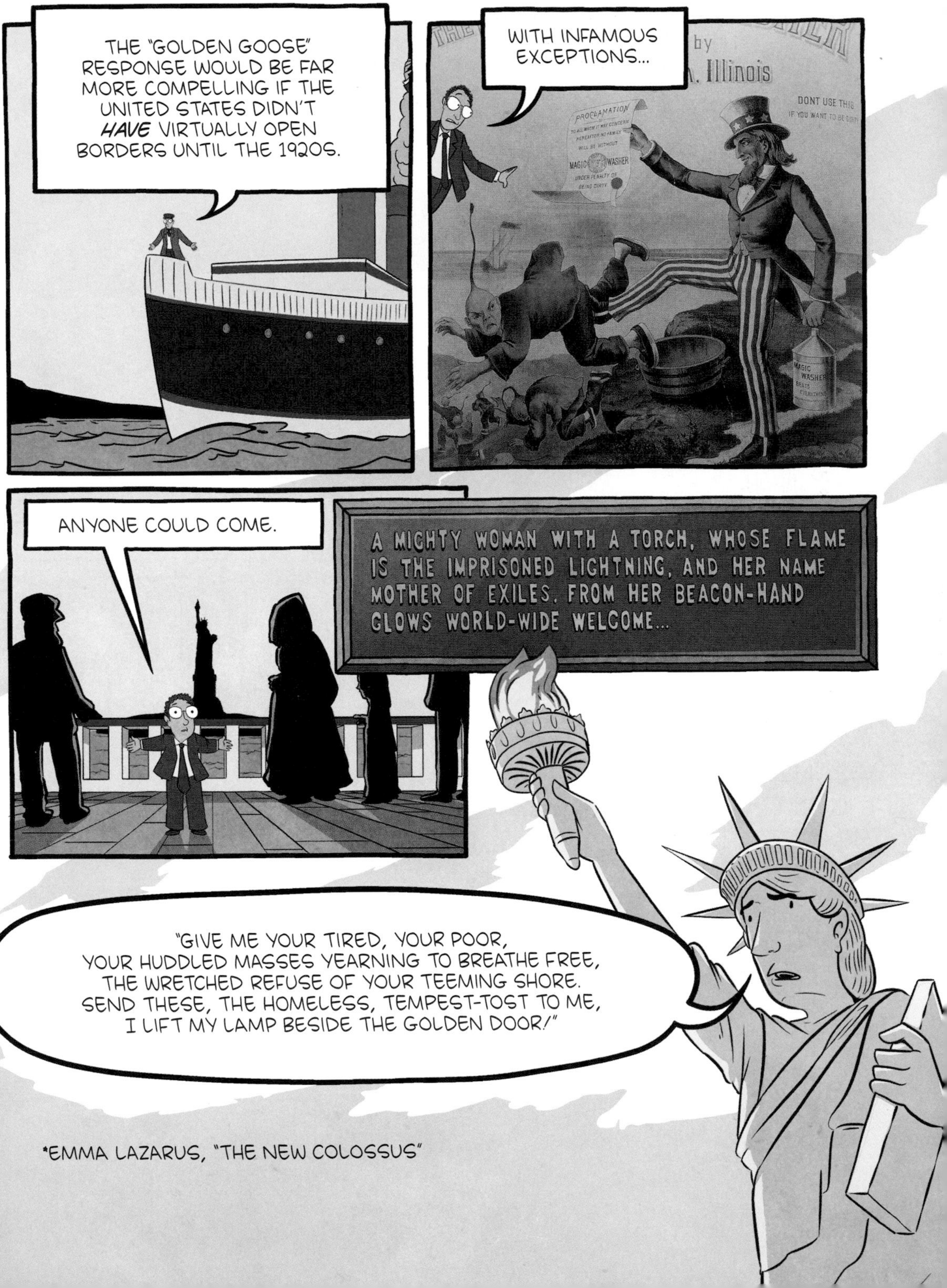

THE "GOLDEN GOOSE" RESPONSE WOULD BE FAR MORE COMPELLING IF THE UNITED STATES DIDN'T *HAVE* VIRTUALLY OPEN BORDERS UNTIL THE 1920S.
WITH INFAMOUS EXCEPTIONS...
Illinois
DONT USE THIS IF YOU WANT TO BE DIRTY
PROCLAMATION
MAGIC WASHER
ANYONE COULD COME.
A MIGHTY WOMAN WITH A TORCH, WHOSE FLAME IS THE IMPRISONED LIGHTNING, AND HER NAME MOTHER OF EXILES. FROM HER BEACON-HAND GLOWS WORLD-WIDE WELCOME...
"GIVE ME YOUR TIRED, YOUR POOR, YOUR HUDDLED MASSES YEARNING TO BREATHE FREE, THE WRETCHED REFUSE OF YOUR TEEMING SHORE. SEND THESE, THE HOMELESS, TEMPEST-TOST TO ME, I LIFT MY LAMP BESIDE THE GOLDEN DOOR!"
*EMMA LAZARUS, "THE NEW COLOSSUS"

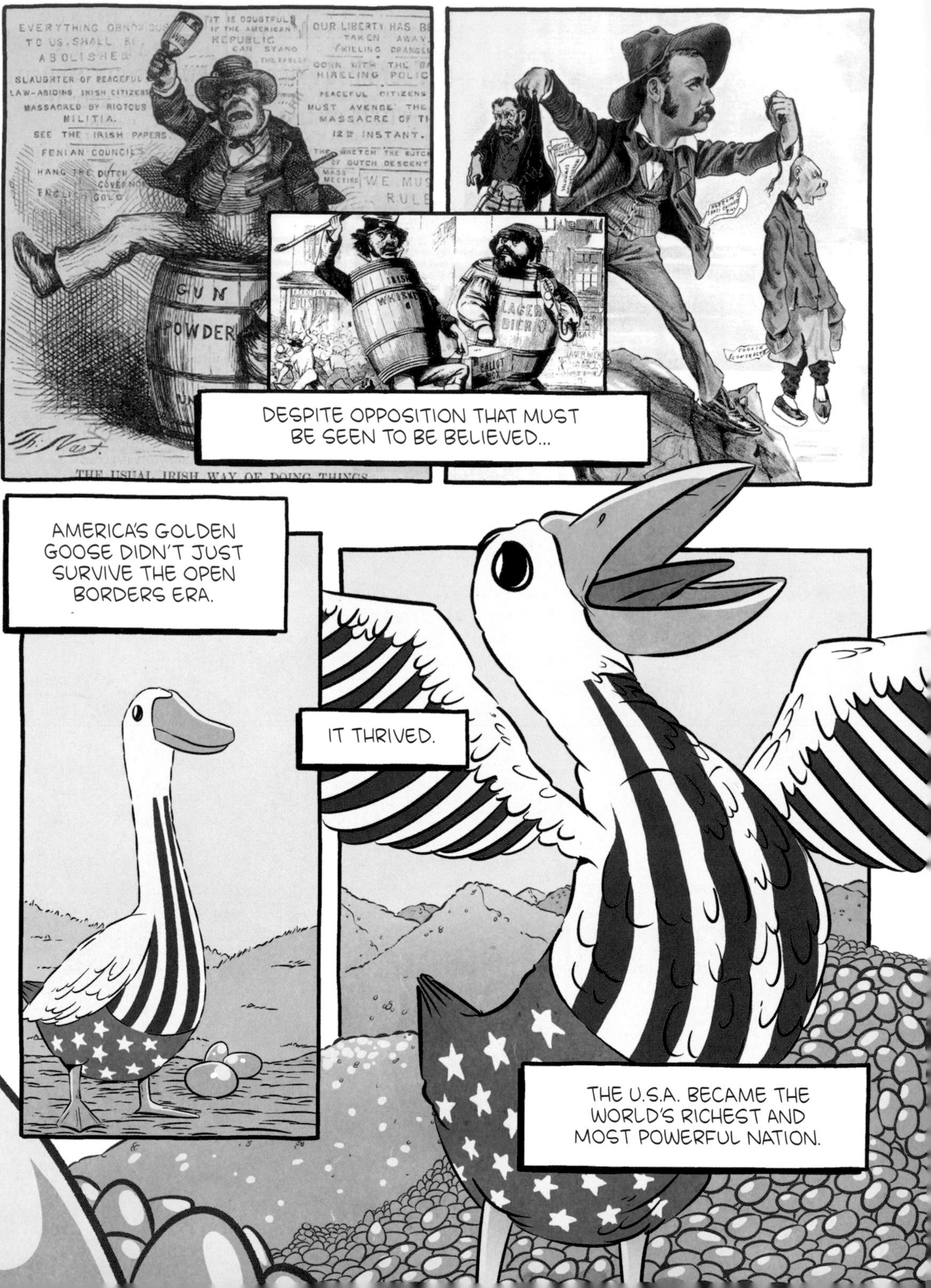
EVERYTHING OBNOXIOUS TO US, SHALL BE ABOLISHED
SLAUGHTER OF PEACEFUL LAW-ABIDING IRISH CITIZENS MASSACRED BY RIOTOUS MILITIA.
SEE THE IRISH PAPERS.
FENIAN COUNCILS
HANG THE DUTCH GOVERNOR
IT IS DOUBTFUL IF THE AMERICAN REPUBLIC CAN STAND
OUR LIBERTY HAS BEEN TAKEN AWAY
DOWN WITH THE BASE HIRELING POLICE
PEACEFUL CITIZENS
MUST AVENGE THE MASSACRE OF THE 12TH INSTANT.
MASS MEETING
WE MUST RULE
GUN POWDER
Th. Nast
THE USUAL IRISH WAY OF DOING THINGS
IRISH WHISKEY
LAGER BIER
BALLOT BOX
DESPITE OPPOSITION THAT MUST BE SEEN TO BE BELIEVED...
AMERICA'S GOLDEN GOOSE DIDN'T JUST SURVIVE THE OPEN BORDERS ERA.
IT THRIVED.
THE U.S.A. BECAME THE WORLD'S RICHEST AND MOST POWERFUL NATION.

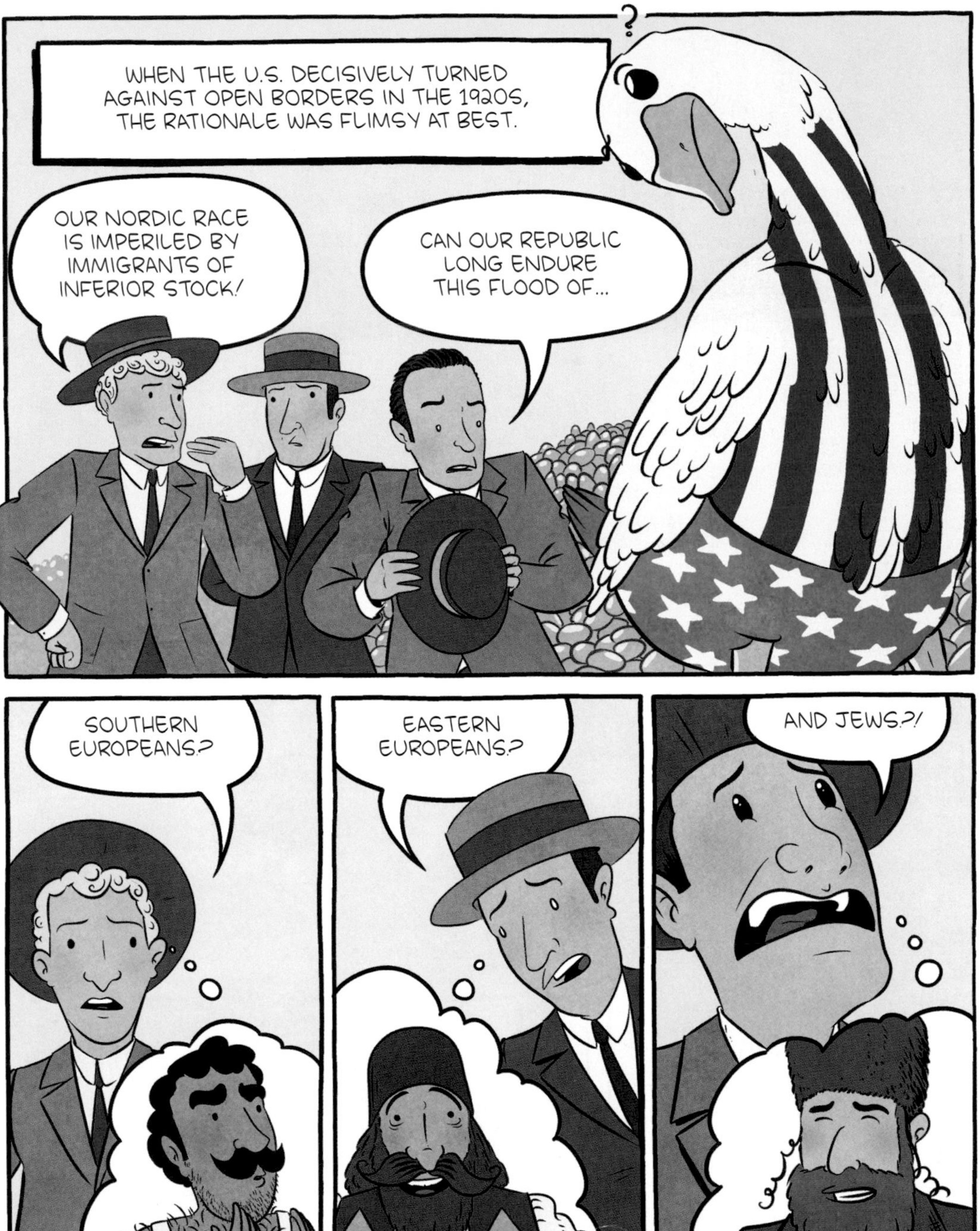
WHEN THE U.S. DECISIVELY TURNED AGAINST OPEN BORDERS IN THE 1920S, THE RATIONALE WAS FLIMSY AT BEST.
?
OUR NORDIC RACE IS IMPERILED BY IMMIGRANTS OF INFERIOR STOCK!
CAN OUR REPUBLIC LONG ENDURE THIS FLOOD OF...
SOUTHERN EUROPEANS?
EASTERN EUROPEANS?
AND JEWS?!

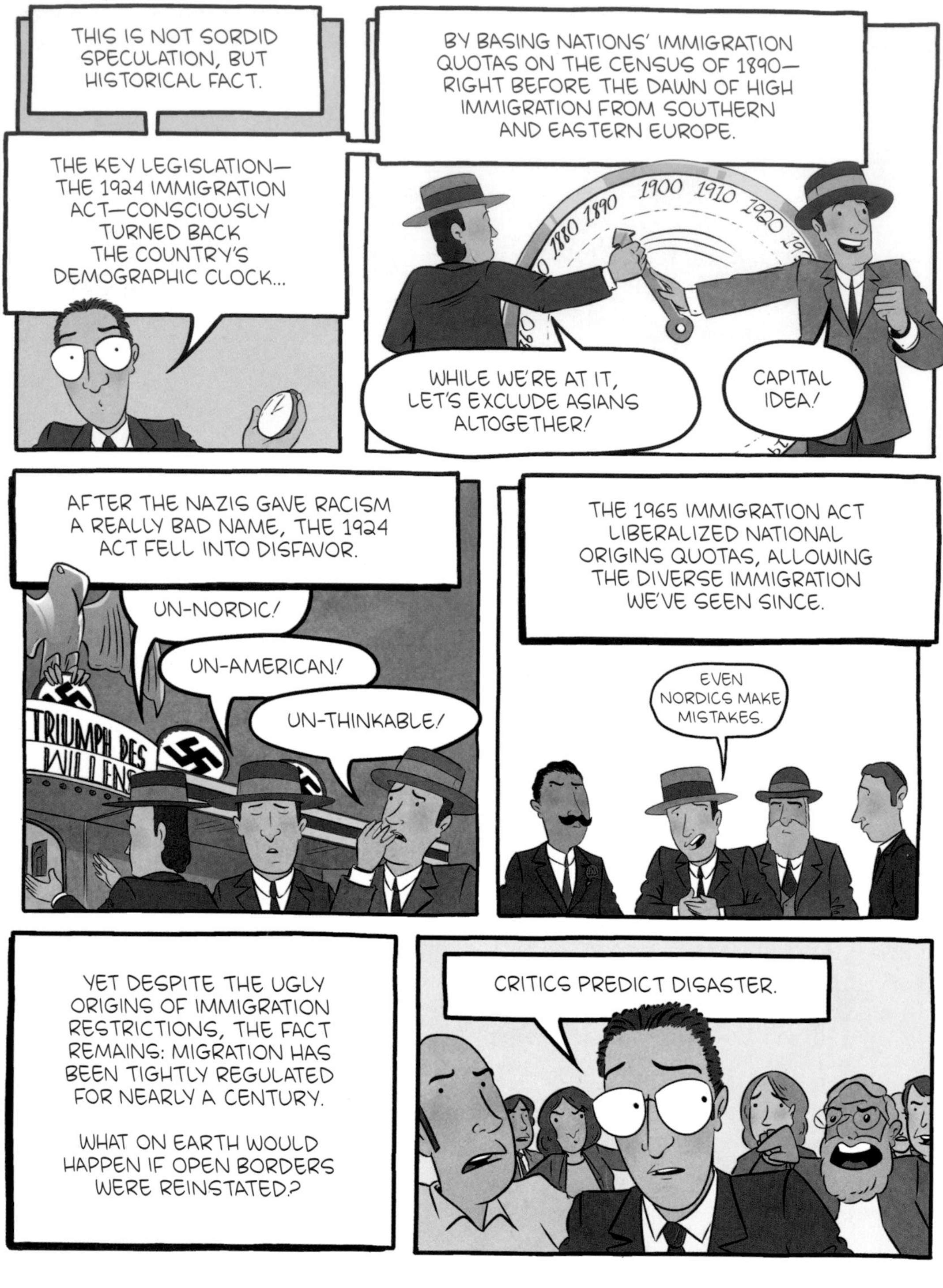
THIS IS NOT SORDID SPECULATION, BUT HISTORICAL FACT.
THE KEY LEGISLATION—THE 1924 IMMIGRATION ACT—CONSCIOUSLY TURNED BACK THE COUNTRY'S DEMOGRAPHIC CLOCK...
BY BASING NATIONS' IMMIGRATION QUOTAS ON THE CENSUS OF 1890—RIGHT BEFORE THE DAWN OF HIGH IMMIGRATION FROM SOUTHERN AND EASTERN EUROPE.
1880 1890 1900 1910 1920
WHILE WE'RE AT IT, LET'S EXCLUDE ASIANS ALTOGETHER!
CAPITAL IDEA!
AFTER THE NAZIS GAVE RACISM A REALLY BAD NAME, THE 1924 ACT FELL INTO DISFAVOR.
UN-NORDIC!
UN-AMERICAN!
UN-THINKABLE!
TRIUMPH DES WILLENS
THE 1965 IMMIGRATION ACT LIBERALIZED NATIONAL ORIGINS QUOTAS, ALLOWING THE DIVERSE IMMIGRATION WE'VE SEEN SINCE.
EVEN NORDICS MAKE MISTAKES.
YET DESPITE THE UGLY ORIGINS OF IMMIGRATION RESTRICTIONS, THE FACT REMAINS: MIGRATION HAS BEEN TIGHTLY REGULATED FOR NEARLY A CENTURY.
WHAT ON EARTH WOULD HAPPEN IF OPEN BORDERS WERE REINSTATED?
CRITICS PREDICT DISASTER.

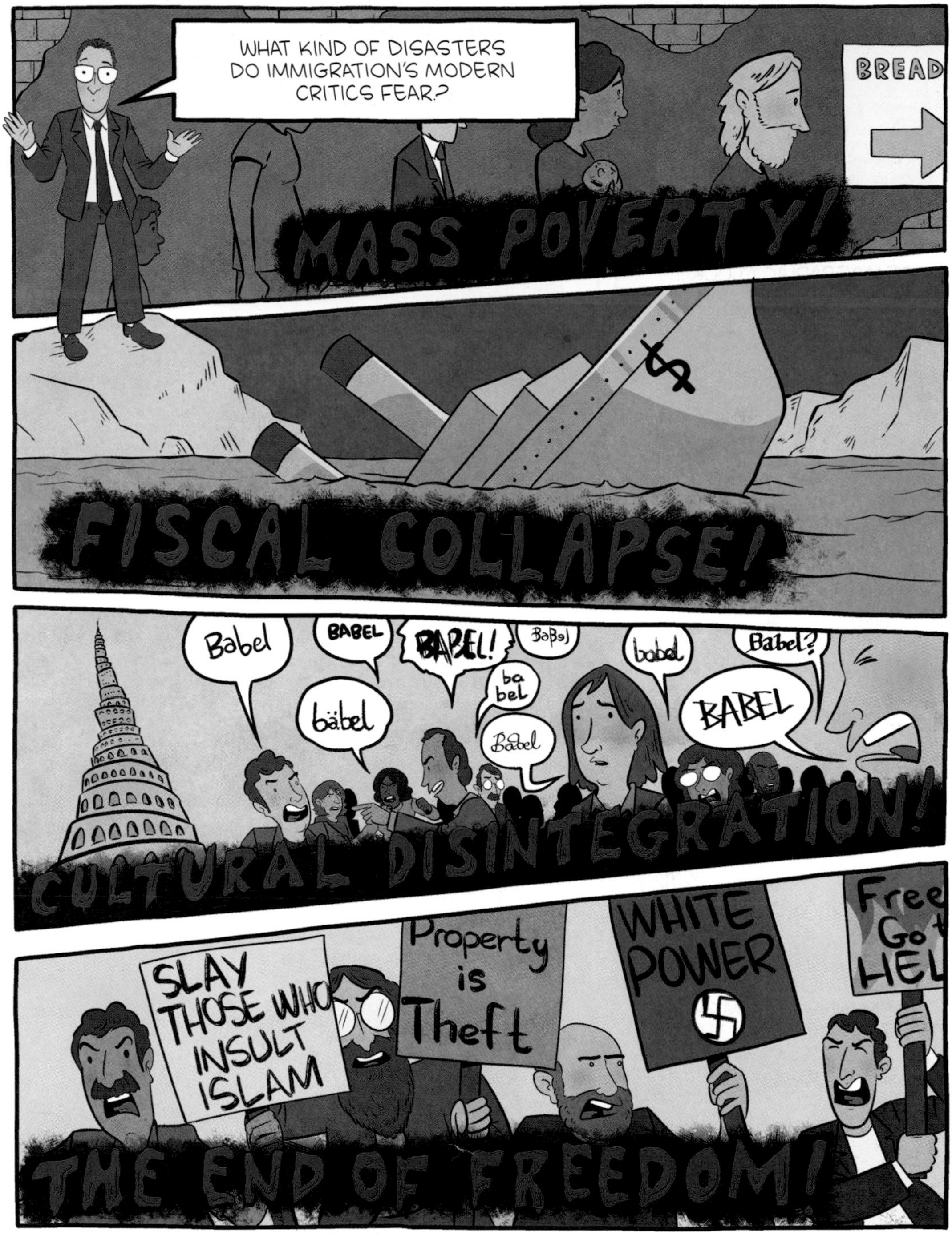

WHAT KIND OF DISASTERS DO IMMIGRATION'S MODERN CRITICS FEAR?
BREAD
MASS POVERTY!
FISCAL COLLAPSE!
Babel
BABEL
BABEL!
bäbel
ba bel
babel
Babel?
BABEL
Babel
CULTURAL DISINTEGRATION!
SLAY THOSE WHO INSULT ISLAM
Property is Theft
WHITE POWER
THE END OF FREEDOM!

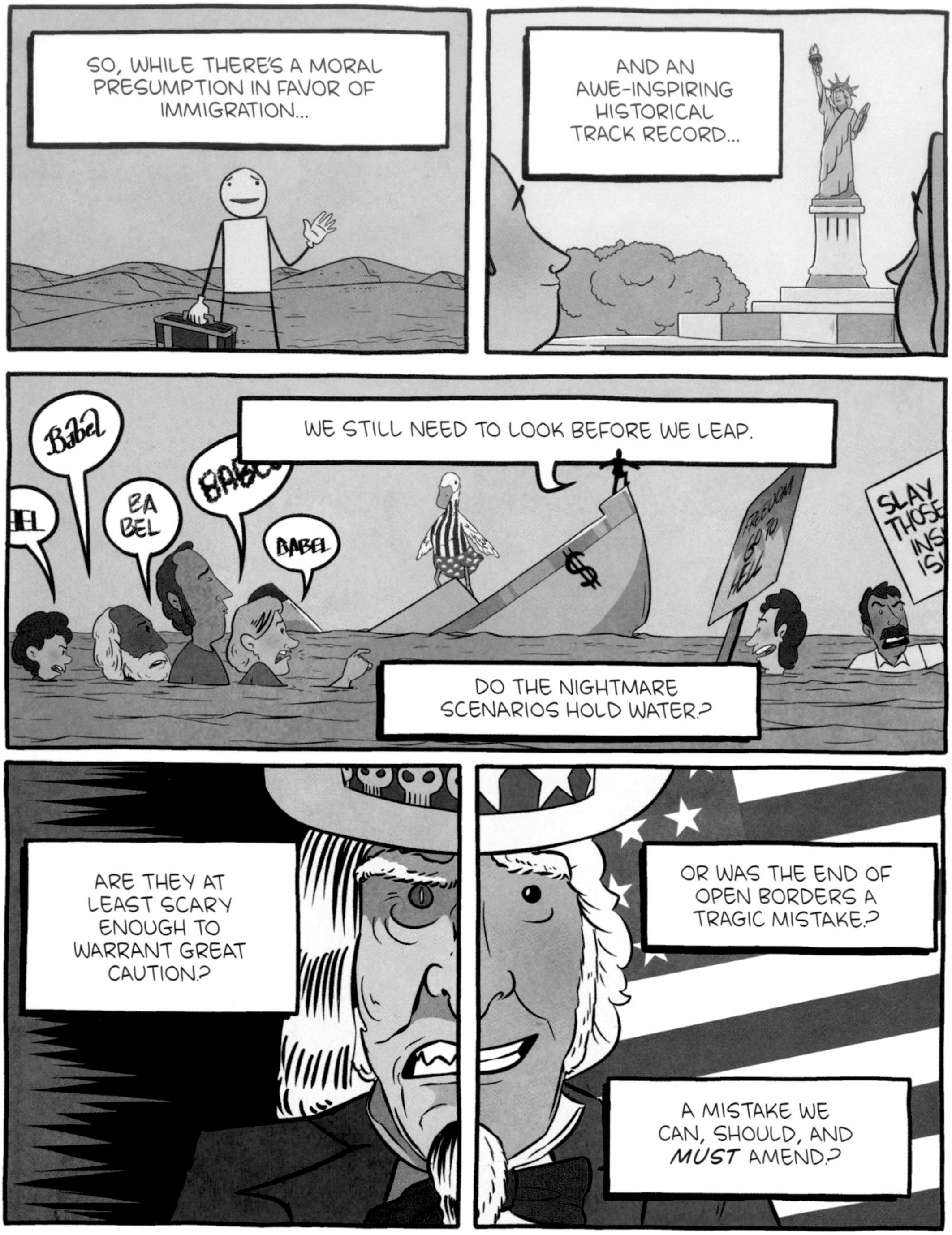
SO, WHILE THERE'S A MORAL PRESUMPTION IN FAVOR OF IMMIGRATION...
AND AN AWE-INSPIRING HISTORICAL TRACK RECORD...
WE STILL NEED TO LOOK BEFORE WE LEAP.
Babel
BA BEL
BABEL
FREEDOM GO TO HELL
DO THE NIGHTMARE SCENARIOS HOLD WATER?
ARE THEY AT LEAST SCARY ENOUGH TO WARRANT GREAT CAUTION?
OR WAS THE END OF OPEN BORDERS A TRAGIC MISTAKE?
A MISTAKE WE CAN, SHOULD, AND *MUST* AMEND?

CHAPTER 2

TRILLION-DOLLAR BILLS ON THE SIDEWALK

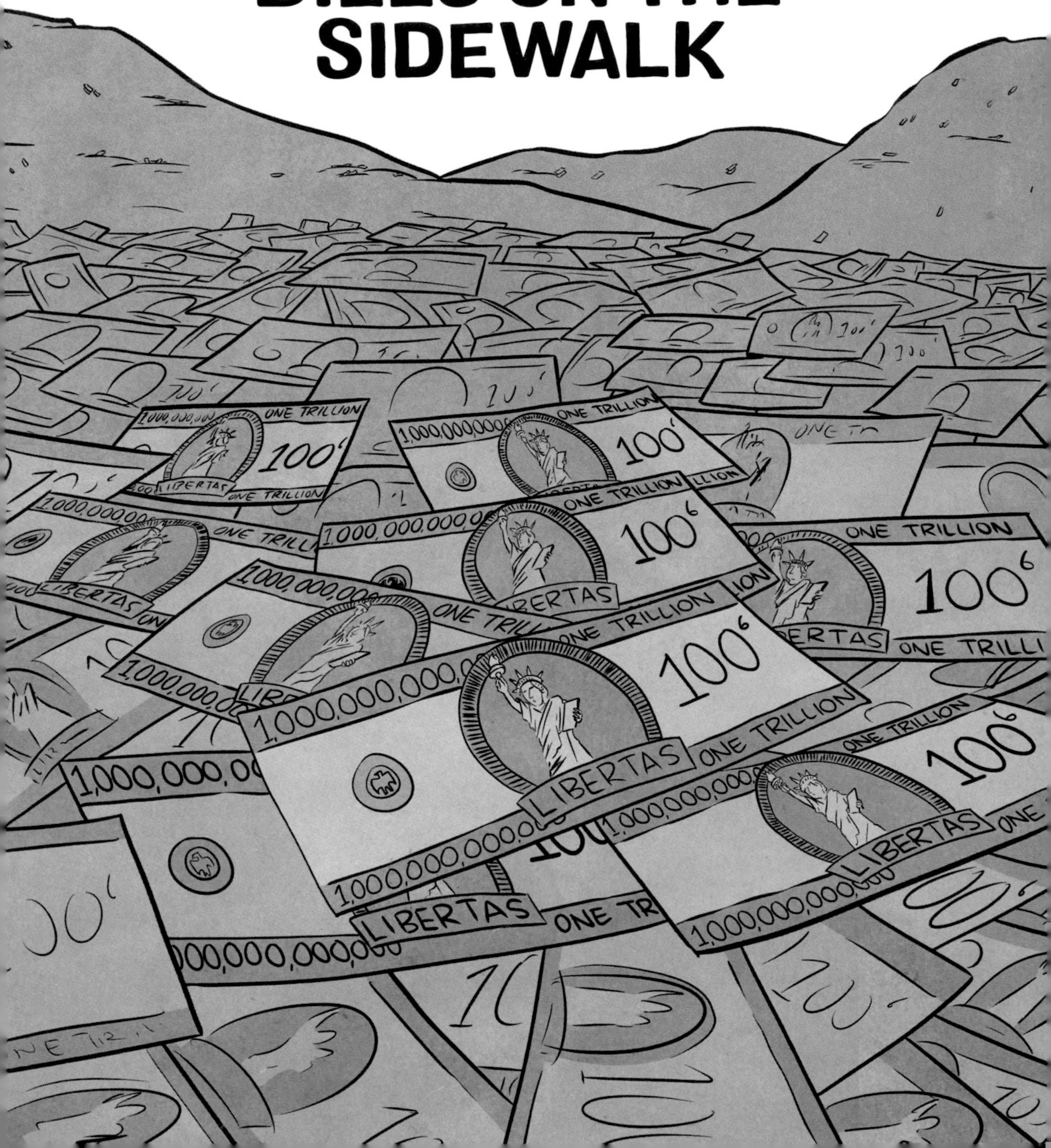
ONE TRILLION
LIBERTAS
100^6

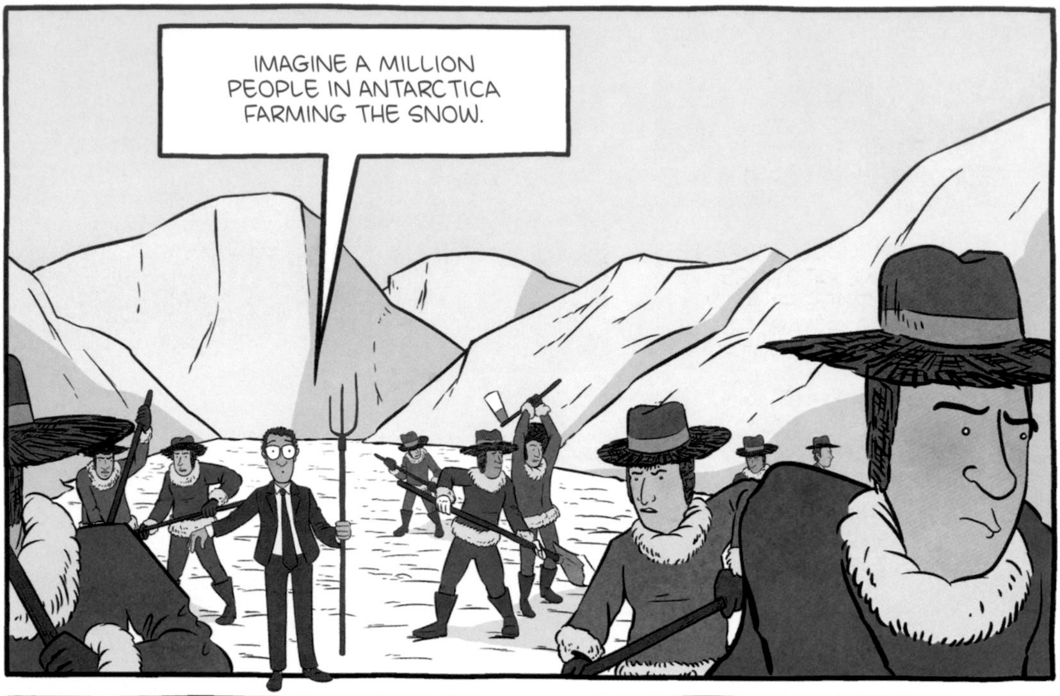
IMAGINE A MILLION PEOPLE IN ANTARCTICA FARMING THE SNOW.

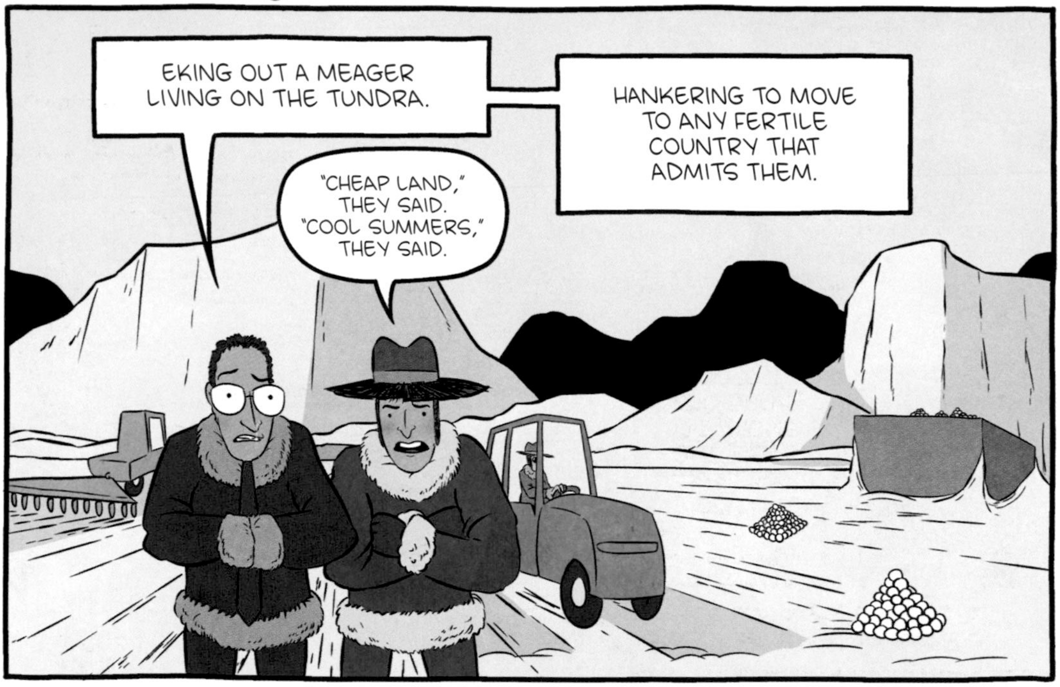
EKING OUT A MEAGER LIVING ON THE TUNDRA.
HANKERING TO MOVE TO ANY FERTILE COUNTRY THAT ADMITS THEM.
"CHEAP LAND," THEY SAID. "COOL SUMMERS," THEY SAID.

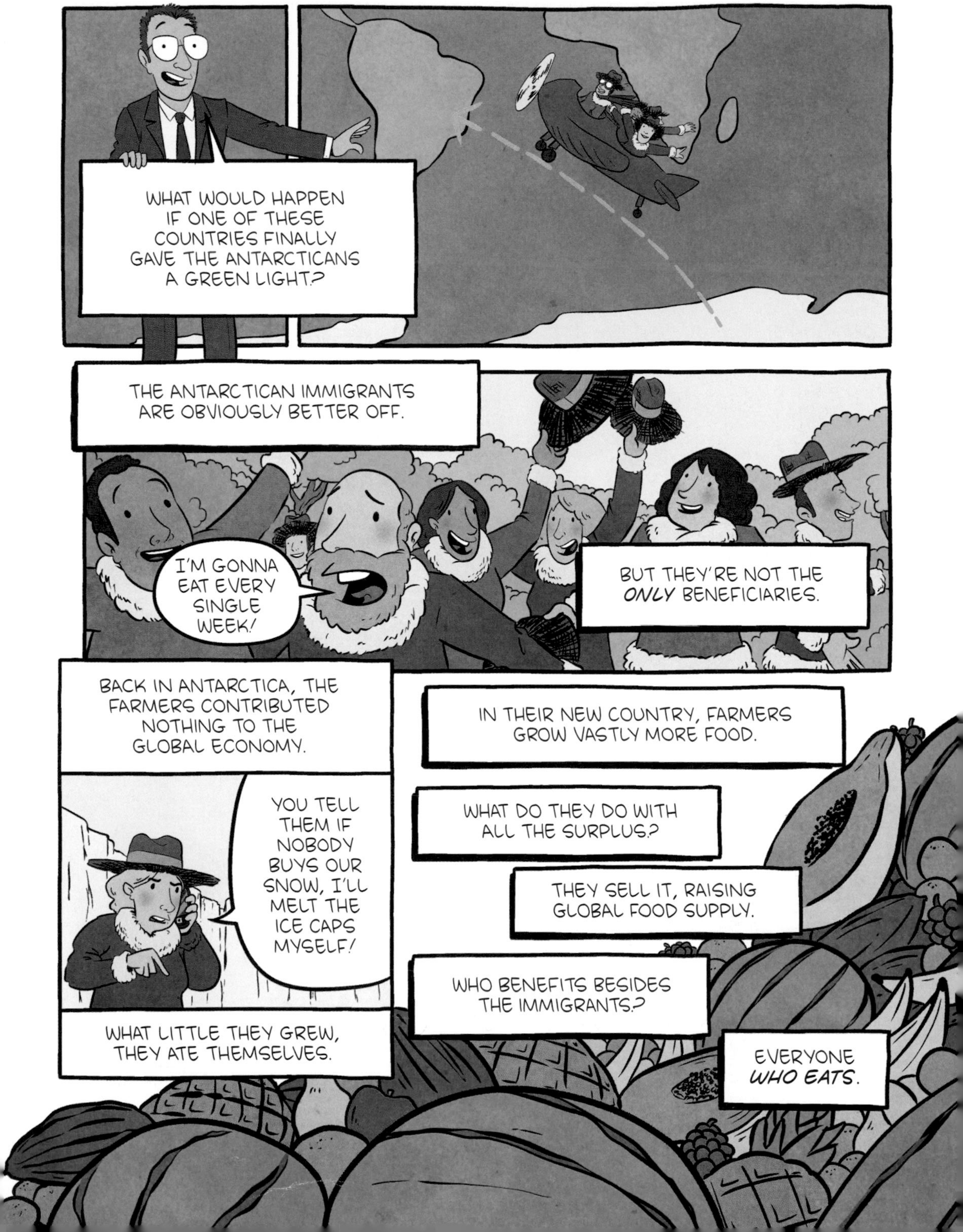

WHAT WOULD HAPPEN IF ONE OF THESE COUNTRIES FINALLY GAVE THE ANTARCTICANS A GREEN LIGHT?
THE ANTARCTICAN IMMIGRANTS ARE OBVIOUSLY BETTER OFF.
I'M GONNA EAT EVERY SINGLE WEEK!
BUT THEY'RE NOT THE *ONLY* BENEFICIARIES.
BACK IN ANTARCTICA, THE FARMERS CONTRIBUTED NOTHING TO THE GLOBAL ECONOMY.
YOU TELL THEM IF NOBODY BUYS OUR SNOW, I'LL MELT THE ICE CAPS MYSELF!
WHAT LITTLE THEY GREW, THEY ATE THEMSELVES.
IN THEIR NEW COUNTRY, FARMERS GROW VASTLY MORE FOOD.
WHAT DO THEY DO WITH ALL THE SURPLUS?
THEY SELL IT, RAISING GLOBAL FOOD SUPPLY.
WHO BENEFITS BESIDES THE IMMIGRANTS?
EVERYONE *WHO EATS*.

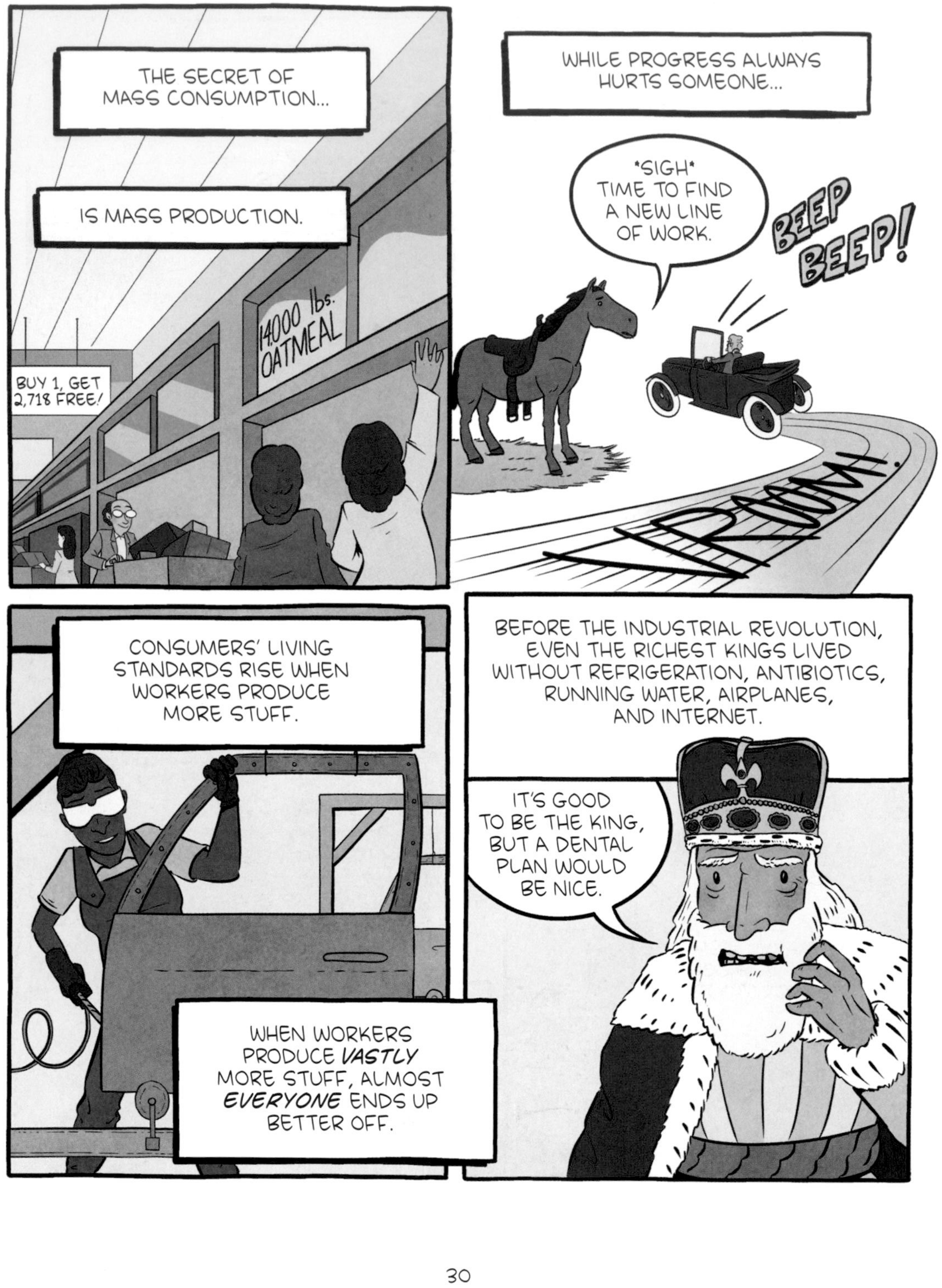
THE SECRET OF MASS CONSUMPTION...
IS MASS PRODUCTION.
14000 lbs. OATMEAL
BUY 1, GET 2,718 FREE!
WHILE PROGRESS ALWAYS HURTS SOMEONE...
SIGH TIME TO FIND A NEW LINE OF WORK.
BEEP BEEP!
VROOM!
CONSUMERS' LIVING STANDARDS RISE WHEN WORKERS PRODUCE MORE STUFF.
WHEN WORKERS PRODUCE *VASTLY* MORE STUFF, ALMOST *EVERYONE* ENDS UP BETTER OFF.
BEFORE THE INDUSTRIAL REVOLUTION, EVEN THE RICHEST KINGS LIVED WITHOUT REFRIGERATION, ANTIBIOTICS, RUNNING WATER, AIRPLANES, AND INTERNET.
IT'S GOOD TO BE THE KING, BUT A DENTAL PLAN WOULD BE NICE.

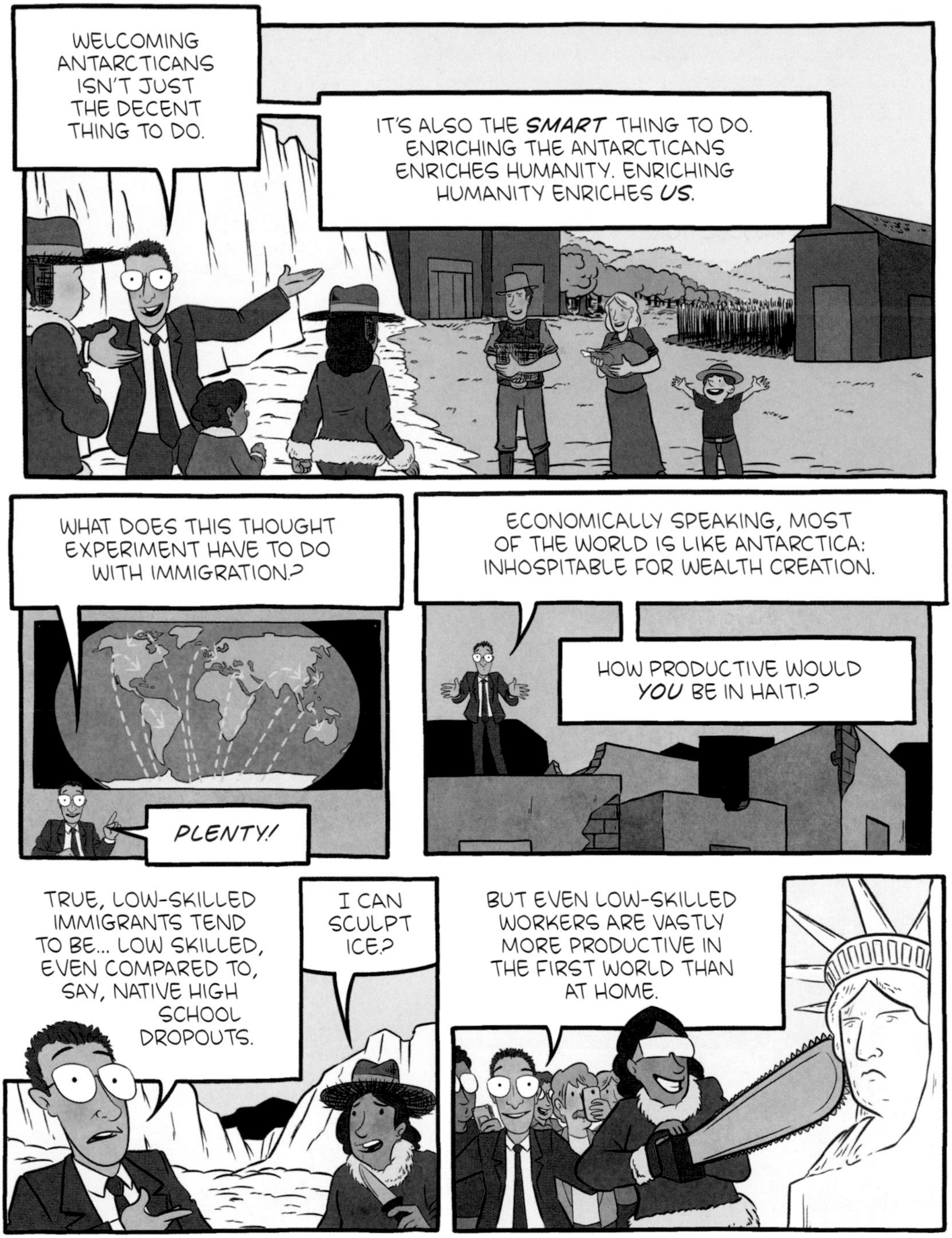
WELCOMING ANTARCTICANS ISN'T JUST THE DECENT THING TO DO.
IT'S ALSO THE **SMART** THING TO DO. ENRICHING THE ANTARCTICANS ENRICHES HUMANITY. ENRICHING HUMANITY ENRICHES **US**.
WHAT DOES THIS THOUGHT EXPERIMENT HAVE TO DO WITH IMMIGRATION?
PLENTY!
ECONOMICALLY SPEAKING, MOST OF THE WORLD IS LIKE ANTARCTICA: INHOSPITABLE FOR WEALTH CREATION.
HOW PRODUCTIVE WOULD **YOU** BE IN HAITI?
TRUE, LOW-SKILLED IMMIGRANTS TEND TO BE... LOW SKILLED, EVEN COMPARED TO, SAY, NATIVE HIGH SCHOOL DROPOUTS.
I CAN SCULPT ICE?
BUT EVEN LOW-SKILLED WORKERS ARE VASTLY MORE PRODUCTIVE IN THE FIRST WORLD THAN AT HOME.

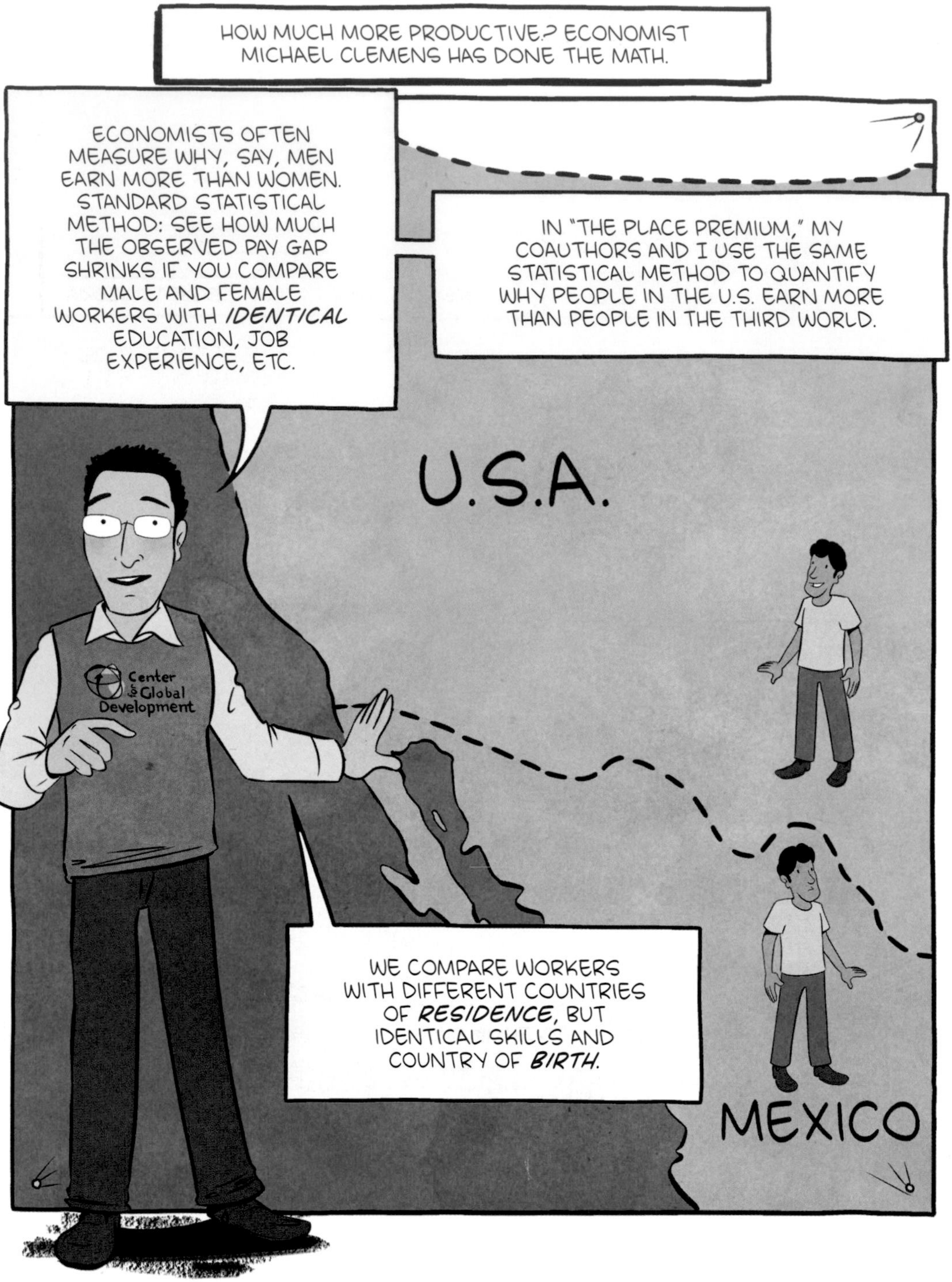
HOW MUCH MORE PRODUCTIVE? ECONOMIST MICHAEL CLEMENS HAS DONE THE MATH.
ECONOMISTS OFTEN MEASURE WHY, SAY, MEN EARN MORE THAN WOMEN. STANDARD STATISTICAL METHOD: SEE HOW MUCH THE OBSERVED PAY GAP SHRINKS IF YOU COMPARE MALE AND FEMALE WORKERS WITH *IDENTICAL* EDUCATION, JOB EXPERIENCE, ETC.
IN "THE PLACE PREMIUM," MY COAUTHORS AND I USE THE SAME STATISTICAL METHOD TO QUANTIFY WHY PEOPLE IN THE U.S. EARN MORE THAN PEOPLE IN THE THIRD WORLD.
U.S.A.
Center for Global Development
WE COMPARE WORKERS WITH DIFFERENT COUNTRIES OF ***RESIDENCE***, BUT IDENTICAL SKILLS AND COUNTRY OF ***BIRTH***.
MEXICO

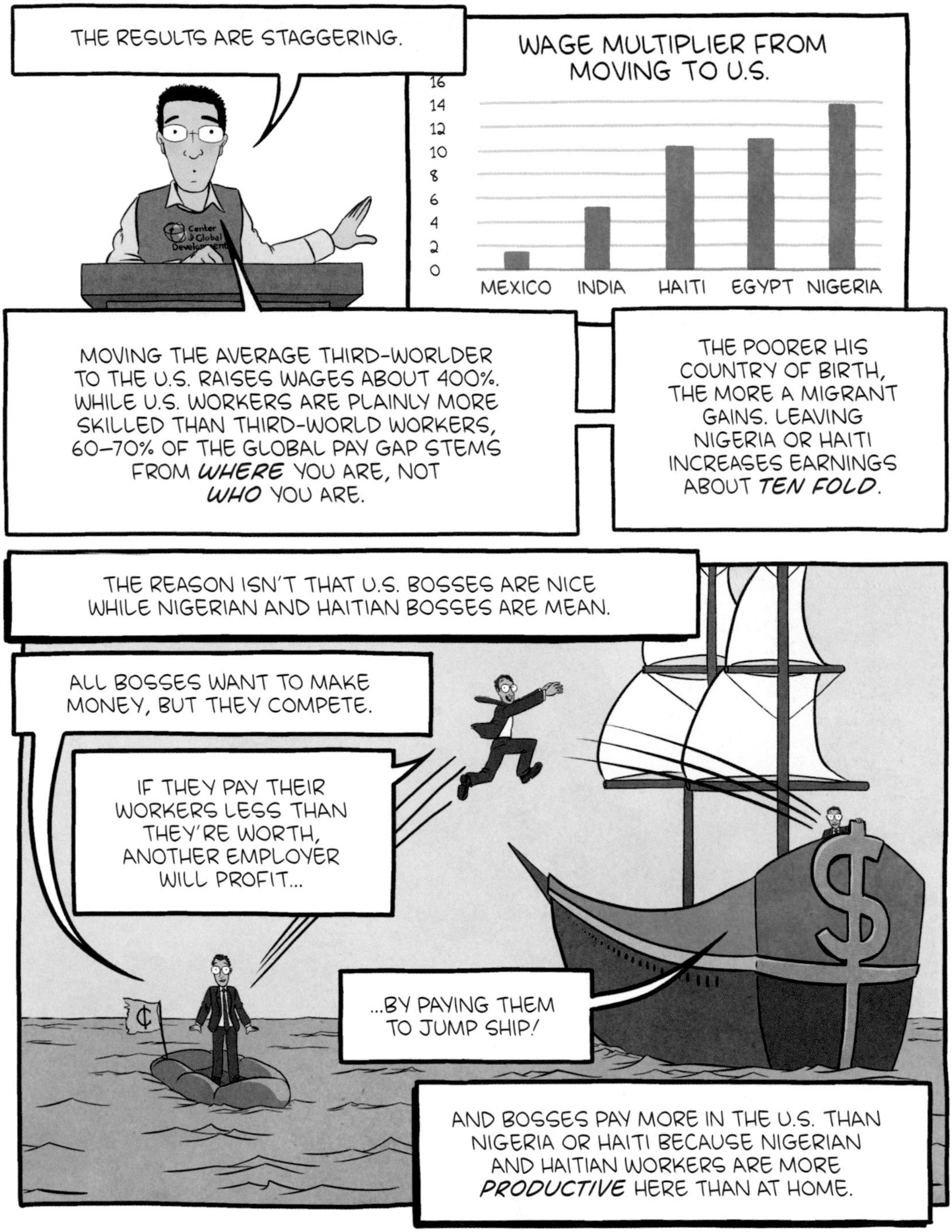
THE RESULTS ARE STAGGERING.
WAGE MULTIPLIER FROM MOVING TO U.S.
16 14 12 10 8 6 4 2 0
MEXICO INDIA HAITI EGYPT NIGERIA
MOVING THE AVERAGE THIRD-WORLDER TO THE U.S. RAISES WAGES ABOUT 400%. WHILE U.S. WORKERS ARE PLAINLY MORE SKILLED THAN THIRD-WORLD WORKERS, 60–70% OF THE GLOBAL PAY GAP STEMS FROM *WHERE* YOU ARE, NOT *WHO* YOU ARE.
THE POORER HIS COUNTRY OF BIRTH, THE MORE A MIGRANT GAINS. LEAVING NIGERIA OR HAITI INCREASES EARNINGS ABOUT *TEN FOLD*.
THE REASON ISN'T THAT U.S. BOSSES ARE NICE WHILE NIGERIAN AND HAITIAN BOSSES ARE MEAN.
ALL BOSSES WANT TO MAKE MONEY, BUT THEY COMPETE.
IF THEY PAY THEIR WORKERS LESS THAN THEY'RE WORTH, ANOTHER EMPLOYER WILL PROFIT...
...BY PAYING THEM TO JUMP SHIP!
AND BOSSES PAY MORE IN THE U.S. THAN NIGERIA OR HAITI BECAUSE NIGERIAN AND HAITIAN WORKERS ARE MORE *PRODUCTIVE* HERE THAN AT HOME.

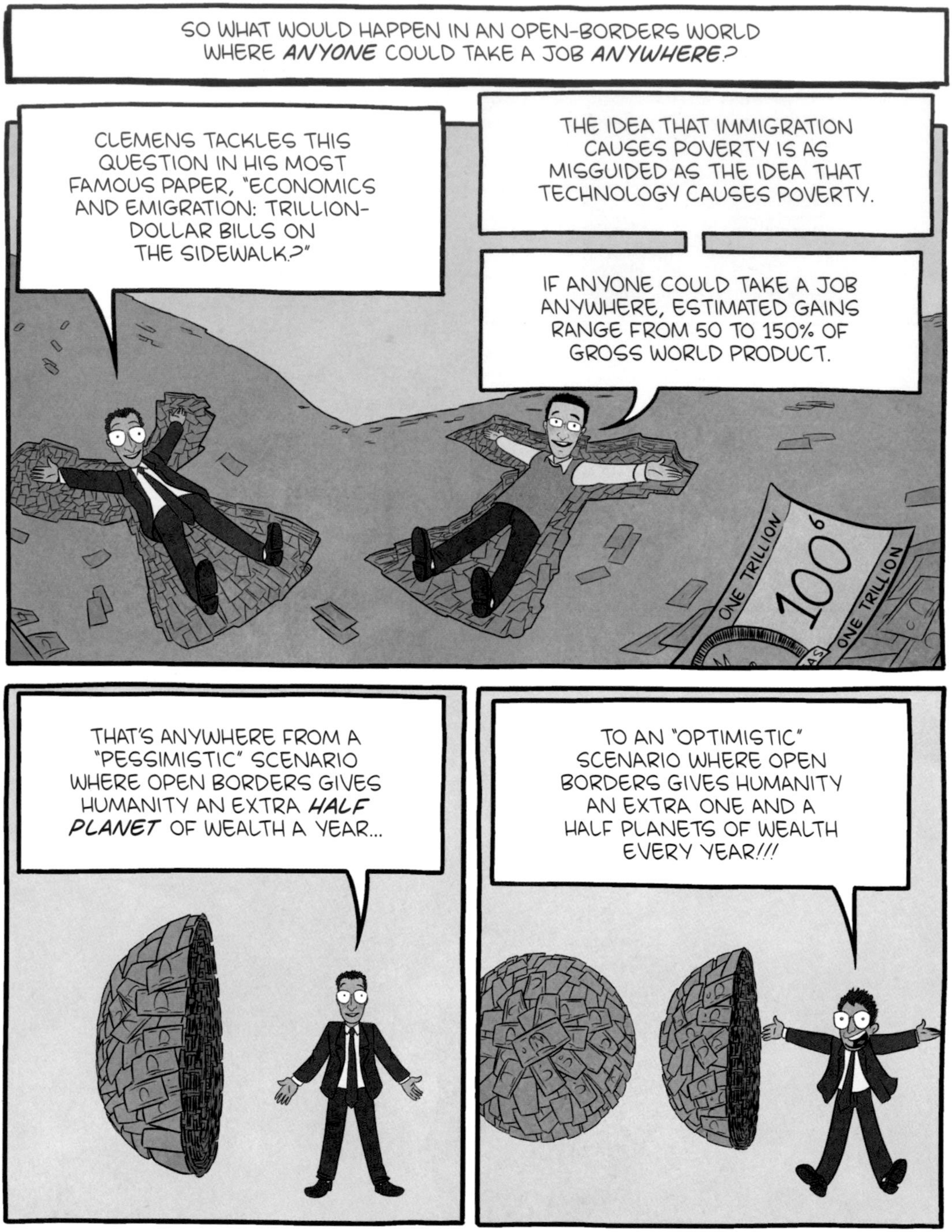
SO WHAT WOULD HAPPEN IN AN OPEN-BORDERS WORLD WHERE *ANYONE* COULD TAKE A JOB *ANYWHERE*?
CLEMENS TACKLES THIS QUESTION IN HIS MOST FAMOUS PAPER, "ECONOMICS AND EMIGRATION: TRILLION-DOLLAR BILLS ON THE SIDEWALK?"
THE IDEA THAT IMMIGRATION CAUSES POVERTY IS AS MISGUIDED AS THE IDEA THAT TECHNOLOGY CAUSES POVERTY.
IF ANYONE COULD TAKE A JOB ANYWHERE, ESTIMATED GAINS RANGE FROM 50 TO 150% OF GROSS WORLD PRODUCT.
ONE TRILLION
ONE TRILLION
THAT'S ANYWHERE FROM A "PESSIMISTIC" SCENARIO WHERE OPEN BORDERS GIVES HUMANITY AN EXTRA *HALF PLANET* OF WEALTH A YEAR...
TO AN "OPTIMISTIC" SCENARIO WHERE OPEN BORDERS GIVES HUMANITY AN EXTRA ONE AND A HALF PLANETS OF WEALTH EVERY YEAR!!!

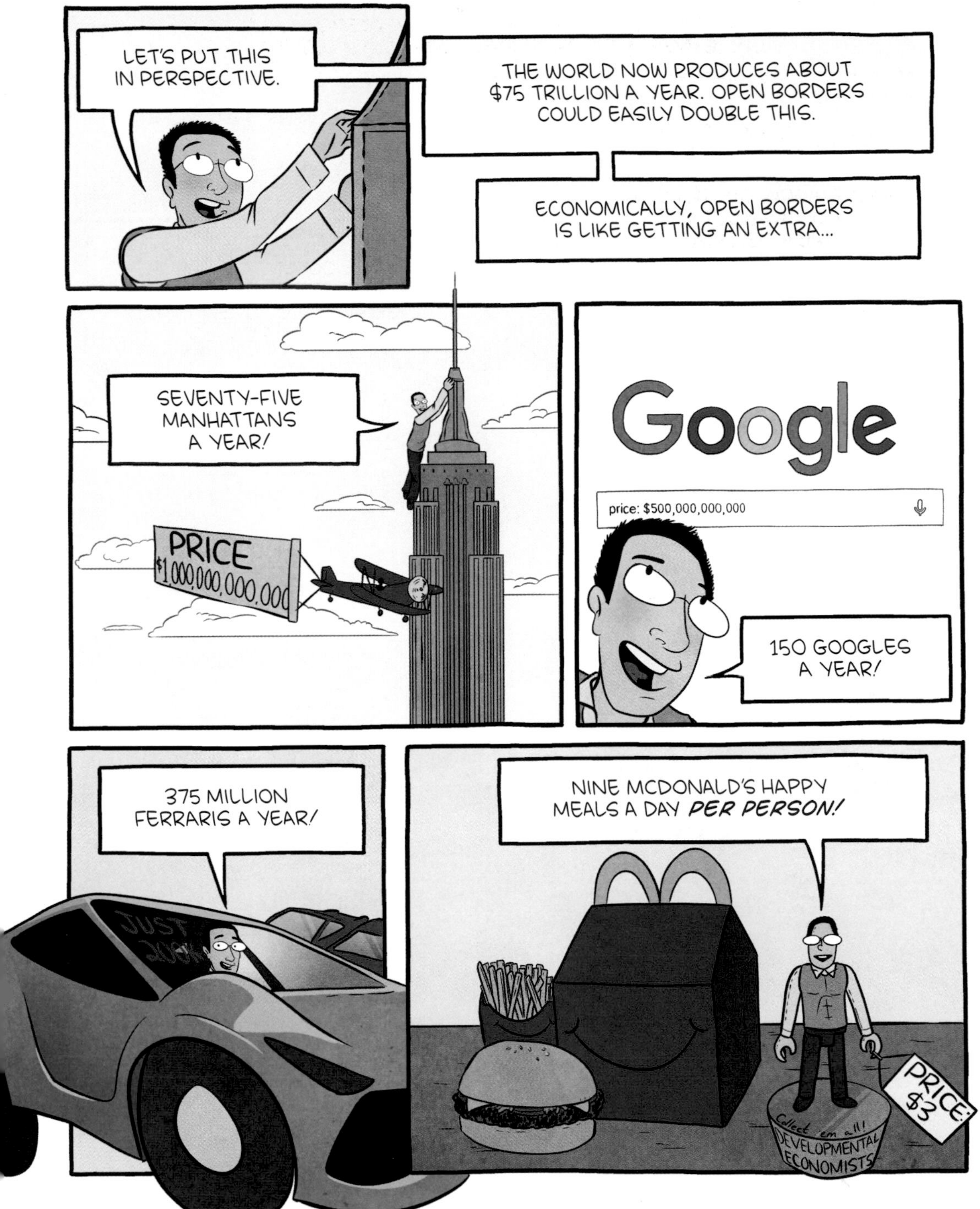
LET'S PUT THIS IN PERSPECTIVE.
THE WORLD NOW PRODUCES ABOUT $75 TRILLION A YEAR. OPEN BORDERS COULD EASILY DOUBLE THIS.
ECONOMICALLY, OPEN BORDERS IS LIKE GETTING AN EXTRA...
SEVENTY-FIVE MANHATTANS A YEAR!
PRICE
$1,000,000,000,000
Google
price: $500,000,000,000
150 GOOGLES A YEAR!
375 MILLION FERRARIS A YEAR!
NINE MCDONALD'S HAPPY MEALS A DAY *PER PERSON!*
PRICE: $3
Collect 'em all!
DEVELOPMENTAL ECONOMISTS

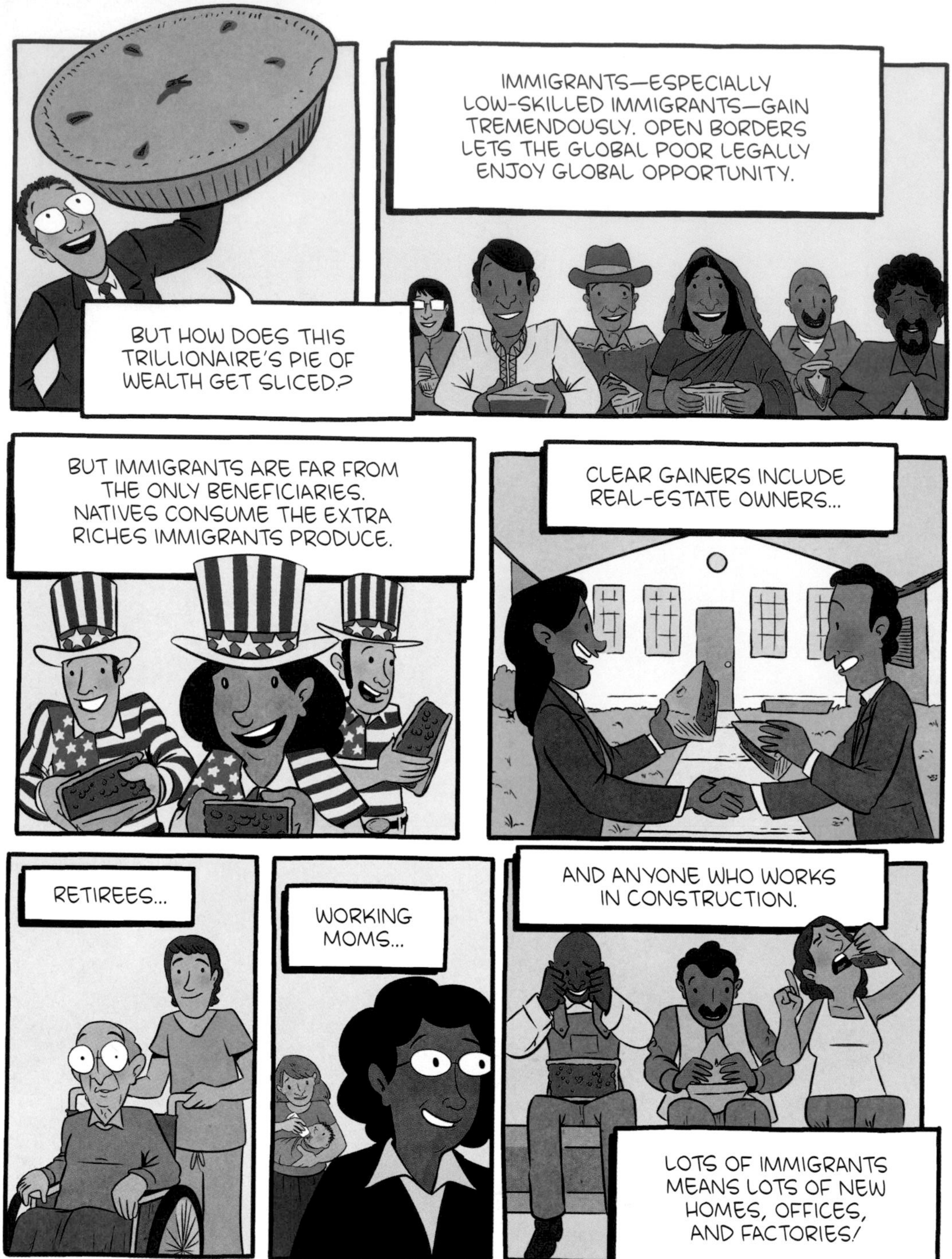
IMMIGRANTS—ESPECIALLY LOW-SKILLED IMMIGRANTS—GAIN TREMENDOUSLY. OPEN BORDERS LETS THE GLOBAL POOR LEGALLY ENJOY GLOBAL OPPORTUNITY.
BUT HOW DOES THIS TRILLIONAIRE'S PIE OF WEALTH GET SLICED?
BUT IMMIGRANTS ARE FAR FROM THE ONLY BENEFICIARIES. NATIVES CONSUME THE EXTRA RICHES IMMIGRANTS PRODUCE.
CLEAR GAINERS INCLUDE REAL-ESTATE OWNERS...
RETIREES...
WORKING MOMS...
AND ANYONE WHO WORKS IN CONSTRUCTION.
LOTS OF IMMIGRANTS MEANS LOTS OF NEW HOMES, OFFICES, AND FACTORIES!

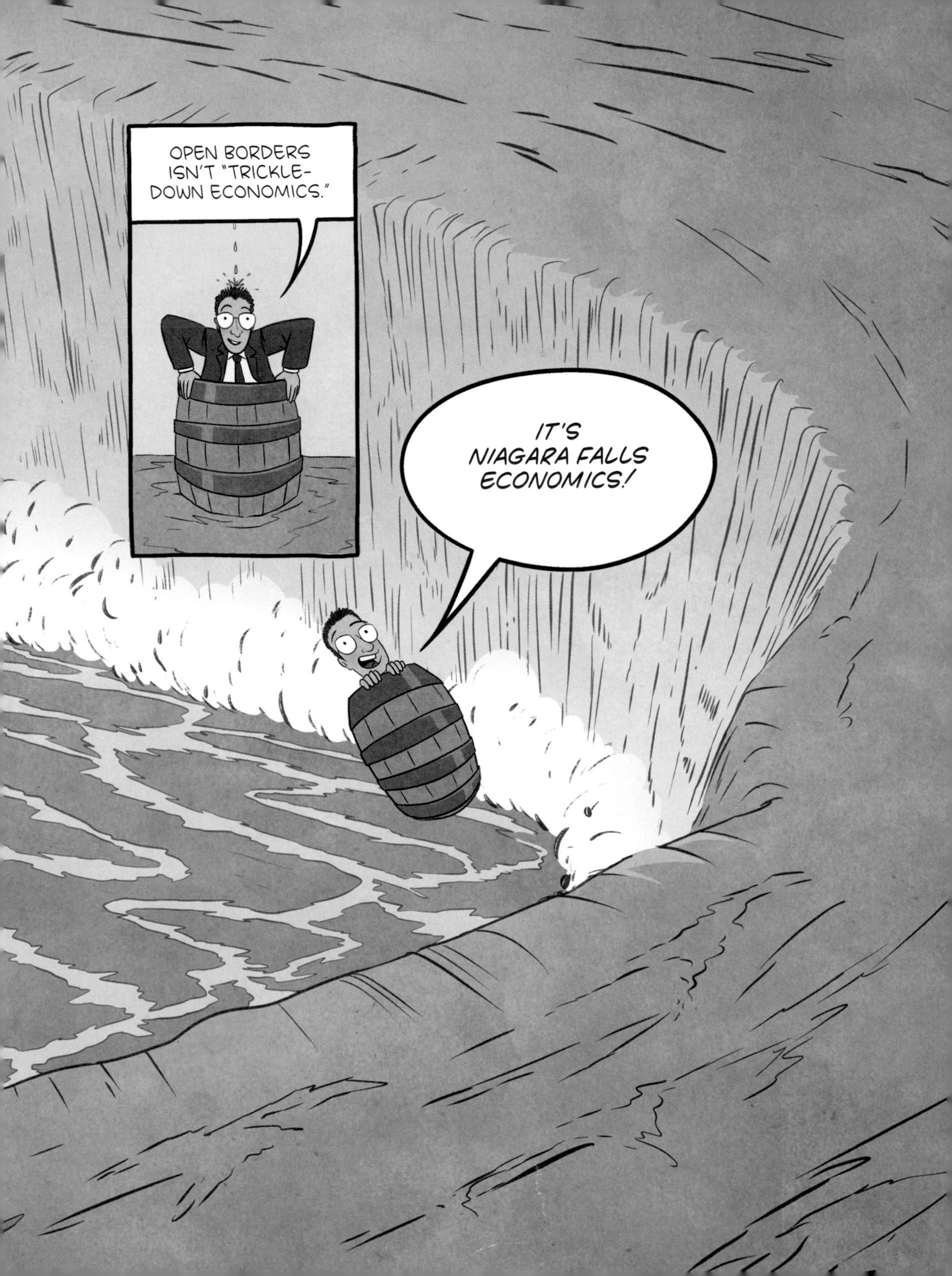
OPEN BORDERS ISN'T "TRICKLE-DOWN ECONOMICS."
IT'S NIAGARA FALLS ECONOMICS!

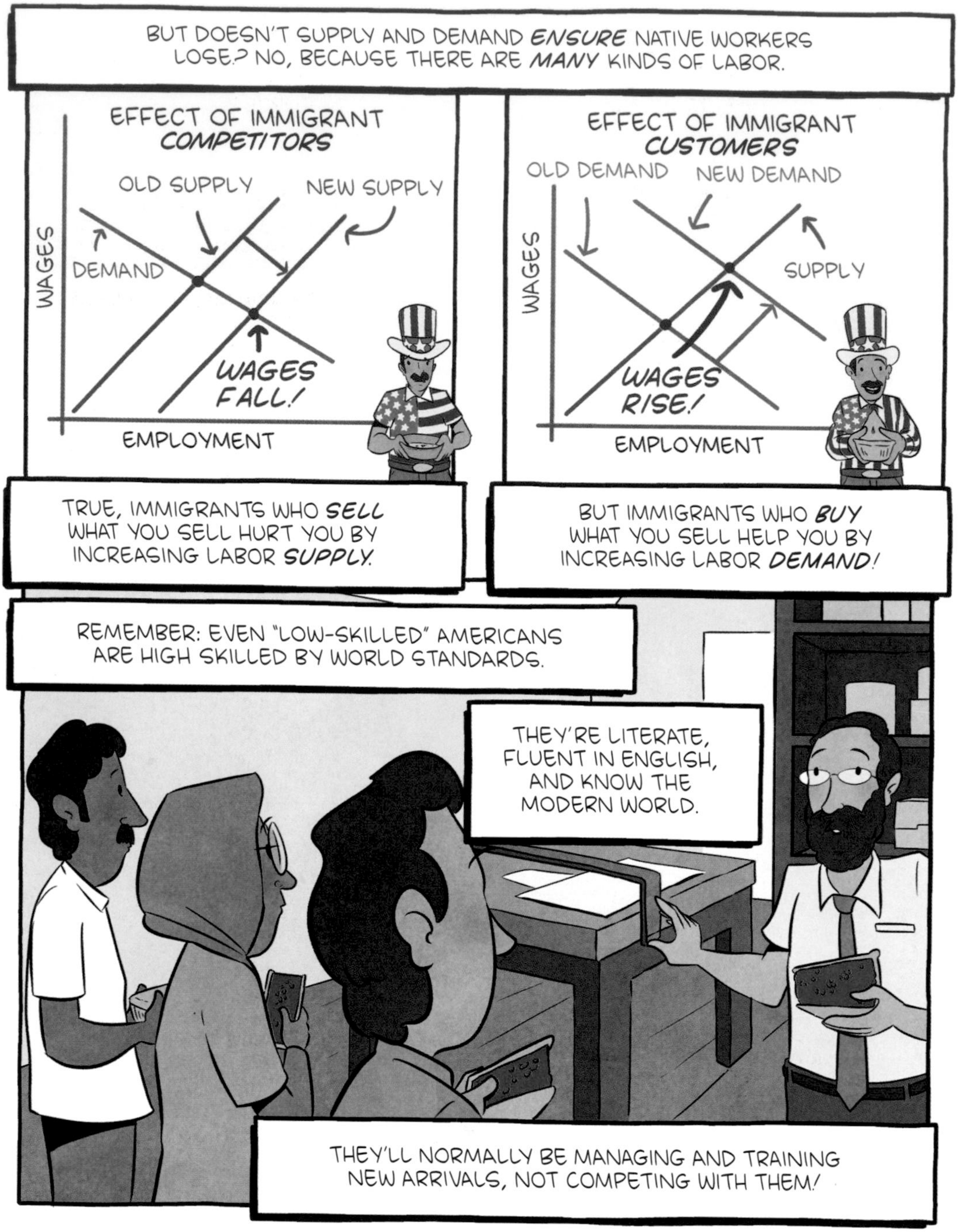

BUT DOESN'T SUPPLY AND DEMAND ENSURE NATIVE WORKERS LOSE? NO, BECAUSE THERE ARE MANY KINDS OF LABOR.
EFFECT OF IMMIGRANT COMPETITORS
OLD SUPPLY
NEW SUPPLY
DEMAND
WAGES
EMPLOYMENT
WAGES FALL!
EFFECT OF IMMIGRANT CUSTOMERS
OLD DEMAND
NEW DEMAND
SUPPLY
WAGES
EMPLOYMENT
WAGES RISE!
TRUE, IMMIGRANTS WHO SELL WHAT YOU SELL HURT YOU BY INCREASING LABOR SUPPLY.
BUT IMMIGRANTS WHO BUY WHAT YOU SELL HELP YOU BY INCREASING LABOR DEMAND!
REMEMBER: EVEN "LOW-SKILLED" AMERICANS ARE HIGH SKILLED BY WORLD STANDARDS.
THEY'RE LITERATE, FLUENT IN ENGLISH, AND KNOW THE MODERN WORLD.
THEY'LL NORMALLY BE MANAGING AND TRAINING NEW ARRIVALS, NOT COMPETING WITH THEM!

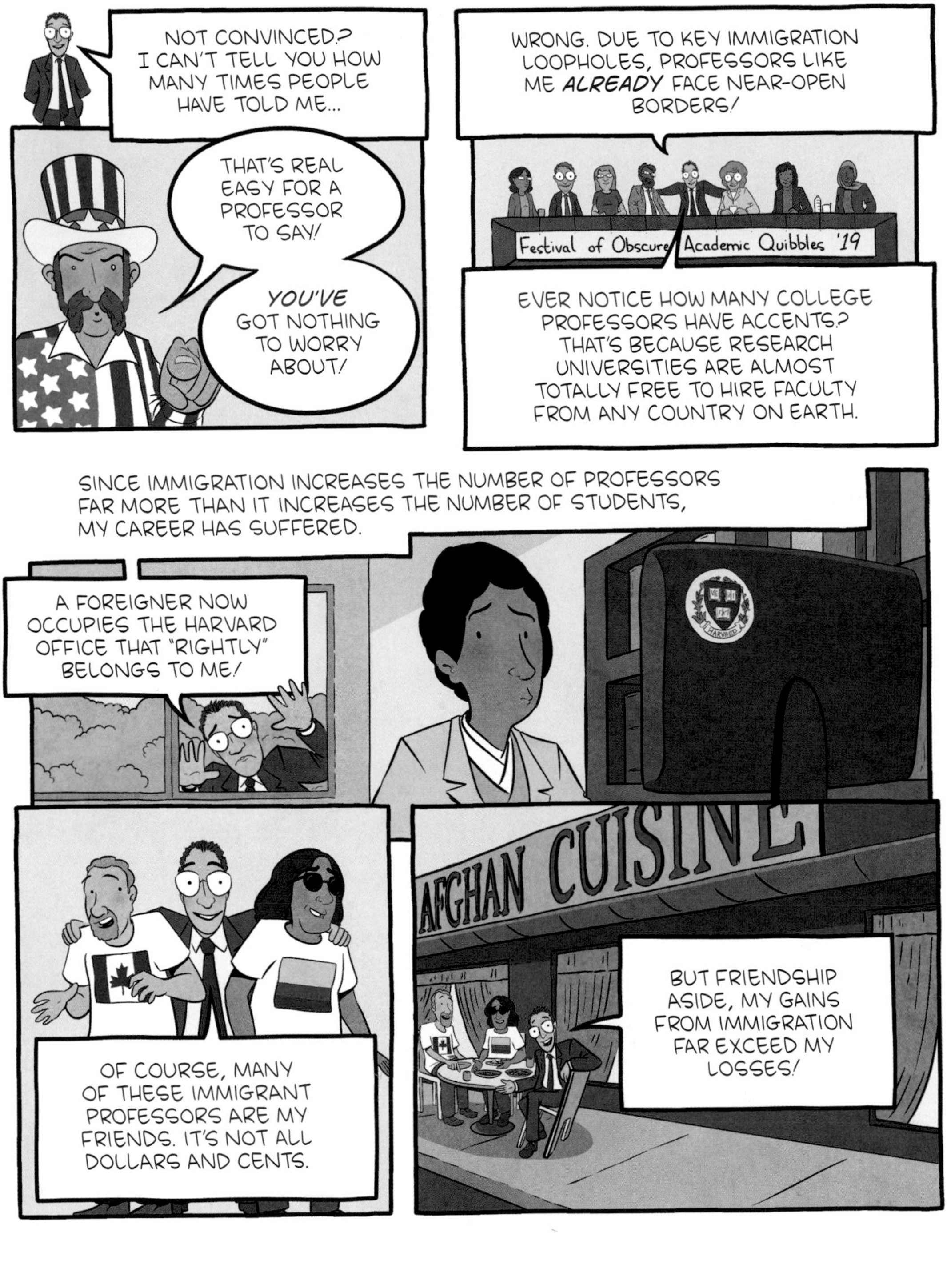
NOT CONVINCED? I CAN'T TELL YOU HOW MANY TIMES PEOPLE HAVE TOLD ME...
THAT'S REAL EASY FOR A PROFESSOR TO SAY!
YOU'VE GOT NOTHING TO WORRY ABOUT!
WRONG. DUE TO KEY IMMIGRATION LOOPHOLES, PROFESSORS LIKE ME ALREADY FACE NEAR-OPEN BORDERS!
Festival of Obscure Academic Quibbles '19
EVER NOTICE HOW MANY COLLEGE PROFESSORS HAVE ACCENTS? THAT'S BECAUSE RESEARCH UNIVERSITIES ARE ALMOST TOTALLY FREE TO HIRE FACULTY FROM ANY COUNTRY ON EARTH.
SINCE IMMIGRATION INCREASES THE NUMBER OF PROFESSORS FAR MORE THAN IT INCREASES THE NUMBER OF STUDENTS, MY CAREER HAS SUFFERED.
A FOREIGNER NOW OCCUPIES THE HARVARD OFFICE THAT "RIGHTLY" BELONGS TO ME!
HARVARD
OF COURSE, MANY OF THESE IMMIGRANT PROFESSORS ARE MY FRIENDS. IT'S NOT ALL DOLLARS AND CENTS.
AFGHAN CUISINE
BUT FRIENDSHIP ASIDE, MY GAINS FROM IMMIGRATION FAR EXCEED MY LOSSES!

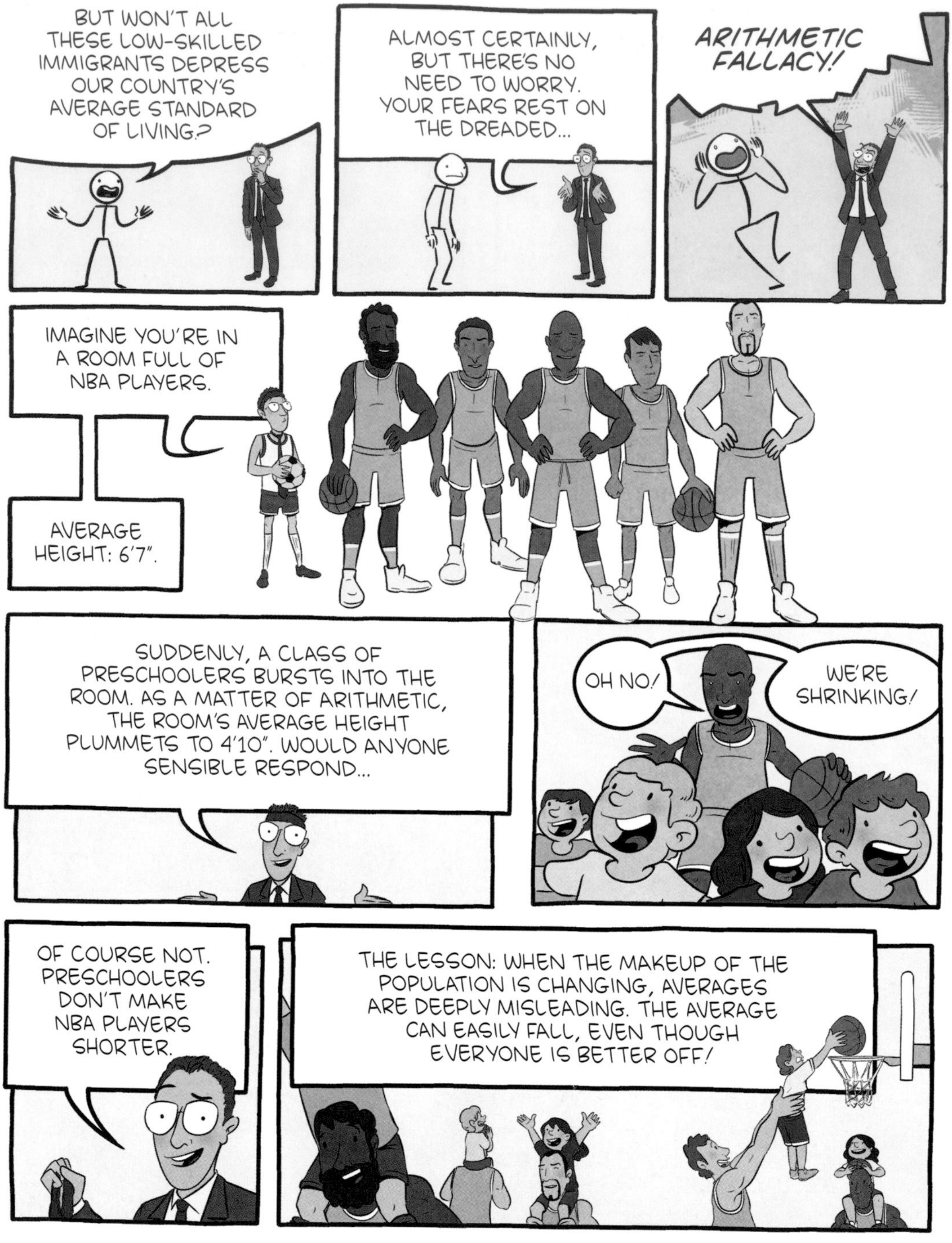
BUT WON'T ALL THESE LOW-SKILLED IMMIGRANTS DEPRESS OUR COUNTRY'S AVERAGE STANDARD OF LIVING?
ALMOST CERTAINLY, BUT THERE'S NO NEED TO WORRY. YOUR FEARS REST ON THE DREADED...
ARITHMETIC FALLACY!
IMAGINE YOU'RE IN A ROOM FULL OF NBA PLAYERS.
AVERAGE HEIGHT: 6'7".
SUDDENLY, A CLASS OF PRESCHOOLERS BURSTS INTO THE ROOM. AS A MATTER OF ARITHMETIC, THE ROOM'S AVERAGE HEIGHT PLUMMETS TO 4'10". WOULD ANYONE SENSIBLE RESPOND...
OH NO!
WE'RE SHRINKING!
OF COURSE NOT. PRESCHOOLERS DON'T MAKE NBA PLAYERS SHORTER.
THE LESSON: WHEN THE MAKEUP OF THE POPULATION IS CHANGING, AVERAGES ARE DEEPLY MISLEADING. THE AVERAGE CAN EASILY FALL, EVEN THOUGH EVERYONE IS BETTER OFF!

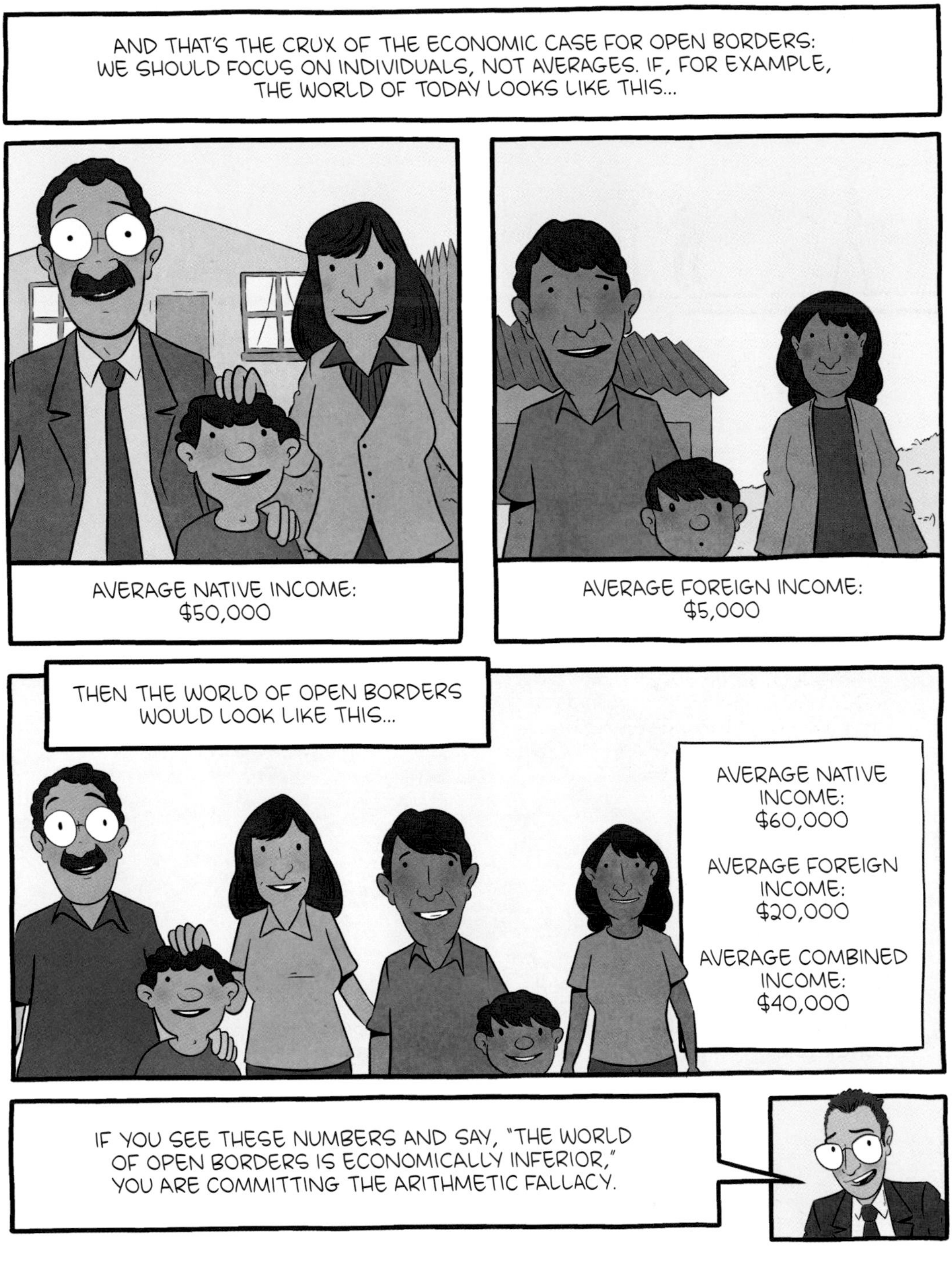
AND THAT'S THE CRUX OF THE ECONOMIC CASE FOR OPEN BORDERS: WE SHOULD FOCUS ON INDIVIDUALS, NOT AVERAGES. IF, FOR EXAMPLE, THE WORLD OF TODAY LOOKS LIKE THIS...
AVERAGE NATIVE INCOME: $50,000
AVERAGE FOREIGN INCOME: $5,000
THEN THE WORLD OF OPEN BORDERS WOULD LOOK LIKE THIS...
AVERAGE NATIVE INCOME: $60,000
AVERAGE FOREIGN INCOME: $20,000
AVERAGE COMBINED INCOME: $40,000
IF YOU SEE THESE NUMBERS AND SAY, "THE WORLD OF OPEN BORDERS IS ECONOMICALLY INFERIOR," YOU ARE COMMITTING THE ARITHMETIC FALLACY.

WHAT WOULD OPEN BORDERS EVEN LOOK LIKE? IS IT REALLY PHYSICALLY POSSIBLE FOR MIGRATION TO MAKE HUMANITY TRILLIONS OF DOLLARS RICHER?

THE CLOSEST MODERN PARALLEL IS THE MASSIVE MIGRATION-FUELED GROWTH *WITHIN* CHINA AND INDIA OVER THE LAST FEW DECADES.

IN 1976, CHINA'S GDP WAS A WRETCHED $504 BILLION; INDIA'S JUST $348 BILLION.

NOW, CHINA EXCEEDS $10 TRILLION. INDIA, $2 TRILLION.

HOW DOES THIS PROSPERITY EXPLOSION HAPPEN? MARKET REFORMS GOT THE BALL ROLLING.

CAPITALIST ROAD

BUT THE BALL COULDN'T HAVE ROLLED VERY FAR IF HUNDREDS OF MILLIONS OF FARMERS HADN'T MOVED TO CITIES TO TAKE ADVANTAGE OF NEW OPPORTUNITIES.

CHINESE AND INDIAN CITIES DIDN'T JUST GROW OVER THE LAST FOUR DECADES; THEY MULTIPLIED.

MIGRANTS MAKE PROSPERITY. YOU CAN SEE IT FROM SPACE!

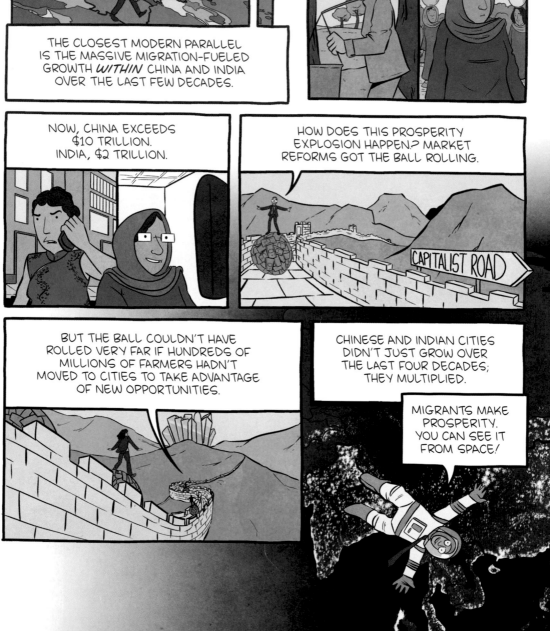

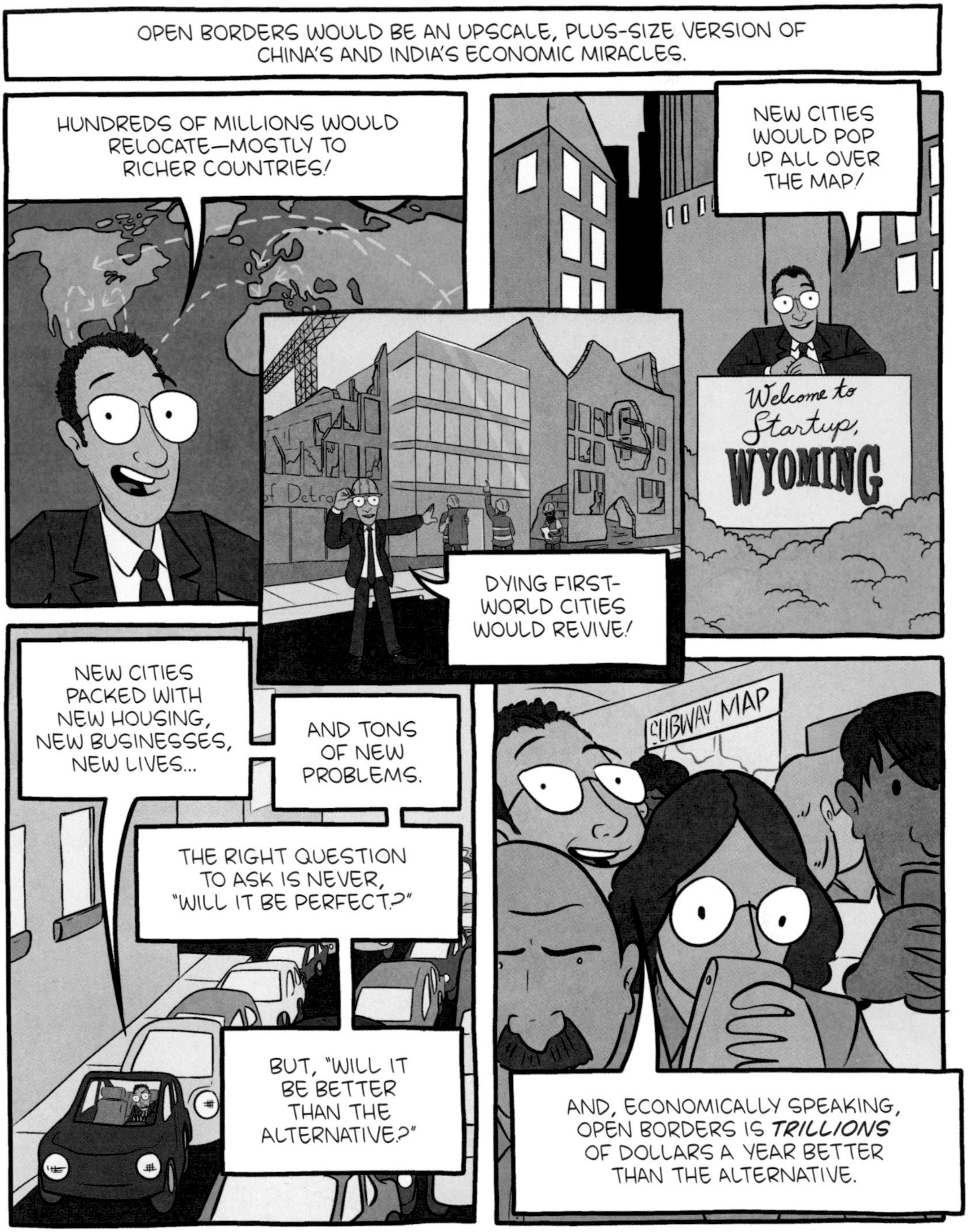
OPEN BORDERS WOULD BE AN UPSCALE, PLUS-SIZE VERSION OF CHINA'S AND INDIA'S ECONOMIC MIRACLES.
HUNDREDS OF MILLIONS WOULD RELOCATE—MOSTLY TO RICHER COUNTRIES!
DYING FIRST-WORLD CITIES WOULD REVIVE!
NEW CITIES WOULD POP UP ALL OVER THE MAP!
Welcome to Startup, WYOMING
NEW CITIES PACKED WITH NEW HOUSING, NEW BUSINESSES, NEW LIVES...
AND TONS OF NEW PROBLEMS.
THE RIGHT QUESTION TO ASK IS NEVER, "WILL IT BE PERFECT?"
BUT, "WILL IT BE BETTER THAN THE ALTERNATIVE?"
SUBWAY MAP
AND, ECONOMICALLY SPEAKING, OPEN BORDERS IS *TRILLIONS* OF DOLLARS A YEAR BETTER THAN THE ALTERNATIVE.

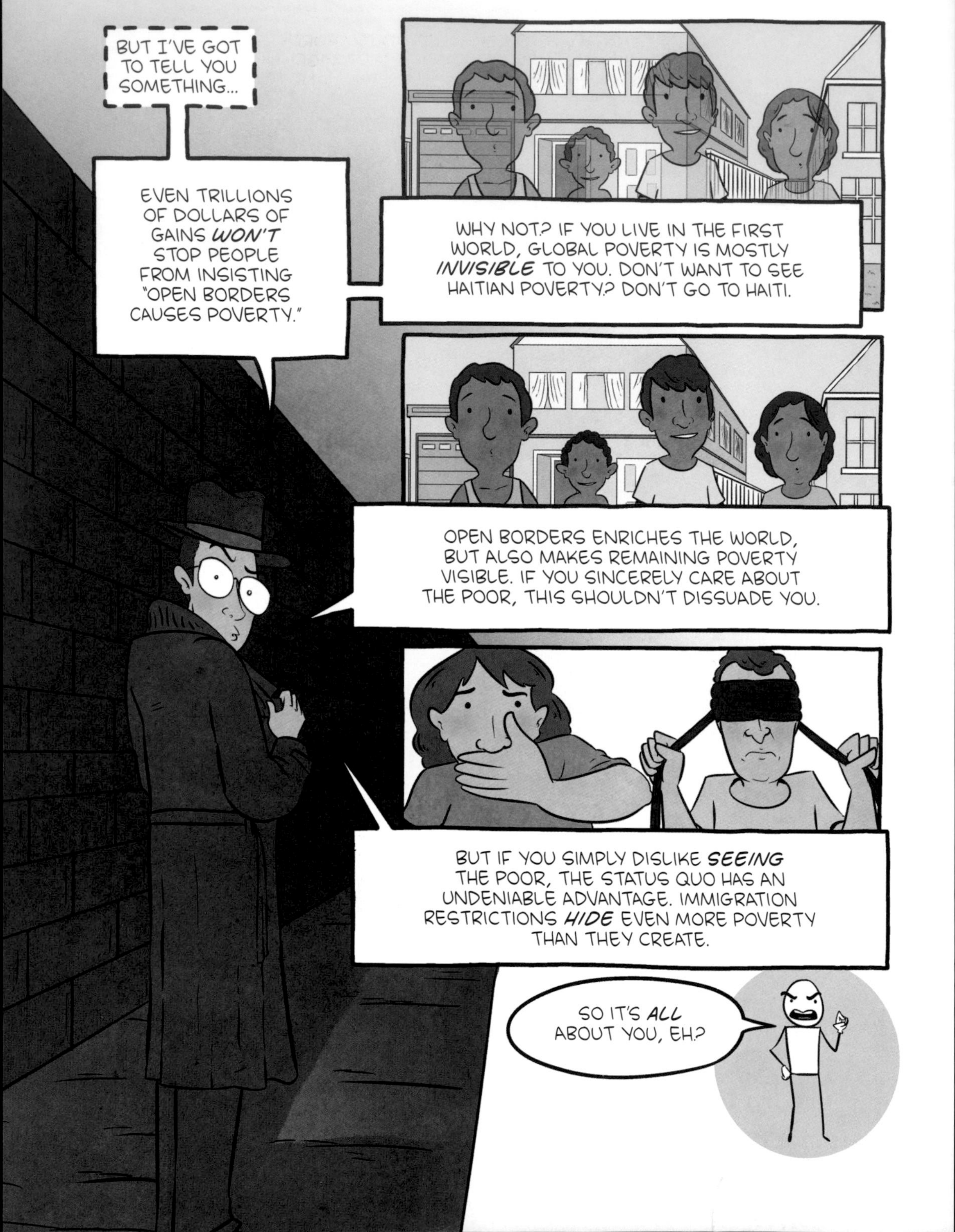

BUT I'VE GOT TO TELL YOU SOMETHING...
EVEN TRILLIONS OF DOLLARS OF GAINS *WON'T* STOP PEOPLE FROM INSISTING "OPEN BORDERS CAUSES POVERTY."
WHY NOT? IF YOU LIVE IN THE FIRST WORLD, GLOBAL POVERTY IS MOSTLY *INVISIBLE* TO YOU. DON'T WANT TO SEE HAITIAN POVERTY? DON'T GO TO HAITI.
OPEN BORDERS ENRICHES THE WORLD, BUT ALSO MAKES REMAINING POVERTY VISIBLE. IF YOU SINCERELY CARE ABOUT THE POOR, THIS SHOULDN'T DISSUADE YOU.
BUT IF YOU SIMPLY DISLIKE *SEEING* THE POOR, THE STATUS QUO HAS AN UNDENIABLE ADVANTAGE. IMMIGRATION RESTRICTIONS *HIDE* EVEN MORE POVERTY THAN THEY CREATE.
SO IT'S *ALL* ABOUT YOU, EH?

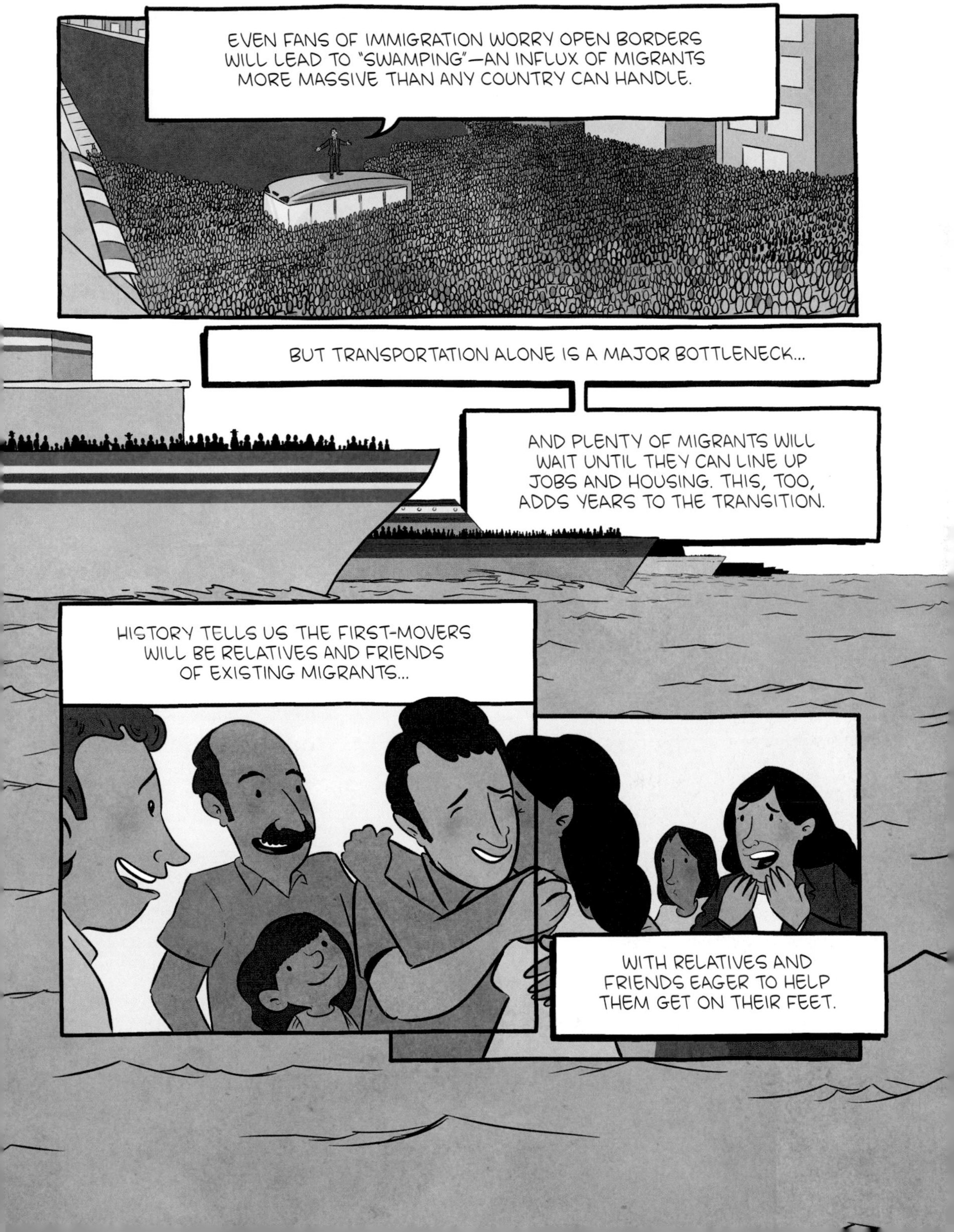
EVEN FANS OF IMMIGRATION WORRY OPEN BORDERS WILL LEAD TO "SWAMPING"—AN INFLUX OF MIGRANTS MORE MASSIVE THAN ANY COUNTRY CAN HANDLE.
BUT TRANSPORTATION ALONE IS A MAJOR BOTTLENECK...
AND PLENTY OF MIGRANTS WILL WAIT UNTIL THEY CAN LINE UP JOBS AND HOUSING. THIS, TOO, ADDS YEARS TO THE TRANSITION.
HISTORY TELLS US THE FIRST-MOVERS WILL BE RELATIVES AND FRIENDS OF EXISTING MIGRANTS...
WITH RELATIVES AND FRIENDS EAGER TO HELP THEM GET ON THEIR FEET.

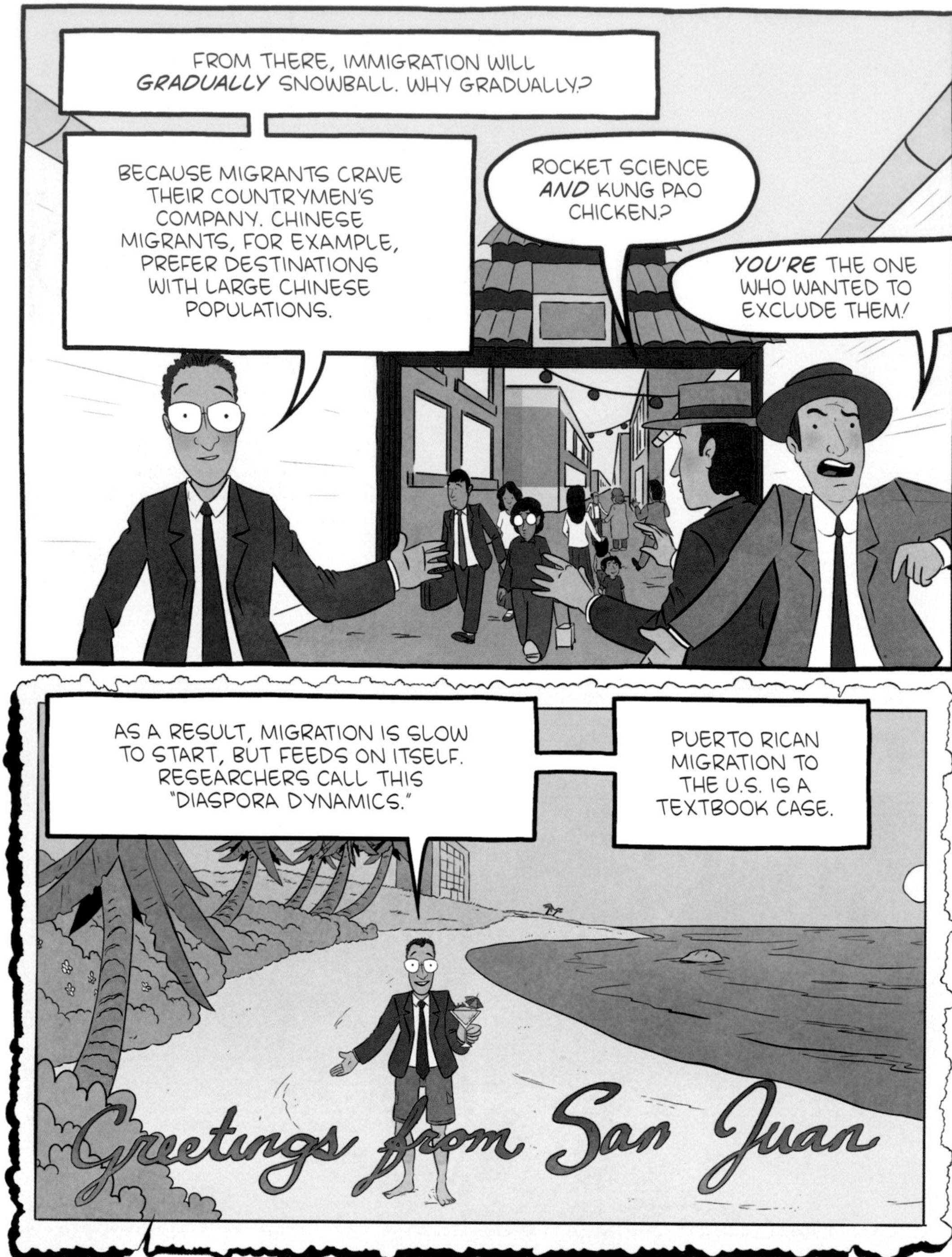
FROM THERE, IMMIGRATION WILL *GRADUALLY* SNOWBALL. WHY GRADUALLY?
BECAUSE MIGRANTS CRAVE THEIR COUNTRYMEN'S COMPANY. CHINESE MIGRANTS, FOR EXAMPLE, PREFER DESTINATIONS WITH LARGE CHINESE POPULATIONS.
ROCKET SCIENCE *AND* KUNG PAO CHICKEN?
YOU'RE THE ONE WHO WANTED TO EXCLUDE THEM!
AS A RESULT, MIGRATION IS SLOW TO START, BUT FEEDS ON ITSELF. RESEARCHERS CALL THIS "DIASPORA DYNAMICS."
PUERTO RICAN MIGRATION TO THE U.S. IS A TEXTBOOK CASE.
Greetings from San Juan

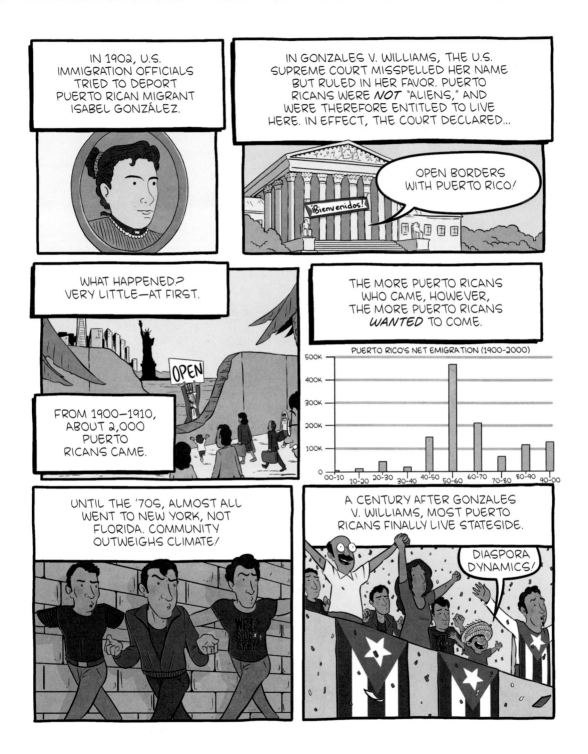

IN 1902, U.S. IMMIGRATION OFFICIALS TRIED TO DEPORT PUERTO RICAN MIGRANT ISABEL GONZÁLEZ.

IN GONZALES V. WILLIAMS, THE U.S. SUPREME COURT MISSPELLED HER NAME BUT RULED IN HER FAVOR. PUERTO RICANS WERE *NOT* "ALIENS," AND WERE THEREFORE ENTITLED TO LIVE HERE. IN EFFECT, THE COURT DECLARED...

¡Bienvenidos!

OPEN BORDERS WITH PUERTO RICO!

WHAT HAPPENED? VERY LITTLE—AT FIRST.

THE MORE PUERTO RICANS WHO CAME, HOWEVER, THE MORE PUERTO RICANS *WANTED* TO COME.

OPEN

FROM 1900–1910, ABOUT 2,000 PUERTO RICANS CAME.

PUERTO RICO'S NET EMIGRATION (1900–2000)

500K
400K
300K
200K
100K
0

00-10 10-20 20-30 30-40 40-50 50-60 60-70 70-80 80-90 90-00

UNTIL THE '70S, ALMOST ALL WENT TO NEW YORK, NOT FLORIDA. COMMUNITY OUTWEIGHS CLIMATE!

WEST SIDE STORY

A CENTURY AFTER GONZALES V. WILLIAMS, MOST PUERTO RICANS FINALLY LIVE STATESIDE.

DIASPORA DYNAMICS!

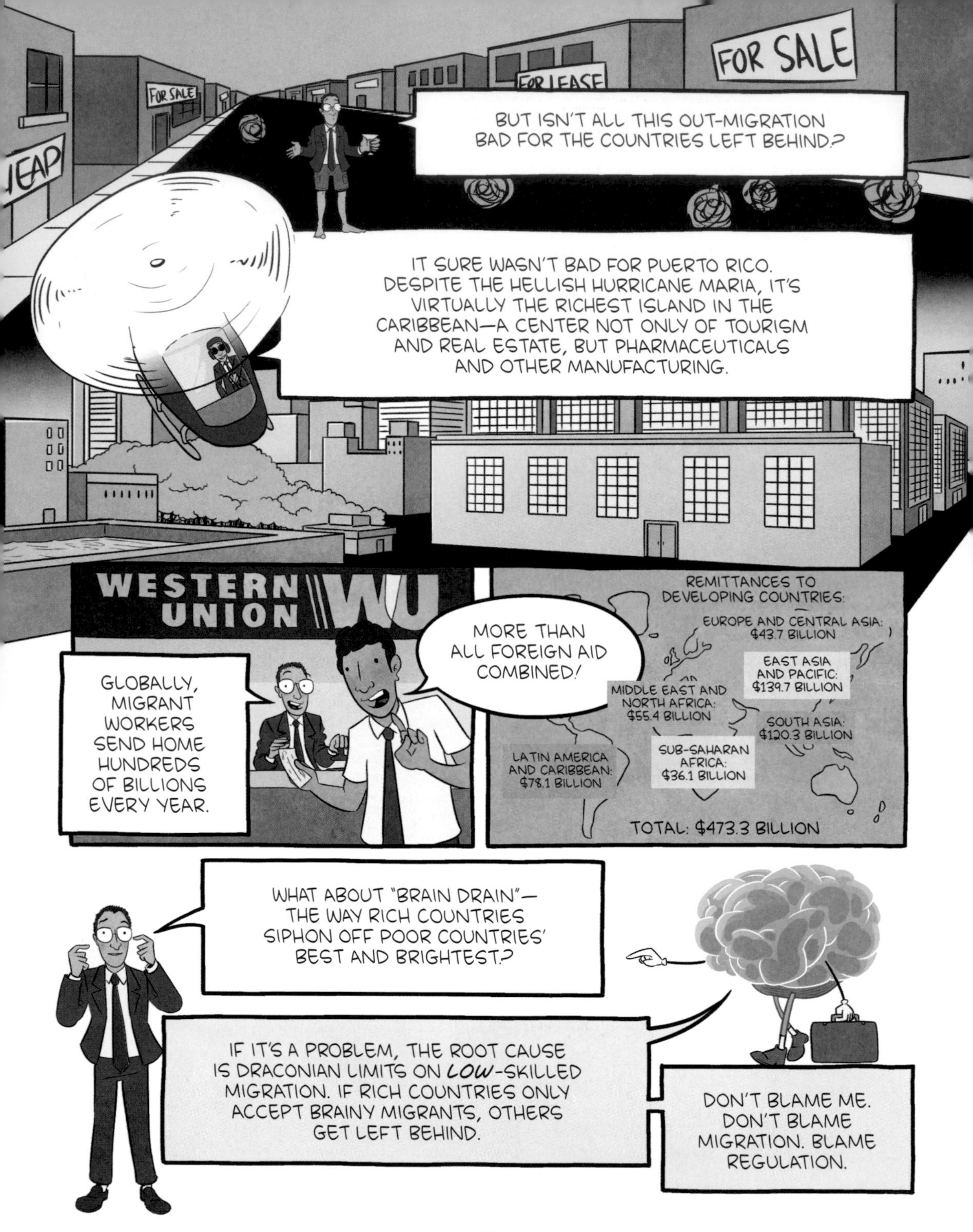
FOR SALE
FOR LEASE
FOR SALE
BUT ISN'T ALL THIS OUT-MIGRATION BAD FOR THE COUNTRIES LEFT BEHIND?
IT SURE WASN'T BAD FOR PUERTO RICO. DESPITE THE HELLISH HURRICANE MARIA, IT'S VIRTUALLY THE RICHEST ISLAND IN THE CARIBBEAN—A CENTER NOT ONLY OF TOURISM AND REAL ESTATE, BUT PHARMACEUTICALS AND OTHER MANUFACTURING.
WESTERN UNION
WU
GLOBALLY, MIGRANT WORKERS SEND HOME HUNDREDS OF BILLIONS EVERY YEAR.
MORE THAN ALL FOREIGN AID COMBINED!
REMITTANCES TO DEVELOPING COUNTRIES:
EUROPE AND CENTRAL ASIA: $43.7 BILLION
EAST ASIA AND PACIFIC: $139.7 BILLION
MIDDLE EAST AND NORTH AFRICA: $55.4 BILLION
SOUTH ASIA: $120.3 BILLION
LATIN AMERICA AND CARIBBEAN: $78.1 BILLION
SUB-SAHARAN AFRICA: $36.1 BILLION
TOTAL: $473.3 BILLION
WHAT ABOUT "BRAIN DRAIN"—THE WAY RICH COUNTRIES SIPHON OFF POOR COUNTRIES' BEST AND BRIGHTEST?
IF IT'S A PROBLEM, THE ROOT CAUSE IS DRACONIAN LIMITS ON *LOW*-SKILLED MIGRATION. IF RICH COUNTRIES ONLY ACCEPT BRAINY MIGRANTS, OTHERS GET LEFT BEHIND.
DON'T BLAME ME. DON'T BLAME MIGRATION. BLAME REGULATION.

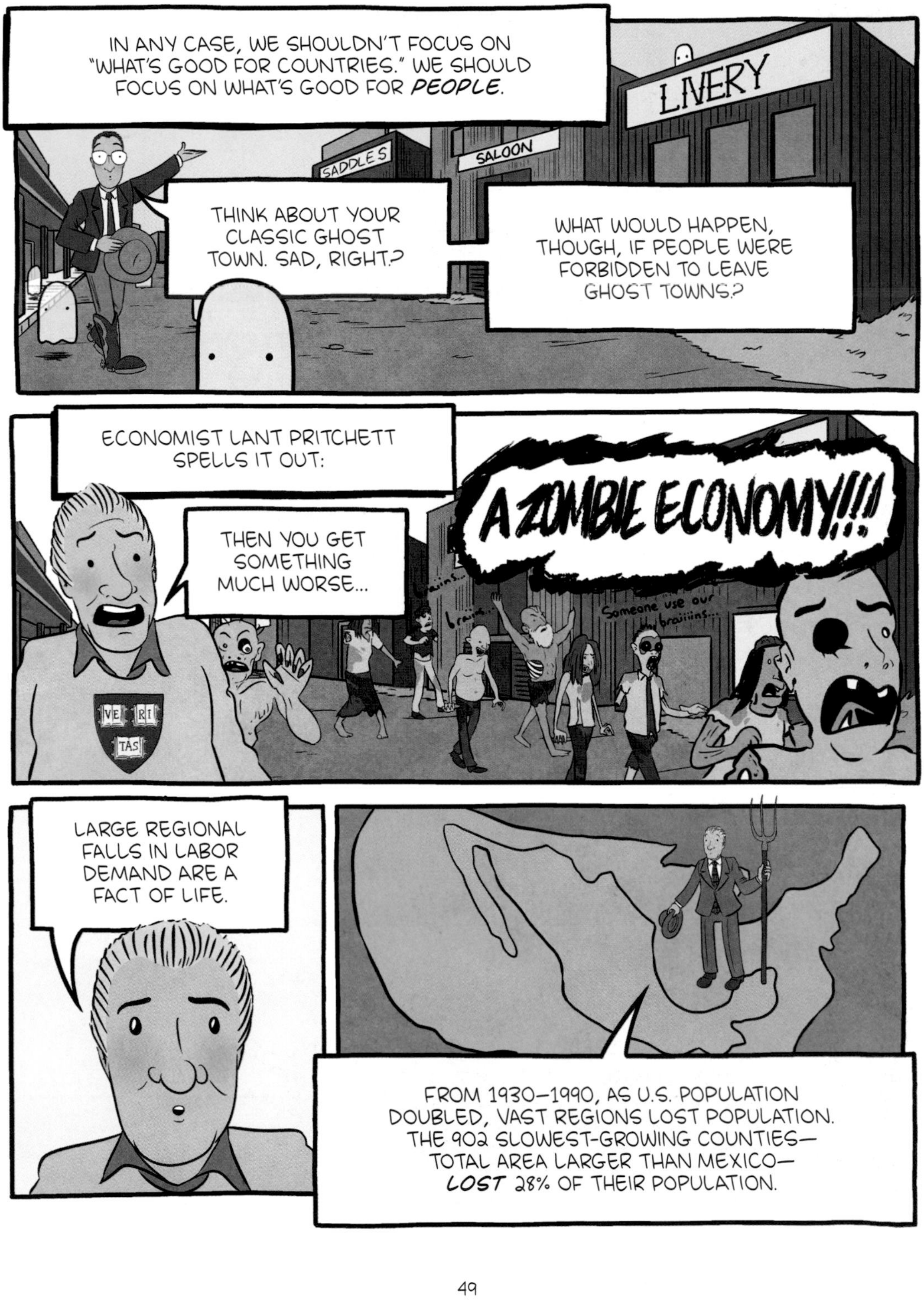
IN ANY CASE, WE SHOULDN'T FOCUS ON "WHAT'S GOOD FOR COUNTRIES." WE SHOULD FOCUS ON WHAT'S GOOD FOR *PEOPLE*.
LIVERY
SADDLES
SALOON
THINK ABOUT YOUR CLASSIC GHOST TOWN. SAD, RIGHT?
WHAT WOULD HAPPEN, THOUGH, IF PEOPLE WERE FORBIDDEN TO LEAVE GHOST TOWNS?
ECONOMIST LANT PRITCHETT SPELLS IT OUT:
THEN YOU GET SOMETHING MUCH WORSE...
A ZOMBIE ECONOMY!!!!
Someone use our braiiins...
VE RI TAS
LARGE REGIONAL FALLS IN LABOR DEMAND ARE A FACT OF LIFE.
FROM 1930–1990, AS U.S. POPULATION DOUBLED, VAST REGIONS LOST POPULATION. THE 902 SLOWEST-GROWING COUNTIES— TOTAL AREA LARGER THAN MEXICO— ***LOST*** 28% OF THEIR POPULATION.

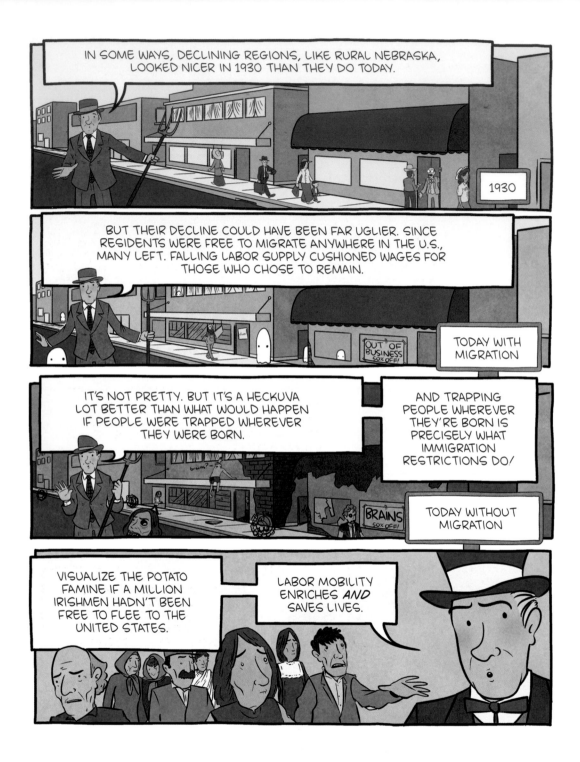

IN SOME WAYS, DECLINING REGIONS, LIKE RURAL NEBRASKA, LOOKED NICER IN 1930 THAN THEY DO TODAY.

1930

BUT THEIR DECLINE COULD HAVE BEEN FAR UGLIER. SINCE RESIDENTS WERE FREE TO MIGRATE ANYWHERE IN THE U.S., MANY LEFT. FALLING LABOR SUPPLY CUSHIONED WAGES FOR THOSE WHO CHOSE TO REMAIN.

OUT OF BUSINESS 50% OFF!

TODAY WITH MIGRATION

IT'S NOT PRETTY. BUT IT'S A HECKUVA LOT BETTER THAN WHAT WOULD HAPPEN IF PEOPLE WERE TRAPPED WHEREVER THEY WERE BORN.

AND TRAPPING PEOPLE WHEREVER THEY'RE BORN IS PRECISELY WHAT IMMIGRATION RESTRICTIONS DO!

BRAINS 50% OFF!

TODAY WITHOUT MIGRATION

VISUALIZE THE POTATO FAMINE IF A MILLION IRISHMEN HADN'T BEEN FREE TO FLEE TO THE UNITED STATES.

LABOR MOBILITY ENRICHES *AND* SAVES LIVES.

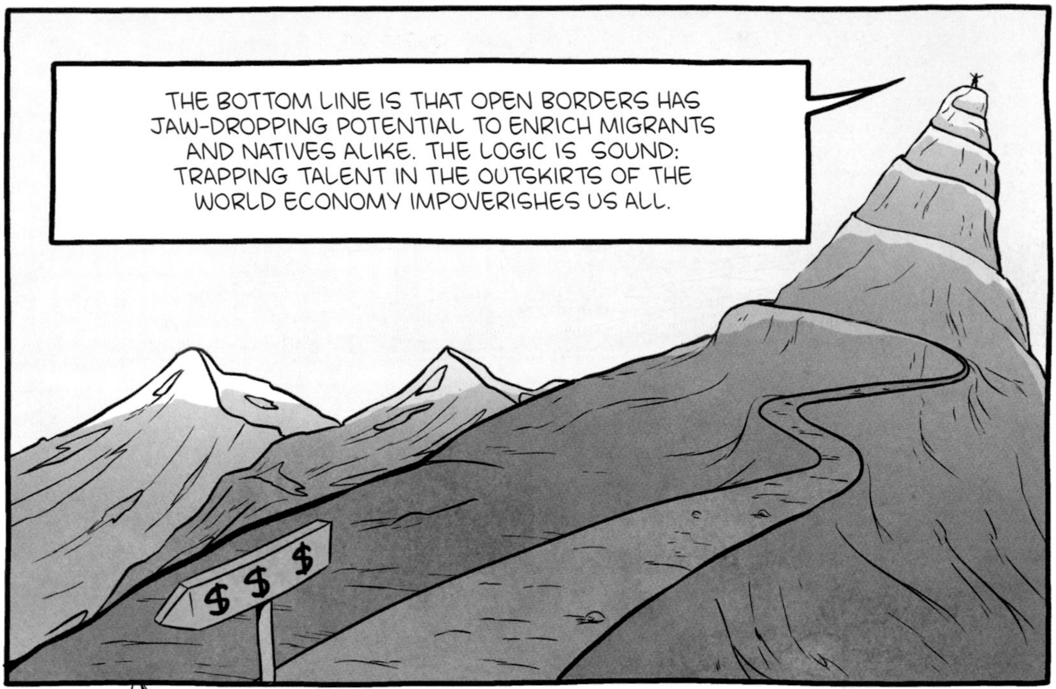
THE BOTTOM LINE IS THAT OPEN BORDERS HAS JAW-DROPPING POTENTIAL TO ENRICH MIGRANTS AND NATIVES ALIKE. THE LOGIC IS SOUND: TRAPPING TALENT IN THE OUTSKIRTS OF THE WORLD ECONOMY IMPOVERISHES US ALL.
$ $ $

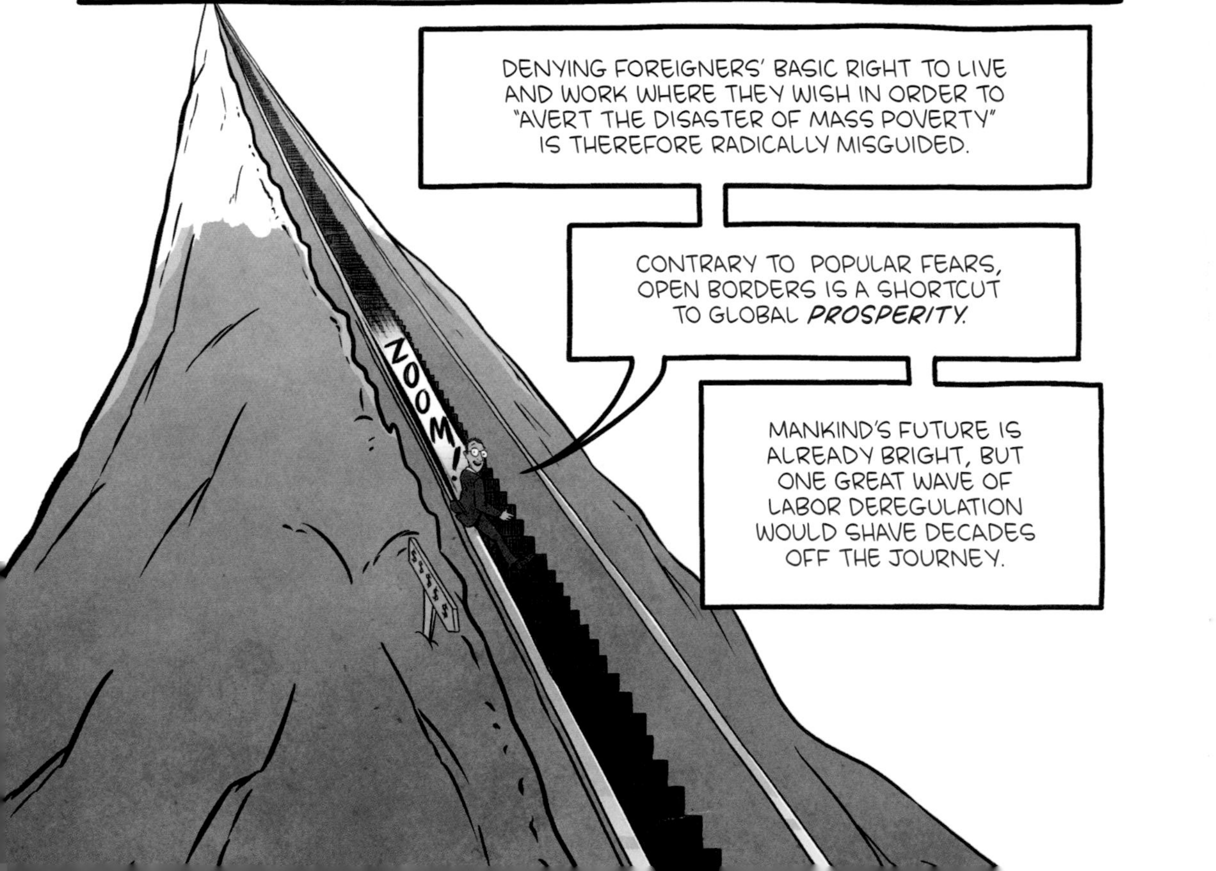
DENYING FOREIGNERS' BASIC RIGHT TO LIVE AND WORK WHERE THEY WISH IN ORDER TO "AVERT THE DISASTER OF MASS POVERTY" IS THEREFORE RADICALLY MISGUIDED.
CONTRARY TO POPULAR FEARS, OPEN BORDERS IS A SHORTCUT TO GLOBAL *PROSPERITY*.
MANKIND'S FUTURE IS ALREADY BRIGHT, BUT ONE GREAT WAVE OF LABOR DEREGULATION WOULD SHAVE DECADES OFF THE JOURNEY.
ZOOM!

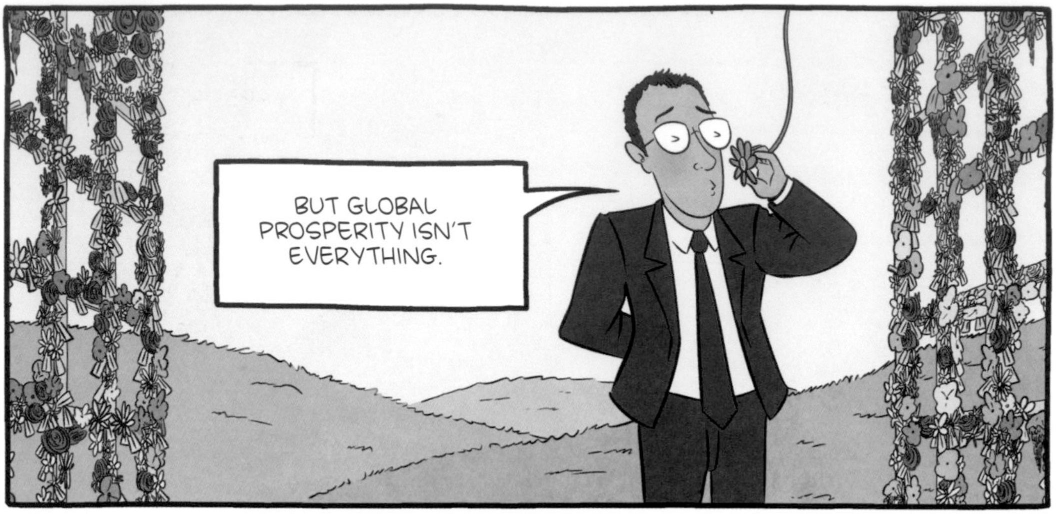
BUT GLOBAL PROSPERITY ISN'T EVERYTHING.

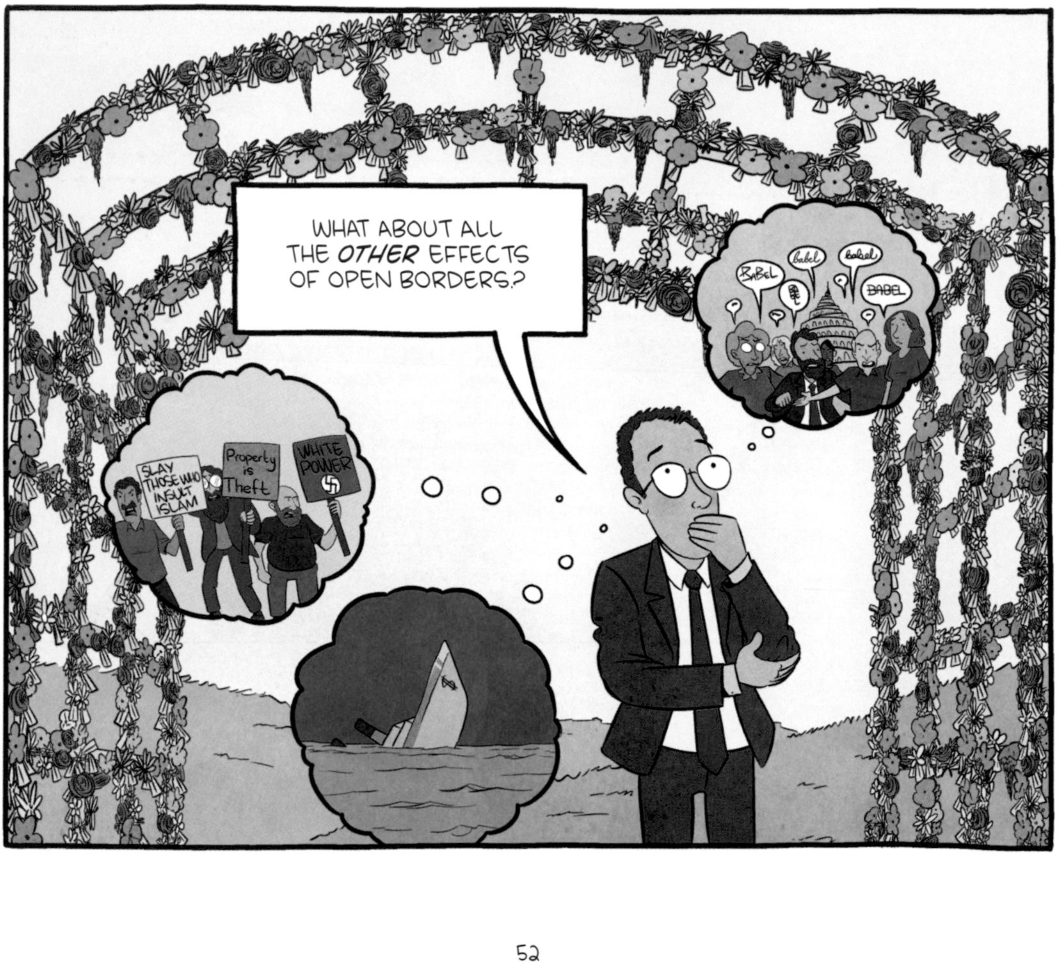
WHAT ABOUT ALL THE *OTHER* EFFECTS OF OPEN BORDERS?
BABEL
babel
babel
BABEL
SLAY THOSE WHO INSULT ISLAM
Property is Theft
WHITE POWER

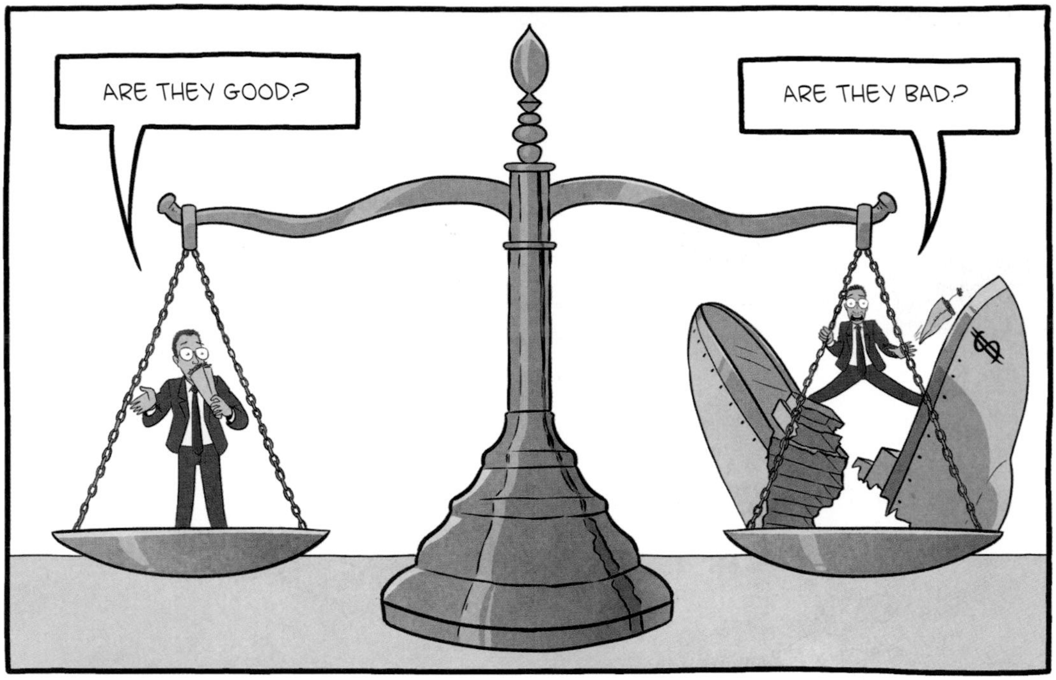
ARE THEY GOOD?
ARE THEY BAD?

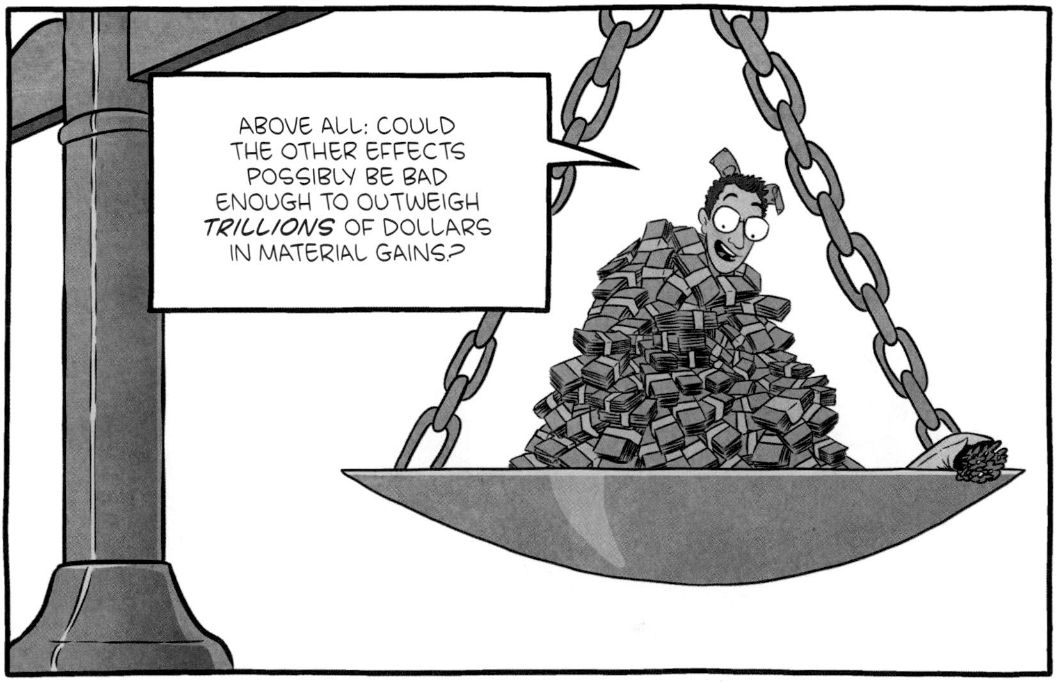
ABOVE ALL: COULD THE OTHER EFFECTS POSSIBLY BE BAD ENOUGH TO OUTWEIGH *TRILLIONS* OF DOLLARS IN MATERIAL GAINS?

CHAPTER 3

THE NATIVE'S BURDEN?

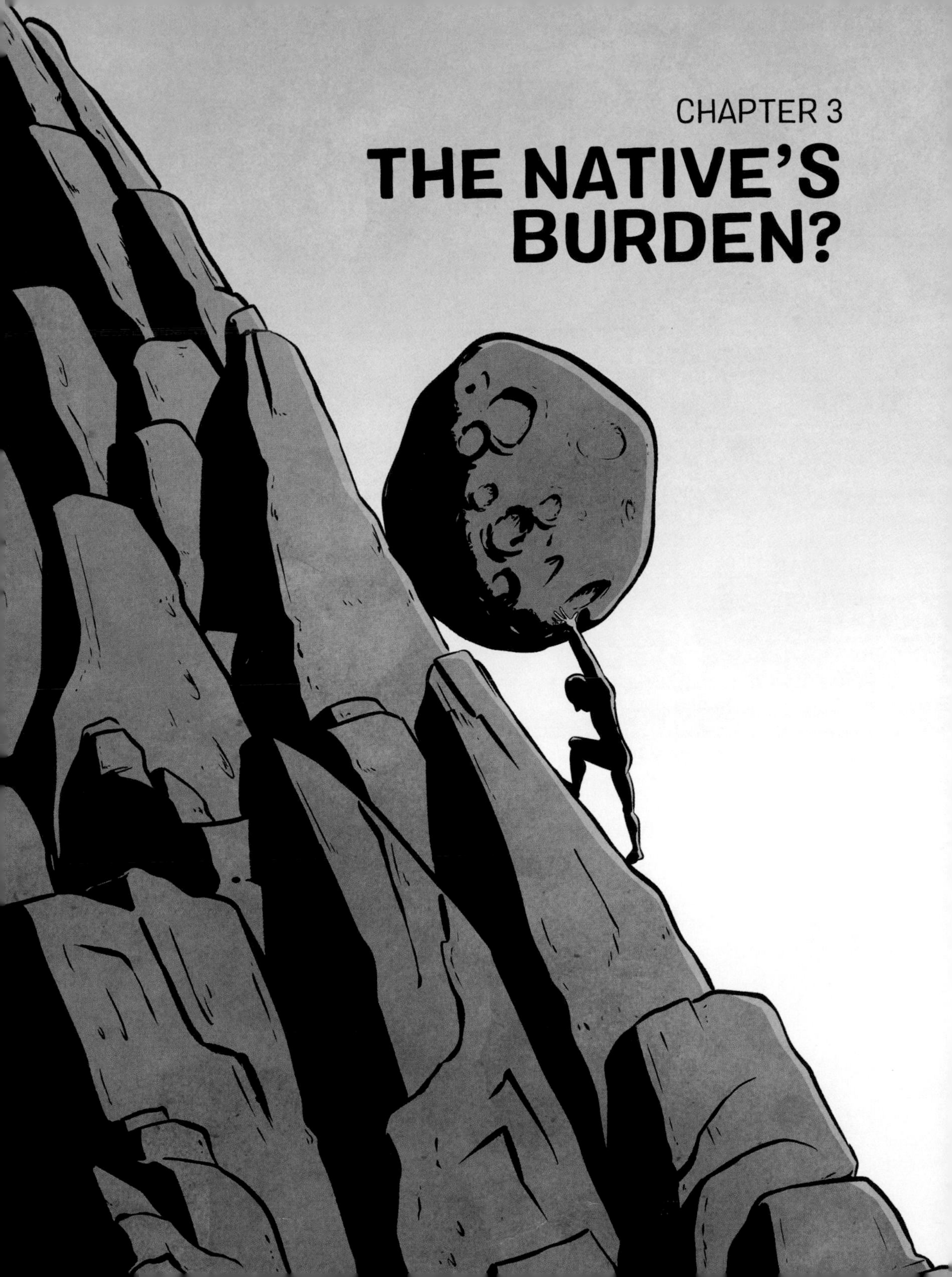

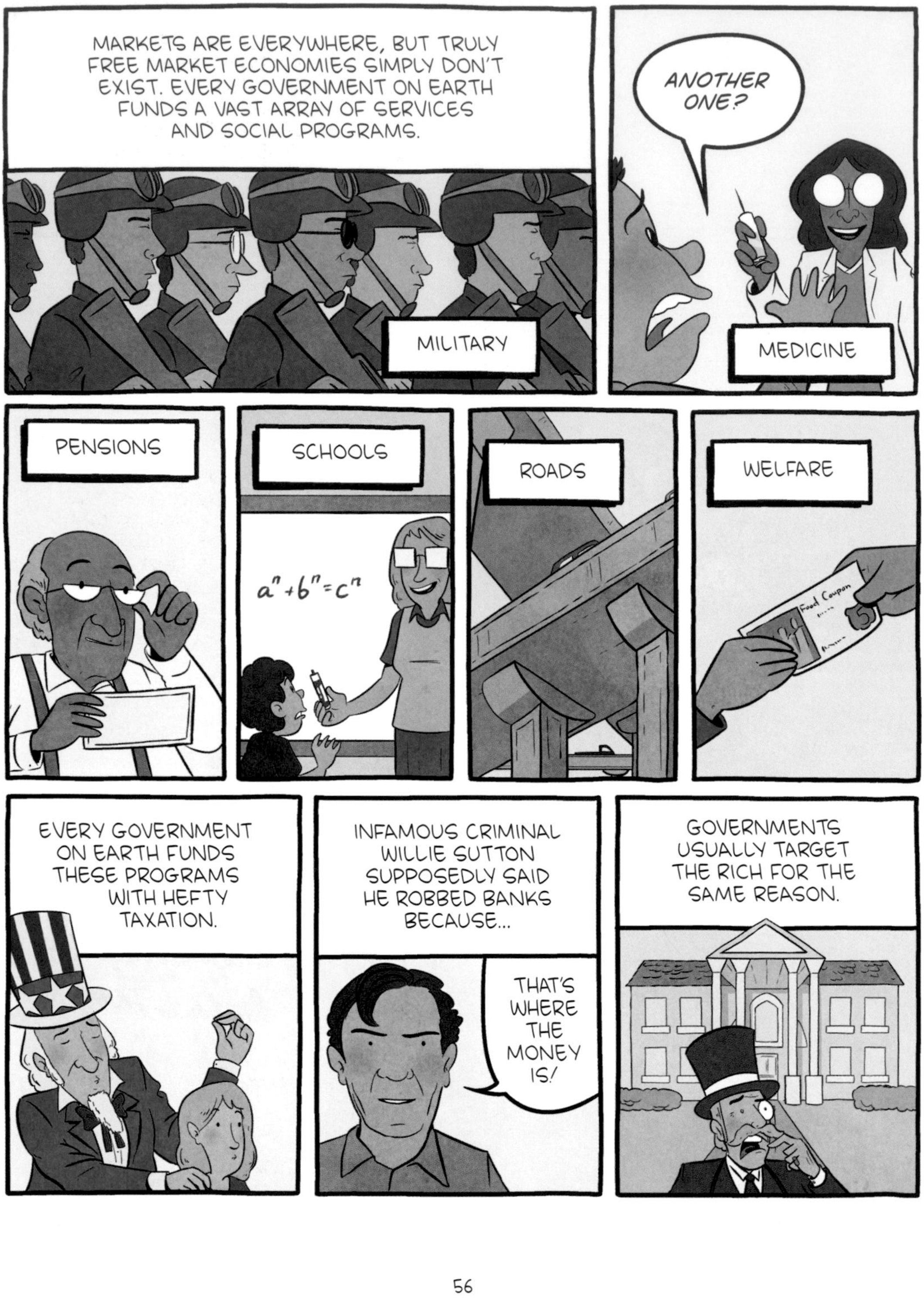
MARKETS ARE EVERYWHERE, BUT TRULY FREE MARKET ECONOMIES SIMPLY DON'T EXIST. EVERY GOVERNMENT ON EARTH FUNDS A VAST ARRAY OF SERVICES AND SOCIAL PROGRAMS.
MILITARY
ANOTHER ONE?
MEDICINE
PENSIONS
SCHOOLS
$a^n + b^n = c^n$
ROADS
WELFARE
Food Coupon
EVERY GOVERNMENT ON EARTH FUNDS THESE PROGRAMS WITH HEFTY TAXATION.
INFAMOUS CRIMINAL WILLIE SUTTON SUPPOSEDLY SAID HE ROBBED BANKS BECAUSE...
THAT'S WHERE THE MONEY IS!
GOVERNMENTS USUALLY TARGET THE RICH FOR THE SAME REASON.

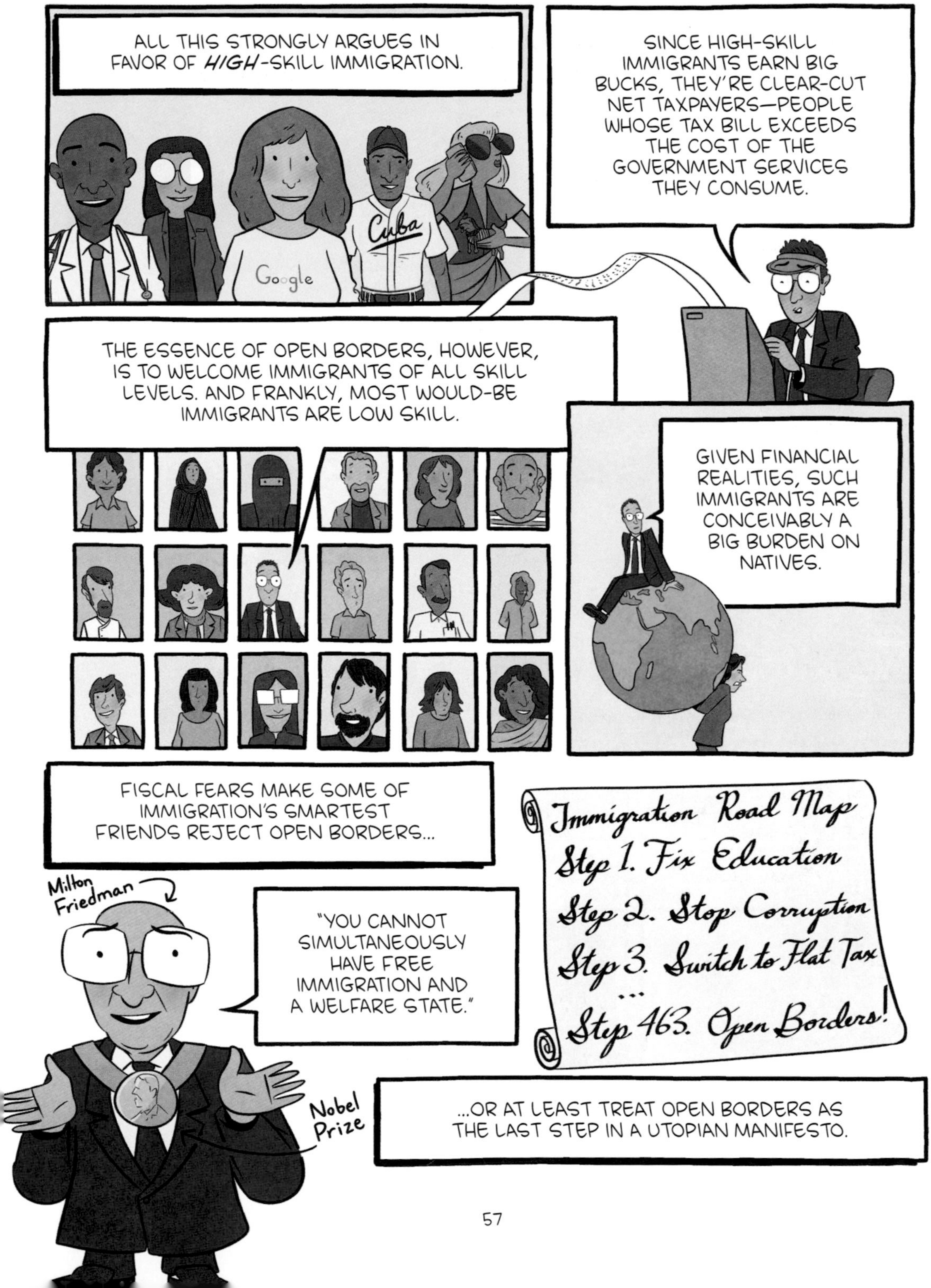
ALL THIS STRONGLY ARGUES IN FAVOR OF *HIGH*-SKILL IMMIGRATION.
Google
Cuba
SINCE HIGH-SKILL IMMIGRANTS EARN BIG BUCKS, THEY'RE CLEAR-CUT NET TAXPAYERS—PEOPLE WHOSE TAX BILL EXCEEDS THE COST OF THE GOVERNMENT SERVICES THEY CONSUME.
THE ESSENCE OF OPEN BORDERS, HOWEVER, IS TO WELCOME IMMIGRANTS OF ALL SKILL LEVELS. AND FRANKLY, MOST WOULD-BE IMMIGRANTS ARE LOW SKILL.
GIVEN FINANCIAL REALITIES, SUCH IMMIGRANTS ARE CONCEIVABLY A BIG BURDEN ON NATIVES.
FISCAL FEARS MAKE SOME OF IMMIGRATION'S SMARTEST FRIENDS REJECT OPEN BORDERS...
Milton Friedman
"YOU CANNOT SIMULTANEOUSLY HAVE FREE IMMIGRATION AND A WELFARE STATE."
Nobel Prize
Immigration Road Map
Step 1. Fix Education
Step 2. Stop Corruption
Step 3. Switch to Flat Tax
...
Step 463. Open Borders!
...OR AT LEAST TREAT OPEN BORDERS AS THE LAST STEP IN A UTOPIAN MANIFESTO.

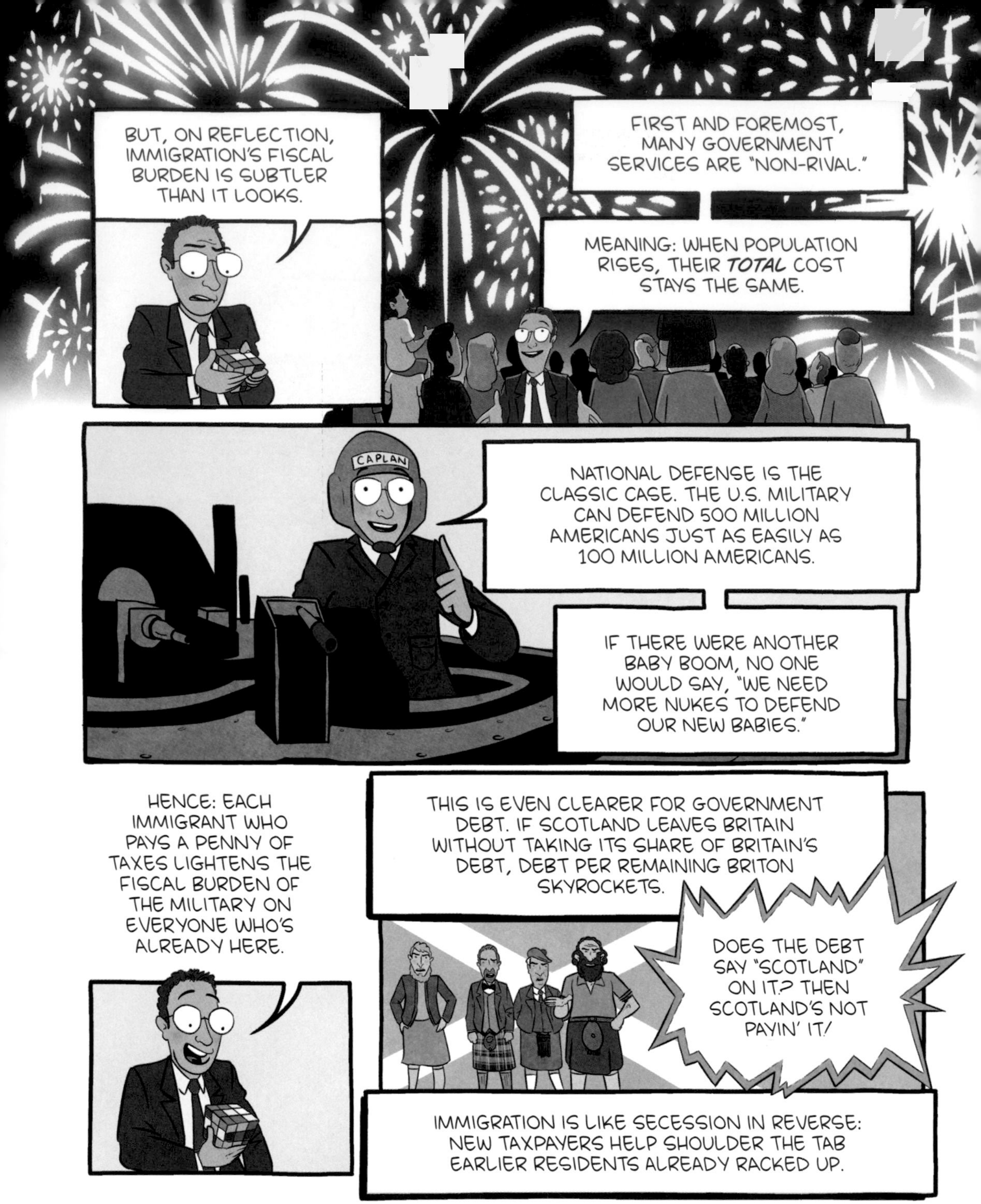
BUT, ON REFLECTION, IMMIGRATION'S FISCAL BURDEN IS SUBTLER THAN IT LOOKS.
FIRST AND FOREMOST, MANY GOVERNMENT SERVICES ARE "NON-RIVAL."
MEANING: WHEN POPULATION RISES, THEIR *TOTAL* COST STAYS THE SAME.
CAPLAN
NATIONAL DEFENSE IS THE CLASSIC CASE. THE U.S. MILITARY CAN DEFEND 500 MILLION AMERICANS JUST AS EASILY AS 100 MILLION AMERICANS.
IF THERE WERE ANOTHER BABY BOOM, NO ONE WOULD SAY, "WE NEED MORE NUKES TO DEFEND OUR NEW BABIES."
HENCE: EACH IMMIGRANT WHO PAYS A PENNY OF TAXES LIGHTENS THE FISCAL BURDEN OF THE MILITARY ON EVERYONE WHO'S ALREADY HERE.
THIS IS EVEN CLEARER FOR GOVERNMENT DEBT. IF SCOTLAND LEAVES BRITAIN WITHOUT TAKING ITS SHARE OF BRITAIN'S DEBT, DEBT PER REMAINING BRITON SKYROCKETS.
DOES THE DEBT SAY "SCOTLAND" ON IT? THEN SCOTLAND'S NOT PAYIN' IT!
IMMIGRATION IS LIKE SECESSION IN REVERSE: NEW TAXPAYERS HELP SHOULDER THE TAB EARLIER RESIDENTS ALREADY RACKED UP.

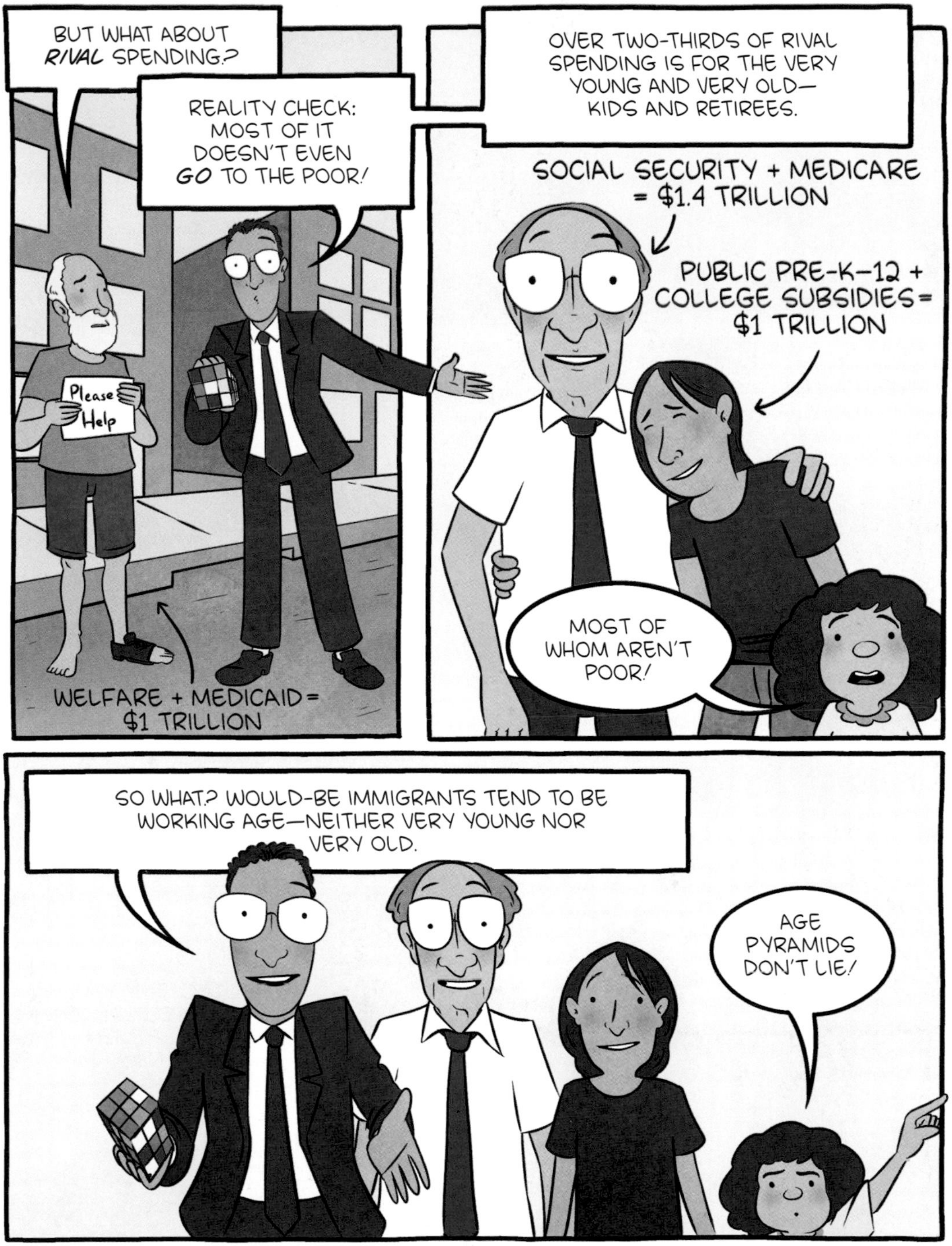

BUT WHAT ABOUT *RIVAL* SPENDING?
REALITY CHECK: MOST OF IT DOESN'T EVEN *GO* TO THE POOR!
Please Help
WELFARE + MEDICAID = $1 TRILLION
OVER TWO-THIRDS OF RIVAL SPENDING IS FOR THE VERY YOUNG AND VERY OLD—KIDS AND RETIREES.
SOCIAL SECURITY + MEDICARE = $1.4 TRILLION
PUBLIC PRE-K–12 + COLLEGE SUBSIDIES = $1 TRILLION
MOST OF WHOM AREN'T POOR!
SO WHAT? WOULD-BE IMMIGRANTS TEND TO BE WORKING AGE—NEITHER VERY YOUNG NOR VERY OLD.
AGE PYRAMIDS DON'T LIE!

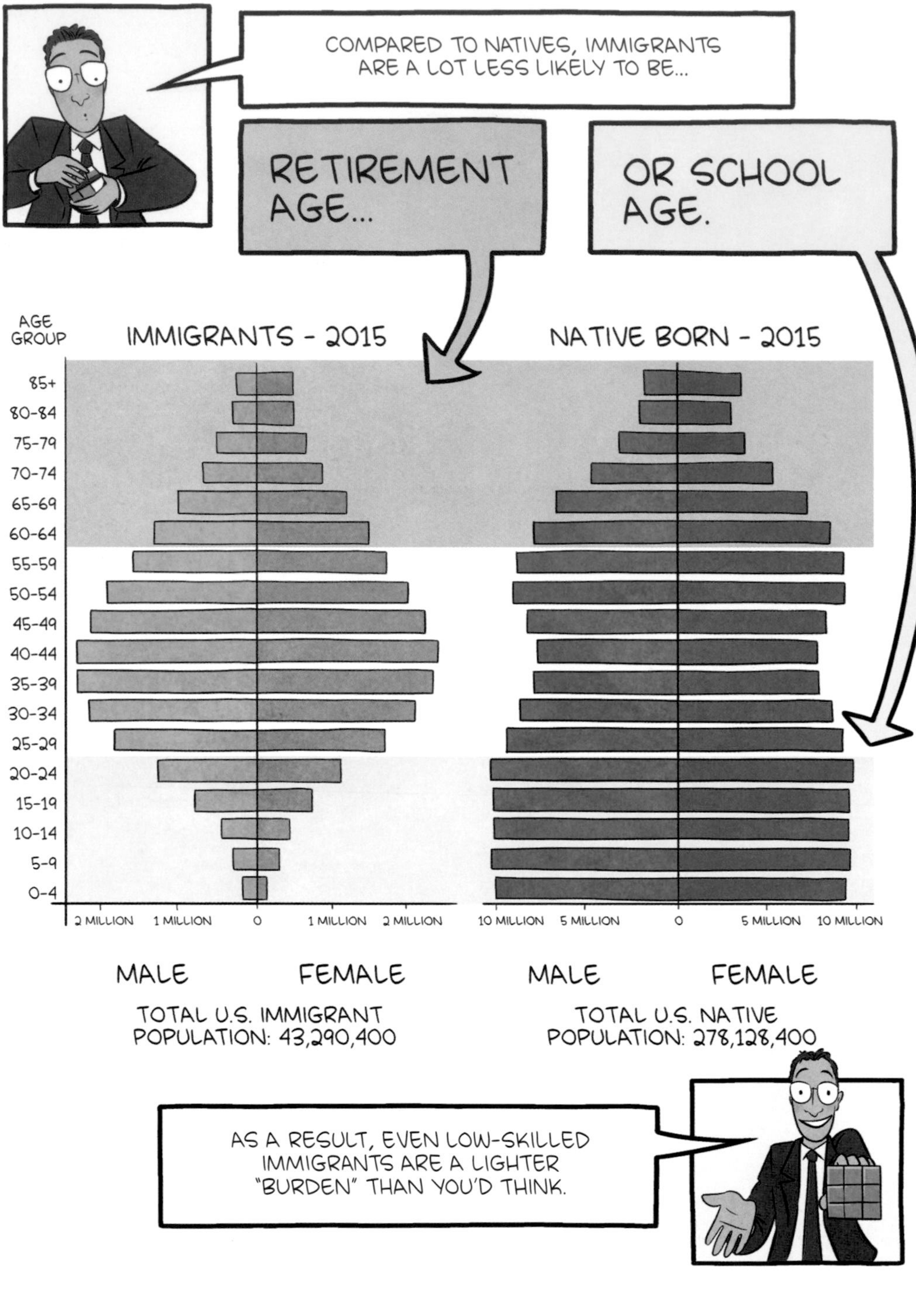
COMPARED TO NATIVES, IMMIGRANTS ARE A LOT LESS LIKELY TO BE...
RETIREMENT AGE...
OR SCHOOL AGE.
AGE GROUP
IMMIGRANTS - 2015
NATIVE BORN - 2015
85+
80-84
75-79
70-74
65-69
60-64
55-59
50-54
45-49
40-44
35-39
30-34
25-29
20-24
15-19
10-14
5-9
0-4
2 MILLION 1 MILLION 0 1 MILLION 2 MILLION
10 MILLION 5 MILLION 0 5 MILLION 10 MILLION
MALE
FEMALE
MALE
FEMALE
TOTAL U.S. IMMIGRANT POPULATION: 43,290,400
TOTAL U.S. NATIVE POPULATION: 278,128,400
AS A RESULT, EVEN LOW-SKILLED IMMIGRANTS ARE A LIGHTER "BURDEN" THAN YOU'D THINK.

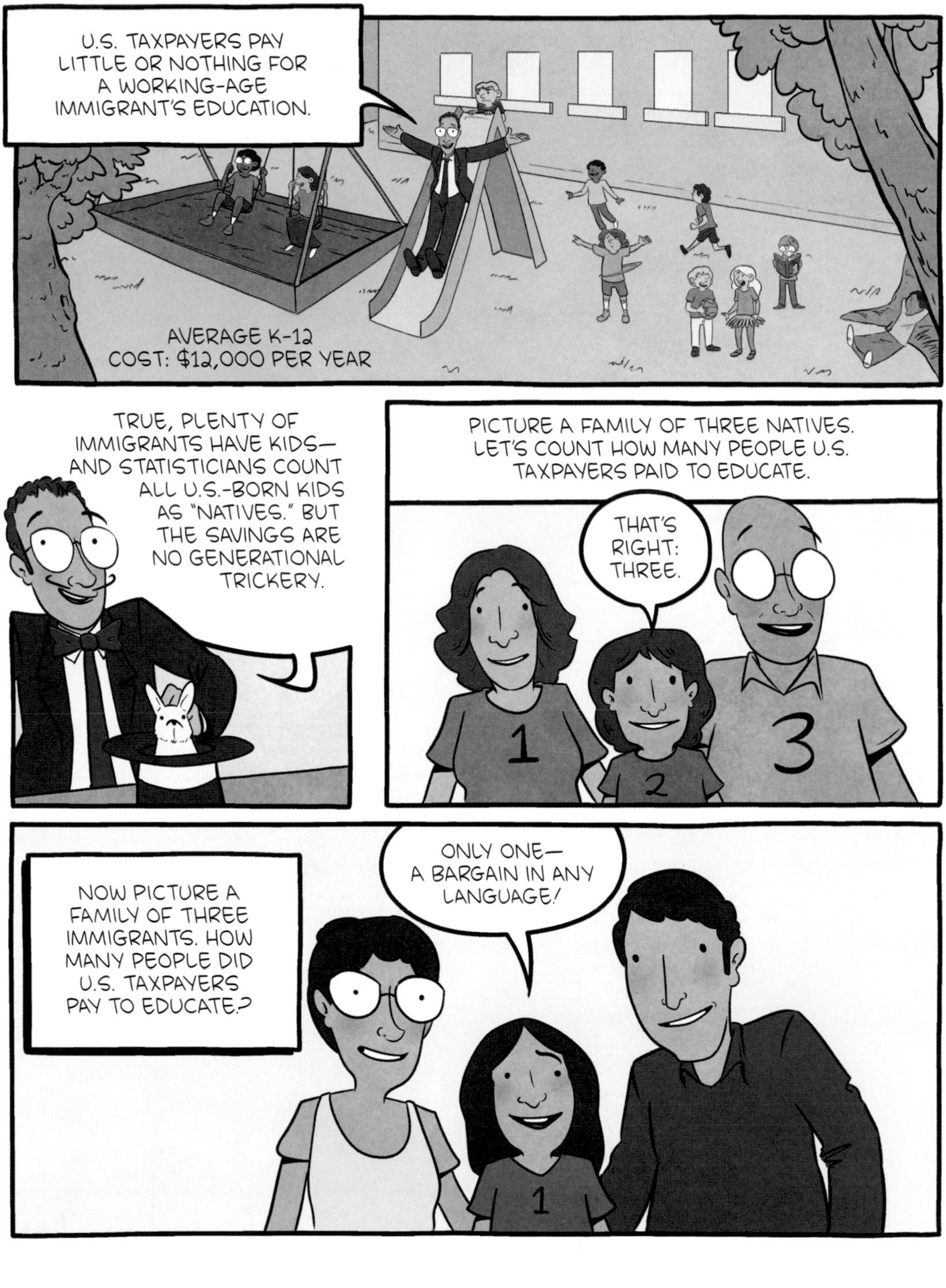
U.S. TAXPAYERS PAY LITTLE OR NOTHING FOR A WORKING-AGE IMMIGRANT'S EDUCATION.
AVERAGE K-12 COST: $12,000 PER YEAR
TRUE, PLENTY OF IMMIGRANTS HAVE KIDS—AND STATISTICIANS COUNT ALL U.S.-BORN KIDS AS "NATIVES." BUT THE SAVINGS ARE NO GENERATIONAL TRICKERY.
PICTURE A FAMILY OF THREE NATIVES. LET'S COUNT HOW MANY PEOPLE U.S. TAXPAYERS PAID TO EDUCATE.
THAT'S RIGHT: THREE.
1
2
3
NOW PICTURE A FAMILY OF THREE IMMIGRANTS. HOW MANY PEOPLE DID U.S. TAXPAYERS PAY TO EDUCATE?
ONLY ONE—A BARGAIN IN ANY LANGUAGE!
1

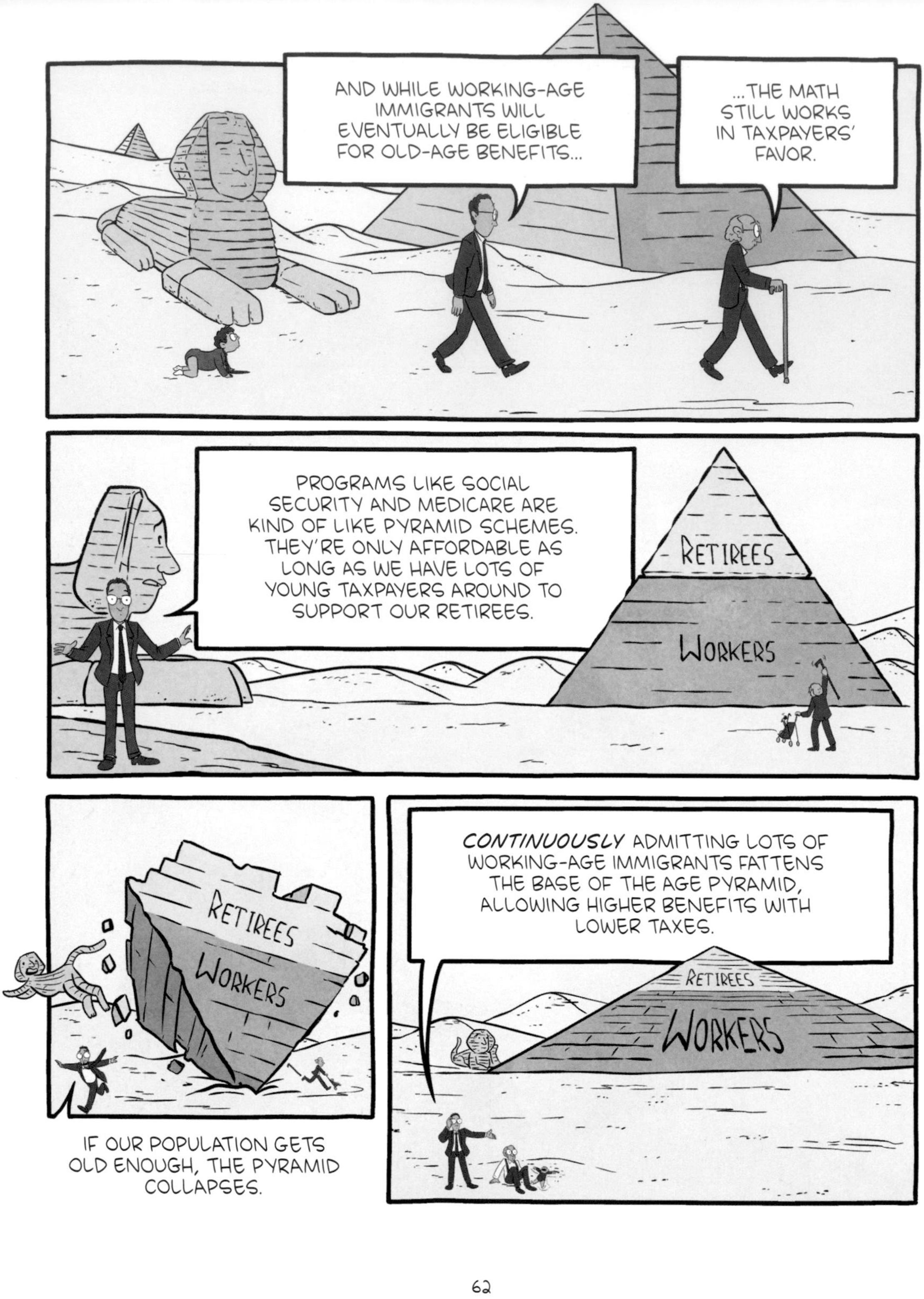
AND WHILE WORKING-AGE IMMIGRANTS WILL EVENTUALLY BE ELIGIBLE FOR OLD-AGE BENEFITS...
...THE MATH STILL WORKS IN TAXPAYERS' FAVOR.
PROGRAMS LIKE SOCIAL SECURITY AND MEDICARE ARE KIND OF LIKE PYRAMID SCHEMES. THEY'RE ONLY AFFORDABLE AS LONG AS WE HAVE LOTS OF YOUNG TAXPAYERS AROUND TO SUPPORT OUR RETIREES.
RETIREES
WORKERS
RETIREES
WORKERS
IF OUR POPULATION GETS OLD ENOUGH, THE PYRAMID COLLAPSES.
CONTINUOUSLY ADMITTING LOTS OF WORKING-AGE IMMIGRANTS FATTENS THE BASE OF THE AGE PYRAMID, ALLOWING HIGHER BENEFITS WITH LOWER TAXES.
RETIREES
WORKERS

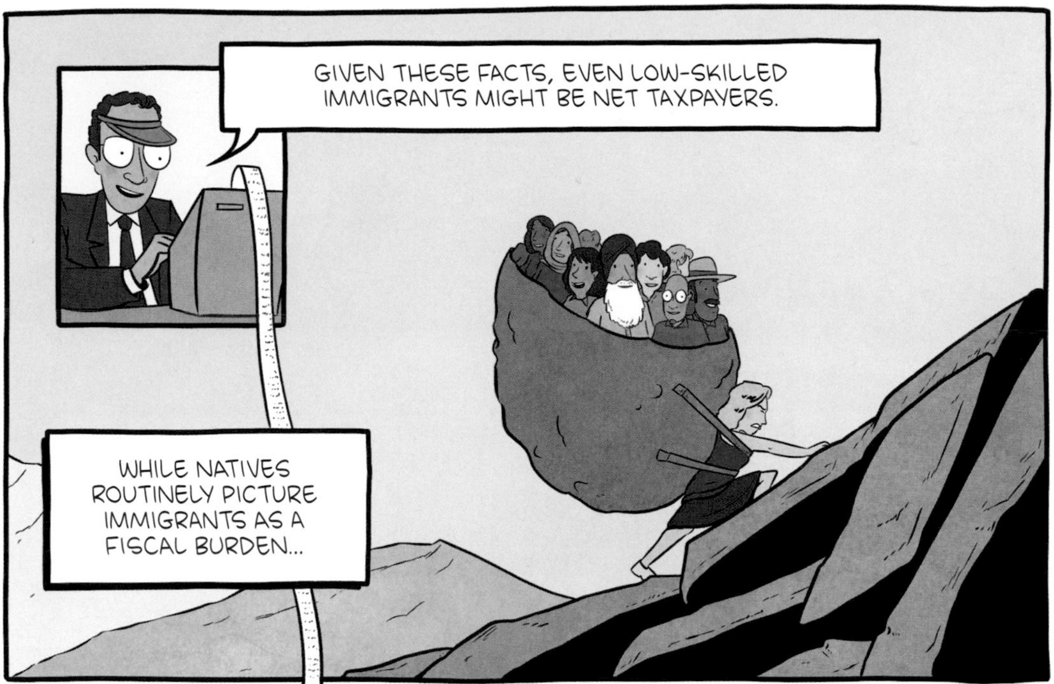
GIVEN THESE FACTS, EVEN LOW-SKILLED IMMIGRANTS MIGHT BE NET TAXPAYERS.
WHILE NATIVES ROUTINELY PICTURE IMMIGRANTS AS A FISCAL BURDEN...

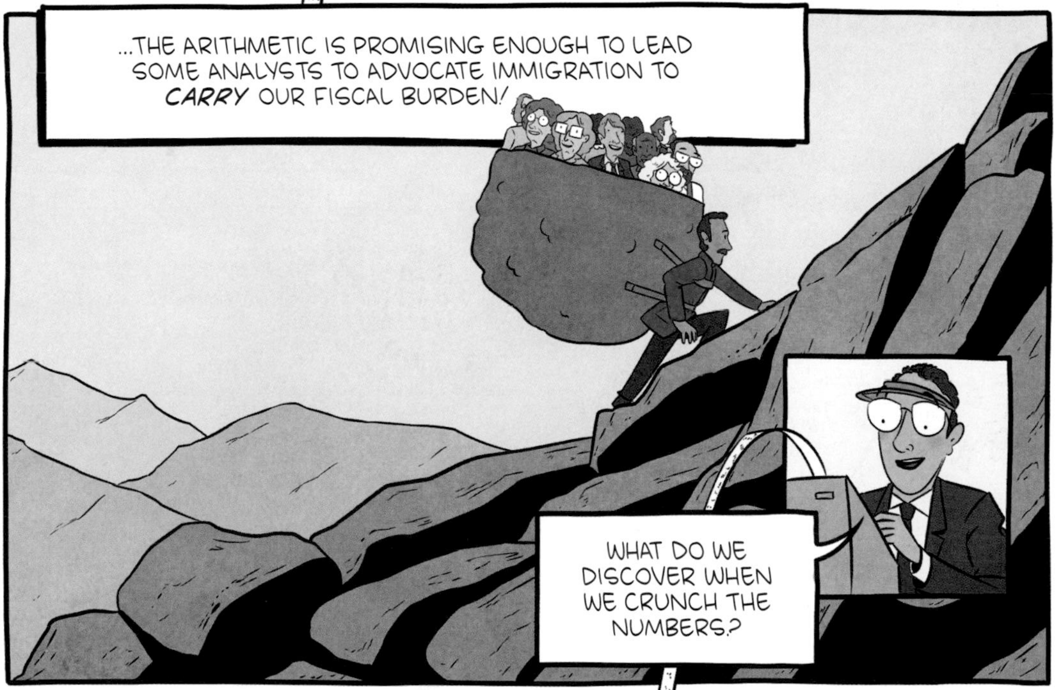
...THE ARITHMETIC IS PROMISING ENOUGH TO LEAD SOME ANALYSTS TO ADVOCATE IMMIGRATION TO *CARRY* OUR FISCAL BURDEN!
WHAT DO WE DISCOVER WHEN WE CRUNCH THE NUMBERS?

THIS 2016 REPORT FROM THE NATIONAL ACADEMY OF SCIENCES THOROUGHLY REVIEWS DECADES OF RESEARCH, THEN METICULOUSLY ESTIMATES IMMIGRATION'S ***OVERALL, LONG-RUN*** FISCAL EFFECT.

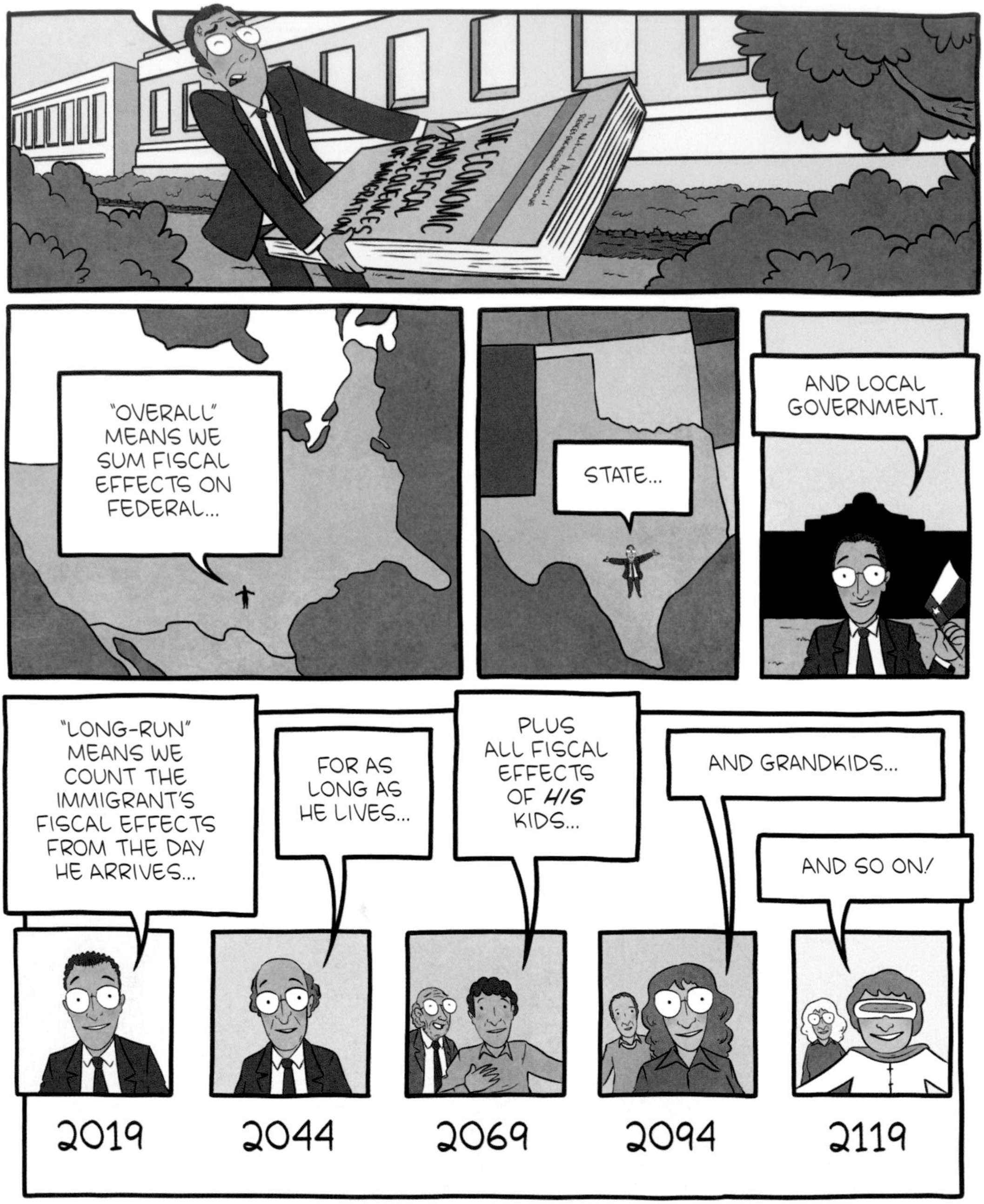
THE ECONOMIC AND FISCAL CONSEQUENCES OF IMMIGRATION
"OVERALL" MEANS WE SUM FISCAL EFFECTS ON FEDERAL...
STATE...
AND LOCAL GOVERNMENT.
"LONG-RUN" MEANS WE COUNT THE IMMIGRANT'S FISCAL EFFECTS FROM THE DAY HE ARRIVES...
FOR AS LONG AS HE LIVES...
PLUS ALL FISCAL EFFECTS OF *HIS* KIDS...
AND GRANDKIDS...
AND SO ON!
2019
2044
2069
2094
2119

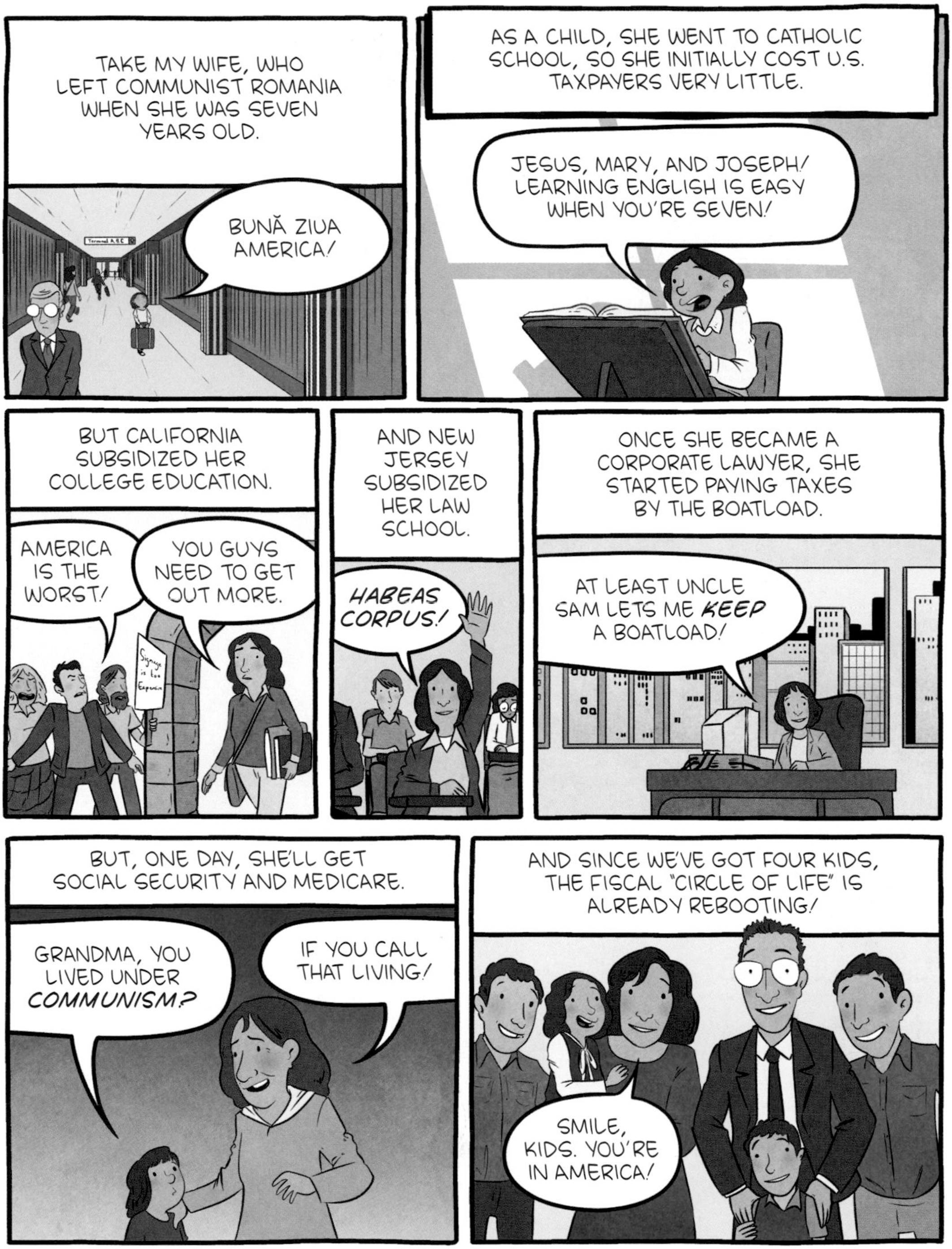
TAKE MY WIFE, WHO LEFT COMMUNIST ROMANIA WHEN SHE WAS SEVEN YEARS OLD.
BUNĂ ZIUA AMERICA!
AS A CHILD, SHE WENT TO CATHOLIC SCHOOL, SO SHE INITIALLY COST U.S. TAXPAYERS VERY LITTLE.
JESUS, MARY, AND JOSEPH! LEARNING ENGLISH IS EASY WHEN YOU'RE SEVEN!
BUT CALIFORNIA SUBSIDIZED HER COLLEGE EDUCATION.
AMERICA IS THE WORST!
YOU GUYS NEED TO GET OUT MORE.
AND NEW JERSEY SUBSIDIZED HER LAW SCHOOL.
HABEAS CORPUS!
ONCE SHE BECAME A CORPORATE LAWYER, SHE STARTED PAYING TAXES BY THE BOATLOAD.
AT LEAST UNCLE SAM LETS ME KEEP A BOATLOAD!
BUT, ONE DAY, SHE'LL GET SOCIAL SECURITY AND MEDICARE.
GRANDMA, YOU LIVED UNDER COMMUNISM?
IF YOU CALL THAT LIVING!
AND SINCE WE'VE GOT FOUR KIDS, THE FISCAL "CIRCLE OF LIFE" IS ALREADY REBOOTING!
SMILE, KIDS. YOU'RE IN AMERICA!

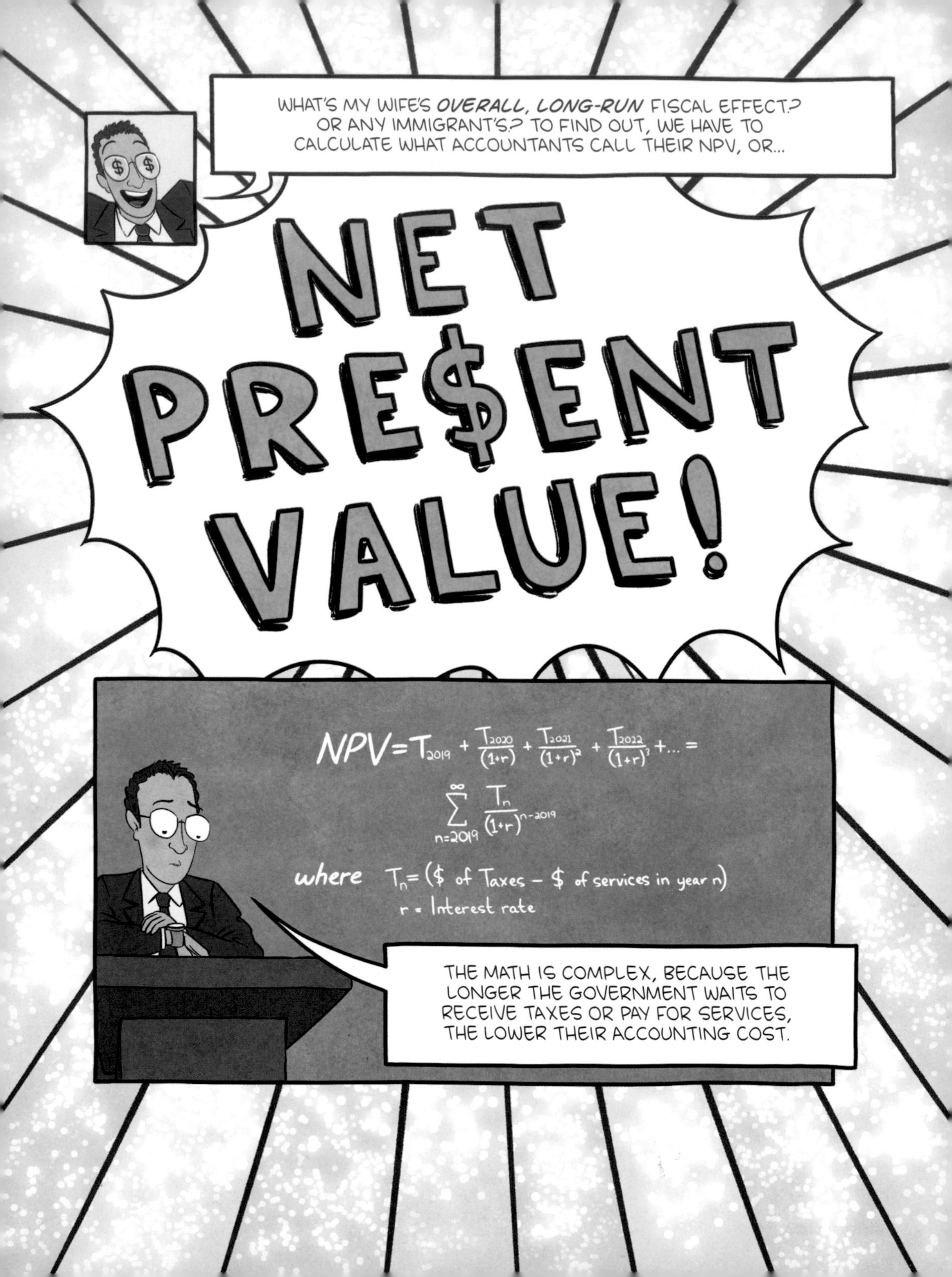

WHAT'S MY WIFE'S *OVERALL, LONG-RUN* FISCAL EFFECT? OR ANY IMMIGRANT'S? TO FIND OUT, WE HAVE TO CALCULATE WHAT ACCOUNTANTS CALL THEIR NPV, OR...
NET PRE$ENT VALUE!
$NPV = T_{2019} + \frac{T_{2020}}{(1+r)} + \frac{T_{2021}}{(1+r)^2} + \frac{T_{2022}}{(1+r)^3} + \ldots = \sum_{n=2019}^{\infty} \frac{T_n}{(1+r)^{n-2019}}$
where T_n = ($ of Taxes – $ of services in year n)
r = Interest rate
THE MATH IS COMPLEX, BECAUSE THE LONGER THE GOVERNMENT WAITS TO RECEIVE TAXES OR PAY FOR SERVICES, THE LOWER THEIR ACCOUNTING COST.

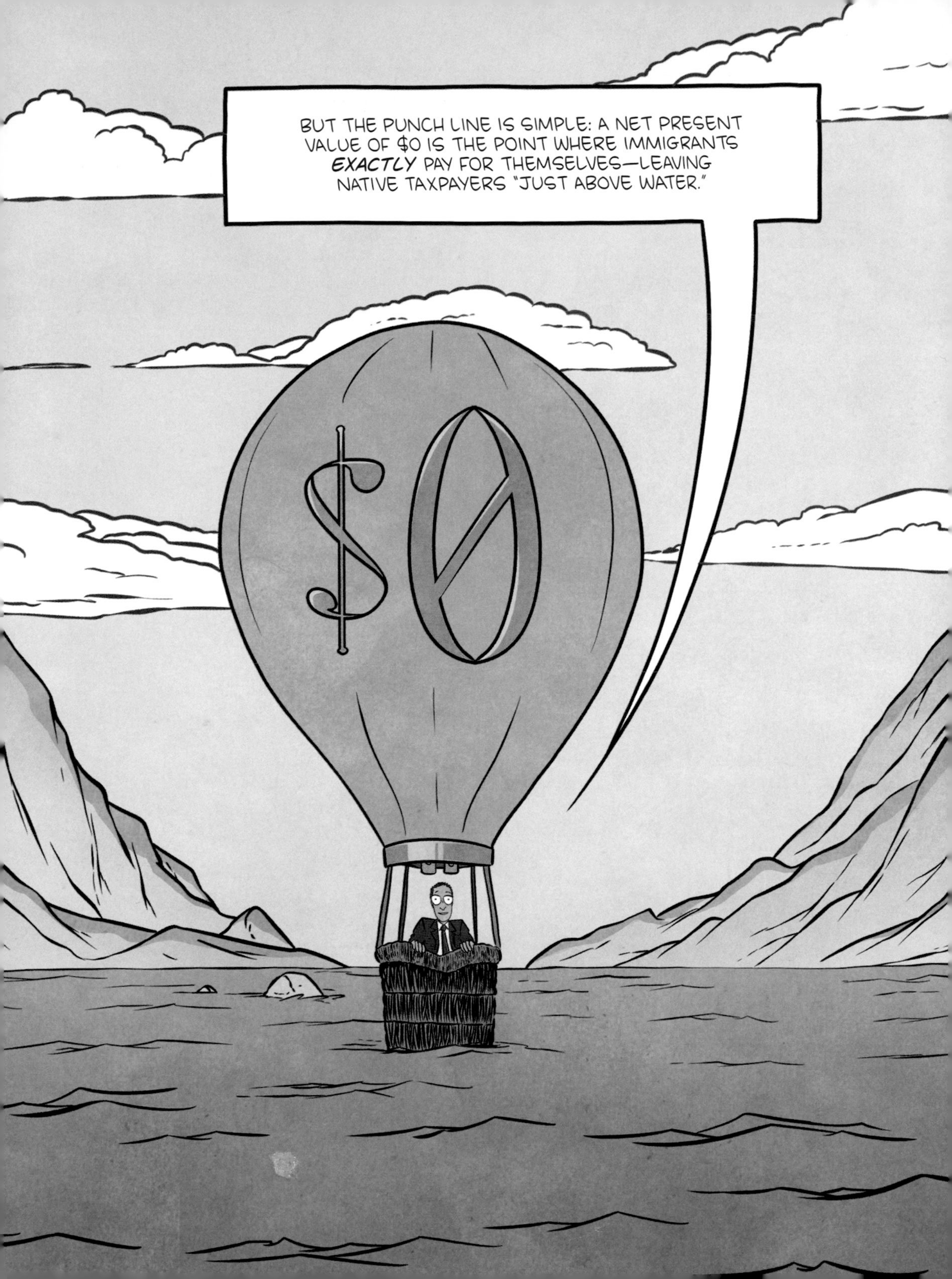
BUT THE PUNCH LINE IS SIMPLE: A NET PRESENT VALUE OF $0 IS THE POINT WHERE IMMIGRANTS *EXACTLY* PAY FOR THEMSELVES—LEAVING NATIVE TAXPAYERS "JUST ABOVE WATER."
$0

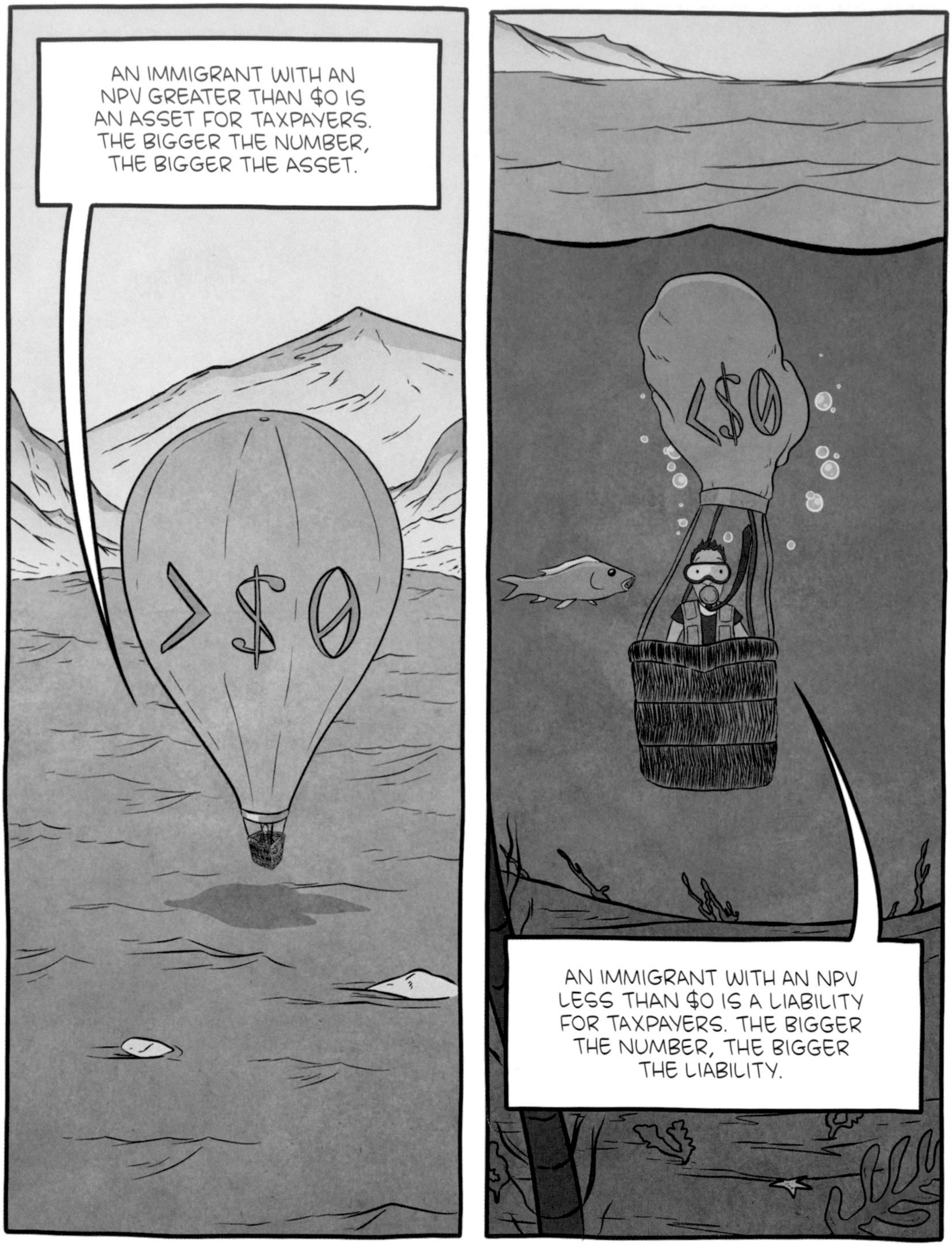
AN IMMIGRANT WITH AN NPV GREATER THAN $0 IS AN ASSET FOR TAXPAYERS. THE BIGGER THE NUMBER, THE BIGGER THE ASSET.
>$0
<$0
AN IMMIGRANT WITH AN NPV LESS THAN $0 IS A LIABILITY FOR TAXPAYERS. THE BIGGER THE NUMBER, THE BIGGER THE LIABILITY.

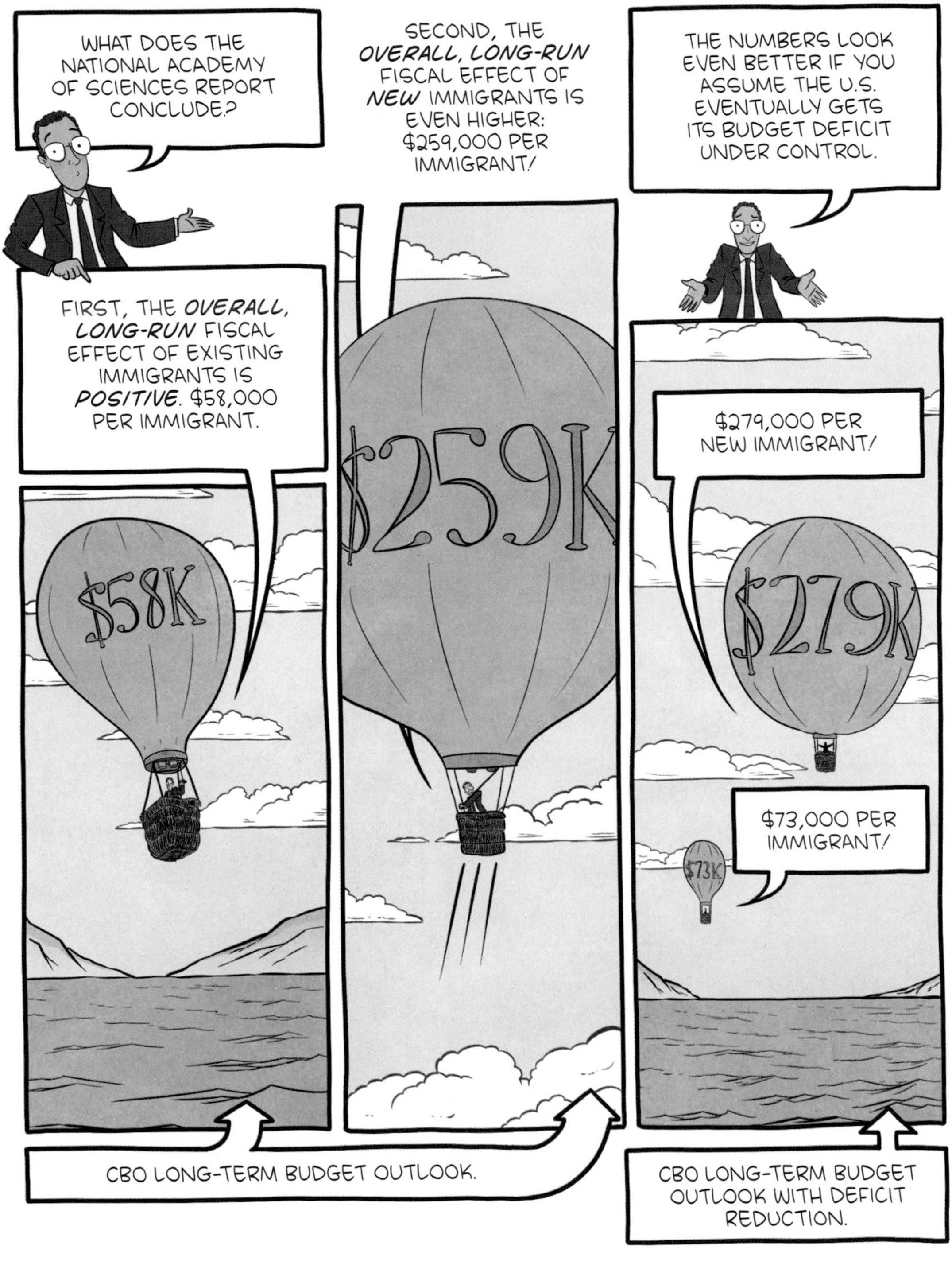

WHAT DOES THE NATIONAL ACADEMY OF SCIENCES REPORT CONCLUDE?
FIRST, THE *OVERALL, LONG-RUN* FISCAL EFFECT OF EXISTING IMMIGRANTS IS *POSITIVE*. $58,000 PER IMMIGRANT.
$58K
SECOND, THE *OVERALL, LONG-RUN* FISCAL EFFECT OF *NEW* IMMIGRANTS IS EVEN HIGHER: $259,000 PER IMMIGRANT!
$259K
THE NUMBERS LOOK EVEN BETTER IF YOU ASSUME THE U.S. EVENTUALLY GETS ITS BUDGET DEFICIT UNDER CONTROL.
$279,000 PER NEW IMMIGRANT!
$279K
$73,000 PER IMMIGRANT!
$73K
CBO LONG-TERM BUDGET OUTLOOK.
CBO LONG-TERM BUDGET OUTLOOK WITH DEFICIT REDUCTION.

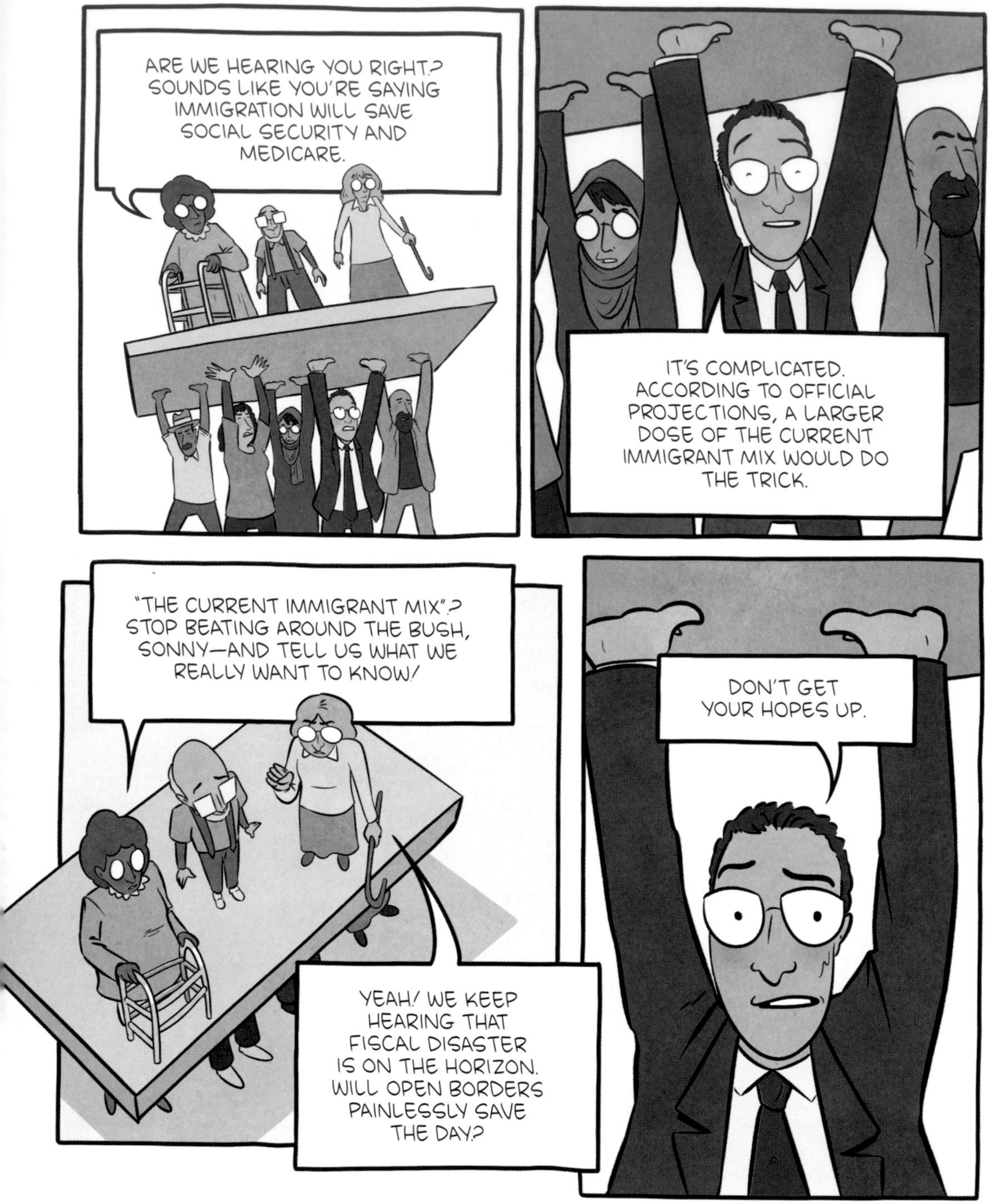
ARE WE HEARING YOU RIGHT? SOUNDS LIKE YOU'RE SAYING IMMIGRATION WILL SAVE SOCIAL SECURITY AND MEDICARE.
IT'S COMPLICATED. ACCORDING TO OFFICIAL PROJECTIONS, A LARGER DOSE OF THE CURRENT IMMIGRANT MIX WOULD DO THE TRICK.
"THE CURRENT IMMIGRANT MIX"? STOP BEATING AROUND THE BUSH, SONNY—AND TELL US WHAT WE REALLY WANT TO KNOW!
YEAH! WE KEEP HEARING THAT FISCAL DISASTER IS ON THE HORIZON. WILL OPEN BORDERS PAINLESSLY SAVE THE DAY?
DON'T GET YOUR HOPES UP.

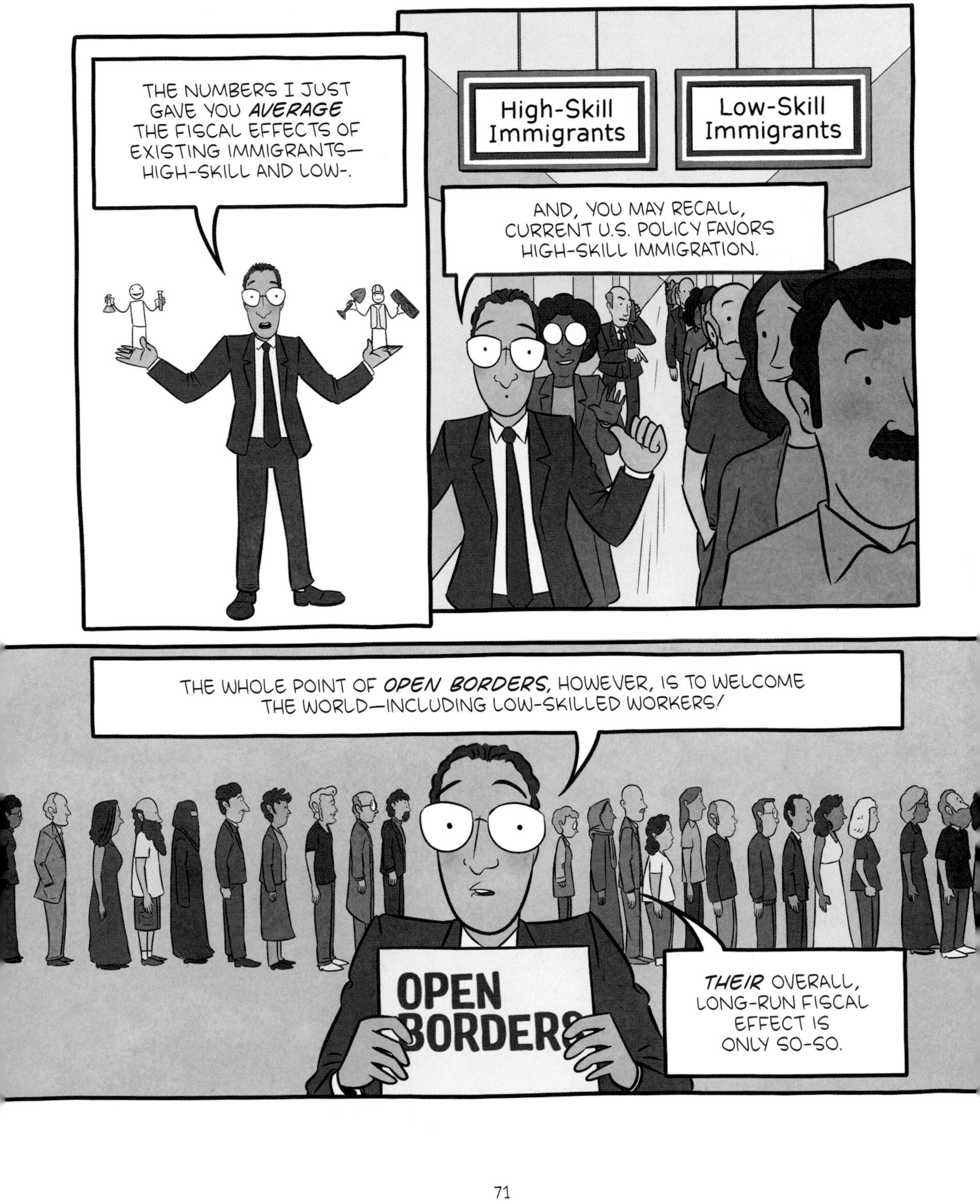
THE NUMBERS I JUST GAVE YOU *AVERAGE* THE FISCAL EFFECTS OF EXISTING IMMIGRANTS—HIGH-SKILL AND LOW-.
High-Skill Immigrants
Low-Skill Immigrants
AND, YOU MAY RECALL, CURRENT U.S. POLICY FAVORS HIGH-SKILL IMMIGRATION.
THE WHOLE POINT OF *OPEN BORDERS*, HOWEVER, IS TO WELCOME THE WORLD—INCLUDING LOW-SKILLED WORKERS!
OPEN BORDERS
THEIR OVERALL, LONG-RUN FISCAL EFFECT IS ONLY SO-SO.

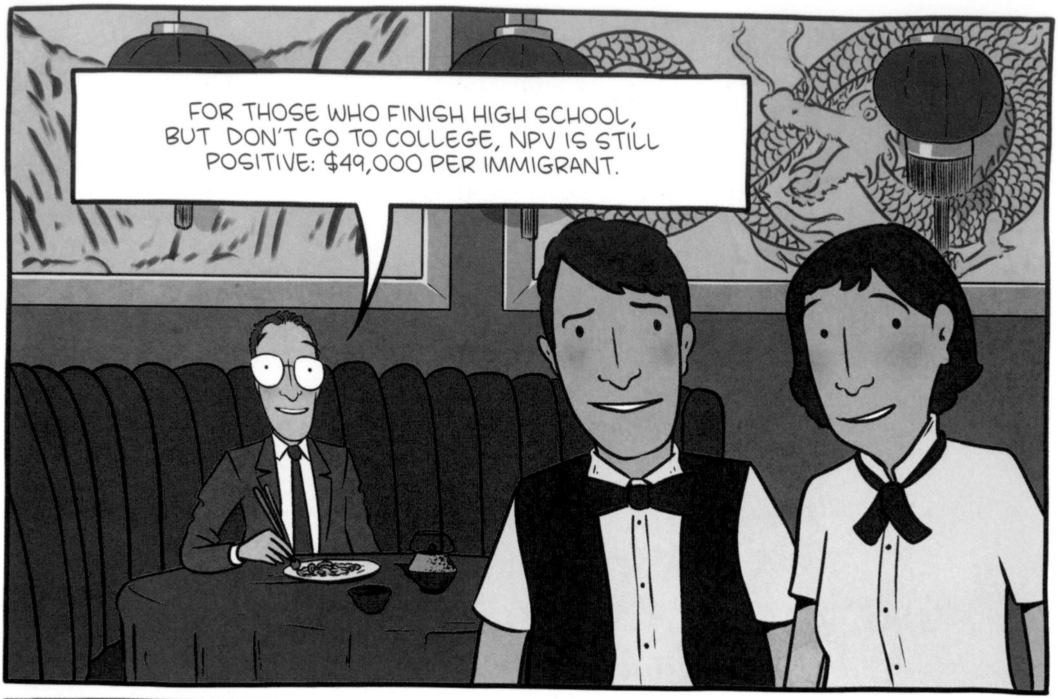
FOR THOSE WHO FINISH HIGH SCHOOL, BUT DON'T GO TO COLLEGE, NPV IS STILL POSITIVE: $49,000 PER IMMIGRANT.

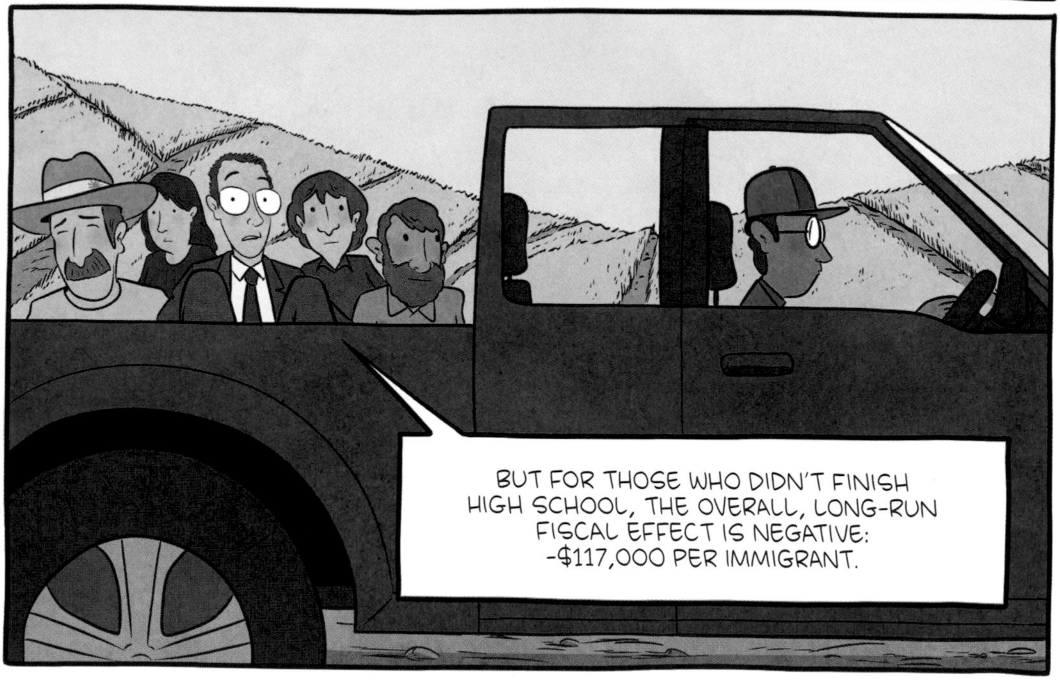
BUT FOR THOSE WHO DIDN'T FINISH HIGH SCHOOL, THE OVERALL, LONG-RUN FISCAL EFFECT IS NEGATIVE: -$117,000 PER IMMIGRANT.

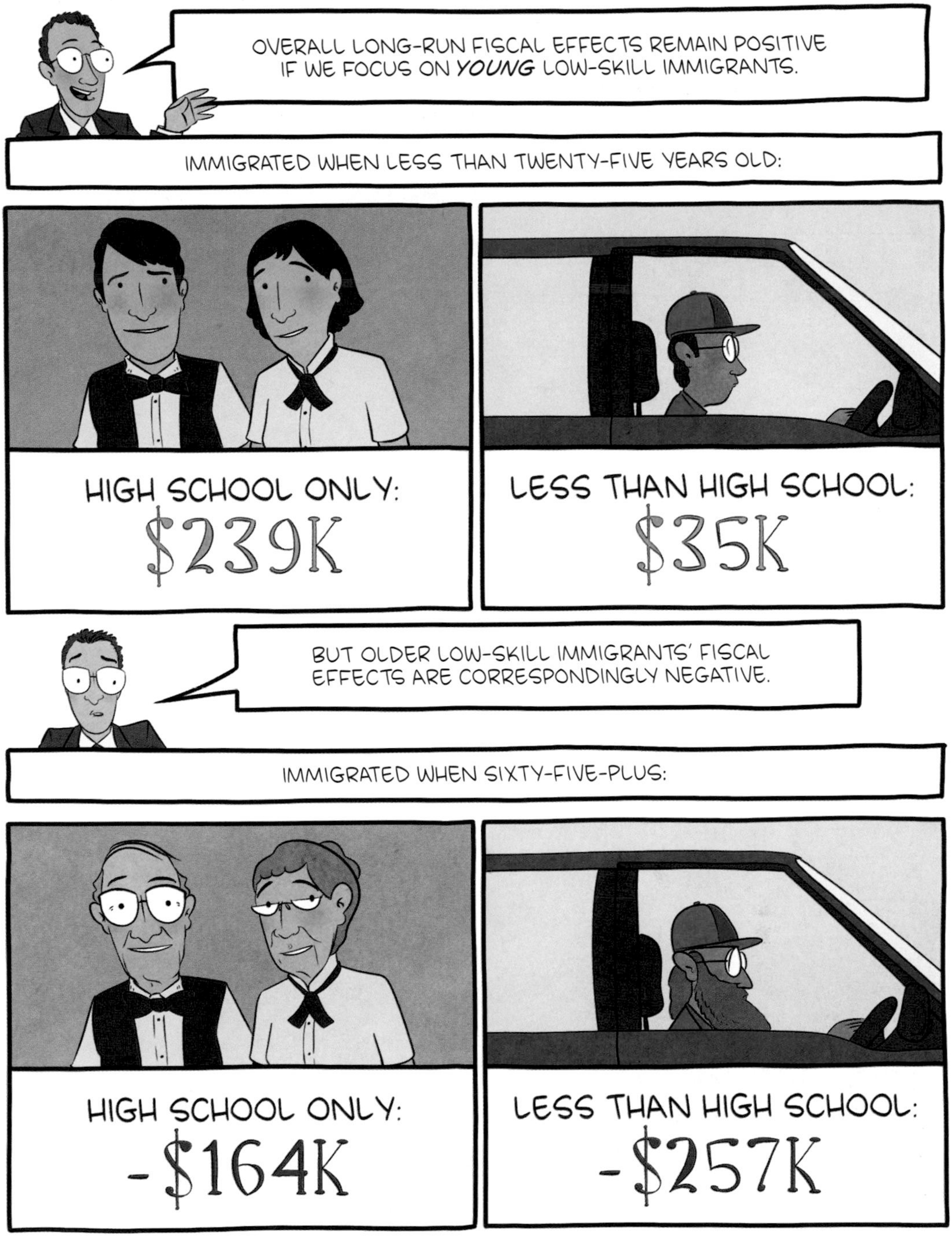

OVERALL LONG-RUN FISCAL EFFECTS REMAIN POSITIVE IF WE FOCUS ON YOUNG LOW-SKILL IMMIGRANTS.
IMMIGRATED WHEN LESS THAN TWENTY-FIVE YEARS OLD:
HIGH SCHOOL ONLY:
$239K
LESS THAN HIGH SCHOOL:
$35K
BUT OLDER LOW-SKILL IMMIGRANTS' FISCAL EFFECTS ARE CORRESPONDINGLY NEGATIVE.
IMMIGRATED WHEN SIXTY-FIVE-PLUS:
HIGH SCHOOL ONLY:
-$164K
LESS THAN HIGH SCHOOL:
-$257K

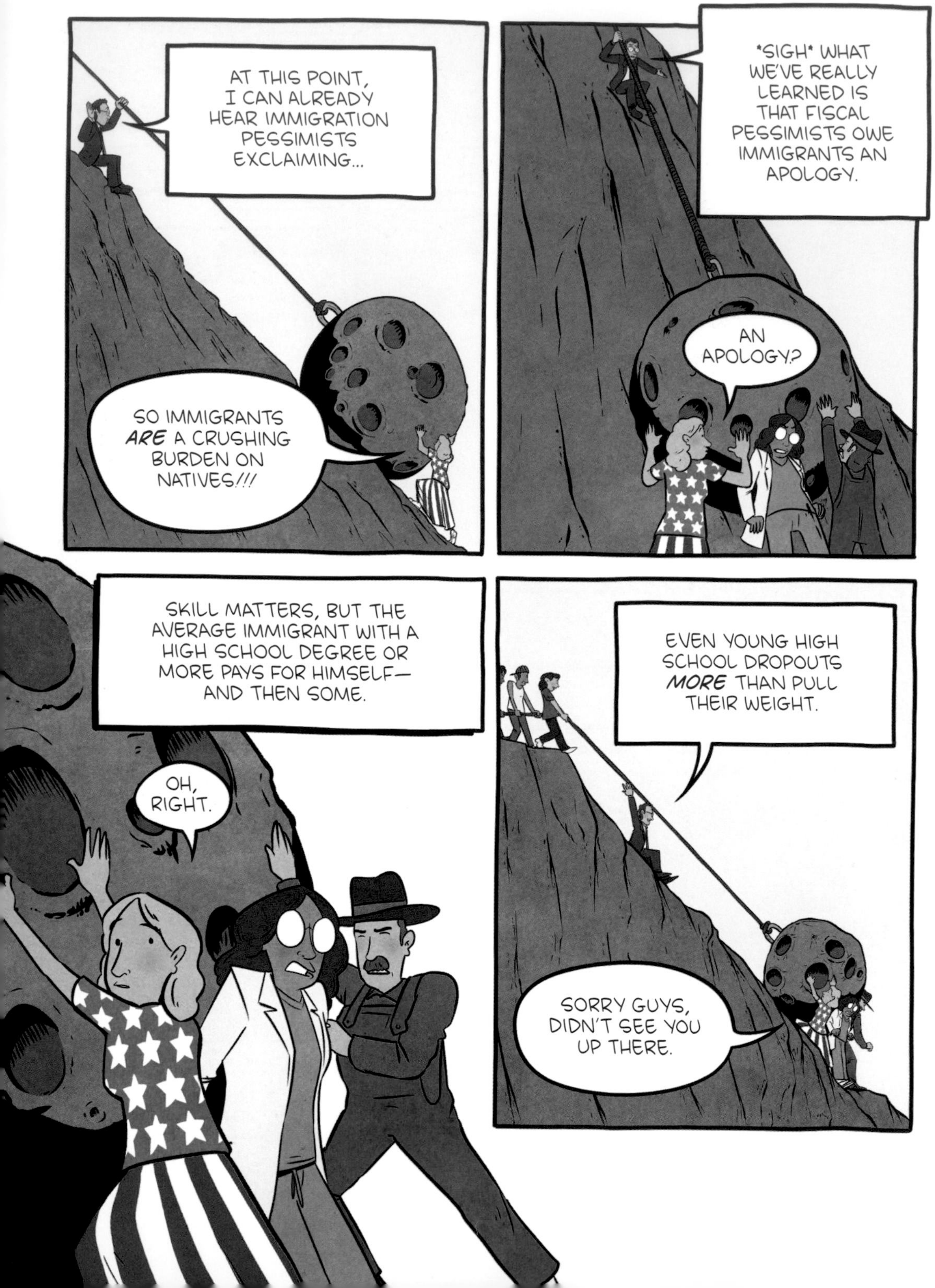
AT THIS POINT, I CAN ALREADY HEAR IMMIGRATION PESSIMISTS EXCLAIMING...
SO IMMIGRANTS *ARE* A CRUSHING BURDEN ON NATIVES!!!
SIGH WHAT WE'VE REALLY LEARNED IS THAT FISCAL PESSIMISTS OWE IMMIGRANTS AN APOLOGY.
AN APOLOGY?
SKILL MATTERS, BUT THE AVERAGE IMMIGRANT WITH A HIGH SCHOOL DEGREE OR MORE PAYS FOR HIMSELF— AND THEN SOME.
OH, RIGHT.
EVEN YOUNG HIGH SCHOOL DROPOUTS *MORE* THAN PULL THEIR WEIGHT.
SORRY GUYS, DIDN'T SEE YOU UP THERE.

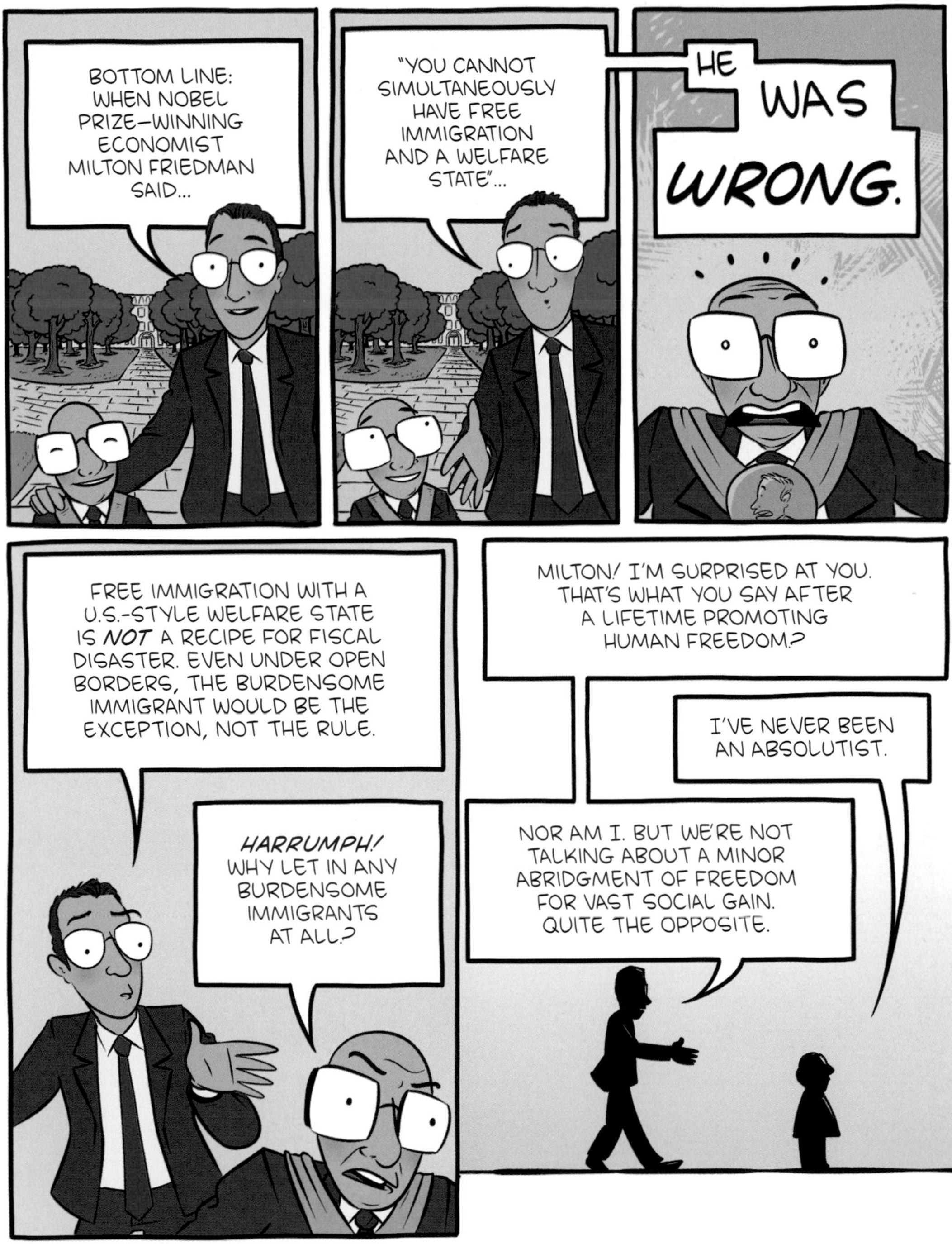
BOTTOM LINE: WHEN NOBEL PRIZE-WINNING ECONOMIST MILTON FRIEDMAN SAID...
"YOU CANNOT SIMULTANEOUSLY HAVE FREE IMMIGRATION AND A WELFARE STATE"...
HE WAS *WRONG.*
FREE IMMIGRATION WITH A U.S.-STYLE WELFARE STATE IS ***NOT*** A RECIPE FOR FISCAL DISASTER. EVEN UNDER OPEN BORDERS, THE BURDENSOME IMMIGRANT WOULD BE THE EXCEPTION, NOT THE RULE.
HARRUMPH! WHY LET IN ANY BURDENSOME IMMIGRANTS AT ALL?
MILTON! I'M SURPRISED AT YOU. THAT'S WHAT YOU SAY AFTER A LIFETIME PROMOTING HUMAN FREEDOM?
I'VE NEVER BEEN AN ABSOLUTIST.
NOR AM I. BUT WE'RE NOT TALKING ABOUT A MINOR ABRIDGMENT OF FREEDOM FOR VAST SOCIAL GAIN. QUITE THE OPPOSITE.

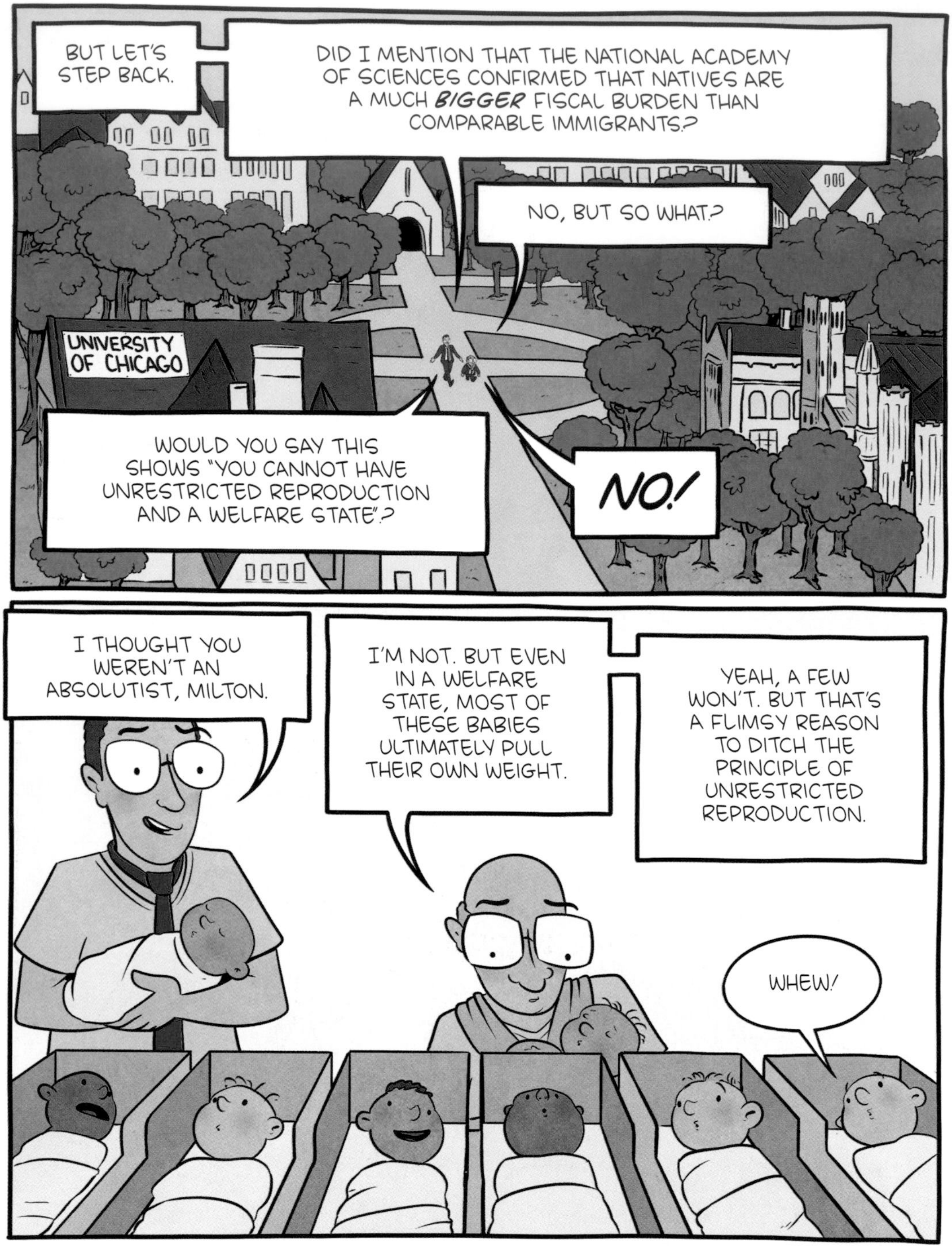
BUT LET'S STEP BACK.
DID I MENTION THAT THE NATIONAL ACADEMY OF SCIENCES CONFIRMED THAT NATIVES ARE A MUCH BIGGER FISCAL BURDEN THAN COMPARABLE IMMIGRANTS?
NO, BUT SO WHAT?
UNIVERSITY OF CHICAGO
WOULD YOU SAY THIS SHOWS "YOU CANNOT HAVE UNRESTRICTED REPRODUCTION AND A WELFARE STATE"?
NO!
I THOUGHT YOU WEREN'T AN ABSOLUTIST, MILTON.
I'M NOT. BUT EVEN IN A WELFARE STATE, MOST OF THESE BABIES ULTIMATELY PULL THEIR OWN WEIGHT.
YEAH, A FEW WON'T. BUT THAT'S A FLIMSY REASON TO DITCH THE PRINCIPLE OF UNRESTRICTED REPRODUCTION.
WHEW!

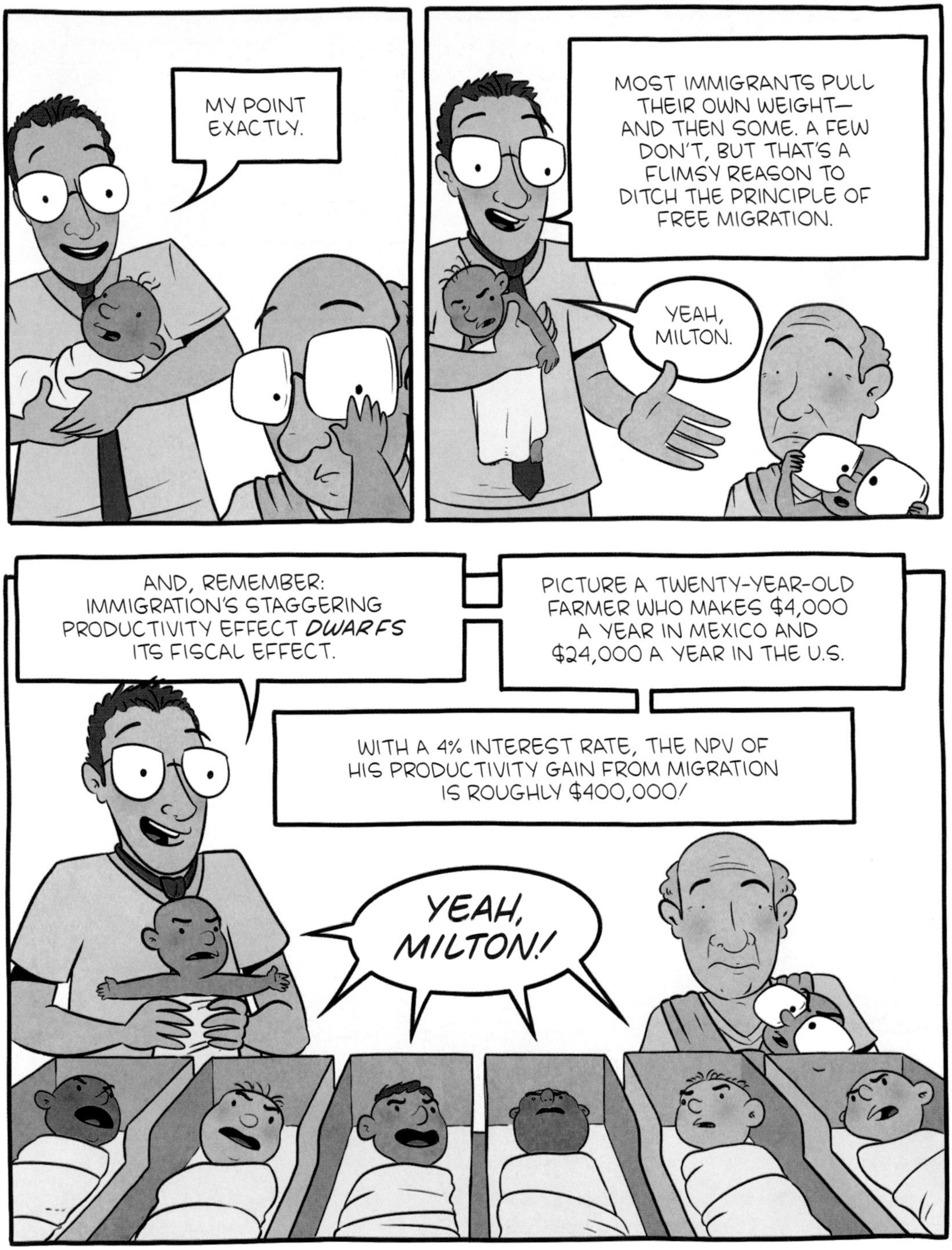
MY POINT EXACTLY.
MOST IMMIGRANTS PULL THEIR OWN WEIGHT— AND THEN SOME. A FEW DON'T, BUT THAT'S A FLIMSY REASON TO DITCH THE PRINCIPLE OF FREE MIGRATION.
YEAH, MILTON.
AND, REMEMBER: IMMIGRATION'S STAGGERING PRODUCTIVITY EFFECT *DWARFS* ITS FISCAL EFFECT.
PICTURE A TWENTY-YEAR-OLD FARMER WHO MAKES $4,000 A YEAR IN MEXICO AND $24,000 A YEAR IN THE U.S.
WITH A 4% INTEREST RATE, THE NPV OF HIS PRODUCTIVITY GAIN FROM MIGRATION IS ROUGHLY $400,000!
YEAH, MILTON!

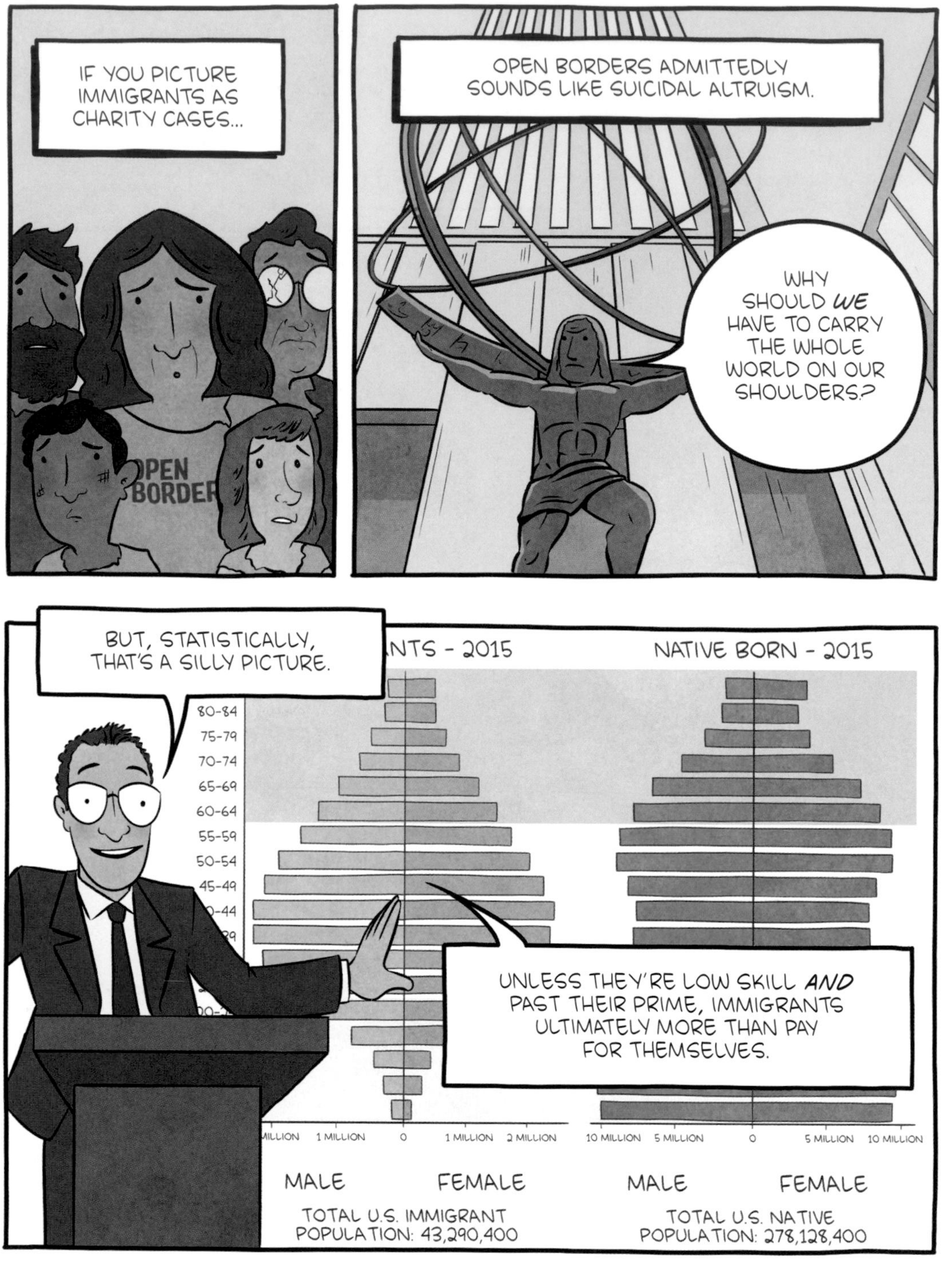
IF YOU PICTURE IMMIGRANTS AS CHARITY CASES...
OPEN BORDERS
OPEN BORDERS ADMITTEDLY SOUNDS LIKE SUICIDAL ALTRUISM.
WHY SHOULD *WE* HAVE TO CARRY THE WHOLE WORLD ON OUR SHOULDERS?
BUT, STATISTICALLY, THAT'S A SILLY PICTURE.
NTS - 2015
NATIVE BORN - 2015
80-84
75-79
70-74
65-69
60-64
55-59
50-54
45-49
UNLESS THEY'RE LOW SKILL *AND* PAST THEIR PRIME, IMMIGRANTS ULTIMATELY MORE THAN PAY FOR THEMSELVES.
1 MILLION 0 1 MILLION 2 MILLION
10 MILLION 5 MILLION 0 5 MILLION 10 MILLION
MALE FEMALE
MALE FEMALE
TOTAL U.S. IMMIGRANT POPULATION: 43,290,400
TOTAL U.S. NATIVE POPULATION: 278,128,400

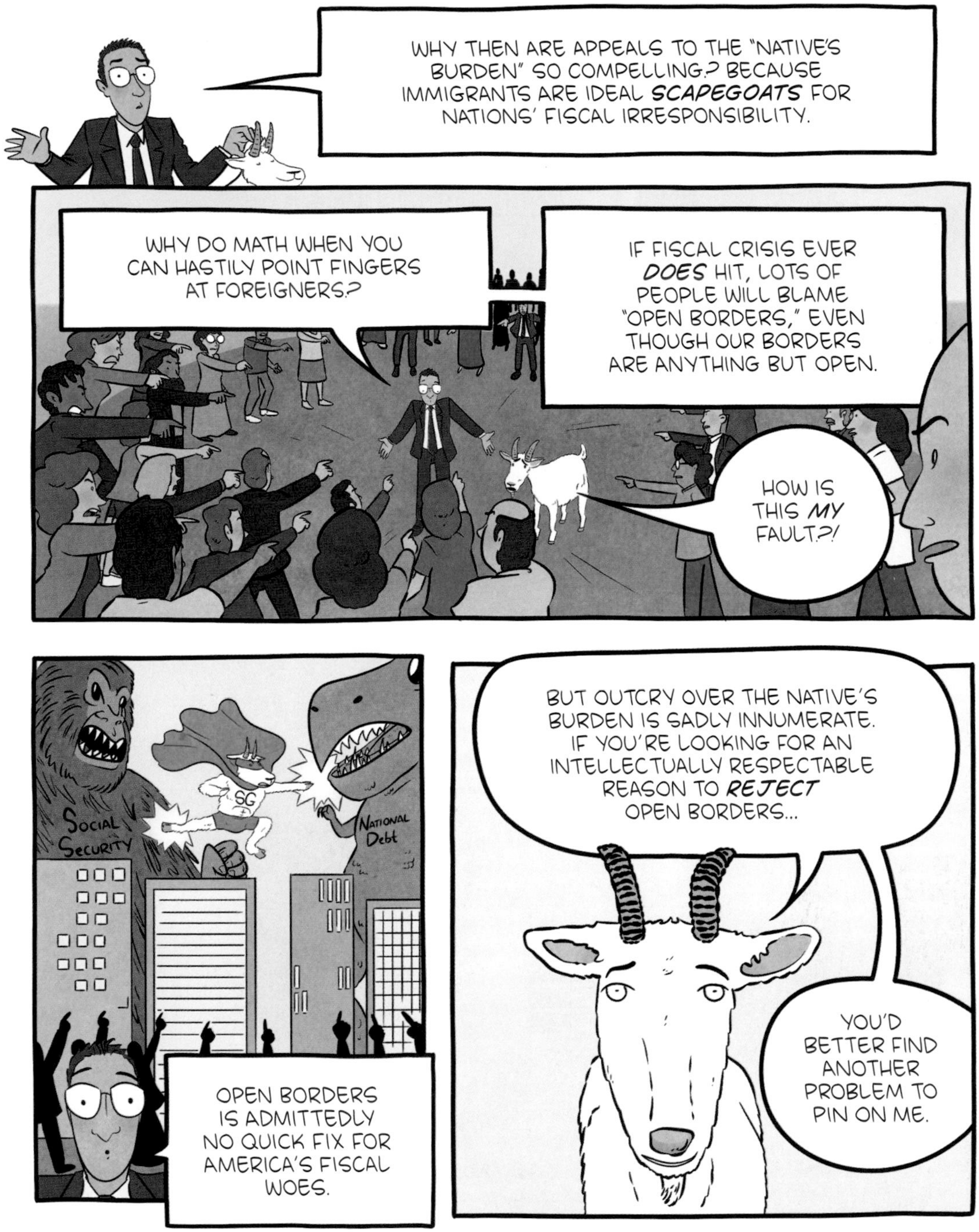
WHY THEN ARE APPEALS TO THE "NATIVE'S BURDEN" SO COMPELLING? BECAUSE IMMIGRANTS ARE IDEAL **SCAPEGOATS** FOR NATIONS' FISCAL IRRESPONSIBILITY.
WHY DO MATH WHEN YOU CAN HASTILY POINT FINGERS AT FOREIGNERS?
IF FISCAL CRISIS EVER **DOES** HIT, LOTS OF PEOPLE WILL BLAME "OPEN BORDERS," EVEN THOUGH OUR BORDERS ARE ANYTHING BUT OPEN.
HOW IS THIS *MY* FAULT?!
SOCIAL SECURITY
SG
NATIONAL Debt
OPEN BORDERS IS ADMITTEDLY NO QUICK FIX FOR AMERICA'S FISCAL WOES.
BUT OUTCRY OVER THE NATIVE'S BURDEN IS SADLY INNUMERATE. IF YOU'RE LOOKING FOR AN INTELLECTUALLY RESPECTABLE REASON TO ***REJECT*** OPEN BORDERS...
YOU'D BETTER FIND ANOTHER PROBLEM TO PIN ON ME.

CHAPTER 4

CRIMES AGAINST CULTURE

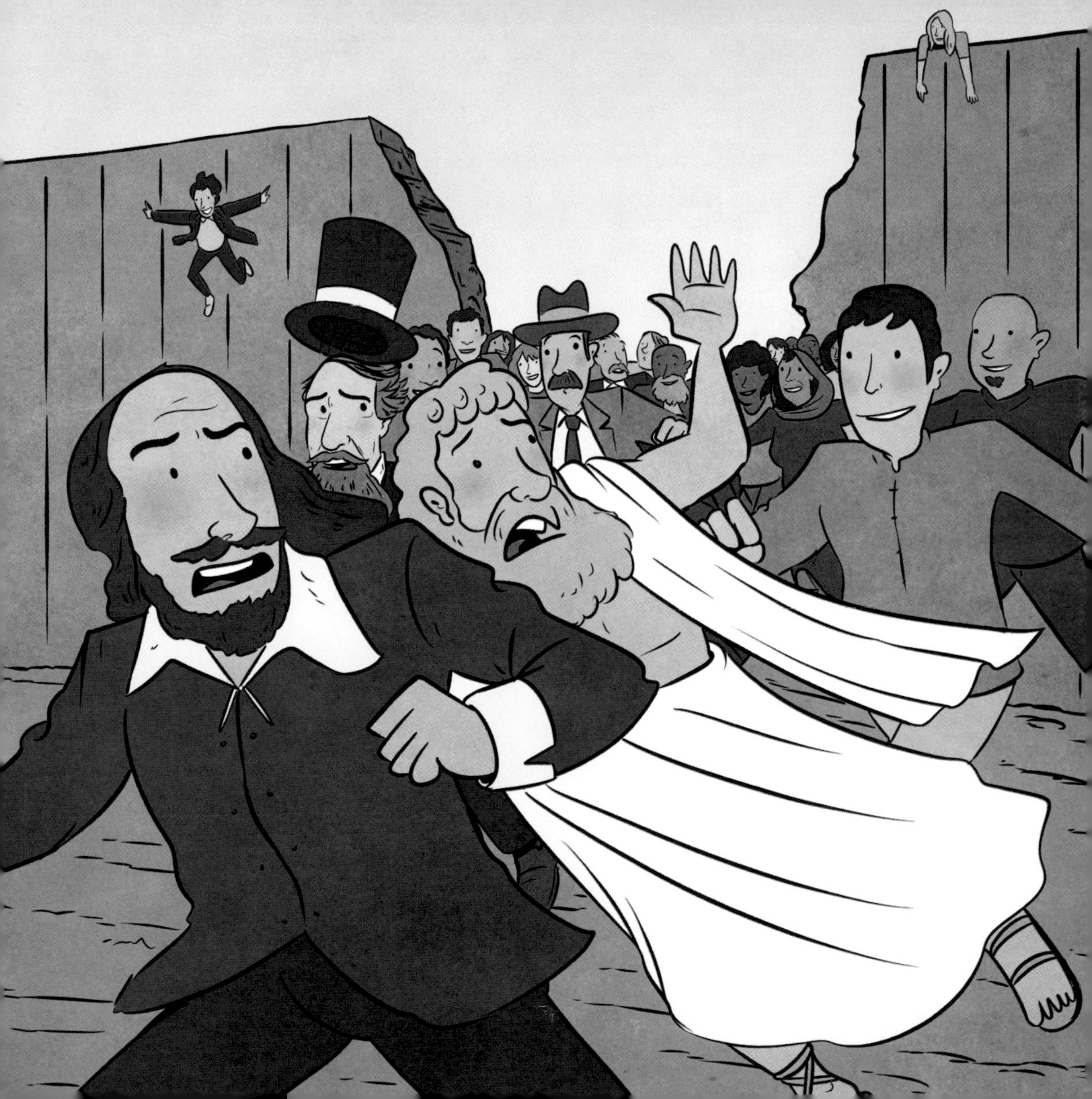

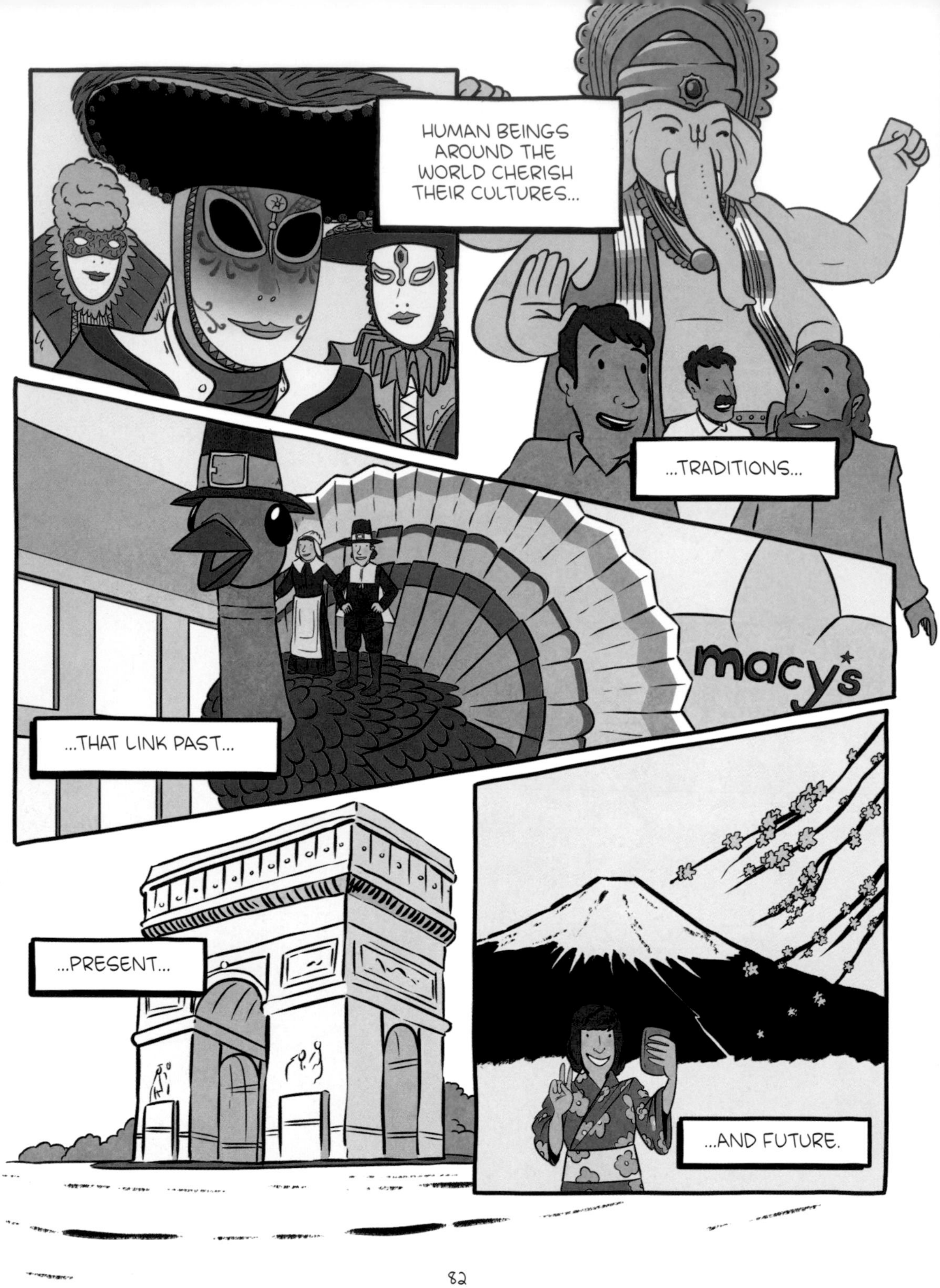
HUMAN BEINGS AROUND THE WORLD CHERISH THEIR CULTURES...
...TRADITIONS...
macy's
...THAT LINK PAST...
...PRESENT...
...AND FUTURE.

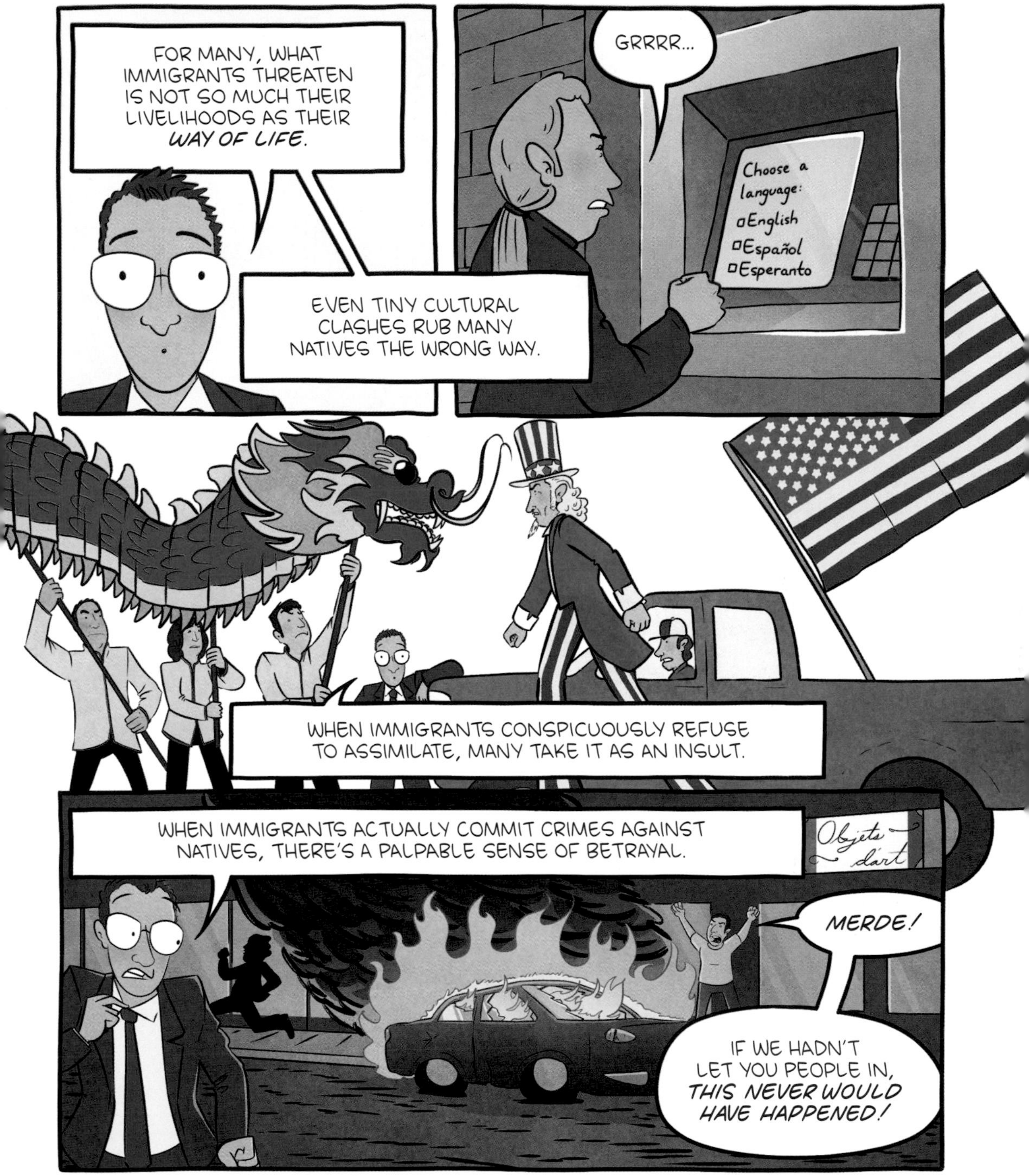

FOR MANY, WHAT IMMIGRANTS THREATEN IS NOT SO MUCH THEIR LIVELIHOODS AS THEIR *WAY OF LIFE*.
EVEN TINY CULTURAL CLASHES RUB MANY NATIVES THE WRONG WAY.
GRRRR...
Choose a language:
English
Español
Esperanto
WHEN IMMIGRANTS CONSPICUOUSLY REFUSE TO ASSIMILATE, MANY TAKE IT AS AN INSULT.
WHEN IMMIGRANTS ACTUALLY COMMIT CRIMES AGAINST NATIVES, THERE'S A PALPABLE SENSE OF BETRAYAL.
Objets d'art
MERDE!
IF WE HADN'T LET YOU PEOPLE IN, ***THIS NEVER WOULD HAVE HAPPENED!***

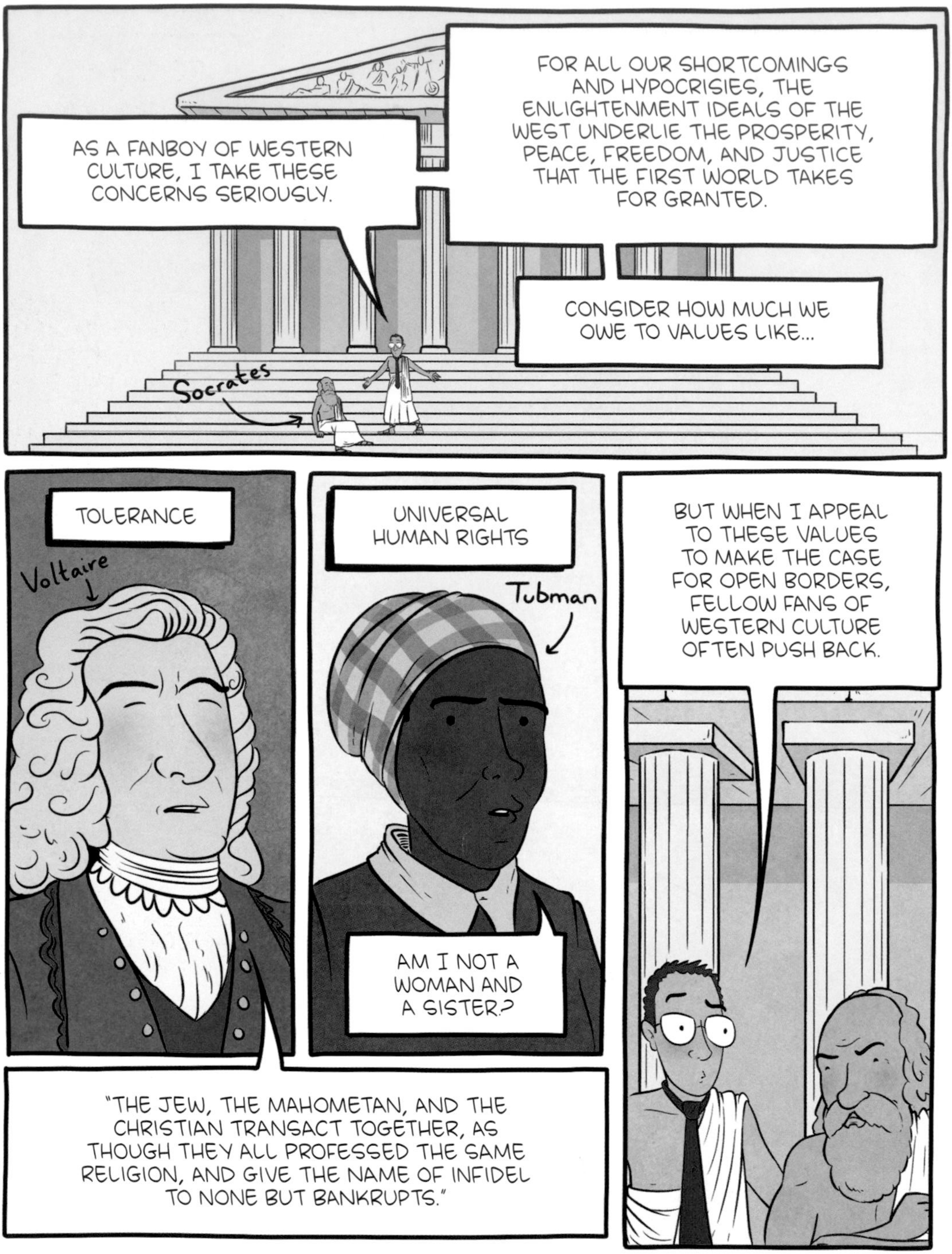
AS A FANBOY OF WESTERN CULTURE, I TAKE THESE CONCERNS SERIOUSLY.
FOR ALL OUR SHORTCOMINGS AND HYPOCRISIES, THE ENLIGHTENMENT IDEALS OF THE WEST UNDERLIE THE PROSPERITY, PEACE, FREEDOM, AND JUSTICE THAT THE FIRST WORLD TAKES FOR GRANTED.
CONSIDER HOW MUCH WE OWE TO VALUES LIKE...
Socrates
TOLERANCE
Voltaire
"THE JEW, THE MAHOMETAN, AND THE CHRISTIAN TRANSACT TOGETHER, AS THOUGH THEY ALL PROFESSED THE SAME RELIGION, AND GIVE THE NAME OF INFIDEL TO NONE BUT BANKRUPTS."
UNIVERSAL HUMAN RIGHTS
Tubman
AM I NOT A WOMAN AND A SISTER?
BUT WHEN I APPEAL TO THESE VALUES TO MAKE THE CASE FOR OPEN BORDERS, FELLOW FANS OF WESTERN CULTURE OFTEN PUSH BACK.

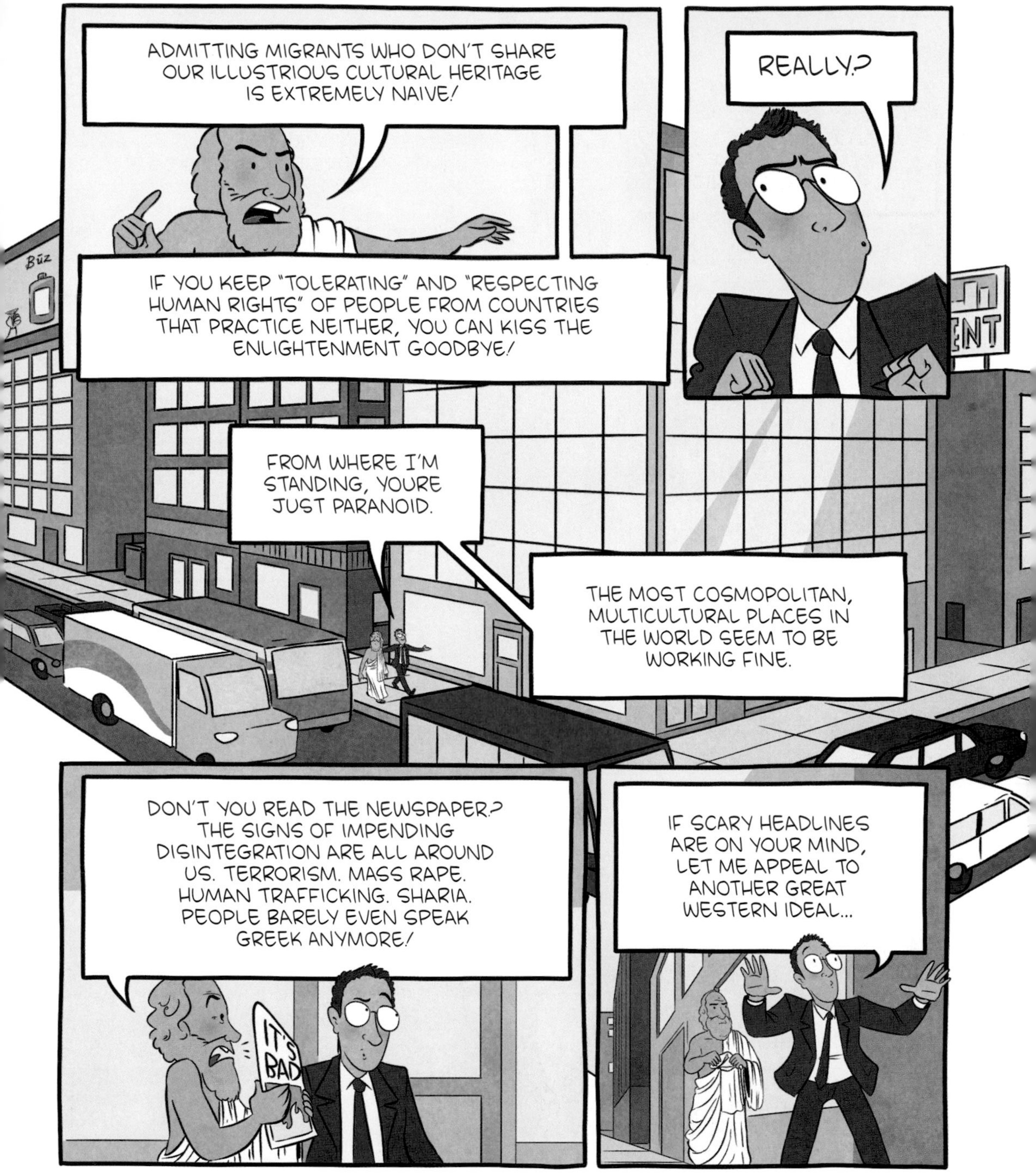
ADMITTING MIGRANTS WHO DON'T SHARE OUR ILLUSTRIOUS CULTURAL HERITAGE IS EXTREMELY NAIVE!
IF YOU KEEP "TOLERATING" AND "RESPECTING HUMAN RIGHTS" OF PEOPLE FROM COUNTRIES THAT PRACTICE NEITHER, YOU CAN KISS THE ENLIGHTENMENT GOODBYE!
REALLY?
FROM WHERE I'M STANDING, YOURE JUST PARANOID.
THE MOST COSMOPOLITAN, MULTICULTURAL PLACES IN THE WORLD SEEM TO BE WORKING FINE.
DON'T YOU READ THE NEWSPAPER? THE SIGNS OF IMPENDING DISINTEGRATION ARE ALL AROUND US. TERRORISM. MASS RAPE. HUMAN TRAFFICKING. SHARIA. PEOPLE BARELY EVEN SPEAK GREEK ANYMORE!
IT'S BAD
IF SCARY HEADLINES ARE ON YOUR MIND, LET ME APPEAL TO ANOTHER GREAT WESTERN IDEAL...

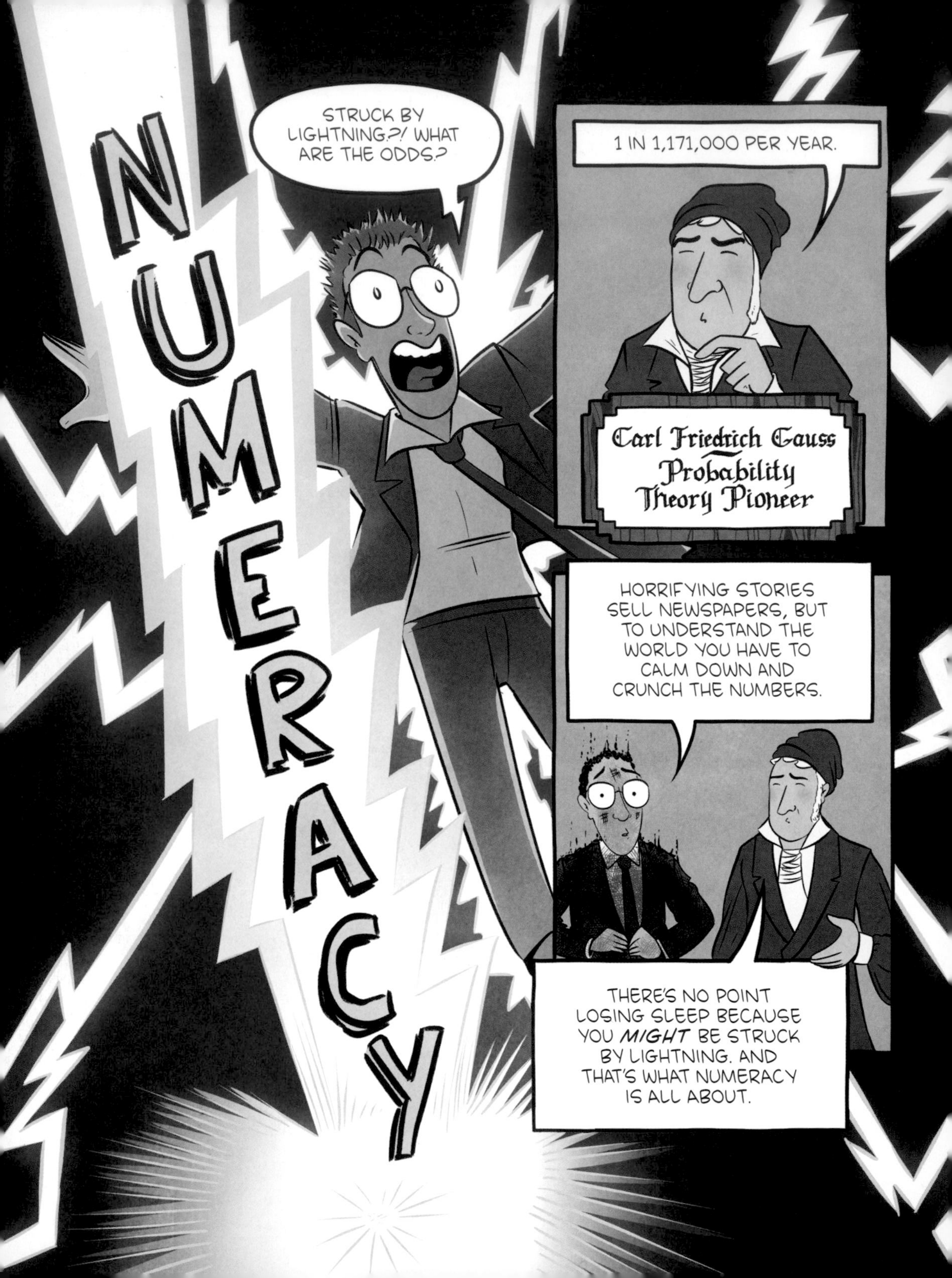
NUMERACY
STRUCK BY LIGHTNING?! WHAT ARE THE ODDS?
1 IN 1,171,000 PER YEAR.
Carl Friedrich Gauss
Probability Theory Pioneer
HORRIFYING STORIES SELL NEWSPAPERS, BUT TO UNDERSTAND THE WORLD YOU HAVE TO CALM DOWN AND CRUNCH THE NUMBERS.
THERE'S NO POINT LOSING SLEEP BECAUSE YOU *MIGHT* BE STRUCK BY LIGHTNING. AND THAT'S WHAT NUMERACY IS ALL ABOUT.

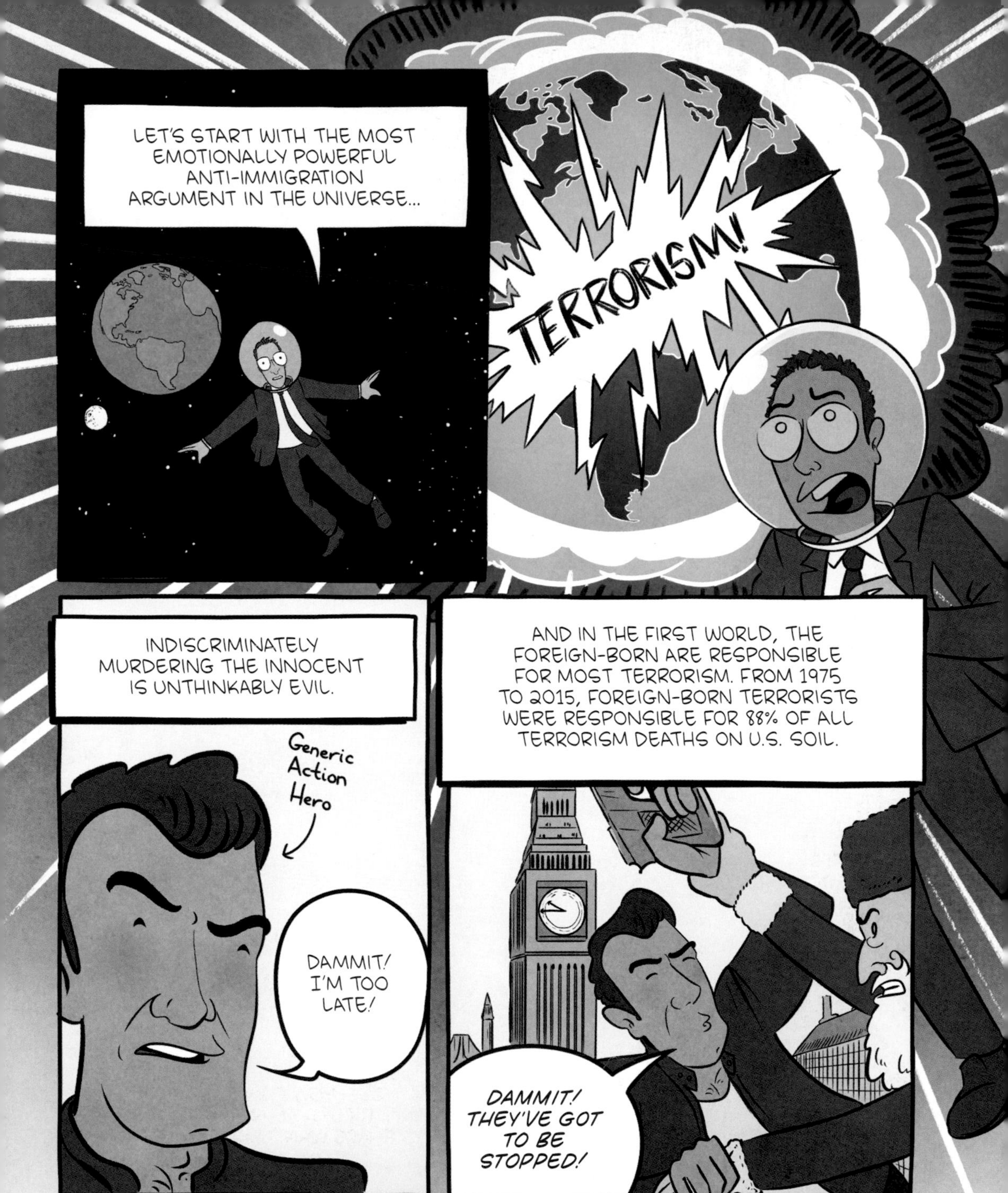
LET'S START WITH THE MOST EMOTIONALLY POWERFUL ANTI-IMMIGRATION ARGUMENT IN THE UNIVERSE...
TERRORISM!
INDISCRIMINATELY MURDERING THE INNOCENT IS UNTHINKABLY EVIL.
Generic Action Hero
DAMMIT! I'M TOO LATE!
AND IN THE FIRST WORLD, THE FOREIGN-BORN ARE RESPONSIBLE FOR MOST TERRORISM. FROM 1975 TO 2015, FOREIGN-BORN TERRORISTS WERE RESPONSIBLE FOR 88% OF ALL TERRORISM DEATHS ON U.S. SOIL.
DAMMIT! THEY'VE GOT TO BE STOPPED!

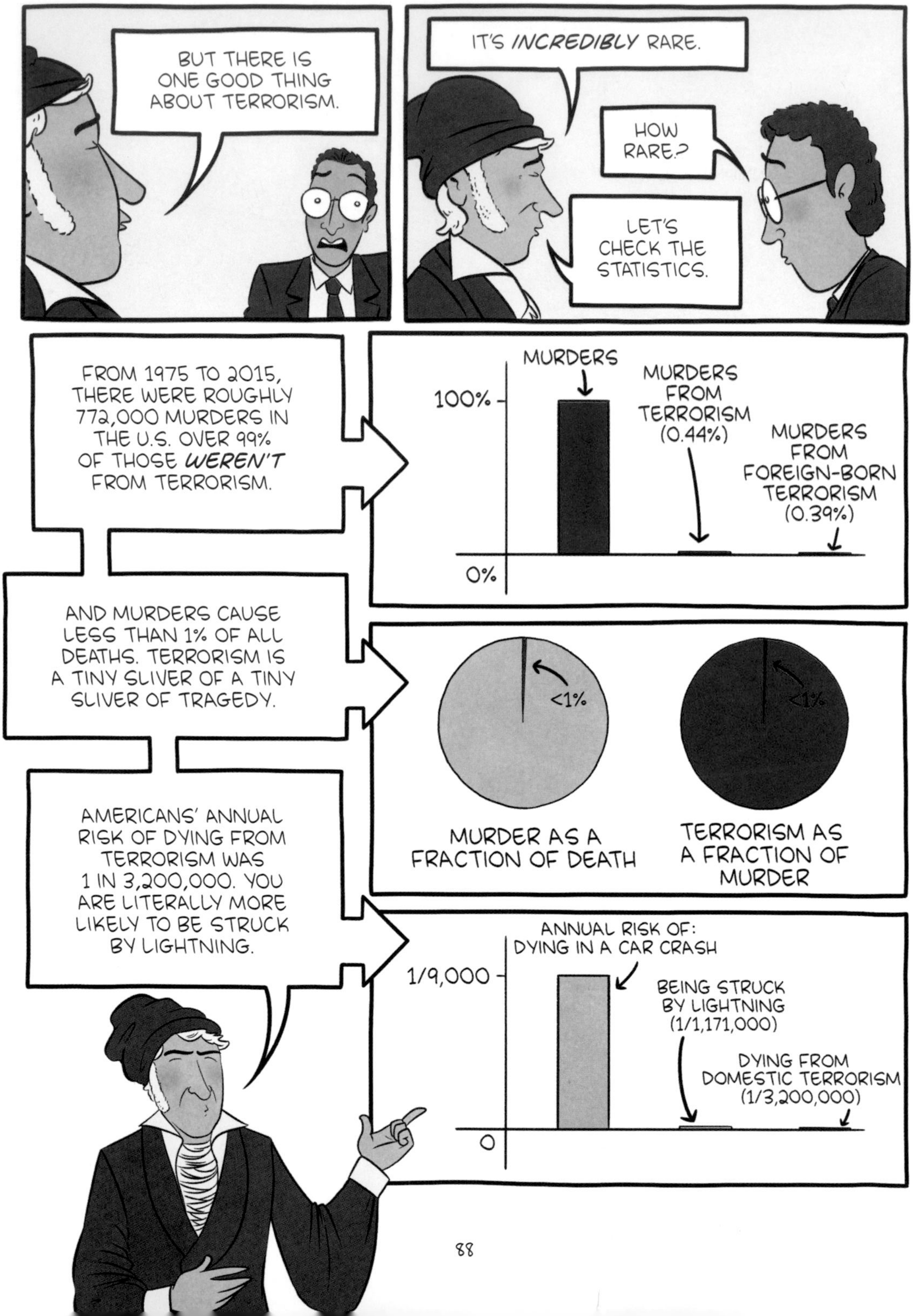
BUT THERE IS ONE GOOD THING ABOUT TERRORISM.
IT'S *INCREDIBLY* RARE.
HOW RARE?
LET'S CHECK THE STATISTICS.
FROM 1975 TO 2015, THERE WERE ROUGHLY 772,000 MURDERS IN THE U.S. OVER 99% OF THOSE *WEREN'T* FROM TERRORISM.
MURDERS
100%
0%
MURDERS FROM TERRORISM (0.44%)
MURDERS FROM FOREIGN-BORN TERRORISM (0.39%)
AND MURDERS CAUSE LESS THAN 1% OF ALL DEATHS. TERRORISM IS A TINY SLIVER OF A TINY SLIVER OF TRAGEDY.
<1%
MURDER AS A FRACTION OF DEATH
<1%
TERRORISM AS A FRACTION OF MURDER
AMERICANS' ANNUAL RISK OF DYING FROM TERRORISM WAS 1 IN 3,200,000. YOU ARE LITERALLY MORE LIKELY TO BE STRUCK BY LIGHTNING.
ANNUAL RISK OF: DYING IN A CAR CRASH
1/9,000
0
BEING STRUCK BY LIGHTNING (1/1,171,000)
DYING FROM DOMESTIC TERRORISM (1/3,200,000)

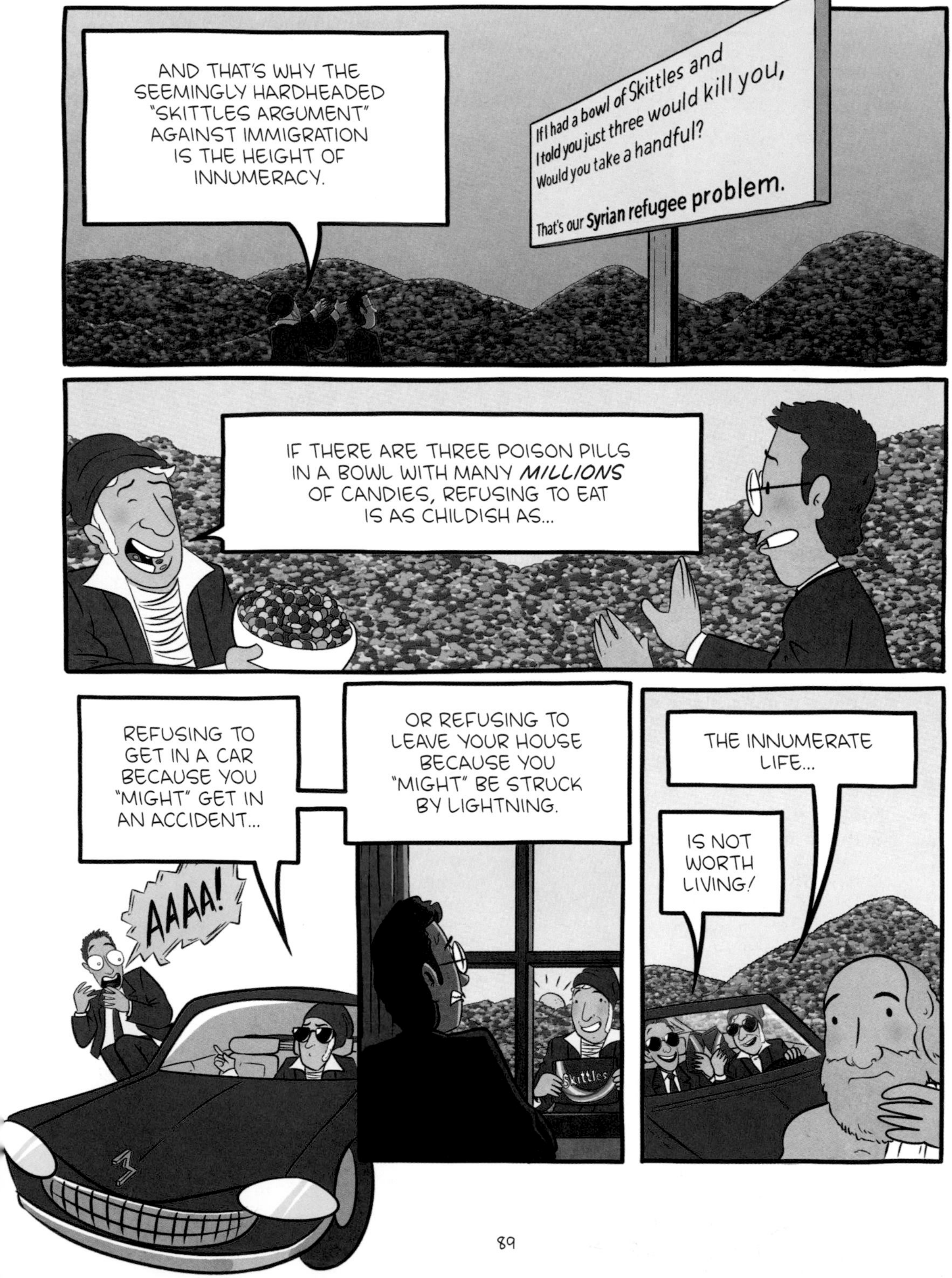
AND THAT'S WHY THE SEEMINGLY HARDHEADED "SKITTLES ARGUMENT" AGAINST IMMIGRATION IS THE HEIGHT OF INNUMERACY.
If I had a bowl of Skittles and I told you just three would kill you, Would you take a handful?
That's our Syrian refugee problem.
IF THERE ARE THREE POISON PILLS IN A BOWL WITH MANY *MILLIONS* OF CANDIES, REFUSING TO EAT IS AS CHILDISH AS...
REFUSING TO GET IN A CAR BECAUSE YOU "MIGHT" GET IN AN ACCIDENT...
AAAA!
OR REFUSING TO LEAVE YOUR HOUSE BECAUSE YOU "MIGHT" BE STRUCK BY LIGHTNING.
Skittles
THE INNUMERATE LIFE...
IS NOT WORTH LIVING!

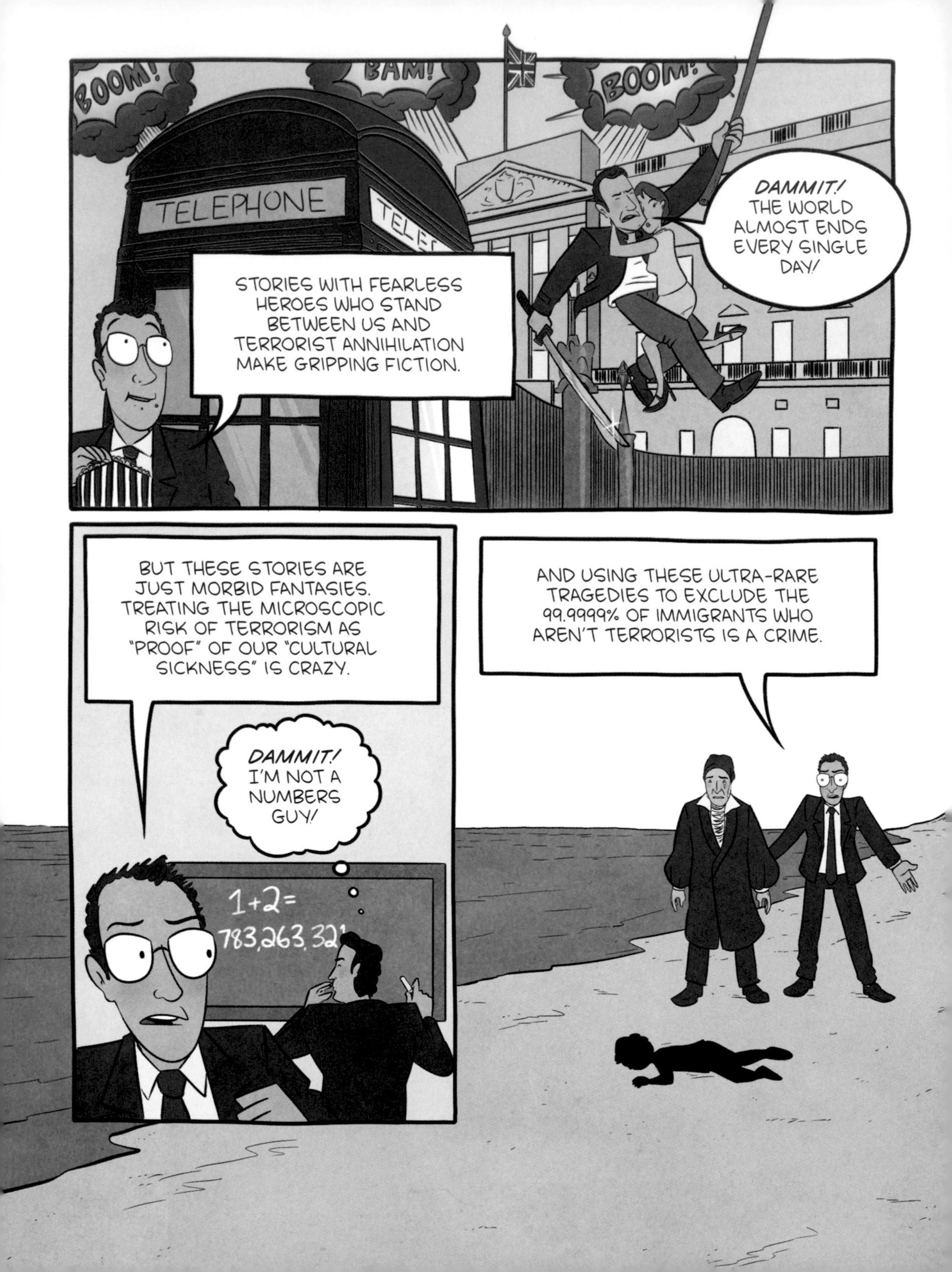
BOOM!
BAM!
BOOM!
TELEPHONE
STORIES WITH FEARLESS HEROES WHO STAND BETWEEN US AND TERRORIST ANNIHILATION MAKE GRIPPING FICTION.
DAMMIT! THE WORLD ALMOST ENDS EVERY SINGLE DAY!
BUT THESE STORIES ARE JUST MORBID FANTASIES. TREATING THE MICROSCOPIC RISK OF TERRORISM AS "PROOF" OF OUR "CULTURAL SICKNESS" IS CRAZY.
DAMMIT! I'M NOT A NUMBERS GUY!
1+2=
AND USING THESE ULTRA-RARE TRAGEDIES TO EXCLUDE THE 99.9999% OF IMMIGRANTS WHO AREN'T TERRORISTS IS A CRIME.

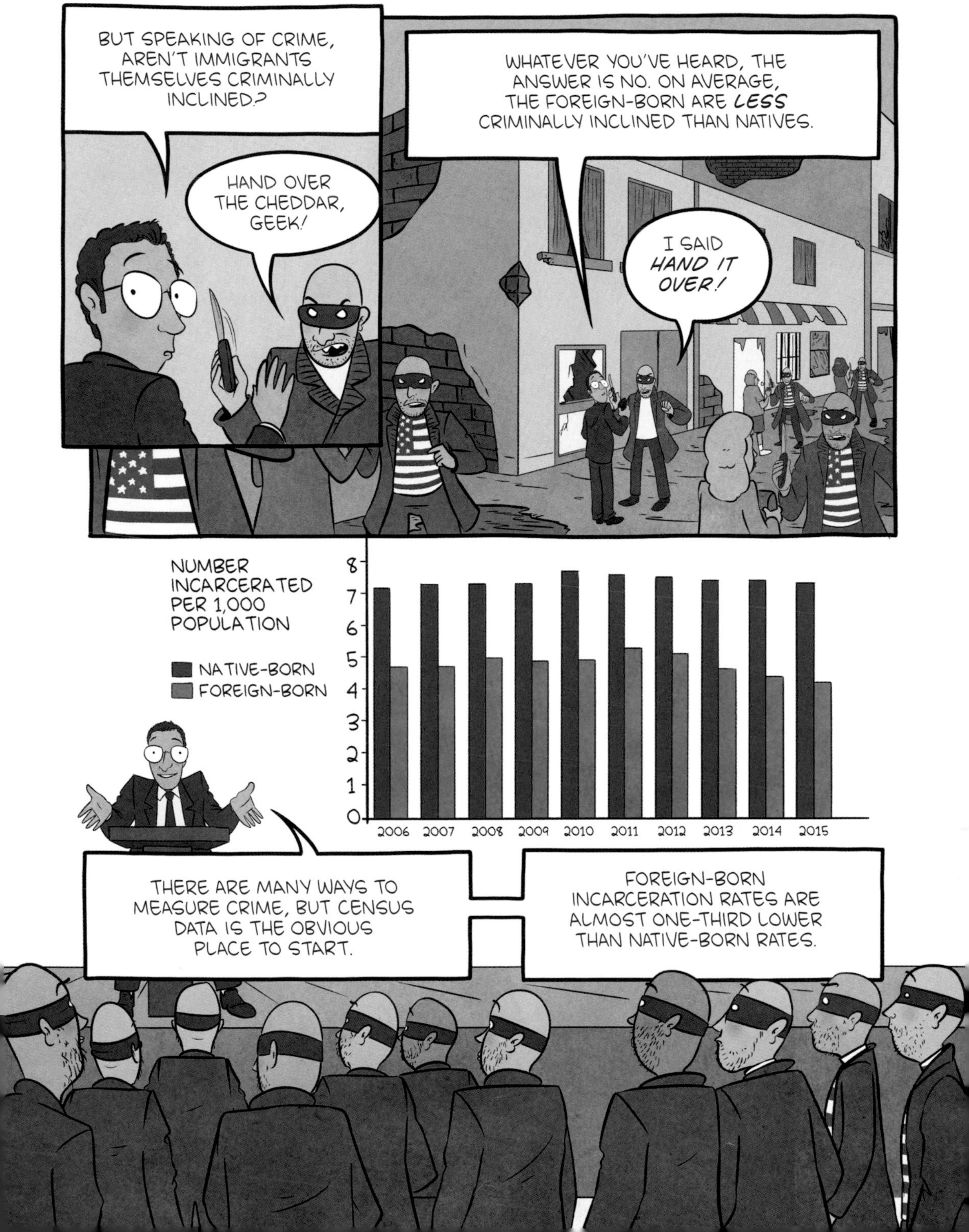
BUT SPEAKING OF CRIME, AREN'T IMMIGRANTS THEMSELVES CRIMINALLY INCLINED?
HAND OVER THE CHEDDAR, GEEK!
WHATEVER YOU'VE HEARD, THE ANSWER IS NO. ON AVERAGE, THE FOREIGN-BORN ARE *LESS* CRIMINALLY INCLINED THAN NATIVES.
I SAID *HAND IT OVER!*
NUMBER INCARCERATED PER 1,000 POPULATION
NATIVE-BORN
FOREIGN-BORN
0
1
2
3
4
5
6
7
8
2006 2007 2008 2009 2010 2011 2012 2013 2014 2015
THERE ARE MANY WAYS TO MEASURE CRIME, BUT CENSUS DATA IS THE OBVIOUS PLACE TO START.
FOREIGN-BORN INCARCERATION RATES ARE ALMOST ONE-THIRD LOWER THAN NATIVE-BORN RATES.

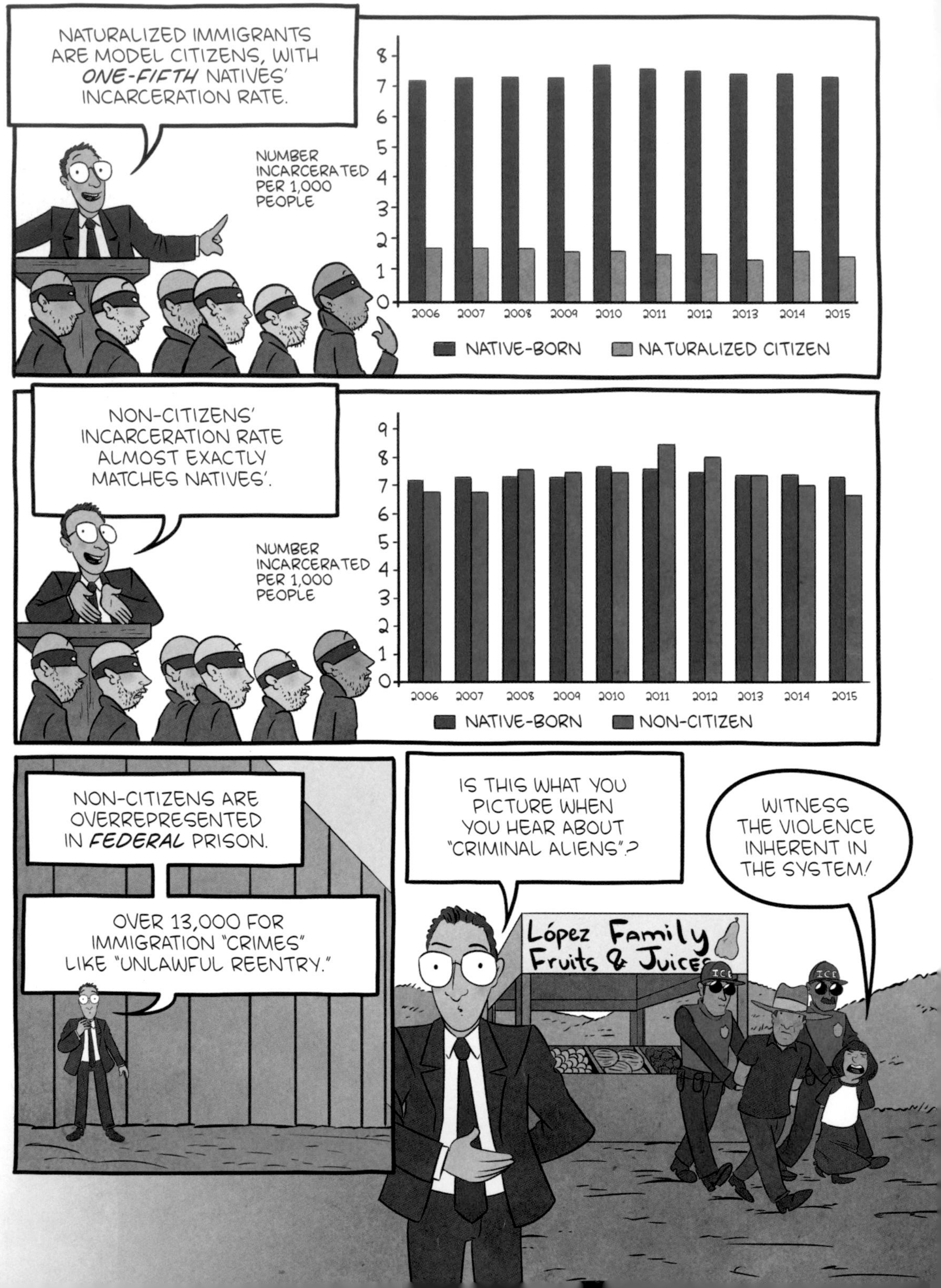
NATURALIZED IMMIGRANTS ARE MODEL CITIZENS, WITH *ONE-FIFTH* NATIVES' INCARCERATION RATE.
NUMBER INCARCERATED PER 1,000 PEOPLE
0 1 2 3 4 5 6 7 8
2006 2007 2008 2009 2010 2011 2012 2013 2014 2015
NATIVE-BORN
NATURALIZED CITIZEN
NON-CITIZENS' INCARCERATION RATE ALMOST EXACTLY MATCHES NATIVES'.
NUMBER INCARCERATED PER 1,000 PEOPLE
0 1 2 3 4 5 6 7 8 9
2006 2007 2008 2009 2010 2011 2012 2013 2014 2015
NATIVE-BORN
NON-CITIZEN
NON-CITIZENS ARE OVERREPRESENTED IN *FEDERAL* PRISON.
OVER 13,000 FOR IMMIGRATION "CRIMES" LIKE "UNLAWFUL REENTRY."
IS THIS WHAT YOU PICTURE WHEN YOU HEAR ABOUT "CRIMINAL ALIENS"?
López Family Fruits & Juices
ICE
ICE
WITNESS THE VIOLENCE INHERENT IN THE SYSTEM!

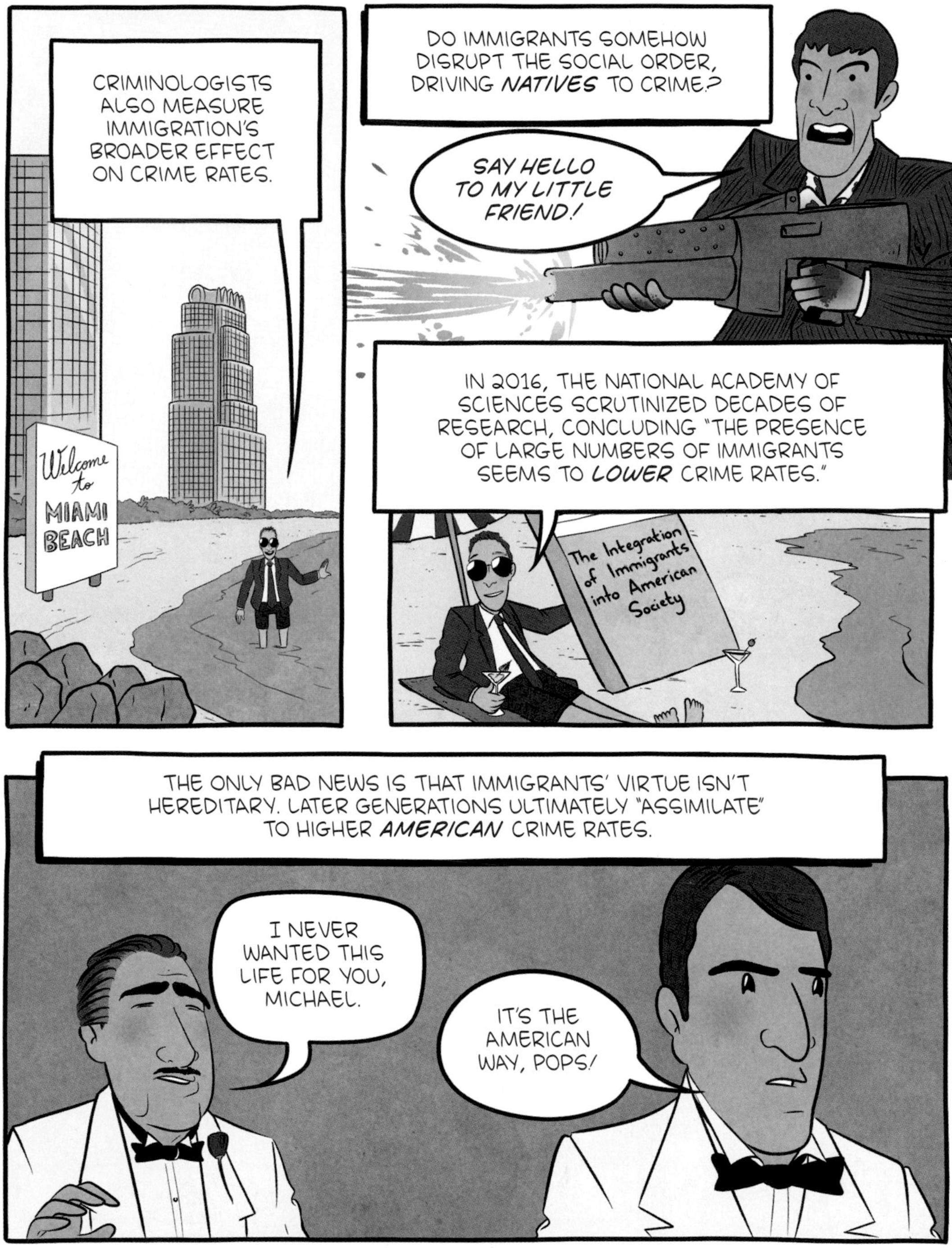
CRIMINOLOGISTS ALSO MEASURE IMMIGRATION'S BROADER EFFECT ON CRIME RATES.
Welcome to MIAMI BEACH
DO IMMIGRANTS SOMEHOW DISRUPT THE SOCIAL ORDER, DRIVING *NATIVES* TO CRIME?
SAY HELLO TO MY LITTLE FRIEND!
IN 2016, THE NATIONAL ACADEMY OF SCIENCES SCRUTINIZED DECADES OF RESEARCH, CONCLUDING "THE PRESENCE OF LARGE NUMBERS OF IMMIGRANTS SEEMS TO *LOWER* CRIME RATES."
The Integration of Immigrants into American Society
THE ONLY BAD NEWS IS THAT IMMIGRANTS' VIRTUE ISN'T HEREDITARY. LATER GENERATIONS ULTIMATELY "ASSIMILATE" TO HIGHER *AMERICAN* CRIME RATES.
I NEVER WANTED THIS LIFE FOR YOU, MICHAEL.
IT'S THE AMERICAN WAY, POPS!

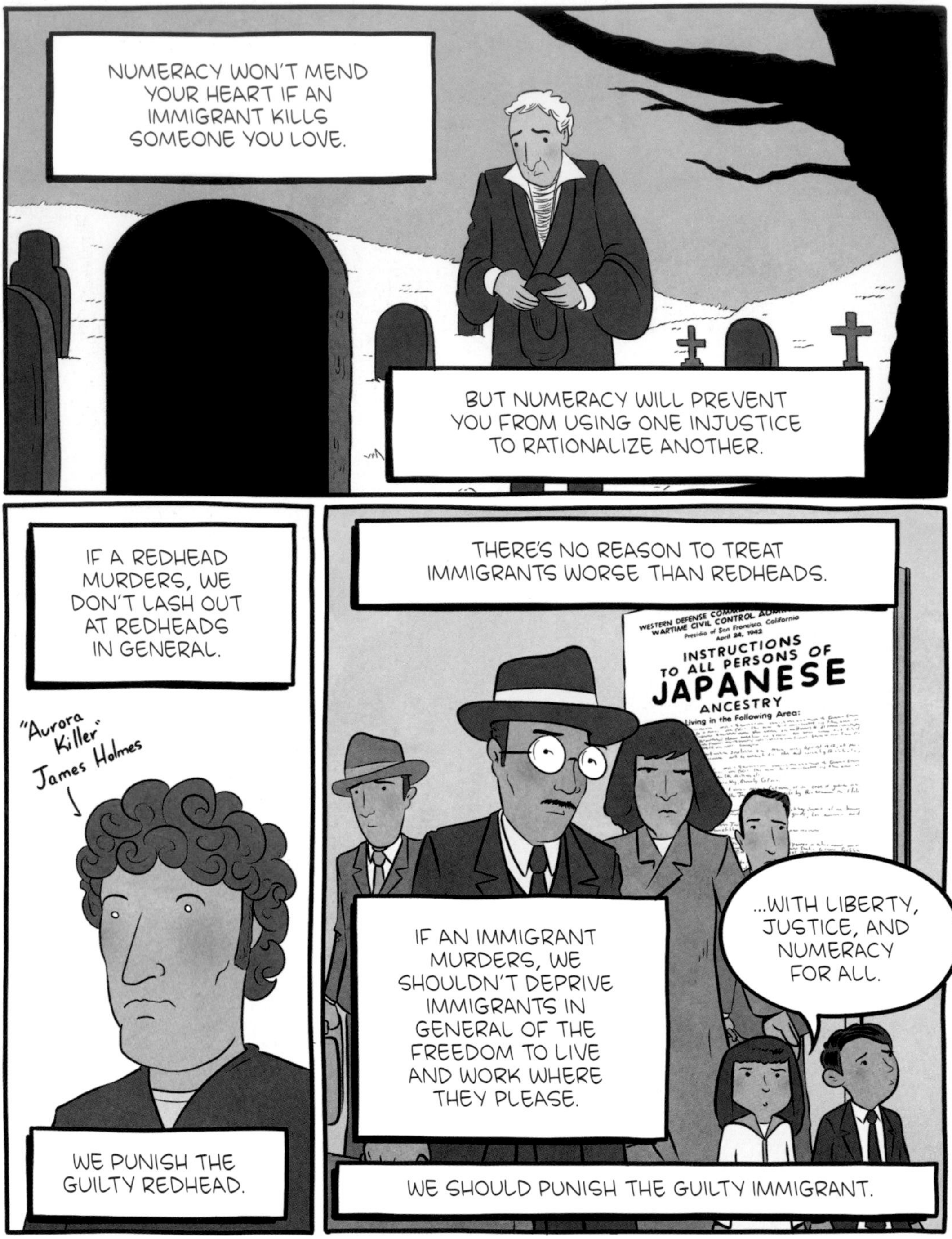

NUMERACY WON'T MEND YOUR HEART IF AN IMMIGRANT KILLS SOMEONE YOU LOVE.
BUT NUMERACY WILL PREVENT YOU FROM USING ONE INJUSTICE TO RATIONALIZE ANOTHER.
IF A REDHEAD MURDERS, WE DON'T LASH OUT AT REDHEADS IN GENERAL.
"Aurora Killer" James Holmes
WE PUNISH THE GUILTY REDHEAD.
THERE'S NO REASON TO TREAT IMMIGRANTS WORSE THAN REDHEADS.
Presidio of San Francisco, California
April 24, 1942
INSTRUCTIONS TO ALL PERSONS OF JAPANESE ANCESTRY
Living in the Following Area:
IF AN IMMIGRANT MURDERS, WE SHOULDN'T DEPRIVE IMMIGRANTS IN GENERAL OF THE FREEDOM TO LIVE AND WORK WHERE THEY PLEASE.
...WITH LIBERTY, JUSTICE, AND NUMERACY FOR ALL.
WE SHOULD PUNISH THE GUILTY IMMIGRANT.

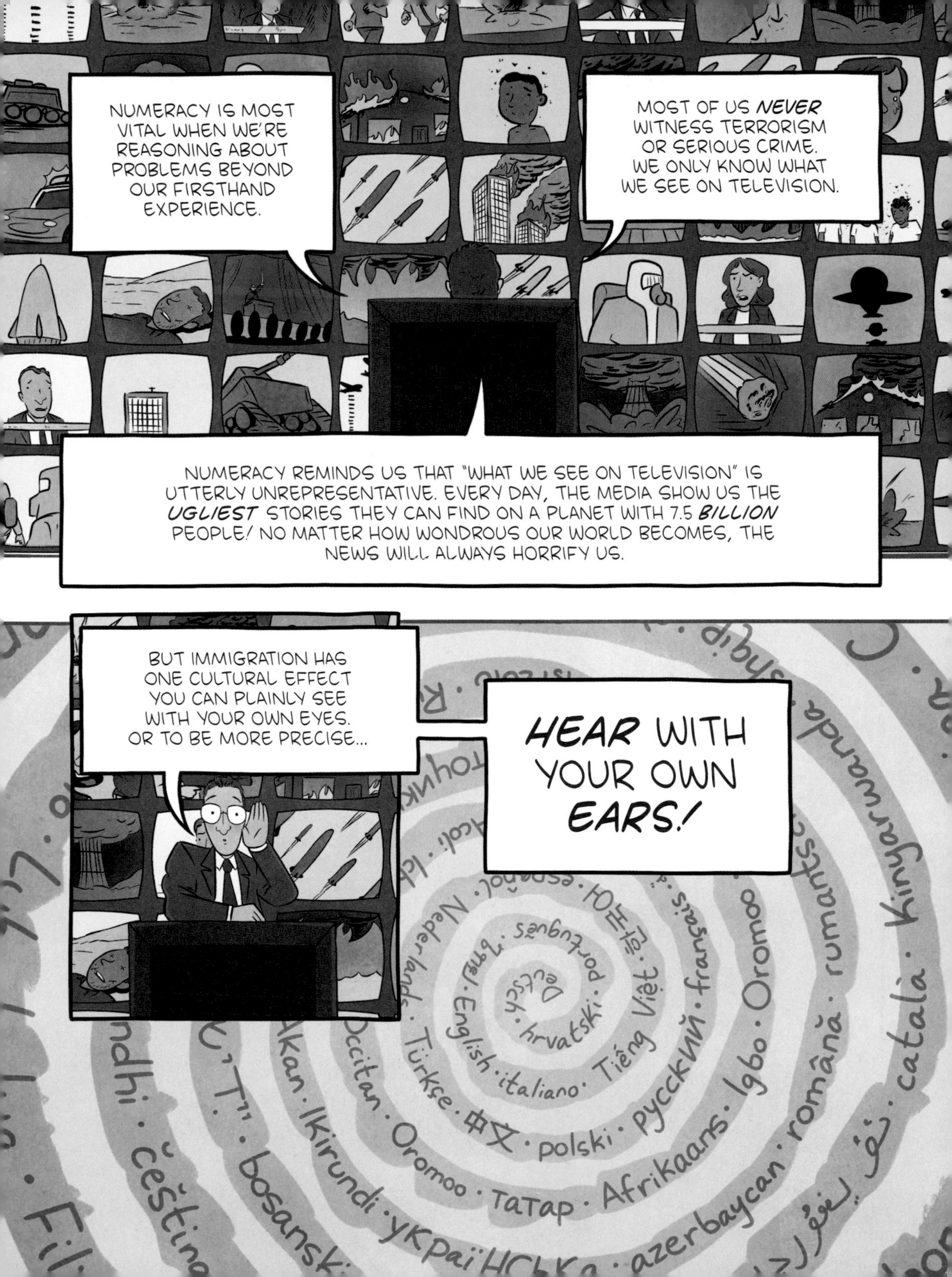
NUMERACY IS MOST VITAL WHEN WE'RE REASONING ABOUT PROBLEMS BEYOND OUR FIRSTHAND EXPERIENCE.
MOST OF US *NEVER* WITNESS TERRORISM OR SERIOUS CRIME. WE ONLY KNOW WHAT WE SEE ON TELEVISION.
NUMERACY REMINDS US THAT "WHAT WE SEE ON TELEVISION" IS UTTERLY UNREPRESENTATIVE. EVERY DAY, THE MEDIA SHOW US THE *UGLIEST* STORIES THEY CAN FIND ON A PLANET WITH 7.5 *BILLION* PEOPLE! NO MATTER HOW WONDROUS OUR WORLD BECOMES, THE NEWS WILL ALWAYS HORRIFY US.
BUT IMMIGRATION HAS ONE CULTURAL EFFECT YOU CAN PLAINLY SEE WITH YOUR OWN EYES. OR TO BE MORE PRECISE...
HEAR WITH YOUR OWN *EARS!*

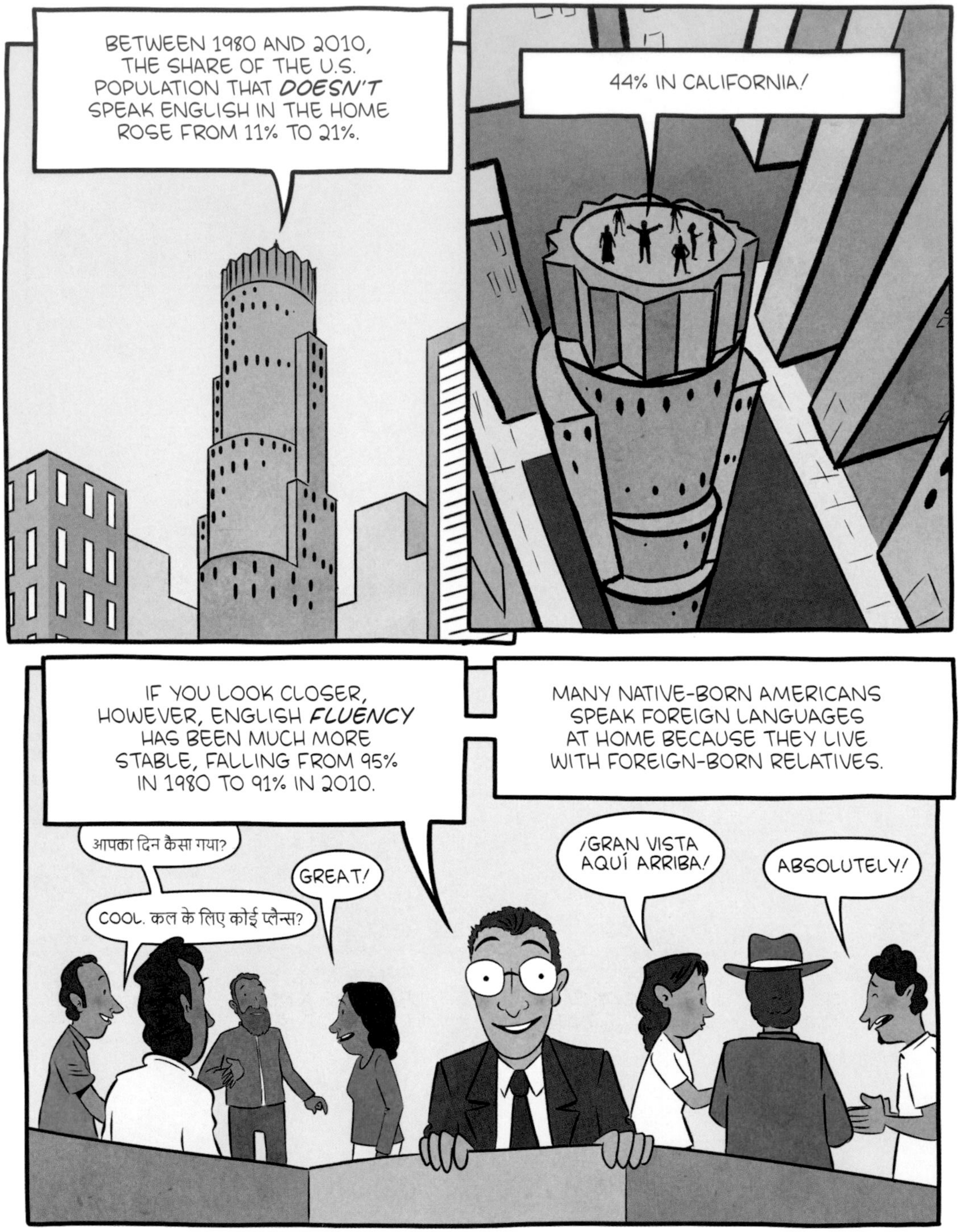
BETWEEN 1980 AND 2010, THE SHARE OF THE U.S. POPULATION THAT *DOESN'T* SPEAK ENGLISH IN THE HOME ROSE FROM 11% TO 21%.
44% IN CALIFORNIA!
IF YOU LOOK CLOSER, HOWEVER, ENGLISH *FLUENCY* HAS BEEN MUCH MORE STABLE, FALLING FROM 95% IN 1980 TO 91% IN 2010.
MANY NATIVE-BORN AMERICANS SPEAK FOREIGN LANGUAGES AT HOME BECAUSE THEY LIVE WITH FOREIGN-BORN RELATIVES.
आपका दिन कैसा गया?
GREAT!
COOL. कल के लिए कोई प्लैन्स?
¡GRAN VISTA AQUÍ ARRIBA!
ABSOLUTELY!

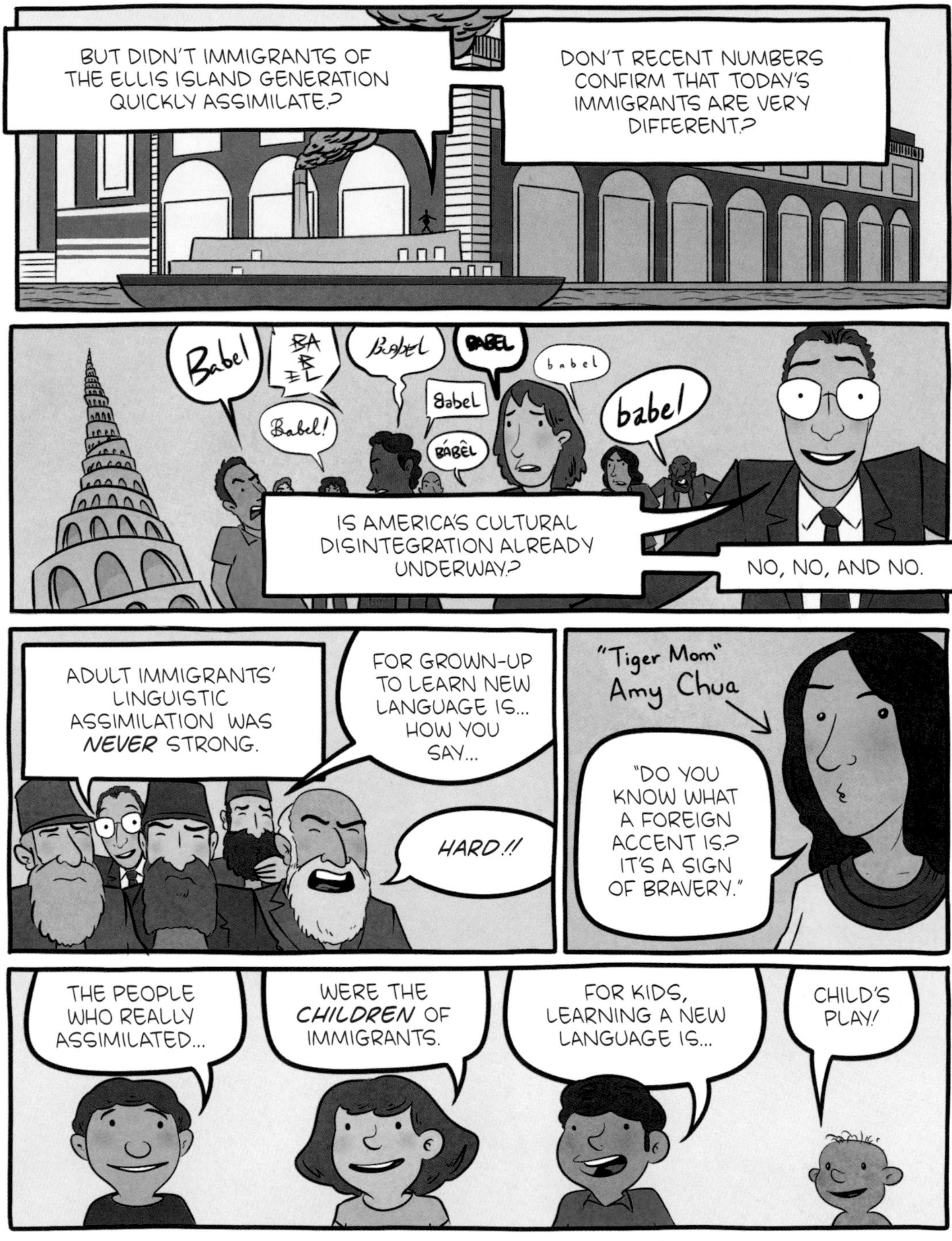
BUT DIDN'T IMMIGRANTS OF THE ELLIS ISLAND GENERATION QUICKLY ASSIMILATE?
DON'T RECENT NUMBERS CONFIRM THAT TODAY'S IMMIGRANTS ARE VERY DIFFERENT?
Babel
BA B EL
Babel
BABEL
babel
Babel!
Babel
BÁBÊL
babel
IS AMERICA'S CULTURAL DISINTEGRATION ALREADY UNDERWAY?
NO, NO, AND NO.
ADULT IMMIGRANTS' LINGUISTIC ASSIMILATION WAS *NEVER* STRONG.
FOR GROWN-UP TO LEARN NEW LANGUAGE IS... HOW YOU SAY...
HARD!!
"Tiger Mom" Amy Chua
"DO YOU KNOW WHAT A FOREIGN ACCENT IS? IT'S A SIGN OF BRAVERY."
THE PEOPLE WHO REALLY ASSIMILATED...
WERE THE *CHILDREN* OF IMMIGRANTS.
FOR KIDS, LEARNING A NEW LANGUAGE IS...
CHILD'S PLAY!

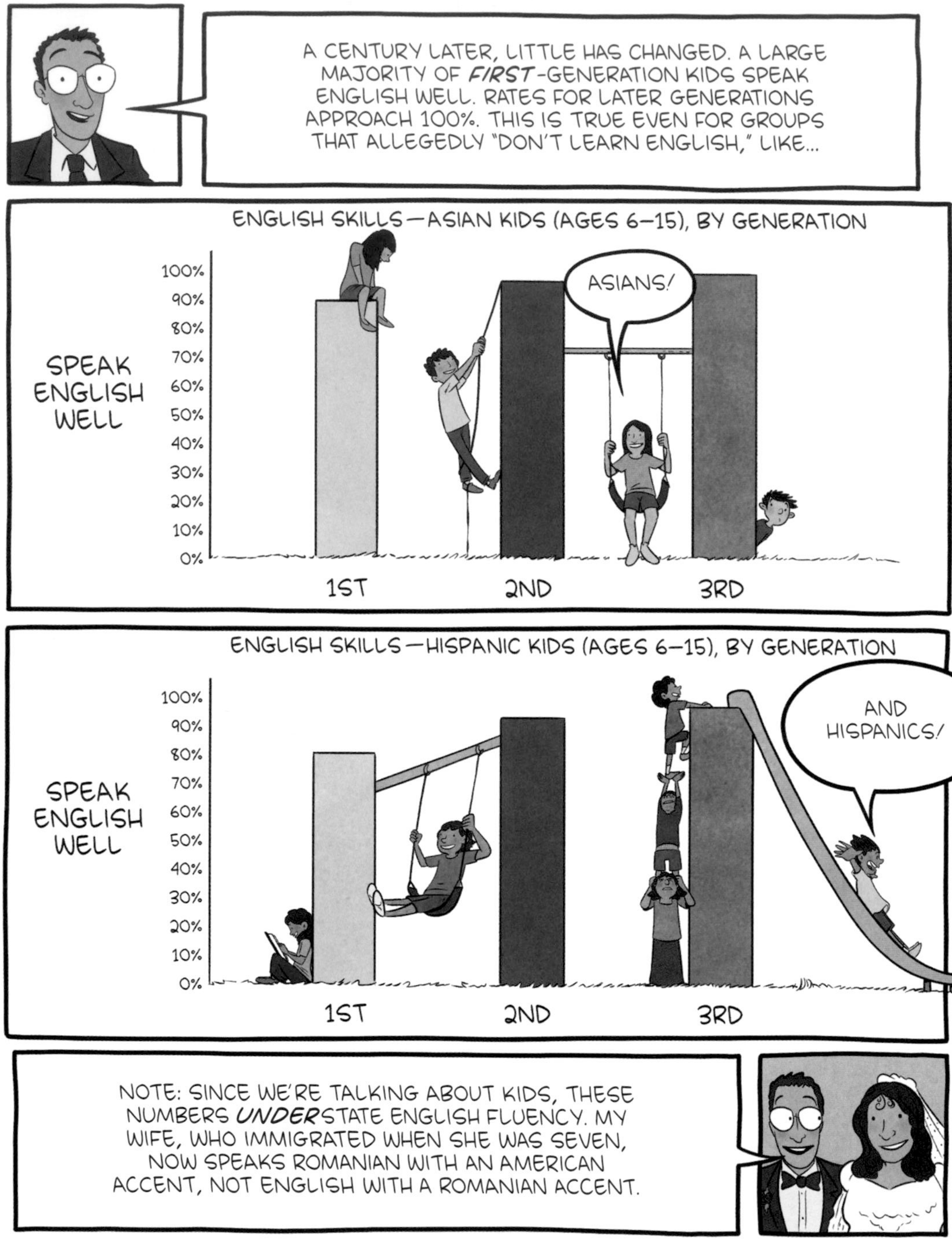
A CENTURY LATER, LITTLE HAS CHANGED. A LARGE MAJORITY OF *FIRST*-GENERATION KIDS SPEAK ENGLISH WELL. RATES FOR LATER GENERATIONS APPROACH 100%. THIS IS TRUE EVEN FOR GROUPS THAT ALLEGEDLY "DON'T LEARN ENGLISH," LIKE...
ENGLISH SKILLS—ASIAN KIDS (AGES 6–15), BY GENERATION
SPEAK ENGLISH WELL
100%
90%
80%
70%
60%
50%
40%
30%
20%
10%
0%
1ST
2ND
3RD
ASIANS!
ENGLISH SKILLS—HISPANIC KIDS (AGES 6–15), BY GENERATION
SPEAK ENGLISH WELL
100%
90%
80%
70%
60%
50%
40%
30%
20%
10%
0%
1ST
2ND
3RD
AND HISPANICS!
NOTE: SINCE WE'RE TALKING ABOUT KIDS, THESE NUMBERS *UNDER*STATE ENGLISH FLUENCY. MY WIFE, WHO IMMIGRATED WHEN SHE WAS SEVEN, NOW SPEAKS ROMANIAN WITH AN AMERICAN ACCENT, NOT ENGLISH WITH A ROMANIAN ACCENT.

IF YOU WANT THE *REAL* STORY OF ASSIMILATION, ASK AN IMMIGRANT PARENT...

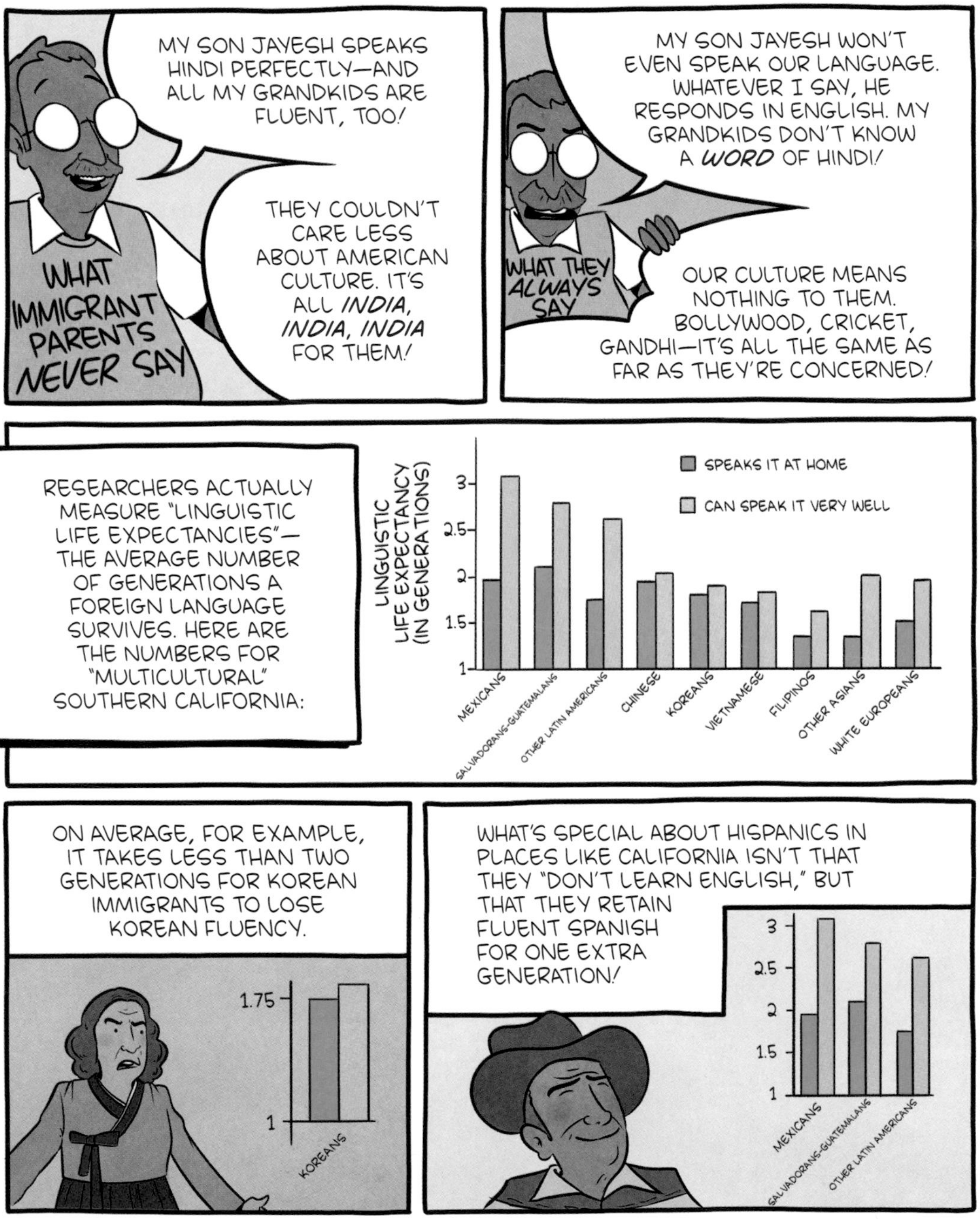
WHAT IMMIGRANT PARENTS NEVER SAY
MY SON JAYESH SPEAKS HINDI PERFECTLY—AND ALL MY GRANDKIDS ARE FLUENT, TOO!
THEY COULDN'T CARE LESS ABOUT AMERICAN CULTURE. IT'S ALL *INDIA, INDIA, INDIA* FOR THEM!
WHAT THEY ALWAYS SAY
MY SON JAYESH WON'T EVEN SPEAK OUR LANGUAGE. WHATEVER I SAY, HE RESPONDS IN ENGLISH. MY GRANDKIDS DON'T KNOW A *WORD* OF HINDI!
OUR CULTURE MEANS NOTHING TO THEM. BOLLYWOOD, CRICKET, GANDHI—IT'S ALL THE SAME AS FAR AS THEY'RE CONCERNED!
RESEARCHERS ACTUALLY MEASURE "LINGUISTIC LIFE EXPECTANCIES"—THE AVERAGE NUMBER OF GENERATIONS A FOREIGN LANGUAGE SURVIVES. HERE ARE THE NUMBERS FOR "MULTICULTURAL" SOUTHERN CALIFORNIA:
LINGUISTIC LIFE EXPECTANCY (IN GENERATIONS)
SPEAKS IT AT HOME
CAN SPEAK IT VERY WELL
3
2.5
2
1.5
1
MEXICANS
SALVADORANS-GUATEMALANS
OTHER LATIN AMERICANS
CHINESE
KOREANS
VIETNAMESE
FILIPINOS
OTHER ASIANS
WHITE EUROPEANS
ON AVERAGE, FOR EXAMPLE, IT TAKES LESS THAN TWO GENERATIONS FOR KOREAN IMMIGRANTS TO LOSE KOREAN FLUENCY.
1.75
1
KOREANS
WHAT'S SPECIAL ABOUT HISPANICS IN PLACES LIKE CALIFORNIA ISN'T THAT THEY "DON'T LEARN ENGLISH," BUT THAT THEY RETAIN FLUENT SPANISH FOR ONE EXTRA GENERATION!
3
2.5
2
1.5
1
MEXICANS
SALVADORANS-GUATEMALANS
OTHER LATIN AMERICANS

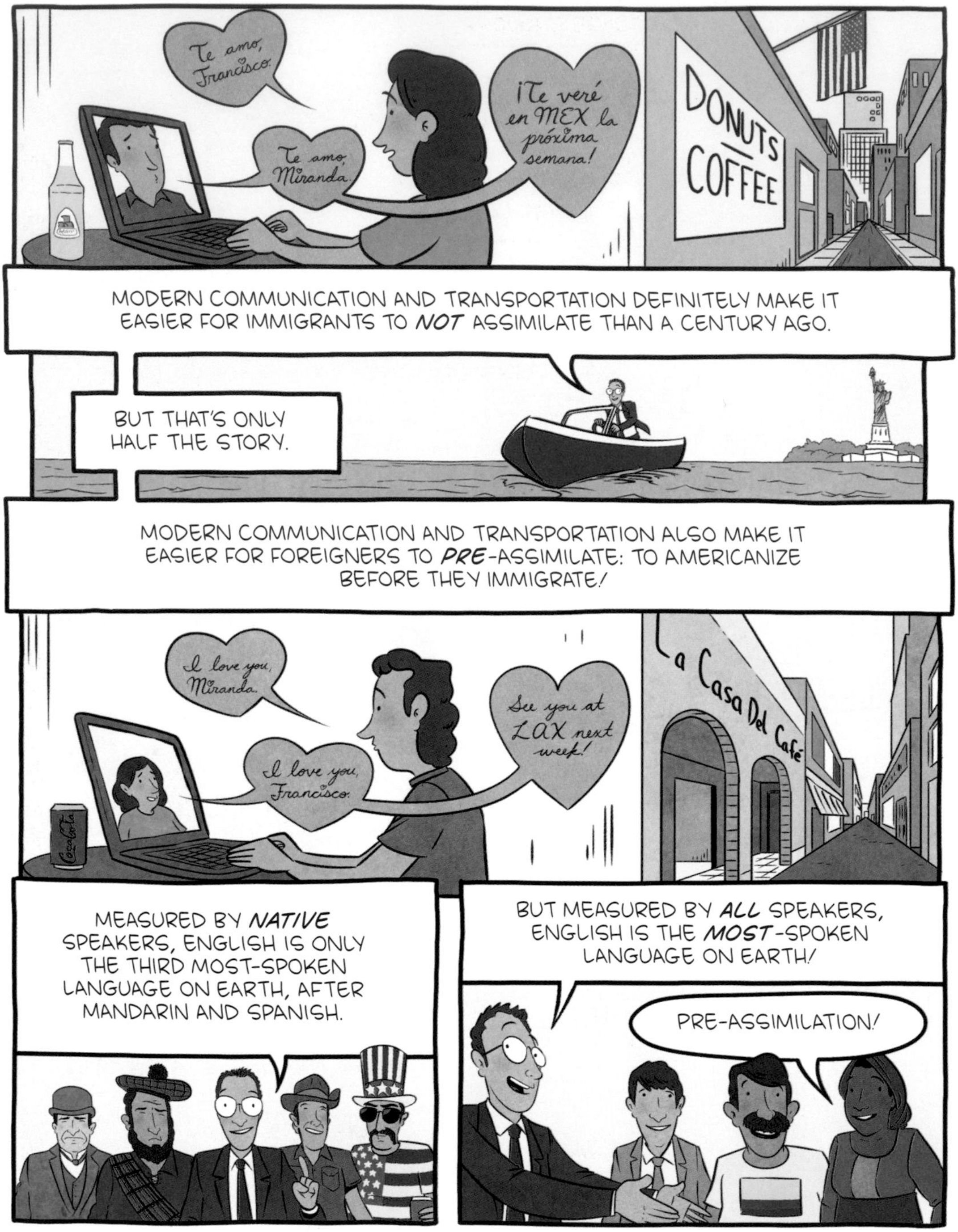
Te amo, Francisco.
Te amo, Miranda.
¡Te veré en MEX la próxima semana!
DONUTS
COFFEE
MODERN COMMUNICATION AND TRANSPORTATION DEFINITELY MAKE IT EASIER FOR IMMIGRANTS TO *NOT* ASSIMILATE THAN A CENTURY AGO.
BUT THAT'S ONLY HALF THE STORY.
MODERN COMMUNICATION AND TRANSPORTATION ALSO MAKE IT EASIER FOR FOREIGNERS TO *PRE*-ASSIMILATE: TO AMERICANIZE BEFORE THEY IMMIGRATE!
I love you, Miranda.
I love you, Francisco.
See you at LAX next week!
La Casa Del Café
MEASURED BY *NATIVE* SPEAKERS, ENGLISH IS ONLY THE THIRD MOST-SPOKEN LANGUAGE ON EARTH, AFTER MANDARIN AND SPANISH.
BUT MEASURED BY *ALL* SPEAKERS, ENGLISH IS THE *MOST*-SPOKEN LANGUAGE ON EARTH!
PRE-ASSIMILATION!

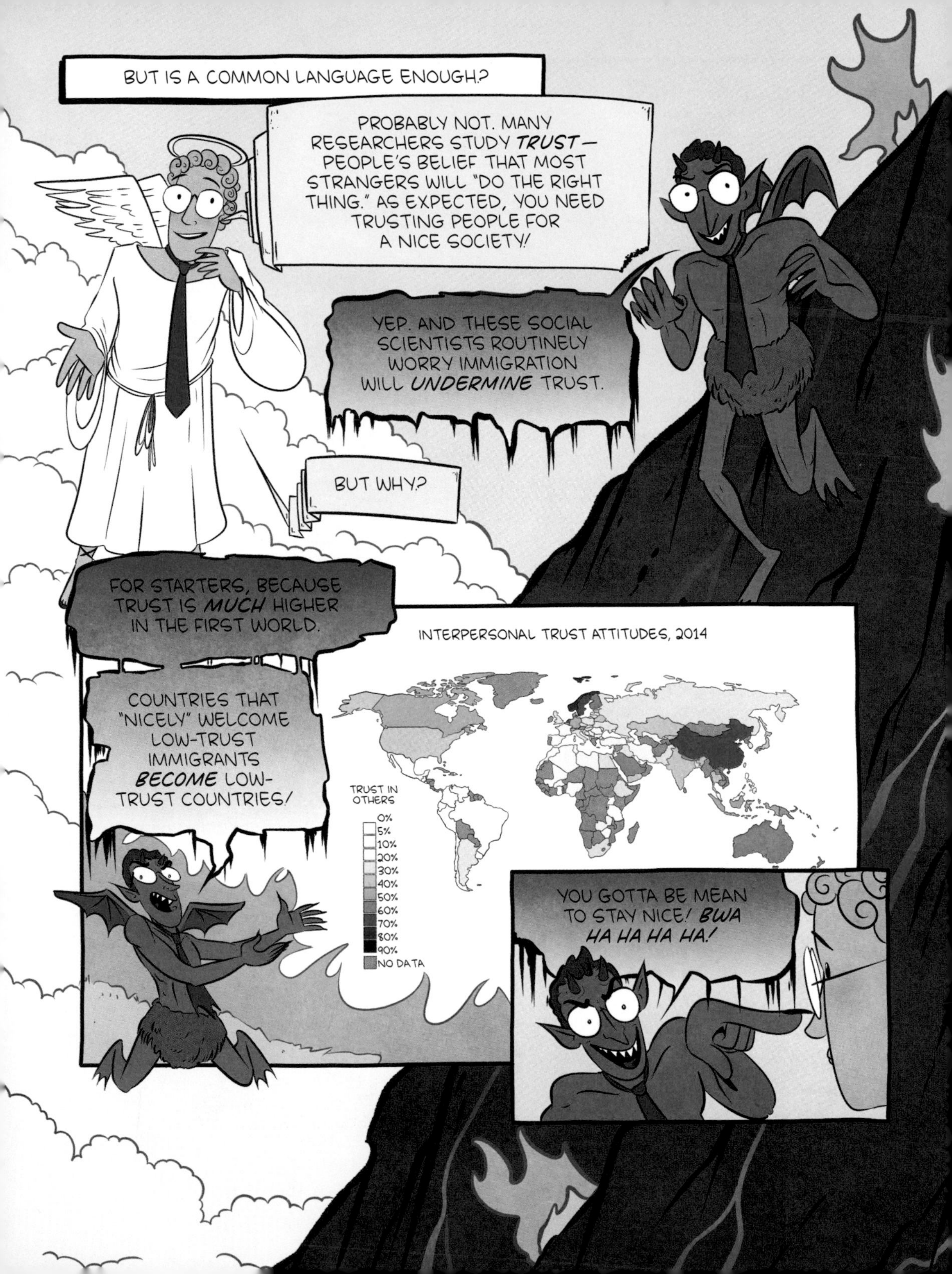
BUT IS A COMMON LANGUAGE ENOUGH?
PROBABLY NOT. MANY RESEARCHERS STUDY TRUST— PEOPLE'S BELIEF THAT MOST STRANGERS WILL "DO THE RIGHT THING." AS EXPECTED, YOU NEED TRUSTING PEOPLE FOR A NICE SOCIETY!
YEP. AND THESE SOCIAL SCIENTISTS ROUTINELY WORRY IMMIGRATION WILL UNDERMINE TRUST.
BUT WHY?
FOR STARTERS, BECAUSE TRUST IS MUCH HIGHER IN THE FIRST WORLD.
COUNTRIES THAT "NICELY" WELCOME LOW-TRUST IMMIGRANTS BECOME LOW-TRUST COUNTRIES!
INTERPERSONAL TRUST ATTITUDES, 2014
TRUST IN OTHERS
0%
5%
10%
20%
30%
40%
50%
60%
70%
80%
90%
NO DATA
YOU GOTTA BE MEAN TO STAY NICE! BWA HA HA HA HA!

BUT WHAT ABOUT ASSIMILATION?

IT WON'T SAVE YOU. TRUST IS SHOCKINGLY STABLE.

SWEDEN'S WAY MORE TRUSTING THAN THE U.S., BUT SWEDISH AMERICANS ARE ABOUT AS TRUSTING AS HOME-GROWN SWEDES!

STOCKHOLM

MINNEAPOLIS

ARE YOU SERIOUSLY GOING TO *TRUST* THIS GUY? LET'S LOOK AT THE DATA.

WHILE TRUST IS FAIRLY PERSISTENT, FOLKS WHO LEAVE LOW-TRUST COUNTRIES HAVE MARKEDLY HIGHER TRUST THAN FOLKS WHO STAY BEHIND.

LET THE ST

WE

Everyone needs a HOME

Refugees Welcome!

CHANGING THE PEOPLE YOU SEE CHANGES THE WAY YOU SEE PEOPLE.

FOR DESCENDANTS OF WILLING IMMIGRANTS, TRUST ASSIMILATION IS ALMOST COMPLETE.

"MOST PEOPLE CAN BE TRUSTED"

HOW PERFECT TRUST *PERSISTENCE* WOULD WORK

% U.S. NATIVES WHO SAY YES

100
80
60
40
20

HOW TRUST *ASSIMILATION* ACTUALLY WORKS

20   40   60   80   100

% IN ANCESTRAL COUNTRY WHO SAY YES

HERE'S WHAT HAPPENS IF WE USE AVERAGE TRUST IN YOUR ANCESTRAL COUNTRY TO PREDICT YOUR TRUST IN THE U.S.

SWEDISH AMERICANS *ARE* UNUSUALLY TRUSTING. BUT AS A RULE, TRUST IS A LOT MORE LIKE LANGUAGE THAN HAIR COLOR.

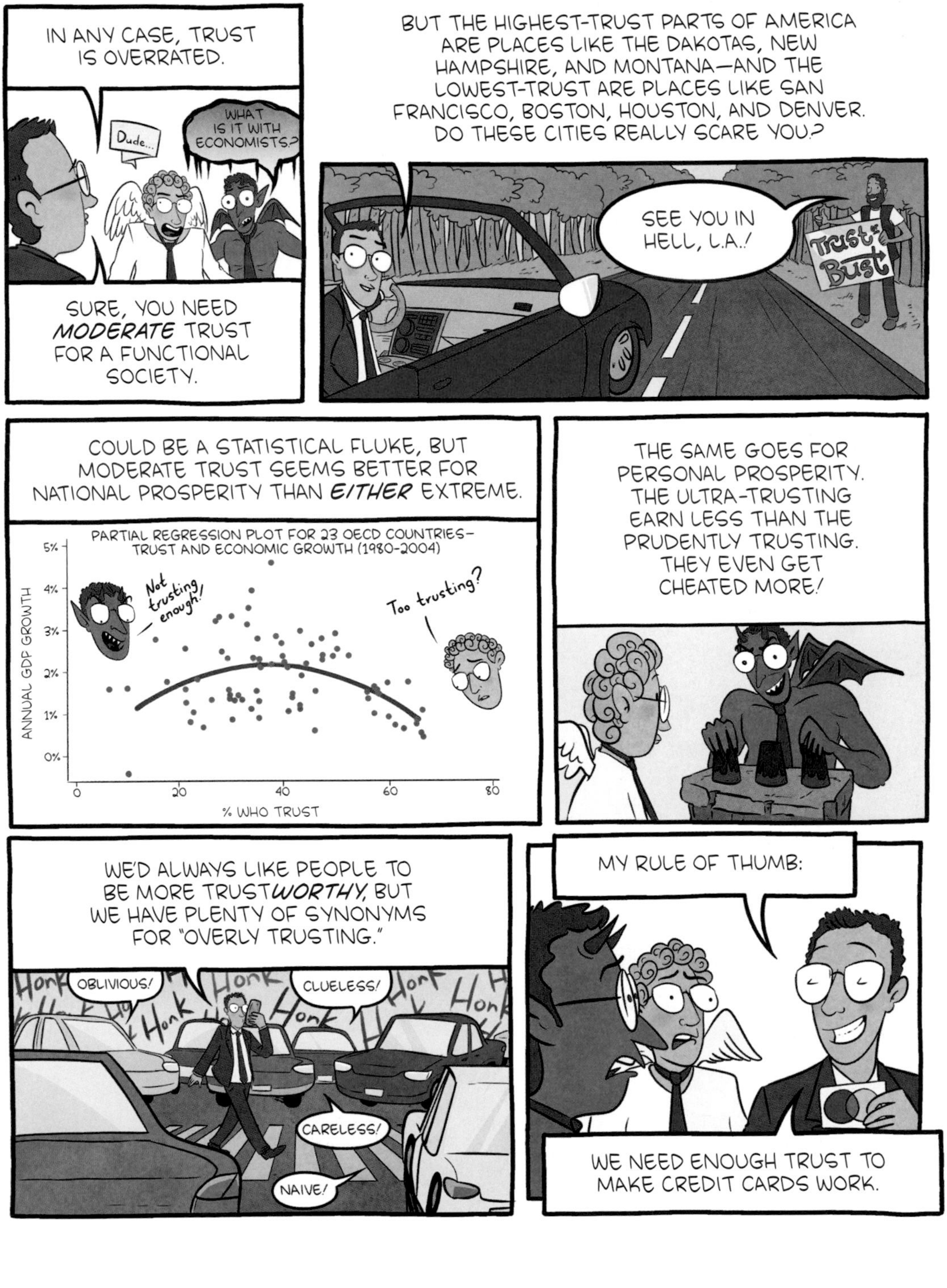

IN ANY CASE, TRUST IS OVERRATED.
Dude...
WHAT IS IT WITH ECONOMISTS?
SURE, YOU NEED *MODERATE* TRUST FOR A FUNCTIONAL SOCIETY.
BUT THE HIGHEST-TRUST PARTS OF AMERICA ARE PLACES LIKE THE DAKOTAS, NEW HAMPSHIRE, AND MONTANA—AND THE LOWEST-TRUST ARE PLACES LIKE SAN FRANCISCO, BOSTON, HOUSTON, AND DENVER. DO THESE CITIES REALLY SCARE YOU?
SEE YOU IN HELL, L.A.!
Trust or Bust
COULD BE A STATISTICAL FLUKE, BUT MODERATE TRUST SEEMS BETTER FOR NATIONAL PROSPERITY THAN *EITHER* EXTREME.
PARTIAL REGRESSION PLOT FOR 23 OECD COUNTRIES—TRUST AND ECONOMIC GROWTH (1980-2004)
ANNUAL GDP GROWTH
5%
4%
3%
2%
1%
0%
0
20
40
60
80
% WHO TRUST
Not trusting enough!
Too trusting?
THE SAME GOES FOR PERSONAL PROSPERITY. THE ULTRA-TRUSTING EARN LESS THAN THE PRUDENTLY TRUSTING. THEY EVEN GET CHEATED MORE!
WE'D ALWAYS LIKE PEOPLE TO BE MORE TRUST*WORTHY*, BUT WE HAVE PLENTY OF SYNONYMS FOR "OVERLY TRUSTING."
OBLIVIOUS!
CLUELESS!
CARELESS!
NAIVE!
Honk Honk Honk Honk
MY RULE OF THUMB:
WE NEED ENOUGH TRUST TO MAKE CREDIT CARDS WORK.

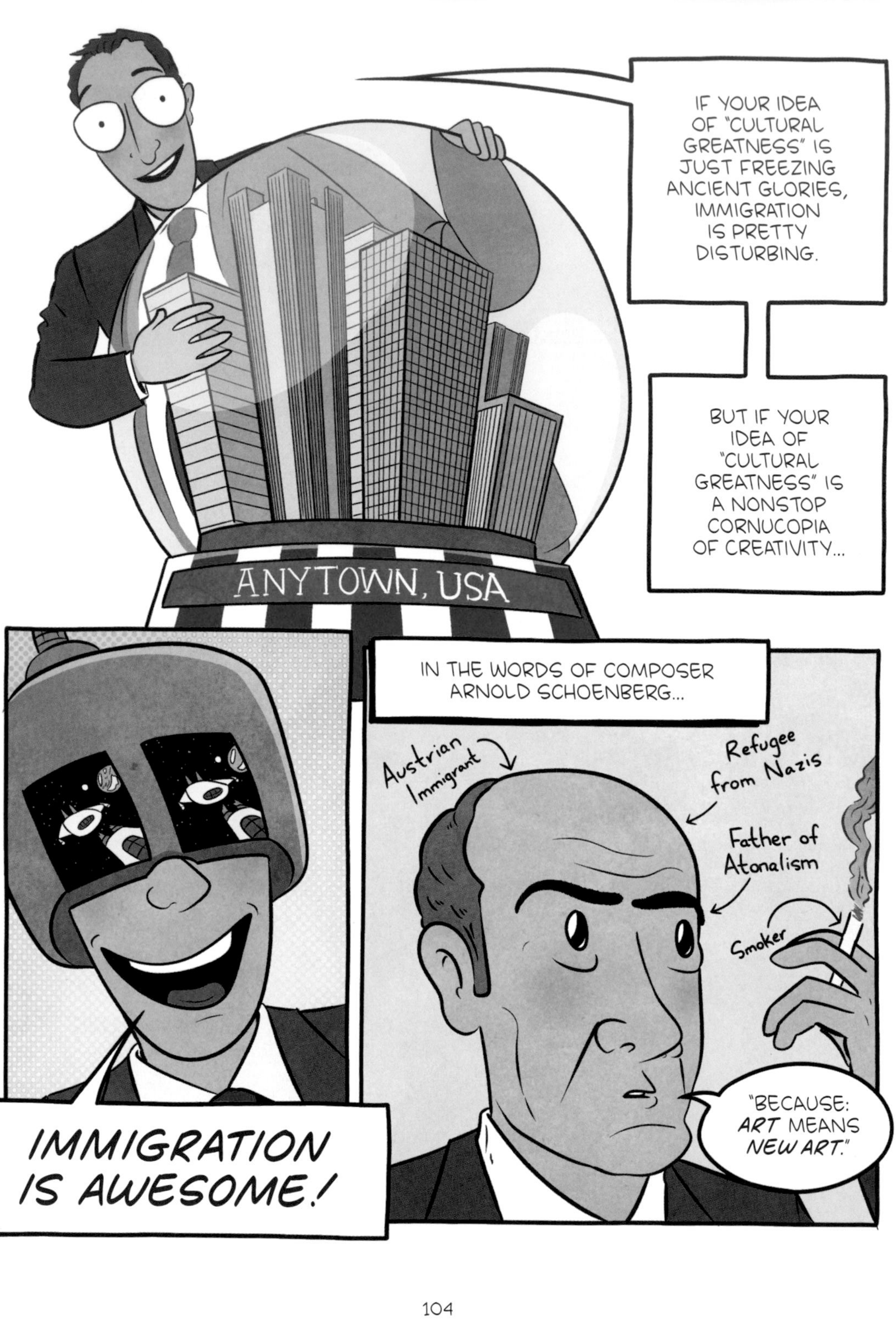
IF YOUR IDEA OF "CULTURAL GREATNESS" IS JUST FREEZING ANCIENT GLORIES, IMMIGRATION IS PRETTY DISTURBING.
BUT IF YOUR IDEA OF "CULTURAL GREATNESS" IS A NONSTOP CORNUCOPIA OF CREATIVITY...
ANYTOWN, USA
IMMIGRATION IS AWESOME!
IN THE WORDS OF COMPOSER ARNOLD SCHOENBERG...
Austrian Immigrant
Refugee from Nazis
Father of Atonalism
Smoker
"BECAUSE: *ART* MEANS *NEW ART*."

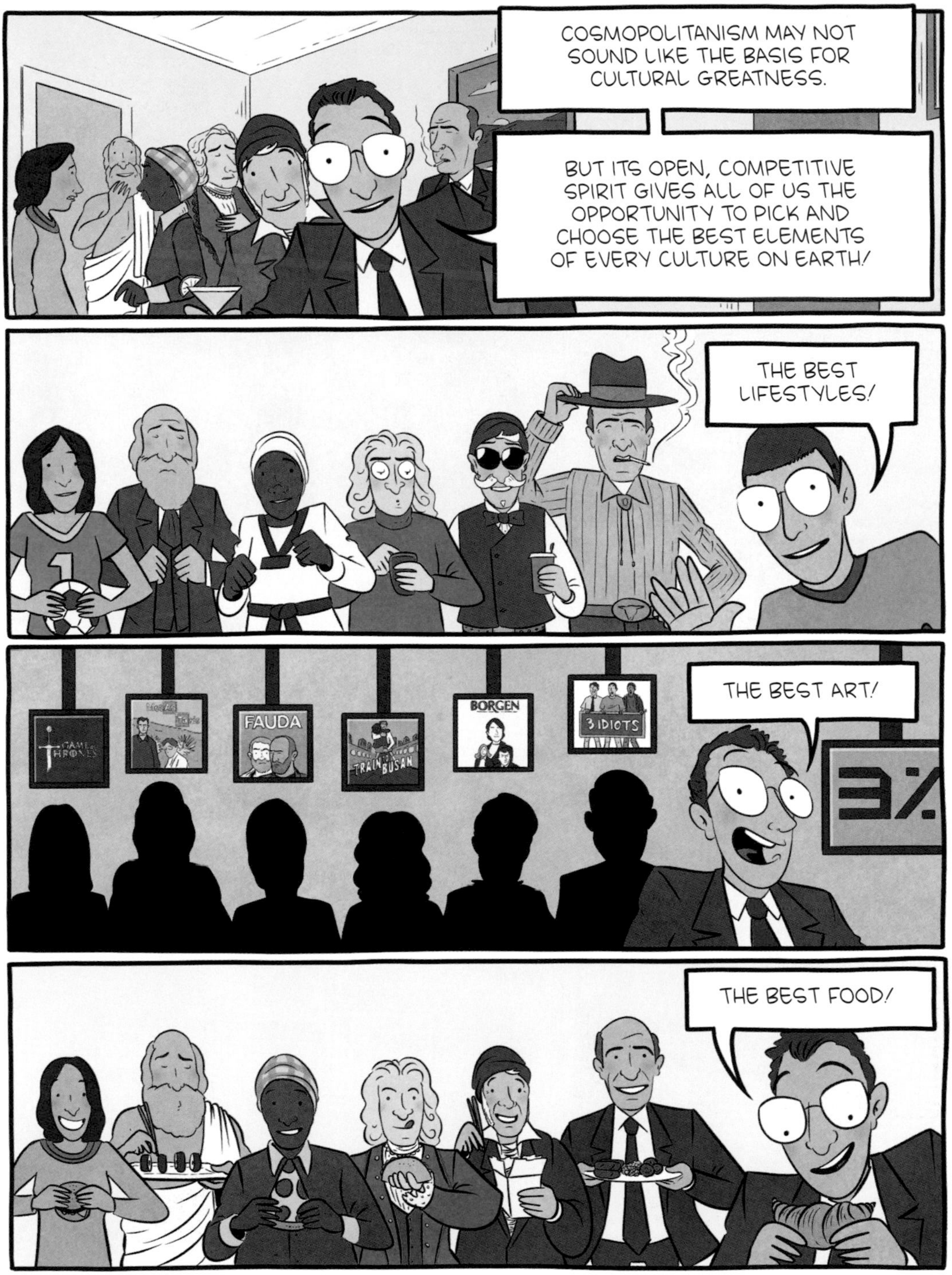
COSMOPOLITANISM MAY NOT SOUND LIKE THE BASIS FOR CULTURAL GREATNESS.
BUT ITS OPEN, COMPETITIVE SPIRIT GIVES ALL OF US THE OPPORTUNITY TO PICK AND CHOOSE THE BEST ELEMENTS OF EVERY CULTURE ON EARTH!
THE BEST LIFESTYLES!
FAUDA
BORGEN
3 IDIOTS
3%
THE BEST ART!
THE BEST FOOD!

WE SHOULD EXPECT THE ENEMIES OF WESTERN CULTURE TO PREDICT ITS DEMISE.

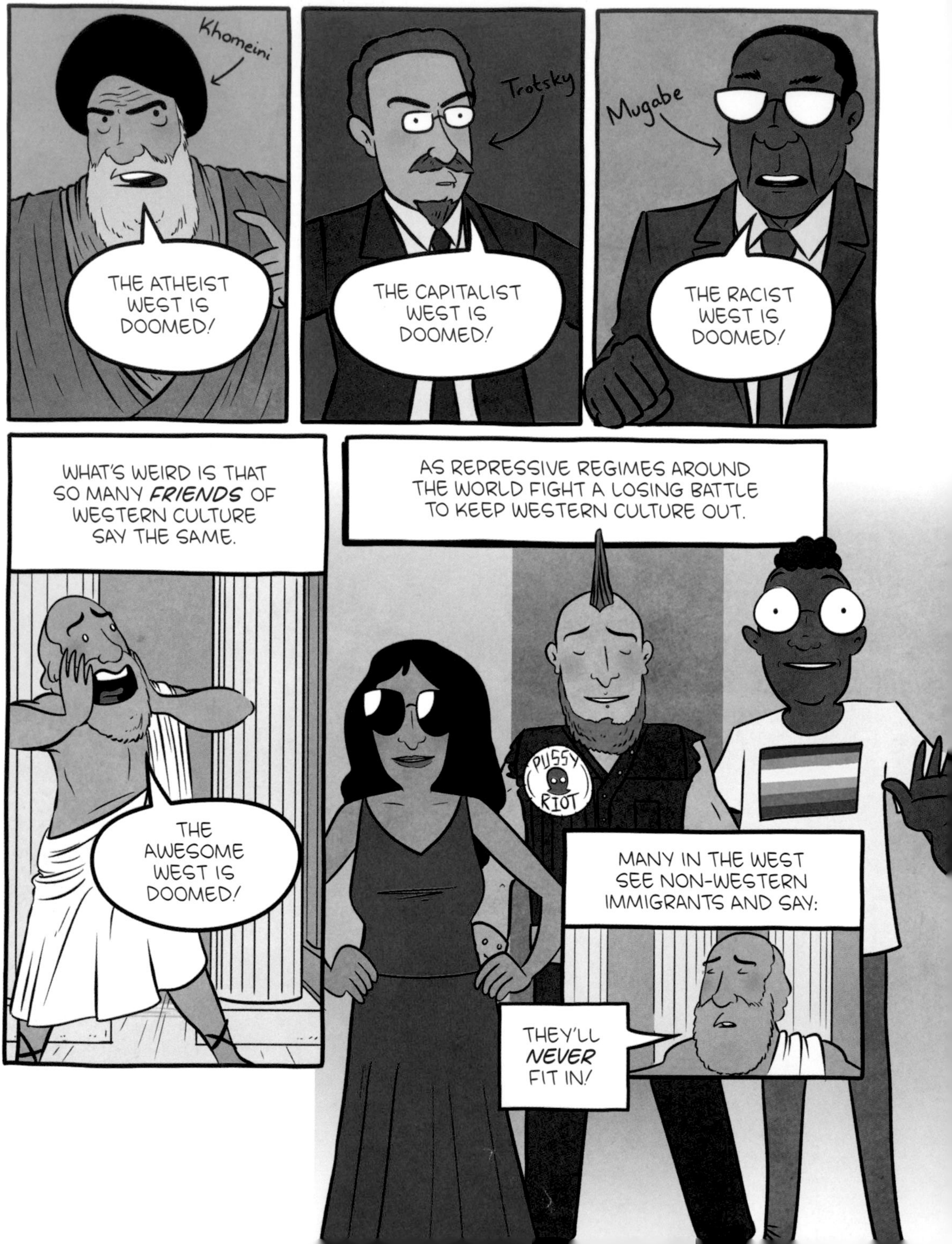
Khomeini
THE ATHEIST WEST IS DOOMED!
Trotsky
THE CAPITALIST WEST IS DOOMED!
Mugabe
THE RACIST WEST IS DOOMED!
WHAT'S WEIRD IS THAT SO MANY ***FRIENDS*** OF WESTERN CULTURE SAY THE SAME.
THE AWESOME WEST IS DOOMED!
AS REPRESSIVE REGIMES AROUND THE WORLD FIGHT A LOSING BATTLE TO KEEP WESTERN CULTURE OUT.
PUSSY RIOT
MANY IN THE WEST SEE NON-WESTERN IMMIGRANTS AND SAY:
THEY'LL ***NEVER*** FIT IN!

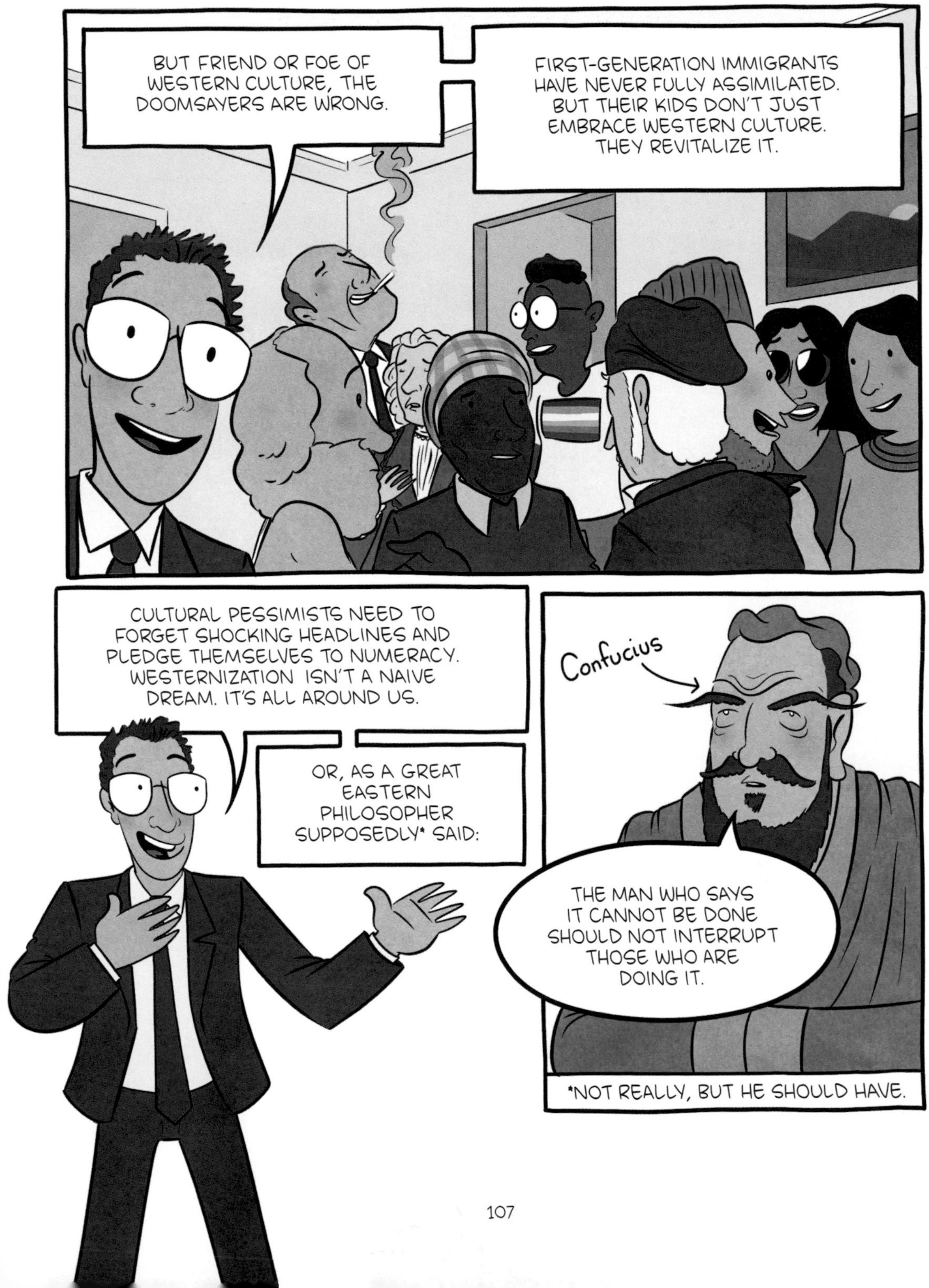
BUT FRIEND OR FOE OF WESTERN CULTURE, THE DOOMSAYERS ARE WRONG.
FIRST-GENERATION IMMIGRANTS HAVE NEVER FULLY ASSIMILATED. BUT THEIR KIDS DON'T JUST EMBRACE WESTERN CULTURE. THEY REVITALIZE IT.
CULTURAL PESSIMISTS NEED TO FORGET SHOCKING HEADLINES AND PLEDGE THEMSELVES TO NUMERACY. WESTERNIZATION ISN'T A NAIVE DREAM. IT'S ALL AROUND US.
OR, AS A GREAT EASTERN PHILOSOPHER SUPPOSEDLY* SAID:
Confucius
THE MAN WHO SAYS IT CANNOT BE DONE SHOULD NOT INTERRUPT THOSE WHO ARE DOING IT.
*NOT REALLY, BUT HE SHOULD HAVE.

CHAPTER 5

THE GOLDEN GOOSE ON TRIAL

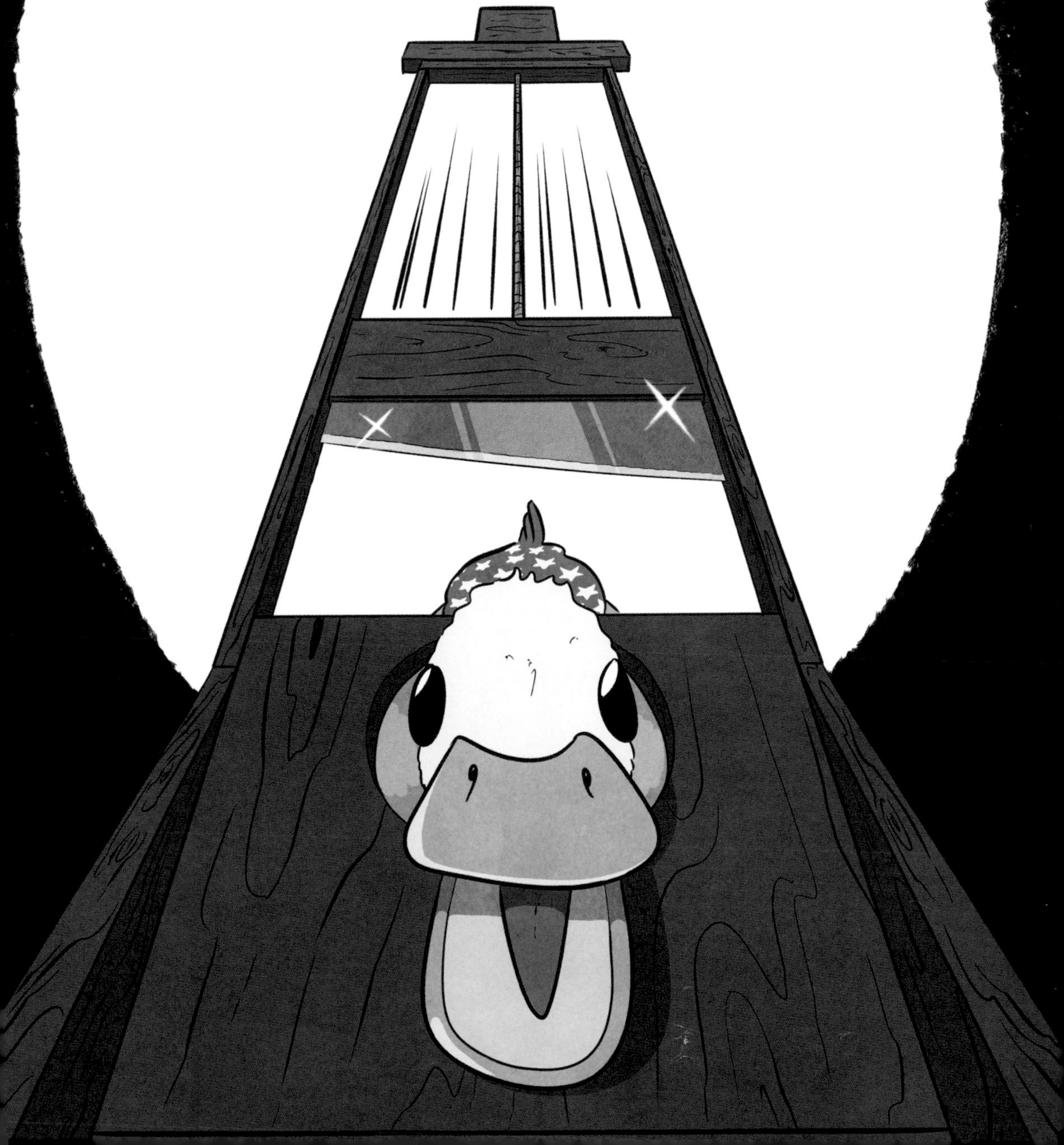

BY HISTORICAL AND WORLD STANDARDS, CITIZENS OF THE FIRST WORLD ENJOY MANY FREEDOMS.

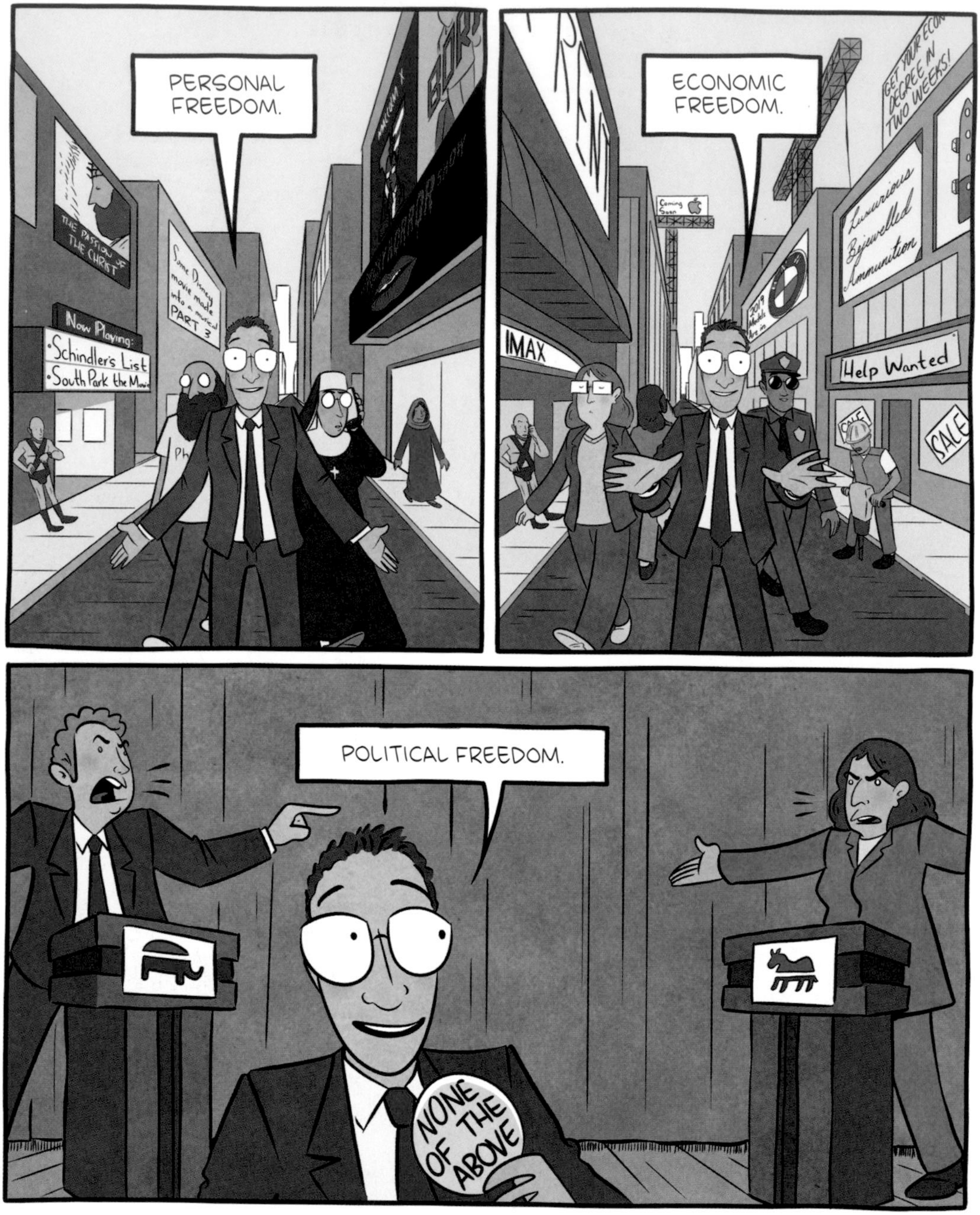
PERSONAL FREEDOM.
THE PASSION OF THE CHRIST
Now Playing:
Schindler's List
Some Disney movie made into a musical PART 3
ECONOMIC FREEDOM.
Coming Soon
IMAX
Luxurious Bejewelled Ammunition
Help Wanted
SALE
SALE
POLITICAL FREEDOM.
NONE OF THE ABOVE

IN HISTORY BOOKS, THESE FREEDOMS ARE A POWERFUL MAGNET FOR IMMIGRATION. FOREIGNERS VENTURE HERE TO ENJOY THE BLESSINGS OF LIBERTY.

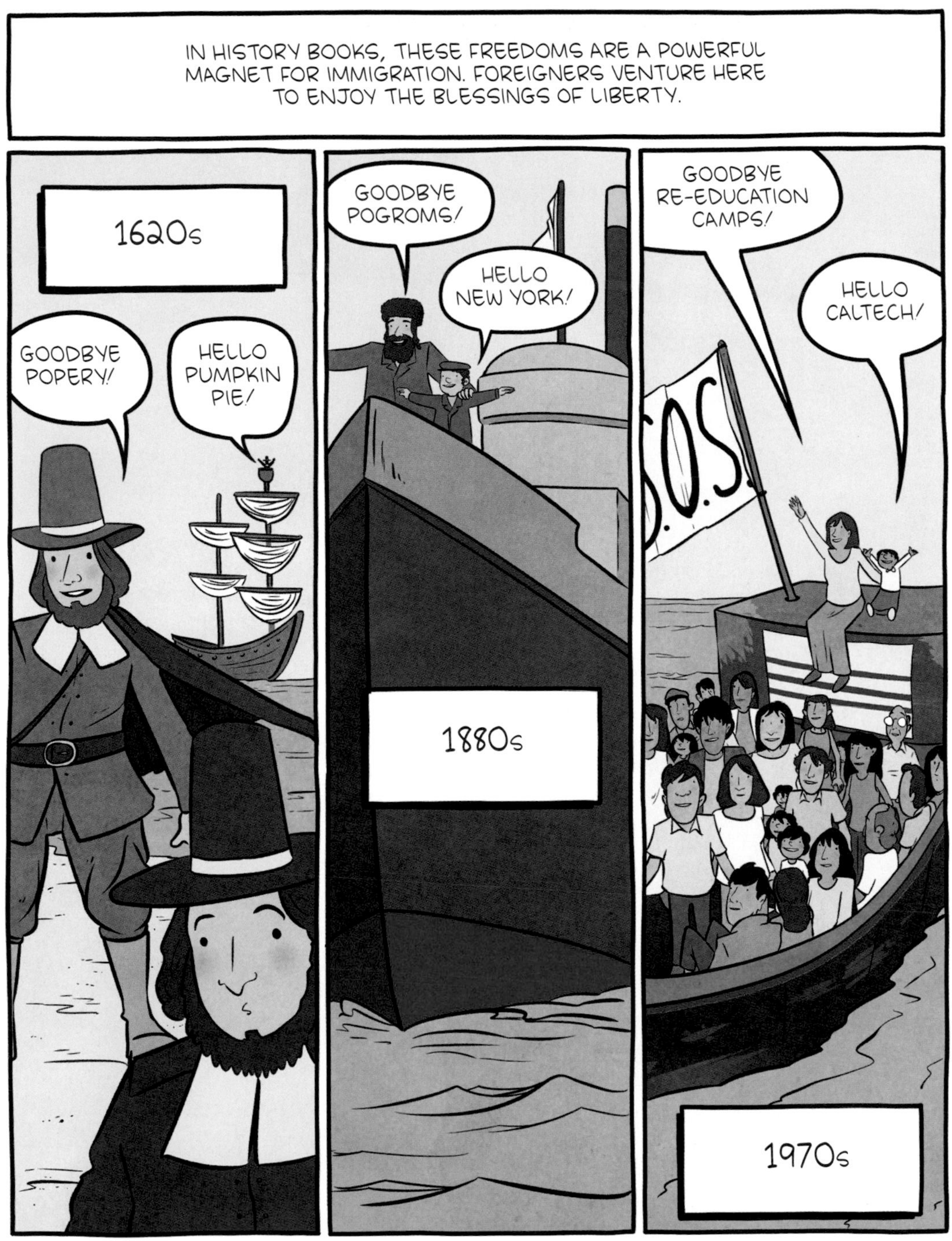
1620s
GOODBYE POPERY!
HELLO PUMPKIN PIE!
GOODBYE POGROMS!
HELLO NEW YORK!
1880s
GOODBYE RE-EDUCATION CAMPS!
HELLO CALTECH!
S.O.S.
1970s

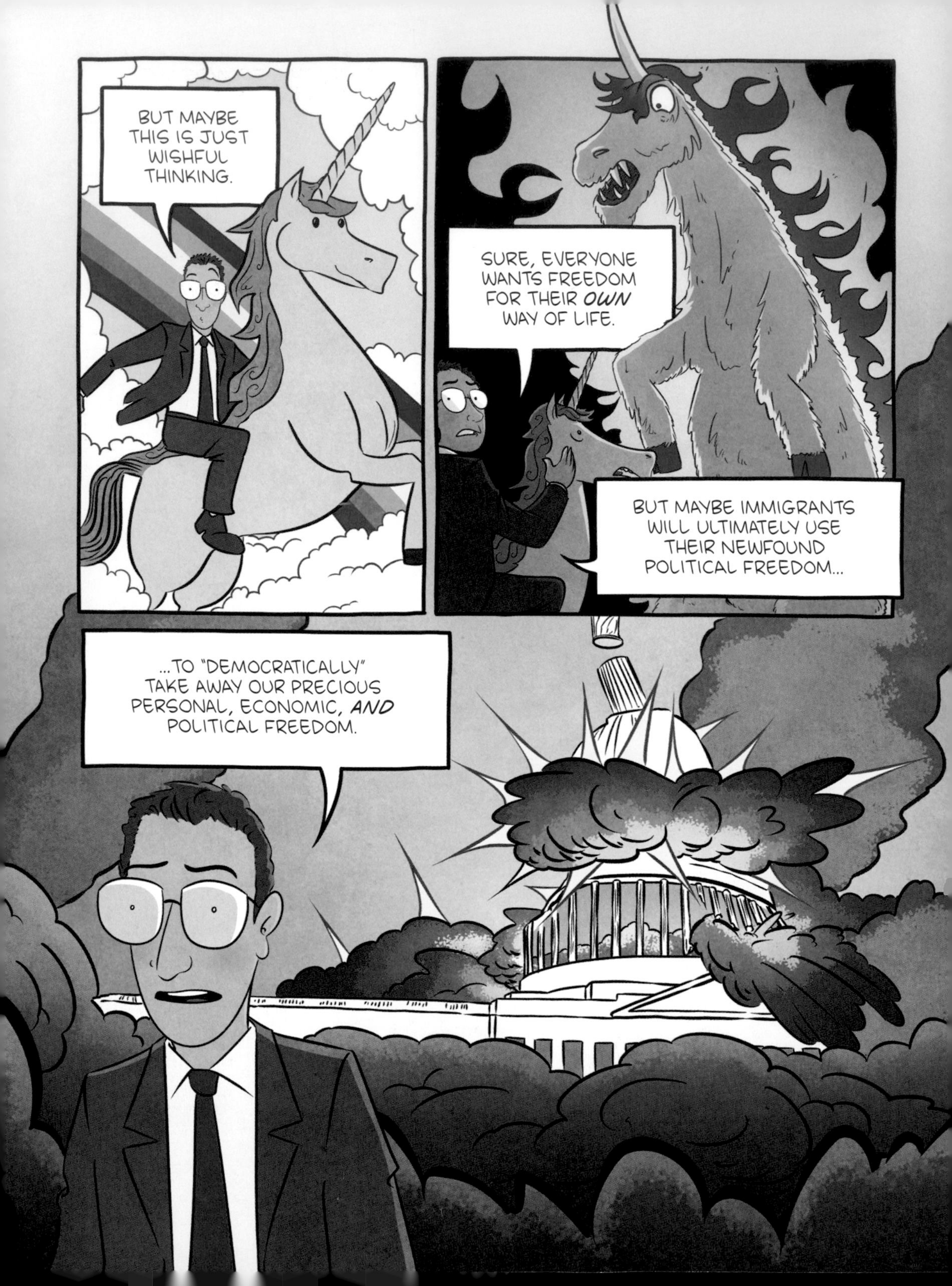
BUT MAYBE THIS IS JUST WISHFUL THINKING.
SURE, EVERYONE WANTS FREEDOM FOR THEIR *OWN* WAY OF LIFE.
BUT MAYBE IMMIGRANTS WILL ULTIMATELY USE THEIR NEWFOUND POLITICAL FREEDOM...
...TO "DEMOCRATICALLY" TAKE AWAY OUR PRECIOUS PERSONAL, ECONOMIC, *AND* POLITICAL FREEDOM.

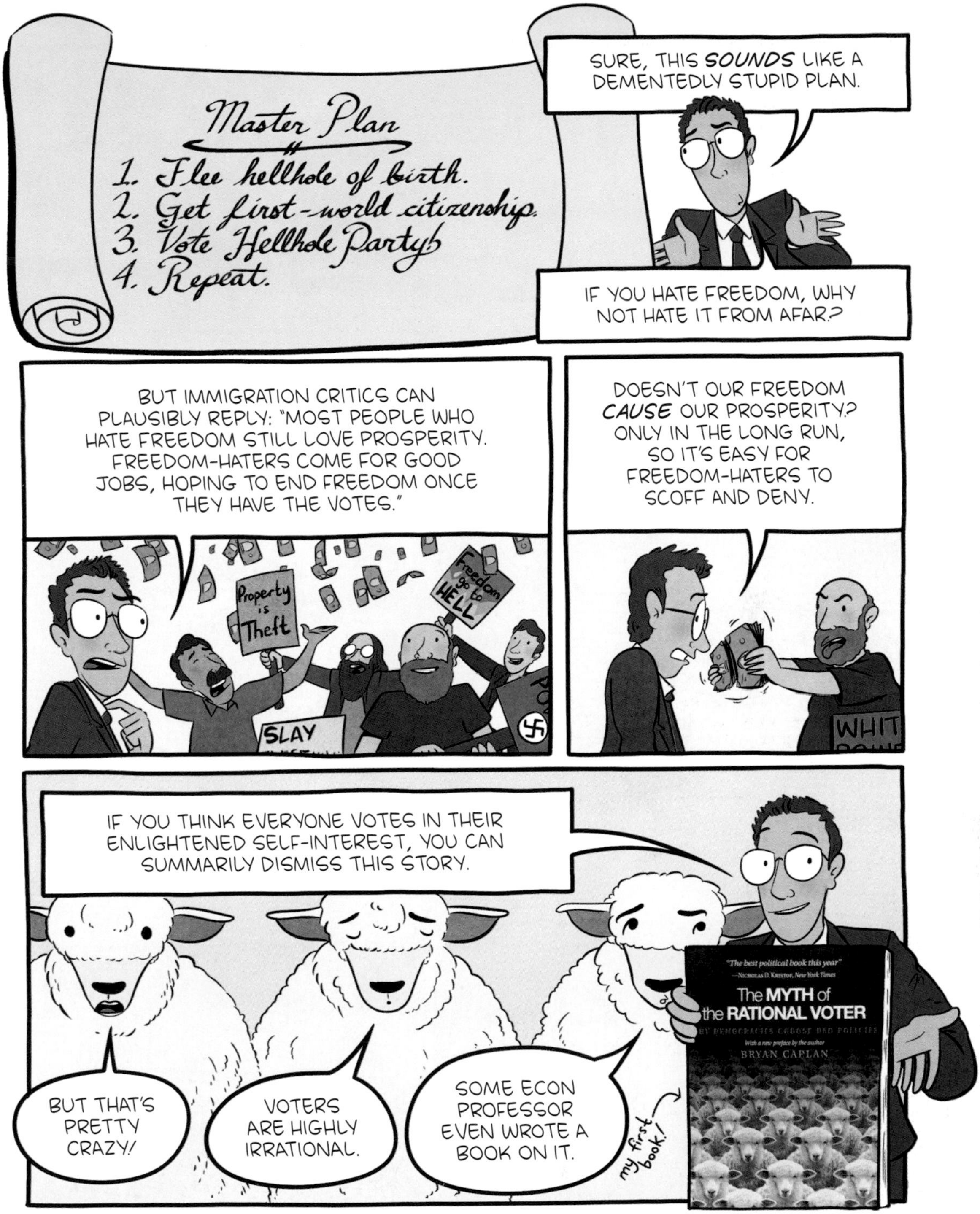
Master Plan
1. Flee hellhole of birth.
2. Get first-world citizenship.
3. Vote Hellhole Party!
4. Repeat.
SURE, THIS **SOUNDS** LIKE A DEMENTEDLY STUPID PLAN.
IF YOU HATE FREEDOM, WHY NOT HATE IT FROM AFAR?
BUT IMMIGRATION CRITICS CAN PLAUSIBLY REPLY: "MOST PEOPLE WHO HATE FREEDOM STILL LOVE PROSPERITY. FREEDOM-HATERS COME FOR GOOD JOBS, HOPING TO END FREEDOM ONCE THEY HAVE THE VOTES."
Property is Theft
Freedom go to HELL
SLAY
DOESN'T OUR FREEDOM **CAUSE** OUR PROSPERITY? ONLY IN THE LONG RUN, SO IT'S EASY FOR FREEDOM-HATERS TO SCOFF AND DENY.
IF YOU THINK EVERYONE VOTES IN THEIR ENLIGHTENED SELF-INTEREST, YOU CAN SUMMARILY DISMISS THIS STORY.
BUT THAT'S PRETTY CRAZY!
VOTERS ARE HIGHLY IRRATIONAL.
SOME ECON PROFESSOR EVEN WROTE A BOOK ON IT.
my first book!
"The best political book this year" —Nicholas D. Kristof, New York Times
The MYTH of the RATIONAL VOTER
With a new preface by the author
BRYAN CAPLAN

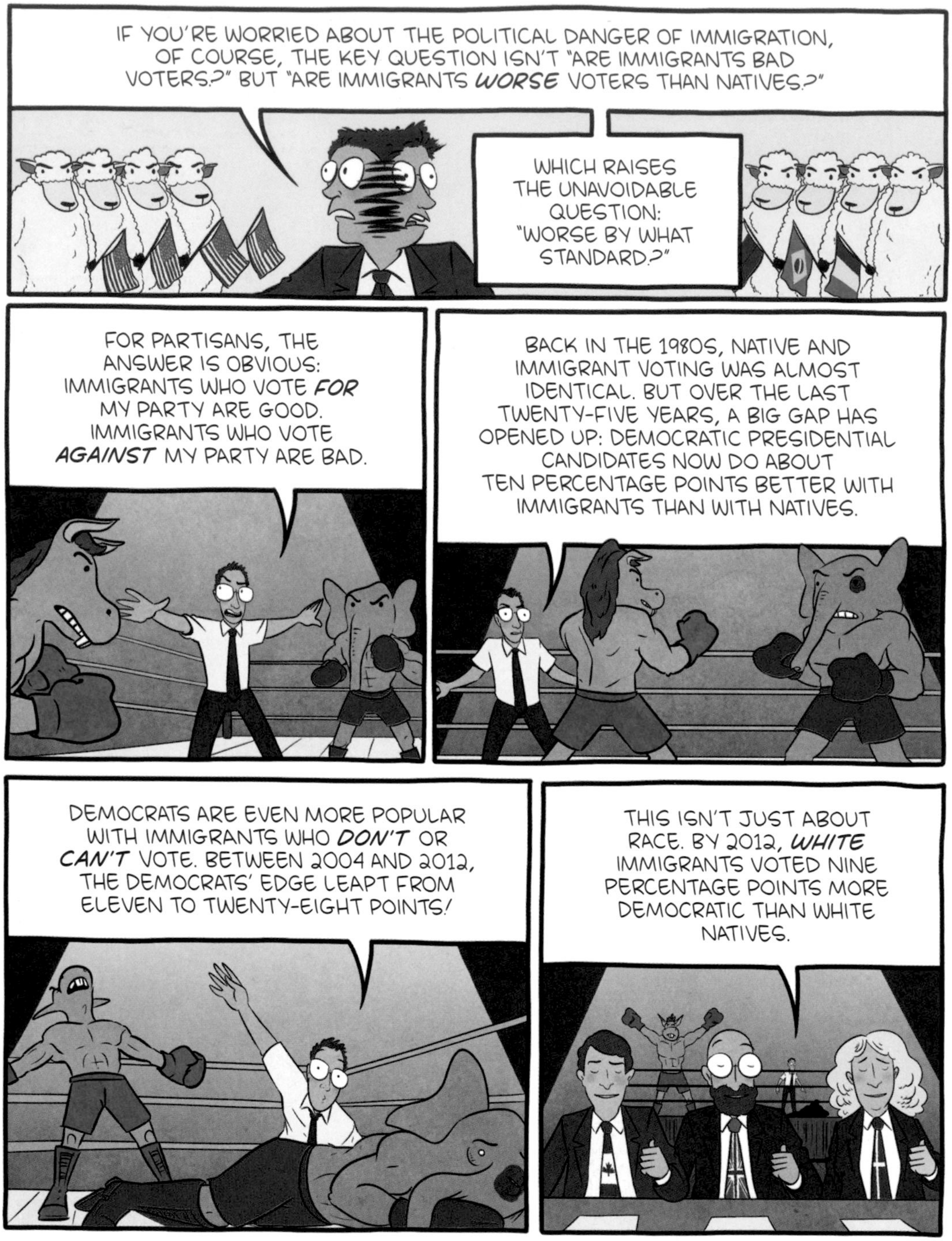
IF YOU'RE WORRIED ABOUT THE POLITICAL DANGER OF IMMIGRATION, OF COURSE, THE KEY QUESTION ISN'T "ARE IMMIGRANTS BAD VOTERS?" BUT "ARE IMMIGRANTS *WORSE* VOTERS THAN NATIVES?"
WHICH RAISES THE UNAVOIDABLE QUESTION: "WORSE BY WHAT STANDARD?"
FOR PARTISANS, THE ANSWER IS OBVIOUS: IMMIGRANTS WHO VOTE *FOR* MY PARTY ARE GOOD. IMMIGRANTS WHO VOTE *AGAINST* MY PARTY ARE BAD.
BACK IN THE 1980S, NATIVE AND IMMIGRANT VOTING WAS ALMOST IDENTICAL. BUT OVER THE LAST TWENTY-FIVE YEARS, A BIG GAP HAS OPENED UP: DEMOCRATIC PRESIDENTIAL CANDIDATES NOW DO ABOUT TEN PERCENTAGE POINTS BETTER WITH IMMIGRANTS THAN WITH NATIVES.
DEMOCRATS ARE EVEN MORE POPULAR WITH IMMIGRANTS WHO *DON'T* OR *CAN'T* VOTE. BETWEEN 2004 AND 2012, THE DEMOCRATS' EDGE LEAPT FROM ELEVEN TO TWENTY-EIGHT POINTS!
THIS ISN'T JUST ABOUT RACE. BY 2012, *WHITE* IMMIGRANTS VOTED NINE PERCENTAGE POINTS MORE DEMOCRATIC THAN WHITE NATIVES.

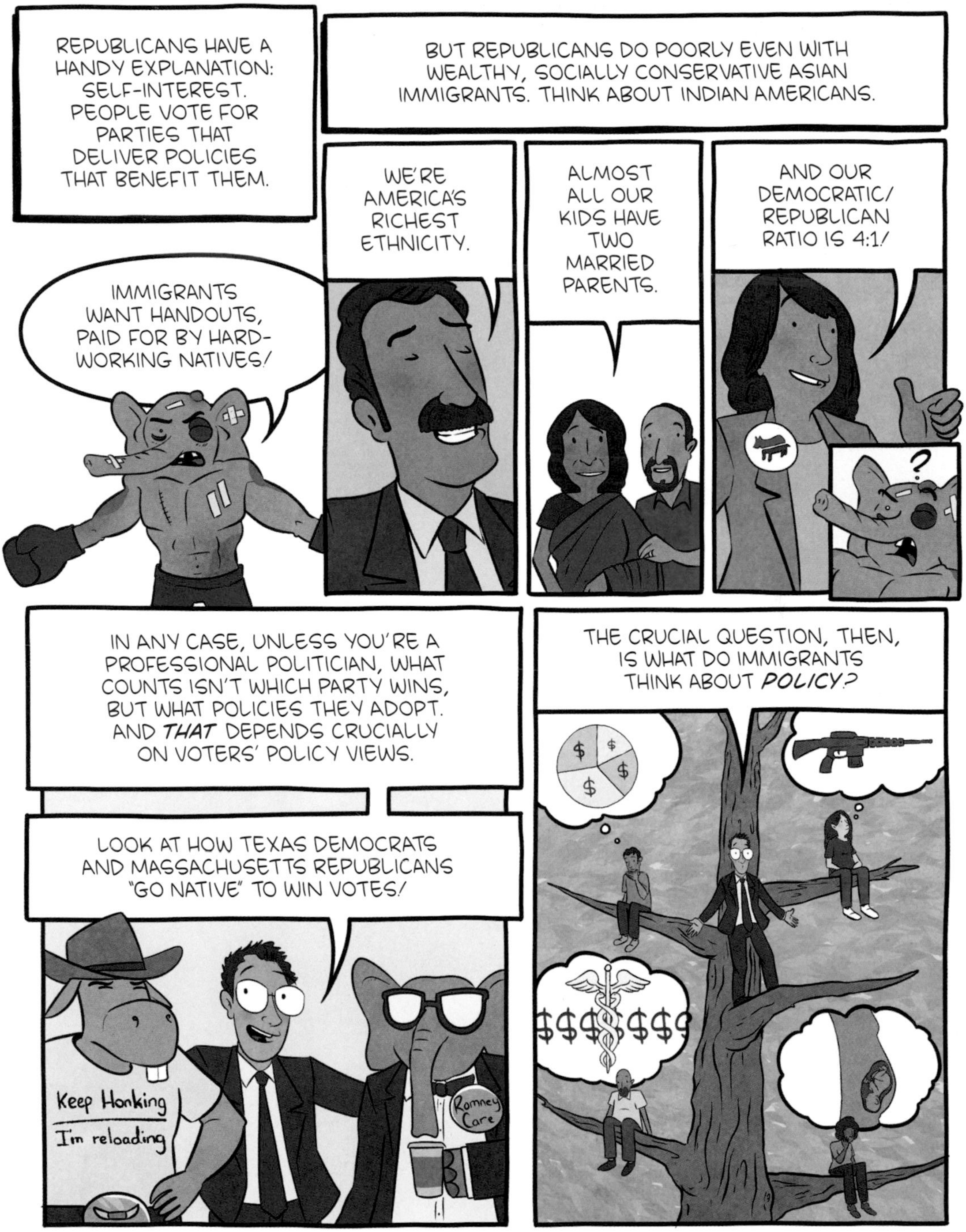

REPUBLICANS HAVE A HANDY EXPLANATION: SELF-INTEREST. PEOPLE VOTE FOR PARTIES THAT DELIVER POLICIES THAT BENEFIT THEM.
IMMIGRANTS WANT HANDOUTS, PAID FOR BY HARD-WORKING NATIVES!
BUT REPUBLICANS DO POORLY EVEN WITH WEALTHY, SOCIALLY CONSERVATIVE ASIAN IMMIGRANTS. THINK ABOUT INDIAN AMERICANS.
WE'RE AMERICA'S RICHEST ETHNICITY.
ALMOST ALL OUR KIDS HAVE TWO MARRIED PARENTS.
AND OUR DEMOCRATIC/ REPUBLICAN RATIO IS 4:1!
?
IN ANY CASE, UNLESS YOU'RE A PROFESSIONAL POLITICIAN, WHAT COUNTS ISN'T WHICH PARTY WINS, BUT WHAT POLICIES THEY ADOPT. AND *THAT* DEPENDS CRUCIALLY ON VOTERS' POLICY VIEWS.
LOOK AT HOW TEXAS DEMOCRATS AND MASSACHUSETTS REPUBLICANS "GO NATIVE" TO WIN VOTES!
Keep Honking
I'm reloading
Romney Care
THE CRUCIAL QUESTION, THEN, IS WHAT DO IMMIGRANTS THINK ABOUT *POLICY*?
$ $ $ $
$$$$$$

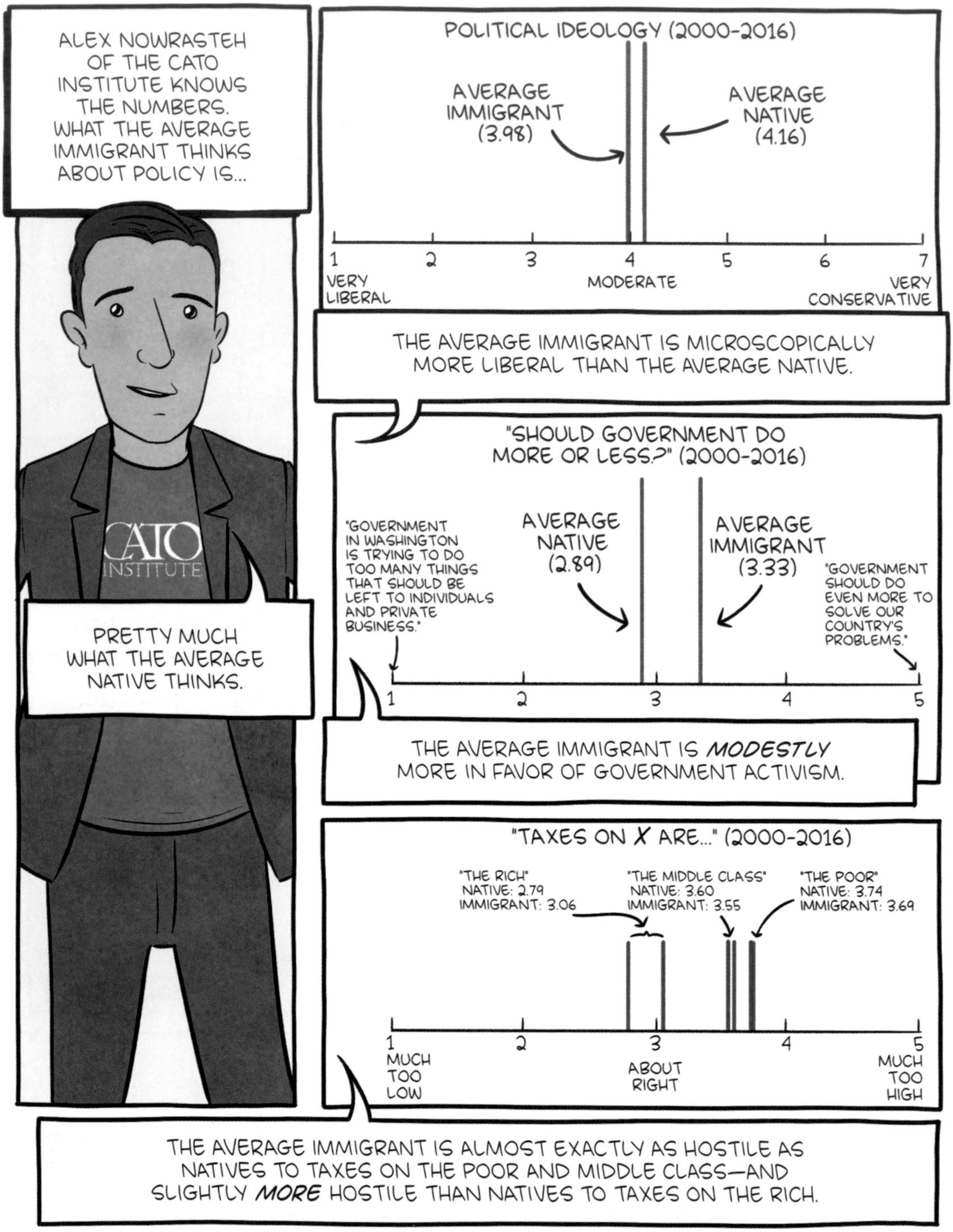
ALEX NOWRASTEH OF THE CATO INSTITUTE KNOWS THE NUMBERS. WHAT THE AVERAGE IMMIGRANT THINKS ABOUT POLICY IS...
POLITICAL IDEOLOGY (2000-2016)
AVERAGE IMMIGRANT (3.98)
AVERAGE NATIVE (4.16)
1 VERY LIBERAL
2
3
4 MODERATE
5
6
7 VERY CONSERVATIVE
THE AVERAGE IMMIGRANT IS MICROSCOPICALLY MORE LIBERAL THAN THE AVERAGE NATIVE.
CATO INSTITUTE
"SHOULD GOVERNMENT DO MORE OR LESS?" (2000-2016)
"GOVERNMENT IN WASHINGTON IS TRYING TO DO TOO MANY THINGS THAT SHOULD BE LEFT TO INDIVIDUALS AND PRIVATE BUSINESS."
AVERAGE NATIVE (2.89)
AVERAGE IMMIGRANT (3.33)
"GOVERNMENT SHOULD DO EVEN MORE TO SOLVE OUR COUNTRY'S PROBLEMS."
1
2
3
4
5
PRETTY MUCH WHAT THE AVERAGE NATIVE THINKS.
THE AVERAGE IMMIGRANT IS *MODESTLY* MORE IN FAVOR OF GOVERNMENT ACTIVISM.
"TAXES ON *X* ARE..." (2000-2016)
"THE RICH" NATIVE: 2.79 IMMIGRANT: 3.06
"THE MIDDLE CLASS" NATIVE: 3.60 IMMIGRANT: 3.55
"THE POOR" NATIVE: 3.74 IMMIGRANT: 3.69
1 MUCH TOO LOW
2
3 ABOUT RIGHT
4
5 MUCH TOO HIGH
THE AVERAGE IMMIGRANT IS ALMOST EXACTLY AS HOSTILE AS NATIVES TO TAXES ON THE POOR AND MIDDLE CLASS—AND SLIGHTLY ***MORE*** HOSTILE THAN NATIVES TO TAXES ON THE RICH.

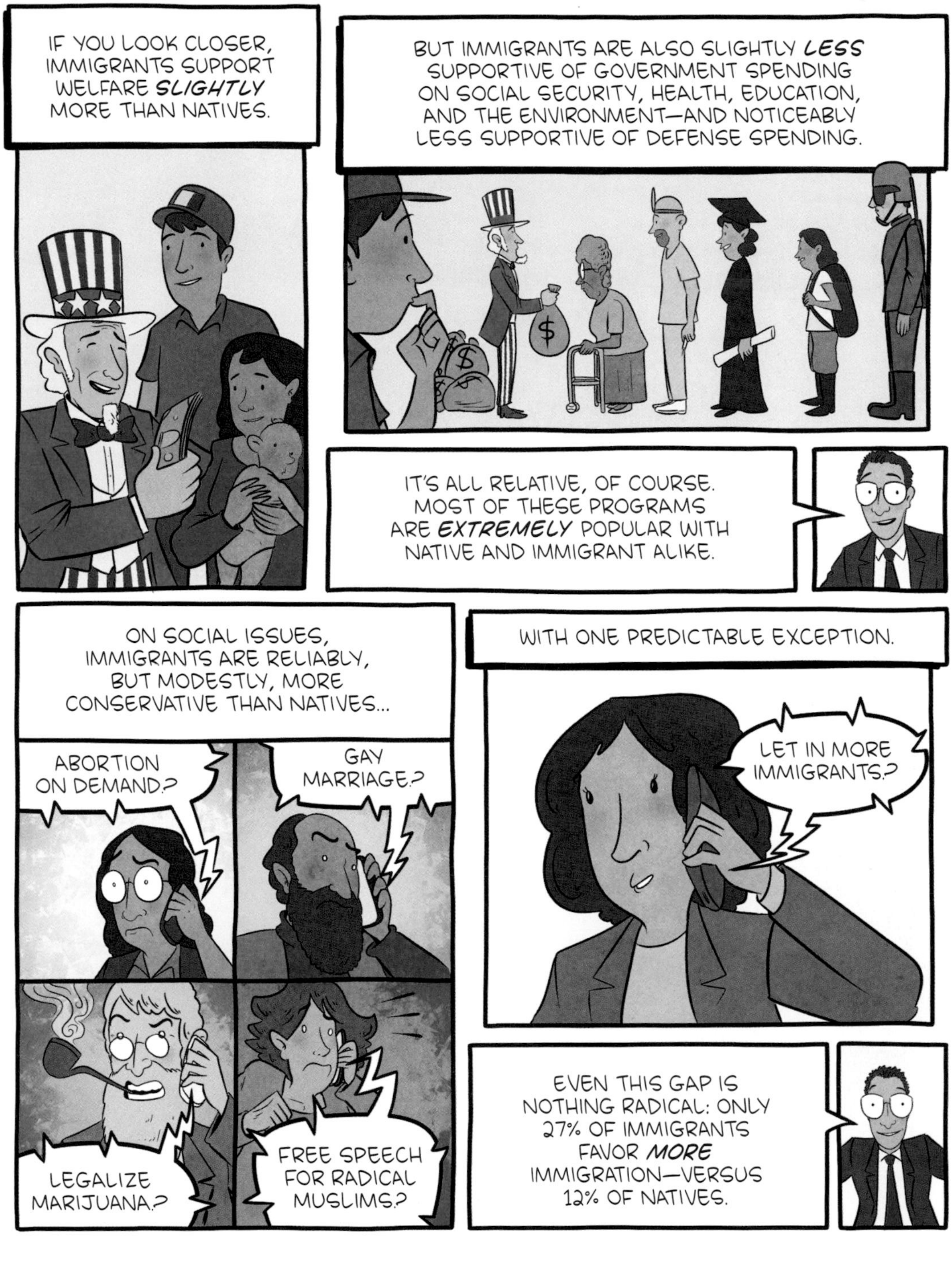
IF YOU LOOK CLOSER, IMMIGRANTS SUPPORT WELFARE *SLIGHTLY* MORE THAN NATIVES.
BUT IMMIGRANTS ARE ALSO SLIGHTLY *LESS* SUPPORTIVE OF GOVERNMENT SPENDING ON SOCIAL SECURITY, HEALTH, EDUCATION, AND THE ENVIRONMENT—AND NOTICEABLY LESS SUPPORTIVE OF DEFENSE SPENDING.
$
$
IT'S ALL RELATIVE, OF COURSE. MOST OF THESE PROGRAMS ARE *EXTREMELY* POPULAR WITH NATIVE AND IMMIGRANT ALIKE.
ON SOCIAL ISSUES, IMMIGRANTS ARE RELIABLY, BUT MODESTLY, MORE CONSERVATIVE THAN NATIVES...
ABORTION ON DEMAND?
GAY MARRIAGE?
LEGALIZE MARIJUANA?
FREE SPEECH FOR RADICAL MUSLIMS?
WITH ONE PREDICTABLE EXCEPTION.
LET IN MORE IMMIGRANTS?
EVEN THIS GAP IS NOTHING RADICAL: ONLY 27% OF IMMIGRANTS FAVOR *MORE* IMMIGRATION—VERSUS 12% OF NATIVES.

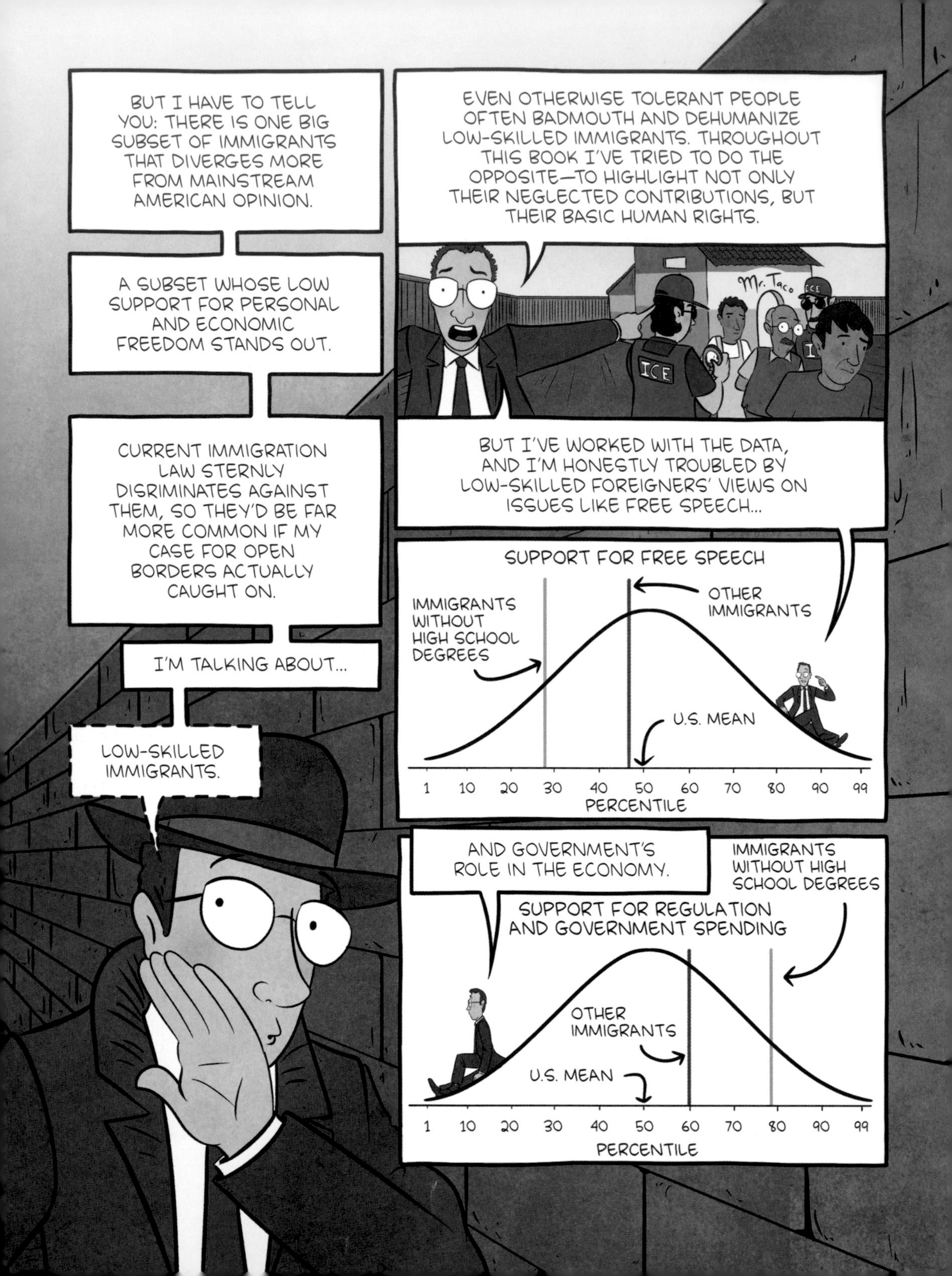
BUT I HAVE TO TELL YOU: THERE IS ONE BIG SUBSET OF IMMIGRANTS THAT DIVERGES MORE FROM MAINSTREAM AMERICAN OPINION.
A SUBSET WHOSE LOW SUPPORT FOR PERSONAL AND ECONOMIC FREEDOM STANDS OUT.
CURRENT IMMIGRATION LAW STERNLY DISRIMINATES AGAINST THEM, SO THEY'D BE FAR MORE COMMON IF MY CASE FOR OPEN BORDERS ACTUALLY CAUGHT ON.
I'M TALKING ABOUT...
LOW-SKILLED IMMIGRANTS.
EVEN OTHERWISE TOLERANT PEOPLE OFTEN BADMOUTH AND DEHUMANIZE LOW-SKILLED IMMIGRANTS. THROUGHOUT THIS BOOK I'VE TRIED TO DO THE OPPOSITE—TO HIGHLIGHT NOT ONLY THEIR NEGLECTED CONTRIBUTIONS, BUT THEIR BASIC HUMAN RIGHTS.
Mr. Taco
ICE
ICE
BUT I'VE WORKED WITH THE DATA, AND I'M HONESTLY TROUBLED BY LOW-SKILLED FOREIGNERS' VIEWS ON ISSUES LIKE FREE SPEECH...
SUPPORT FOR FREE SPEECH
IMMIGRANTS WITHOUT HIGH SCHOOL DEGREES
OTHER IMMIGRANTS
U.S. MEAN
1 10 20 30 40 50 60 70 80 90 99
PERCENTILE
AND GOVERNMENT'S ROLE IN THE ECONOMY.
IMMIGRANTS WITHOUT HIGH SCHOOL DEGREES
SUPPORT FOR REGULATION AND GOVERNMENT SPENDING
OTHER IMMIGRANTS
U.S. MEAN
1 10 20 30 40 50 60 70 80 90 99
PERCENTILE

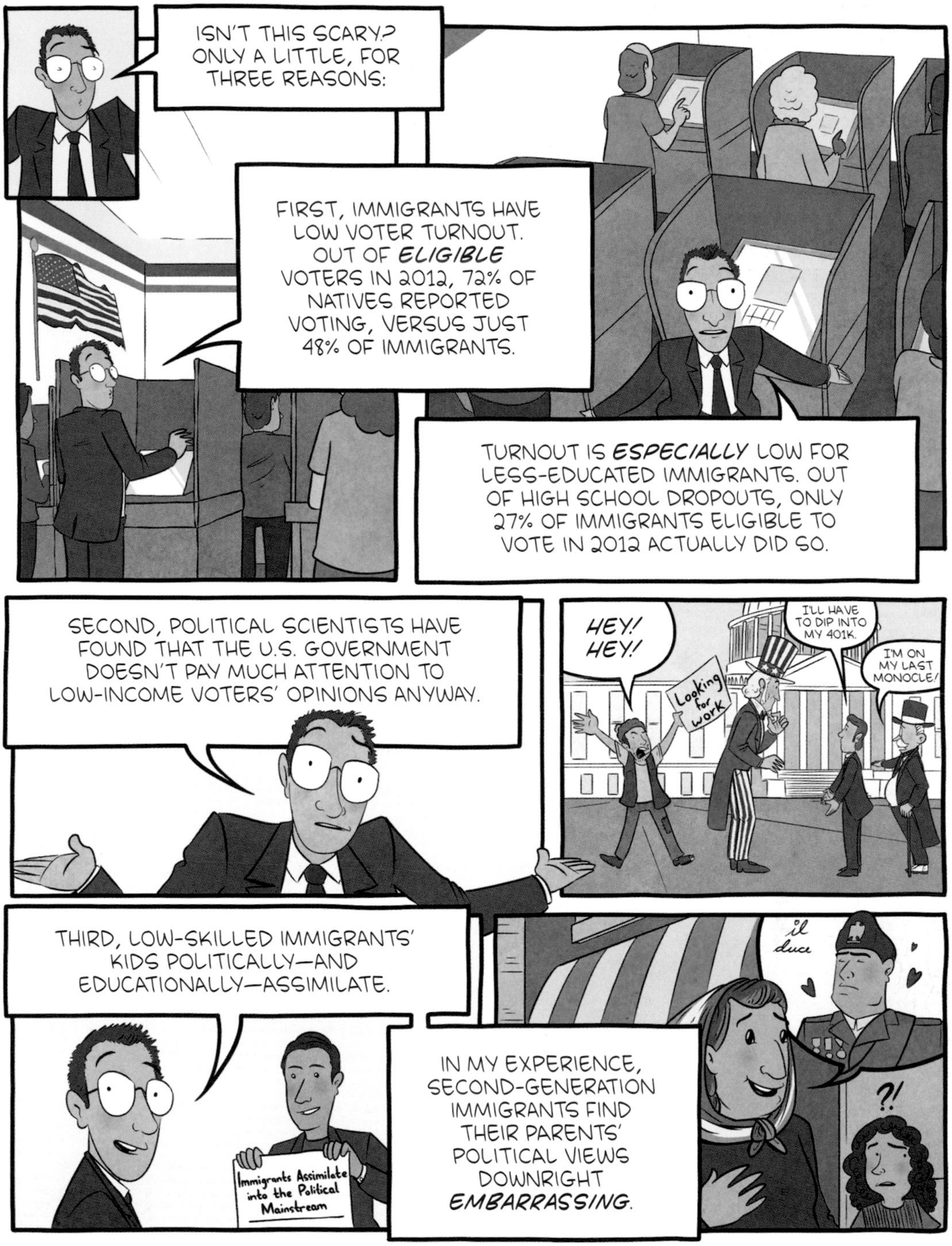
ISN'T THIS SCARY? ONLY A LITTLE, FOR THREE REASONS:
FIRST, IMMIGRANTS HAVE LOW VOTER TURNOUT. OUT OF *ELIGIBLE* VOTERS IN 2012, 72% OF NATIVES REPORTED VOTING, VERSUS JUST 48% OF IMMIGRANTS.
TURNOUT IS *ESPECIALLY* LOW FOR LESS-EDUCATED IMMIGRANTS. OUT OF HIGH SCHOOL DROPOUTS, ONLY 27% OF IMMIGRANTS ELIGIBLE TO VOTE IN 2012 ACTUALLY DID SO.
SECOND, POLITICAL SCIENTISTS HAVE FOUND THAT THE U.S. GOVERNMENT DOESN'T PAY MUCH ATTENTION TO LOW-INCOME VOTERS' OPINIONS ANYWAY.
HEY! HEY!
Looking for work
I'LL HAVE TO DIP INTO MY 401K.
I'M ON MY LAST MONOCLE!
THIRD, LOW-SKILLED IMMIGRANTS' KIDS POLITICALLY—AND EDUCATIONALLY—ASSIMILATE.
Immigrants Assimilate into the Political Mainstream
IN MY EXPERIENCE, SECOND-GENERATION IMMIGRANTS FIND THEIR PARENTS' POLITICAL VIEWS DOWNRIGHT *EMBARRASSING*.
il duce
?!

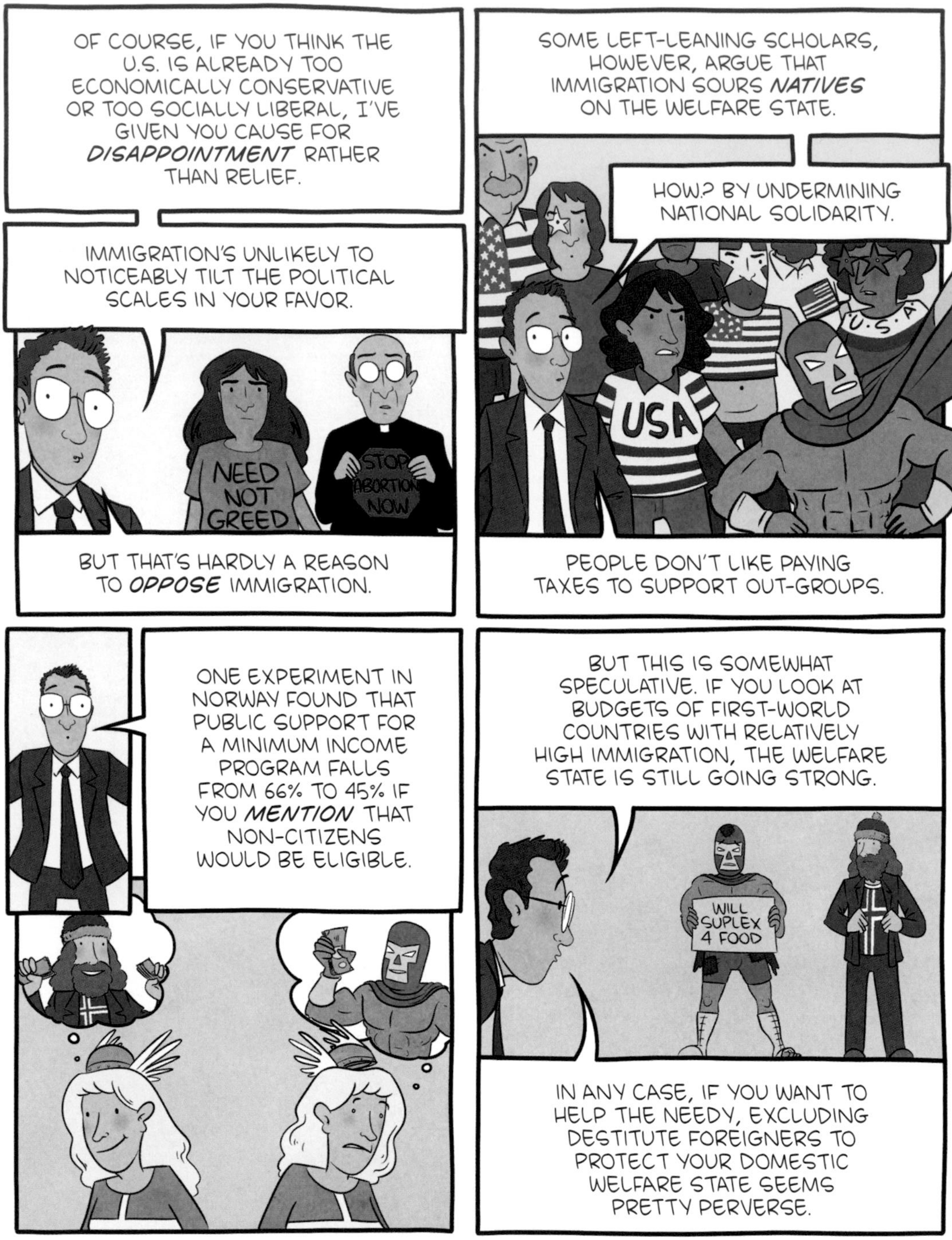
OF COURSE, IF YOU THINK THE U.S. IS ALREADY TOO ECONOMICALLY CONSERVATIVE OR TOO SOCIALLY LIBERAL, I'VE GIVEN YOU CAUSE FOR *DISAPPOINTMENT* RATHER THAN RELIEF.
IMMIGRATION'S UNLIKELY TO NOTICEABLY TILT THE POLITICAL SCALES IN YOUR FAVOR.
NEED NOT GREED
STOP ABORTION NOW
BUT THAT'S HARDLY A REASON TO *OPPOSE* IMMIGRATION.
SOME LEFT-LEANING SCHOLARS, HOWEVER, ARGUE THAT IMMIGRATION SOURS *NATIVES* ON THE WELFARE STATE.
HOW? BY UNDERMINING NATIONAL SOLIDARITY.
USA
U.S.A
PEOPLE DON'T LIKE PAYING TAXES TO SUPPORT OUT-GROUPS.
ONE EXPERIMENT IN NORWAY FOUND THAT PUBLIC SUPPORT FOR A MINIMUM INCOME PROGRAM FALLS FROM 66% TO 45% IF YOU *MENTION* THAT NON-CITIZENS WOULD BE ELIGIBLE.
BUT THIS IS SOMEWHAT SPECULATIVE. IF YOU LOOK AT BUDGETS OF FIRST-WORLD COUNTRIES WITH RELATIVELY HIGH IMMIGRATION, THE WELFARE STATE IS STILL GOING STRONG.
WILL SUPLEX 4 FOOD
IN ANY CASE, IF YOU WANT TO HELP THE NEEDY, EXCLUDING DESTITUTE FOREIGNERS TO PROTECT YOUR DOMESTIC WELFARE STATE SEEMS PRETTY PERVERSE.

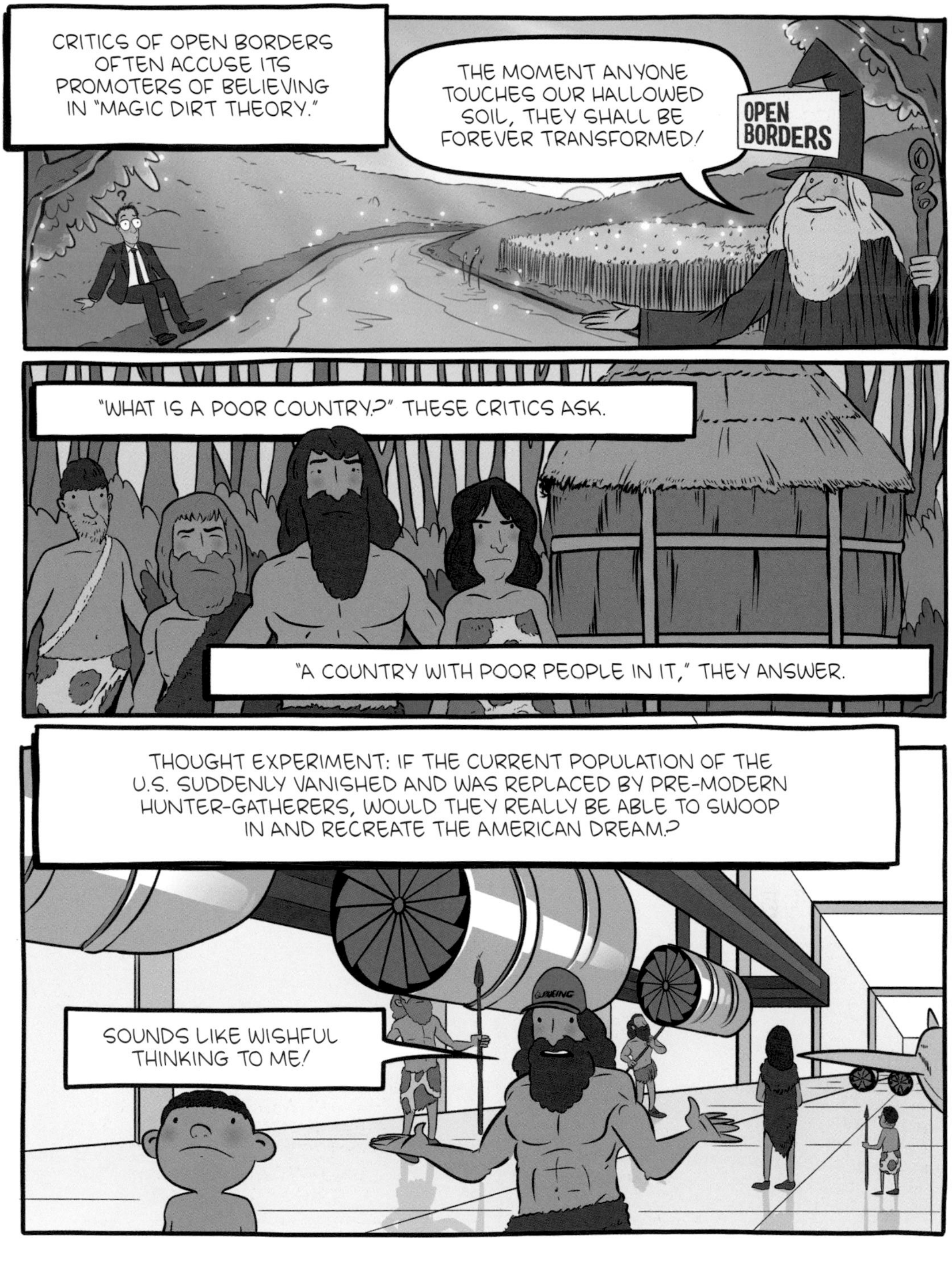
CRITICS OF OPEN BORDERS OFTEN ACCUSE ITS PROMOTERS OF BELIEVING IN "MAGIC DIRT THEORY."
THE MOMENT ANYONE TOUCHES OUR HALLOWED SOIL, THEY SHALL BE FOREVER TRANSFORMED!
OPEN BORDERS
"WHAT IS A POOR COUNTRY?" THESE CRITICS ASK.
"A COUNTRY WITH POOR PEOPLE IN IT," THEY ANSWER.
THOUGHT EXPERIMENT: IF THE CURRENT POPULATION OF THE U.S. SUDDENLY VANISHED AND WAS REPLACED BY PRE-MODERN HUNTER-GATHERERS, WOULD THEY REALLY BE ABLE TO SWOOP IN AND RECREATE THE AMERICAN DREAM?
SOUNDS LIKE WISHFUL THINKING TO ME!
BOEING

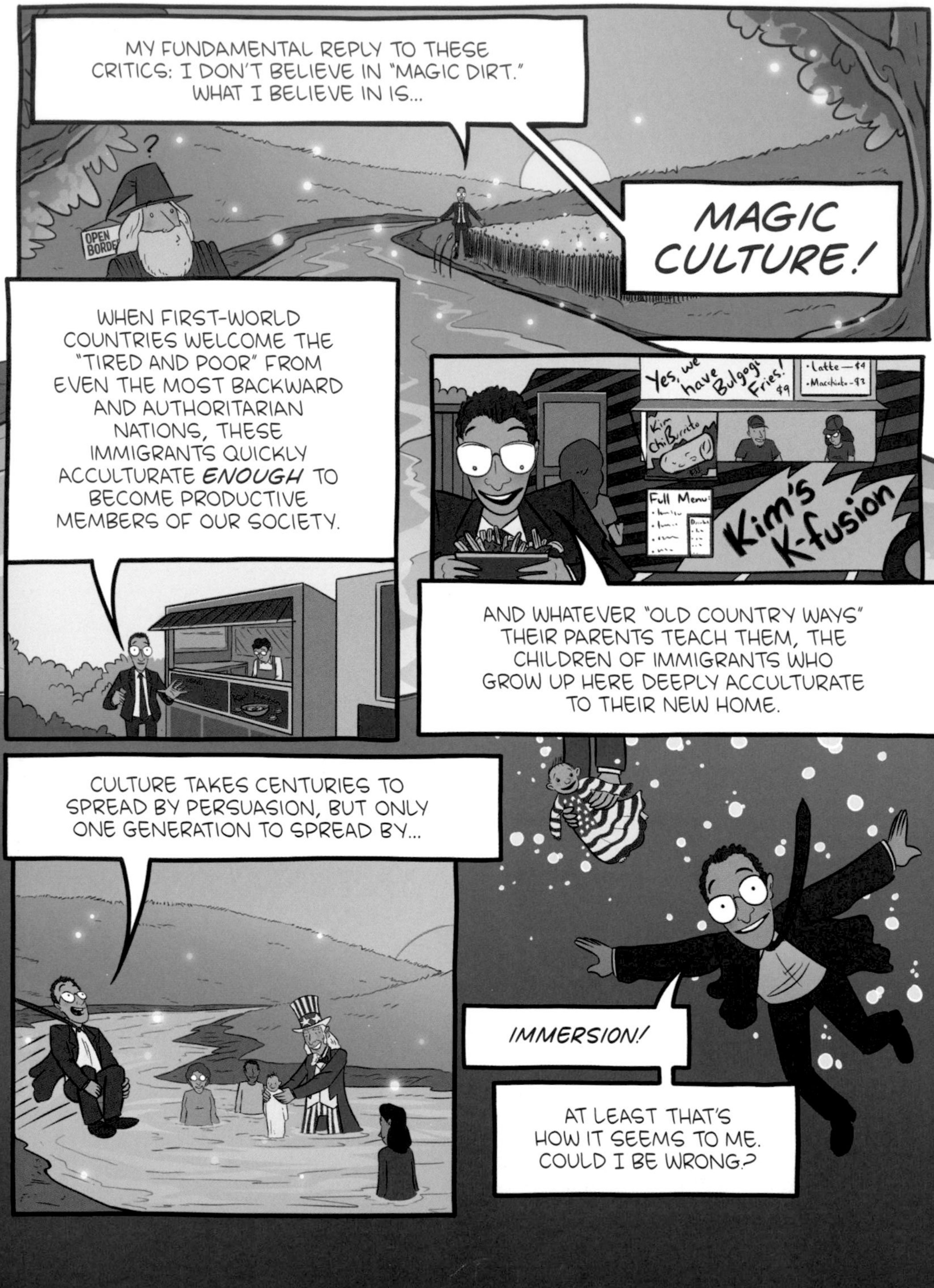

MY FUNDAMENTAL REPLY TO THESE CRITICS: I DON'T BELIEVE IN "MAGIC DIRT." WHAT I BELIEVE IN IS...
?
OPEN BORDE
MAGIC CULTURE!
WHEN FIRST-WORLD COUNTRIES WELCOME THE "TIRED AND POOR" FROM EVEN THE MOST BACKWARD AND AUTHORITARIAN NATIONS, THESE IMMIGRANTS QUICKLY ACCULTURATE ***ENOUGH*** TO BECOME PRODUCTIVE MEMBERS OF OUR SOCIETY.
Yes, we have Bulgogi Fries! $9
•Latte — $4
•Macchiato - $3
Kim ChiBurrito
Full Menu:
Kim's K-fusion
AND WHATEVER "OLD COUNTRY WAYS" THEIR PARENTS TEACH THEM, THE CHILDREN OF IMMIGRANTS WHO GROW UP HERE DEEPLY ACCULTURATE TO THEIR NEW HOME.
CULTURE TAKES CENTURIES TO SPREAD BY PERSUASION, BUT ONLY ONE GENERATION TO SPREAD BY...
IMMERSION!
AT LEAST THAT'S HOW IT SEEMS TO ME. COULD I BE WRONG?

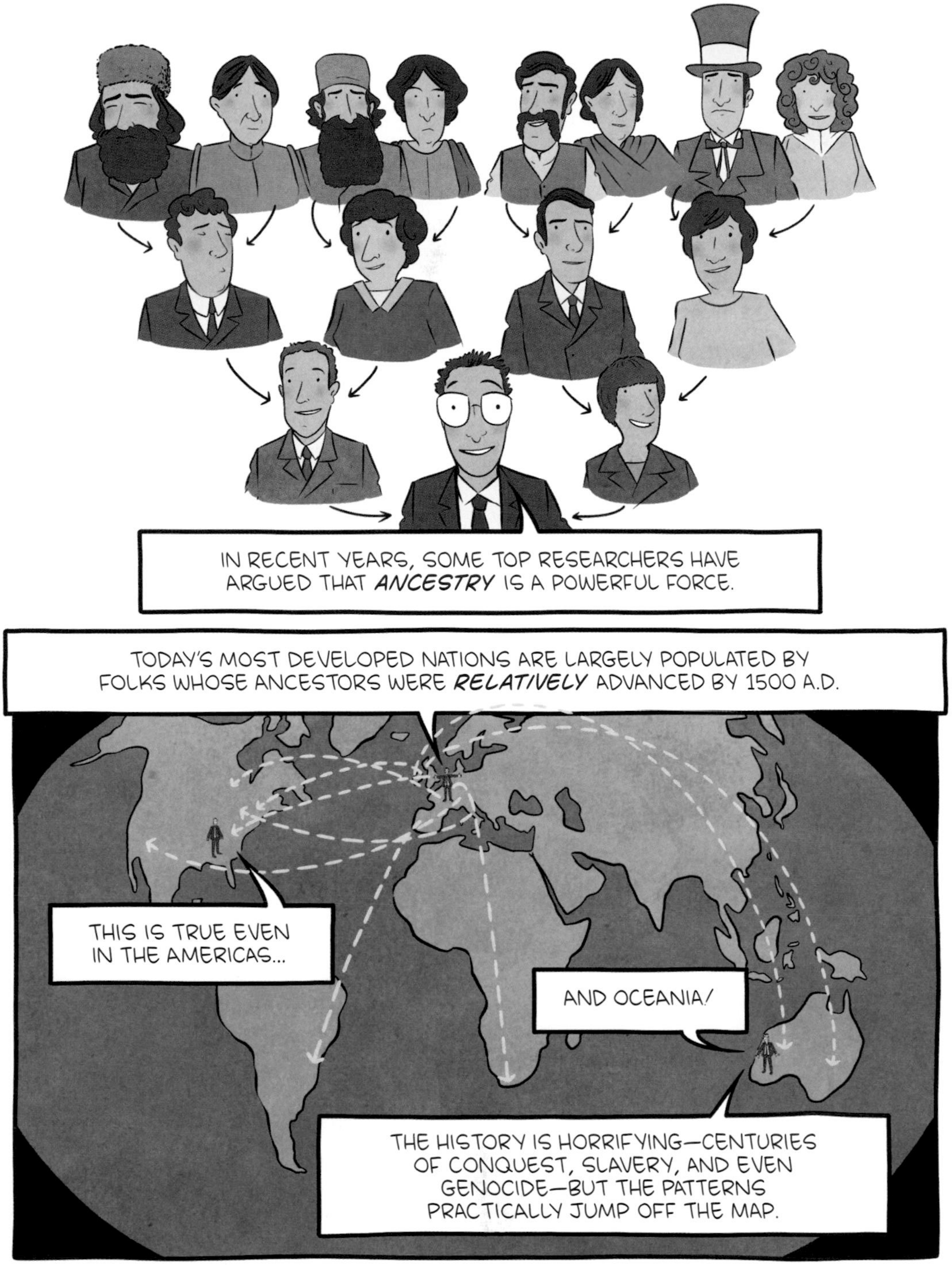
IN RECENT YEARS, SOME TOP RESEARCHERS HAVE ARGUED THAT *ANCESTRY* IS A POWERFUL FORCE.
TODAY'S MOST DEVELOPED NATIONS ARE LARGELY POPULATED BY FOLKS WHOSE ANCESTORS WERE ***RELATIVELY*** ADVANCED BY 1500 A.D.
THIS IS TRUE EVEN IN THE AMERICAS...
AND OCEANIA!
THE HISTORY IS HORRIFYING—CENTURIES OF CONQUEST, SLAVERY, AND EVEN GENOCIDE—BUT THE PATTERNS PRACTICALLY JUMP OFF THE MAP.

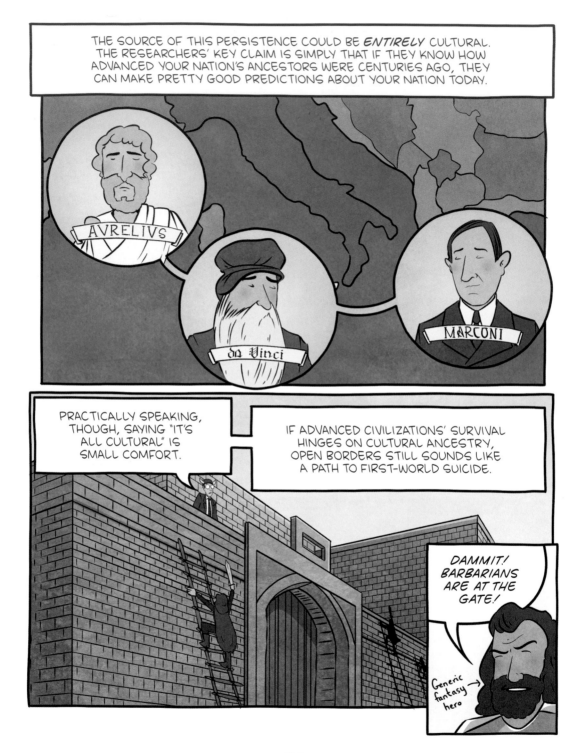

THE SOURCE OF THIS PERSISTENCE COULD BE *ENTIRELY* CULTURAL. THE RESEARCHERS' KEY CLAIM IS SIMPLY THAT IF THEY KNOW HOW ADVANCED YOUR NATION'S ANCESTORS WERE CENTURIES AGO, THEY CAN MAKE PRETTY GOOD PREDICTIONS ABOUT YOUR NATION TODAY.

AVRELIVS

da Vinci

MARCONI

PRACTICALLY SPEAKING, THOUGH, SAYING "IT'S ALL CULTURAL" IS SMALL COMFORT.

IF ADVANCED CIVILIZATIONS' SURVIVAL HINGES ON CULTURAL ANCESTRY, OPEN BORDERS STILL SOUNDS LIKE A PATH TO FIRST-WORLD SUICIDE.

DAMMIT! BARBARIANS ARE AT THE GATE!

Generic fantasy hero →

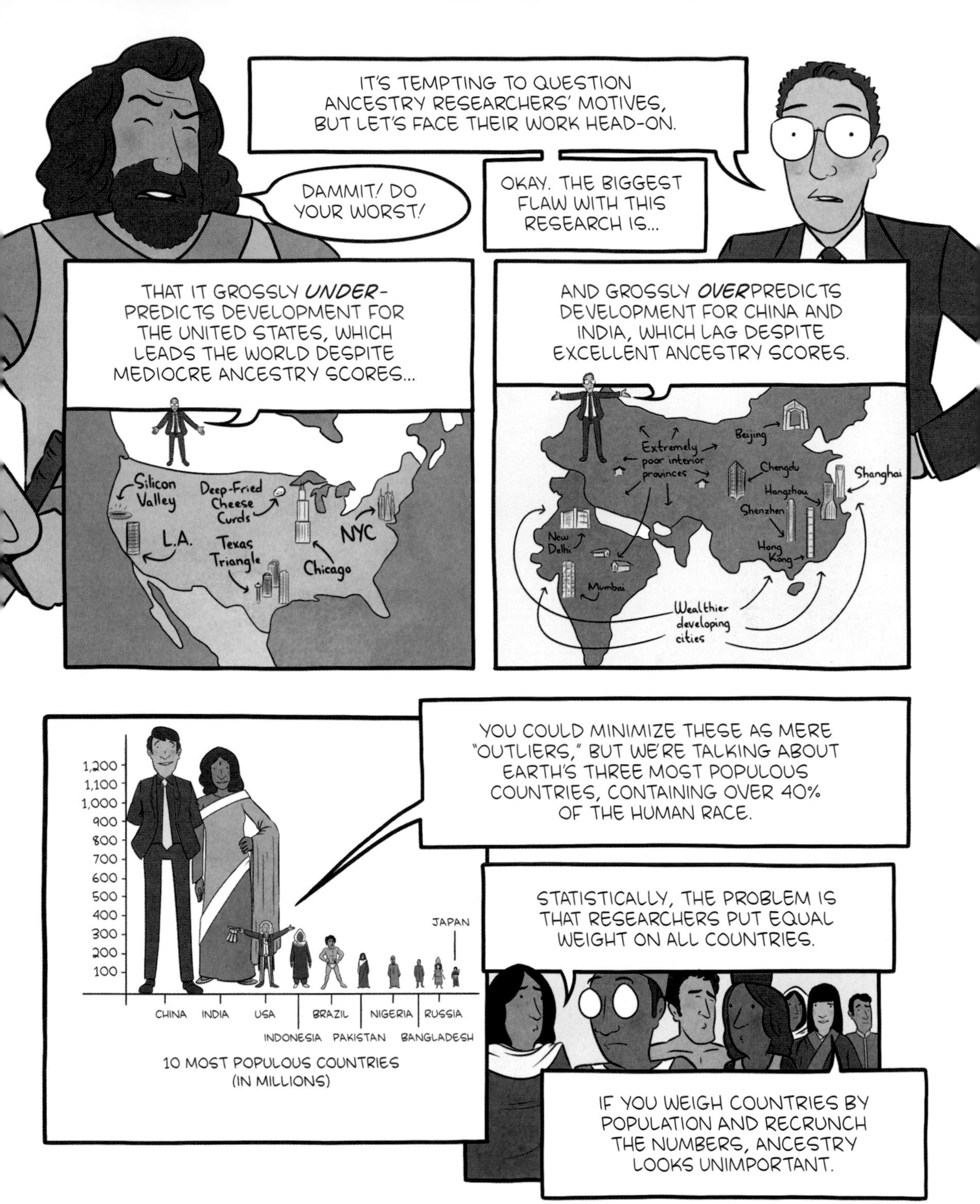
IT'S TEMPTING TO QUESTION ANCESTRY RESEARCHERS' MOTIVES, BUT LET'S FACE THEIR WORK HEAD-ON.
DAMMIT! DO YOUR WORST!
OKAY. THE BIGGEST FLAW WITH THIS RESEARCH IS...
THAT IT GROSSLY *UNDER*-PREDICTS DEVELOPMENT FOR THE UNITED STATES, WHICH LEADS THE WORLD DESPITE MEDIOCRE ANCESTRY SCORES...
Silicon Valley
Deep-Fried Cheese Curds
L.A.
Texas Triangle
Chicago
NYC
AND GROSSLY *OVER*PREDICTS DEVELOPMENT FOR CHINA AND INDIA, WHICH LAG DESPITE EXCELLENT ANCESTRY SCORES.
Extremely poor interior provinces
Beijing
Chengdu
Shanghai
Hangzhou
Shenzhen
Hong Kong
New Delhi
Mumbai
Wealthier developing cities
1,200
1,100
1,000
900
800
700
600
500
400
300
200
100
JAPAN
CHINA
INDIA
USA
INDONESIA
BRAZIL
PAKISTAN
NIGERIA
BANGLADESH
RUSSIA
10 MOST POPULOUS COUNTRIES (IN MILLIONS)
YOU COULD MINIMIZE THESE AS MERE "OUTLIERS," BUT WE'RE TALKING ABOUT EARTH'S THREE MOST POPULOUS COUNTRIES, CONTAINING OVER 40% OF THE HUMAN RACE.
STATISTICALLY, THE PROBLEM IS THAT RESEARCHERS PUT EQUAL WEIGHT ON ALL COUNTRIES.
IF YOU WEIGH COUNTRIES BY POPULATION AND RECRUNCH THE NUMBERS, ANCESTRY LOOKS UNIMPORTANT.

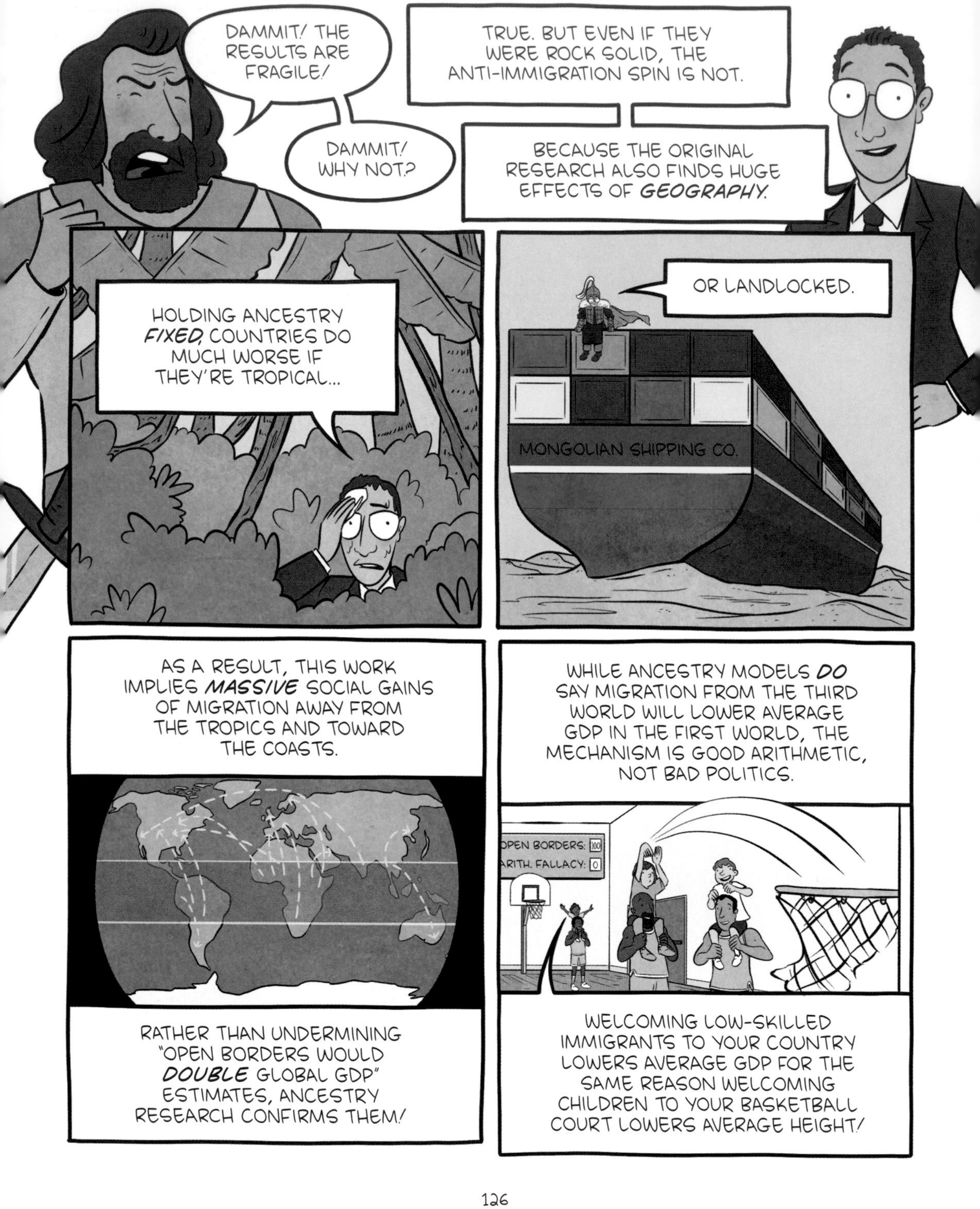

DAMMIT! THE RESULTS ARE FRAGILE!
DAMMIT! WHY NOT?
TRUE. BUT EVEN IF THEY WERE ROCK SOLID, THE ANTI-IMMIGRATION SPIN IS NOT.
BECAUSE THE ORIGINAL RESEARCH ALSO FINDS HUGE EFFECTS OF GEOGRAPHY.
HOLDING ANCESTRY FIXED, COUNTRIES DO MUCH WORSE IF THEY'RE TROPICAL...
OR LANDLOCKED.
MONGOLIAN SHIPPING CO.
AS A RESULT, THIS WORK IMPLIES MASSIVE SOCIAL GAINS OF MIGRATION AWAY FROM THE TROPICS AND TOWARD THE COASTS.
RATHER THAN UNDERMINING "OPEN BORDERS WOULD DOUBLE GLOBAL GDP" ESTIMATES, ANCESTRY RESEARCH CONFIRMS THEM!
WHILE ANCESTRY MODELS DO SAY MIGRATION FROM THE THIRD WORLD WILL LOWER AVERAGE GDP IN THE FIRST WORLD, THE MECHANISM IS GOOD ARITHMETIC, NOT BAD POLITICS.
OPEN BORDERS: 100
ARITH. FALLACY: 0
WELCOMING LOW-SKILLED IMMIGRANTS TO YOUR COUNTRY LOWERS AVERAGE GDP FOR THE SAME REASON WELCOMING CHILDREN TO YOUR BASKETBALL COURT LOWERS AVERAGE HEIGHT!

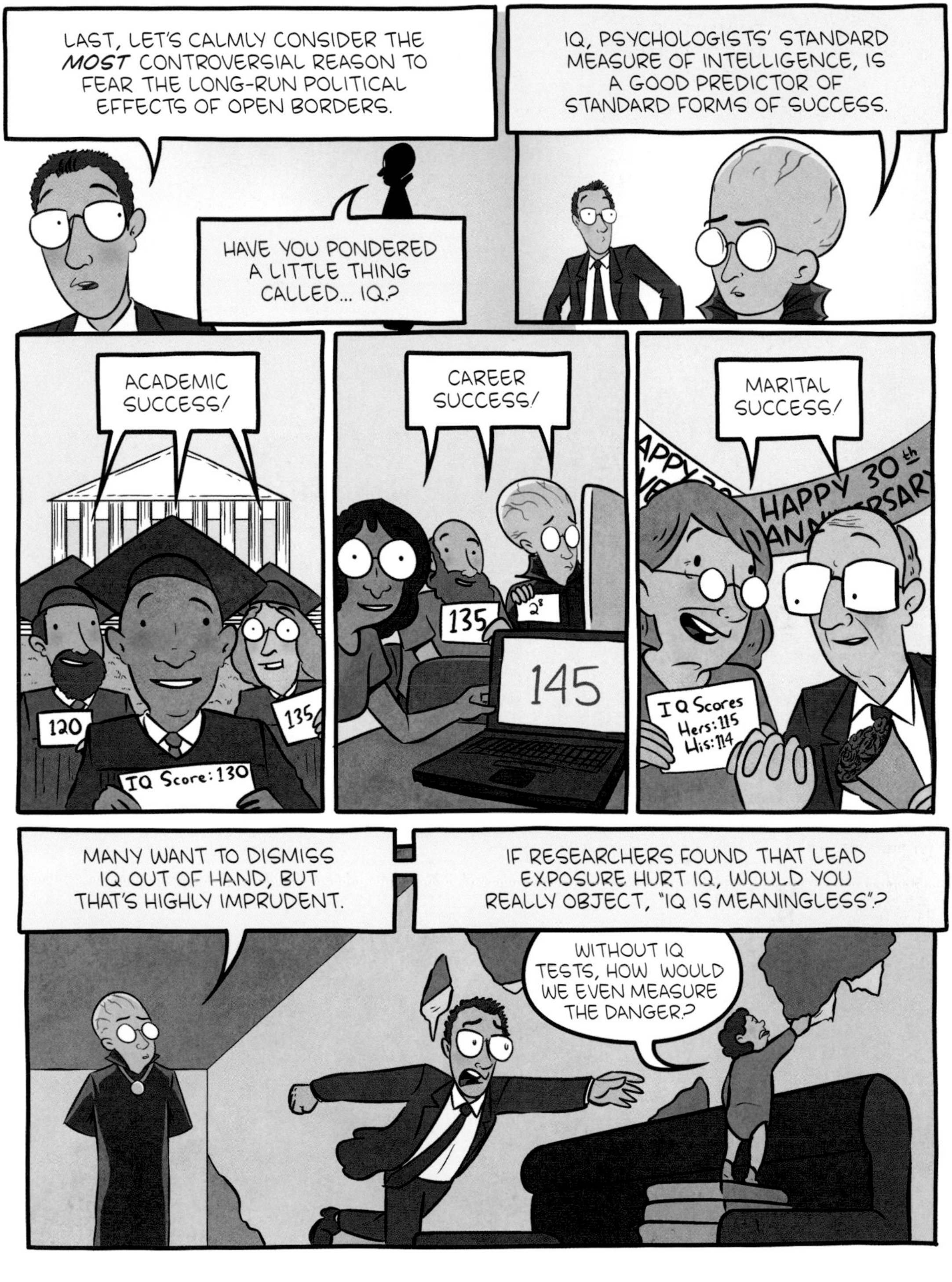
LAST, LET'S CALMLY CONSIDER THE *MOST* CONTROVERSIAL REASON TO FEAR THE LONG-RUN POLITICAL EFFECTS OF OPEN BORDERS.
HAVE YOU PONDERED A LITTLE THING CALLED... IQ?
IQ, PSYCHOLOGISTS' STANDARD MEASURE OF INTELLIGENCE, IS A GOOD PREDICTOR OF STANDARD FORMS OF SUCCESS.
ACADEMIC SUCCESS!
120
IQ Score: 130
135
CAREER SUCCESS!
135
2^8
145
MARITAL SUCCESS!
HAPPY 30th ANNIVERSARY
I Q Scores Hers: 115 His: 114
MANY WANT TO DISMISS IQ OUT OF HAND, BUT THAT'S HIGHLY IMPRUDENT.
IF RESEARCHERS FOUND THAT LEAD EXPOSURE HURT IQ, WOULD YOU REALLY OBJECT, "IQ IS MEANINGLESS"?
WITHOUT IQ TESTS, HOW WOULD WE EVEN MEASURE THE DANGER?

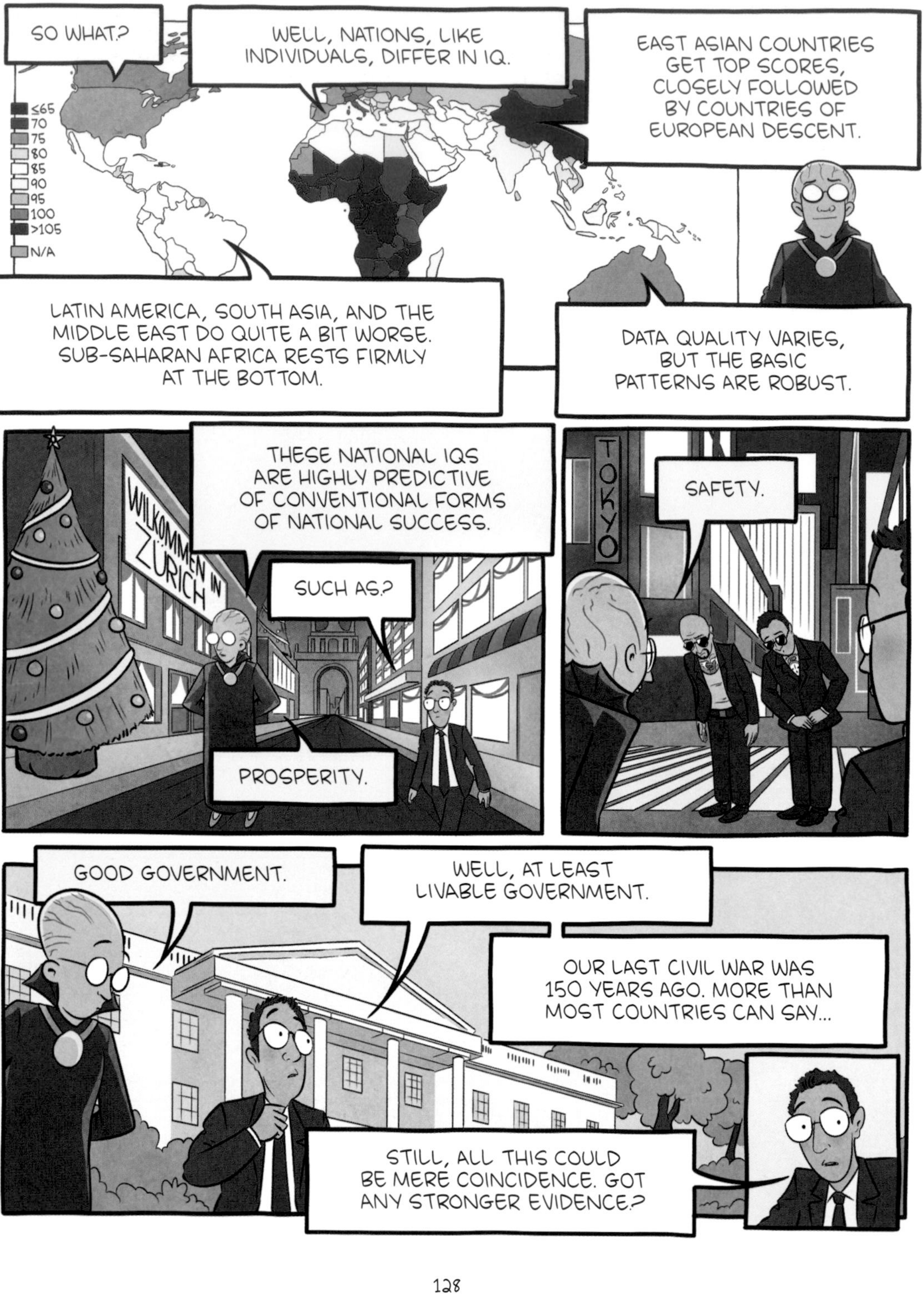
SO WHAT?
WELL, NATIONS, LIKE INDIVIDUALS, DIFFER IN IQ.
EAST ASIAN COUNTRIES GET TOP SCORES, CLOSELY FOLLOWED BY COUNTRIES OF EUROPEAN DESCENT.
≤65
70
75
80
85
90
95
100
>105
N/A
LATIN AMERICA, SOUTH ASIA, AND THE MIDDLE EAST DO QUITE A BIT WORSE. SUB-SAHARAN AFRICA RESTS FIRMLY AT THE BOTTOM.
DATA QUALITY VARIES, BUT THE BASIC PATTERNS ARE ROBUST.
WILKOMMEN IN ZÜRICH
THESE NATIONAL IQS ARE HIGHLY PREDICTIVE OF CONVENTIONAL FORMS OF NATIONAL SUCCESS.
SUCH AS?
PROSPERITY.
TOKYO
SAFETY.
GOOD GOVERNMENT.
WELL, AT LEAST LIVABLE GOVERNMENT.
OUR LAST CIVIL WAR WAS 150 YEARS AGO. MORE THAN MOST COUNTRIES CAN SAY...
STILL, ALL THIS COULD BE MERE COINCIDENCE. GOT ANY STRONGER EVIDENCE?

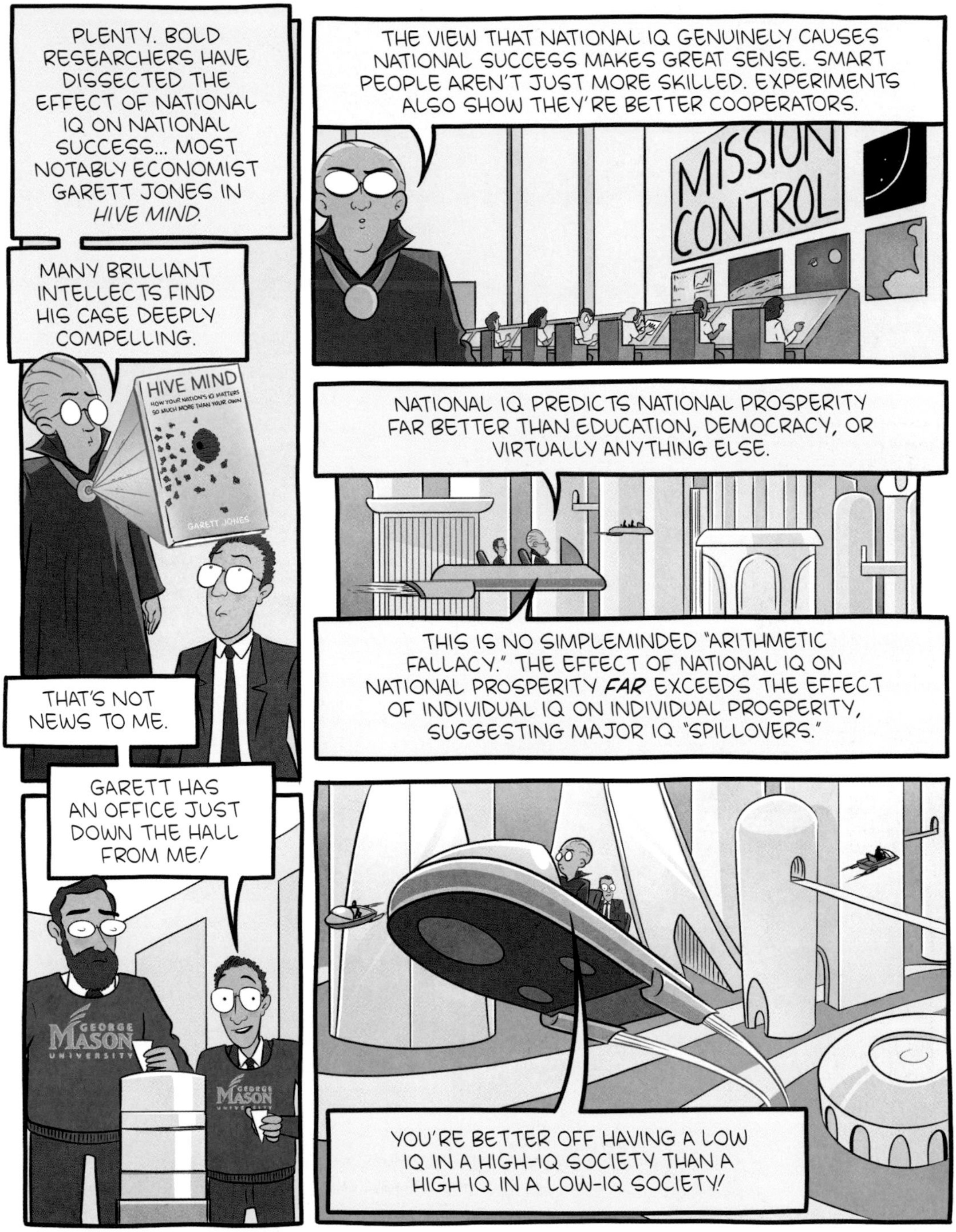
PLENTY. BOLD RESEARCHERS HAVE DISSECTED THE EFFECT OF NATIONAL IQ ON NATIONAL SUCCESS... MOST NOTABLY ECONOMIST GARETT JONES IN *HIVE MIND*.
MANY BRILLIANT INTELLECTS FIND HIS CASE DEEPLY COMPELLING.
HIVE MIND
HOW YOUR NATION'S IQ MATTERS SO MUCH MORE THAN YOUR OWN
GARETT JONES
THAT'S NOT NEWS TO ME.
GARETT HAS AN OFFICE JUST DOWN THE HALL FROM ME!
GEORGE MASON UNIVERSITY
GEORGE MASON UNIVERSITY
THE VIEW THAT NATIONAL IQ GENUINELY CAUSES NATIONAL SUCCESS MAKES GREAT SENSE. SMART PEOPLE AREN'T JUST MORE SKILLED. EXPERIMENTS ALSO SHOW THEY'RE BETTER COOPERATORS.
MISSION CONTROL
NATIONAL IQ PREDICTS NATIONAL PROSPERITY FAR BETTER THAN EDUCATION, DEMOCRACY, OR VIRTUALLY ANYTHING ELSE.
THIS IS NO SIMPLEMINDED "ARITHMETIC FALLACY." THE EFFECT OF NATIONAL IQ ON NATIONAL PROSPERITY ***FAR*** EXCEEDS THE EFFECT OF INDIVIDUAL IQ ON INDIVIDUAL PROSPERITY, SUGGESTING MAJOR IQ "SPILLOVERS."
YOU'RE BETTER OFF HAVING A LOW IQ IN A HIGH-IQ SOCIETY THAN A HIGH IQ IN A LOW-IQ SOCIETY!

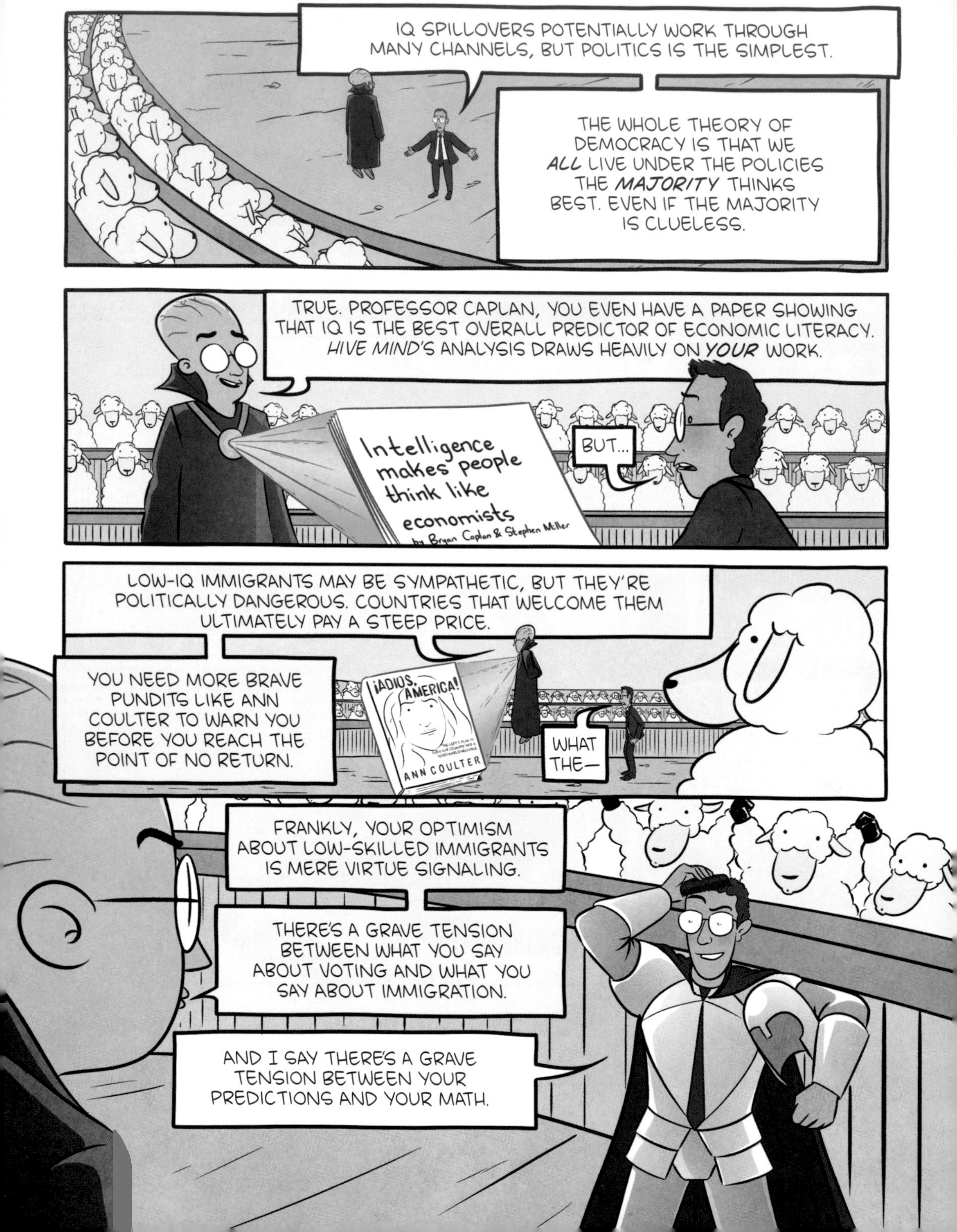
IQ SPILLOVERS POTENTIALLY WORK THROUGH MANY CHANNELS, BUT POLITICS IS THE SIMPLEST.
THE WHOLE THEORY OF DEMOCRACY IS THAT WE *ALL* LIVE UNDER THE POLICIES THE *MAJORITY* THINKS BEST. EVEN IF THE MAJORITY IS CLUELESS.
TRUE. PROFESSOR CAPLAN, YOU EVEN HAVE A PAPER SHOWING THAT IQ IS THE BEST OVERALL PREDICTOR OF ECONOMIC LITERACY. *HIVE MIND*'S ANALYSIS DRAWS HEAVILY ON *YOUR* WORK.
Intelligence makes people think like economists
by Bryan Caplan & Stephen Miller
BUT...
LOW-IQ IMMIGRANTS MAY BE SYMPATHETIC, BUT THEY'RE POLITICALLY DANGEROUS. COUNTRIES THAT WELCOME THEM ULTIMATELY PAY A STEEP PRICE.
YOU NEED MORE BRAVE PUNDITS LIKE ANN COULTER TO WARN YOU BEFORE YOU REACH THE POINT OF NO RETURN.
¡ADIOS, AMERICA!
ANN COULTER
WHAT THE—
FRANKLY, YOUR OPTIMISM ABOUT LOW-SKILLED IMMIGRANTS IS MERE VIRTUE SIGNALING.
THERE'S A GRAVE TENSION BETWEEN WHAT YOU SAY ABOUT VOTING AND WHAT YOU SAY ABOUT IMMIGRATION.
AND I SAY THERE'S A GRAVE TENSION BETWEEN YOUR PREDICTIONS AND YOUR MATH.

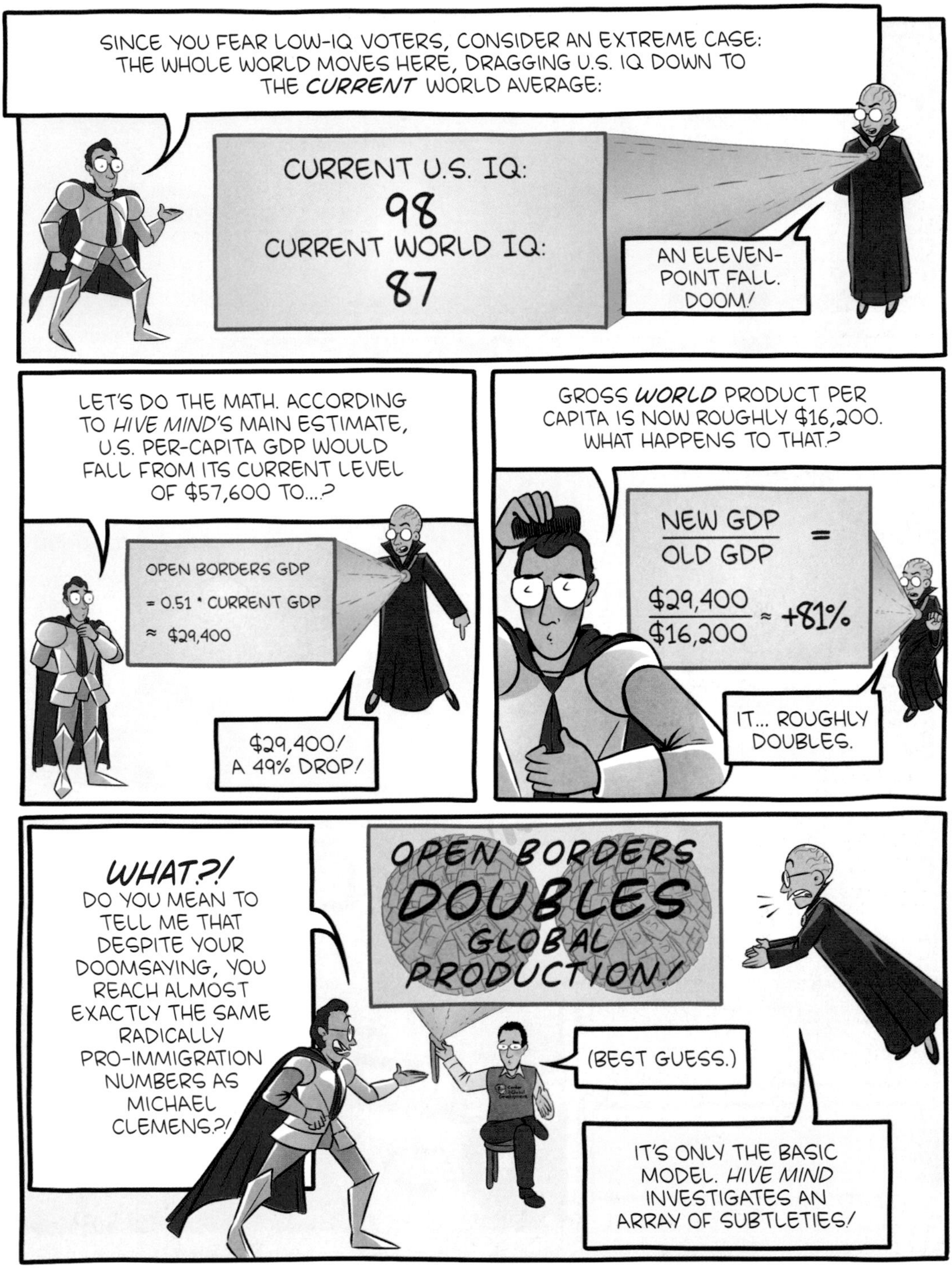
SINCE YOU FEAR LOW-IQ VOTERS, CONSIDER AN EXTREME CASE: THE WHOLE WORLD MOVES HERE, DRAGGING U.S. IQ DOWN TO THE CURRENT WORLD AVERAGE:
CURRENT U.S. IQ: 98
CURRENT WORLD IQ: 87
AN ELEVEN-POINT FALL. DOOM!
LET'S DO THE MATH. ACCORDING TO HIVE MIND'S MAIN ESTIMATE, U.S. PER-CAPITA GDP WOULD FALL FROM ITS CURRENT LEVEL OF $57,600 TO...?
OPEN BORDERS GDP = 0.51 * CURRENT GDP ≈ $29,400
$29,400! A 49% DROP!
GROSS WORLD PRODUCT PER CAPITA IS NOW ROUGHLY $16,200. WHAT HAPPENS TO THAT?
NEW GDP / OLD GDP = $29,400 / $16,200 ≈ +81%
IT... ROUGHLY DOUBLES.
WHAT?! DO YOU MEAN TO TELL ME THAT DESPITE YOUR DOOMSAYING, YOU REACH ALMOST EXACTLY THE SAME RADICALLY PRO-IMMIGRATION NUMBERS AS MICHAEL CLEMENS?!
OPEN BORDERS DOUBLES GLOBAL PRODUCTION!
(BEST GUESS.)
IT'S ONLY THE BASIC MODEL. HIVE MIND INVESTIGATES AN ARRAY OF SUBTLETIES!

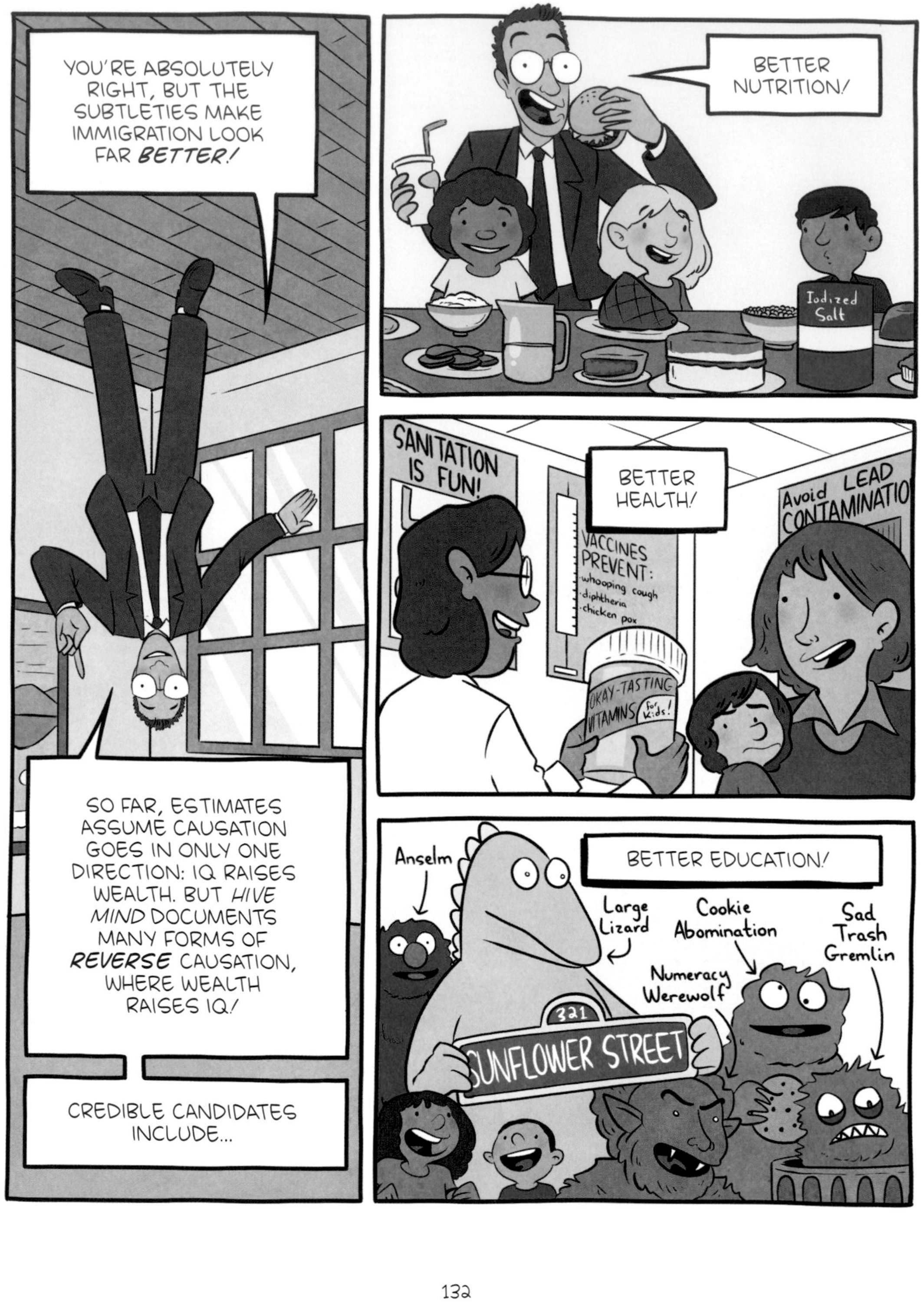

YOU'RE ABSOLUTELY RIGHT, BUT THE SUBTLETIES MAKE IMMIGRATION LOOK FAR *BETTER!*
SO FAR, ESTIMATES ASSUME CAUSATION GOES IN ONLY ONE DIRECTION: IQ RAISES WEALTH. BUT *HIVE MIND* DOCUMENTS MANY FORMS OF ***REVERSE*** CAUSATION, WHERE WEALTH RAISES IQ!
CREDIBLE CANDIDATES INCLUDE...
BETTER NUTRITION!
Iodized Salt
BETTER HEALTH!
SANITATION IS FUN!
VACCINES PREVENT:
·whooping cough
·diphtheria
·chicken pox
Avoid LEAD CONTAMINATIO
OKAY-TASTING VITAMINS for kids!
BETTER EDUCATION!
Anselm
Large Lizard
Cookie Abomination
Sad Trash Gremlin
Numeracy Werewolf
321
SUNFLOWER STREET

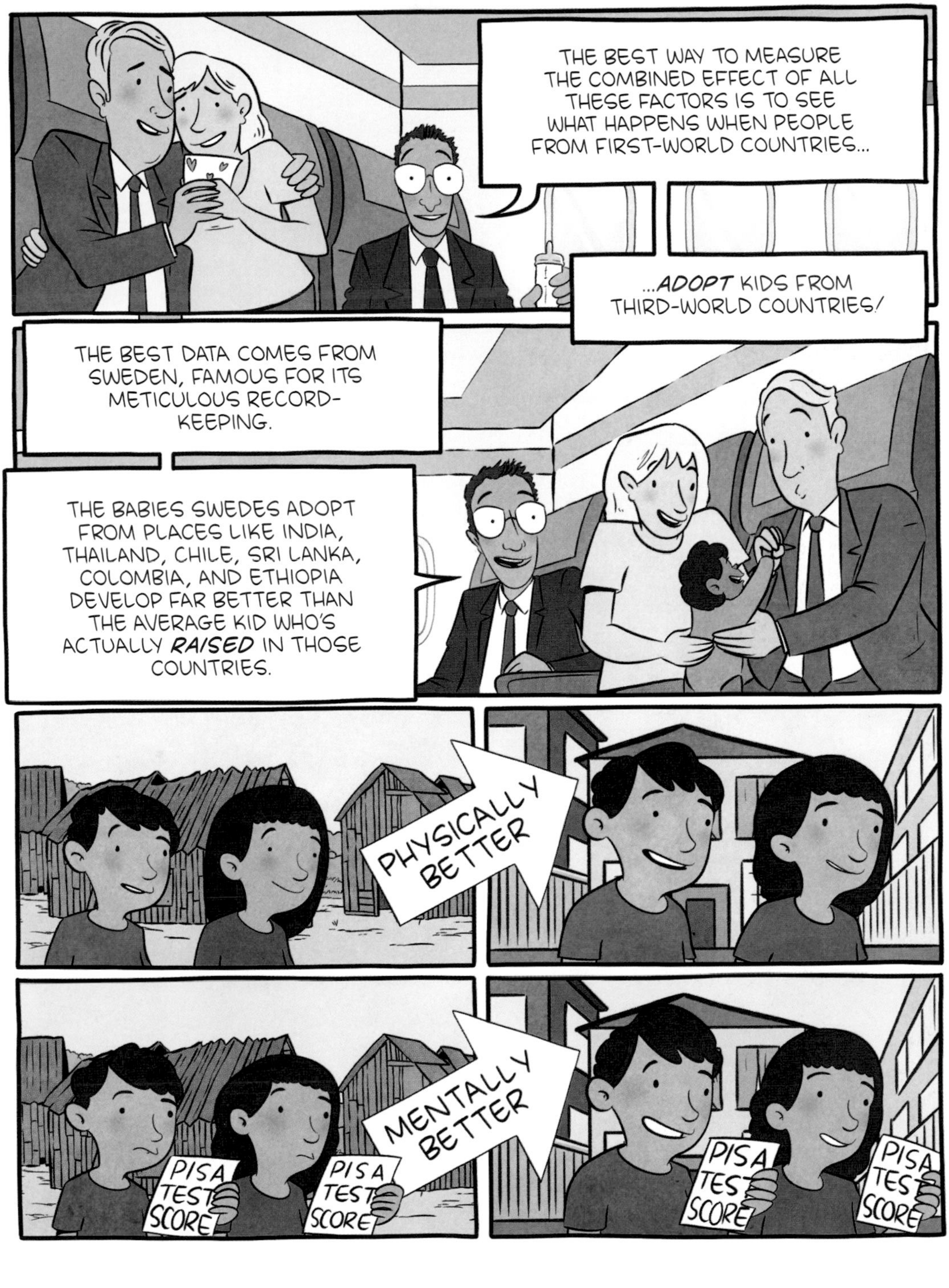
THE BEST WAY TO MEASURE THE COMBINED EFFECT OF ALL THESE FACTORS IS TO SEE WHAT HAPPENS WHEN PEOPLE FROM FIRST-WORLD COUNTRIES...
...ADOPT KIDS FROM THIRD-WORLD COUNTRIES!
THE BEST DATA COMES FROM SWEDEN, FAMOUS FOR ITS METICULOUS RECORD-KEEPING.
THE BABIES SWEDES ADOPT FROM PLACES LIKE INDIA, THAILAND, CHILE, SRI LANKA, COLOMBIA, AND ETHIOPIA DEVELOP FAR BETTER THAN THE AVERAGE KID WHO'S ACTUALLY RAISED IN THOSE COUNTRIES.
PHYSICALLY BETTER
MENTALLY BETTER
PISA TEST SCORE
PISA TEST SCORE
PISA TEST SCORE
PISA TEST SCORE

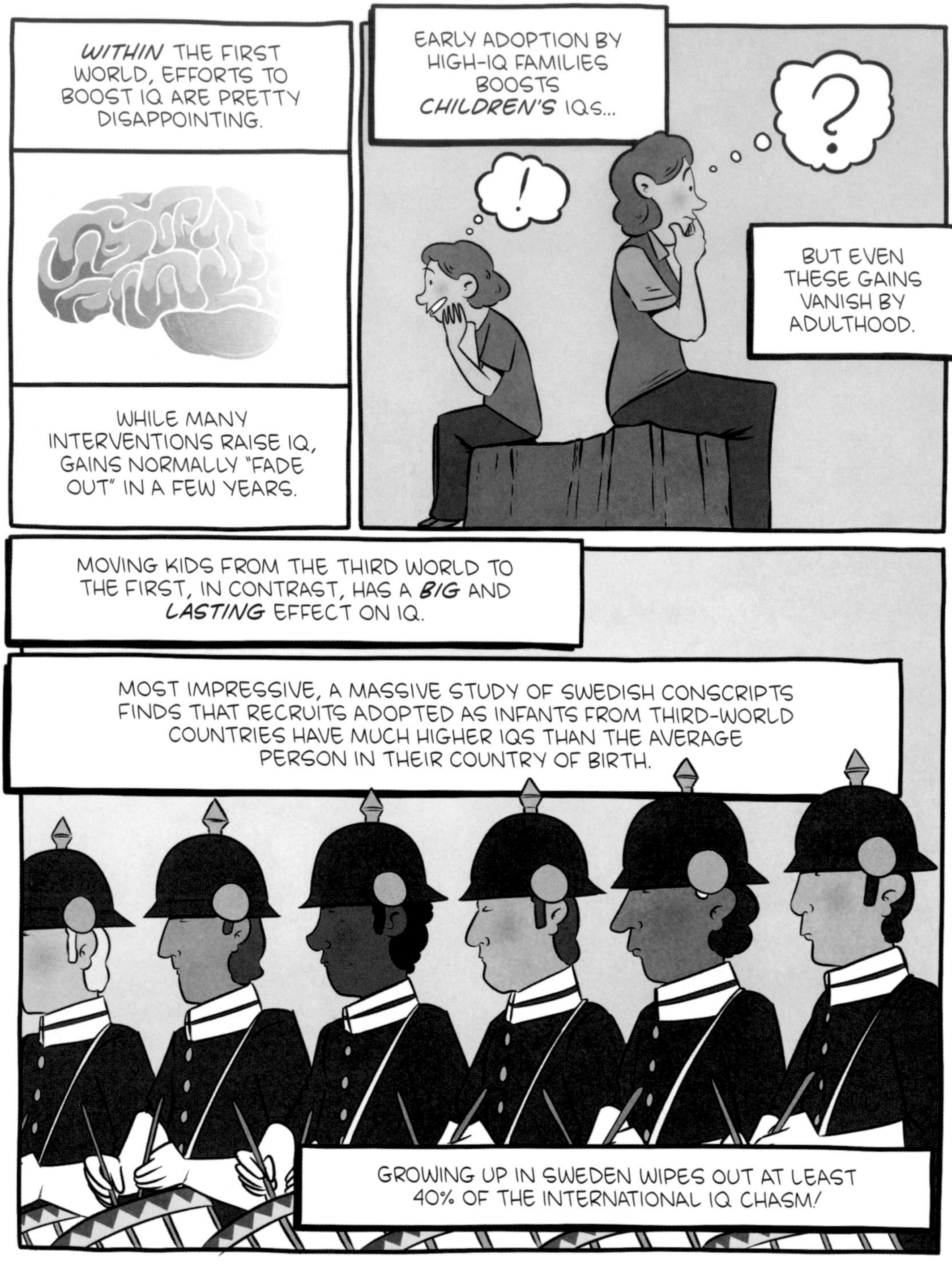
WITHIN THE FIRST WORLD, EFFORTS TO BOOST IQ ARE PRETTY DISAPPOINTING.
WHILE MANY INTERVENTIONS RAISE IQ, GAINS NORMALLY "FADE OUT" IN A FEW YEARS.
EARLY ADOPTION BY HIGH-IQ FAMILIES BOOSTS *CHILDREN'S* IQS...
!
?
BUT EVEN THESE GAINS VANISH BY ADULTHOOD.
MOVING KIDS FROM THE THIRD WORLD TO THE FIRST, IN CONTRAST, HAS A *BIG* AND *LASTING* EFFECT ON IQ.
MOST IMPRESSIVE, A MASSIVE STUDY OF SWEDISH CONSCRIPTS FINDS THAT RECRUITS ADOPTED AS INFANTS FROM THIRD-WORLD COUNTRIES HAVE MUCH HIGHER IQS THAN THE AVERAGE PERSON IN THEIR COUNTRY OF BIRTH.
GROWING UP IN SWEDEN WIPES OUT AT LEAST 40% OF THE INTERNATIONAL IQ CHASM!

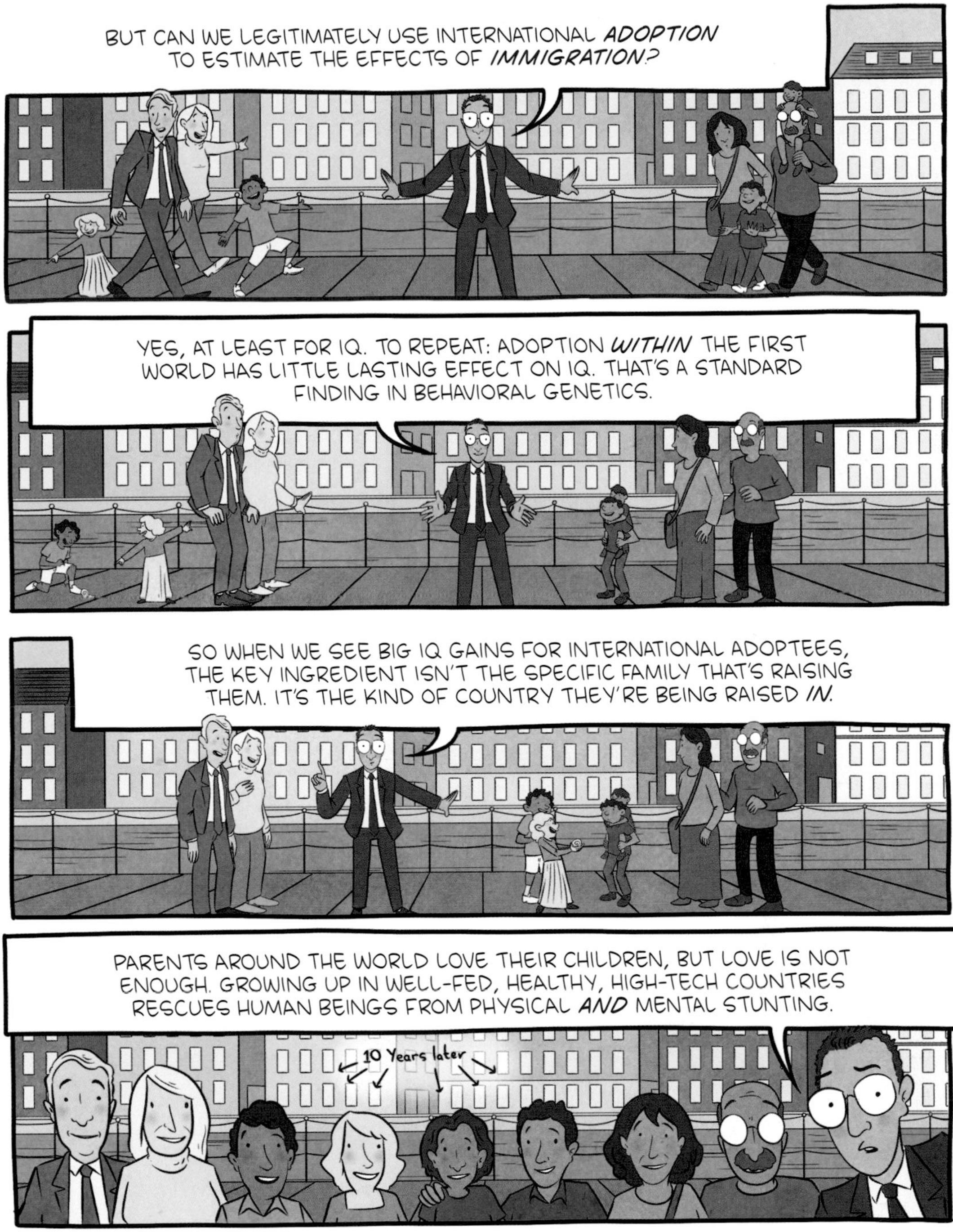
BUT CAN WE LEGITIMATELY USE INTERNATIONAL *ADOPTION* TO ESTIMATE THE EFFECTS OF *IMMIGRATION*?
YES, AT LEAST FOR IQ. TO REPEAT: ADOPTION *WITHIN* THE FIRST WORLD HAS LITTLE LASTING EFFECT ON IQ. THAT'S A STANDARD FINDING IN BEHAVIORAL GENETICS.
SO WHEN WE SEE BIG IQ GAINS FOR INTERNATIONAL ADOPTEES, THE KEY INGREDIENT ISN'T THE SPECIFIC FAMILY THAT'S RAISING THEM. IT'S THE KIND OF COUNTRY THEY'RE BEING RAISED *IN*.
PARENTS AROUND THE WORLD LOVE THEIR CHILDREN, BUT LOVE IS NOT ENOUGH. GROWING UP IN WELL-FED, HEALTHY, HIGH-TECH COUNTRIES RESCUES HUMAN BEINGS FROM PHYSICAL *AND* MENTAL STUNTING.
10 Years later

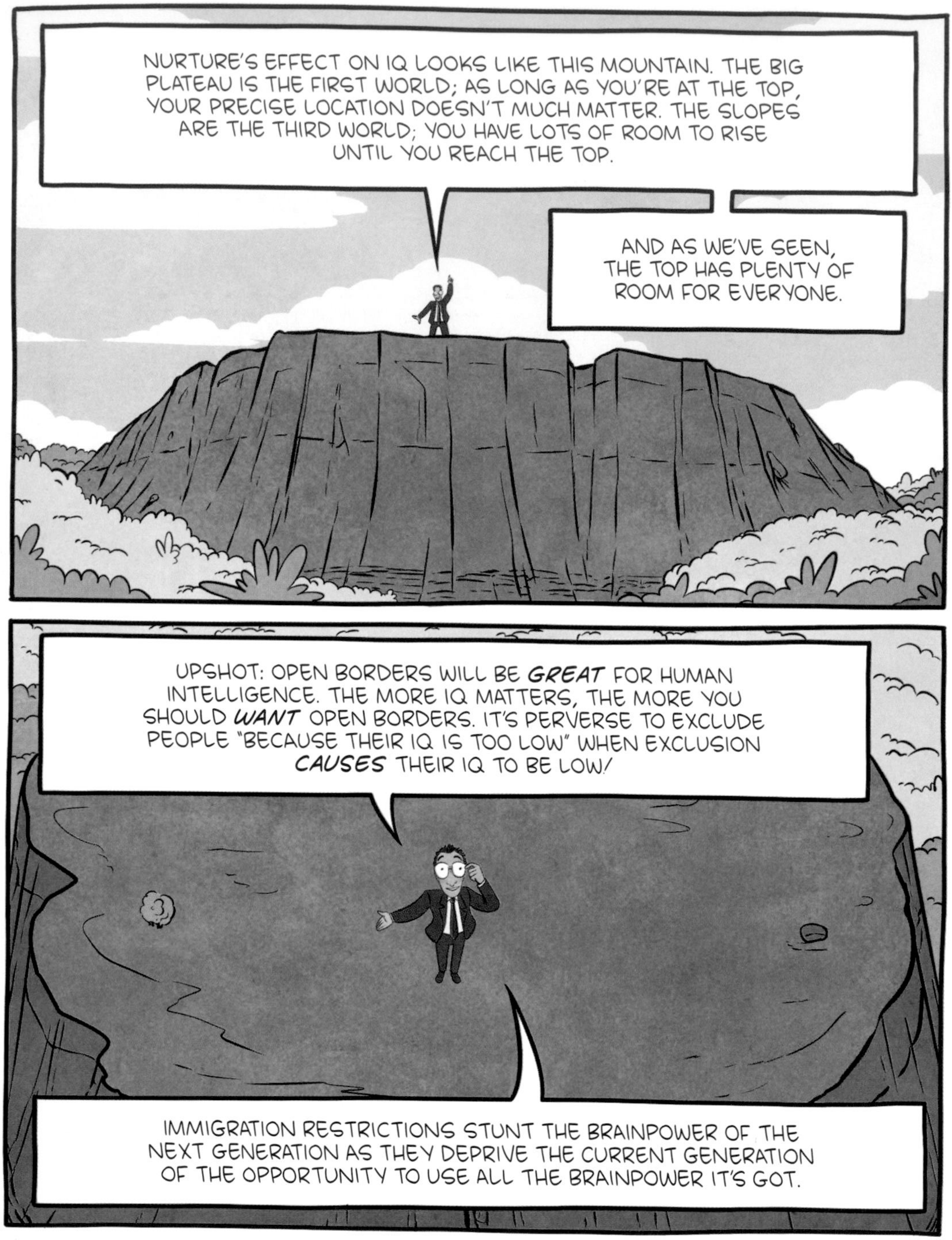
NURTURE'S EFFECT ON IQ LOOKS LIKE THIS MOUNTAIN. THE BIG PLATEAU IS THE FIRST WORLD; AS LONG AS YOU'RE AT THE TOP, YOUR PRECISE LOCATION DOESN'T MUCH MATTER. THE SLOPES ARE THE THIRD WORLD; YOU HAVE LOTS OF ROOM TO RISE UNTIL YOU REACH THE TOP.
AND AS WE'VE SEEN, THE TOP HAS PLENTY OF ROOM FOR EVERYONE.
UPSHOT: OPEN BORDERS WILL BE *GREAT* FOR HUMAN INTELLIGENCE. THE MORE IQ MATTERS, THE MORE YOU SHOULD *WANT* OPEN BORDERS. IT'S PERVERSE TO EXCLUDE PEOPLE "BECAUSE THEIR IQ IS TOO LOW" WHEN EXCLUSION *CAUSES* THEIR IQ TO BE LOW!
IMMIGRATION RESTRICTIONS STUNT THE BRAINPOWER OF THE NEXT GENERATION AS THEY DEPRIVE THE CURRENT GENERATION OF THE OPPORTUNITY TO USE ALL THE BRAINPOWER IT'S GOT.

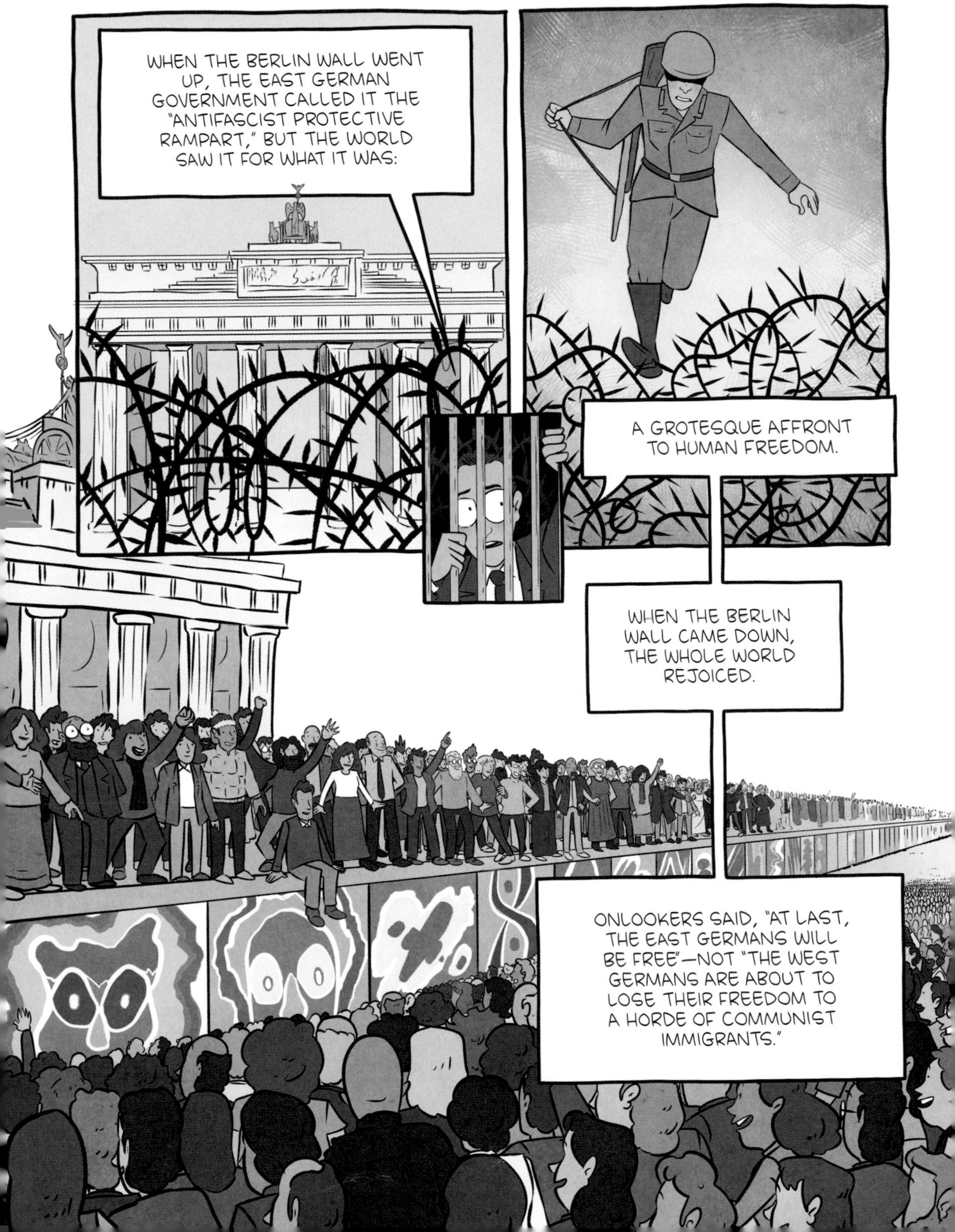

WHEN THE BERLIN WALL WENT UP, THE EAST GERMAN GOVERNMENT CALLED IT THE "ANTIFASCIST PROTECTIVE RAMPART," BUT THE WORLD SAW IT FOR WHAT IT WAS:
A GROTESQUE AFFRONT TO HUMAN FREEDOM.
WHEN THE BERLIN WALL CAME DOWN, THE WHOLE WORLD REJOICED.
ONLOOKERS SAID, "AT LAST, THE EAST GERMANS WILL BE FREE"—NOT "THE WEST GERMANS ARE ABOUT TO LOSE THEIR FREEDOM TO A HORDE OF COMMUNIST IMMIGRANTS."

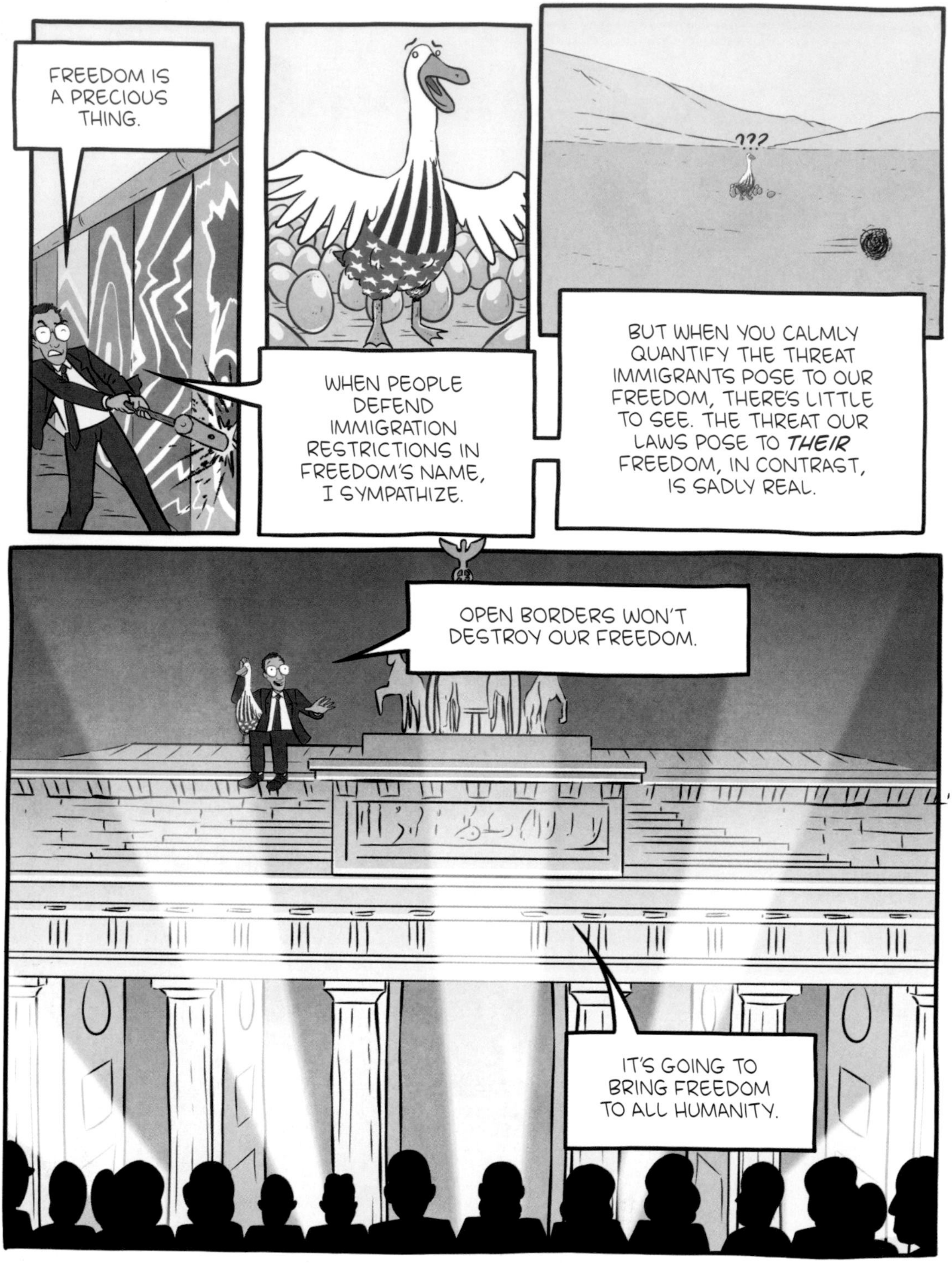

FREEDOM IS A PRECIOUS THING.
WHEN PEOPLE DEFEND IMMIGRATION RESTRICTIONS IN FREEDOM'S NAME, I SYMPATHIZE.
???
BUT WHEN YOU CALMLY QUANTIFY THE THREAT IMMIGRANTS POSE TO OUR FREEDOM, THERE'S LITTLE TO SEE. THE THREAT OUR LAWS POSE TO *THEIR* FREEDOM, IN CONTRAST, IS SADLY REAL.
OPEN BORDERS WON'T DESTROY OUR FREEDOM.
IT'S GOING TO BRING FREEDOM TO ALL HUMANITY.

CHAPTER 6

KEYHOLE SOLUTIONS

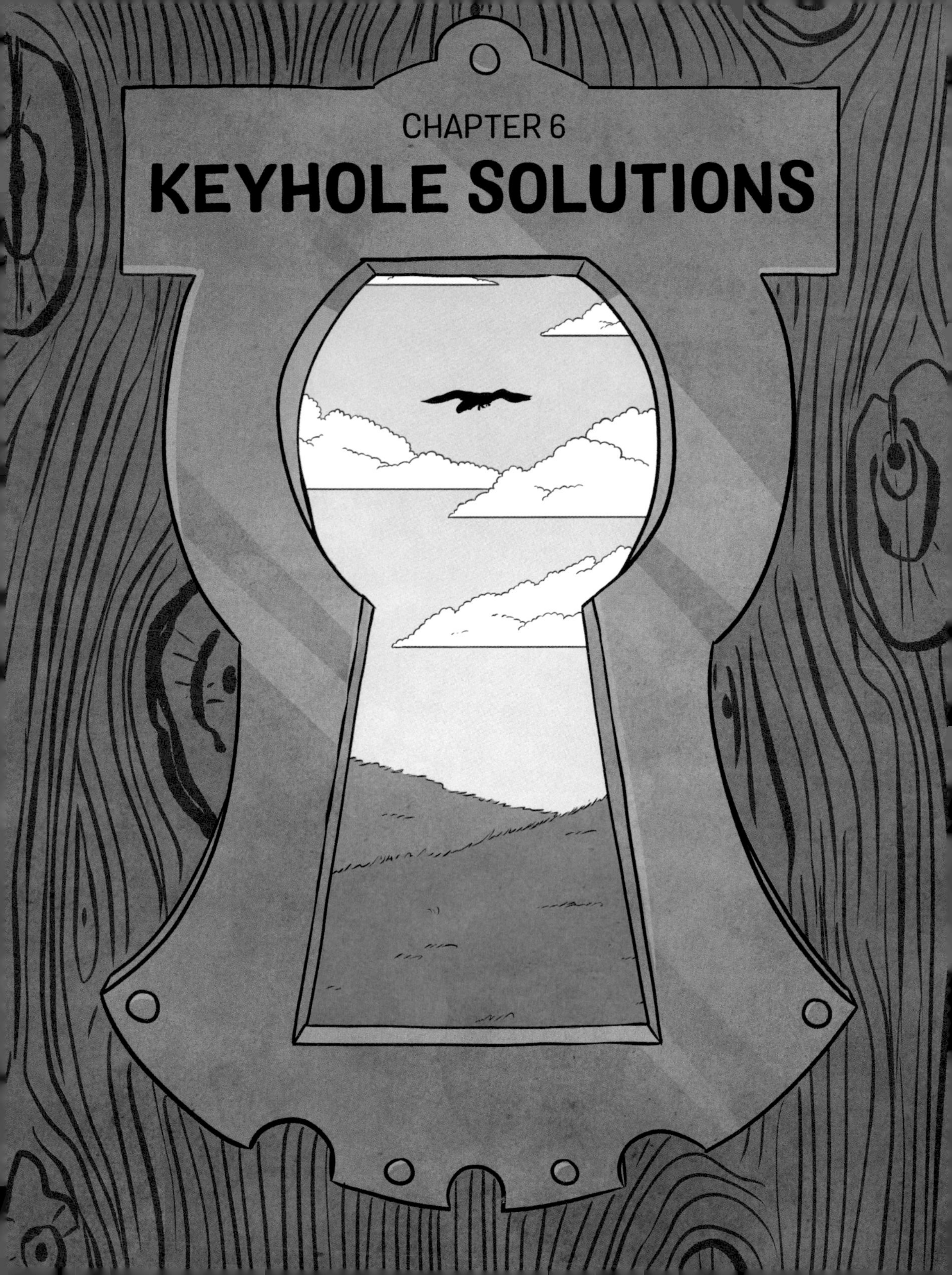

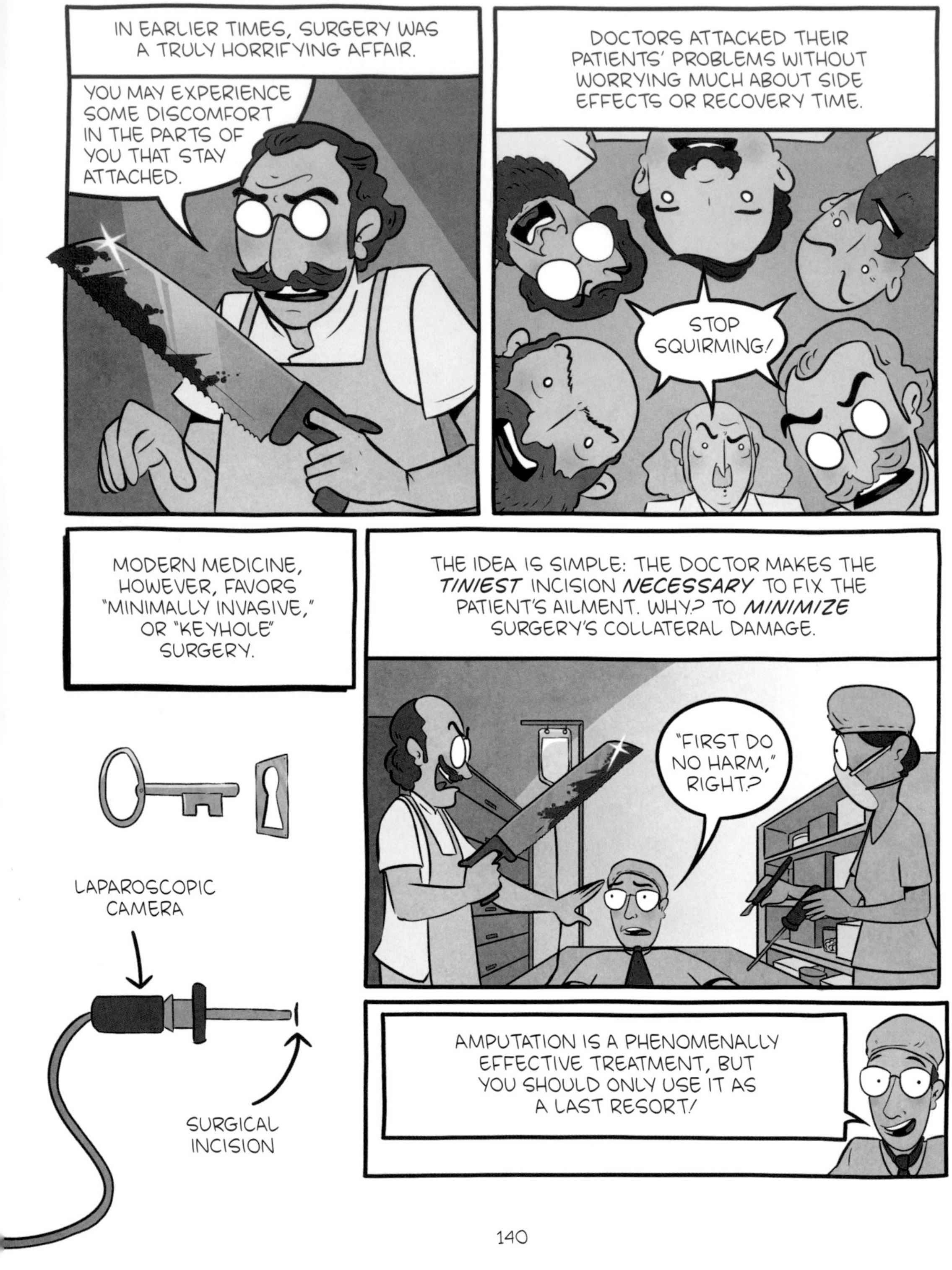
IN EARLIER TIMES, SURGERY WAS A TRULY HORRIFYING AFFAIR.
YOU MAY EXPERIENCE SOME DISCOMFORT IN THE PARTS OF YOU THAT STAY ATTACHED.
DOCTORS ATTACKED THEIR PATIENTS' PROBLEMS WITHOUT WORRYING MUCH ABOUT SIDE EFFECTS OR RECOVERY TIME.
STOP SQUIRMING!
MODERN MEDICINE, HOWEVER, FAVORS "MINIMALLY INVASIVE," OR "KEYHOLE" SURGERY.
THE IDEA IS SIMPLE: THE DOCTOR MAKES THE *TINIEST* INCISION *NECESSARY* TO FIX THE PATIENT'S AILMENT. WHY? TO *MINIMIZE* SURGERY'S COLLATERAL DAMAGE.
"FIRST DO NO HARM," RIGHT?
LAPAROSCOPIC CAMERA
SURGICAL INCISION
AMPUTATION IS A PHENOMENALLY EFFECTIVE TREATMENT, BUT YOU SHOULD ONLY USE IT AS A LAST RESORT!

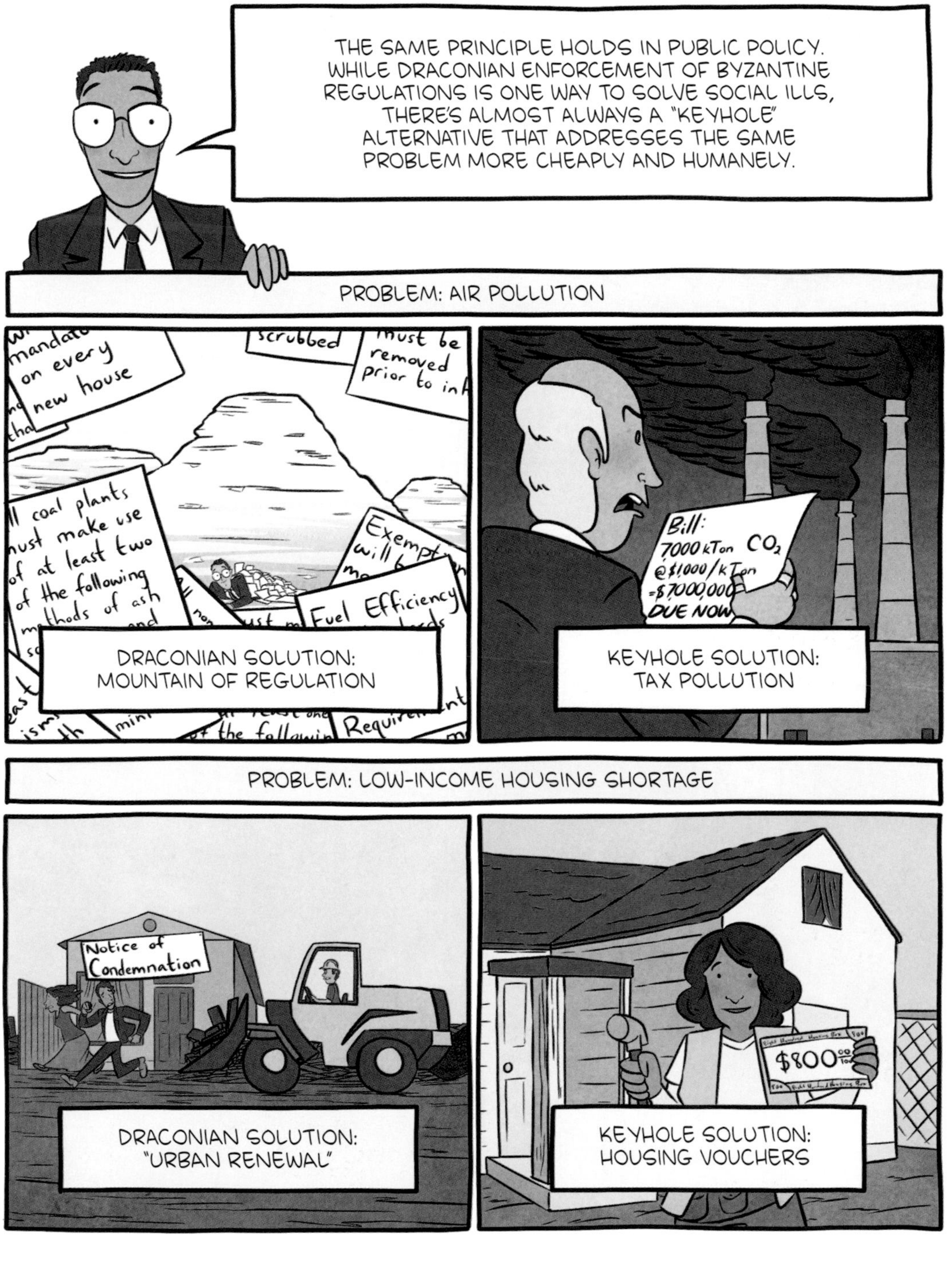

THE SAME PRINCIPLE HOLDS IN PUBLIC POLICY. WHILE DRACONIAN ENFORCEMENT OF BYZANTINE REGULATIONS IS ONE WAY TO SOLVE SOCIAL ILLS, THERE'S ALMOST ALWAYS A "KEYHOLE" ALTERNATIVE THAT ADDRESSES THE SAME PROBLEM MORE CHEAPLY AND HUMANELY.
PROBLEM: AIR POLLUTION
on every new house
scrubbed
must be removed
coal plants
make use
of at least two
of the following
methods of ash
Fuel Efficiency
DRACONIAN SOLUTION: MOUNTAIN OF REGULATION
Bill:
7,000 kTon CO_2
@$1,000/kTon
=$7,000,000
DUE NOW
KEYHOLE SOLUTION: TAX POLLUTION
PROBLEM: LOW-INCOME HOUSING SHORTAGE
Notice of Condemnation
DRACONIAN SOLUTION: "URBAN RENEWAL"
$800
KEYHOLE SOLUTION: HOUSING VOUCHERS

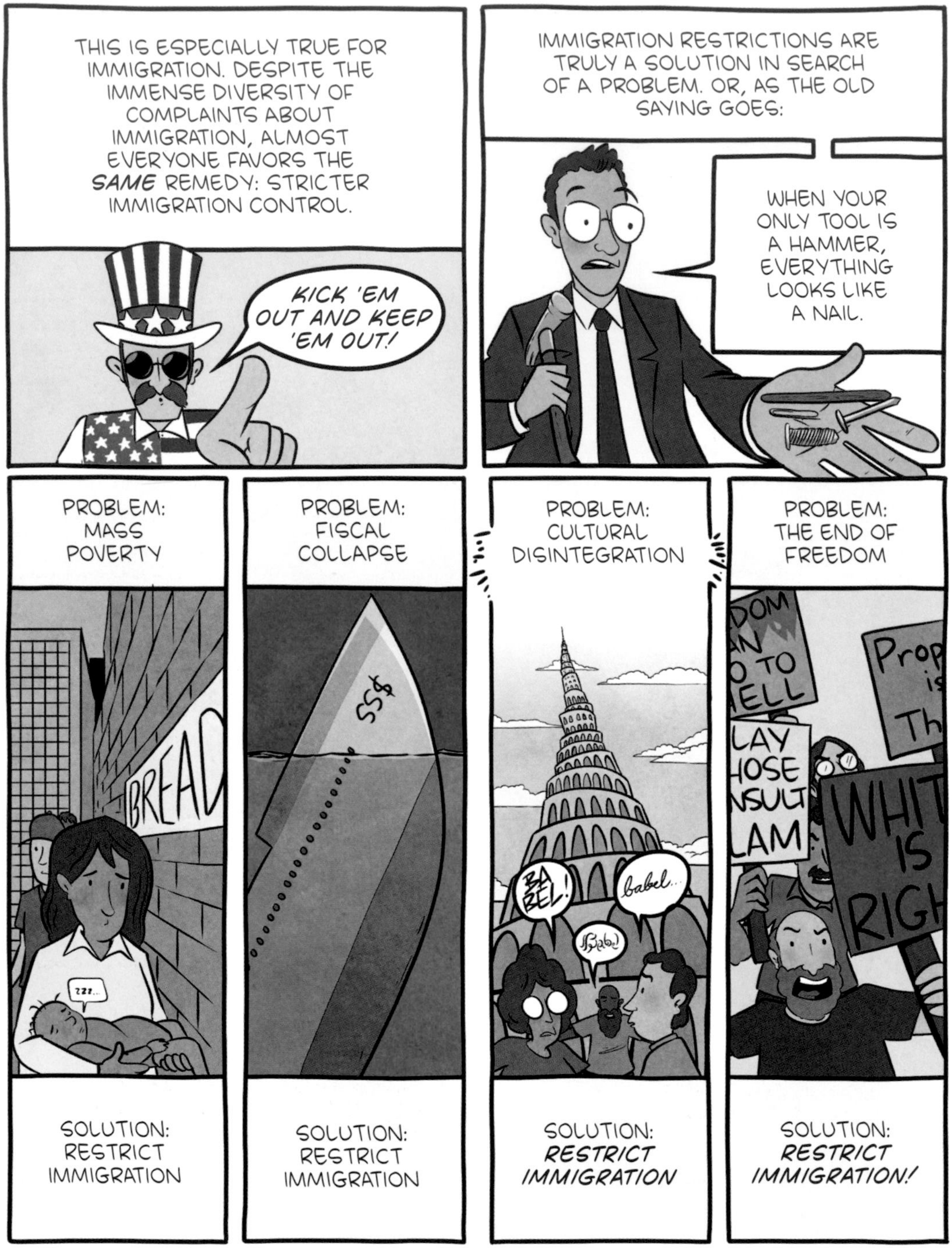
THIS IS ESPECIALLY TRUE FOR IMMIGRATION. DESPITE THE IMMENSE DIVERSITY OF COMPLAINTS ABOUT IMMIGRATION, ALMOST EVERYONE FAVORS THE *SAME* REMEDY: STRICTER IMMIGRATION CONTROL.
KICK 'EM OUT AND KEEP 'EM OUT!
IMMIGRATION RESTRICTIONS ARE TRULY A SOLUTION IN SEARCH OF A PROBLEM. OR, AS THE OLD SAYING GOES:
WHEN YOUR ONLY TOOL IS A HAMMER, EVERYTHING LOOKS LIKE A NAIL.
PROBLEM: MASS POVERTY
BREAD
zzz...
SOLUTION: RESTRICT IMMIGRATION
PROBLEM: FISCAL COLLAPSE
$$$
SOLUTION: RESTRICT IMMIGRATION
PROBLEM: CULTURAL DISINTEGRATION
BA BEL!
babel...
SOLUTION: *RESTRICT IMMIGRATION*
PROBLEM: THE END OF FREEDOM
SOLUTION: *RESTRICT IMMIGRATION!*

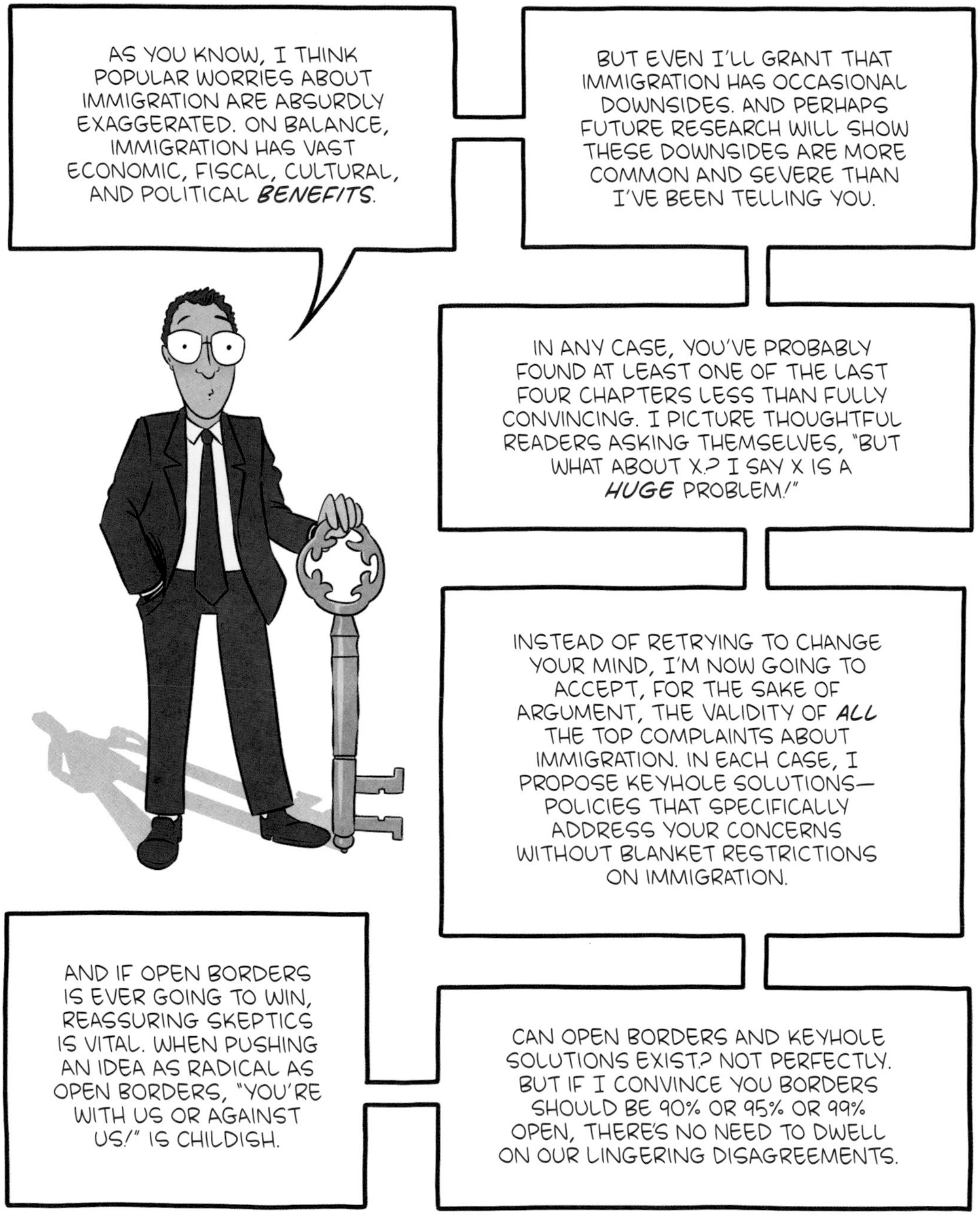
AS YOU KNOW, I THINK POPULAR WORRIES ABOUT IMMIGRATION ARE ABSURDLY EXAGGERATED. ON BALANCE, IMMIGRATION HAS VAST ECONOMIC, FISCAL, CULTURAL, AND POLITICAL ***BENEFITS***.
BUT EVEN I'LL GRANT THAT IMMIGRATION HAS OCCASIONAL DOWNSIDES. AND PERHAPS FUTURE RESEARCH WILL SHOW THESE DOWNSIDES ARE MORE COMMON AND SEVERE THAN I'VE BEEN TELLING YOU.
IN ANY CASE, YOU'VE PROBABLY FOUND AT LEAST ONE OF THE LAST FOUR CHAPTERS LESS THAN FULLY CONVINCING. I PICTURE THOUGHTFUL READERS ASKING THEMSELVES, "BUT WHAT ABOUT X? I SAY X IS A ***HUGE*** PROBLEM!"
INSTEAD OF RETRYING TO CHANGE YOUR MIND, I'M NOW GOING TO ACCEPT, FOR THE SAKE OF ARGUMENT, THE VALIDITY OF ***ALL*** THE TOP COMPLAINTS ABOUT IMMIGRATION. IN EACH CASE, I PROPOSE KEYHOLE SOLUTIONS—POLICIES THAT SPECIFICALLY ADDRESS YOUR CONCERNS WITHOUT BLANKET RESTRICTIONS ON IMMIGRATION.
CAN OPEN BORDERS AND KEYHOLE SOLUTIONS EXIST? NOT PERFECTLY. BUT IF I CONVINCE YOU BORDERS SHOULD BE 90% OR 95% OR 99% OPEN, THERE'S NO NEED TO DWELL ON OUR LINGERING DISAGREEMENTS.
AND IF OPEN BORDERS IS EVER GOING TO WIN, REASSURING SKEPTICS IS VITAL. WHEN PUSHING AN IDEA AS RADICAL AS OPEN BORDERS, "YOU'RE WITH US OR AGAINST US!" IS CHILDISH.

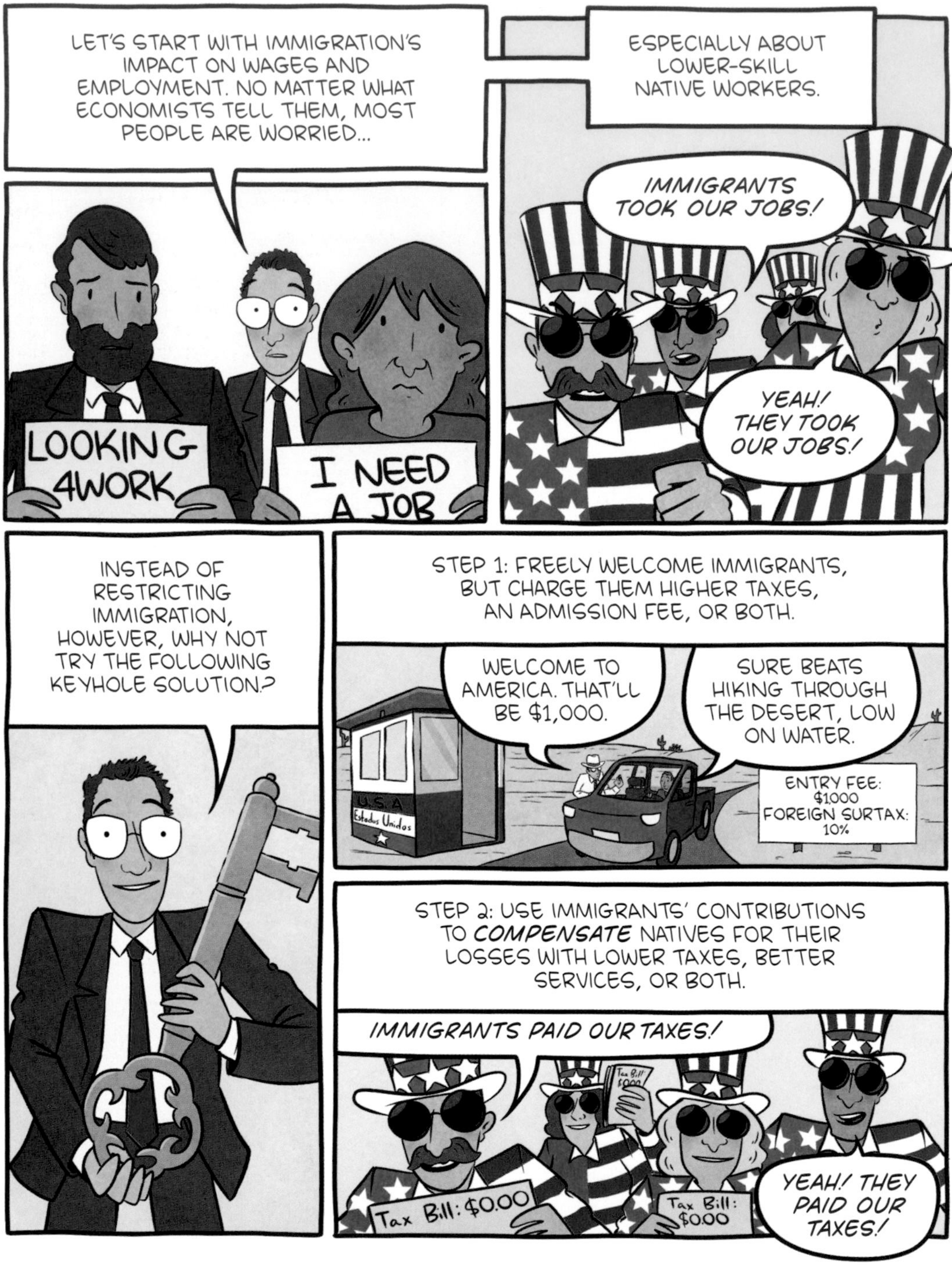
LET'S START WITH IMMIGRATION'S IMPACT ON WAGES AND EMPLOYMENT. NO MATTER WHAT ECONOMISTS TELL THEM, MOST PEOPLE ARE WORRIED...
LOOKING 4WORK
I NEED A JOB
ESPECIALLY ABOUT LOWER-SKILL NATIVE WORKERS.
IMMIGRANTS TOOK OUR JOBS!
YEAH! THEY TOOK OUR JOBS!
INSTEAD OF RESTRICTING IMMIGRATION, HOWEVER, WHY NOT TRY THE FOLLOWING KEYHOLE SOLUTION?
STEP 1: FREELY WELCOME IMMIGRANTS, BUT CHARGE THEM HIGHER TAXES, AN ADMISSION FEE, OR BOTH.
WELCOME TO AMERICA. THAT'LL BE $1,000.
SURE BEATS HIKING THROUGH THE DESERT, LOW ON WATER.
U.S.A
Estados Unidos
ENTRY FEE: $1,000
FOREIGN SURTAX: 10%
STEP 2: USE IMMIGRANTS' CONTRIBUTIONS TO *COMPENSATE* NATIVES FOR THEIR LOSSES WITH LOWER TAXES, BETTER SERVICES, OR BOTH.
IMMIGRANTS PAID OUR TAXES!
Tax Bill: $0.00
Tax Bill: $0.00
YEAH! THEY PAID OUR TAXES!

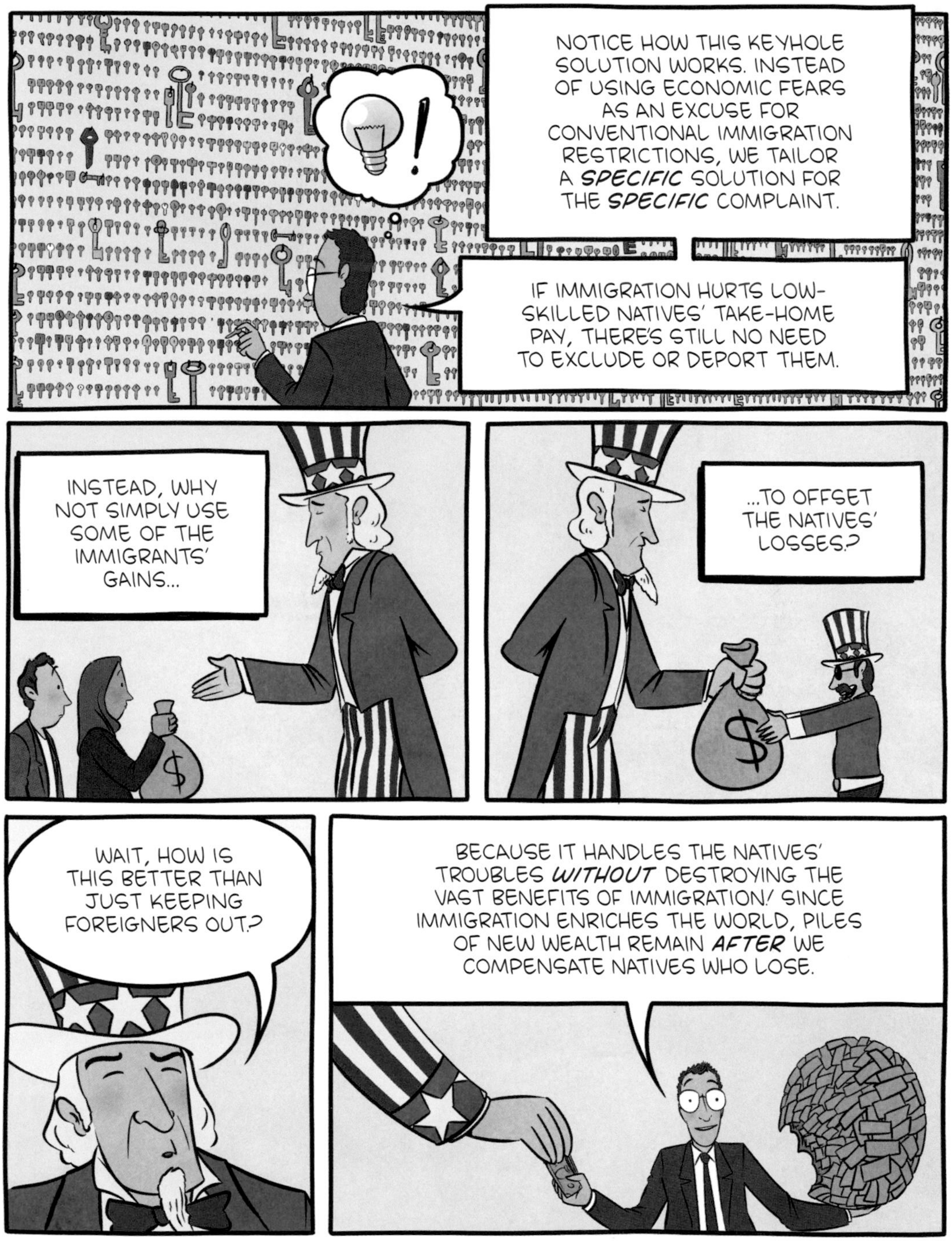
NOTICE HOW THIS KEYHOLE SOLUTION WORKS. INSTEAD OF USING ECONOMIC FEARS AS AN EXCUSE FOR CONVENTIONAL IMMIGRATION RESTRICTIONS, WE TAILOR A *SPECIFIC* SOLUTION FOR THE *SPECIFIC* COMPLAINT.
IF IMMIGRATION HURTS LOW-SKILLED NATIVES' TAKE-HOME PAY, THERE'S STILL NO NEED TO EXCLUDE OR DEPORT THEM.
INSTEAD, WHY NOT SIMPLY USE SOME OF THE IMMIGRANTS' GAINS...
...TO OFFSET THE NATIVES' LOSSES?
WAIT, HOW IS THIS BETTER THAN JUST KEEPING FOREIGNERS OUT?
BECAUSE IT HANDLES THE NATIVES' TROUBLES ***WITHOUT*** DESTROYING THE VAST BENEFITS OF IMMIGRATION! SINCE IMMIGRATION ENRICHES THE WORLD, PILES OF NEW WEALTH REMAIN ***AFTER*** WE COMPENSATE NATIVES WHO LOSE.

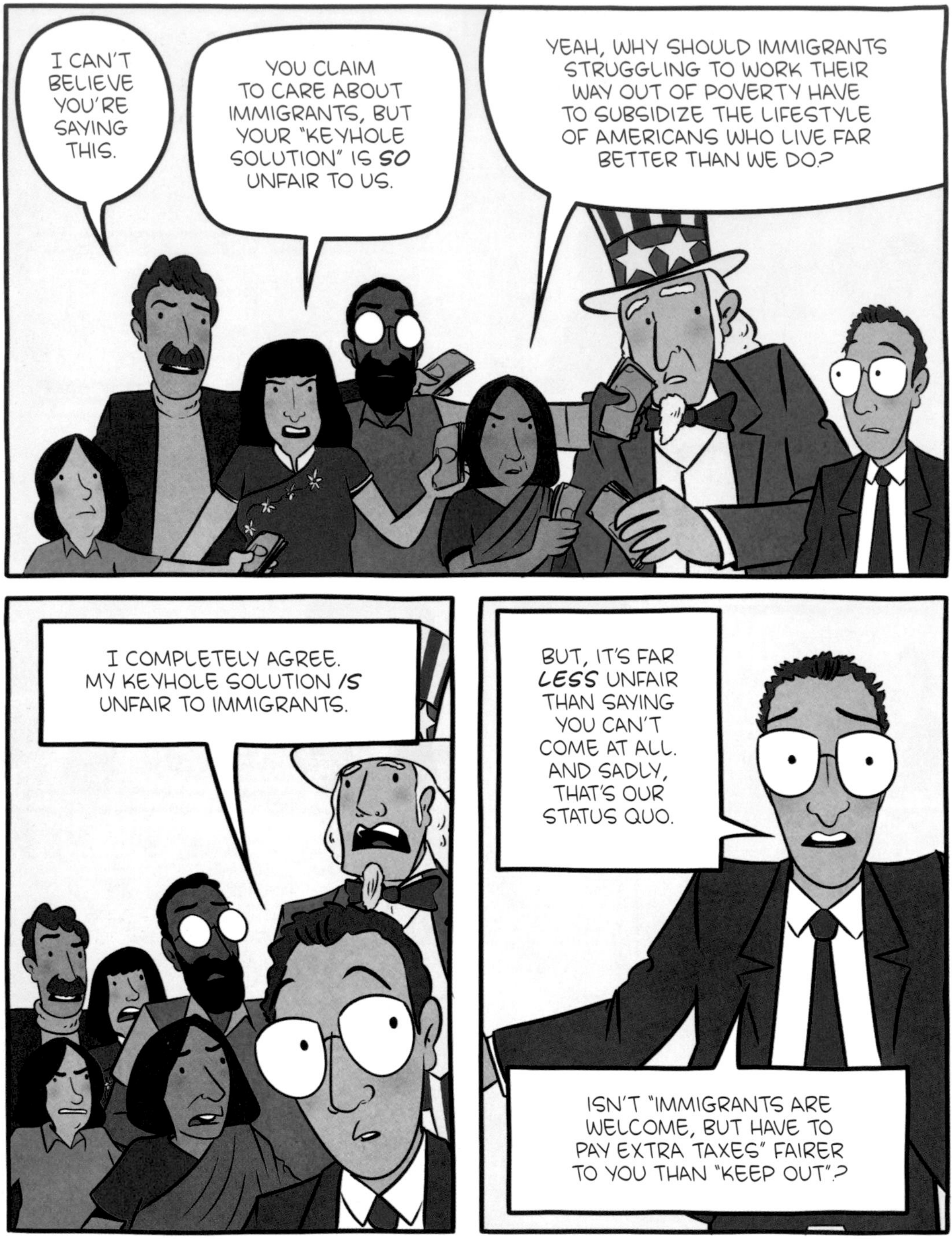
I CAN'T BELIEVE YOU'RE SAYING THIS.
YOU CLAIM TO CARE ABOUT IMMIGRANTS, BUT YOUR "KEYHOLE SOLUTION" IS *SO* UNFAIR TO US.
YEAH, WHY SHOULD IMMIGRANTS STRUGGLING TO WORK THEIR WAY OUT OF POVERTY HAVE TO SUBSIDIZE THE LIFESTYLE OF AMERICANS WHO LIVE FAR BETTER THAN WE DO?
I COMPLETELY AGREE. MY KEYHOLE SOLUTION *IS* UNFAIR TO IMMIGRANTS.
BUT, IT'S FAR *LESS* UNFAIR THAN SAYING YOU CAN'T COME AT ALL. AND SADLY, THAT'S OUR STATUS QUO.
ISN'T "IMMIGRANTS ARE WELCOME, BUT HAVE TO PAY EXTRA TAXES" FAIRER TO YOU THAN "KEEP OUT"?

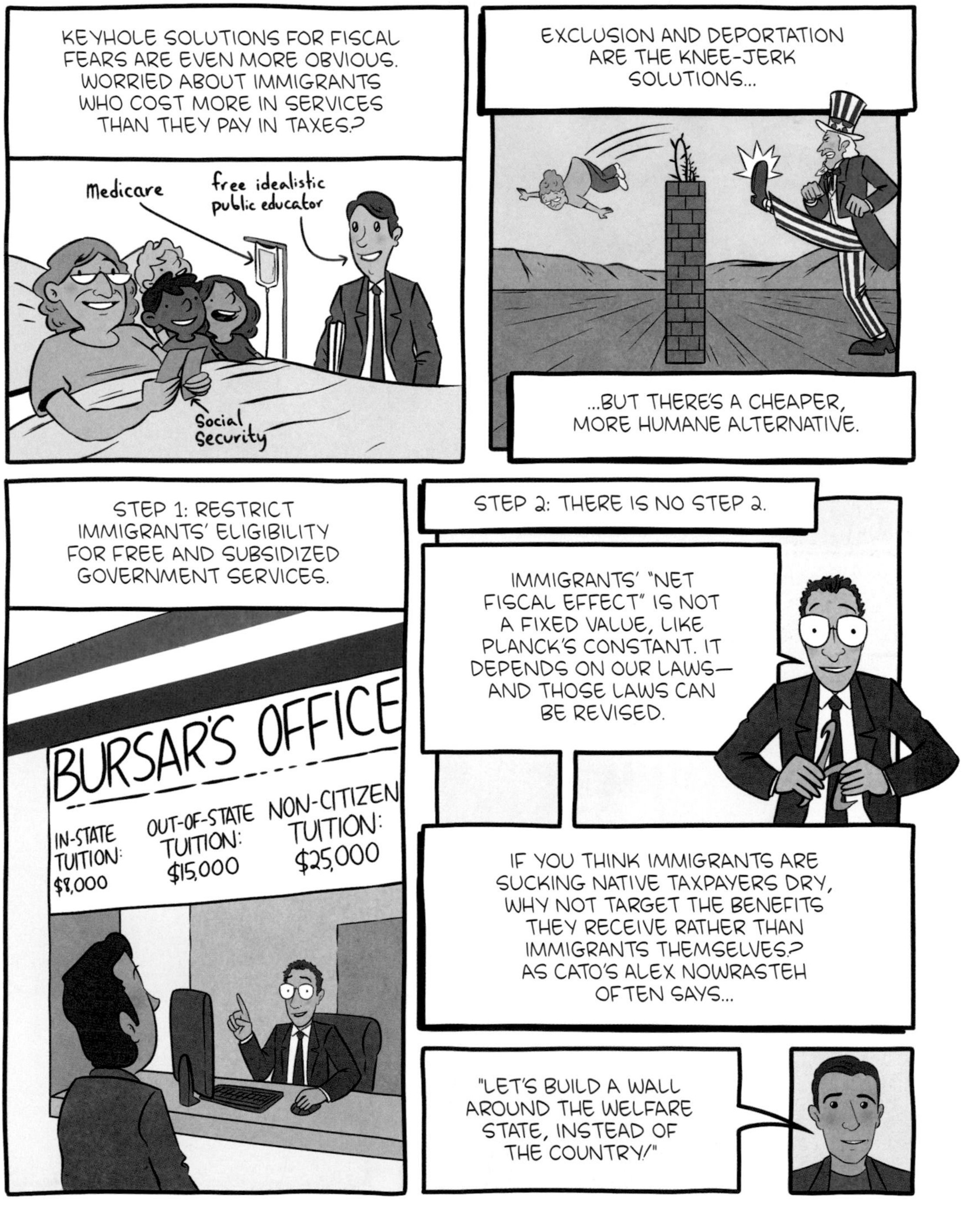
KEYHOLE SOLUTIONS FOR FISCAL FEARS ARE EVEN MORE OBVIOUS. WORRIED ABOUT IMMIGRANTS WHO COST MORE IN SERVICES THAN THEY PAY IN TAXES?
Medicare
free idealistic public educator
Social Security
EXCLUSION AND DEPORTATION ARE THE KNEE-JERK SOLUTIONS...
...BUT THERE'S A CHEAPER, MORE HUMANE ALTERNATIVE.
STEP 1: RESTRICT IMMIGRANTS' ELIGIBILITY FOR FREE AND SUBSIDIZED GOVERNMENT SERVICES.
BURSAR'S OFFICE
IN-STATE TUITION: $8,000
OUT-OF-STATE TUITION: $15,000
NON-CITIZEN TUITION: $25,000
STEP 2: THERE IS NO STEP 2.
IMMIGRANTS' "NET FISCAL EFFECT" IS NOT A FIXED VALUE, LIKE PLANCK'S CONSTANT. IT DEPENDS ON OUR LAWS— AND THOSE LAWS CAN BE REVISED.
IF YOU THINK IMMIGRANTS ARE SUCKING NATIVE TAXPAYERS DRY, WHY NOT TARGET THE BENEFITS THEY RECEIVE RATHER THAN IMMIGRANTS THEMSELVES? AS CATO'S ALEX NOWRASTEH OFTEN SAYS...
"LET'S BUILD A WALL AROUND THE WELFARE STATE, INSTEAD OF THE COUNTRY!"

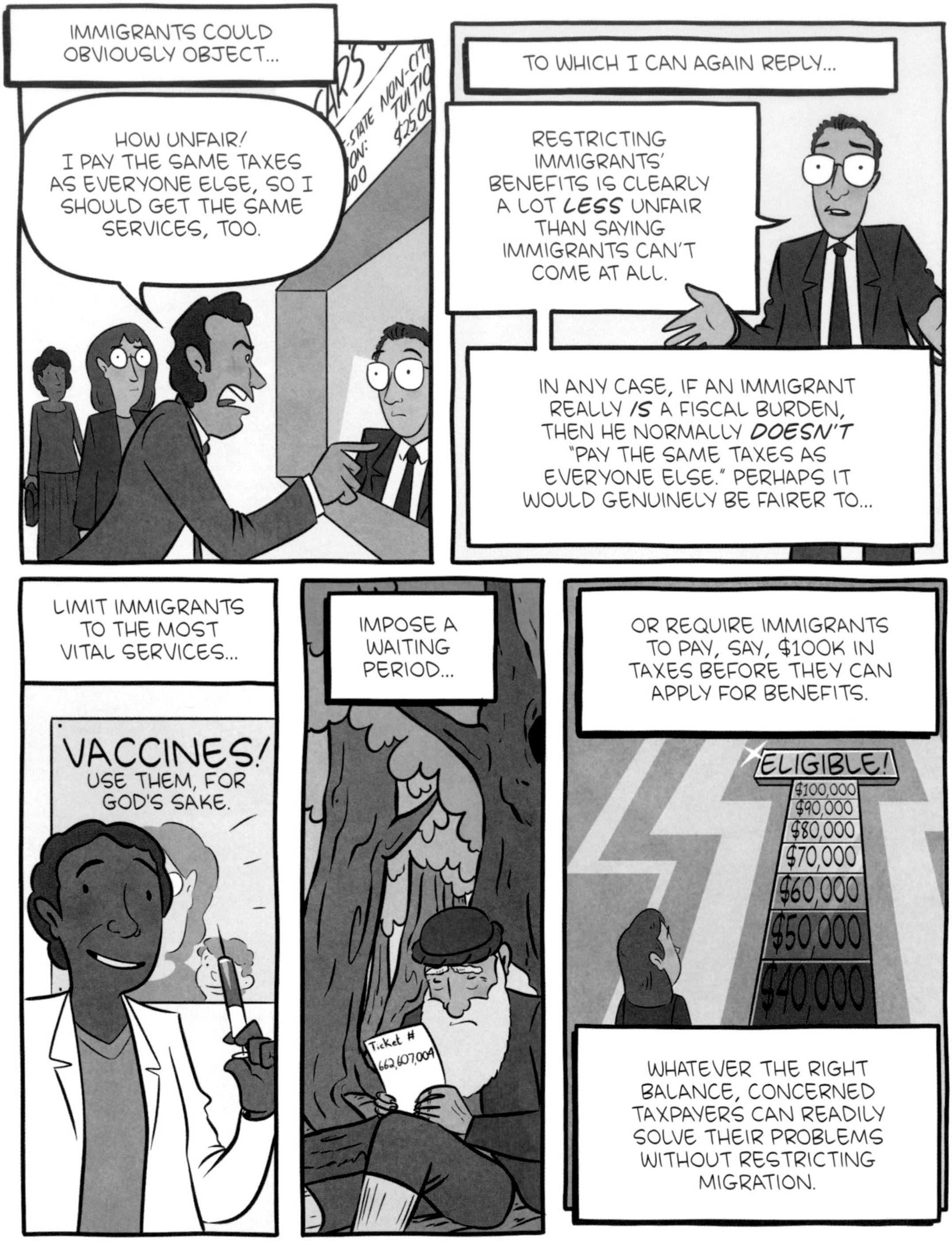
IMMIGRANTS COULD OBVIOUSLY OBJECT...
HOW UNFAIR! I PAY THE SAME TAXES AS EVERYONE ELSE, SO I SHOULD GET THE SAME SERVICES, TOO.
TO WHICH I CAN AGAIN REPLY...
RESTRICTING IMMIGRANTS' BENEFITS IS CLEARLY A LOT *LESS* UNFAIR THAN SAYING IMMIGRANTS CAN'T COME AT ALL.
IN ANY CASE, IF AN IMMIGRANT REALLY *IS* A FISCAL BURDEN, THEN HE NORMALLY *DOESN'T* "PAY THE SAME TAXES AS EVERYONE ELSE." PERHAPS IT WOULD GENUINELY BE FAIRER TO...
LIMIT IMMIGRANTS TO THE MOST VITAL SERVICES...
VACCINES! USE THEM, FOR GOD'S SAKE.
IMPOSE A WAITING PERIOD...
Ticket # 662,607,004
OR REQUIRE IMMIGRANTS TO PAY, SAY, $100K IN TAXES BEFORE THEY CAN APPLY FOR BENEFITS.
ELIGIBLE!
$100,000
$90,000
$80,000
$70,000
$60,000
$50,000
$40,000
WHATEVER THE RIGHT BALANCE, CONCERNED TAXPAYERS CAN READILY SOLVE THEIR PROBLEMS WITHOUT RESTRICTING MIGRATION.

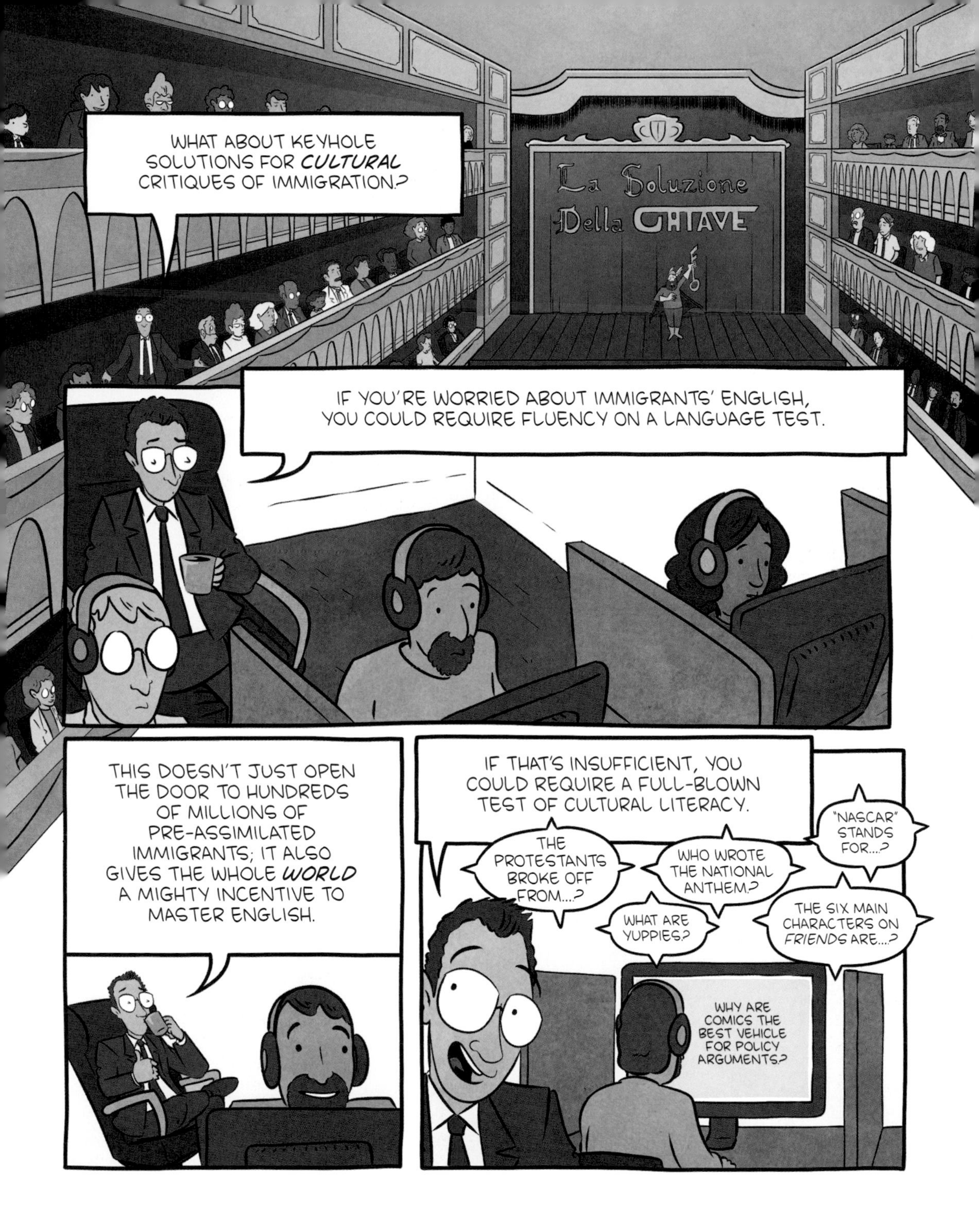
WHAT ABOUT KEYHOLE SOLUTIONS FOR CULTURAL CRITIQUES OF IMMIGRATION?
La Soluzione Della CHIAVE
IF YOU'RE WORRIED ABOUT IMMIGRANTS' ENGLISH, YOU COULD REQUIRE FLUENCY ON A LANGUAGE TEST.
THIS DOESN'T JUST OPEN THE DOOR TO HUNDREDS OF MILLIONS OF PRE-ASSIMILATED IMMIGRANTS; IT ALSO GIVES THE WHOLE WORLD A MIGHTY INCENTIVE TO MASTER ENGLISH.
IF THAT'S INSUFFICIENT, YOU COULD REQUIRE A FULL-BLOWN TEST OF CULTURAL LITERACY.
THE PROTESTANTS BROKE OFF FROM...?
WHO WROTE THE NATIONAL ANTHEM?
"NASCAR" STANDS FOR...?
WHAT ARE YUPPIES?
THE SIX MAIN CHARACTERS ON FRIENDS ARE...?
WHY ARE COMICS THE BEST VEHICLE FOR POLICY ARGUMENTS?

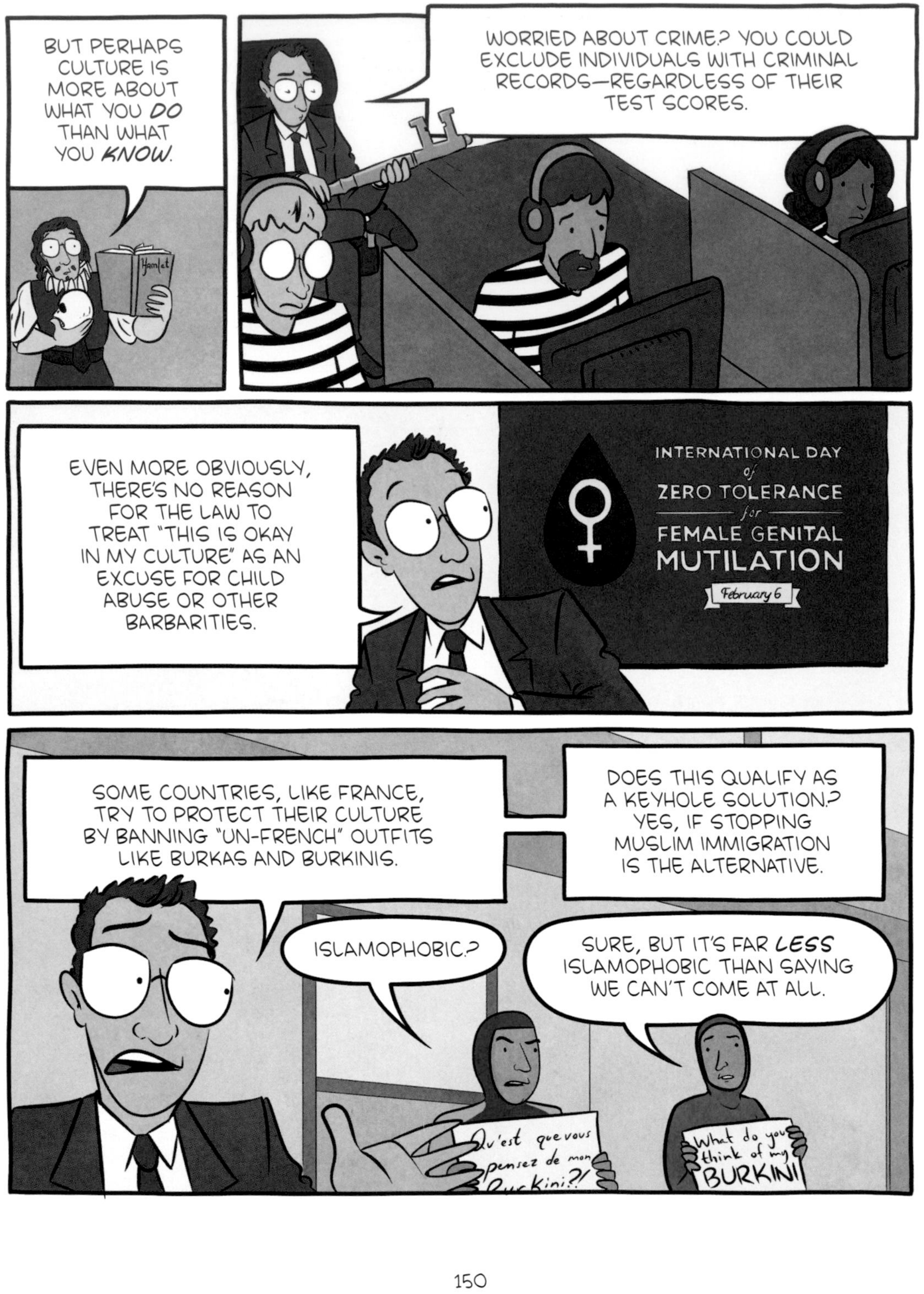
BUT PERHAPS CULTURE IS MORE ABOUT WHAT YOU *DO* THAN WHAT YOU *KNOW*.
Hamlet
WORRIED ABOUT CRIME? YOU COULD EXCLUDE INDIVIDUALS WITH CRIMINAL RECORDS—REGARDLESS OF THEIR TEST SCORES.
EVEN MORE OBVIOUSLY, THERE'S NO REASON FOR THE LAW TO TREAT "THIS IS OKAY IN MY CULTURE" AS AN EXCUSE FOR CHILD ABUSE OR OTHER BARBARITIES.
INTERNATIONAL DAY of ZERO TOLERANCE for FEMALE GENITAL MUTILATION
February 6
SOME COUNTRIES, LIKE FRANCE, TRY TO PROTECT THEIR CULTURE BY BANNING "UN-FRENCH" OUTFITS LIKE BURKAS AND BURKINIS.
DOES THIS QUALIFY AS A KEYHOLE SOLUTION? YES, IF STOPPING MUSLIM IMMIGRATION IS THE ALTERNATIVE.
ISLAMOPHOBIC?
SURE, BUT IT'S FAR *LESS* ISLAMOPHOBIC THAN SAYING WE CAN'T COME AT ALL.
Qu'est que vous pensez de mon
What do you think of my BURKINI

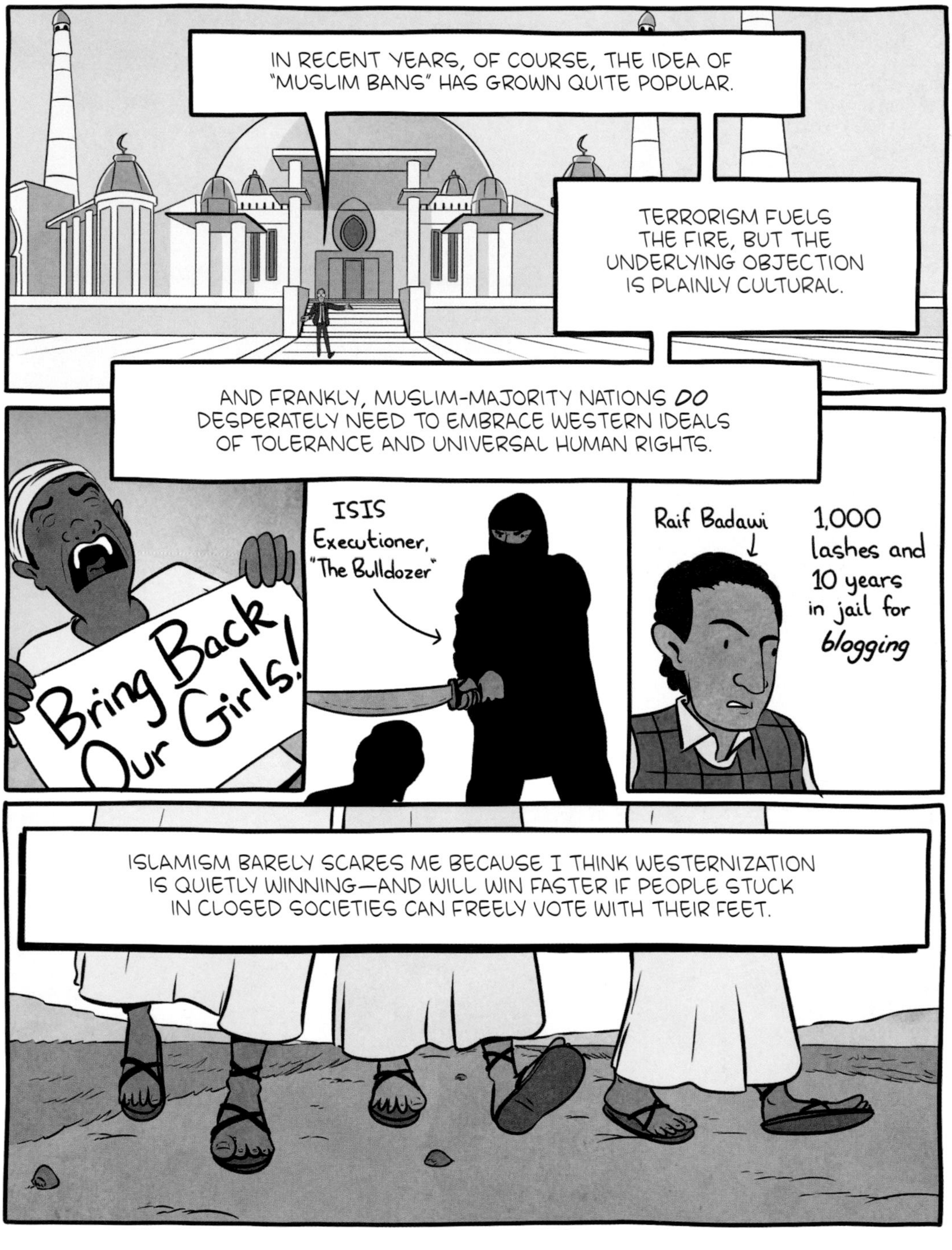
IN RECENT YEARS, OF COURSE, THE IDEA OF "MUSLIM BANS" HAS GROWN QUITE POPULAR.
TERRORISM FUELS THE FIRE, BUT THE UNDERLYING OBJECTION IS PLAINLY CULTURAL.
AND FRANKLY, MUSLIM-MAJORITY NATIONS *DO* DESPERATELY NEED TO EMBRACE WESTERN IDEALS OF TOLERANCE AND UNIVERSAL HUMAN RIGHTS.
Bring Back Our Girls!
ISIS Executioner, "The Bulldozer"
Raif Badawi
1,000 lashes and 10 years in jail for *blogging*
ISLAMISM BARELY SCARES ME BECAUSE I THINK WESTERNIZATION IS QUIETLY WINNING—AND WILL WIN FASTER IF PEOPLE STUCK IN CLOSED SOCIETIES CAN FREELY VOTE WITH THEIR FEET.

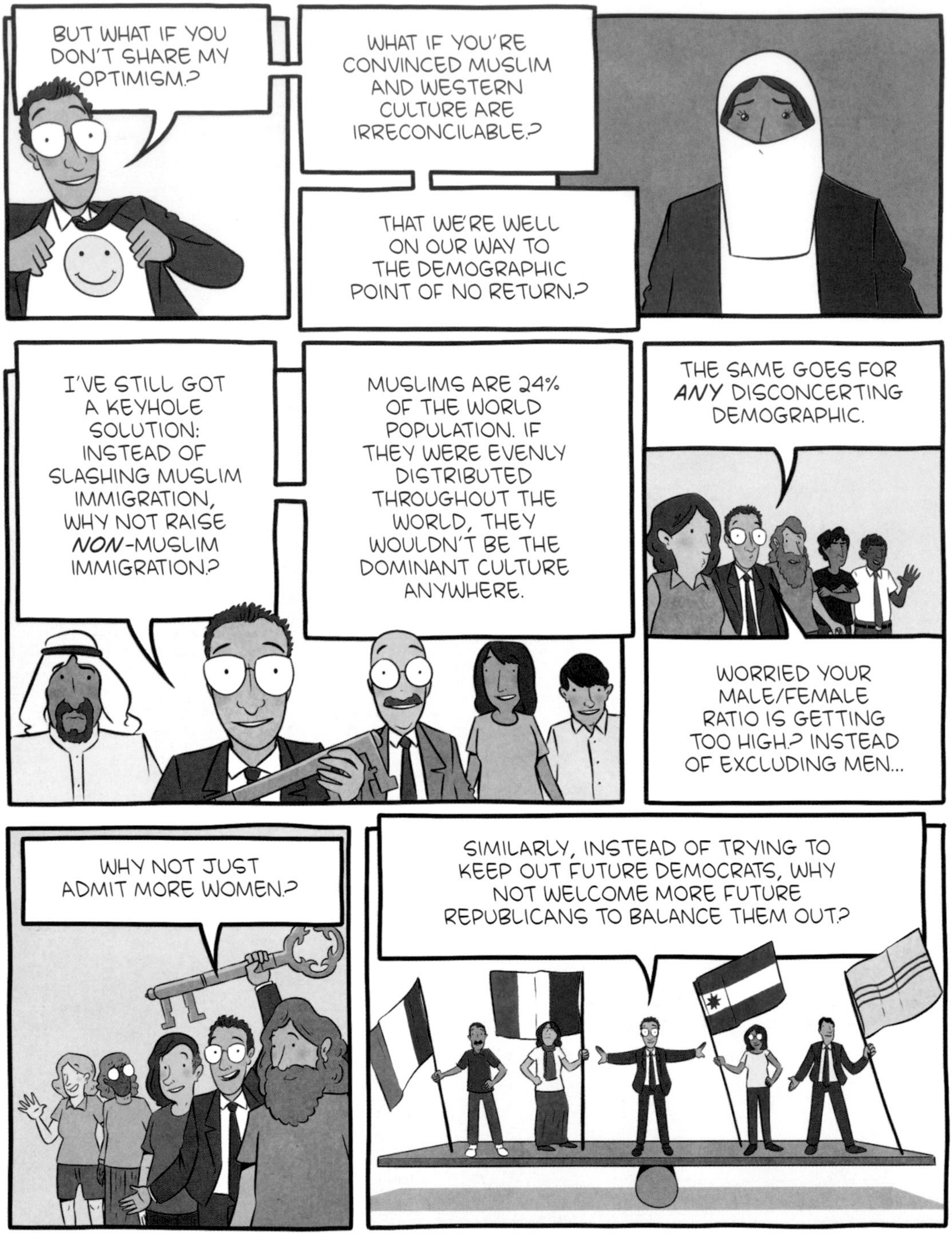

BUT WHAT IF YOU DON'T SHARE MY OPTIMISM?
WHAT IF YOU'RE CONVINCED MUSLIM AND WESTERN CULTURE ARE IRRECONCILABLE?
THAT WE'RE WELL ON OUR WAY TO THE DEMOGRAPHIC POINT OF NO RETURN?
I'VE STILL GOT A KEYHOLE SOLUTION: INSTEAD OF SLASHING MUSLIM IMMIGRATION, WHY NOT RAISE *NON*-MUSLIM IMMIGRATION?
MUSLIMS ARE 24% OF THE WORLD POPULATION. IF THEY WERE EVENLY DISTRIBUTED THROUGHOUT THE WORLD, THEY WOULDN'T BE THE DOMINANT CULTURE ANYWHERE.
THE SAME GOES FOR *ANY* DISCONCERTING DEMOGRAPHIC.
WORRIED YOUR MALE/FEMALE RATIO IS GETTING TOO HIGH? INSTEAD OF EXCLUDING MEN...
WHY NOT JUST ADMIT MORE WOMEN?
SIMILARLY, INSTEAD OF TRYING TO KEEP OUT FUTURE DEMOCRATS, WHY NOT WELCOME MORE FUTURE REPUBLICANS TO BALANCE THEM OUT?

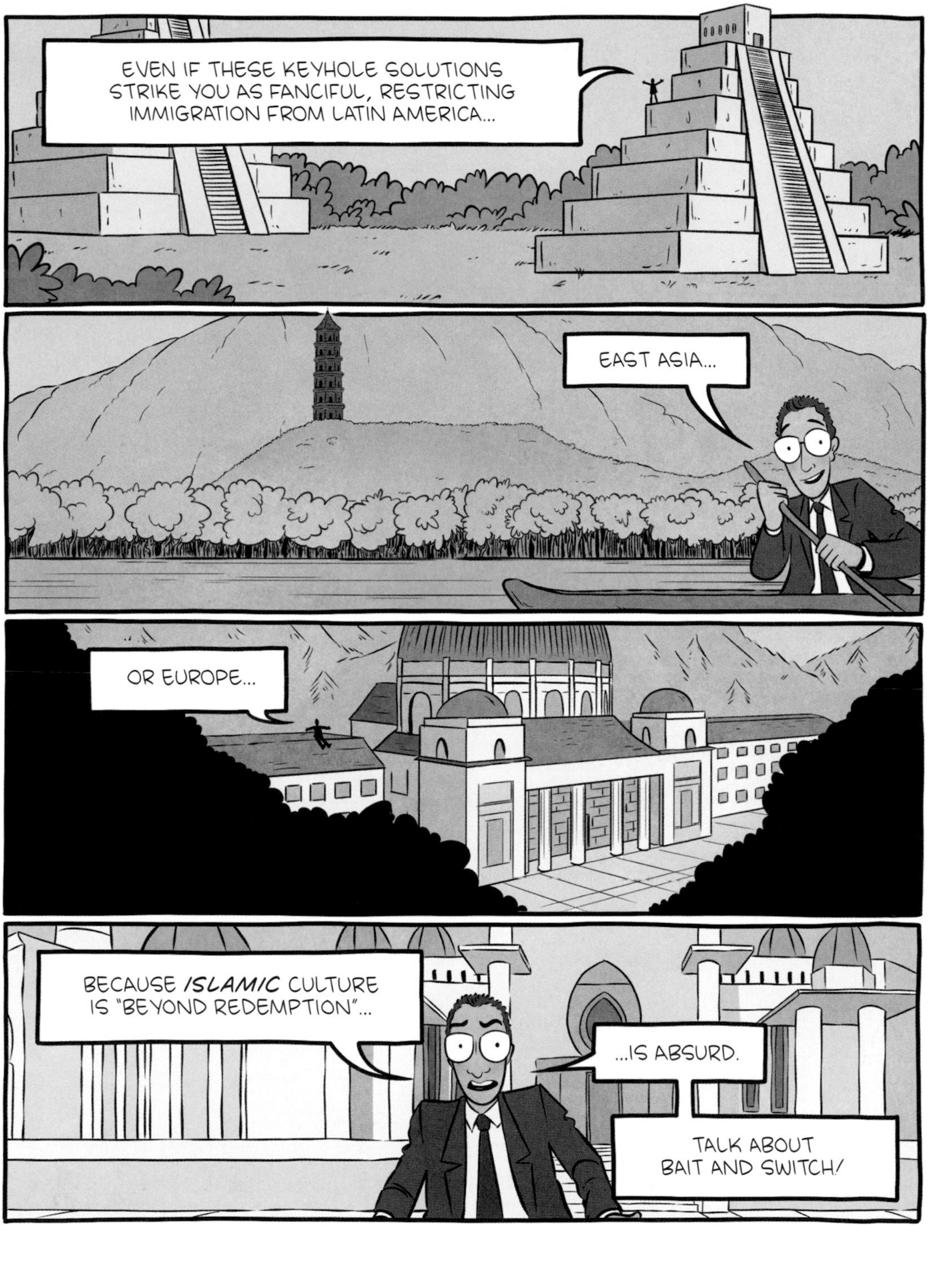
EVEN IF THESE KEYHOLE SOLUTIONS STRIKE YOU AS FANCIFUL, RESTRICTING IMMIGRATION FROM LATIN AMERICA...
EAST ASIA...
OR EUROPE...
BECAUSE *ISLAMIC* CULTURE IS "BEYOND REDEMPTION"...
...IS ABSURD.
TALK ABOUT BAIT AND SWITCH!

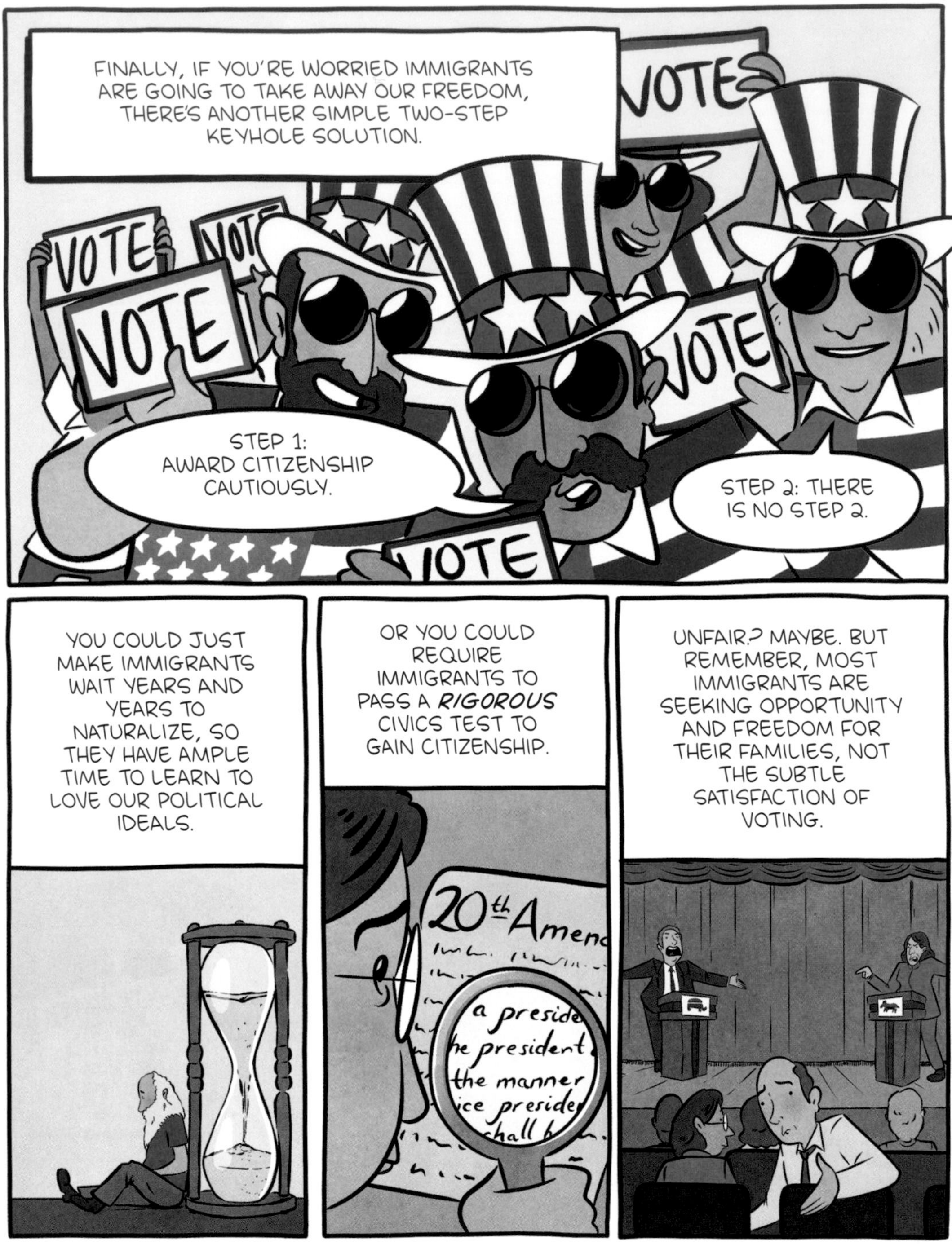
FINALLY, IF YOU'RE WORRIED IMMIGRANTS ARE GOING TO TAKE AWAY OUR FREEDOM, THERE'S ANOTHER SIMPLE TWO-STEP KEYHOLE SOLUTION.
VOTE
VOTE
VOTE
VOTE
VOTE
STEP 1: AWARD CITIZENSHIP CAUTIOUSLY.
STEP 2: THERE IS NO STEP 2.
VOTE
YOU COULD JUST MAKE IMMIGRANTS WAIT YEARS AND YEARS TO NATURALIZE, SO THEY HAVE AMPLE TIME TO LEARN TO LOVE OUR POLITICAL IDEALS.
OR YOU COULD REQUIRE IMMIGRANTS TO PASS A *RIGOROUS* CIVICS TEST TO GAIN CITIZENSHIP.
20th Amen
a preside
he president
the manner
ice preside
UNFAIR? MAYBE. BUT REMEMBER, MOST IMMIGRANTS ARE SEEKING OPPORTUNITY AND FREEDOM FOR THEIR FAMILIES, NOT THE SUBTLE SATISFACTION OF VOTING.

BUT ISN'T THIS JUST PIE IN THE SKY?
ARE ANY OF THESE KEYHOLE SOLUTIONS POLITICALLY POSSIBLE?
ABSOLUTELY, BECAUSE WHAT *EXISTS* IS POSSIBLE. PLENTY OF THESE POLICIES ARE ALREADY ON THE BOOKS!
FOREIGN TOURISTS, MOST OBVIOUSLY, CAN'T VOTE AND ARE INELIGIBLE FOR ALMOST ALL GOVERNMENT BENEFITS.
I HAD APPLE PIE AND A HOT DOG AND I WENT TO DISNEY AND CAN I PLEASE PLEASE PLEASE VOTE IN A CITY COUNCIL ELECTION? MY FRIENDS BACK IN SLOVAKIA WILL BE SO JEALOUS!
YOU PEOPLE NEED NETFLIX.
THE SAME GOES FOR INTERNATIONAL STUDENTS.
DON'T FORGET—THEY ALMOST ALWAYS PAY OUT-OF-STATE TUITION. NO WONDER PUBLIC COLLEGES LOVE THEM!

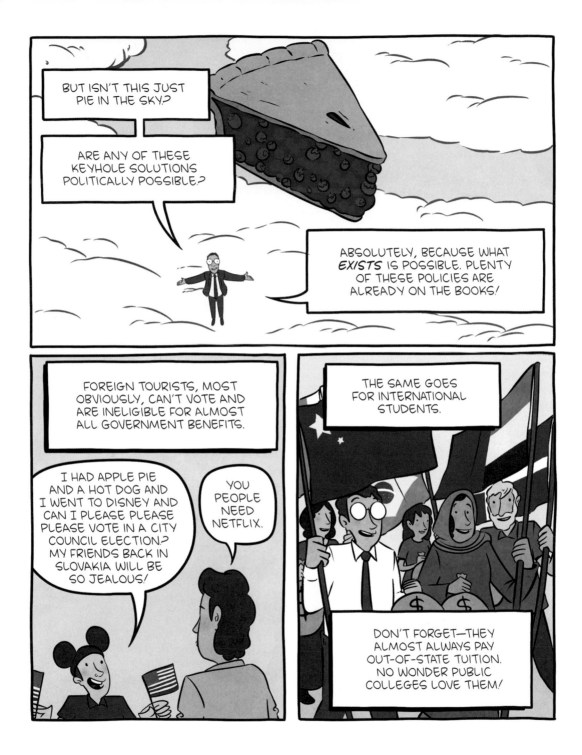

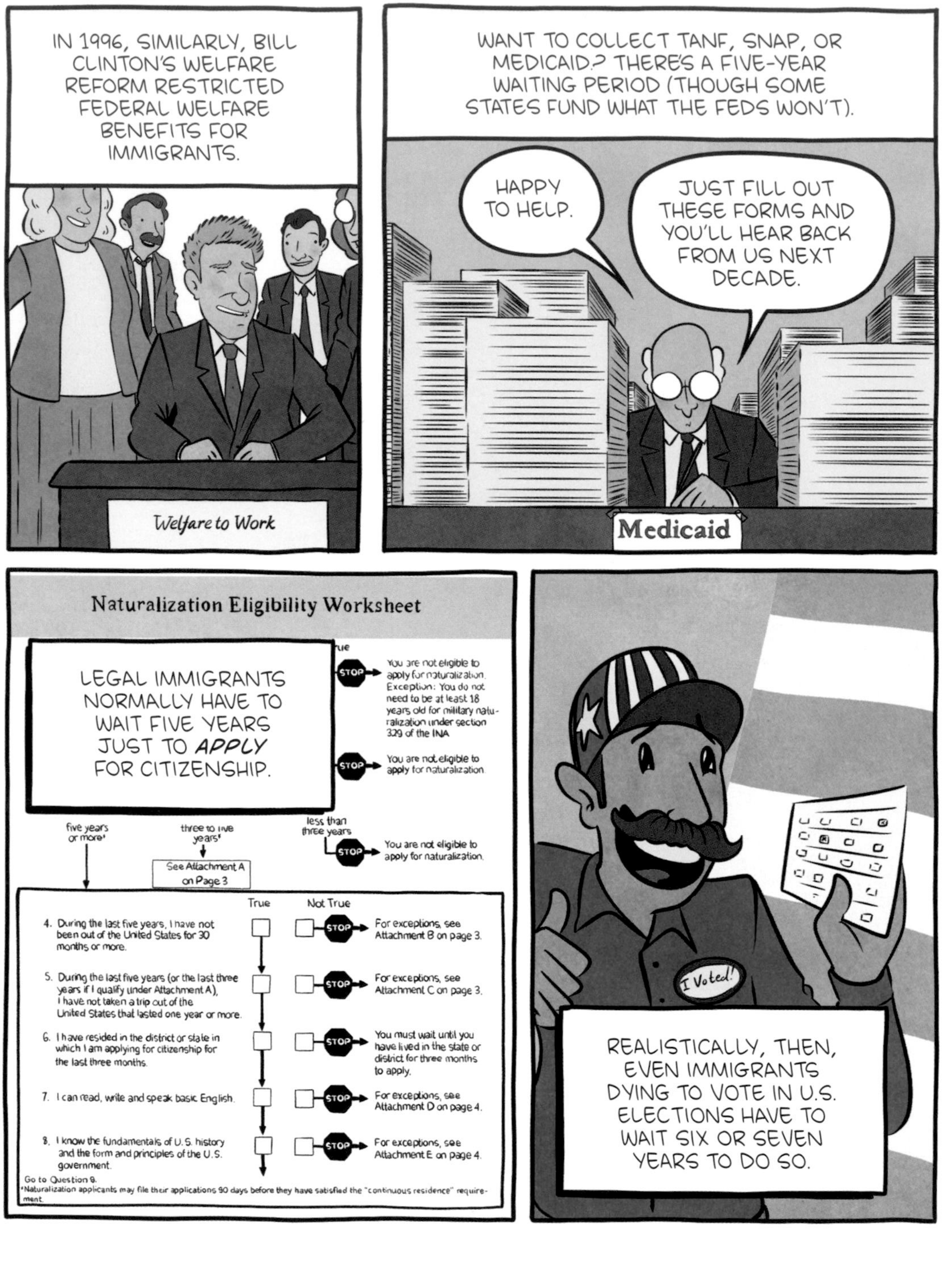
IN 1996, SIMILARLY, BILL CLINTON'S WELFARE REFORM RESTRICTED FEDERAL WELFARE BENEFITS FOR IMMIGRANTS.
Welfare to Work
WANT TO COLLECT TANF, SNAP, OR MEDICAID? THERE'S A FIVE-YEAR WAITING PERIOD (THOUGH SOME STATES FUND WHAT THE FEDS WON'T).
HAPPY TO HELP.
JUST FILL OUT THESE FORMS AND YOU'LL HEAR BACK FROM US NEXT DECADE.
Medicaid
Naturalization Eligibility Worksheet
LEGAL IMMIGRANTS NORMALLY HAVE TO WAIT FIVE YEARS JUST TO *APPLY* FOR CITIZENSHIP.
You are not eligible to apply for naturalization. Exception: You do not need to be at least 18 years old for military naturalization under section 329 of the INA
You are not eligible to apply for naturalization.
five years or more*
three to five years*
See Attachment A on Page 3
less than three years
You are not eligible to apply for naturalization.
True
Not True
4. During the last five years, I have not been out of the United States for 30 months or more.
For exceptions, see Attachment B on page 3.
5. During the last five years (or the last three years if I qualify under Attachment A), I have not taken a trip out of the United States that lasted one year or more.
For exceptions, see Attachment C on page 3.
6. I have resided in the district or state in which I am applying for citizenship for the last three months.
You must wait until you have lived in the state or district for three months to apply.
7. I can read, write and speak basic English.
For exceptions, see Attachment D on page 4.
8. I know the fundamentals of U.S. history and the form and principles of the U.S. government.
For exceptions, see Attachment E on page 4.
Go to Question 9.
*Naturalization applicants may file their applications 90 days before they have satisfied the "continuous residence" requirement.
STOP
I Voted!
REALISTICALLY, THEN, EVEN IMMIGRANTS DYING TO VOTE IN U.S. ELECTIONS HAVE TO WAIT SIX OR SEVEN YEARS TO DO SO.

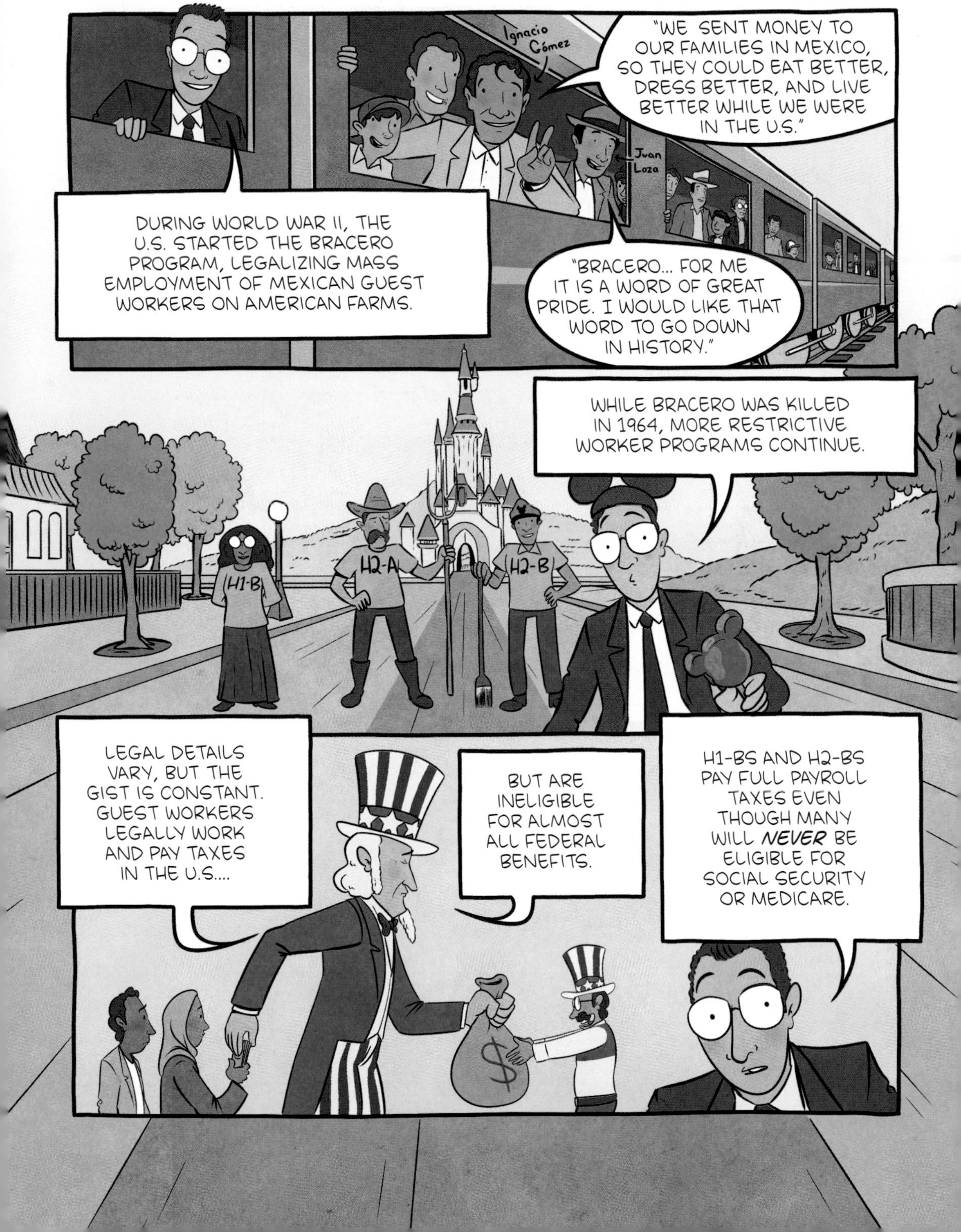
Ignacio Gómez
"WE SENT MONEY TO OUR FAMILIES IN MEXICO, SO THEY COULD EAT BETTER, DRESS BETTER, AND LIVE BETTER WHILE WE WERE IN THE U.S."
Juan Loza
DURING WORLD WAR II, THE U.S. STARTED THE BRACERO PROGRAM, LEGALIZING MASS EMPLOYMENT OF MEXICAN GUEST WORKERS ON AMERICAN FARMS.
"BRACERO... FOR ME IT IS A WORD OF GREAT PRIDE. I WOULD LIKE THAT WORD TO GO DOWN IN HISTORY."
WHILE BRACERO WAS KILLED IN 1964, MORE RESTRICTIVE WORKER PROGRAMS CONTINUE.
H1-B
H2-A
H2-B
LEGAL DETAILS VARY, BUT THE GIST IS CONSTANT. GUEST WORKERS LEGALLY WORK AND PAY TAXES IN THE U.S....
BUT ARE INELIGIBLE FOR ALMOST ALL FEDERAL BENEFITS.
H1-BS AND H2-BS PAY FULL PAYROLL TAXES EVEN THOUGH MANY WILL ***NEVER*** BE ELIGIBLE FOR SOCIAL SECURITY OR MEDICARE.
$

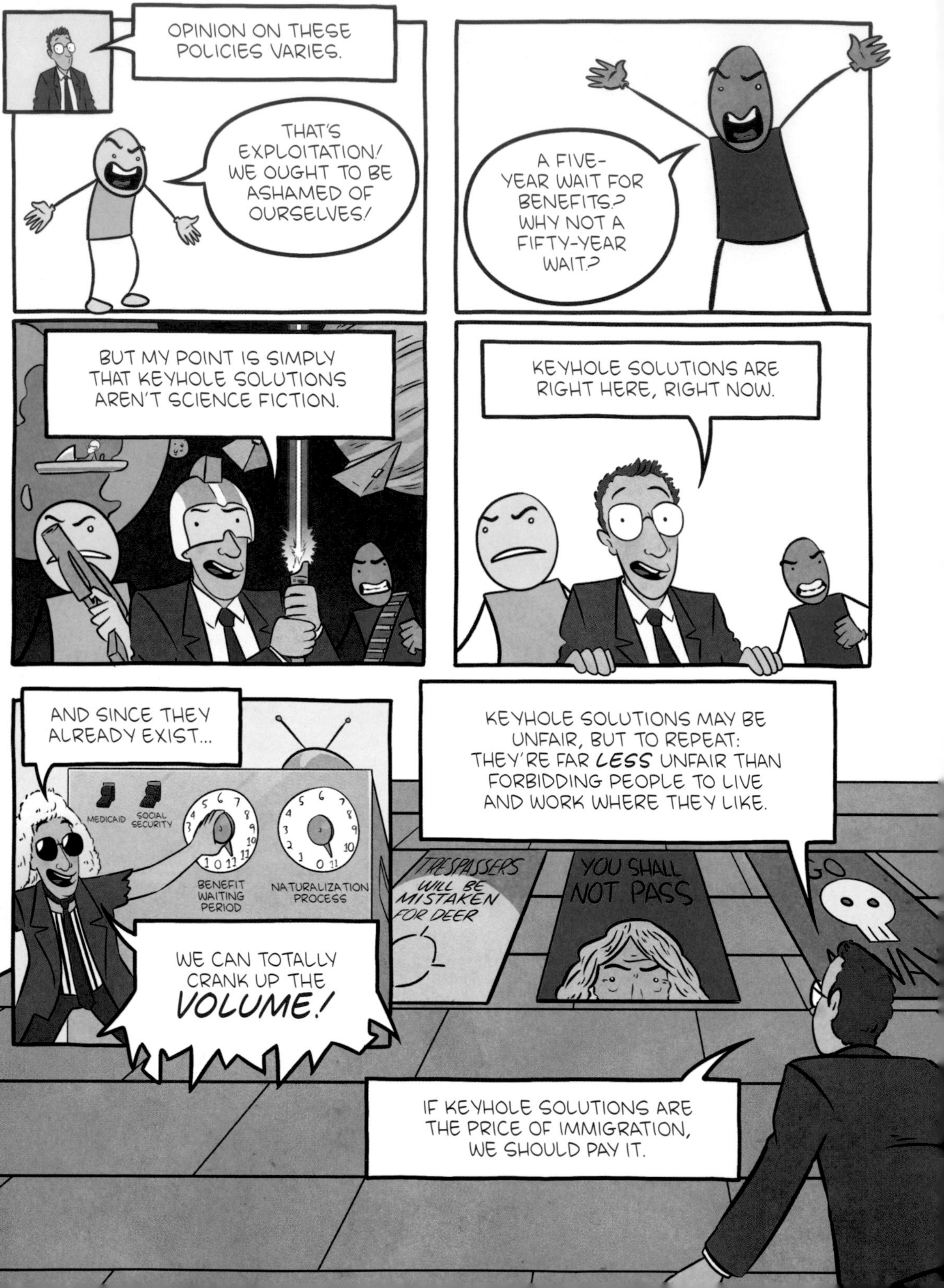
OPINION ON THESE POLICIES VARIES.
THAT'S EXPLOITATION! WE OUGHT TO BE ASHAMED OF OURSELVES!
A FIVE-YEAR WAIT FOR BENEFITS? WHY NOT A FIFTY-YEAR WAIT?
BUT MY POINT IS SIMPLY THAT KEYHOLE SOLUTIONS AREN'T SCIENCE FICTION.
KEYHOLE SOLUTIONS ARE RIGHT HERE, RIGHT NOW.
AND SINCE THEY ALREADY EXIST...
MEDICAID
SOCIAL SECURITY
BENEFIT WAITING PERIOD
NATURALIZATION PROCESS
WE CAN TOTALLY CRANK UP THE *VOLUME!*
KEYHOLE SOLUTIONS MAY BE UNFAIR, BUT TO REPEAT: THEY'RE FAR *LESS* UNFAIR THAN FORBIDDING PEOPLE TO LIVE AND WORK WHERE THEY LIKE.
TRESPASSERS WILL BE MISTAKEN FOR DEER
YOU SHALL NOT PASS
IF KEYHOLE SOLUTIONS ARE THE PRICE OF IMMIGRATION, WE SHOULD PAY IT.

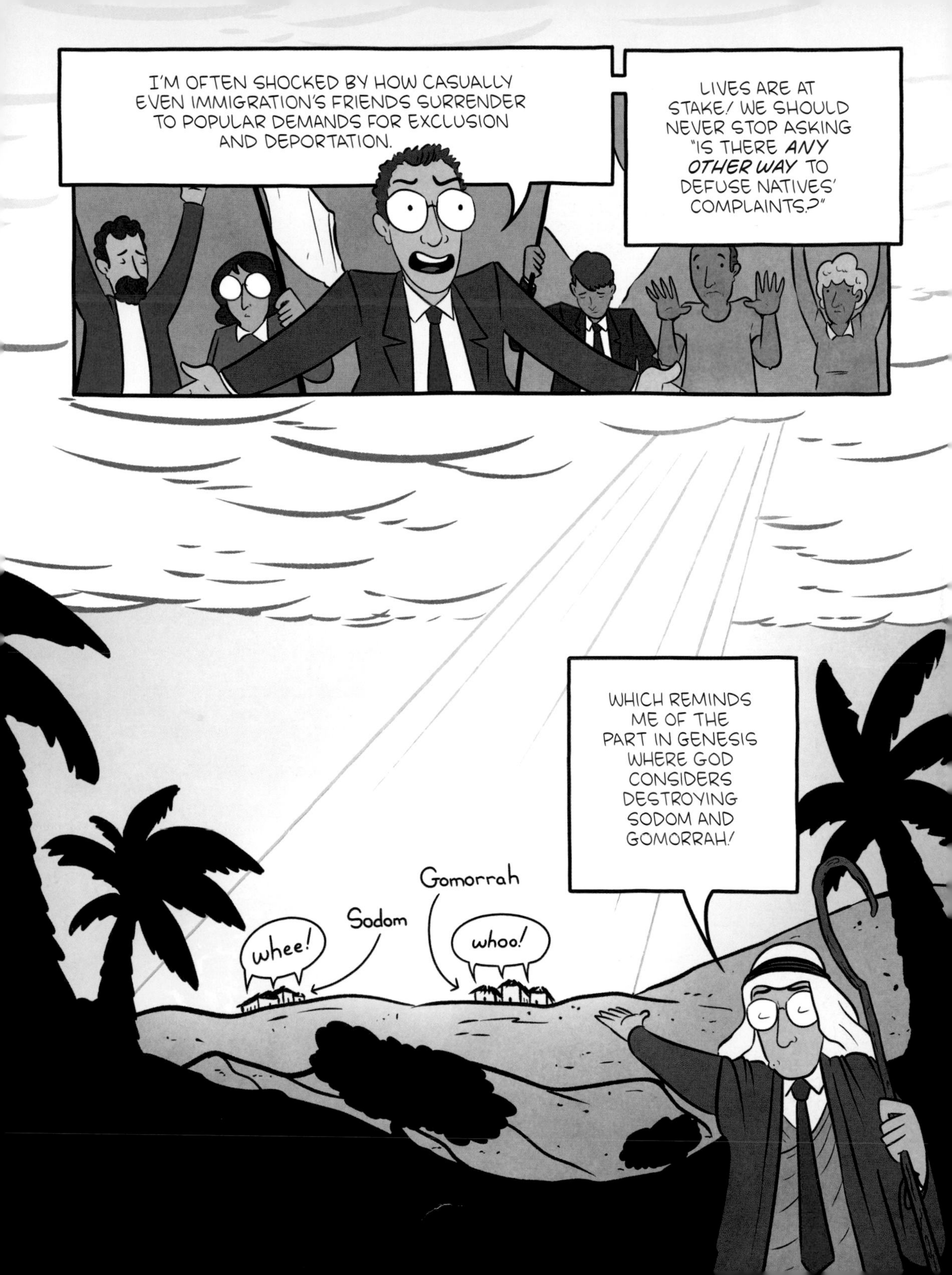
I'M OFTEN SHOCKED BY HOW CASUALLY EVEN IMMIGRATION'S FRIENDS SURRENDER TO POPULAR DEMANDS FOR EXCLUSION AND DEPORTATION.
LIVES ARE AT STAKE! WE SHOULD NEVER STOP ASKING "IS THERE *ANY OTHER WAY* TO DEFUSE NATIVES' COMPLAINTS?"
WHICH REMINDS ME OF THE PART IN GENESIS WHERE GOD CONSIDERS DESTROYING SODOM AND GOMORRAH!
Gomorrah
Sodom
whee!
whoo!

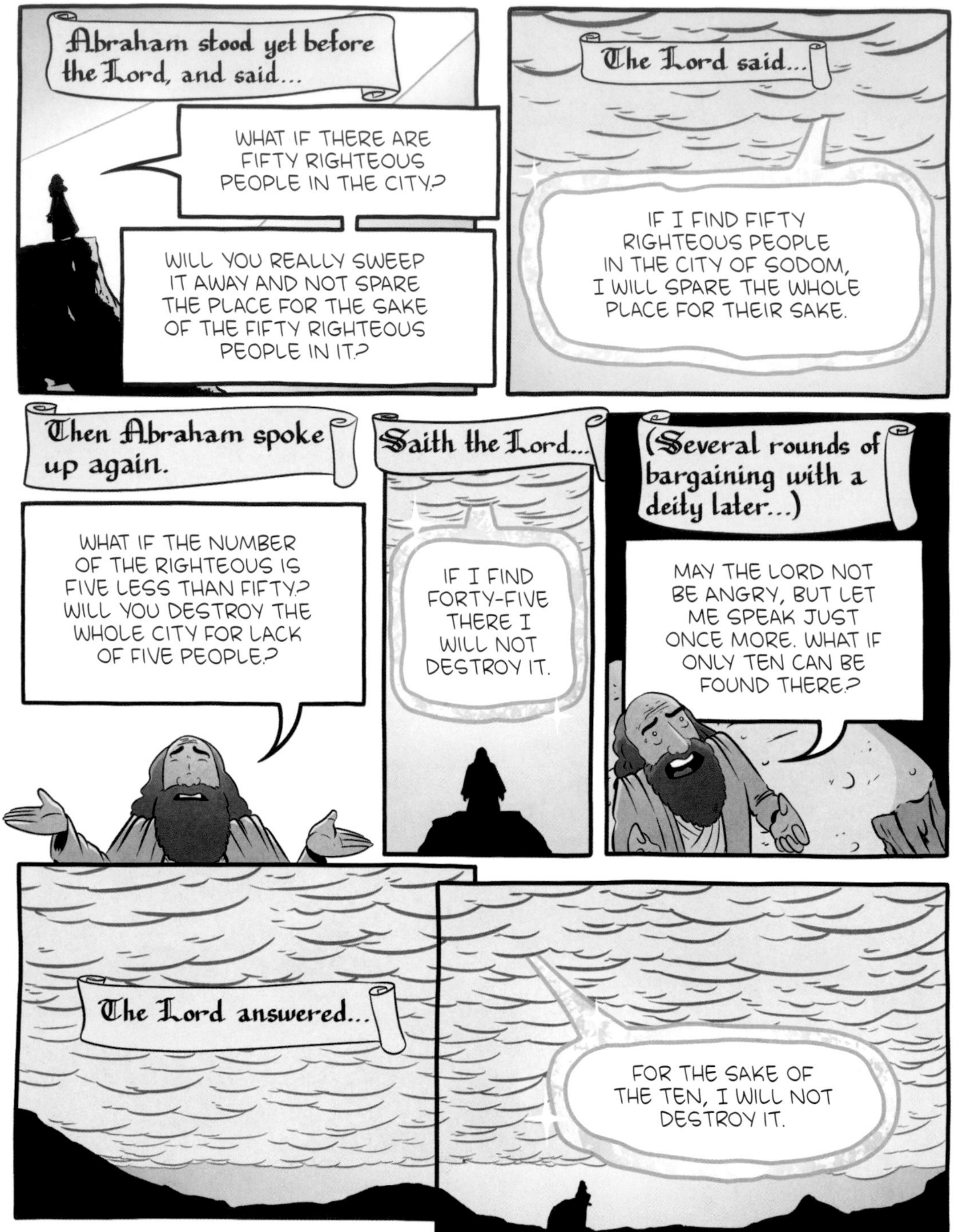
Abraham stood yet before the Lord, and said...
WHAT IF THERE ARE FIFTY RIGHTEOUS PEOPLE IN THE CITY?
WILL YOU REALLY SWEEP IT AWAY AND NOT SPARE THE PLACE FOR THE SAKE OF THE FIFTY RIGHTEOUS PEOPLE IN IT?
The Lord said...
IF I FIND FIFTY RIGHTEOUS PEOPLE IN THE CITY OF SODOM, I WILL SPARE THE WHOLE PLACE FOR THEIR SAKE.
Then Abraham spoke up again.
WHAT IF THE NUMBER OF THE RIGHTEOUS IS FIVE LESS THAN FIFTY? WILL YOU DESTROY THE WHOLE CITY FOR LACK OF FIVE PEOPLE?
Saith the Lord...
IF I FIND FORTY-FIVE THERE I WILL NOT DESTROY IT.
(Several rounds of bargaining with a deity later...)
MAY THE LORD NOT BE ANGRY, BUT LET ME SPEAK JUST ONCE MORE. WHAT IF ONLY TEN CAN BE FOUND THERE?
The Lord answered...
FOR THE SAKE OF THE TEN, I WILL NOT DESTROY IT.

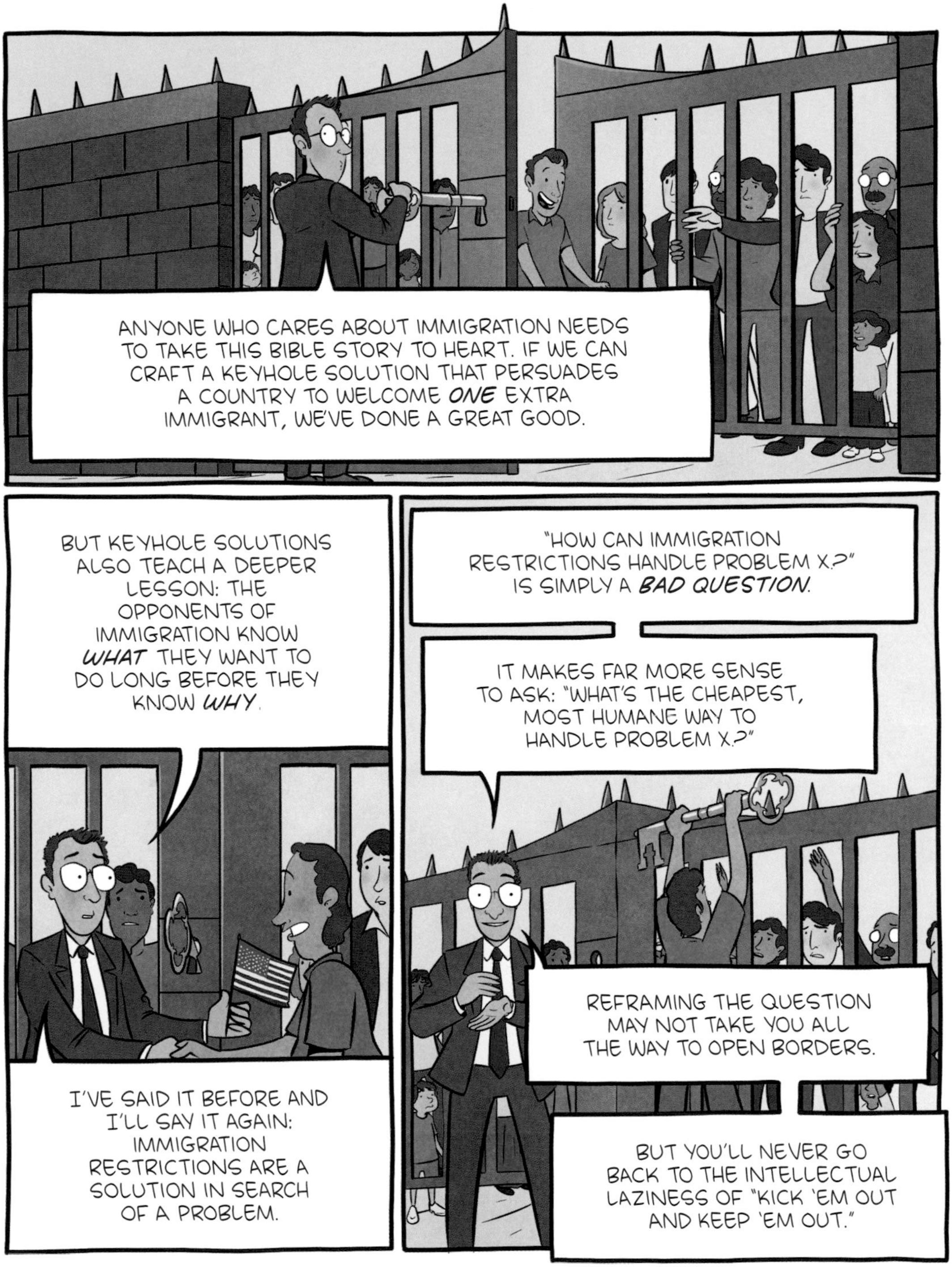
ANYONE WHO CARES ABOUT IMMIGRATION NEEDS TO TAKE THIS BIBLE STORY TO HEART. IF WE CAN CRAFT A KEYHOLE SOLUTION THAT PERSUADES A COUNTRY TO WELCOME ONE EXTRA IMMIGRANT, WE'VE DONE A GREAT GOOD.
BUT KEYHOLE SOLUTIONS ALSO TEACH A DEEPER LESSON: THE OPPONENTS OF IMMIGRATION KNOW WHAT THEY WANT TO DO LONG BEFORE THEY KNOW WHY.
I'VE SAID IT BEFORE AND I'LL SAY IT AGAIN: IMMIGRATION RESTRICTIONS ARE A SOLUTION IN SEARCH OF A PROBLEM.
"HOW CAN IMMIGRATION RESTRICTIONS HANDLE PROBLEM X?" IS SIMPLY A BAD QUESTION.
IT MAKES FAR MORE SENSE TO ASK: "WHAT'S THE CHEAPEST, MOST HUMANE WAY TO HANDLE PROBLEM X?"
REFRAMING THE QUESTION MAY NOT TAKE YOU ALL THE WAY TO OPEN BORDERS.
BUT YOU'LL NEVER GO BACK TO THE INTELLECTUAL LAZINESS OF "KICK 'EM OUT AND KEEP 'EM OUT."

CHAPTER 7

ALL ROADS LEAD TO OPEN BORDERS

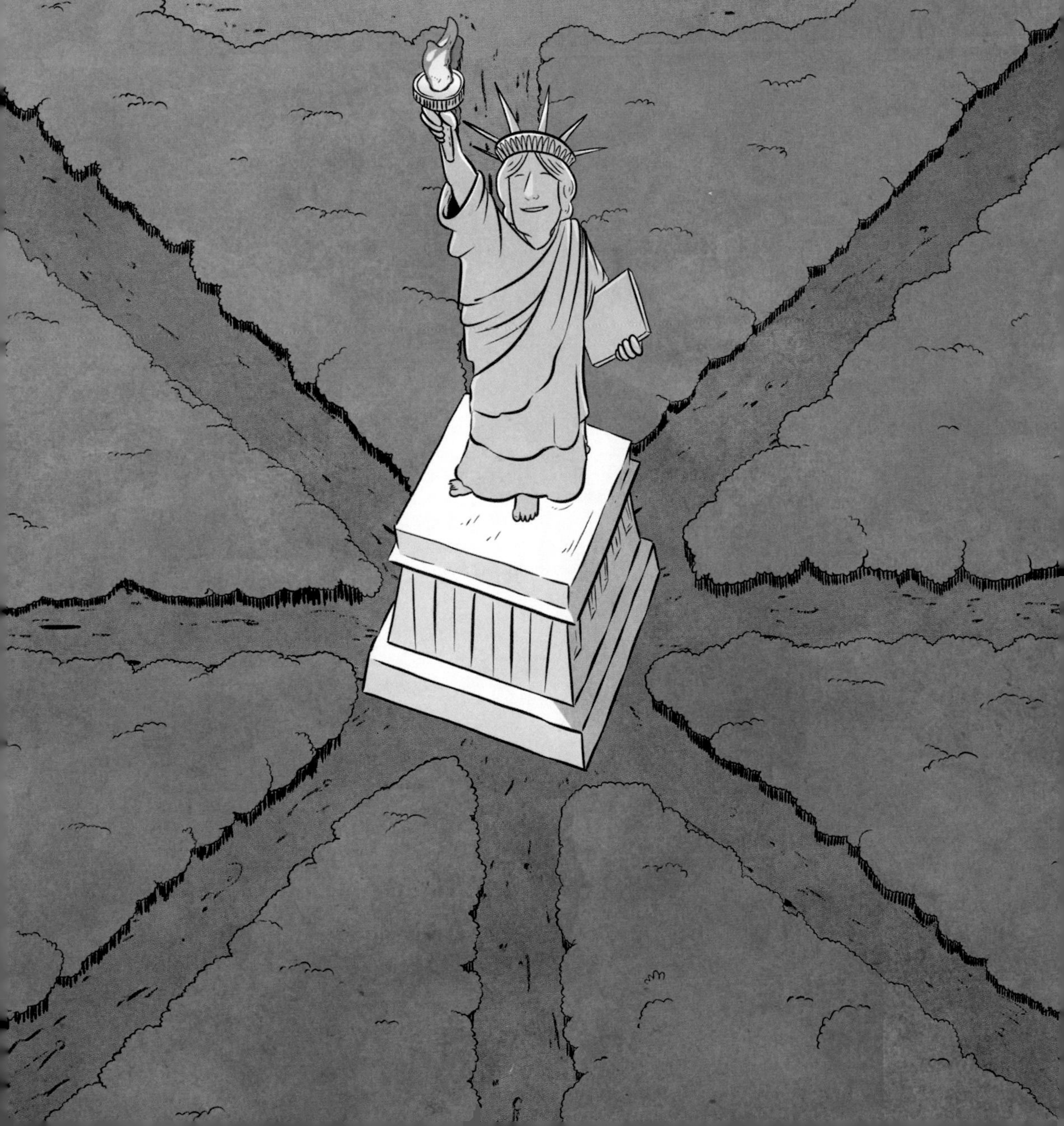

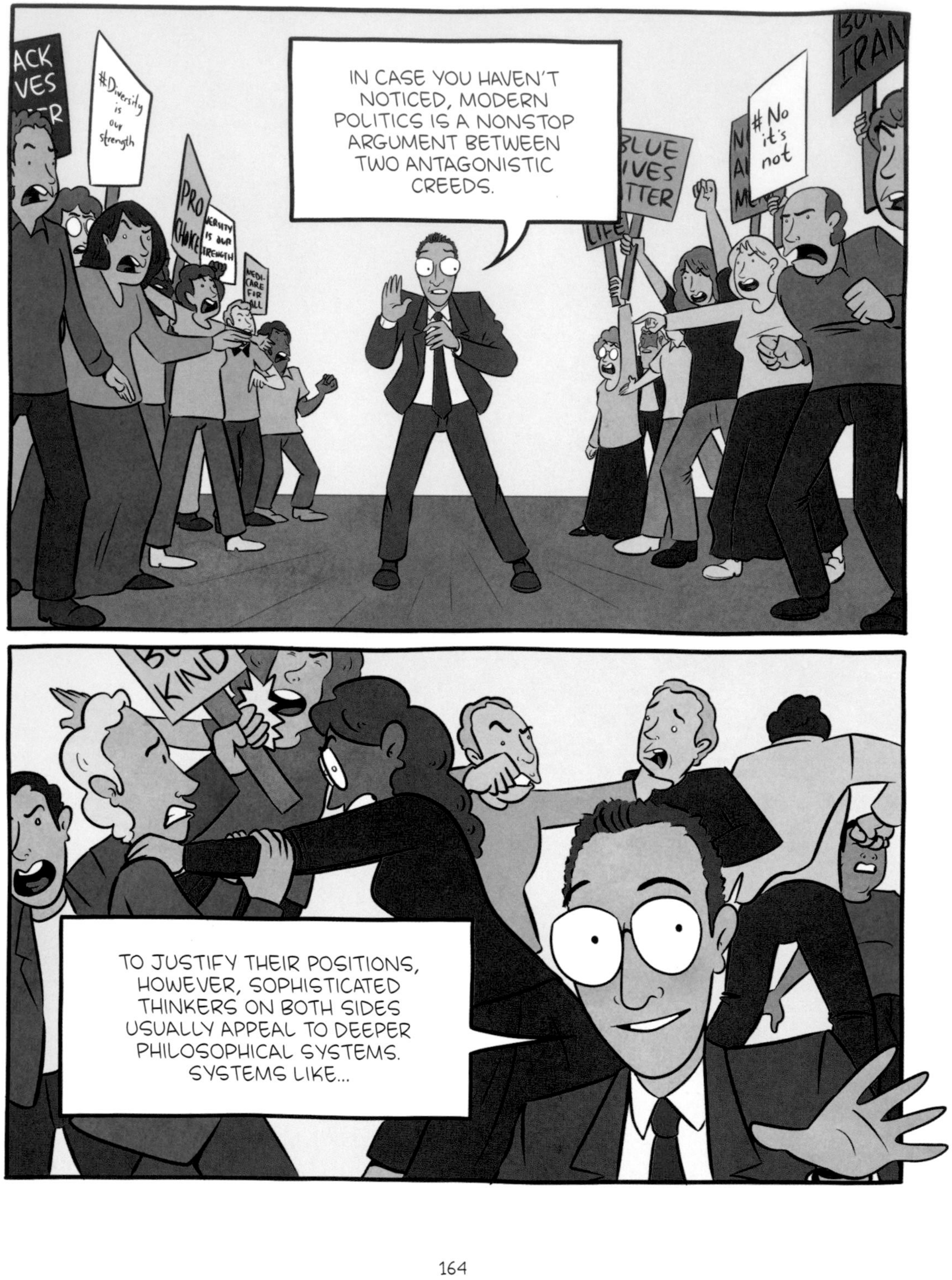
IN CASE YOU HAVEN'T NOTICED, MODERN POLITICS IS A NONSTOP ARGUMENT BETWEEN TWO ANTAGONISTIC CREEDS.
#Diversity is our strength
PRO CHOICE
MEDI-CARE FOR ALL
#No it's not
TO JUSTIFY THEIR POSITIONS, HOWEVER, SOPHISTICATED THINKERS ON BOTH SIDES USUALLY APPEAL TO DEEPER PHILOSOPHICAL SYSTEMS. SYSTEMS LIKE...

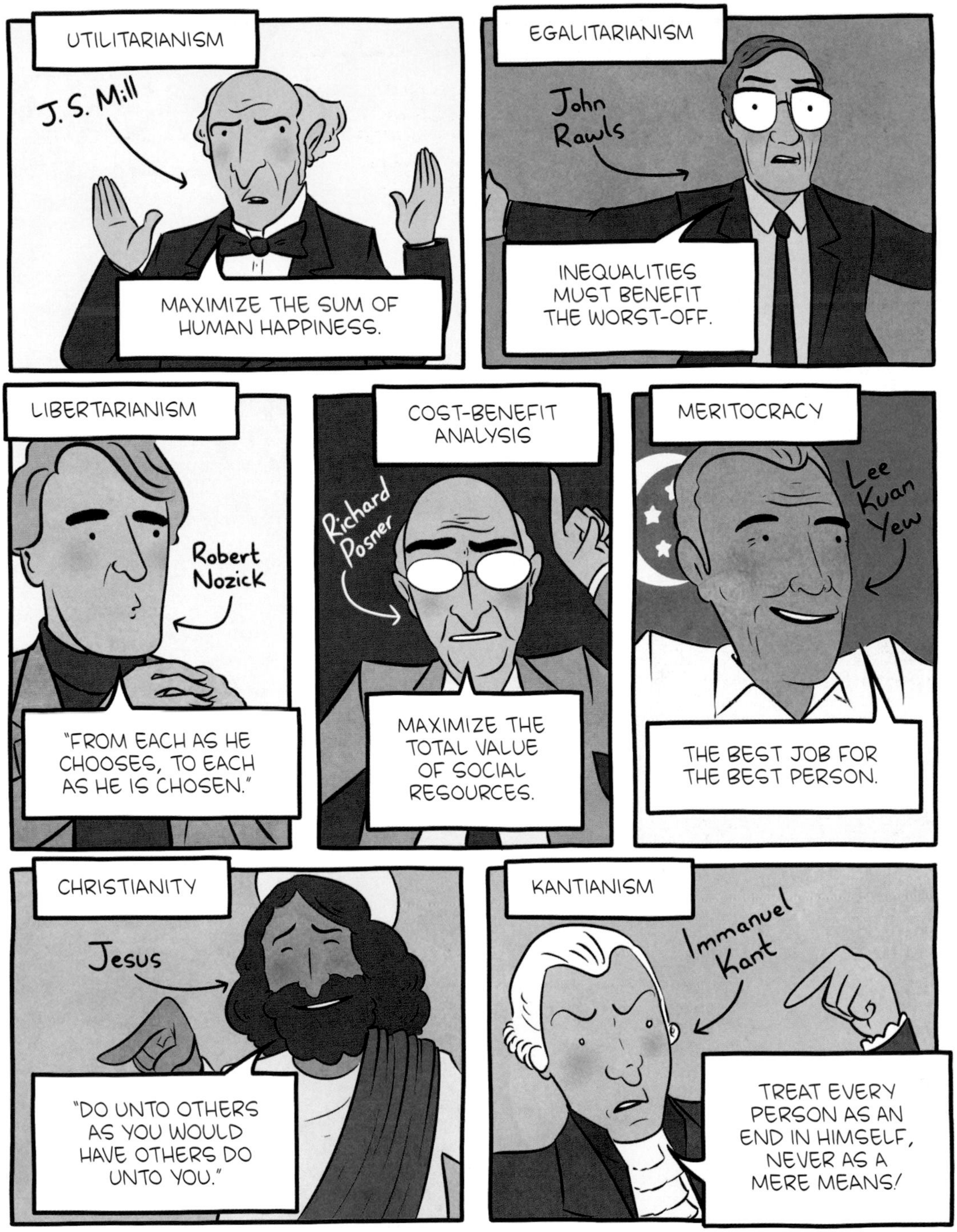
UTILITARIANISM
J. S. Mill
MAXIMIZE THE SUM OF HUMAN HAPPINESS.
EGALITARIANISM
John Rawls
INEQUALITIES MUST BENEFIT THE WORST-OFF.
LIBERTARIANISM
Robert Nozick
"FROM EACH AS HE CHOOSES, TO EACH AS HE IS CHOSEN."
COST-BENEFIT ANALYSIS
Richard Posner
MAXIMIZE THE TOTAL VALUE OF SOCIAL RESOURCES.
MERITOCRACY
Lee Kuan Yew
THE BEST JOB FOR THE BEST PERSON.
CHRISTIANITY
Jesus
"DO UNTO OTHERS AS YOU WOULD HAVE OTHERS DO UNTO YOU."
KANTIANISM
Immanuel Kant
TREAT EVERY PERSON AS AN END IN HIMSELF, NEVER AS A MERE MEANS!

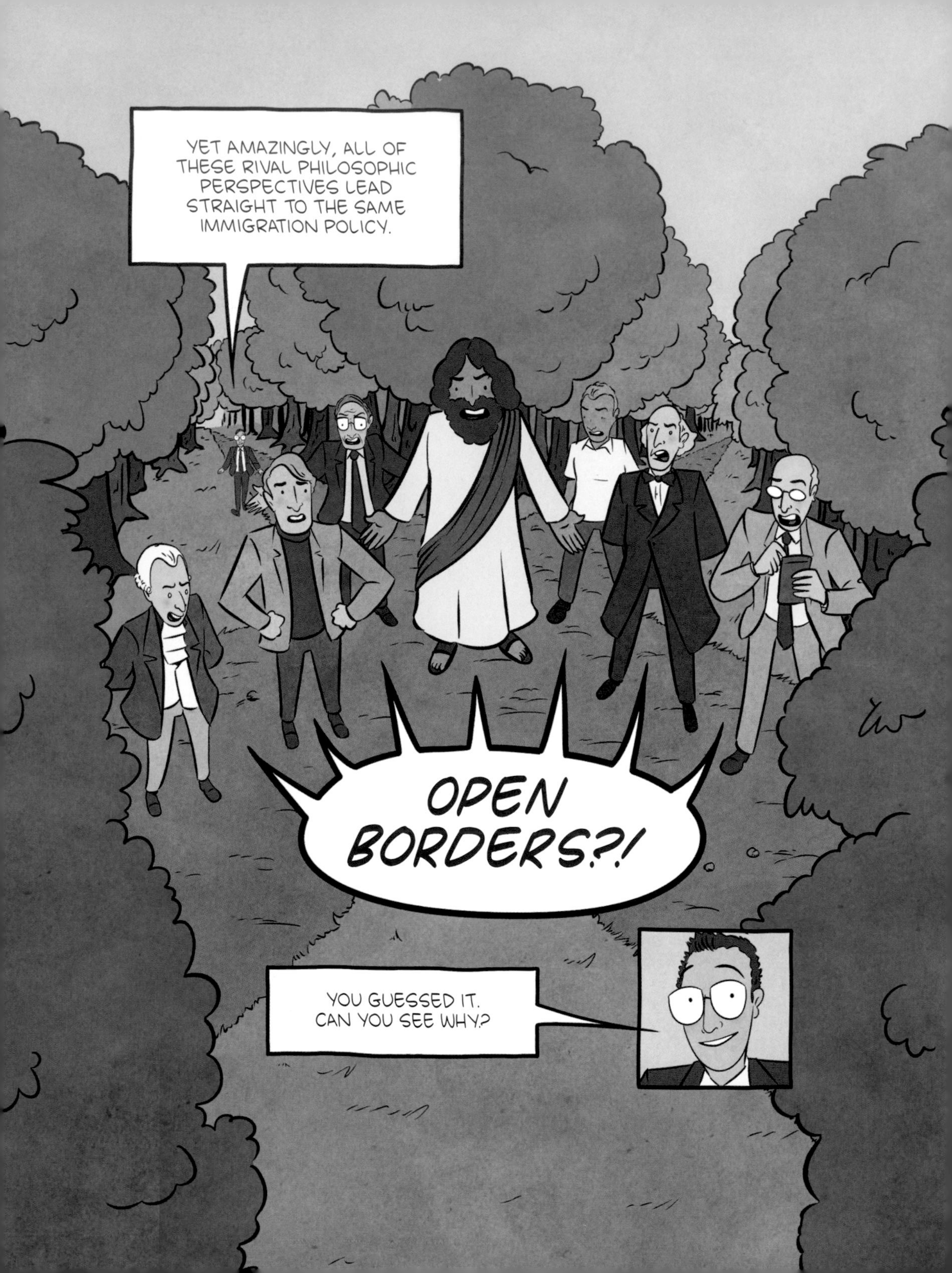
YET AMAZINGLY, ALL OF THESE RIVAL PHILOSOPHIC PERSPECTIVES LEAD STRAIGHT TO THE SAME IMMIGRATION POLICY.
OPEN BORDERS?!
YOU GUESSED IT. CAN YOU SEE WHY?

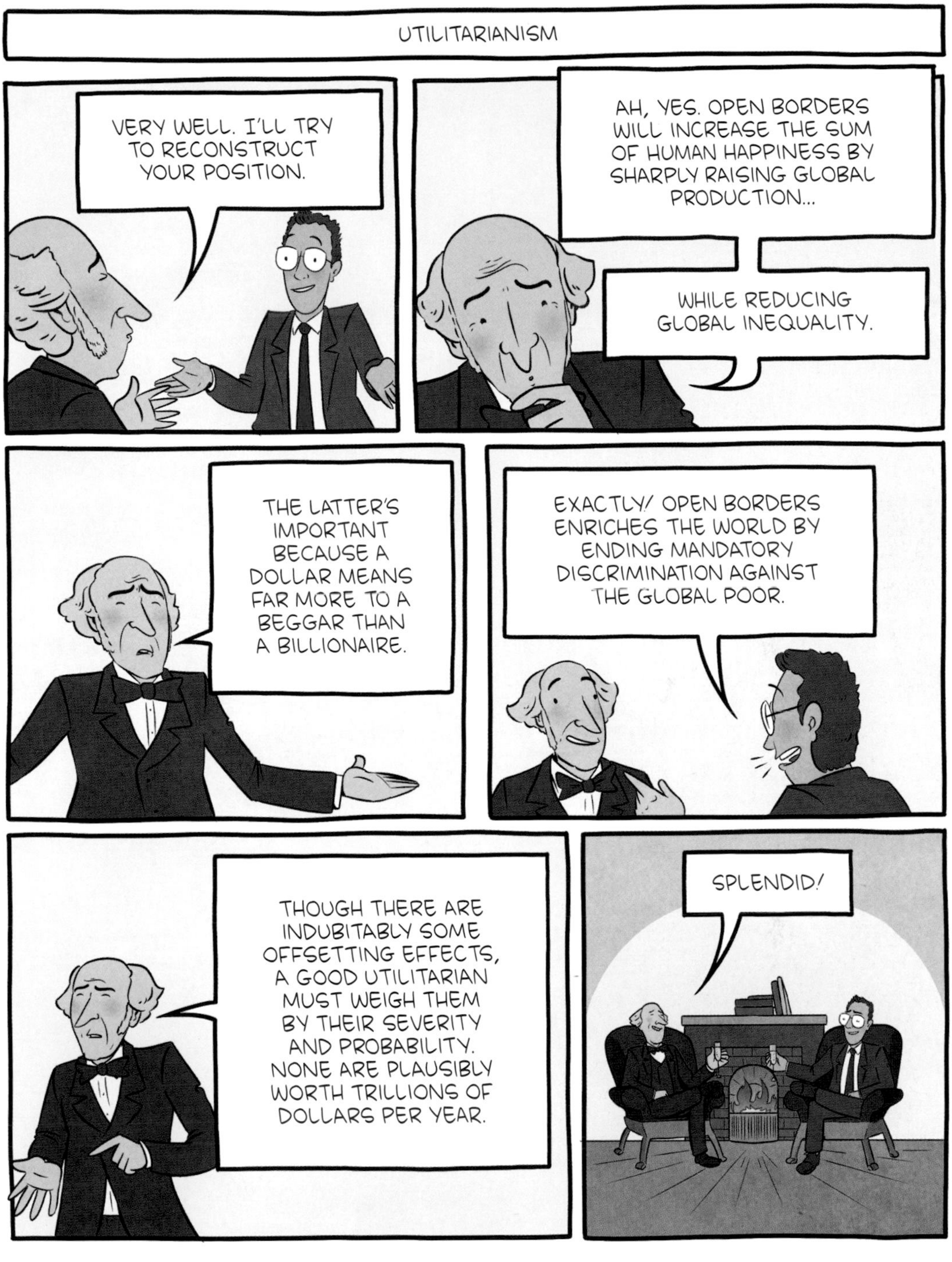
UTILITARIANISM
VERY WELL. I'LL TRY TO RECONSTRUCT YOUR POSITION.
AH, YES. OPEN BORDERS WILL INCREASE THE SUM OF HUMAN HAPPINESS BY SHARPLY RAISING GLOBAL PRODUCTION...
WHILE REDUCING GLOBAL INEQUALITY.
THE LATTER'S IMPORTANT BECAUSE A DOLLAR MEANS FAR MORE TO A BEGGAR THAN A BILLIONAIRE.
EXACTLY! OPEN BORDERS ENRICHES THE WORLD BY ENDING MANDATORY DISCRIMINATION AGAINST THE GLOBAL POOR.
THOUGH THERE ARE INDUBITABLY SOME OFFSETTING EFFECTS, A GOOD UTILITARIAN MUST WEIGH THEM BY THEIR SEVERITY AND PROBABILITY. NONE ARE PLAUSIBLY WORTH TRILLIONS OF DOLLARS PER YEAR.
SPLENDID!

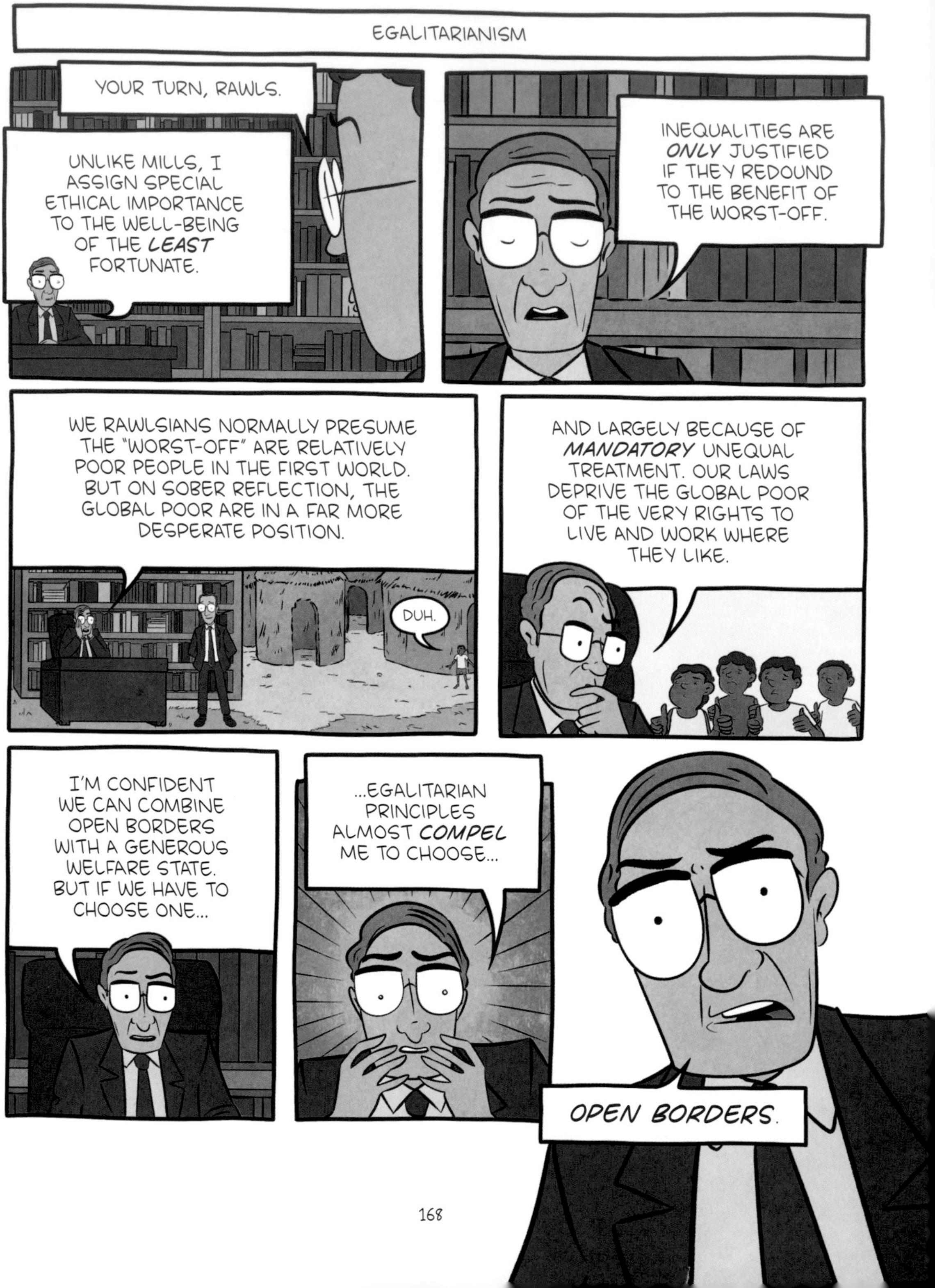
EGALITARIANISM
YOUR TURN, RAWLS.
UNLIKE MILLS, I ASSIGN SPECIAL ETHICAL IMPORTANCE TO THE WELL-BEING OF THE *LEAST* FORTUNATE.
INEQUALITIES ARE *ONLY* JUSTIFIED IF THEY REDOUND TO THE BENEFIT OF THE WORST-OFF.
WE RAWLSIANS NORMALLY PRESUME THE "WORST-OFF" ARE RELATIVELY POOR PEOPLE IN THE FIRST WORLD. BUT ON SOBER REFLECTION, THE GLOBAL POOR ARE IN A FAR MORE DESPERATE POSITION.
DUH.
AND LARGELY BECAUSE OF *MANDATORY* UNEQUAL TREATMENT. OUR LAWS DEPRIVE THE GLOBAL POOR OF THE VERY RIGHTS TO LIVE AND WORK WHERE THEY LIKE.
I'M CONFIDENT WE CAN COMBINE OPEN BORDERS WITH A GENEROUS WELFARE STATE. BUT IF WE HAVE TO CHOOSE ONE...
...EGALITARIAN PRINCIPLES ALMOST *COMPEL* ME TO CHOOSE...
OPEN BORDERS.

LIBERTARIANISM

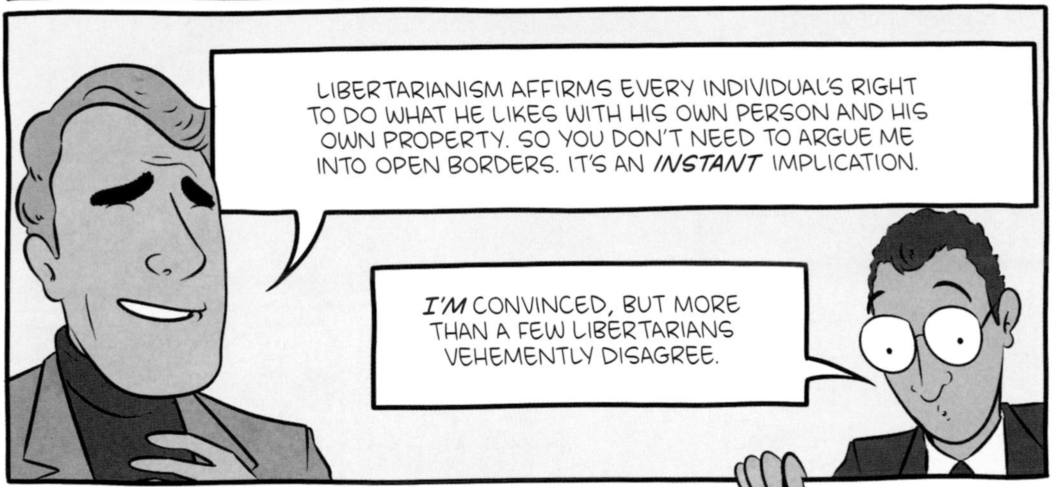
LIBERTARIANISM AFFIRMS EVERY INDIVIDUAL'S RIGHT TO DO WHAT HE LIKES WITH HIS OWN PERSON AND HIS OWN PROPERTY. SO YOU DON'T NEED TO ARGUE ME INTO OPEN BORDERS. IT'S AN *INSTANT* IMPLICATION.
I'M CONVINCED, BUT MORE THAN A FEW LIBERTARIANS VEHEMENTLY DISAGREE.

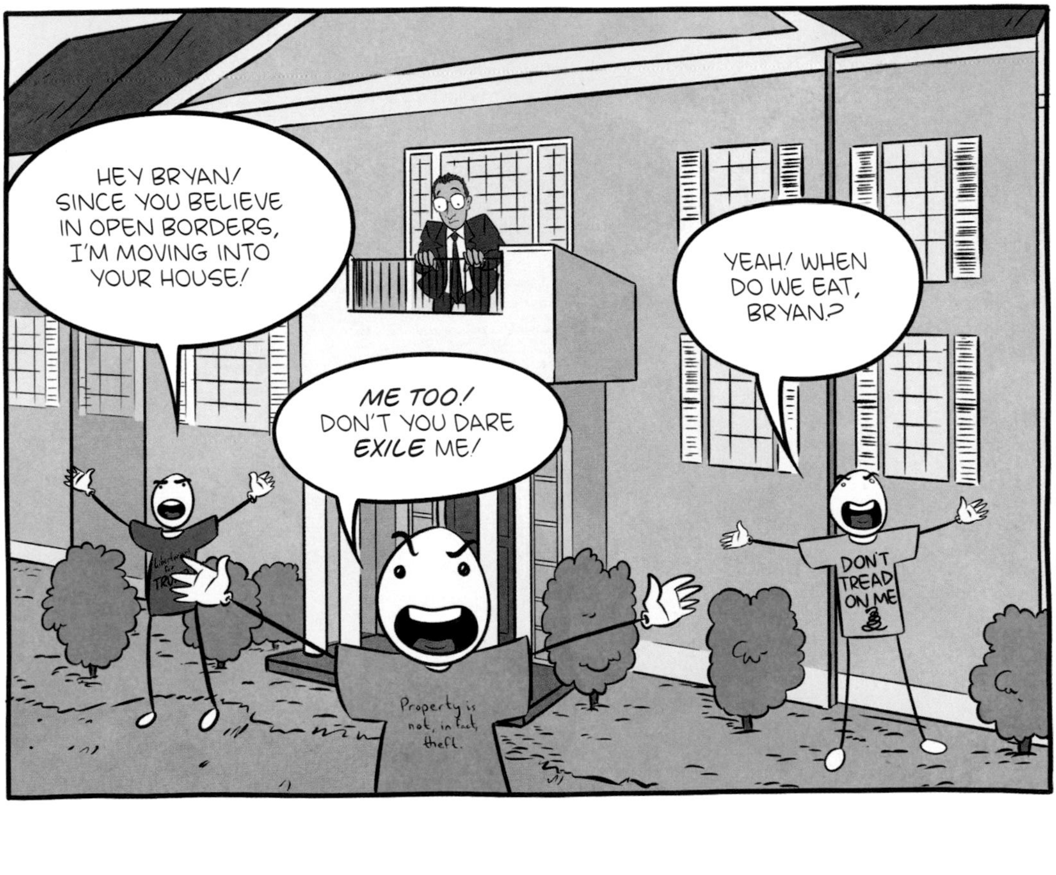
HEY BRYAN! SINCE YOU BELIEVE IN OPEN BORDERS, I'M MOVING INTO YOUR HOUSE!
ME TOO! DON'T YOU DARE *EXILE* ME!
YEAH! WHEN DO WE EAT, BRYAN?
Property is not, in fact, theft.
DON'T TREAD ON ME

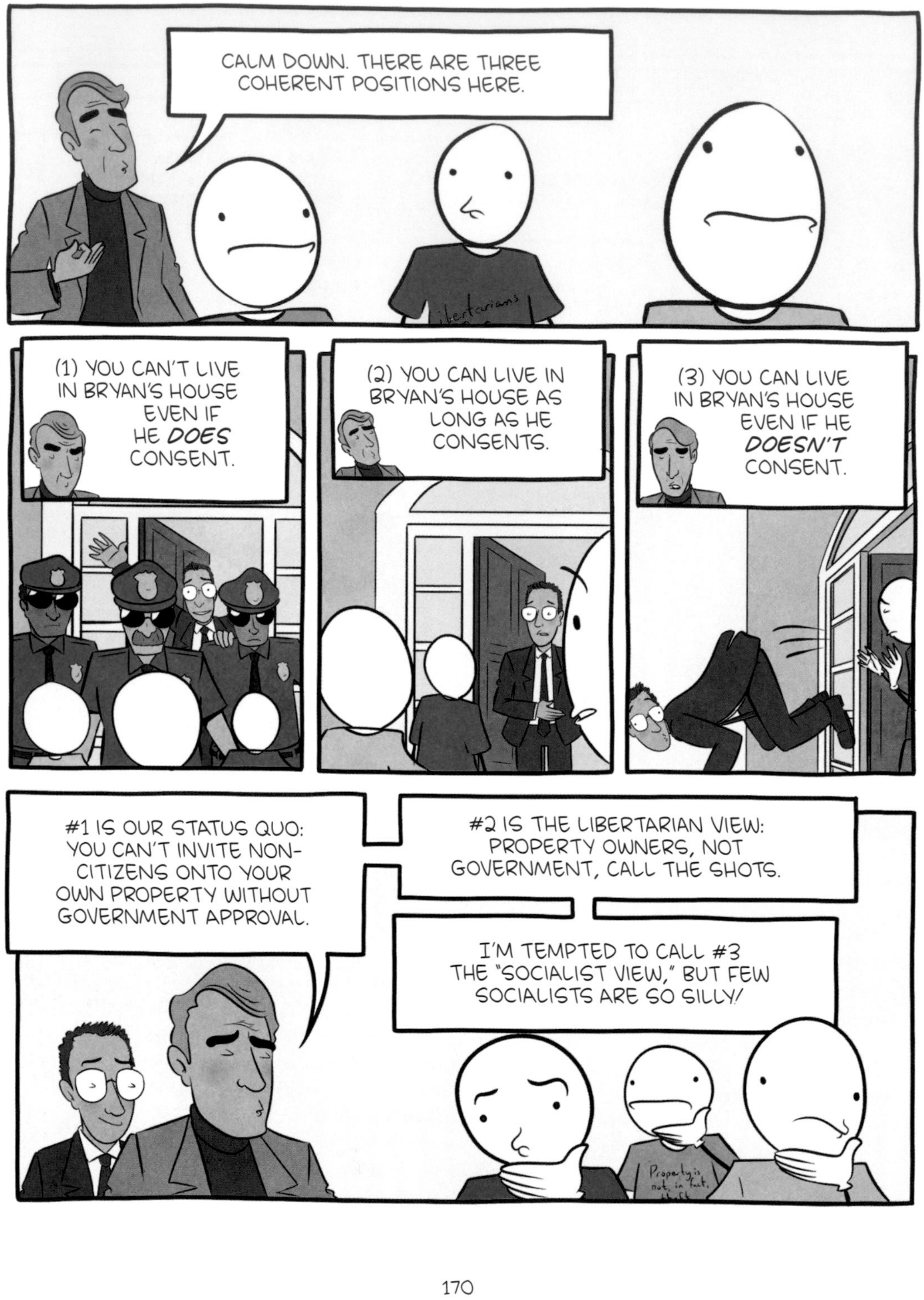

CALM DOWN. THERE ARE THREE COHERENT POSITIONS HERE.
(1) YOU CAN'T LIVE IN BRYAN'S HOUSE EVEN IF HE *DOES* CONSENT.
(2) YOU CAN LIVE IN BRYAN'S HOUSE AS LONG AS HE CONSENTS.
(3) YOU CAN LIVE IN BRYAN'S HOUSE EVEN IF HE *DOESN'T* CONSENT.
#1 IS OUR STATUS QUO: YOU CAN'T INVITE NON-CITIZENS ONTO YOUR OWN PROPERTY WITHOUT GOVERNMENT APPROVAL.
#2 IS THE LIBERTARIAN VIEW: PROPERTY OWNERS, NOT GOVERNMENT, CALL THE SHOTS.
I'M TEMPTED TO CALL #3 THE "SOCIALIST VIEW," BUT FEW SOCIALISTS ARE SO SILLY!

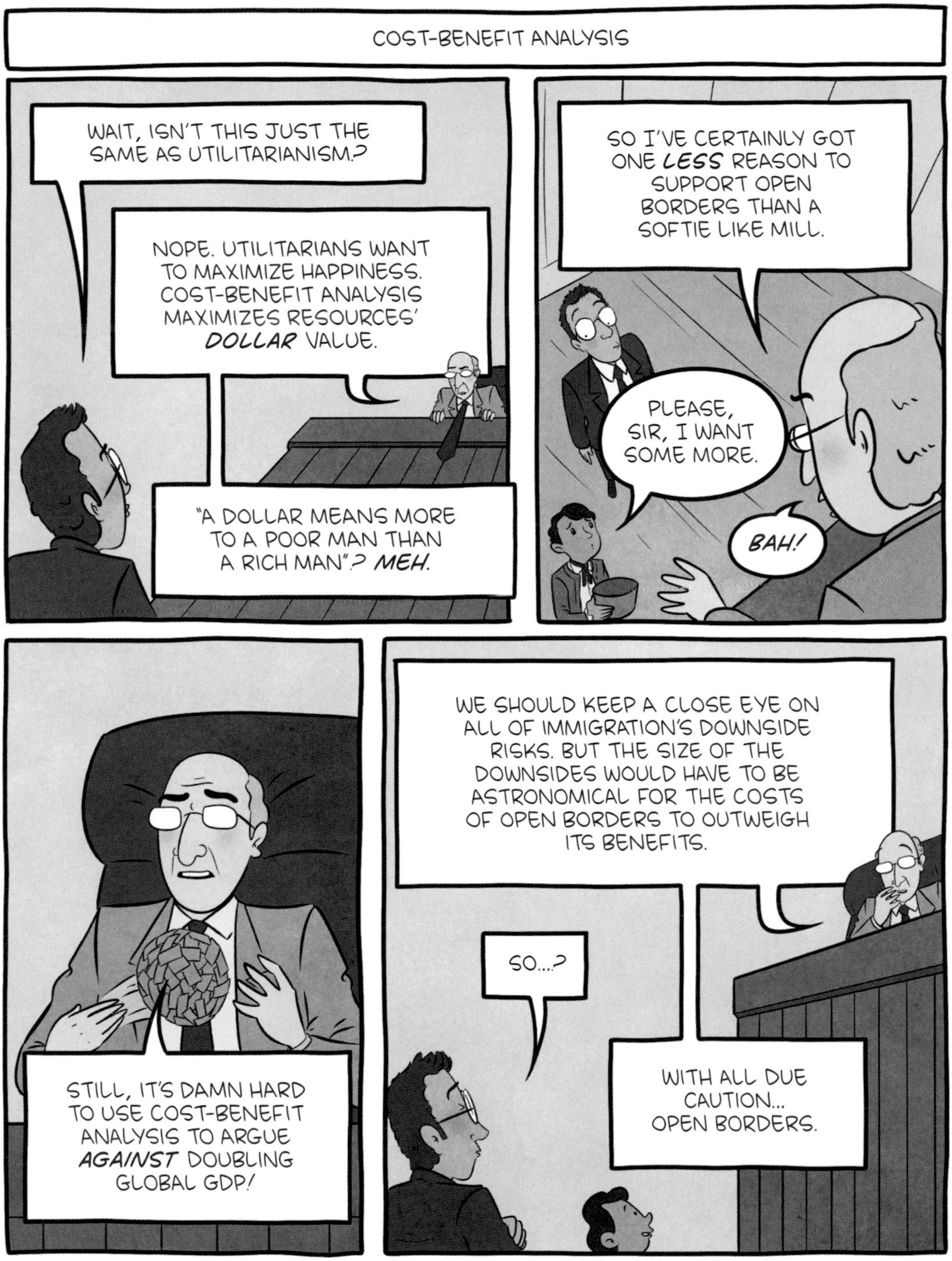
COST-BENEFIT ANALYSIS
WAIT, ISN'T THIS JUST THE SAME AS UTILITARIANISM?
NOPE. UTILITARIANS WANT TO MAXIMIZE HAPPINESS. COST-BENEFIT ANALYSIS MAXIMIZES RESOURCES' *DOLLAR* VALUE.
"A DOLLAR MEANS MORE TO A POOR MAN THAN A RICH MAN"? *MEH.*
SO I'VE CERTAINLY GOT ONE *LESS* REASON TO SUPPORT OPEN BORDERS THAN A SOFTIE LIKE MILL.
PLEASE, SIR, I WANT SOME MORE.
BAH!
STILL, IT'S DAMN HARD TO USE COST-BENEFIT ANALYSIS TO ARGUE *AGAINST* DOUBLING GLOBAL GDP!
WE SHOULD KEEP A CLOSE EYE ON ALL OF IMMIGRATION'S DOWNSIDE RISKS. BUT THE SIZE OF THE DOWNSIDES WOULD HAVE TO BE ASTRONOMICAL FOR THE COSTS OF OPEN BORDERS TO OUTWEIGH ITS BENEFITS.
SO...?
WITH ALL DUE CAUTION... OPEN BORDERS.

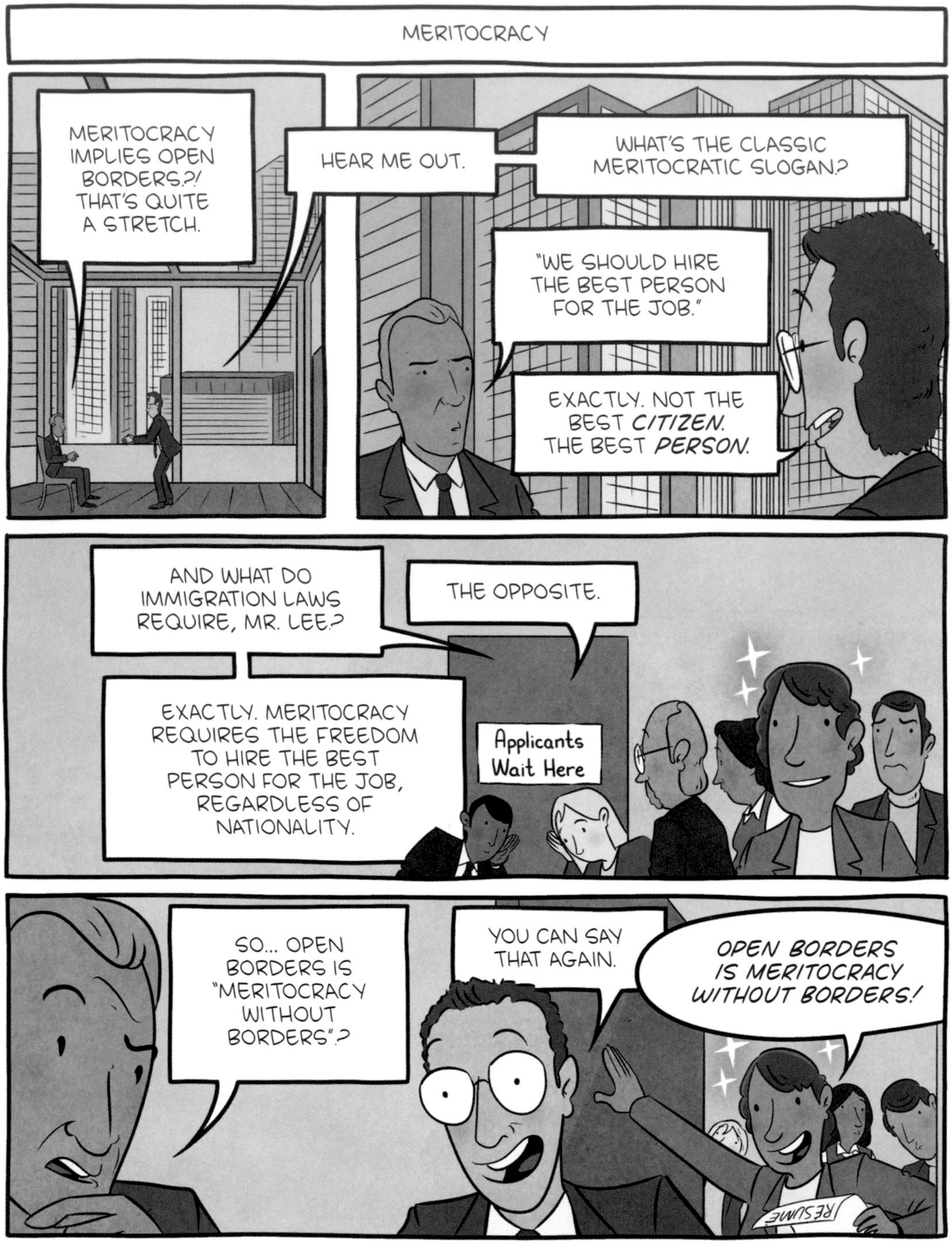
MERITOCRACY
MERITOCRACY IMPLIES OPEN BORDERS?! THAT'S QUITE A STRETCH.
HEAR ME OUT.
WHAT'S THE CLASSIC MERITOCRATIC SLOGAN?
"WE SHOULD HIRE THE BEST PERSON FOR THE JOB."
EXACTLY. NOT THE BEST *CITIZEN*. THE BEST *PERSON*.
AND WHAT DO IMMIGRATION LAWS REQUIRE, MR. LEE?
THE OPPOSITE.
EXACTLY. MERITOCRACY REQUIRES THE FREEDOM TO HIRE THE BEST PERSON FOR THE JOB, REGARDLESS OF NATIONALITY.
Applicants Wait Here
SO... OPEN BORDERS IS "MERITOCRACY WITHOUT BORDERS"?
YOU CAN SAY THAT AGAIN.
OPEN BORDERS IS MERITOCRACY WITHOUT BORDERS!
RESUME

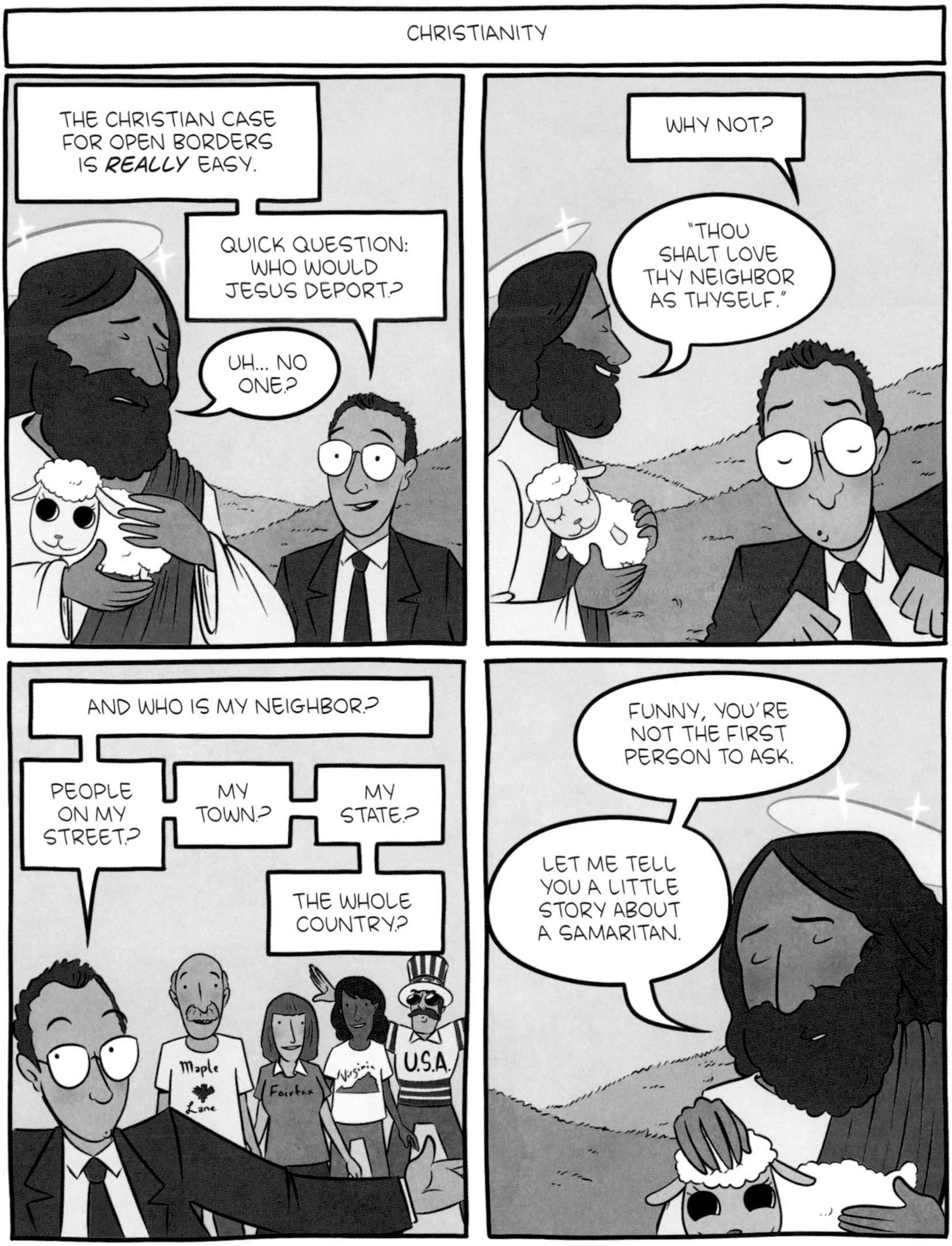
CHRISTIANITY
THE CHRISTIAN CASE FOR OPEN BORDERS IS *REALLY* EASY.
QUICK QUESTION: WHO WOULD JESUS DEPORT?
UH... NO ONE?
WHY NOT?
"THOU SHALT LOVE THY NEIGHBOR AS THYSELF."
AND WHO IS MY NEIGHBOR?
PEOPLE ON MY STREET?
MY TOWN?
MY STATE?
THE WHOLE COUNTRY?
Maple Lane
Fairfax
Virginia
U.S.A.
FUNNY, YOU'RE NOT THE FIRST PERSON TO ASK.
LET ME TELL YOU A LITTLE STORY ABOUT A SAMARITAN.

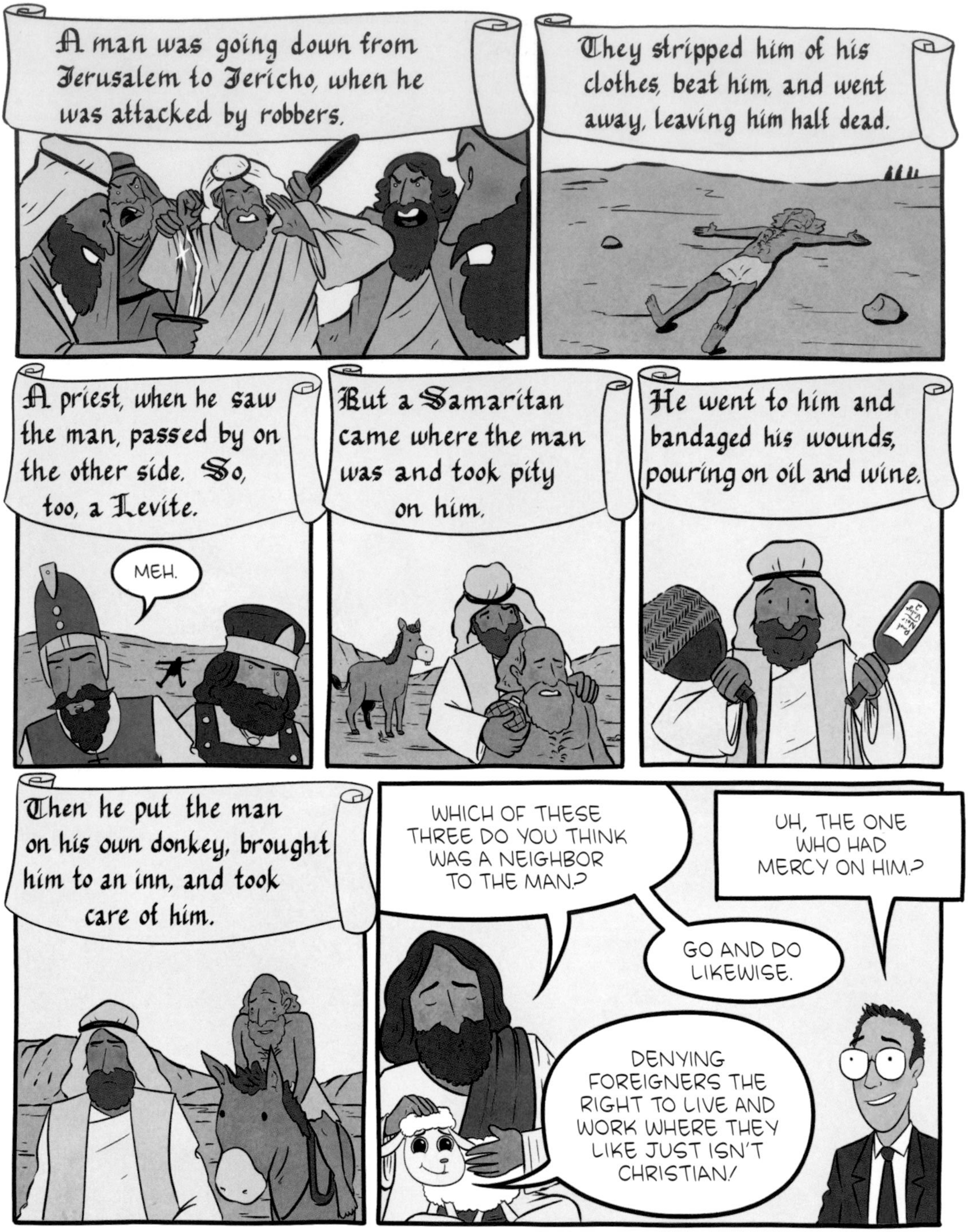
A man was going down from Jerusalem to Jericho, when he was attacked by robbers.
They stripped him of his clothes, beat him, and went away, leaving him half dead.
A priest, when he saw the man, passed by on the other side. So, too, a Levite.
MEH.
But a Samaritan came where the man was and took pity on him.
He went to him and bandaged his wounds, pouring on oil and wine.
Then he put the man on his own donkey, brought him to an inn, and took care of him.
WHICH OF THESE THREE DO YOU THINK WAS A NEIGHBOR TO THE MAN?
UH, THE ONE WHO HAD MERCY ON HIM?
GO AND DO LIKEWISE.
DENYING FOREIGNERS THE RIGHT TO LIVE AND WORK WHERE THEY LIKE JUST ISN'T CHRISTIAN!

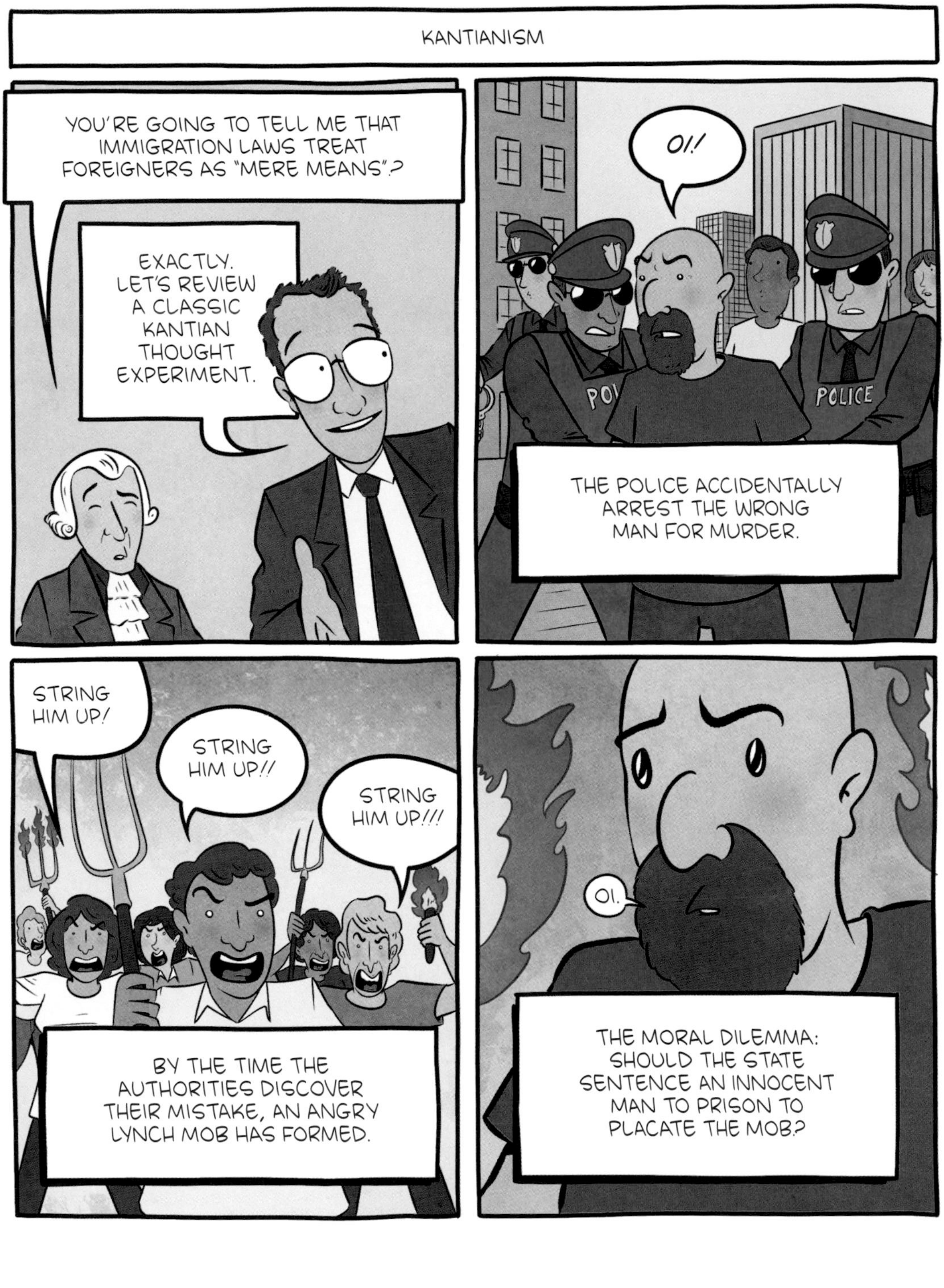
KANTIANISM
YOU'RE GOING TO TELL ME THAT IMMIGRATION LAWS TREAT FOREIGNERS AS "MERE MEANS"?
EXACTLY. LET'S REVIEW A CLASSIC KANTIAN THOUGHT EXPERIMENT.
OI!
POLICE
THE POLICE ACCIDENTALLY ARREST THE WRONG MAN FOR MURDER.
STRING HIM UP!
STRING HIM UP!!
STRING HIM UP!!!
BY THE TIME THE AUTHORITIES DISCOVER THEIR MISTAKE, AN ANGRY LYNCH MOB HAS FORMED.
OI.
THE MORAL DILEMMA: SHOULD THE STATE SENTENCE AN INNOCENT MAN TO PRISON TO PLACATE THE MOB?

I STAND BY THE TEXTBOOK KANTIAN ANSWER:

THE MAN HAS DONE NO WRONG. COME WHAT MAY, THERE IS A MORAL IMPERATIVE *NOT* TO PUNISH HIM.

SUPPOSE THE PUNISHMENT WERE NOT PRISON, BUT BANISHMENT TO THE THIRD WORLD?

IT CHANGES NOTHING. PERSONALLY, I'D RATHER SPEND A FEW YEARS IN JAIL...

THEN HOW CAN IT BE MORALLY PERMISSIBLE TO SO BANISH BILLIONS OF HUMAN BEINGS WHOSE ONLY "CRIME" IS BEING BORN IN THE WRONG COUNTRY?

YOUR ANALOGY IS TROUBLING, BUT NOT FULLY CONVINCING.

COULDN'T YOU JUST AS EASILY ACCUSE ME OF "BANISHING" STRANGERS FROM MY HOUSE?

I KNOW WHERE YOU'RE COMING FROM—AND YOU'RE HARDLY ALONE. CONSERVATIVES ARE ESPECIALLY FOND OF THIS OBJECTION.

TO EVALUATE IT, LET'S RETURN TO MIKE HUEMER'S "STARVING MARVIN" HYPOTHETICAL.

MARVIN TRIES TO BUY FOOD. SAM STOPS HIM. MORALLY SPEAKING, WHAT DO YOU TWO HAVE TO SAY FOR YOURSELVES?

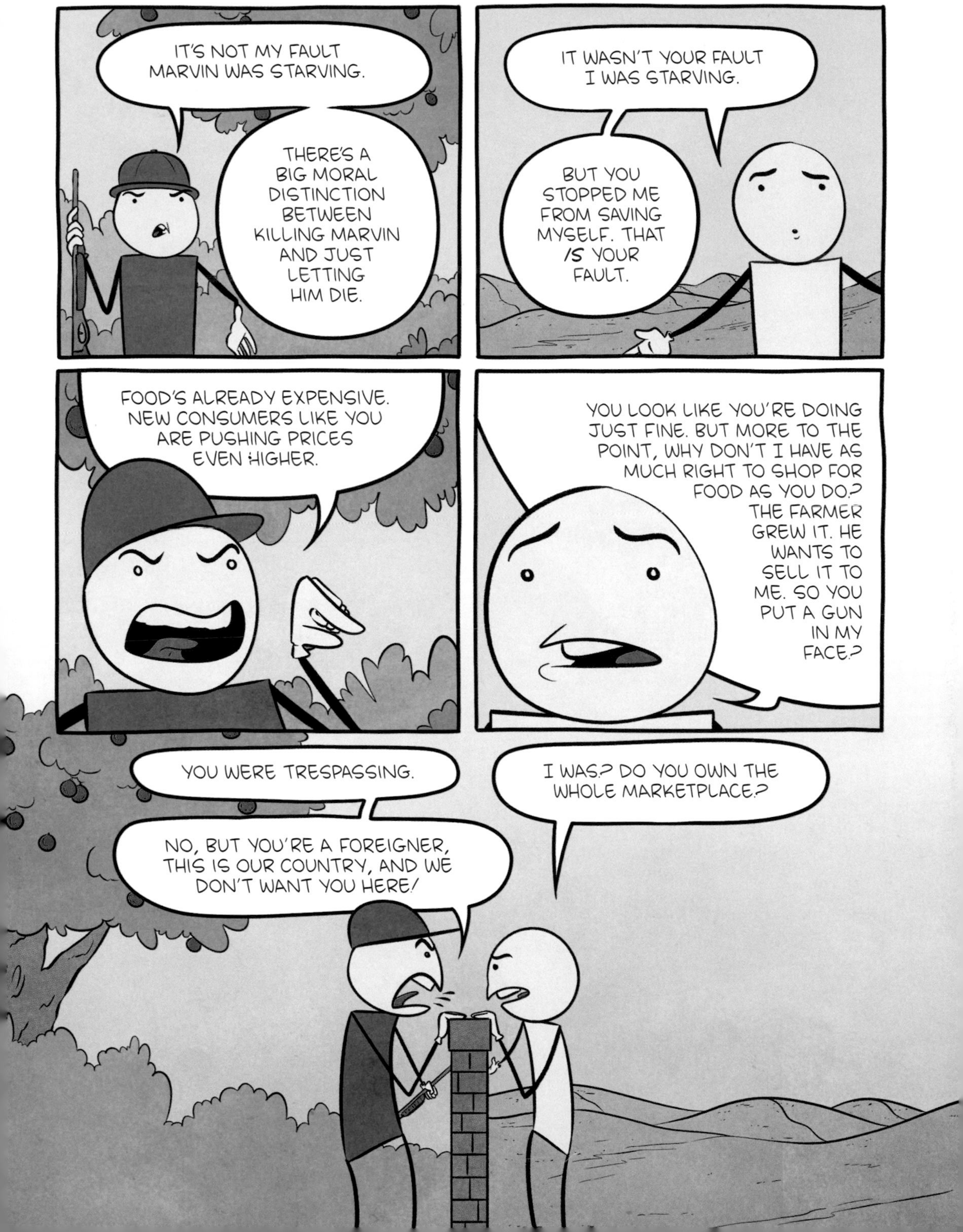
IT'S NOT MY FAULT MARVIN WAS STARVING.
THERE'S A BIG MORAL DISTINCTION BETWEEN KILLING MARVIN AND JUST LETTING HIM DIE.
IT WASN'T YOUR FAULT I WAS STARVING.
BUT YOU STOPPED ME FROM SAVING MYSELF. THAT *IS* YOUR FAULT.
FOOD'S ALREADY EXPENSIVE. NEW CONSUMERS LIKE YOU ARE PUSHING PRICES EVEN HIGHER.
YOU LOOK LIKE YOU'RE DOING JUST FINE. BUT MORE TO THE POINT, WHY DON'T I HAVE AS MUCH RIGHT TO SHOP FOR FOOD AS YOU DO? THE FARMER GREW IT. HE WANTS TO SELL IT TO ME. SO YOU PUT A GUN IN MY FACE?
YOU WERE TRESPASSING.
I WAS? DO YOU OWN THE WHOLE MARKETPLACE?
NO, BUT YOU'RE A FOREIGNER, THIS IS OUR COUNTRY, AND WE DON'T WANT YOU HERE!

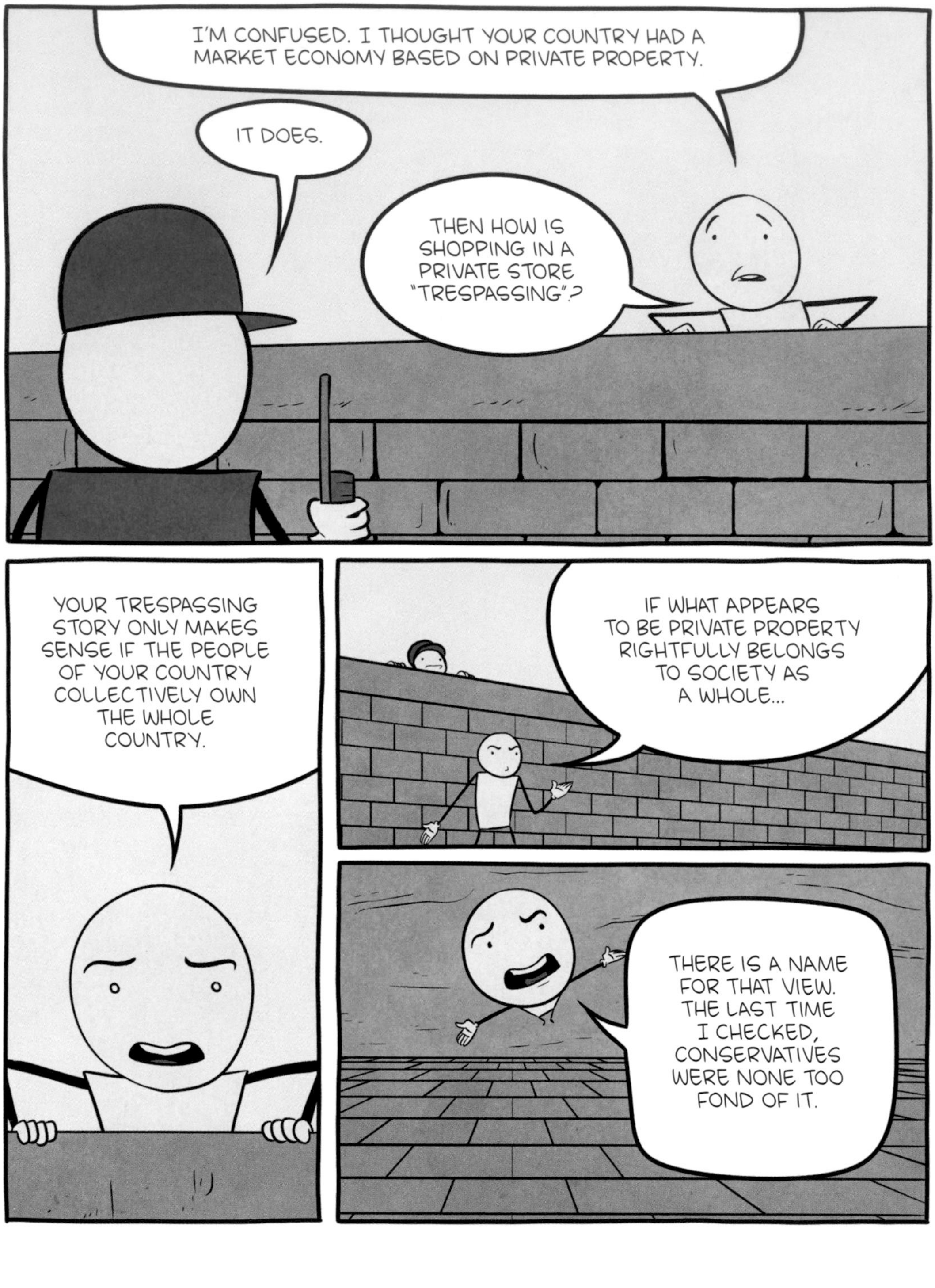
I'M CONFUSED. I THOUGHT YOUR COUNTRY HAD A MARKET ECONOMY BASED ON PRIVATE PROPERTY.
IT DOES.
THEN HOW IS SHOPPING IN A PRIVATE STORE "TRESPASSING"?
YOUR TRESPASSING STORY ONLY MAKES SENSE IF THE PEOPLE OF YOUR COUNTRY COLLECTIVELY OWN THE WHOLE COUNTRY.
IF WHAT APPEARS TO BE PRIVATE PROPERTY RIGHTFULLY BELONGS TO SOCIETY AS A WHOLE...
THERE IS A NAME FOR THAT VIEW. THE LAST TIME I CHECKED, CONSERVATIVES WERE NONE TOO FOND OF IT.

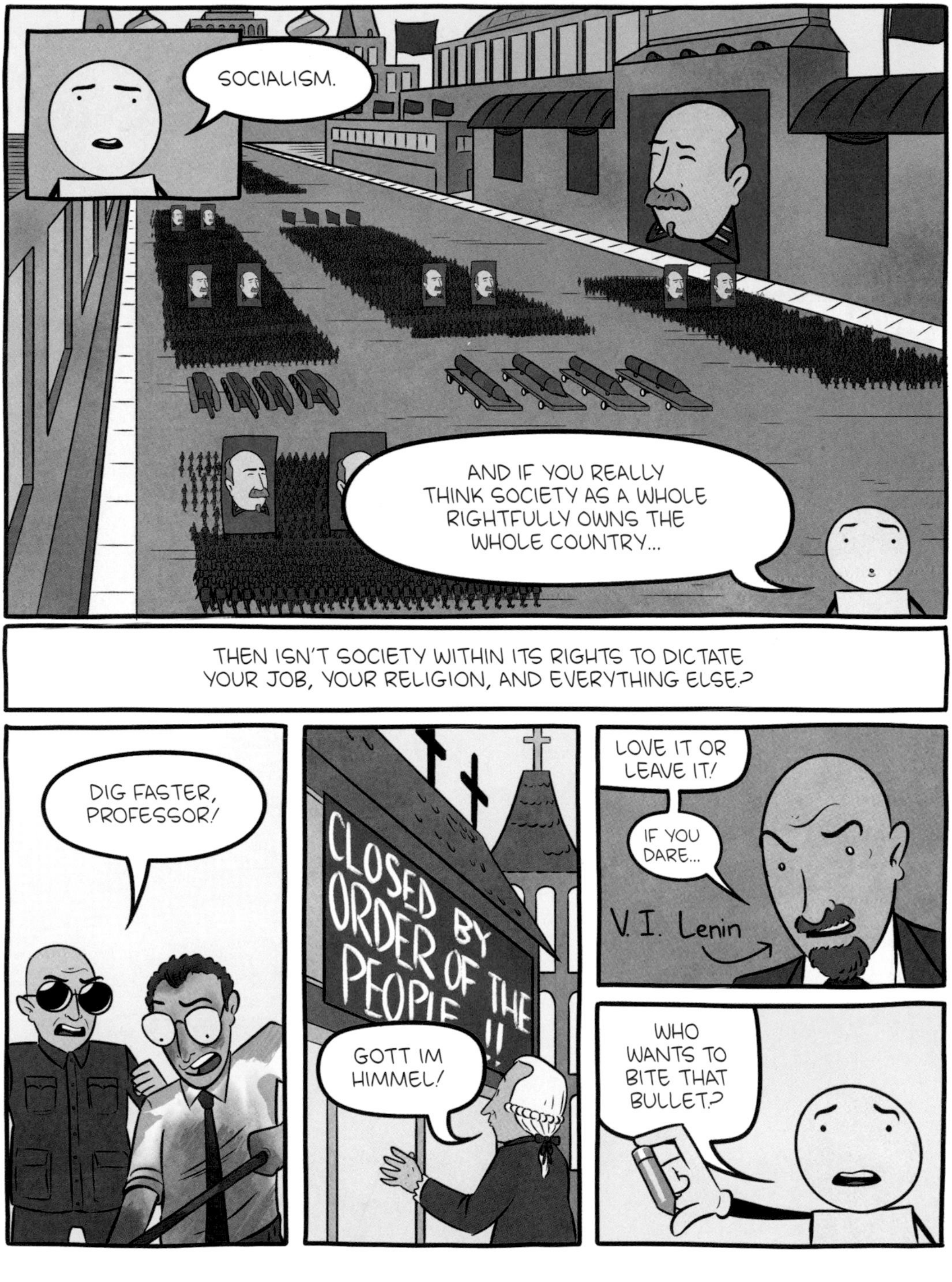
SOCIALISM.
AND IF YOU REALLY THINK SOCIETY AS A WHOLE RIGHTFULLY OWNS THE WHOLE COUNTRY...
THEN ISN'T SOCIETY WITHIN ITS RIGHTS TO DICTATE YOUR JOB, YOUR RELIGION, AND EVERYTHING ELSE?
DIG FASTER, PROFESSOR!
CLOSED BY ORDER OF THE PEOPLE!!
GOTT IM HIMMEL!
LOVE IT OR LEAVE IT!
IF YOU DARE...
V. I. Lenin
WHO WANTS TO BITE THAT BULLET?

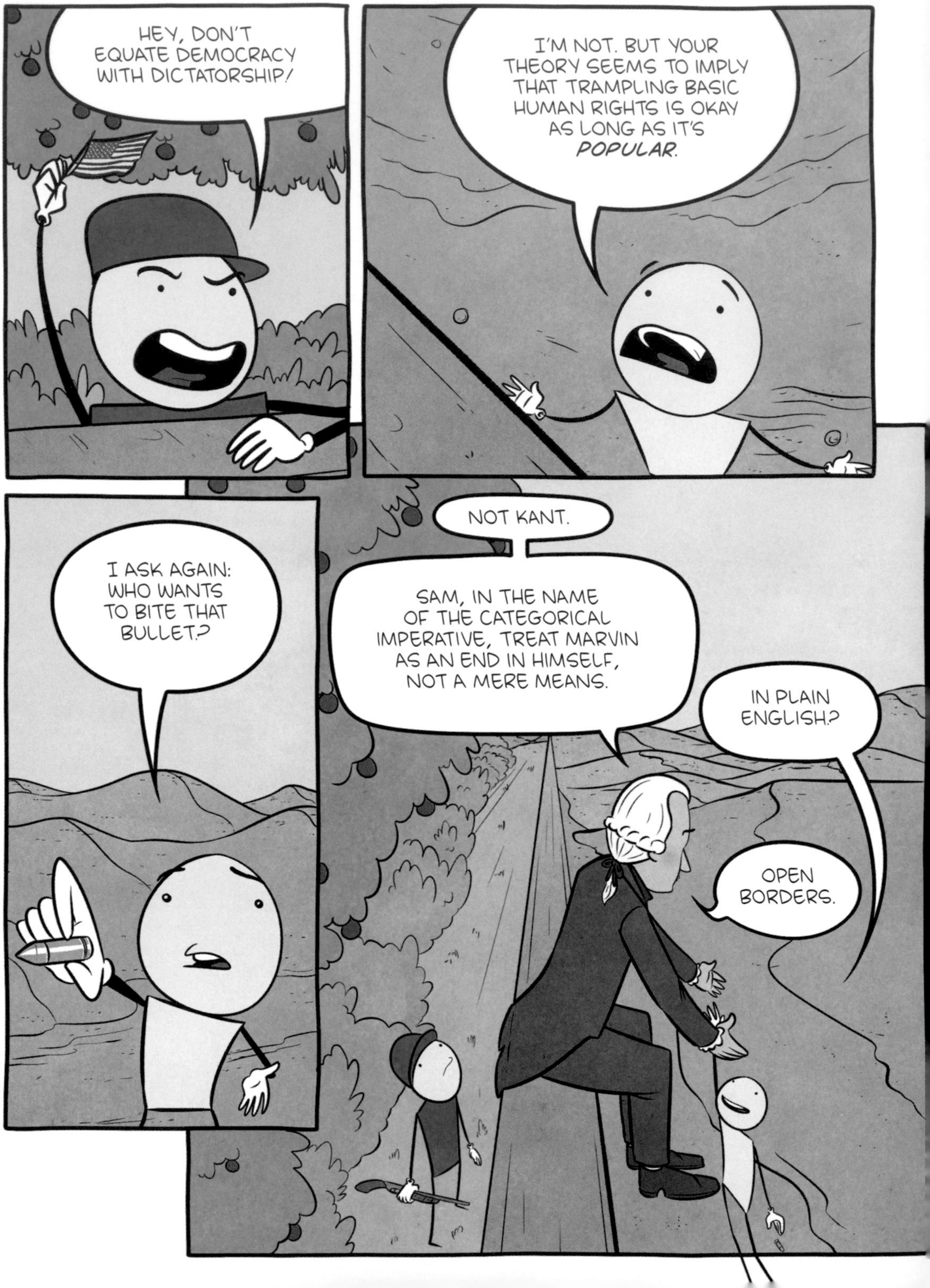
HEY, DON'T EQUATE DEMOCRACY WITH DICTATORSHIP!
I'M NOT. BUT YOUR THEORY SEEMS TO IMPLY THAT TRAMPLING BASIC HUMAN RIGHTS IS OKAY AS LONG AS IT'S *POPULAR*.
I ASK AGAIN: WHO WANTS TO BITE THAT BULLET?
NOT KANT.
SAM, IN THE NAME OF THE CATEGORICAL IMPERATIVE, TREAT MARVIN AS AN END IN HIMSELF, NOT A MERE MEANS.
IN PLAIN ENGLISH?
OPEN BORDERS.

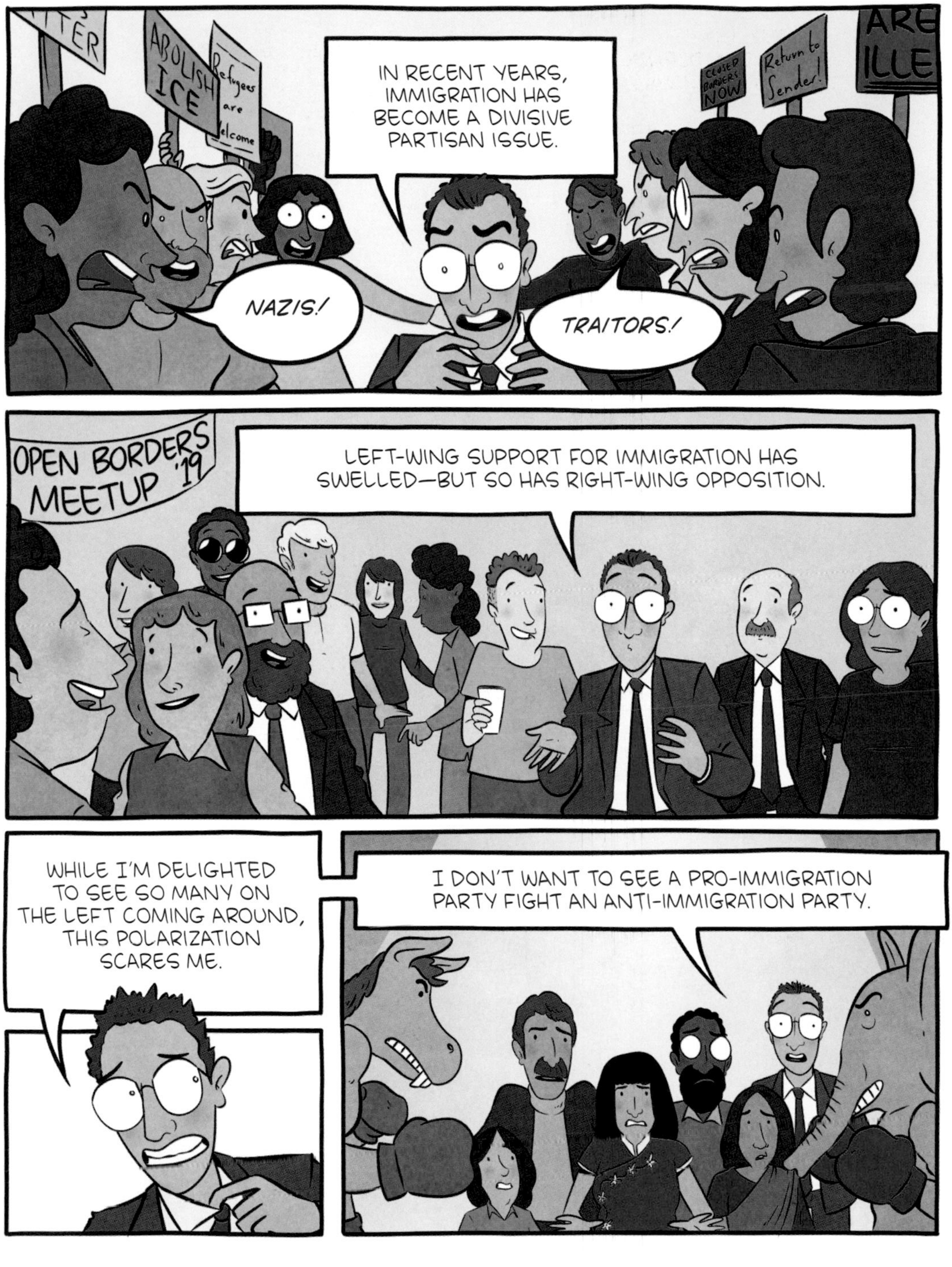

ABOLISH ICE
Refugees are Welcome
CLOSED BORDERS NOW!
Return to Sender!
IN RECENT YEARS, IMMIGRATION HAS BECOME A DIVISIVE PARTISAN ISSUE.
NAZIS!
TRAITORS!
OPEN BORDERS MEETUP '19
LEFT-WING SUPPORT FOR IMMIGRATION HAS SWELLED—BUT SO HAS RIGHT-WING OPPOSITION.
WHILE I'M DELIGHTED TO SEE SO MANY ON THE LEFT COMING AROUND, THIS POLARIZATION SCARES ME.
I DON'T WANT TO SEE A PRO-IMMIGRATION PARTY FIGHT AN ANTI-IMMIGRATION PARTY.

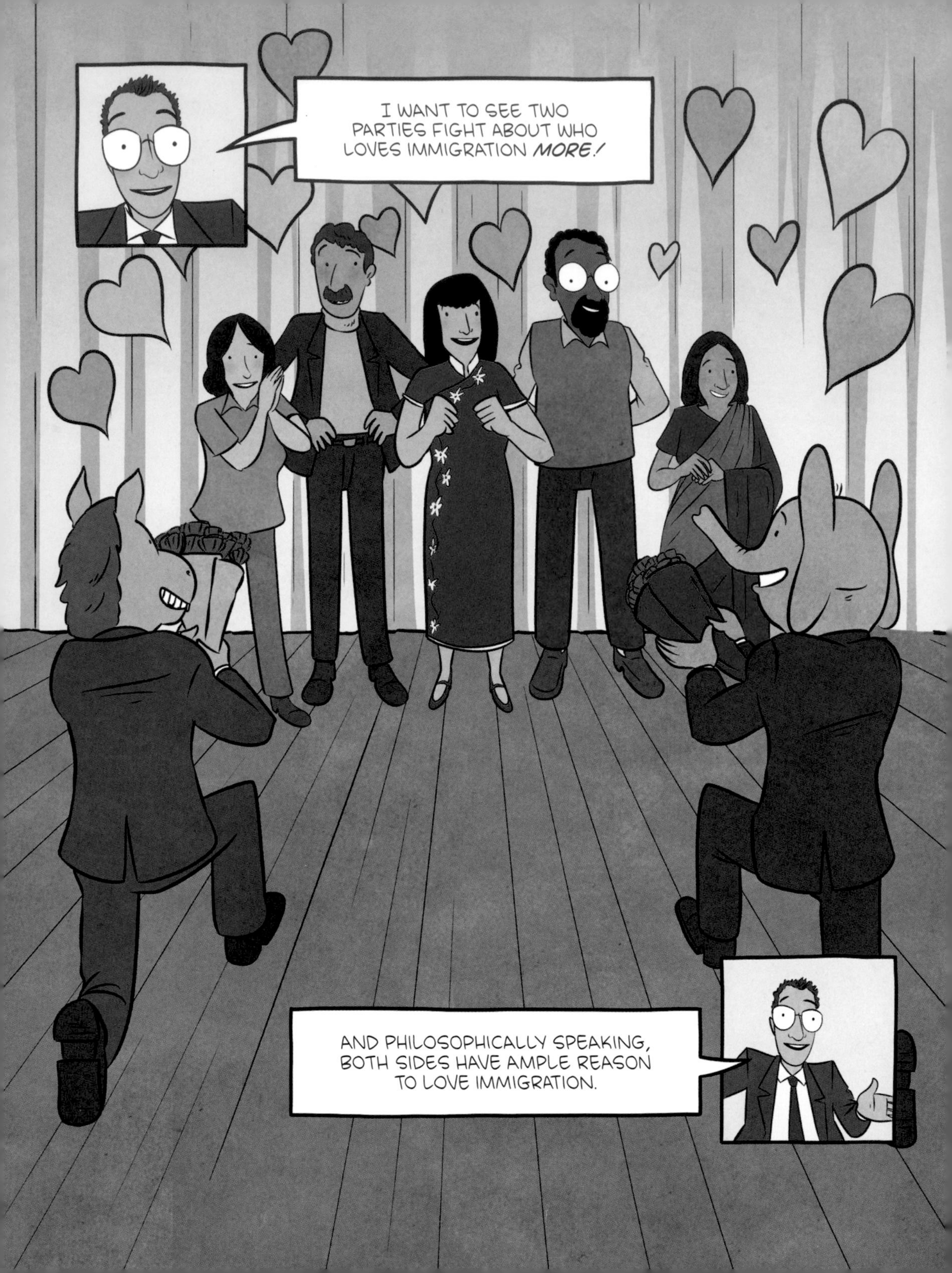
I WANT TO SEE TWO PARTIES FIGHT ABOUT WHO LOVES IMMIGRATION *MORE!*
AND PHILOSOPHICALLY SPEAKING, BOTH SIDES HAVE AMPLE REASON TO LOVE IMMIGRATION.

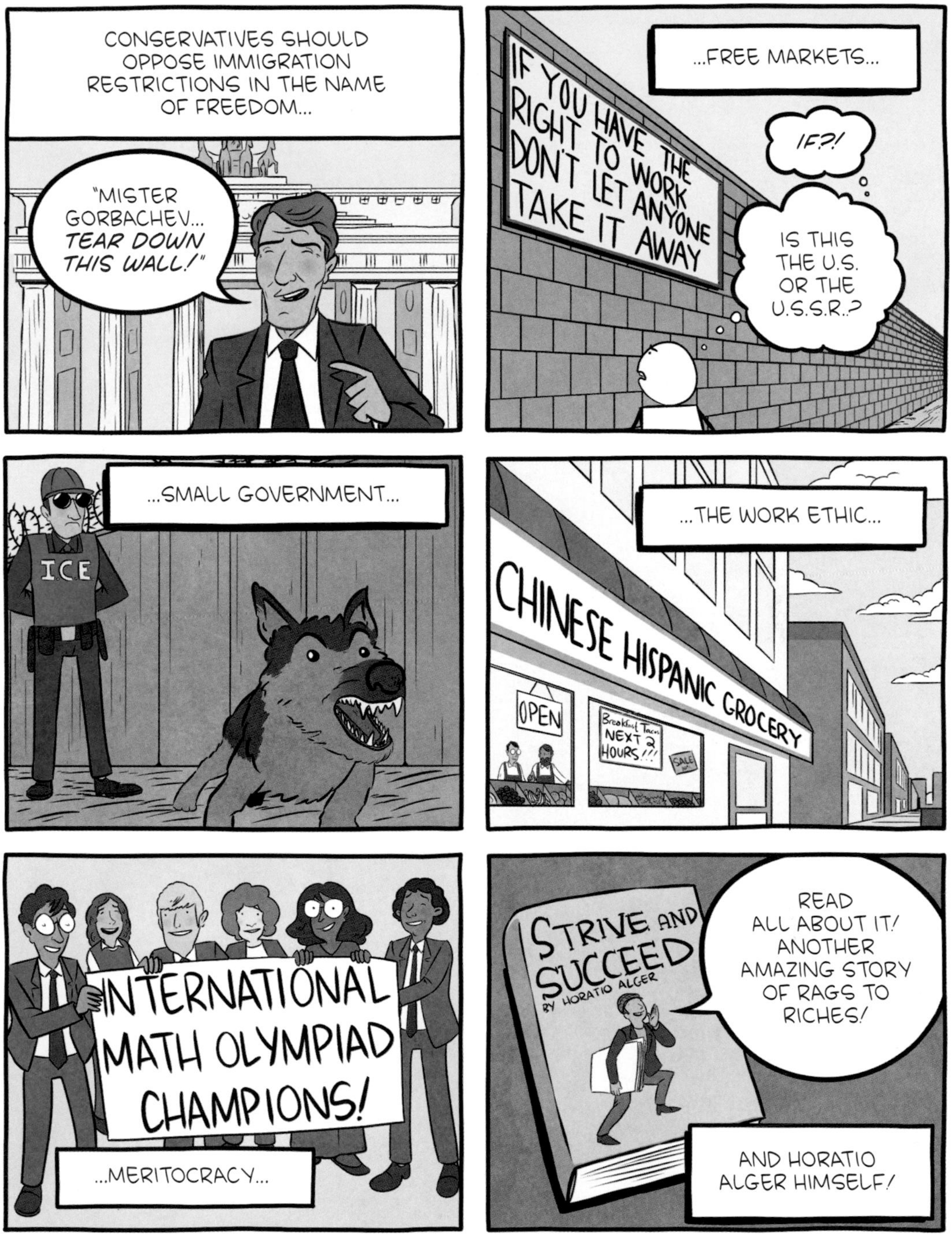
CONSERVATIVES SHOULD OPPOSE IMMIGRATION RESTRICTIONS IN THE NAME OF FREEDOM...
"MISTER GORBACHEV... *TEAR DOWN THIS WALL!*"
...FREE MARKETS...
IF YOU HAVE THE RIGHT TO WORK DON'T LET ANYONE TAKE IT AWAY
IF?!
IS THIS THE U.S. OR THE U.S.S.R.?
...SMALL GOVERNMENT...
ICE
...THE WORK ETHIC...
CHINESE HISPANIC GROCERY
OPEN
Breakfast Tacos NEXT 2 HOURS!!!
SALE
INTERNATIONAL MATH OLYMPIAD CHAMPIONS!
...MERITOCRACY...
STRIVE AND SUCCEED
BY HORATIO ALGER
READ ALL ABOUT IT! ANOTHER AMAZING STORY OF RAGS TO RICHES!
AND HORATIO ALGER HIMSELF!

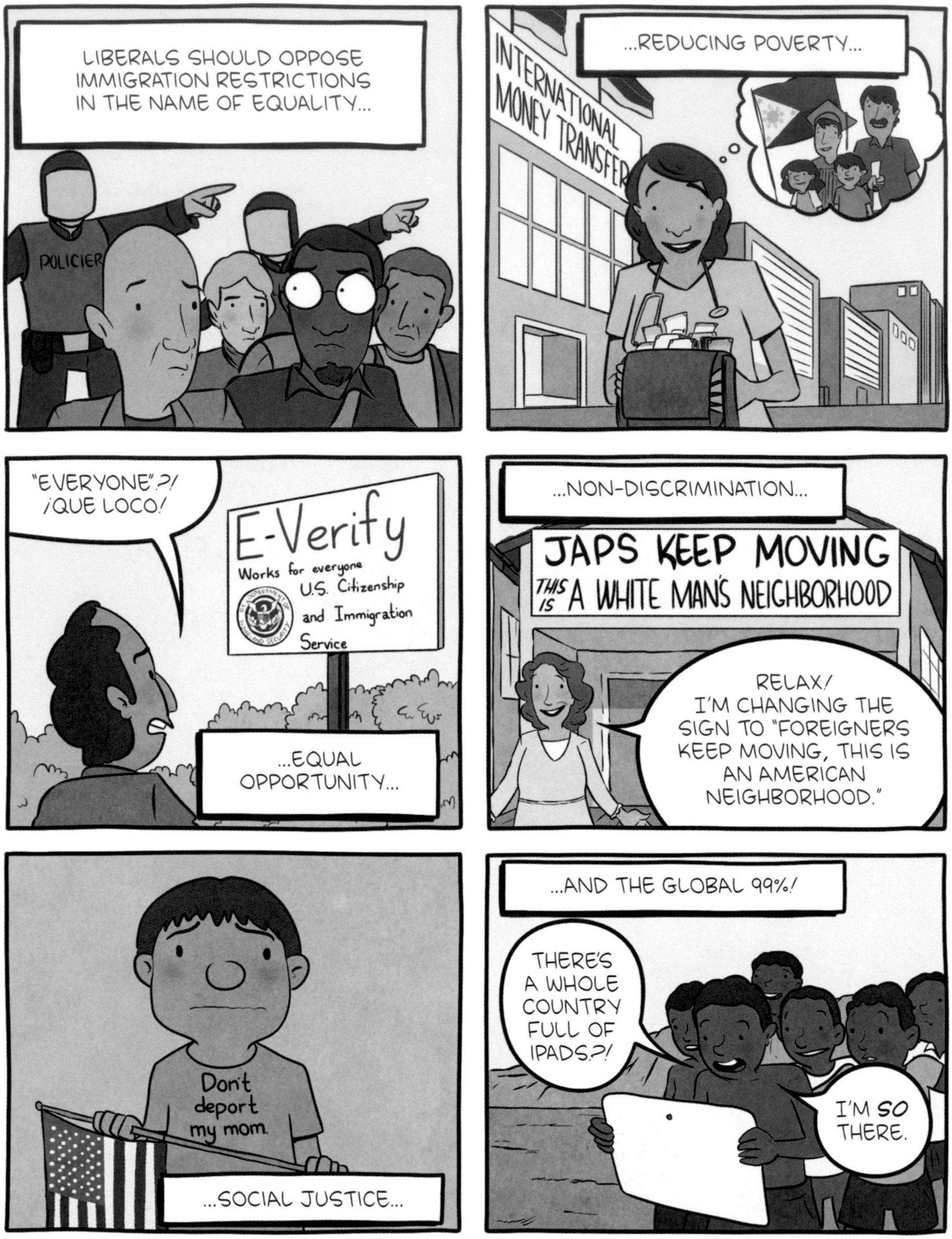
LIBERALS SHOULD OPPOSE IMMIGRATION RESTRICTIONS IN THE NAME OF EQUALITY...
POLICIER
...REDUCING POVERTY...
INTERNATIONAL MONEY TRANSFER
"EVERYONE"?! ¡QUE LOCO!
E-Verify
Works for everyone
U.S. Citizenship and Immigration Service
...EQUAL OPPORTUNITY...
...NON-DISCRIMINATION...
JAPS KEEP MOVING
THIS IS A WHITE MAN'S NEIGHBORHOOD
RELAX! I'M CHANGING THE SIGN TO "FOREIGNERS KEEP MOVING, THIS IS AN AMERICAN NEIGHBORHOOD."
Don't deport my mom.
...SOCIAL JUSTICE...
...AND THE GLOBAL 99%!
THERE'S A WHOLE COUNTRY FULL OF IPADS?!
I'M SO THERE.

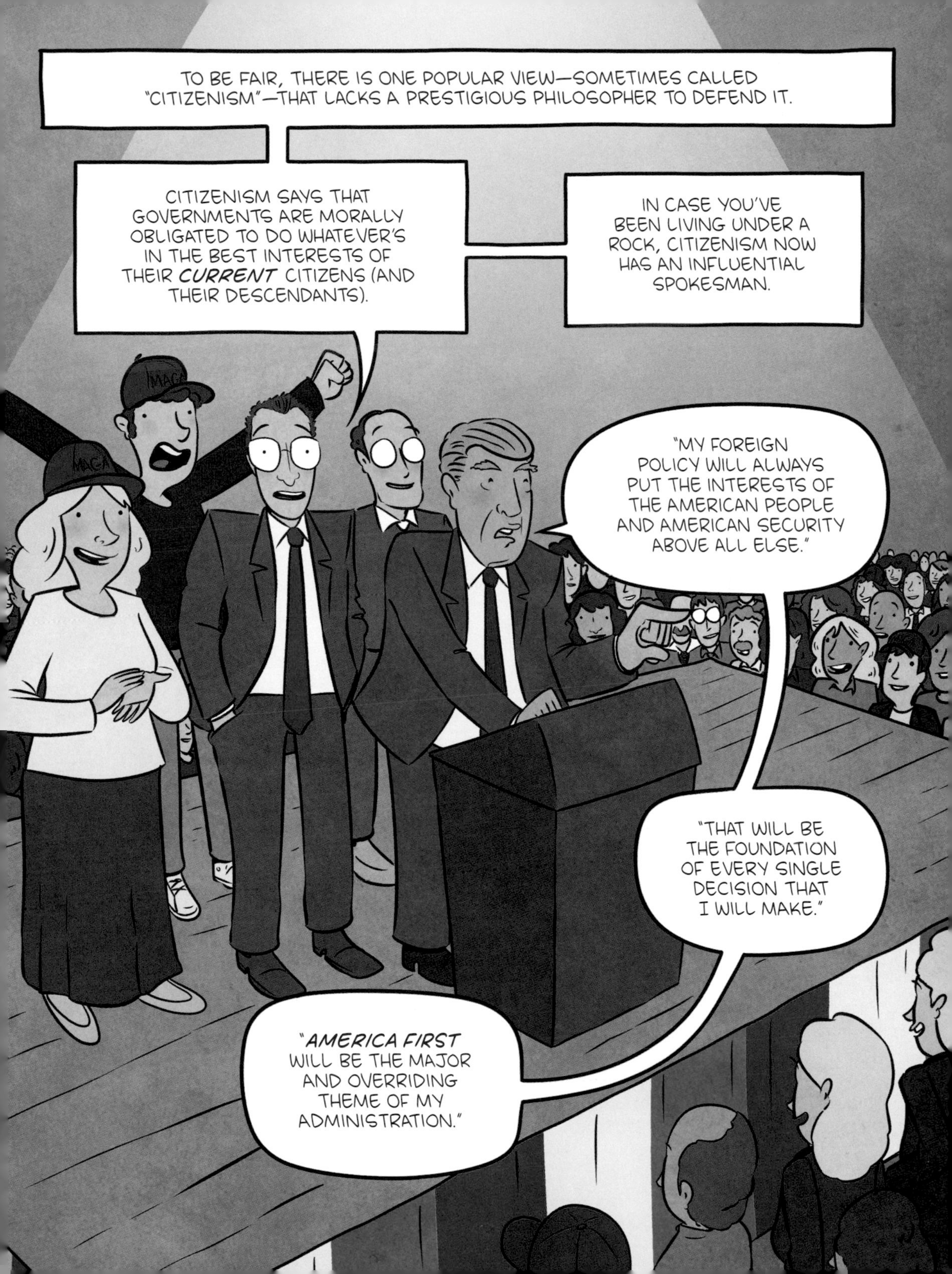
TO BE FAIR, THERE IS ONE POPULAR VIEW—SOMETIMES CALLED "CITIZENISM"—THAT LACKS A PRESTIGIOUS PHILOSOPHER TO DEFEND IT.
CITIZENISM SAYS THAT GOVERNMENTS ARE MORALLY OBLIGATED TO DO WHATEVER'S IN THE BEST INTERESTS OF THEIR *CURRENT* CITIZENS (AND THEIR DESCENDANTS).
IN CASE YOU'VE BEEN LIVING UNDER A ROCK, CITIZENISM NOW HAS AN INFLUENTIAL SPOKESMAN.
"MY FOREIGN POLICY WILL ALWAYS PUT THE INTERESTS OF THE AMERICAN PEOPLE AND AMERICAN SECURITY ABOVE ALL ELSE."
"THAT WILL BE THE FOUNDATION OF EVERY SINGLE DECISION THAT I WILL MAKE."
"*AMERICA FIRST* WILL BE THE MAJOR AND OVERRIDING THEME OF MY ADMINISTRATION."

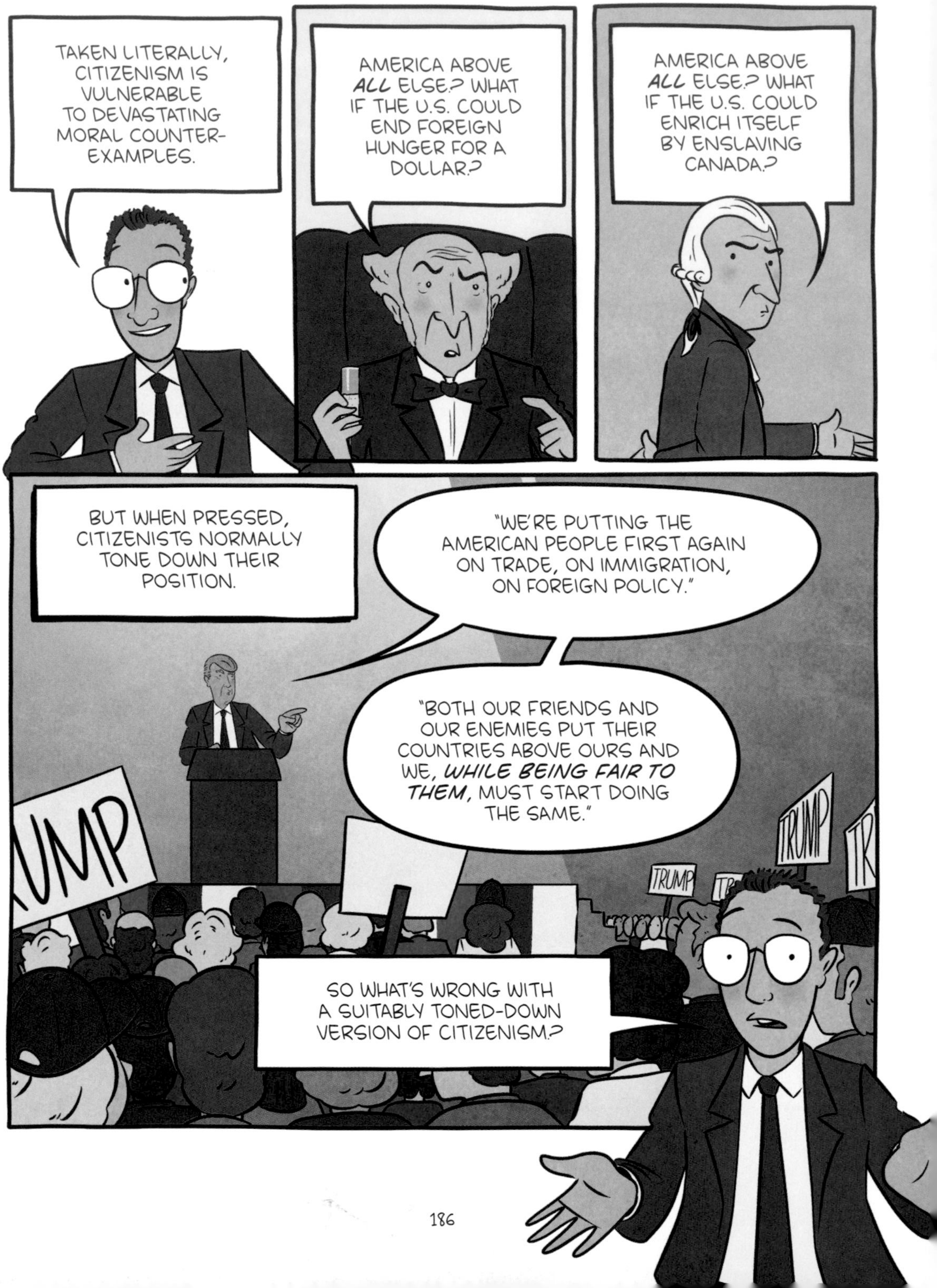
TAKEN LITERALLY, CITIZENISM IS VULNERABLE TO DEVASTATING MORAL COUNTER-EXAMPLES.
AMERICA ABOVE ALL ELSE? WHAT IF THE U.S. COULD END FOREIGN HUNGER FOR A DOLLAR?
AMERICA ABOVE ALL ELSE? WHAT IF THE U.S. COULD ENRICH ITSELF BY ENSLAVING CANADA?
BUT WHEN PRESSED, CITIZENISTS NORMALLY TONE DOWN THEIR POSITION.
"WE'RE PUTTING THE AMERICAN PEOPLE FIRST AGAIN ON TRADE, ON IMMIGRATION, ON FOREIGN POLICY."
"BOTH OUR FRIENDS AND OUR ENEMIES PUT THEIR COUNTRIES ABOVE OURS AND WE, WHILE BEING FAIR TO THEM, MUST START DOING THE SAME."
RUMP
TRUMP
TRUMP
TR
SO WHAT'S WRONG WITH A SUITABLY TONED-DOWN VERSION OF CITIZENISM?

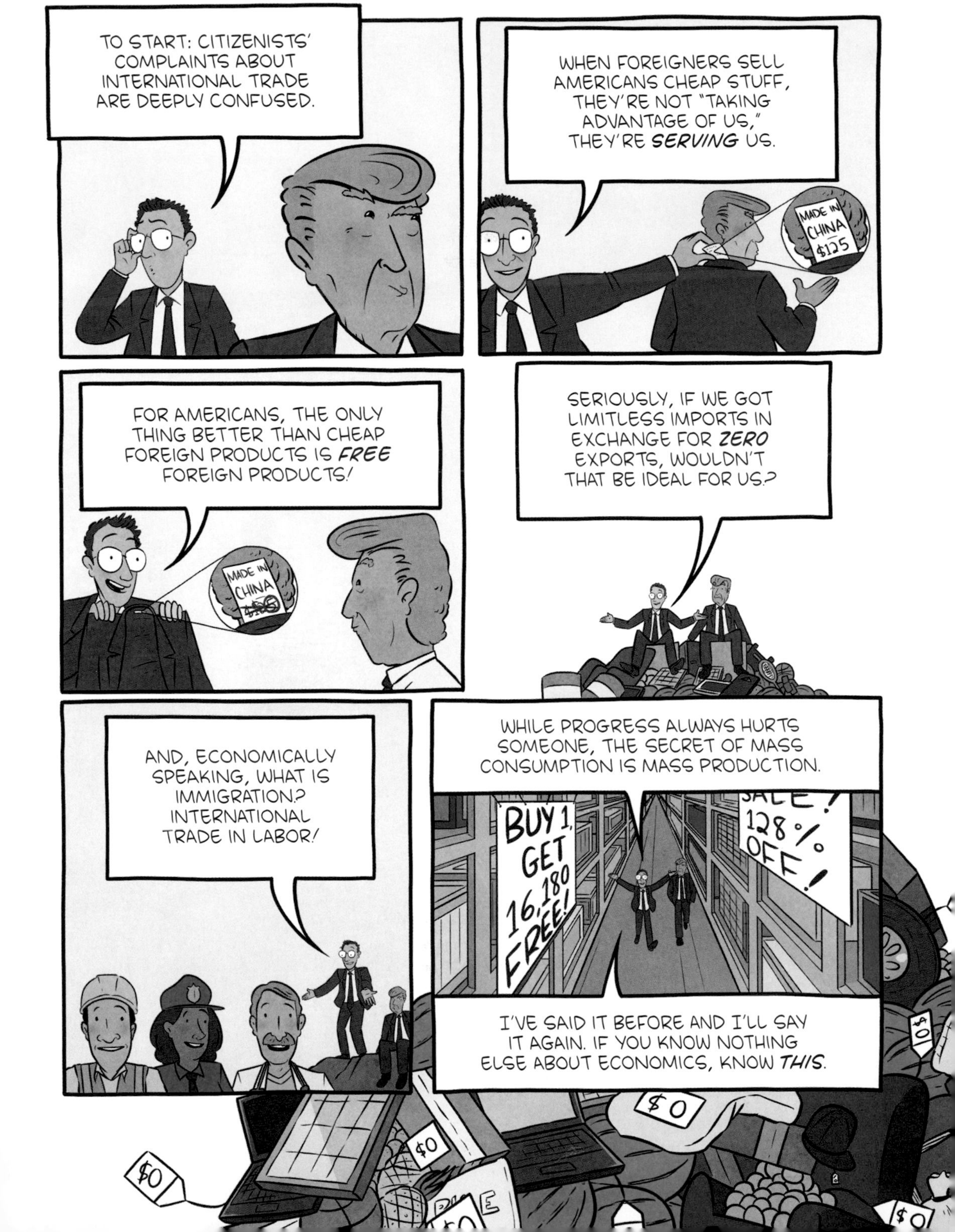
TO START: CITIZENISTS' COMPLAINTS ABOUT INTERNATIONAL TRADE ARE DEEPLY CONFUSED.
WHEN FOREIGNERS SELL AMERICANS CHEAP STUFF, THEY'RE NOT "TAKING ADVANTAGE OF US," THEY'RE *SERVING* US.
MADE IN CHINA $125
FOR AMERICANS, THE ONLY THING BETTER THAN CHEAP FOREIGN PRODUCTS IS *FREE* FOREIGN PRODUCTS!
MADE IN CHINA
SERIOUSLY, IF WE GOT LIMITLESS IMPORTS IN EXCHANGE FOR *ZERO* EXPORTS, WOULDN'T THAT BE IDEAL FOR US?
AND, ECONOMICALLY SPEAKING, WHAT IS IMMIGRATION? INTERNATIONAL TRADE IN LABOR!
WHILE PROGRESS ALWAYS HURTS SOMEONE, THE SECRET OF MASS CONSUMPTION IS MASS PRODUCTION.
BUY 1, GET 16,180 FREE!
128% OFF!
I'VE SAID IT BEFORE AND I'LL SAY IT AGAIN. IF YOU KNOW NOTHING ELSE ABOUT ECONOMICS, KNOW *THIS*.
$0
$0
$0
$0

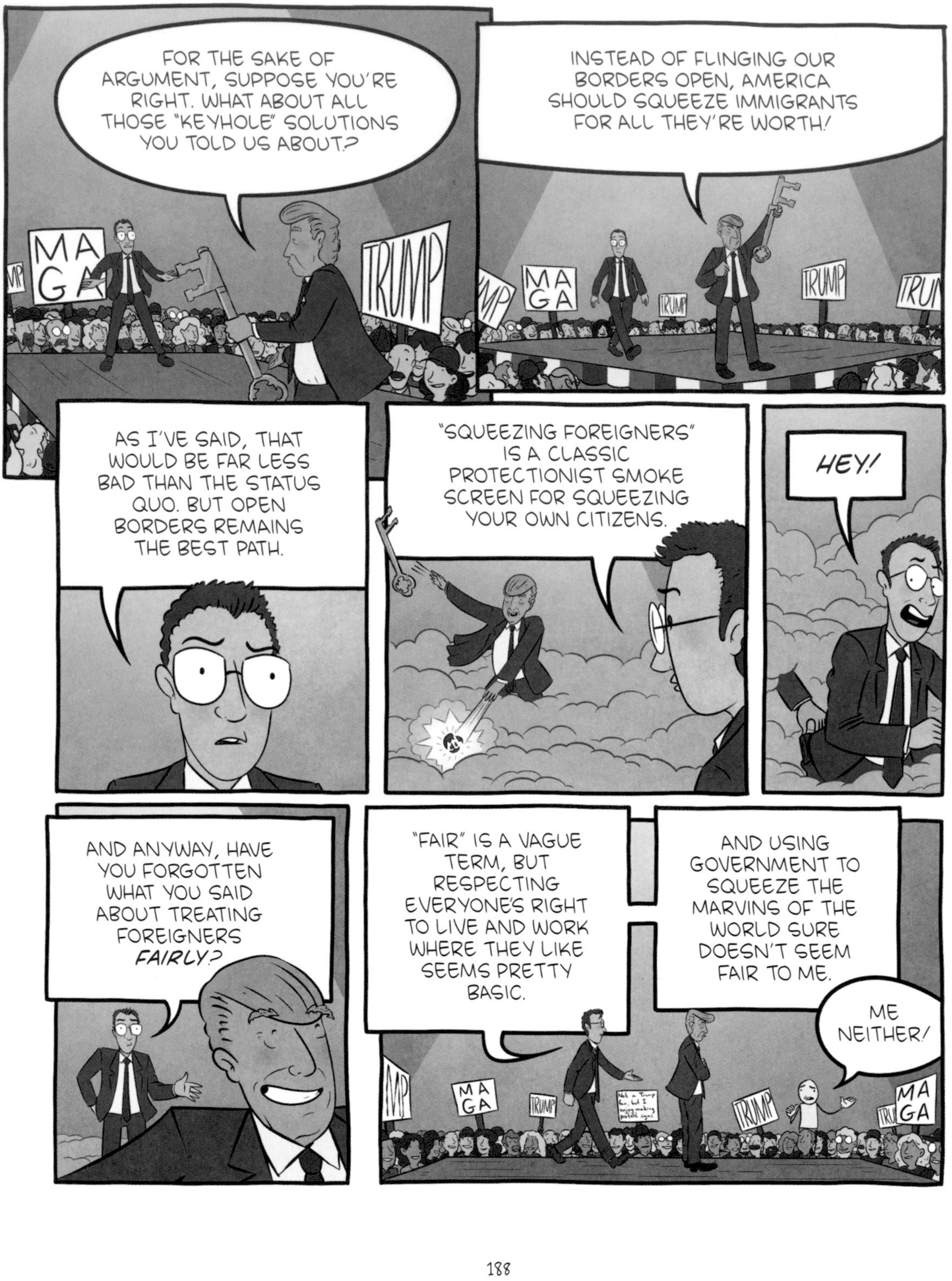
FOR THE SAKE OF ARGUMENT, SUPPOSE YOU'RE RIGHT. WHAT ABOUT ALL THOSE "KEYHOLE" SOLUTIONS YOU TOLD US ABOUT?
MA GA
TRUMP
INSTEAD OF FLINGING OUR BORDERS OPEN, AMERICA SHOULD SQUEEZE IMMIGRANTS FOR ALL THEY'RE WORTH!
AS I'VE SAID, THAT WOULD BE FAR LESS BAD THAN THE STATUS QUO. BUT OPEN BORDERS REMAINS THE BEST PATH.
"SQUEEZING FOREIGNERS" IS A CLASSIC PROTECTIONIST SMOKE SCREEN FOR SQUEEZING YOUR OWN CITIZENS.
HEY!
AND ANYWAY, HAVE YOU FORGOTTEN WHAT YOU SAID ABOUT TREATING FOREIGNERS *FAIRLY*?
"FAIR" IS A VAGUE TERM, BUT RESPECTING EVERYONE'S RIGHT TO LIVE AND WORK WHERE THEY LIKE SEEMS PRETTY BASIC.
AND USING GOVERNMENT TO SQUEEZE THE MARVINS OF THE WORLD SURE DOESN'T SEEM FAIR TO ME.
ME NEITHER!

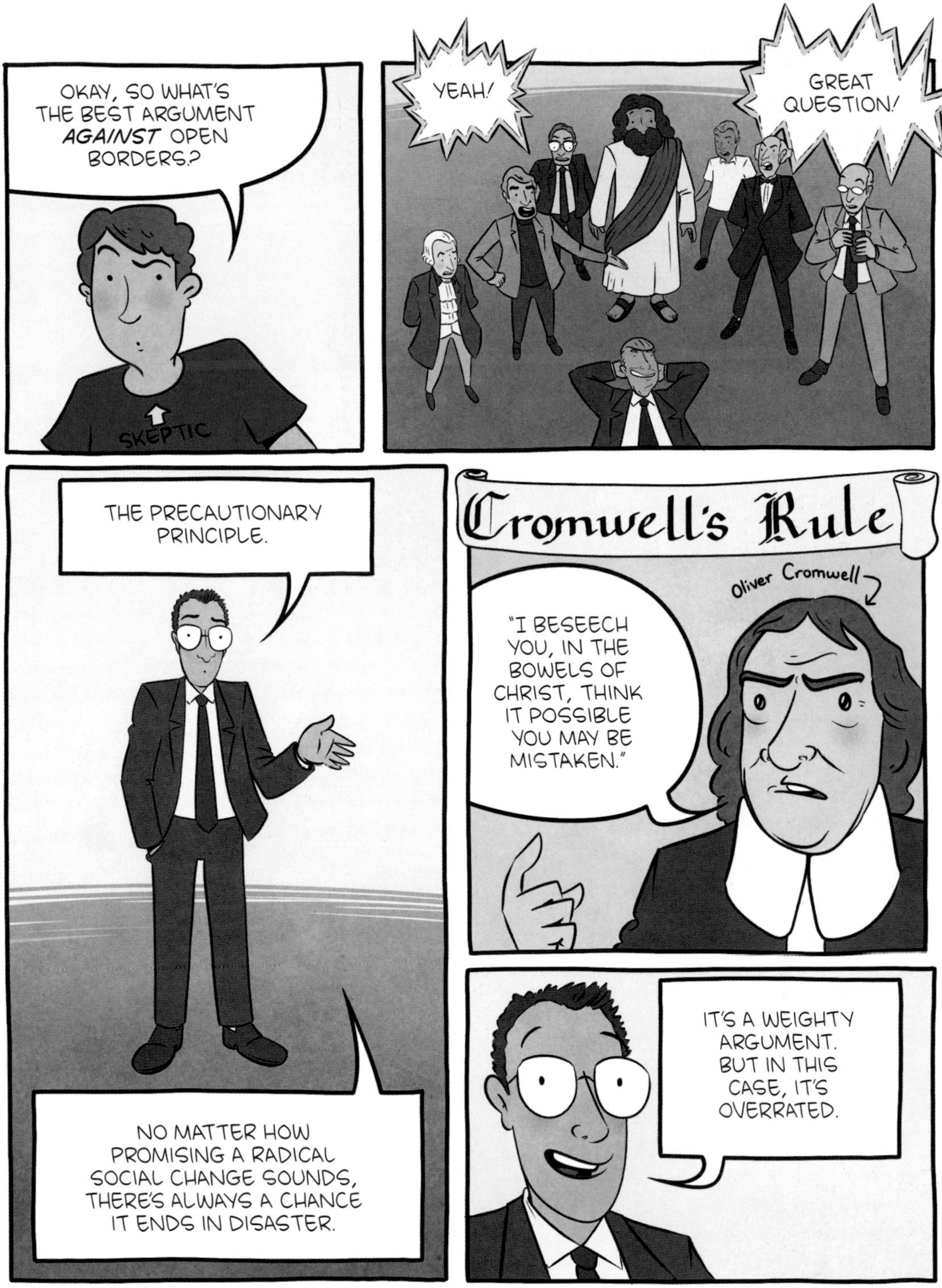
OKAY, SO WHAT'S THE BEST ARGUMENT AGAINST OPEN BORDERS?
SKEPTIC
YEAH!
GREAT QUESTION!
THE PRECAUTIONARY PRINCIPLE.
NO MATTER HOW PROMISING A RADICAL SOCIAL CHANGE SOUNDS, THERE'S ALWAYS A CHANCE IT ENDS IN DISASTER.
Cromwell's Rule
Oliver Cromwell
"I BESEECH YOU, IN THE BOWELS OF CHRIST, THINK IT POSSIBLE YOU MAY BE MISTAKEN."
IT'S A WEIGHTY ARGUMENT. BUT IN THIS CASE, IT'S OVERRATED.

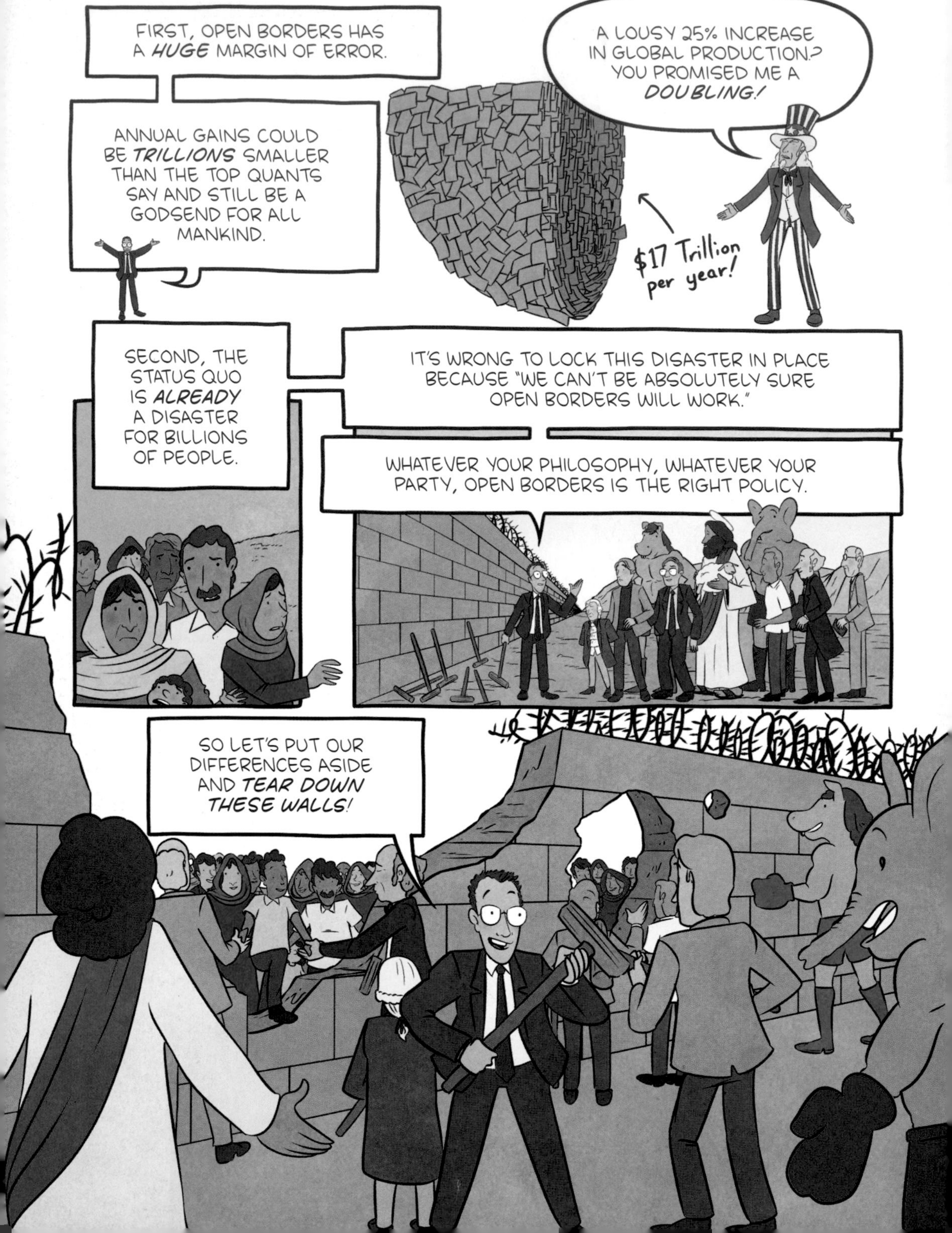
FIRST, OPEN BORDERS HAS A *HUGE* MARGIN OF ERROR.
ANNUAL GAINS COULD BE *TRILLIONS* SMALLER THAN THE TOP QUANTS SAY AND STILL BE A GODSEND FOR ALL MANKIND.
A LOUSY 25% INCREASE IN GLOBAL PRODUCTION? YOU PROMISED ME A *DOUBLING!*
$17 Trillion per year!
SECOND, THE STATUS QUO IS *ALREADY* A DISASTER FOR BILLIONS OF PEOPLE.
IT'S WRONG TO LOCK THIS DISASTER IN PLACE BECAUSE "WE CAN'T BE ABSOLUTELY SURE OPEN BORDERS WILL WORK."
WHATEVER YOUR PHILOSOPHY, WHATEVER YOUR PARTY, OPEN BORDERS IS THE RIGHT POLICY.
SO LET'S PUT OUR DIFFERENCES ASIDE AND *TEAR DOWN THESE WALLS!*

CHAPTER 8

FANTASTIC JOURNEYS...

...AND HOW TO FINISH THEM

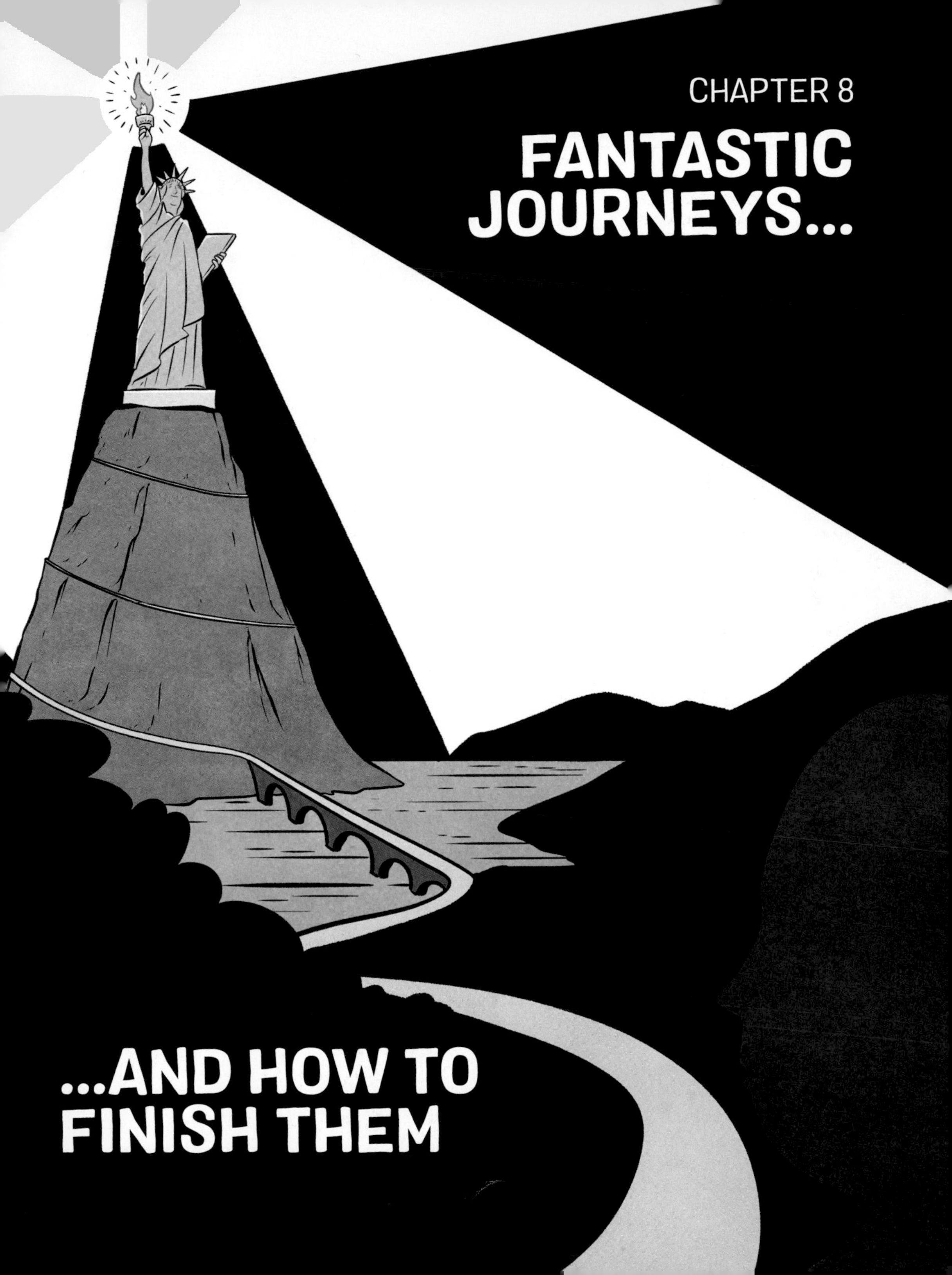

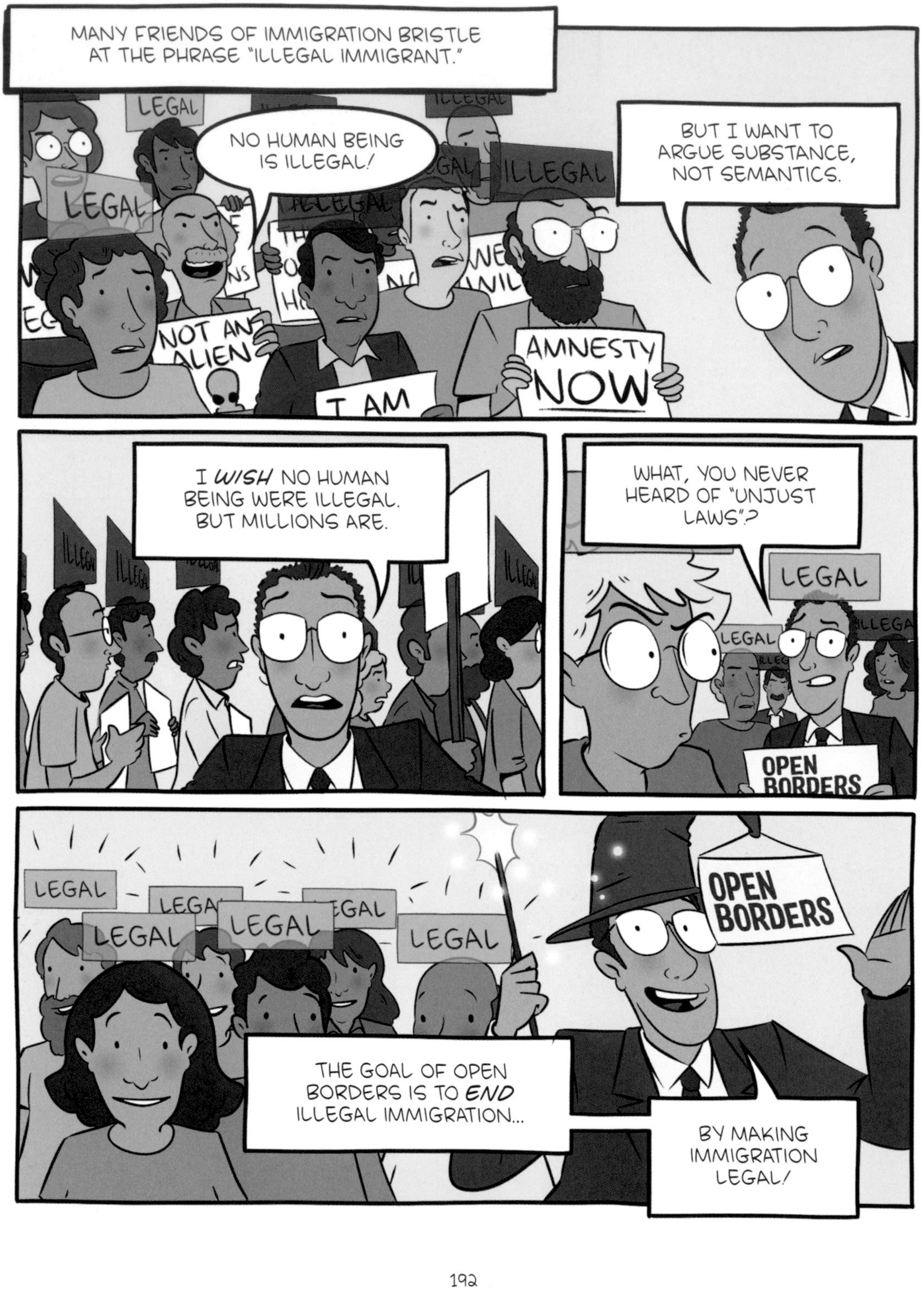
MANY FRIENDS OF IMMIGRATION BRISTLE AT THE PHRASE "ILLEGAL IMMIGRANT."
NO HUMAN BEING IS ILLEGAL!
LEGAL
ILLEGAL
NOT AN ALIEN
I AM
AMNESTY NOW
BUT I WANT TO ARGUE SUBSTANCE, NOT SEMANTICS.
I *WISH* NO HUMAN BEING WERE ILLEGAL. BUT MILLIONS ARE.
WHAT, YOU NEVER HEARD OF "UNJUST LAWS"?
LEGAL
OPEN BORDERS
LEGAL
OPEN BORDERS
THE GOAL OF OPEN BORDERS IS TO *END* ILLEGAL IMMIGRATION...
BY MAKING IMMIGRATION LEGAL!

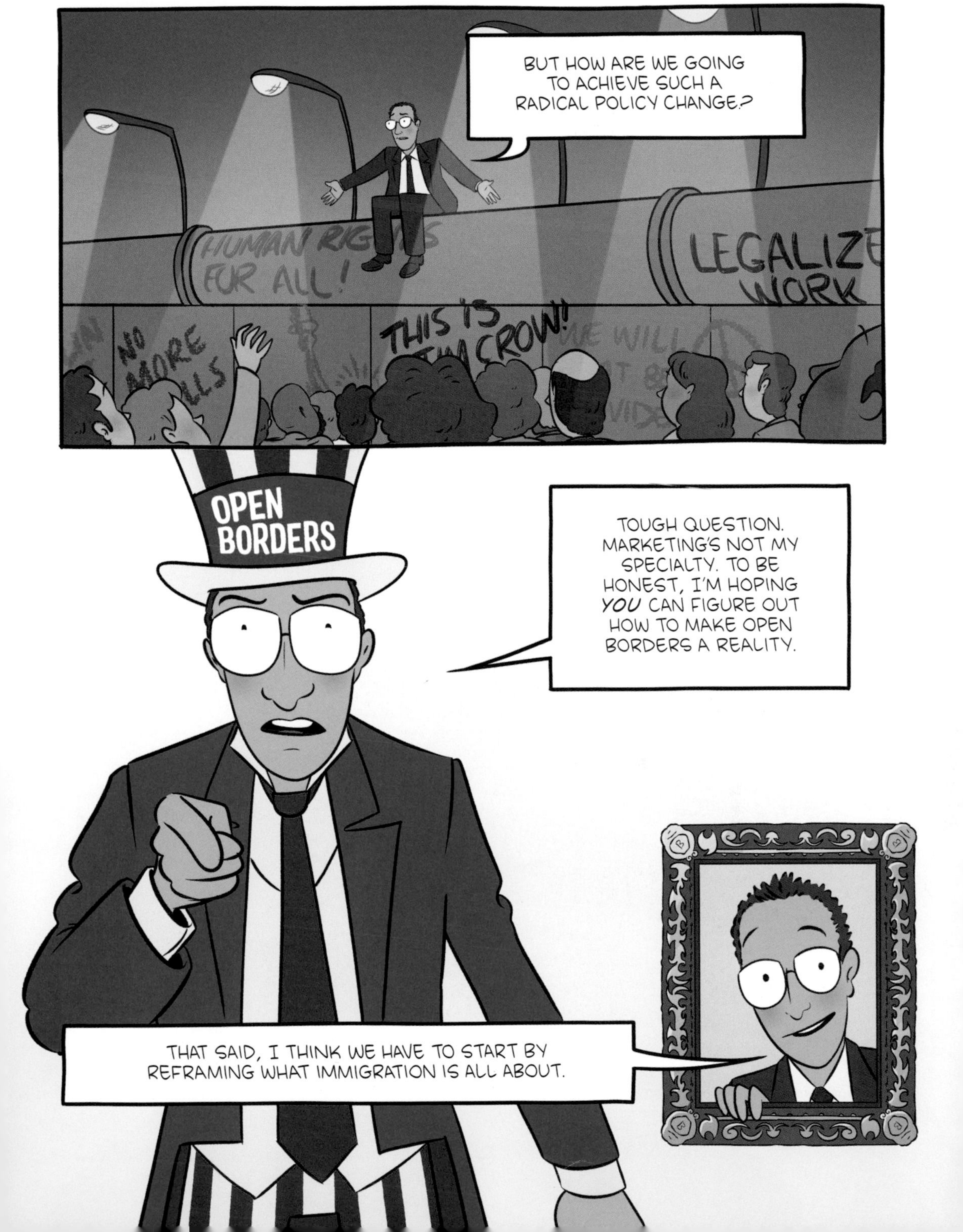

BUT HOW ARE WE GOING TO ACHIEVE SUCH A RADICAL POLICY CHANGE?
HUMAN RIGHTS FOR ALL!
LEGALIZE WORK
NO MORE WALLS
THIS IS JIM CROW!
OPEN BORDERS
TOUGH QUESTION. MARKETING'S NOT MY SPECIALTY. TO BE HONEST, I'M HOPING *YOU* CAN FIGURE OUT HOW TO MAKE OPEN BORDERS A REALITY.
THAT SAID, I THINK WE HAVE TO START BY REFRAMING WHAT IMMIGRATION IS ALL ABOUT.

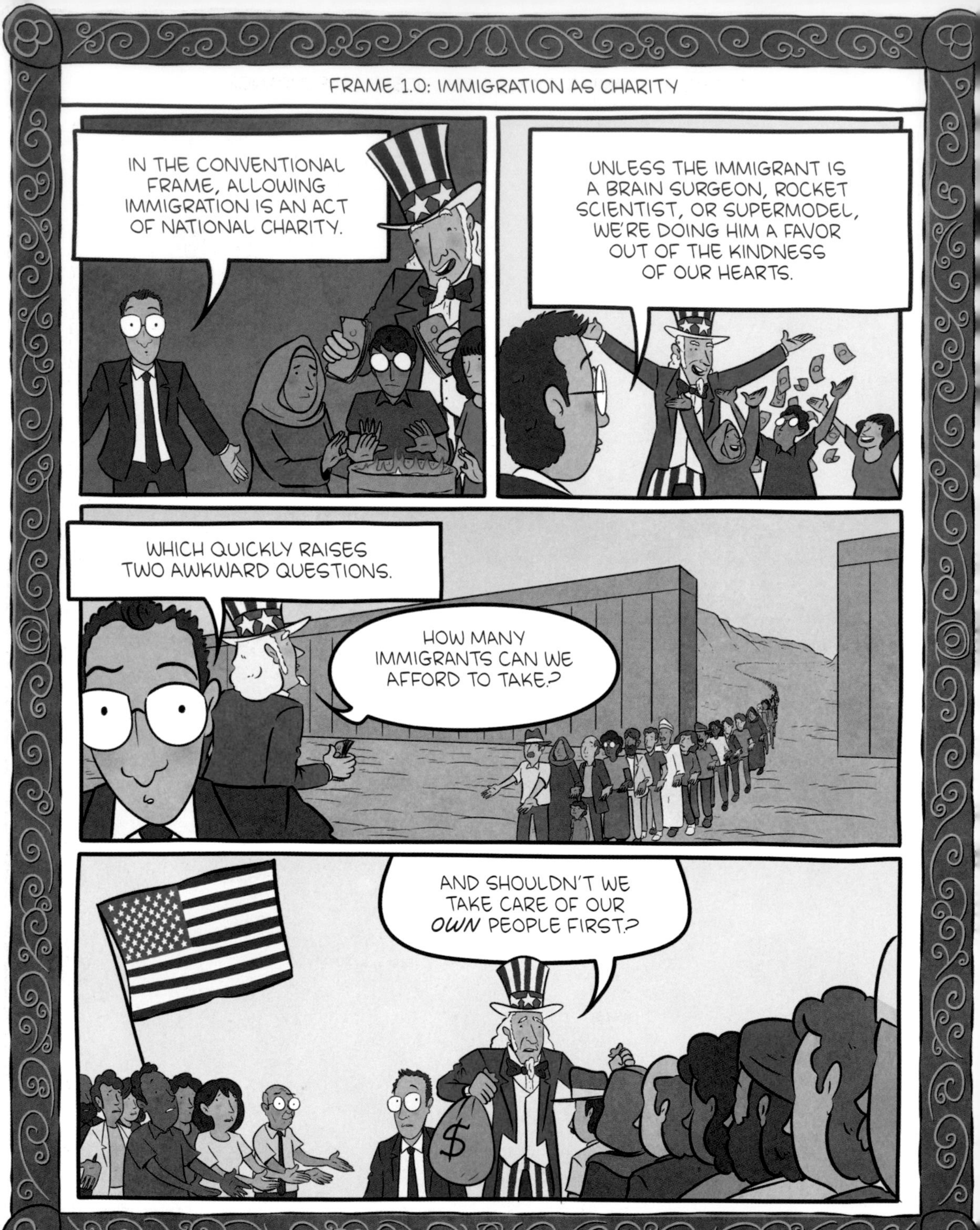
FRAME 1.0: IMMIGRATION AS CHARITY
IN THE CONVENTIONAL FRAME, ALLOWING IMMIGRATION IS AN ACT OF NATIONAL CHARITY.
UNLESS THE IMMIGRANT IS A BRAIN SURGEON, ROCKET SCIENTIST, OR SUPERMODEL, WE'RE DOING HIM A FAVOR OUT OF THE KINDNESS OF OUR HEARTS.
WHICH QUICKLY RAISES TWO AWKWARD QUESTIONS.
HOW MANY IMMIGRANTS CAN WE AFFORD TO TAKE?
AND SHOULDN'T WE TAKE CARE OF OUR *OWN* PEOPLE FIRST?

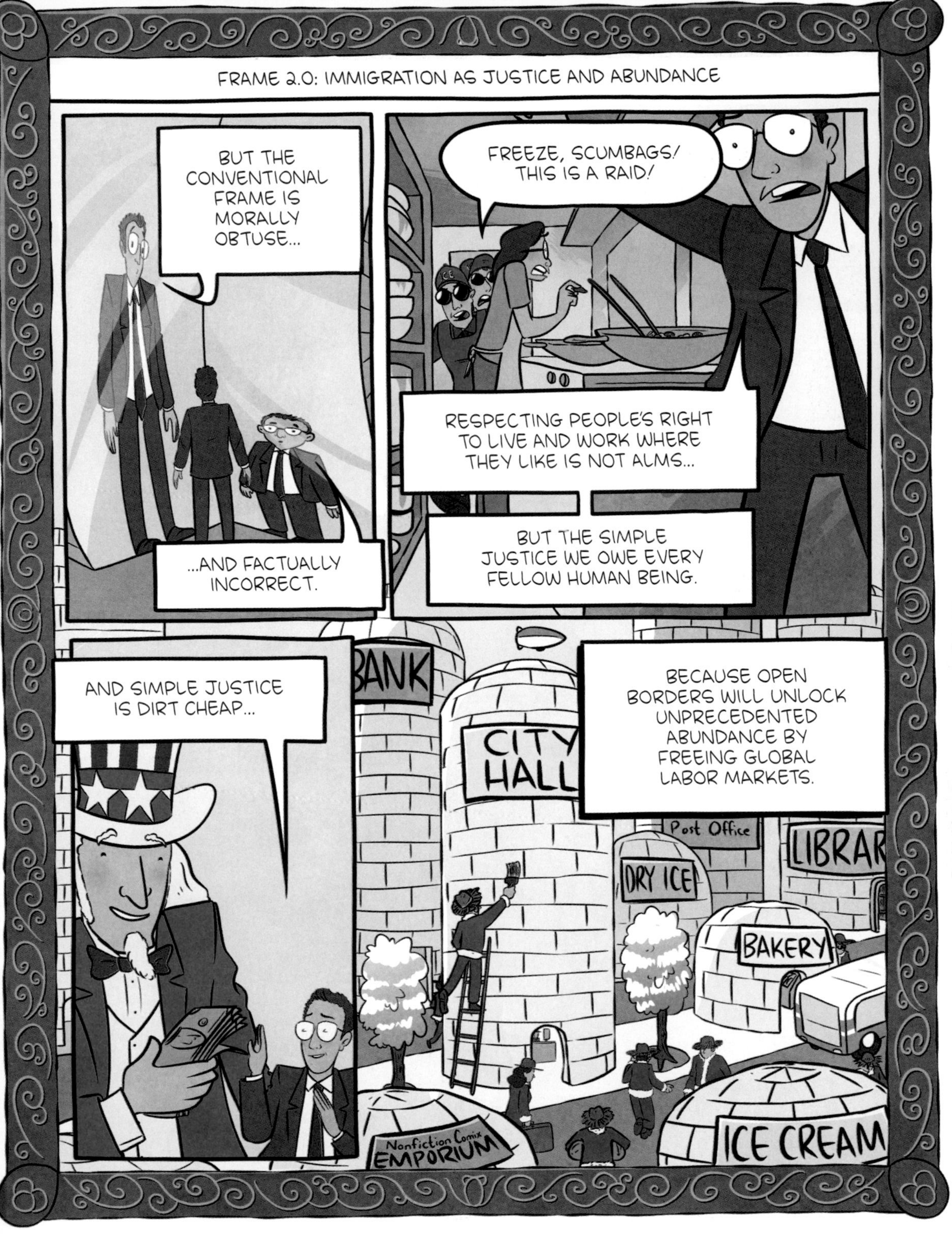
FRAME 2.0: IMMIGRATION AS JUSTICE AND ABUNDANCE
BUT THE CONVENTIONAL FRAME IS MORALLY OBTUSE...
...AND FACTUALLY INCORRECT.
FREEZE, SCUMBAGS! THIS IS A RAID!
ICE
RESPECTING PEOPLE'S RIGHT TO LIVE AND WORK WHERE THEY LIKE IS NOT ALMS...
BUT THE SIMPLE JUSTICE WE OWE EVERY FELLOW HUMAN BEING.
AND SIMPLE JUSTICE IS DIRT CHEAP...
BECAUSE OPEN BORDERS WILL UNLOCK UNPRECEDENTED ABUNDANCE BY FREEING GLOBAL LABOR MARKETS.
BANK
CITY HALL
Post Office
LIBRAR
DRY ICE
BAKERY
ICE CREAM
Nonfiction Comix EMPORIUM

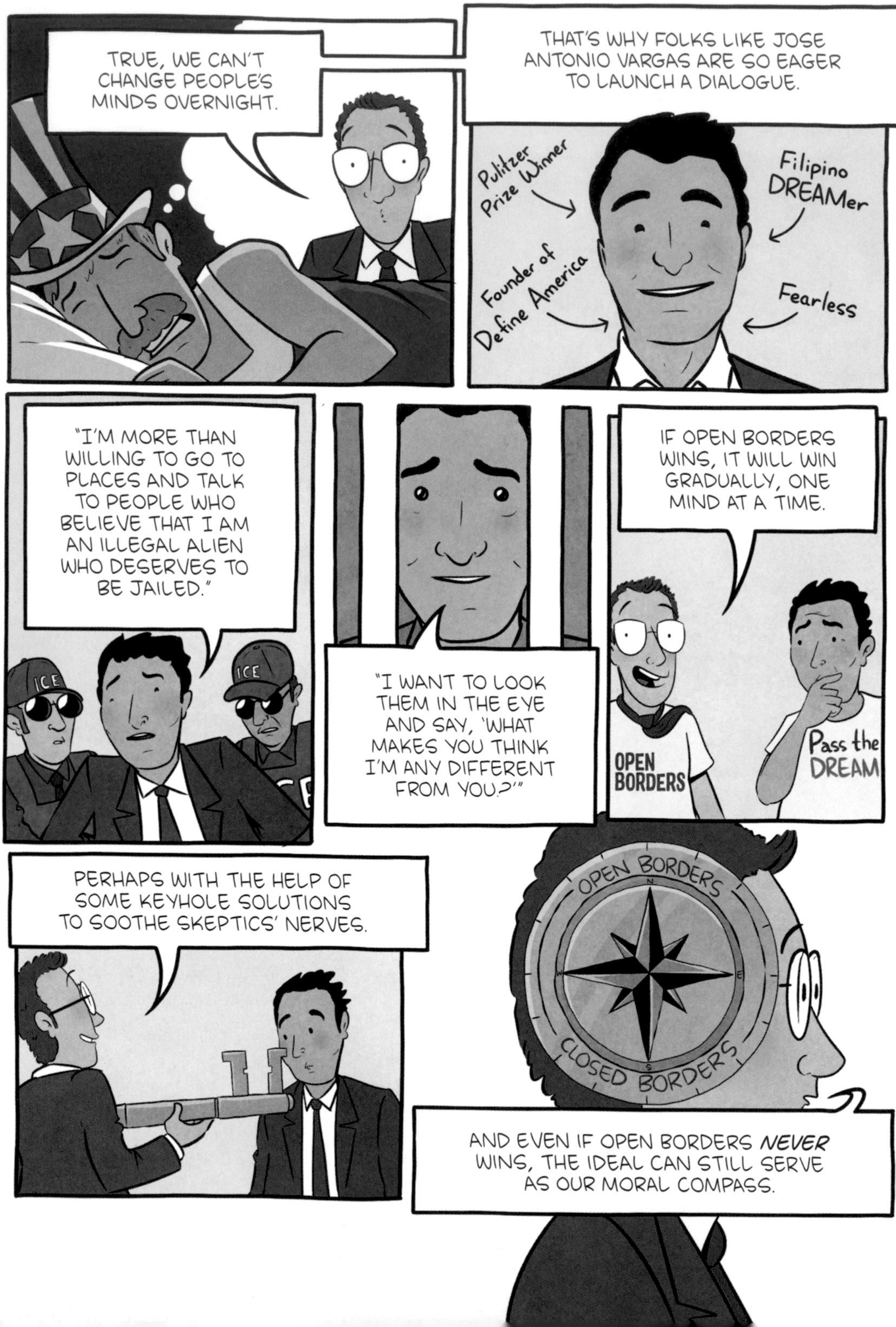
TRUE, WE CAN'T CHANGE PEOPLE'S MINDS OVERNIGHT.
THAT'S WHY FOLKS LIKE JOSE ANTONIO VARGAS ARE SO EAGER TO LAUNCH A DIALOGUE.
Pulitzer Prize Winner
Filipino DREAMer
Founder of Define America
Fearless
"I'M MORE THAN WILLING TO GO TO PLACES AND TALK TO PEOPLE WHO BELIEVE THAT I AM AN ILLEGAL ALIEN WHO DESERVES TO BE JAILED."
ICE
ICE
"I WANT TO LOOK THEM IN THE EYE AND SAY, 'WHAT MAKES YOU THINK I'M ANY DIFFERENT FROM YOU?'"
IF OPEN BORDERS WINS, IT WILL WIN GRADUALLY, ONE MIND AT A TIME.
OPEN BORDERS
Pass the DREAM
PERHAPS WITH THE HELP OF SOME KEYHOLE SOLUTIONS TO SOOTHE SKEPTICS' NERVES.
OPEN BORDERS
CLOSED BORDERS
AND EVEN IF OPEN BORDERS ***NEVER*** WINS, THE IDEAL CAN STILL SERVE AS OUR MORAL COMPASS.

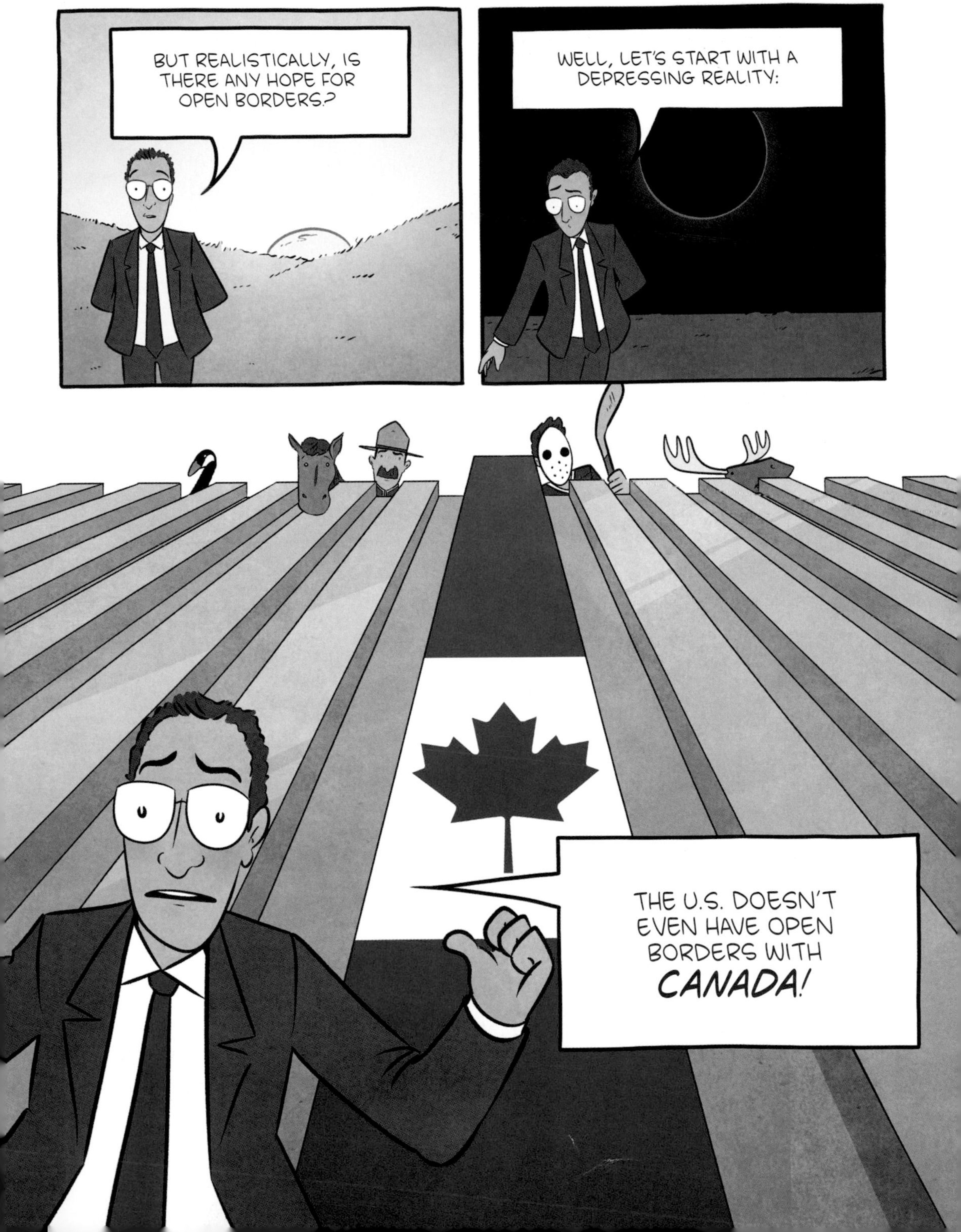
BUT REALISTICALLY, IS THERE ANY HOPE FOR OPEN BORDERS?
WELL, LET'S START WITH A DEPRESSING REALITY:
THE U.S. DOESN'T EVEN HAVE OPEN BORDERS WITH *CANADA*!

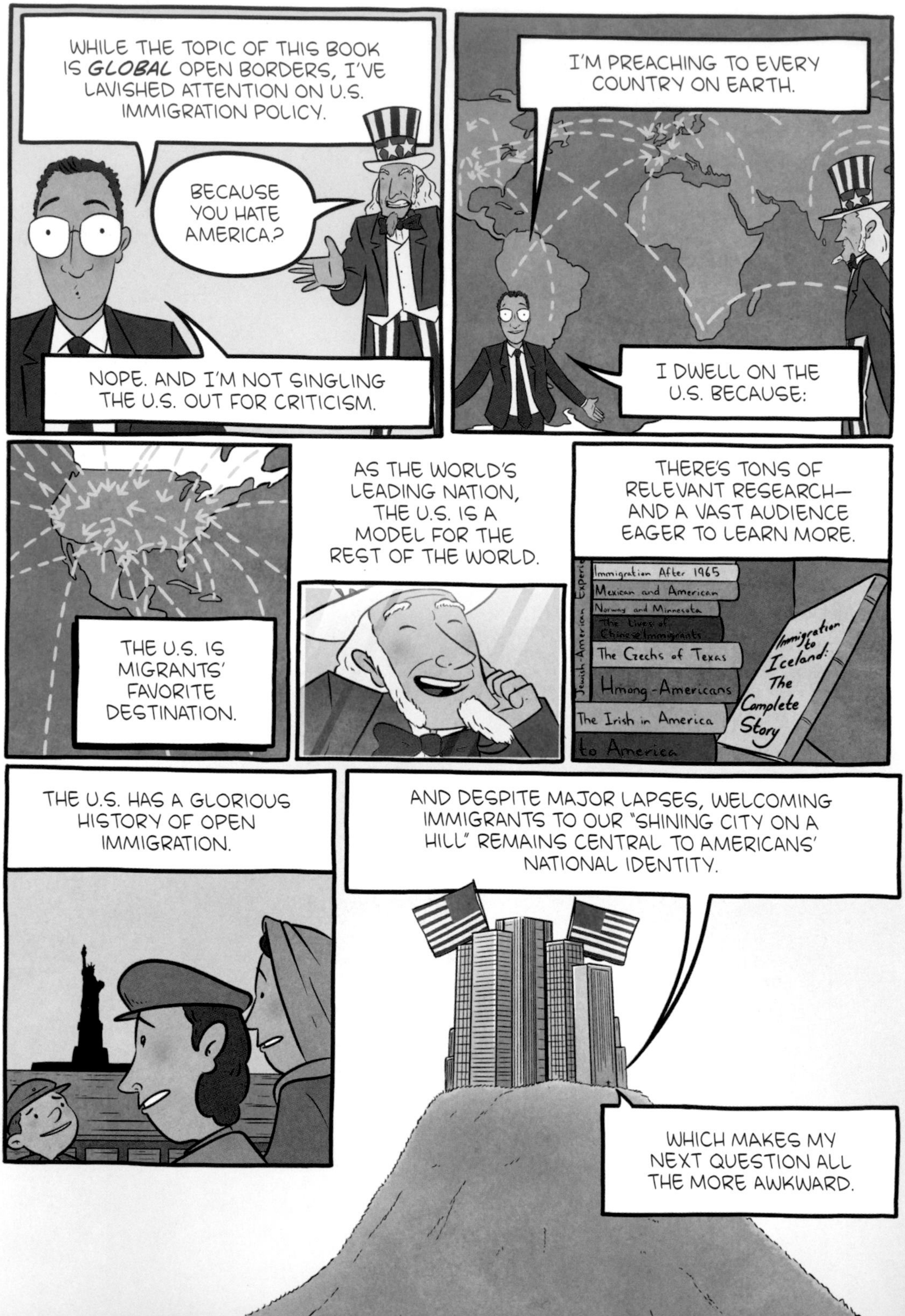
WHILE THE TOPIC OF THIS BOOK IS GLOBAL OPEN BORDERS, I'VE LAVISHED ATTENTION ON U.S. IMMIGRATION POLICY.
BECAUSE YOU HATE AMERICA?
NOPE. AND I'M NOT SINGLING THE U.S. OUT FOR CRITICISM.
I'M PREACHING TO EVERY COUNTRY ON EARTH.
I DWELL ON THE U.S. BECAUSE:
THE U.S. IS MIGRANTS' FAVORITE DESTINATION.
AS THE WORLD'S LEADING NATION, THE U.S. IS A MODEL FOR THE REST OF THE WORLD.
THERE'S TONS OF RELEVANT RESEARCH—AND A VAST AUDIENCE EAGER TO LEARN MORE.
Immigration After 1965
Mexican and American
Norway and Minnesota
The Lives of Chinese Immigrants
The Czechs of Texas
Hmong-Americans
The Irish in America
to America
Immigration to Iceland: The Complete Story
THE U.S. HAS A GLORIOUS HISTORY OF OPEN IMMIGRATION.
AND DESPITE MAJOR LAPSES, WELCOMING IMMIGRANTS TO OUR "SHINING CITY ON A HILL" REMAINS CENTRAL TO AMERICANS' NATIONAL IDENTITY.
WHICH MAKES MY NEXT QUESTION ALL THE MORE AWKWARD.

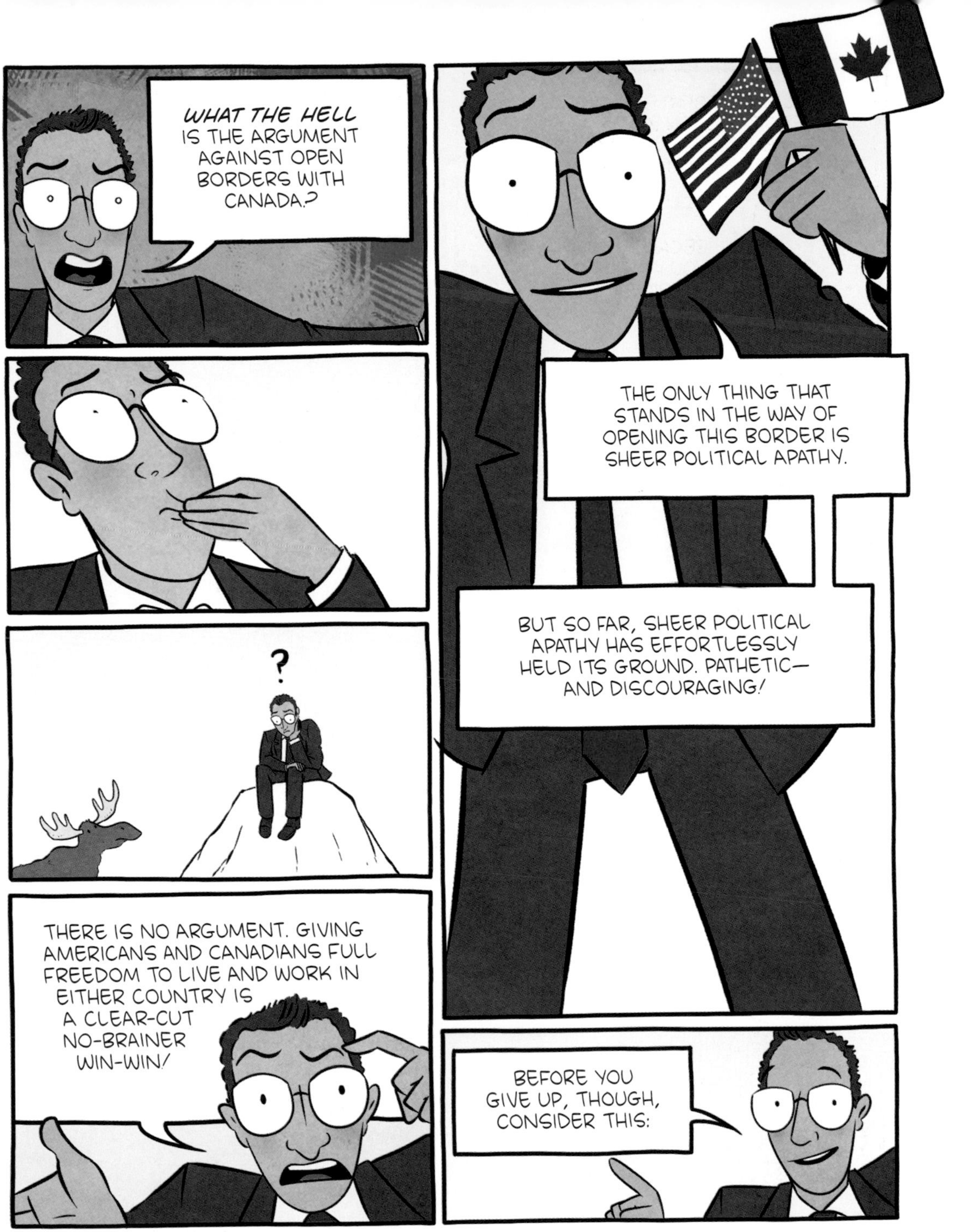

WHAT THE HELL IS THE ARGUMENT AGAINST OPEN BORDERS WITH CANADA?
?
THERE IS NO ARGUMENT. GIVING AMERICANS AND CANADIANS FULL FREEDOM TO LIVE AND WORK IN EITHER COUNTRY IS A CLEAR-CUT NO-BRAINER WIN-WIN!
THE ONLY THING THAT STANDS IN THE WAY OF OPENING THIS BORDER IS SHEER POLITICAL APATHY.
BUT SO FAR, SHEER POLITICAL APATHY HAS EFFORTLESSLY HELD ITS GROUND. PATHETIC— AND DISCOURAGING!
BEFORE YOU GIVE UP, THOUGH, CONSIDER THIS:

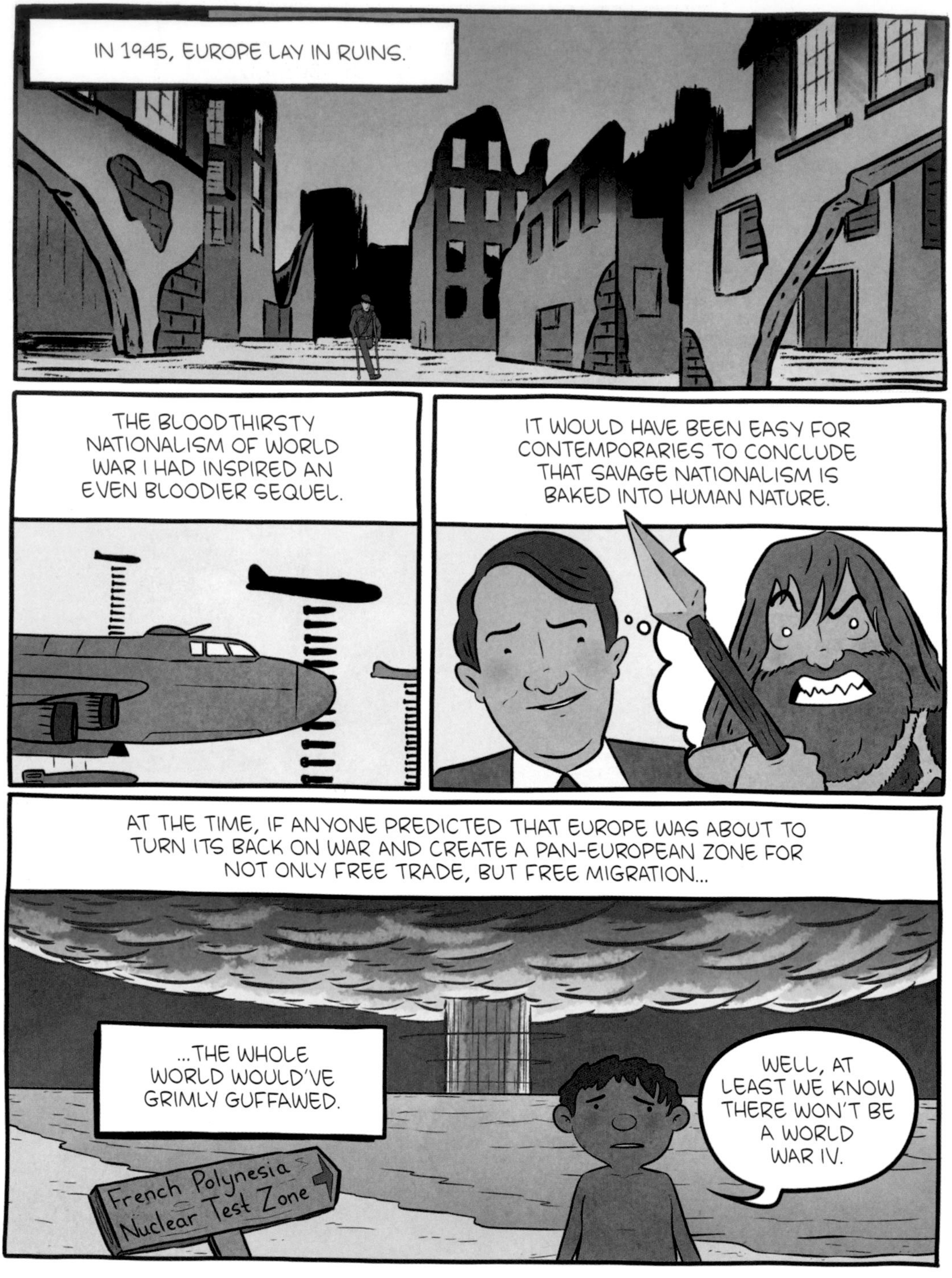
IN 1945, EUROPE LAY IN RUINS.
THE BLOODTHIRSTY NATIONALISM OF WORLD WAR I HAD INSPIRED AN EVEN BLOODIER SEQUEL.
IT WOULD HAVE BEEN EASY FOR CONTEMPORARIES TO CONCLUDE THAT SAVAGE NATIONALISM IS BAKED INTO HUMAN NATURE.
AT THE TIME, IF ANYONE PREDICTED THAT EUROPE WAS ABOUT TO TURN ITS BACK ON WAR AND CREATE A PAN-EUROPEAN ZONE FOR NOT ONLY FREE TRADE, BUT FREE MIGRATION...
...THE WHOLE WORLD WOULD'VE GRIMLY GUFFAWED.
WELL, AT LEAST WE KNOW THERE WON'T BE A WORLD WAR IV.
French Polynesia Nuclear Test Zone

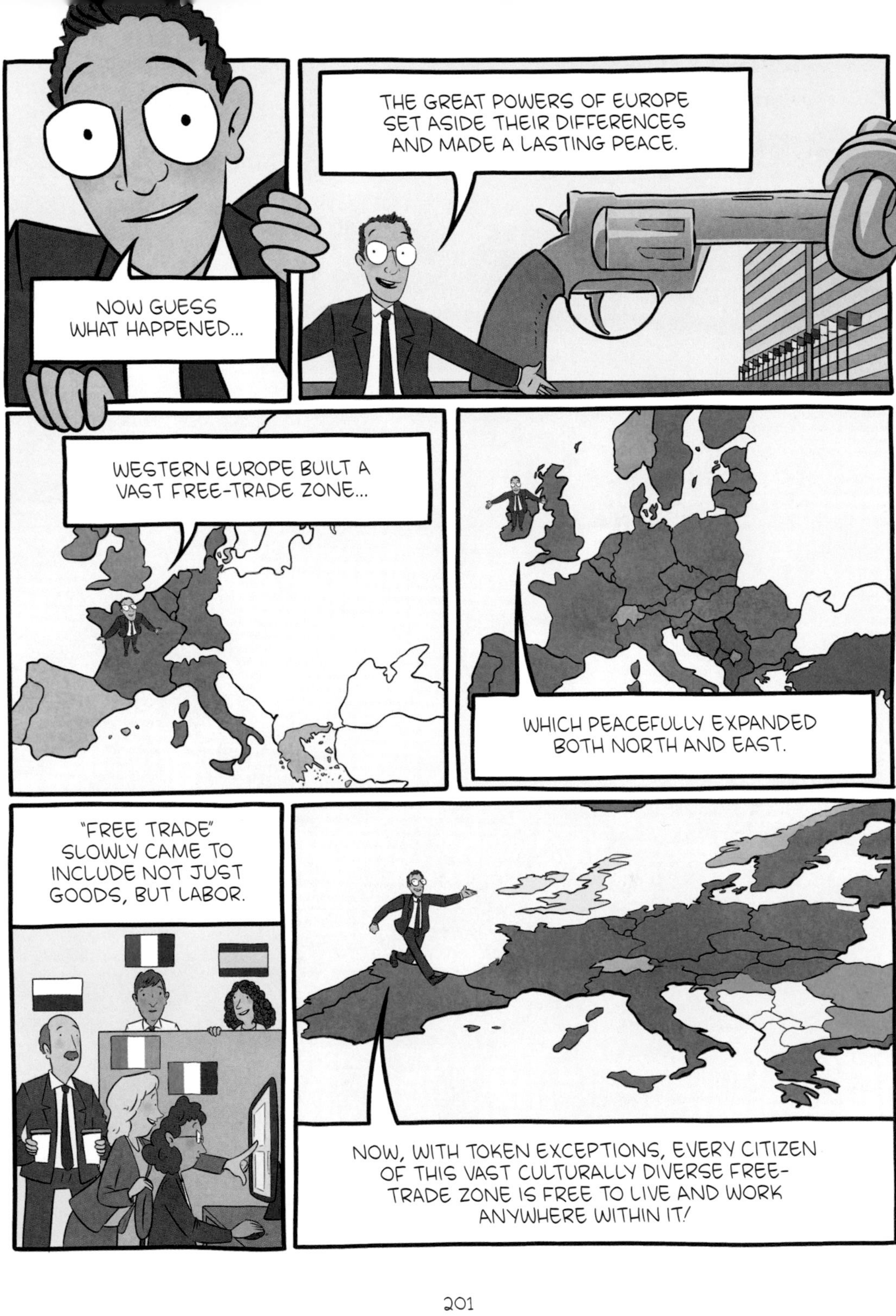
NOW GUESS WHAT HAPPENED...
THE GREAT POWERS OF EUROPE SET ASIDE THEIR DIFFERENCES AND MADE A LASTING PEACE.
WESTERN EUROPE BUILT A VAST FREE-TRADE ZONE...
WHICH PEACEFULLY EXPANDED BOTH NORTH AND EAST.
"FREE TRADE" SLOWLY CAME TO INCLUDE NOT JUST GOODS, BUT LABOR.
NOW, WITH TOKEN EXCEPTIONS, EVERY CITIZEN OF THIS VAST CULTURALLY DIVERSE FREE-TRADE ZONE IS FREE TO LIVE AND WORK ANYWHERE WITHIN IT!

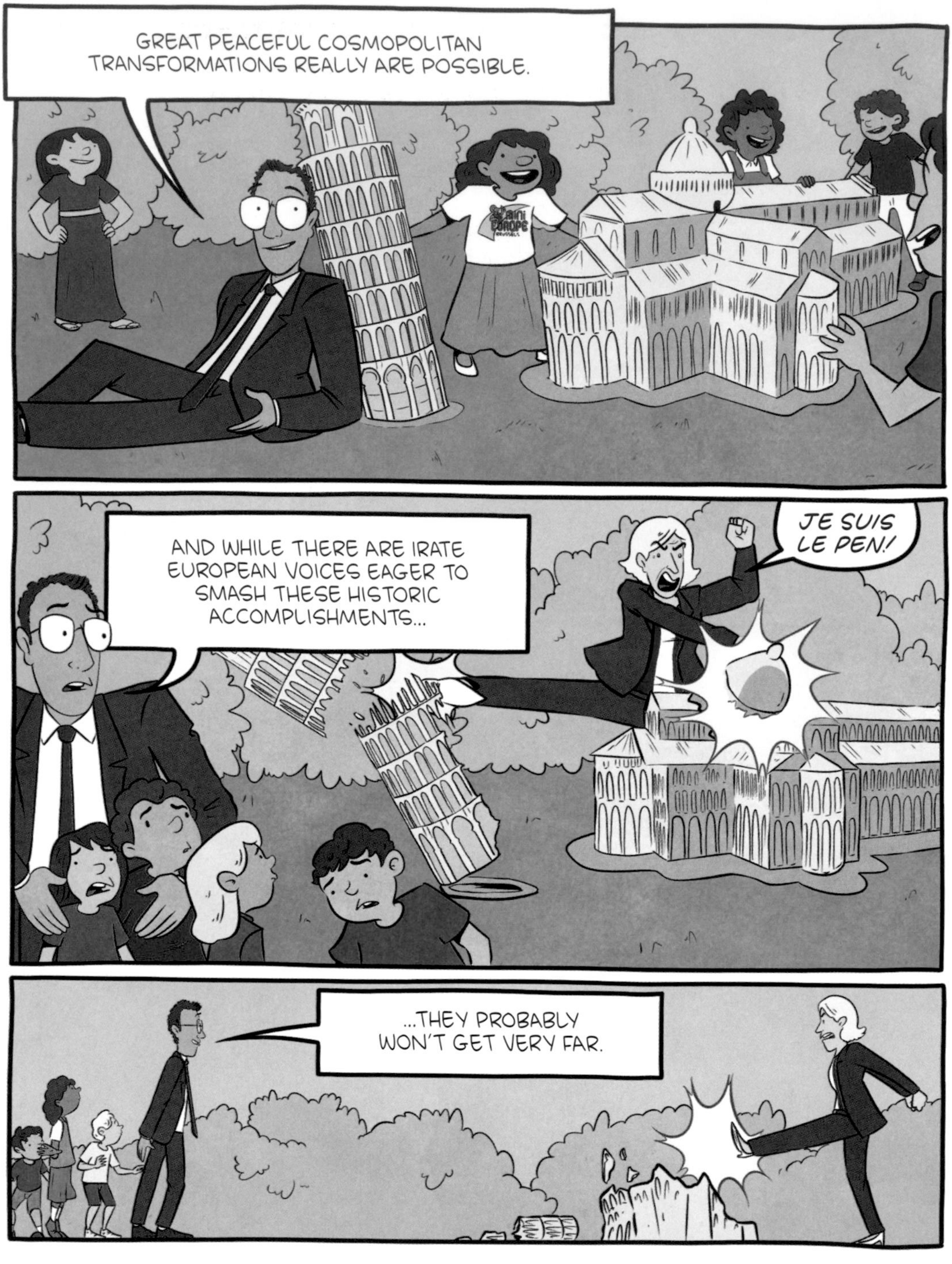
GREAT PEACEFUL COSMOPOLITAN TRANSFORMATIONS REALLY ARE POSSIBLE.
AND WHILE THERE ARE IRATE EUROPEAN VOICES EAGER TO SMASH THESE HISTORIC ACCOMPLISHMENTS...
JE SUIS LE PEN!
...THEY PROBABLY WON'T GET VERY FAR.

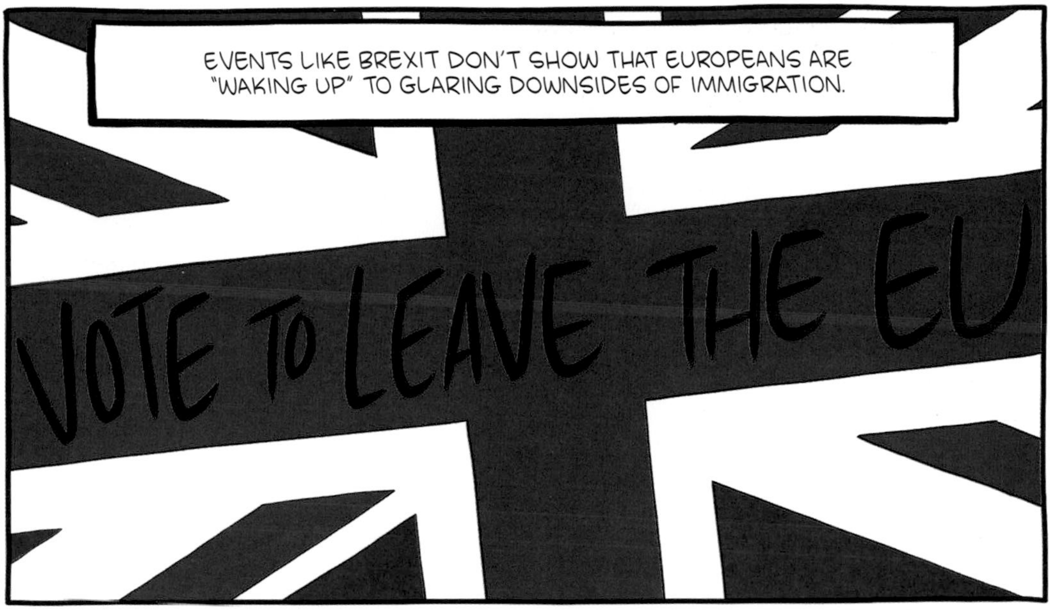
EVENTS LIKE BREXIT DON'T SHOW THAT EUROPEANS ARE "WAKING UP" TO GLARING DOWNSIDES OF IMMIGRATION.
VOTE TO LEAVE THE EU

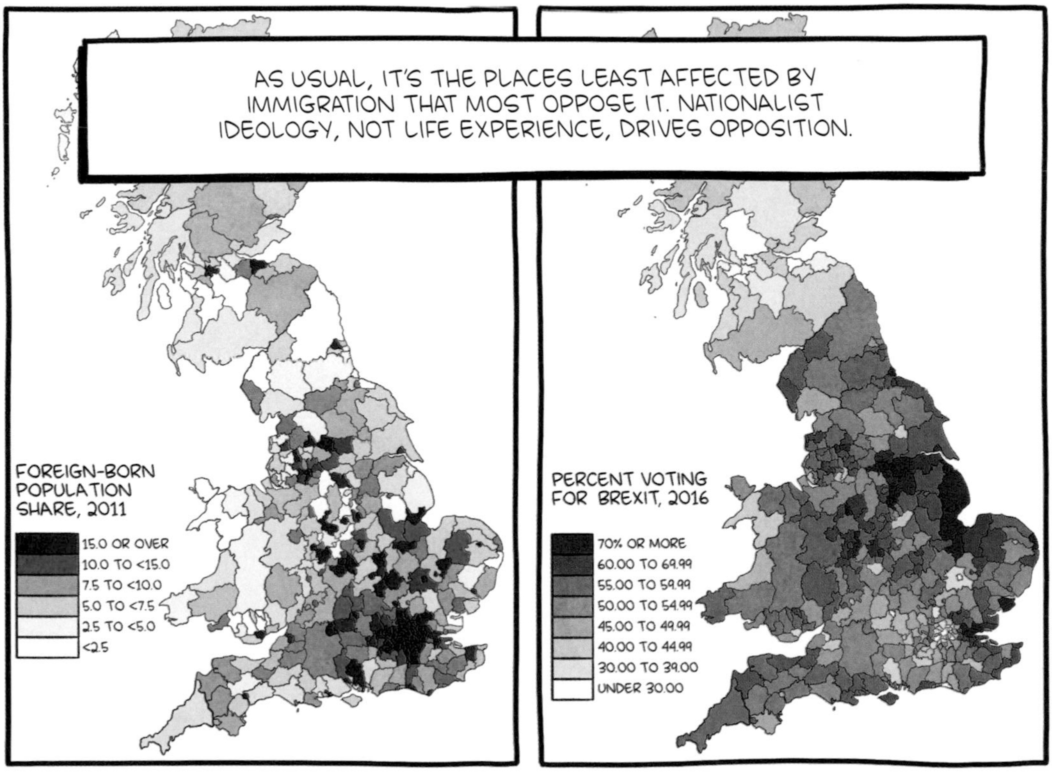
AS USUAL, IT'S THE PLACES LEAST AFFECTED BY IMMIGRATION THAT MOST OPPOSE IT. NATIONALIST IDEOLOGY, NOT LIFE EXPERIENCE, DRIVES OPPOSITION.
FOREIGN-BORN POPULATION SHARE, 2011
15.0 OR OVER
10.0 TO <15.0
7.5 TO <10.0
5.0 TO <7.5
2.5 TO <5.0
<2.5
PERCENT VOTING FOR BREXIT, 2016
70% OR MORE
60.00 TO 69.99
55.00 TO 59.99
50.00 TO 54.99
45.00 TO 49.99
40.00 TO 44.99
30.00 TO 39.00
UNDER 30.00

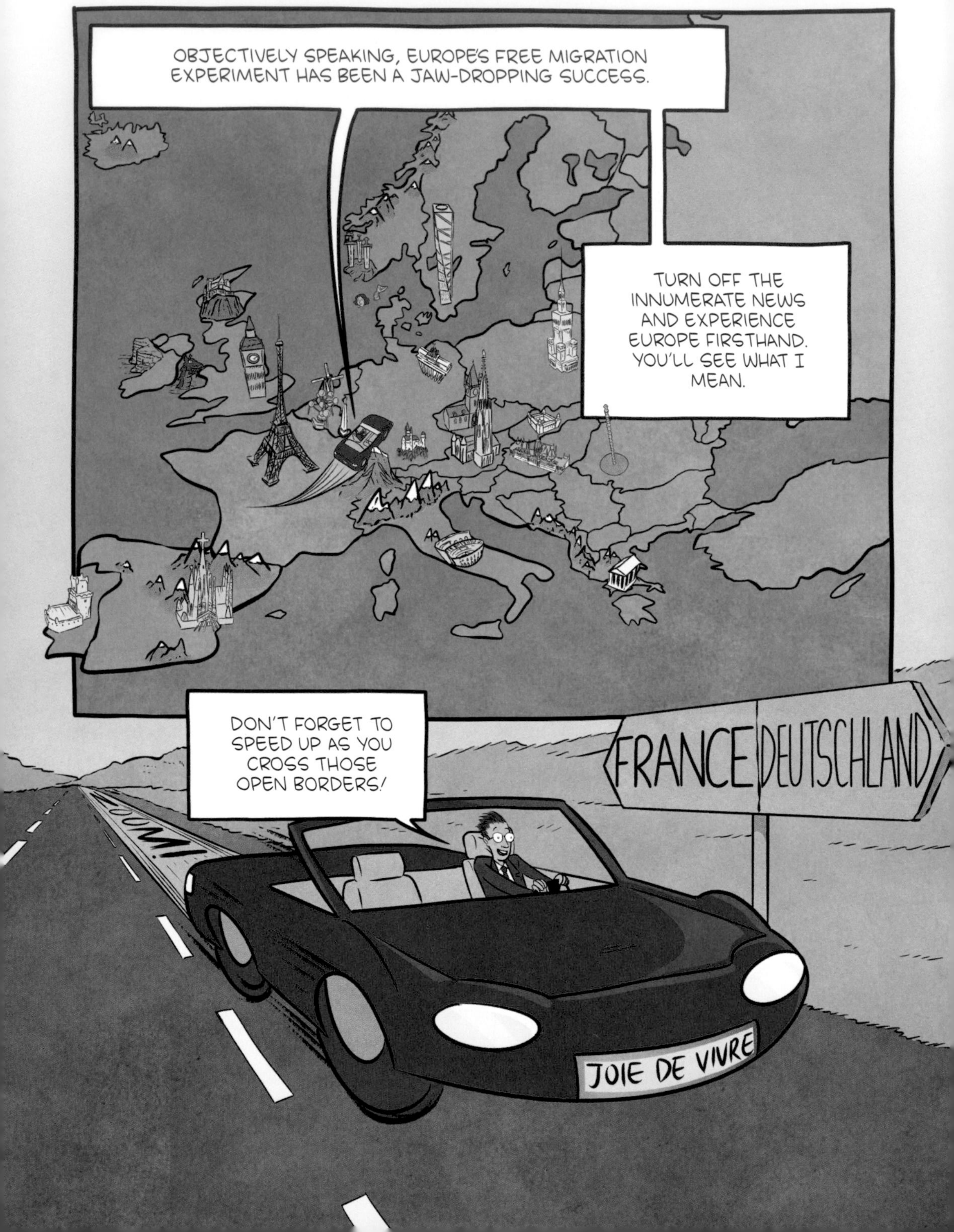

OBJECTIVELY SPEAKING, EUROPE'S FREE MIGRATION EXPERIMENT HAS BEEN A JAW-DROPPING SUCCESS.
TURN OFF THE INNUMERATE NEWS AND EXPERIENCE EUROPE FIRSTHAND. YOU'LL SEE WHAT I MEAN.
DON'T FORGET TO SPEED UP AS YOU CROSS THOSE OPEN BORDERS!
FRANCE
DEUTSCHLAND
ZOOM!
JOIE DE VIVRE

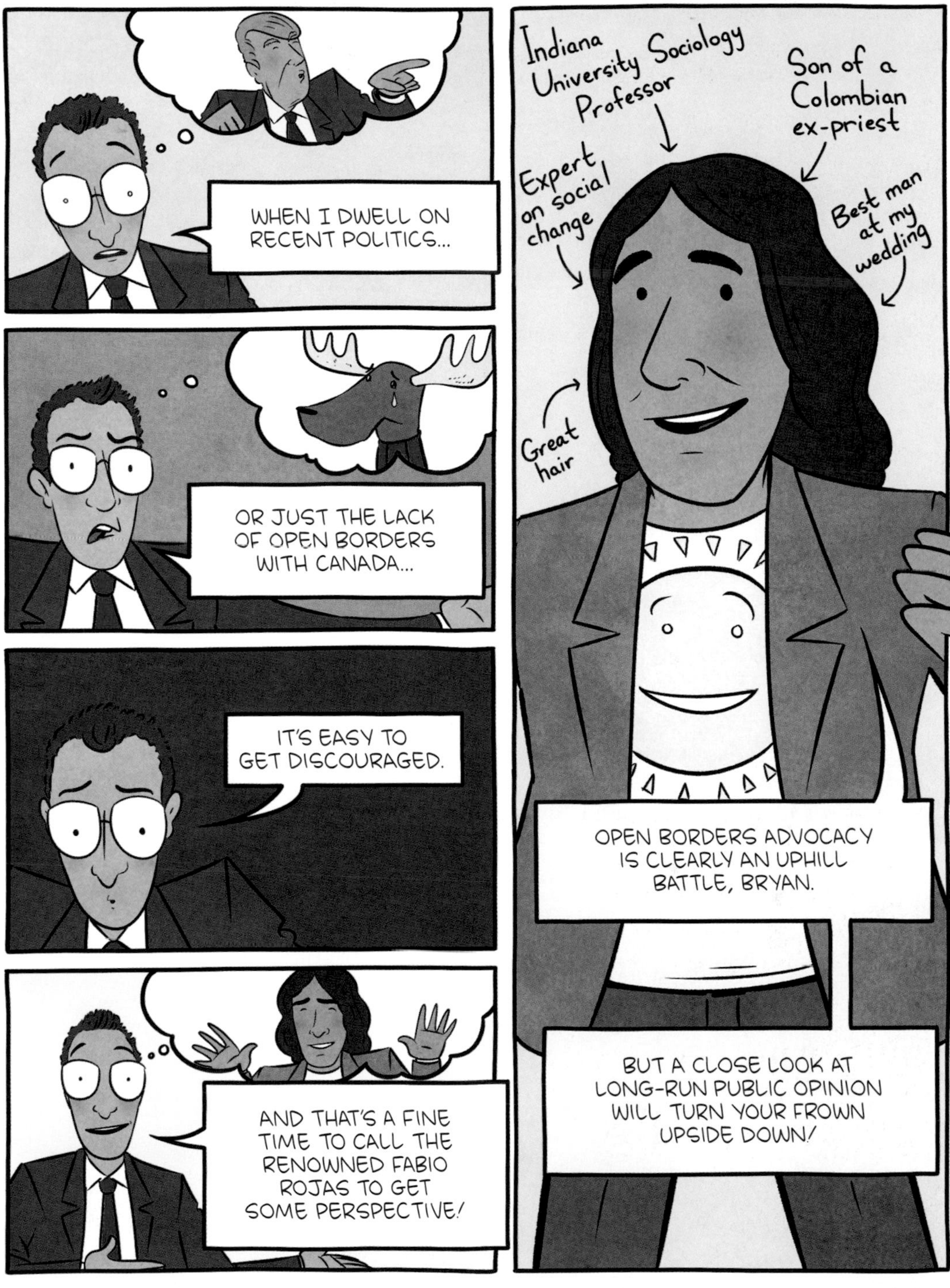
WHEN I DWELL ON RECENT POLITICS...
OR JUST THE LACK OF OPEN BORDERS WITH CANADA...
IT'S EASY TO GET DISCOURAGED.
AND THAT'S A FINE TIME TO CALL THE RENOWNED FABIO ROJAS TO GET SOME PERSPECTIVE!
Indiana University Sociology Professor
Son of a Colombian ex-priest
Expert on social change
Best man at my wedding
Great hair
OPEN BORDERS ADVOCACY IS CLEARLY AN UPHILL BATTLE, BRYAN.
BUT A CLOSE LOOK AT LONG-RUN PUBLIC OPINION WILL TURN YOUR FROWN UPSIDE DOWN!

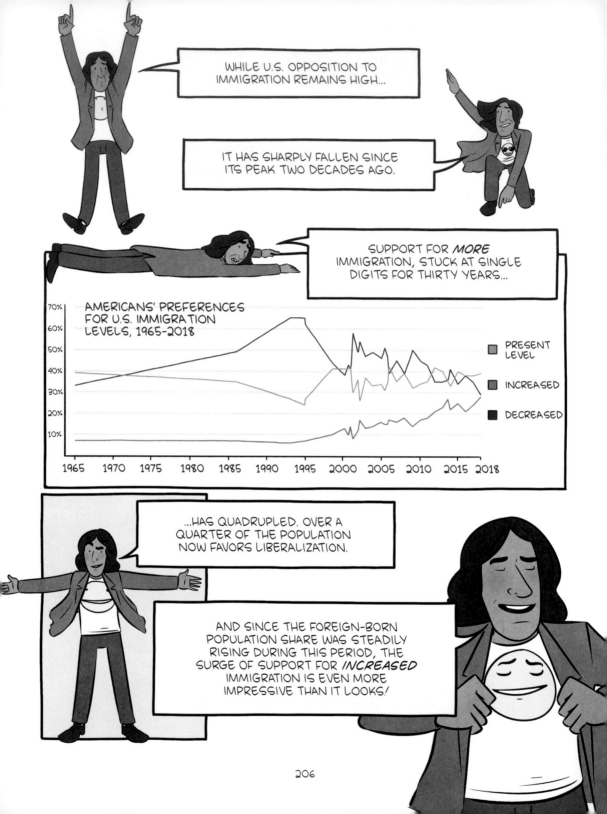

WHILE U.S. OPPOSITION TO IMMIGRATION REMAINS HIGH...

IT HAS SHARPLY FALLEN SINCE ITS PEAK TWO DECADES AGO.

SUPPORT FOR *MORE* IMMIGRATION, STUCK AT SINGLE DIGITS FOR THIRTY YEARS...

AMERICANS' PREFERENCES FOR U.S. IMMIGRATION LEVELS, 1965–2018

70%
60%
50%
40%
30%
20%
10%

1965 1970 1975 1980 1985 1990 1995 2000 2005 2010 2015 2018

PRESENT LEVEL

INCREASED

DECREASED

...HAS QUADRUPLED. OVER A QUARTER OF THE POPULATION NOW FAVORS LIBERALIZATION.

AND SINCE THE FOREIGN-BORN POPULATION SHARE WAS STEADILY RISING DURING THIS PERIOD, THE SURGE OF SUPPORT FOR *INCREASED* IMMIGRATION IS EVEN MORE IMPRESSIVE THAN IT LOOKS!

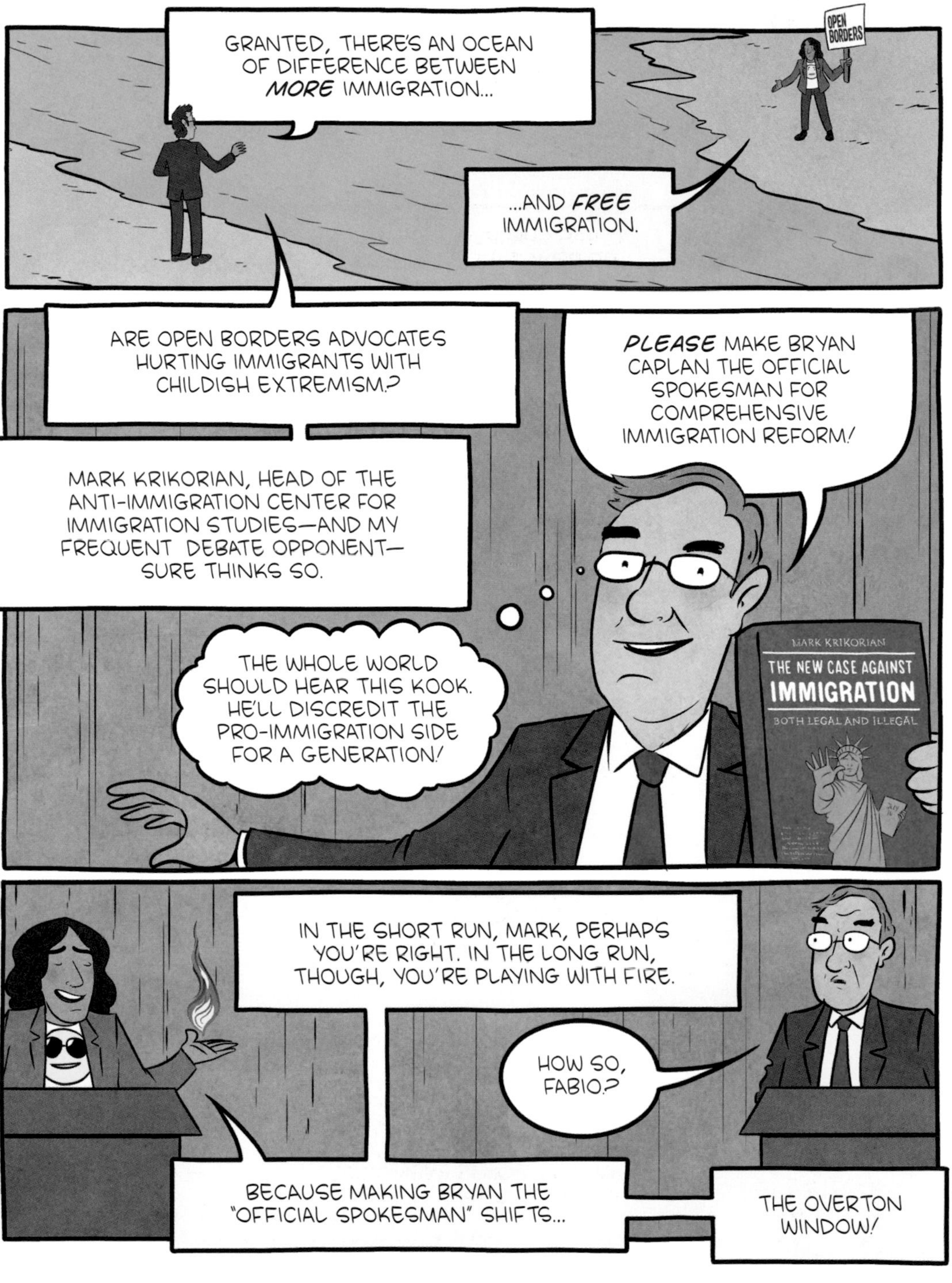

GRANTED, THERE'S AN OCEAN OF DIFFERENCE BETWEEN *MORE* IMMIGRATION...
OPEN BORDERS
...AND *FREE* IMMIGRATION.
ARE OPEN BORDERS ADVOCATES HURTING IMMIGRANTS WITH CHILDISH EXTREMISM?
MARK KRIKORIAN, HEAD OF THE ANTI-IMMIGRATION CENTER FOR IMMIGRATION STUDIES—AND MY FREQUENT DEBATE OPPONENT—SURE THINKS SO.
PLEASE MAKE BRYAN CAPLAN THE OFFICIAL SPOKESMAN FOR COMPREHENSIVE IMMIGRATION REFORM!
THE WHOLE WORLD SHOULD HEAR THIS KOOK. HE'LL DISCREDIT THE PRO-IMMIGRATION SIDE FOR A GENERATION!
MARK KRIKORIAN
THE NEW CASE AGAINST IMMIGRATION
BOTH LEGAL AND ILLEGAL
IN THE SHORT RUN, MARK, PERHAPS YOU'RE RIGHT. IN THE LONG RUN, THOUGH, YOU'RE PLAYING WITH FIRE.
HOW SO, FABIO?
BECAUSE MAKING BRYAN THE "OFFICIAL SPOKESMAN" SHIFTS...
THE OVERTON WINDOW!

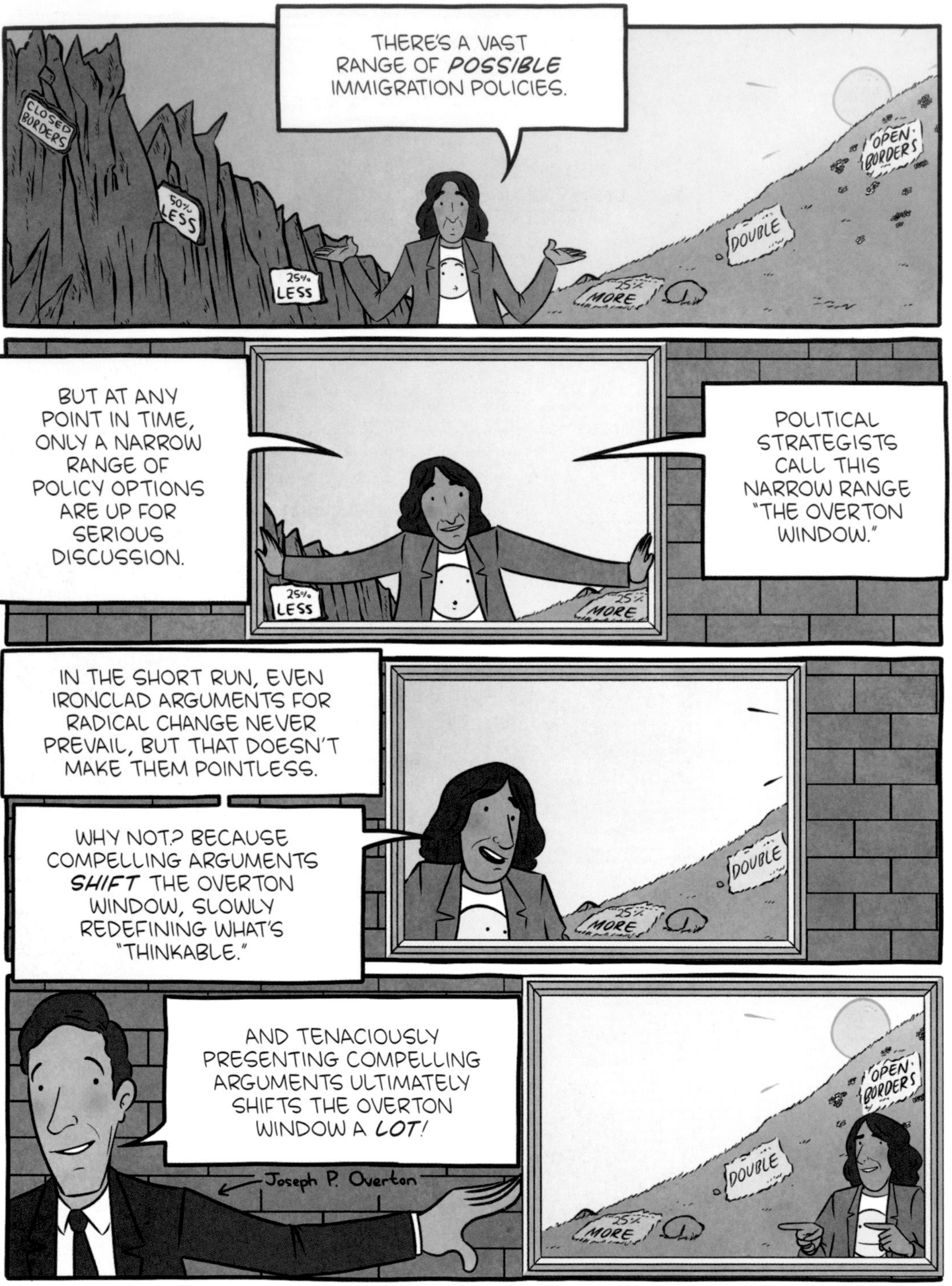
THERE'S A VAST RANGE OF *POSSIBLE* IMMIGRATION POLICIES.
CLOSED BORDERS
50% LESS
25% LESS
25% MORE
DOUBLE
OPEN BORDERS
BUT AT ANY POINT IN TIME, ONLY A NARROW RANGE OF POLICY OPTIONS ARE UP FOR SERIOUS DISCUSSION.
POLITICAL STRATEGISTS CALL THIS NARROW RANGE "THE OVERTON WINDOW."
25% LESS
25% MORE
IN THE SHORT RUN, EVEN IRONCLAD ARGUMENTS FOR RADICAL CHANGE NEVER PREVAIL, BUT THAT DOESN'T MAKE THEM POINTLESS.
WHY NOT? BECAUSE COMPELLING ARGUMENTS *SHIFT* THE OVERTON WINDOW, SLOWLY REDEFINING WHAT'S "THINKABLE."
DOUBLE
25% MORE
AND TENACIOUSLY PRESENTING COMPELLING ARGUMENTS ULTIMATELY SHIFTS THE OVERTON WINDOW A *LOT*!
Joseph P. Overton
OPEN BORDERS
DOUBLE
25% MORE

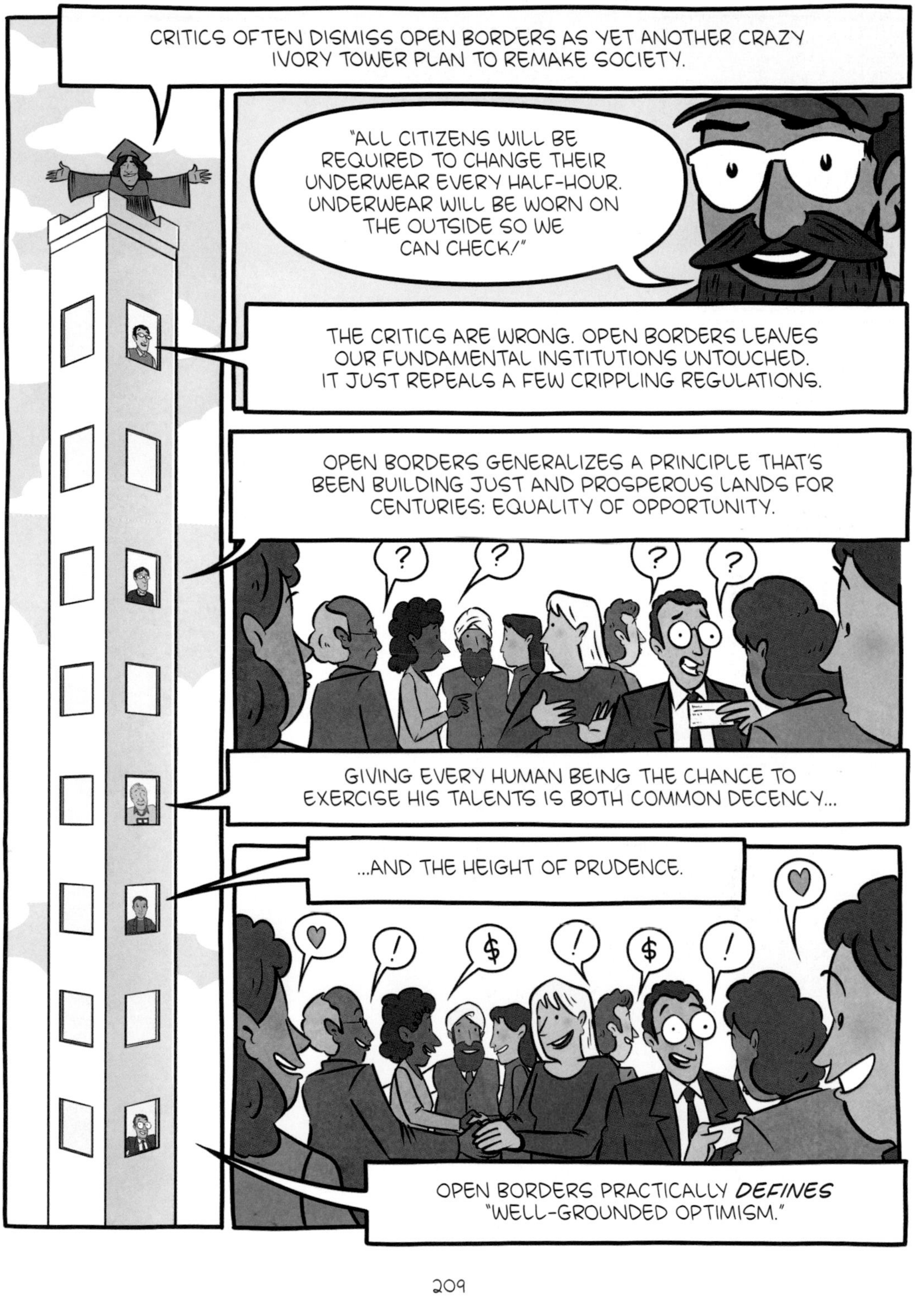
CRITICS OFTEN DISMISS OPEN BORDERS AS YET ANOTHER CRAZY IVORY TOWER PLAN TO REMAKE SOCIETY.
"ALL CITIZENS WILL BE REQUIRED TO CHANGE THEIR UNDERWEAR EVERY HALF-HOUR. UNDERWEAR WILL BE WORN ON THE OUTSIDE SO WE CAN CHECK!"
THE CRITICS ARE WRONG. OPEN BORDERS LEAVES OUR FUNDAMENTAL INSTITUTIONS UNTOUCHED. IT JUST REPEALS A FEW CRIPPLING REGULATIONS.
OPEN BORDERS GENERALIZES A PRINCIPLE THAT'S BEEN BUILDING JUST AND PROSPEROUS LANDS FOR CENTURIES: EQUALITY OF OPPORTUNITY.
?
?
?
?
GIVING EVERY HUMAN BEING THE CHANCE TO EXERCISE HIS TALENTS IS BOTH COMMON DECENCY...
...AND THE HEIGHT OF PRUDENCE.
!
$
!
$
!
OPEN BORDERS PRACTICALLY *DEFINES* "WELL-GROUNDED OPTIMISM."

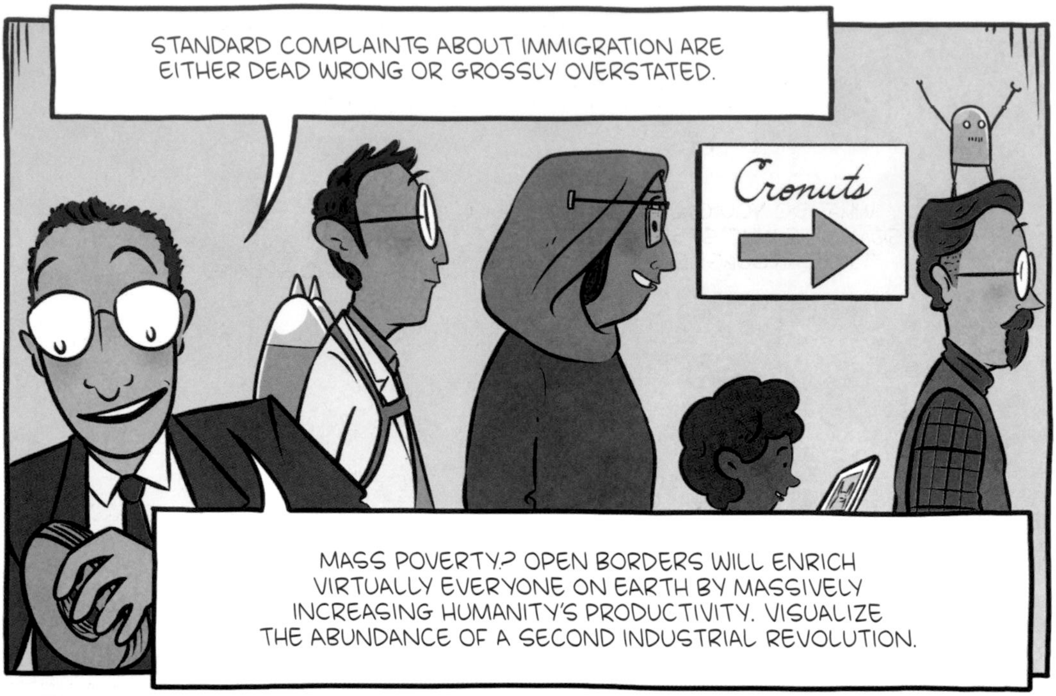
STANDARD COMPLAINTS ABOUT IMMIGRATION ARE EITHER DEAD WRONG OR GROSSLY OVERSTATED.
Cronuts
MASS POVERTY? OPEN BORDERS WILL ENRICH VIRTUALLY EVERYONE ON EARTH BY MASSIVELY INCREASING HUMANITY'S PRODUCTIVITY. VISUALIZE THE ABUNDANCE OF A SECOND INDUSTRIAL REVOLUTION.

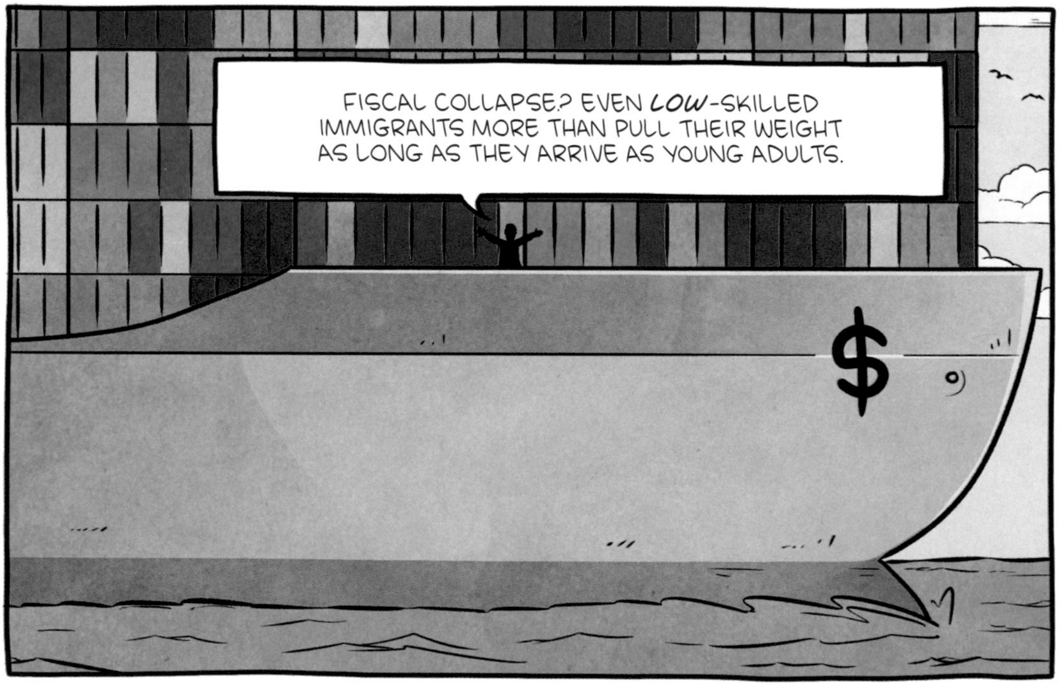
FISCAL COLLAPSE? EVEN ***LOW***-SKILLED IMMIGRANTS MORE THAN PULL THEIR WEIGHT AS LONG AS THEY ARRIVE AS YOUNG ADULTS.
$

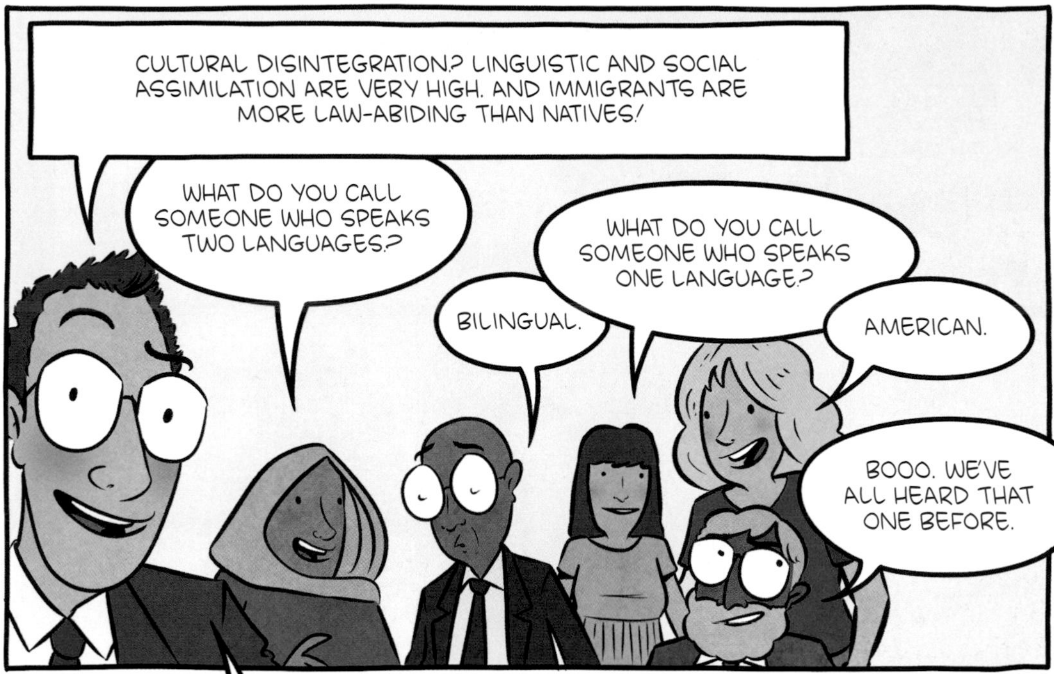
CULTURAL DISINTEGRATION? LINGUISTIC AND SOCIAL ASSIMILATION ARE VERY HIGH. AND IMMIGRANTS ARE MORE LAW-ABIDING THAN NATIVES!
WHAT DO YOU CALL SOMEONE WHO SPEAKS TWO LANGUAGES?
BILINGUAL.
WHAT DO YOU CALL SOMEONE WHO SPEAKS ONE LANGUAGE?
AMERICAN.
BOOO. WE'VE ALL HEARD THAT ONE BEFORE.

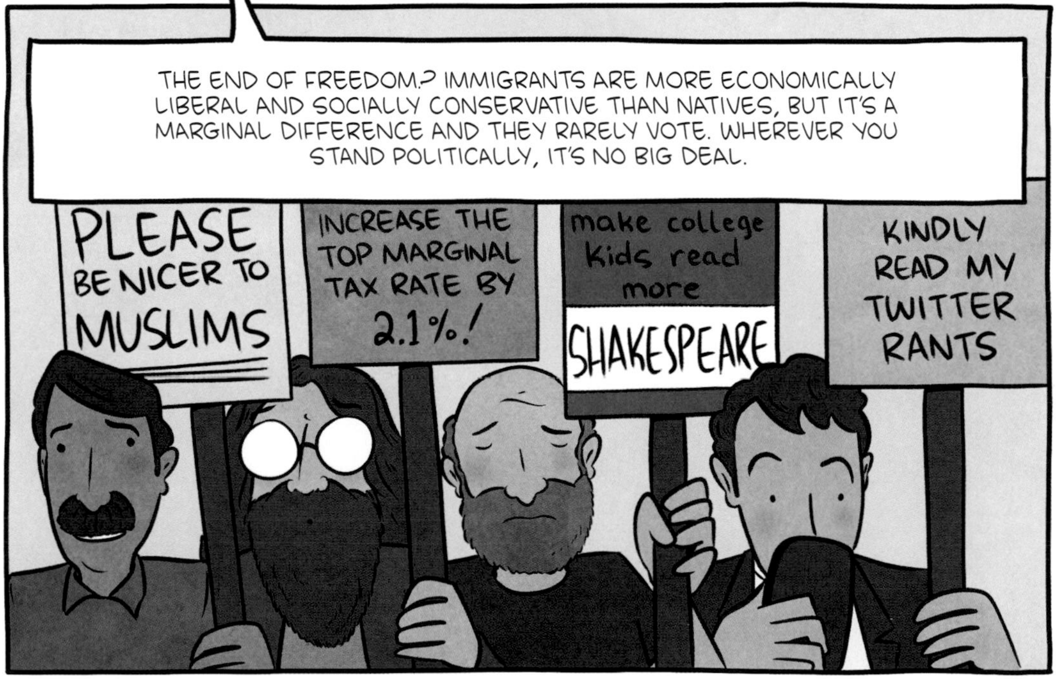
THE END OF FREEDOM? IMMIGRANTS ARE MORE ECONOMICALLY LIBERAL AND SOCIALLY CONSERVATIVE THAN NATIVES, BUT IT'S A MARGINAL DIFFERENCE AND THEY RARELY VOTE. WHEREVER YOU STAND POLITICALLY, IT'S NO BIG DEAL.
PLEASE BE NICER TO MUSLIMS
INCREASE THE TOP MARGINAL TAX RATE BY 2.1%!
make college kids read more SHAKESPEARE
KINDLY READ MY TWITTER RANTS

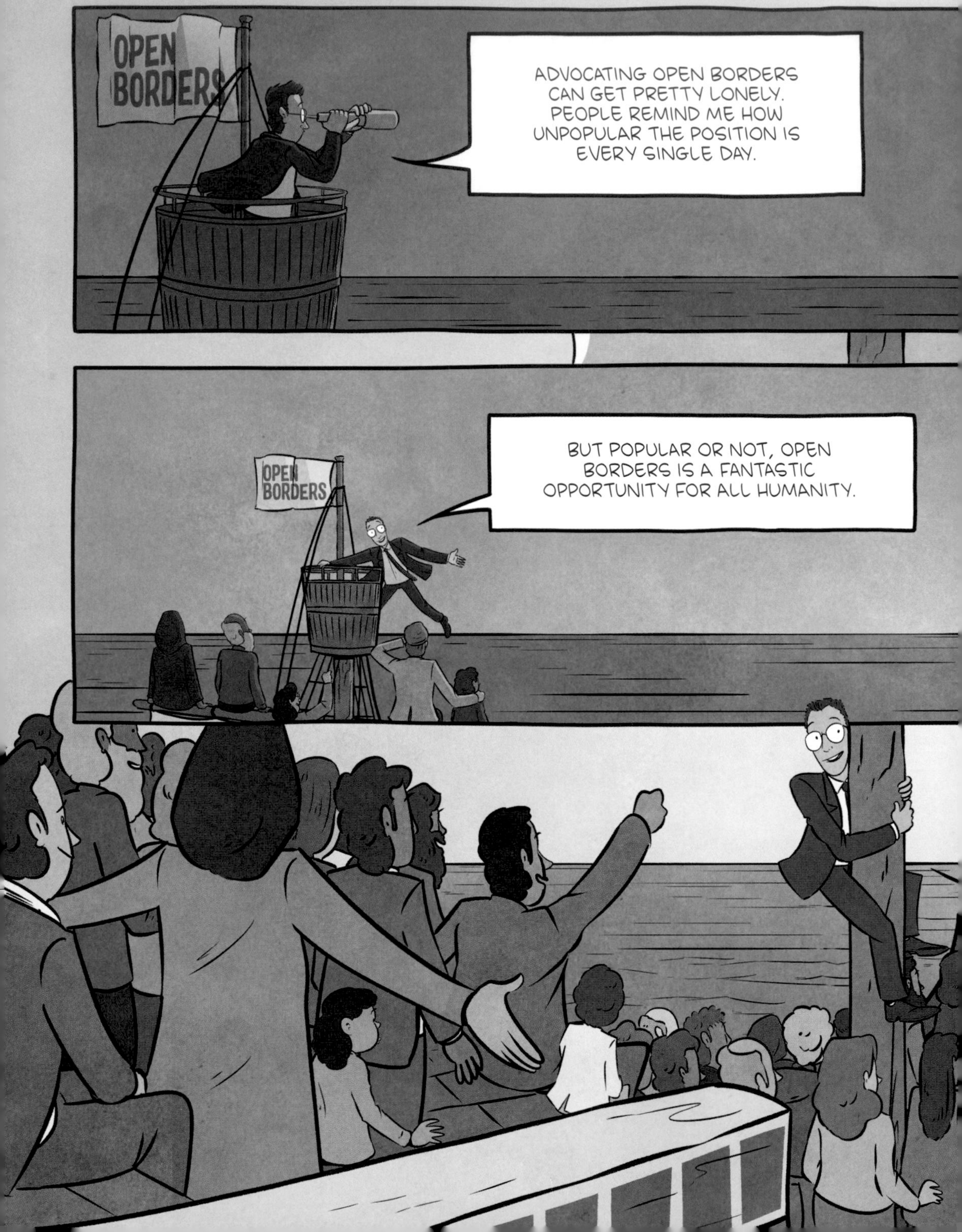
OPEN BORDERS
ADVOCATING OPEN BORDERS CAN GET PRETTY LONELY. PEOPLE REMIND ME HOW UNPOPULAR THE POSITION IS EVERY SINGLE DAY.
OPEN BORDERS
BUT POPULAR OR NOT, OPEN BORDERS IS A FANTASTIC OPPORTUNITY FOR ALL HUMANITY.

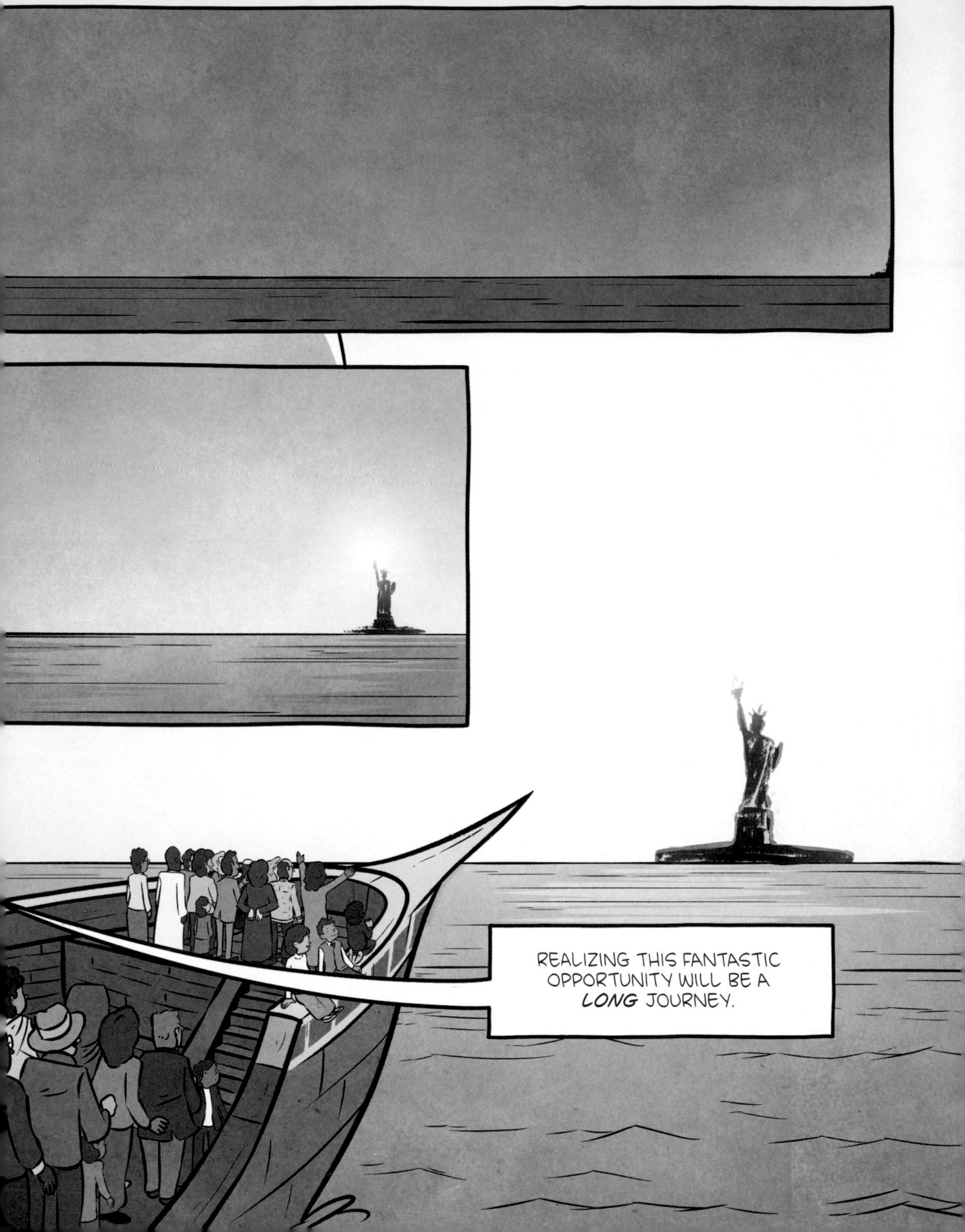
REALIZING THIS FANTASTIC OPPORTUNITY WILL BE A *LONG* JOURNEY.

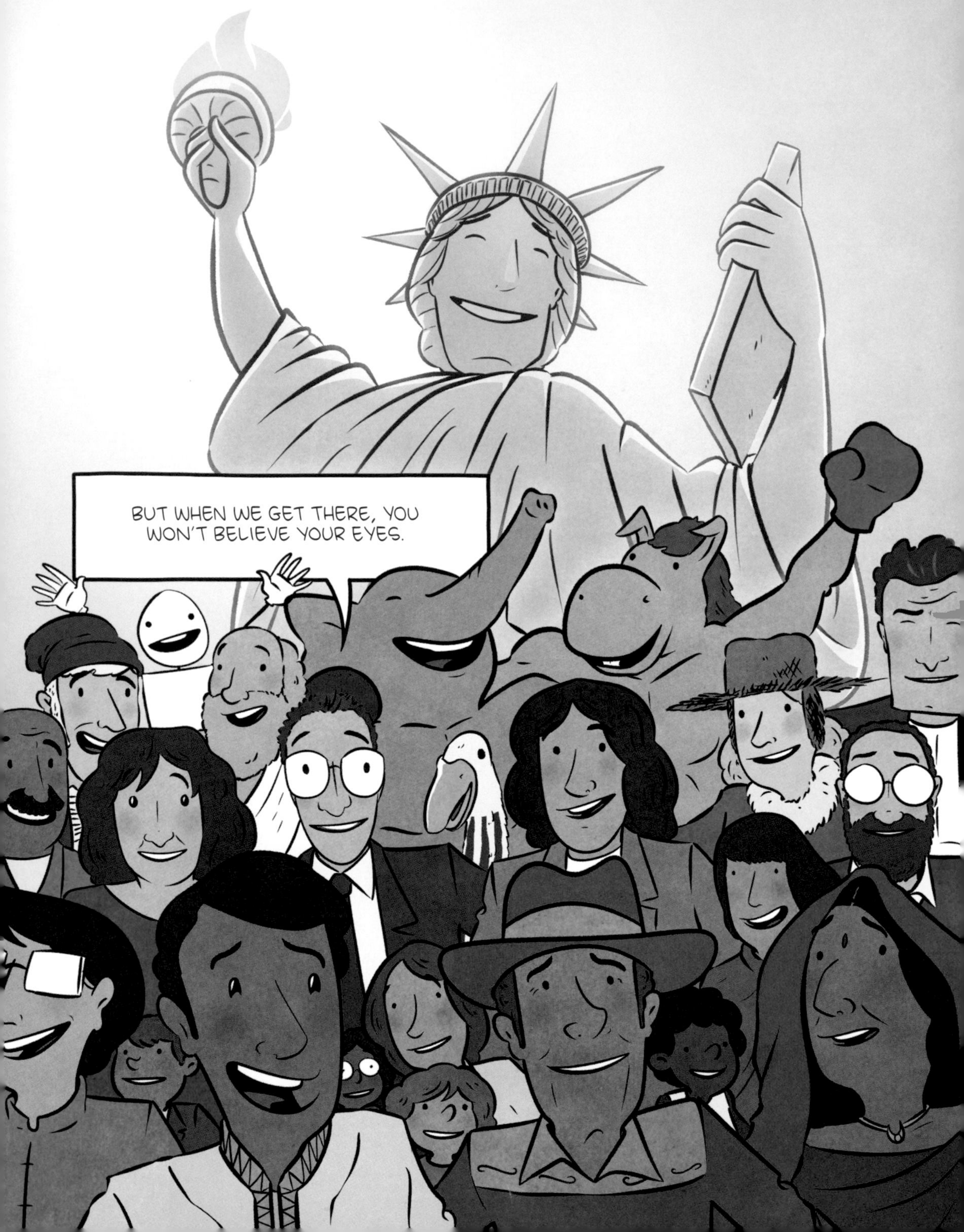
BUT WHEN WE GET THERE, YOU WON'T BELIEVE YOUR EYES.

NOTES

CHAPTER 1:
GLOBAL APARTHEID

p.5, panel 1. This graph uses (a) IMF data for World GDP adjusted for Purchasing Power Parity in international dollars, (b) the CPI to convert international dollars into constant U.S. dollars, and (c) the U.S. Census for global population. Special thanks to Mark J. Perry for performing all calculations.

p.5, panel 2. This graph comes from World Bank Group 2016, p.5.

p.7, panel 3. According to the United Nations, annual migration into OECD countries has ranged from about 4 million in 2000 to about 7 million in 2015. The estimated global migrant population is about 244 million, about 3.3% of global population. In other words, 96.7% of humanity continue to reside in their country of birth. (International Organization for Migration 2017, pps.24, 15). For further information, see Connor et al. 2013.

p.8, panel 2. Clifton 2013. Esipova and Ray 2012 estimates that 600 million globally wish to permanently move to another country, and over a billion wish to seek temporary work abroad. Esipova et al. 2009, 2014, and Esipova 2017 estimate population gain and loss if everyone on Earth migrated to their first-choice destination. Despite the noisiness of the annual estimates, many hundreds of millions clearly desire to move to another country.

p.8, panel 3. According to the last Census (United States Census Bureau 2018a), Los Angeles County has a population density of 2,419 people per square mile. Since the continental United States is 3,119,885 square miles in area, this area would contain about 7.6 billion people, the current world population.

p.8, panel 5. See especially Clemens et al. forthcoming, Pritchett 2006, pp.18–27, and further discussion in chapter 2 of this book.

p.9, panel 2. Some commentators favor an expansive definition of "global apartheid" such as "an international system of minority rule whose attributes include: differential access to basic human rights; wealth and power structured by race and place; structural racism, embedded in global economic processes, political institutions and cultural assumptions; and the international practice of double standards that assume inferior rights to be appropriate for certain 'others,' defined by location, origin, race or gender." (Booker and Minter 2001) But others, notably Lant Pritchett, focus on South African apartheid's most distinctive feature: mobility restrictions. "It is said that fish do not know they are swimming in water. The analogy between apartheid and restrictions on labor mobility is almost exact. People are not allowed to live and work where they please." (Pritchett 2006, p.79; see also Howley 2008)

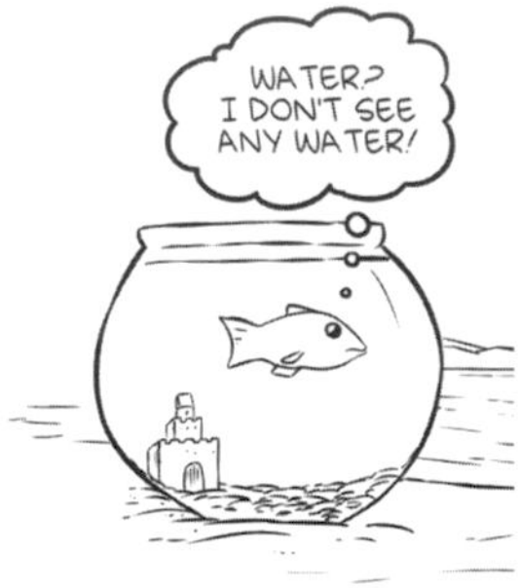
WATER?
I DON'T SEE
ANY WATER!

For a review of the evidence on the strictness and enforcement of immigration laws, see Caplan and Naik 2015, pp.181–3.

p.10, panel 2. For recent international statistics on illegal (or "irregular") immigration, see International Organization for Migration 2017, pp.20–1.

p.11, panels 1–2. For further discussion, see Caplan and Naik 2015, pp.184-5, and Caplan 2012a.

p.12, panels 1–2. For admittedly imperfect estimates of human smuggling fees, see Havocscope 2018. These figures have apparently not been updated since 2014 at the latest; due to inflation, we should expect them to be modestly higher today. Roberts et al. 2010, p.5, reports a lower average Mexican smuggling figure of roughly $2,000 as of 2007.

p.12, panels 3–4. See Roberts et al. 2013, pp.20–5.

p.13. For a more academic version of this common-sense ethical argument, see Chang 2003.

p.14, panel 1. King 1963, p.5.

p.15. For general discussion of open borders, see Caplan 2012b, Caplan and Naik 2015, Van der Vossen and Brennan 2018, Legrain 2007, Pritchett 2006, and the website openborders.info. Critics occasionally equate "open borders" with "no borders," but these are distinct proposals; an open borders regime could still have border checkpoints, require passports, and so on. The acid test, in my view, is that an open borders regime does not subject foreigners to any mobility restrictions *more stringent than natives face.* Thus, if a foreigner commits a crime warranting incarceration, an open borders regime could impose the lesser punishment of exclusion. Similarly, if a foreigner has a contagious disease warranting quarantine, an open borders regime could impose the lesser precaution of exclusion.

p.16. For elaboration of these points, see Caplan 2013a.

pp.17–19. See Huemer 2010 for a full discussion. All quotations from Huemer 2010, pp.431-3.

p.21, panels 1–3. For brief histories of U.S. immigration policy, see Gjelten 2015, pp.79-135 and Gerber 2011, pp.17-64.

p.21, panel 2. This image, "The Magic Washer" 1886, is an advertisement for a laundry detergent.

The fine print reads, "The Chinese must go. We have no use for them since we got this wonderful washer."

p.21, panel 4. See Ratiner 2015, pp.1–39 for a short discussion of the life and work of Emma Lazarus, and pp.202–3 for the text of her poem "The New Colossus," mounted inside the lower level of the pedestal of "Liberty Enlightening the World," better known as the Statue of Liberty.

p.22, panel 1. This image, "The Usual Irish Way of Doing Things," shows a drunken Irish terrorist. (Nast 1871)

p.22, panel 2. This image, "Know-Nothing," c.1850, shows Irish and German immigrants stealing a ballot box.

p.22, panel 3. This image, "What We Would Like to See," 1888, shows the expulsion of an Italian "pauper" and a Chinese "coolie."

p.22, panels 4–5. According to the Maddison Project Database 2018, U.S. per-capita GDP (variable identifier cgdppc) overtook the United Kingdom's to become the world's highest by 1830. It has remained at or very near the top ever since, occasionally losing out to Australia and New Zealand in the 19th century, and low-population, oil-rich states beginning in the late 20th century. Total U.S. GDP surpassed the United Kingdom's by 1860, and both China and India's by 1890. Total GDP calculated by multiplying Maddison variable identifiers pop*cgdppc. In World War I, the United States fielded fewer troops than any of the other major powers, but clearly retained vast untapped military potential due to the total size of its economy.

pp.23–24. On the end of America's open borders era, see Gjelten 2015, pp.79–94. For further discussion, see Ngai 1999, Ludmerer 1972, and Parker 1924. Parker, writing almost immediately after the passage of the 1924 Immigration Act, opines, "While it is by far the most drastic immigration statute ever passed by the United States Congress, it is in numerous respects the most humane measure yet devised." He then declares that, "*The main objects* of the new, as of the old, quota law are: first, a sufficient reduction in the volume of immigration to give assurance that the country will not admit more annually than it can accommodate; and, second, making the reduction fall most heavily on the 'new immigration' countries (of southern and eastern Europe), and most lightly on those countries (of western and northern Europe) from which our earlier immigration was principally derived—this in order to give assurance of the more rapid assimilation of those admitted." (Parker 1924, 737-8) Many other prominent voices, including Calvin Coolidge and Secretary of Labor James Davis, openly praised the racial—rather than merely cultural—superiority of the Nordic race. (Ludmerer 1972, pp.66-70)

Surprisingly, though, early IQ research played almost no role in the exclusionary legislation of the 1920s. As Herrnstein and Snyderman 1983, pp.993 explain:

> Of the total committee hearings and addenda for both House or Senate, then, allegations of innate intellectual inferiority of immigrants represented a minute fraction... The report teems with reasons for keeping "inferior" immigrants out of the country, but it contains no mention whatever of intelligence or intelligence testing. No mention,

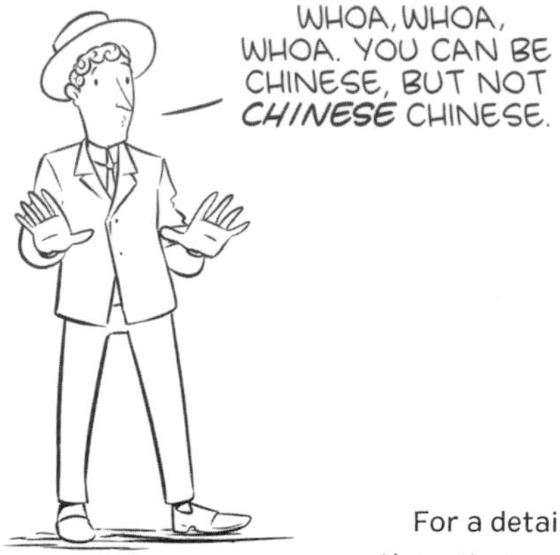
WHOA, WHOA, WHOA. YOU CAN BE CHINESE, BUT NOT CHINESE CHINESE.

either, in the Minority Report, written by Representatives Adolph Sabath and Samuel Dickstein who label the proposed act as racist and discriminatory, and who uphold the worth of the immigrant. Even when the innate characteristics of immigrants were the central issue, as in both of these reports, neither intelligence nor testing came up.

If intelligence testing was of little importance in committee hearings, it played an even smaller role in floor debate. In both chambers of Congress, concern focused on two topics: the influx of cheap labor via immigration and the general, though unspecified, inferiority of immigrants.

For a detailed table of the annual quotas effective in 1929, see Ngai 1999, p.74. Note that east Asian *countries* were given quotas, albeit tiny ones. Yet even these slots were closed to Asian *individuals*: "China, Japan, India, and Siam each received the minimum quota of one hundred, but the law excluded the native citizens of those countries from immigration because they were deemed to be racially ineligible to citizenship. Thus Congress created the oddity of immigration quotas for non-Chinese persons from China, non-Japanese persons from Japan, non-Indian persons from India, and so on." (Ngai 1999, pp.72-3)

p.25. Prominent works criticizing the effects of immigration include Borjas 2001, 2014, 2016, Salam 2018, Krikorian 2008, 2010, Coulter 2015a, and Brimelow 1995. While many interpret Jones 2016 as highly critical of low-skilled immigration, the actual text is strikingly *pro*-immigration:

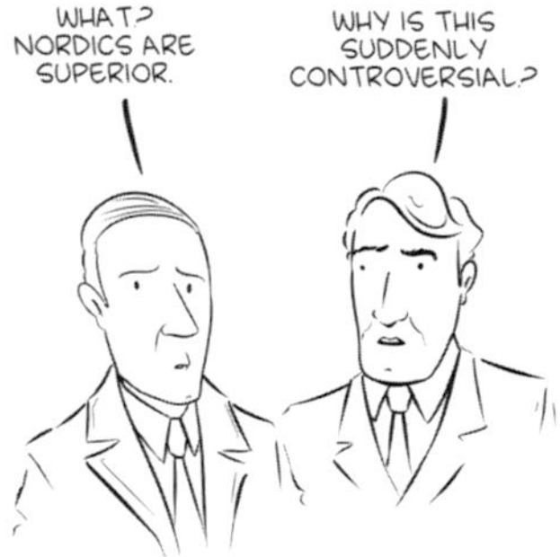
WHAT? NORDICS ARE SUPERIOR.
WHY IS THIS SUDDENLY CONTROVERSIAL?

> About a decade ago, dozens of American economists signed an open letter in support of more immigration. The letter touched on many points: that less-skilled immigrants appear to push down the wages of U.S.-born citizens little if at all, that immigration helps rich-country economies in ways that don't show up in official statistics, and that the biggest beneficiaries of less-skilled immigration are the immigrants themselves... I've always been glad I signed this letter: it sums up the great promise of immigration... For people who care about ending the deepest poverty, migration should be at the top of the list of potential cures. (Jones 2016, pp.160-1)

CHAPTER 2:
TRILLION-DOLLAR BILLS ON THE SIDEWALK

pp.28–29. See Caplan 2013b for the original statement of this thought experiment.

p.30. The world's leading introductory economics textbook includes "A country's standard of living depends on its ability to produce goods and services" on its list of the top ten principles of economics. (Mankiw 2015, p.13; for elaboration, see pp.523-46) Competing textbooks, regardless of the authors' ideology, make the very same point: See e.g. Cowen and Tabarrok 2018, pp.529-51, and Krugman and Wells 2017, pp.407-48.

p.31, panel 3. Leading impediments to wealth creation include bad economic policies (Sachs and Warner 1995a, 1995b; Gwartney et al. 2017, pp.1-26), poor management (Bloom and van Reenen 2010), war (Collier 1999; Blattman and Miguel 2010), geography (Gallup et al. 1999; Sachs 2003), and corruption (Drury et al. 2006; Mo 2001).

pp.32-33. This discussion draws heavily on Clemens et al. forthcoming. While estimates of the gains of migration vary, all leading papers find enormous effects. See Hendricks 2002, Iregui 2005, Bertoli et al. 2008, Clemens and Pritchett 2008, McKenzie et al. 2010, and Abramitzky et al. 2012.

pp.34-35. This discussion draws heavily on Clemens 2011. As usual, estimates of the effect of open borders on Gross World Product vary, but are consistently enormous. See Hamilton and Whalley 1984, Moses and Letnes 2004, 2005, Klein and Ventura 2009, Kennan 2013, and Delogu et al. 2018. Clemens and Pritchett 2016 grant that given pessimistic assumptions, full open borders is no longer economically optimal; the benefits of drastic liberalization, however, remain massive.

Borjas 2014, pp.167-8, offers the only serious quantitative challenge to these eye-popping figures, arguing that they are grossly overstated because they ignore migrants' emotional attachment to their birthplaces. Caplan 2014a shows, however, that Borjas entertains absurdly high monetary values for these attachments. Why absurd? Borjas looks at how many dollars you would have to pay the *average American* to relocate, then imputes similar figures to even the world's poorest and most eager migrants. All the benefits of open borders go away if you "only" assume that Haitian immigrants pay a $140,000 emotional cost to leave Port-au-Prince! Borjas 2015, p.971 repeats his original argument but pleads agnosticism on the numbers: "Of course, we have no idea what the costs of migration will actually be if migration restrictions were to be removed and billions of people from poor countries were on the move." But agnosticism is not warranted; while people around the world feel *some* emotional attachment to their homeland, the monetary value of these attachments is clearly tiny compared to the gains of migration. See Clemens and Pritchett 2016, pp.11-16 for a more extended response to the Borjas challenge.

p.36, panel 4. Researchers find large, positive effects of immigration on housing prices; when immigrants increase regional population by 1%, housing prices rise by roughly 1%. See especially Saiz 2007, as well as Ottaviano and Peri 2006 and Gonzalez and Ortega 2013. Since roughly two-thirds of Americans own their own home, these gains would be widely dispersed. There is, however, some evidence that immigration (especially low-skilled immigration) lowers *local* housing prices by encouraging the exit of wealthier natives. (Saiz and Wachter 2011, Sá 2015) In other words, immigration enriches the *average* homeowner, but some lose nonetheless.

p.36, panel 5. Roughly 25% of direct-care workers are foreign-born (Espinoza 2017), well above the foreign-born share of the workforce.

p.36, panel 6.   See especially Cortés and Tessada 2011.

p.36, panel 7.   Rising home prices standardly lead to large increases in construction, except in regions with strict land-use regulation. For an overview, see Glaeser 2017.

p.38, panel 1.   Even economists who emphasize the negative effects of immigration on native wages report small—and mixed—effects. Borjas and Katz 2007, p.49, estimate that, in the long run, extra Mexican migration from 1980–2000 reduced U.S. native dropouts' wages by a grand total of 4.8%, and college graduates' wages by 0.5%. They also conclude, however, that Mexican immigration *increased* the wages of native high school graduates by 1.2% and those with some college by 0.7%.

p.38, panel 2.   Immigration increases labor demand through two channels—one obvious, the other subtle. The obvious: More immigrants means more potential customers. The subtle: Since migration increases foreigners' productivity, they have more resources to offer in the marketplace. As a rule, sellers profit from more and richer customers.

   Aside: It is equally correct to say that "Immigrants who *sell* what you *buy* help you by increasing labor demand." All else equal, your real wage—the amount of stuff an hour of your labor actually buys—rises whenever the supply of *anything* you consume becomes more abundant. If a new immigrant restaurant opens in my neighborhood, for example, I effectively receive a raise, because my salary now permits me to buy a slightly better basket of goods.

p.38, panel 3.   How can native workers possibly profit when labor supply rises? Through specialization and trade. When the supply of low-skilled workers goes up, so does the demand for higher-skilled workers to manage them. When non-English-speaking immigrants increase the supply of cooks and dishwashers, this increases the demand for English-speaking waiters. See Peri and Sparber 2009 and D'Amuri and Peri 2014 for a careful analysis of this mechanism, and Ottaviano and Peri 2012 for further evidence.

p.39, panel 2.   By 2005–8, roughly 20% of tenure-track faculty at four-year U.S. universities were foreign-born, with the share rising to 33% in the physical sciences and 43% in engineering/computer science. (Kim et al. 2012, pp.28–9)

pp.40–41.   The Arithmetic Fallacy is roughly what statisticians call "Simpson's Paradox." See Wagner 1982 and Kievit et al. 2013 for readable introductions, and Caplan 2005, 2010 for the immigration connection.

pp.41, panel 3.   Why do both groups' incomes rise under open borders? As usual, because migrants' productivity drastically rises—and native consumers share the bounty. The precise figures, to be clear, are merely illustrative, and assume that under open borders, the population ends up half native, half foreign. So, even though average native income rises to $60,000 and average foreign income rises to $20,000, the receiving country's overall average income *falls* to $40,000.

p.42, panels 2–3.   World Bank 2014 estimates of Chinese and Indian GDP in 2014 U.S. dollars, with 1976 figures adjusted for U.S. GDP deflator. (World Bank 2018a, 2018b, 2018c)

p.42, panel 4.   Useful analyses of Chinese and Indian economic liberalization and development include Sachs and Woo 2001, and Kotwal et al. 2011.

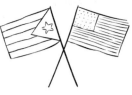

p.42, panel 5-6.   See Woetzel et al. 2009, esp. pp.55-65 and Sankhe 2010, esp. pp.37–51 on internal migration and urbanization in China and India.

p.43.   For further discussion, see Caplan and Naik 2015, pp.185-190.

p.44.   For more, see Caplan and Naik 2015, pp.190-1.

p.46.   For an excellent introduction to diaspora dynamics, see Collier 2013, pps.37-53, 166-8. Caplan 2014b argues that, contrary to Collier, diaspora dynamics bolster the case for open borders.

p.47, panels 1–2.   For the complete ruling in the González case, see FindLaw 2018.

p.47, panels 3–5.   For historical context and data on Puerto Rican migration, see Whalen 2005, esp. pps.2, 11. Caplan 2014c argues that Puerto Rico provides a compelling illustration of diaspora dynamics under open borders.

p.47, panel 6.   The current population of Puerto Rico is roughly 3.3 million. (Wikipedia 2018a) According to Whalen 2005, p.11, 3.4 million people of Puerto Rican descent were already living in the United States in 2000.

p.48, panels 1–2.   Wikipedia 2018b.

p.48, panels 3–4.   Ratha et al. 2016.

p.48, panel 5.   See Gibson and McKenzie 2011 for a review of research on brain drain.

pp.49–50.   This discussion draws heavily on Pritchett 2006, pp.43-62, and Pritchett et al. 2006, as well as Clemens and Pritchett 2008.

p.49, panel 4.   Pritchett et al. 2006, pp.29–30.

CHAPTER 3:
THE NATIVE'S BURDEN?

p.56, panel 8.   According to Snopes 2018, Sutton claims he never actually spoke these words, although he did write a book alluding to the quote.

p.57, panel 5.   Friedman 1999. For context, see Caplan 2008.

p.58, panels 2–5.   See Cowen and Tabarrok 2018, pp.368–371.

p.59, panel 1.   In 2015, combined local, state, and federal spending came to $601.7 billion for means-tested medical care and $447.8 billion for other means-tested spending, bringing total means-tested spending to $1.05 trillion. (USGovernmentSpending 2018)

p.59, panel 2.   In 2015, the U.S. government spent $887.8 billion on Social Security and $546.2 billion on Medicare, summing to $1.434 trillion. (Office of Management and Budget 2017, pp.83) Combined local, state, and federal education spending in the same year comes to $1.03 trillion. (USGovernmentSpending 2018)

p.60.   Migration Policy Institute 2016. Note that this webpage is updated annually.

p.61, panel 1.   In the most recent statistics (2013-4), average U.S. K–12 spending in 2015–16 dollars was $12,000 per pupil in average daily attendance and $11,226 per pupil in fall enrollment. (Snyder et al. 2018, p.382)

p.62.	For an introduction to the demographics of retirement systems, see Schwarz and Arias 2014, esp. pps.1–11, 41–56.
p.64, panel 1.	Blau and Mackie 2016.
p.64, panels 2–5.	For background, see Blau and Mackie 2016, pp.247–75.
pp.66-8.	For an introduction to Net Present Value (also called "Present Discounted Value" or simply "Present Value"), see Mishkin 2016, pp.110–13.
p.69, panel 2.	Blau and Mackie 2016, p.343, "All Immigrants" figures. Disclosure: This section of Blau and Mackie estimates immigrants' fiscal effects in *six* different scenarios.

Scenario #	Forecasting Assumption	Public Goods Assumption
1	CBO Long-term Budget Outlook	Congestible Only
2	CBO Long-term Budget Outlook	With Non-Interest Public Goods
3	CBO Long-term Budget Outlook with Deficit Reduction	Congestible Only
4	CBO Long-term Budget Outlook with Deficit Reduction	With Non-Interest Public Goods
5	No Budget Adjustments	Congestible Only
6	No Budget Adjustments	With Non-Interest Public Goods

Why do I report figures for Scenario #1, when most of the other scenarios are less optimistic?

First, the No Budget Adjustments Assumption, which ignores even readily foreseeable information about future U.S. finances, is clearly the worst forecasting assumption of the bunch. (Blau and Mackie 2016, p.323) Both CBO Long-term Budget Outlook assumptions are superior because they account for foreseeable social and economic changes, such as aging. In this panel, I conservatively rely on the *more* pessimistic of the two CBO scenarios.

Second, the "Congestible Only" assumption is better because it tries to distinguish between rival and non-rival goods. ("Congestible" is a synonym for "rival.") The alternate assumption absurdly treats all spending as fully rival.

p.69, panel 3.	Blau and Mackie 2016, p.343, "All Immigrants" figures. The disclosure in the previous note applies here as well.
p.69, panel 5.	Blau and Mackie 2016, p.343. These figures come from Scenario #3, as explained in the note for p.69, panel 2. All things considered, the figures in this panel are not only the most optimistic; they are also the most credible. The CBO Long-term Budget Outlook accounts for future social and economic changes, but treats existing government policies as immutable. (Blau and Mackie 2016, p.323) Given large recent and expected budget deficits, however, spending cuts and tax increases are both highly likely in the medium term. (Congressional Budget Office 2018) The CBO Long-term Budget Outlook with Deficit Reduction accordingly assumes that the government *slowly* moves in this direction, gradually raising taxes by 3% and cutting spending by 3% by 2035. (Blau and Mackie 2016, p.323)
p.72, panels 1–2.	Blau and Mackie 2016, p.341, "HS" and "<HS" rows, "Average Total Impact" column.

Since we are now considering the fiscal effects of *additional* immigrants, I here use the "Averages Based on Recent Immigrants," Scenario #1. Note: "No public goods included in benefits" is equivalent to the "congestible only" assumption that appears in Blau and Mackie 2016, p.343.

p.73, panels 2–3. Blau and Mackie 2016, p.341, "HS" and "<HS" rows, "0-24" column.

p.73, panels 5–6. Blau and Mackie 2016, p.341, "HS" and "<HS" rows, "65+" column.

p.75, panel 2. Friedman 1999.

p.76, panel 1. "When a marginal cost allocation of public goods is assumed, instead of the average cost allocation, the total net fiscal impact of the first generation group becomes much lower than that of the two native-born groups." (Blau and Mackie 2016, p.320; for details, see Scenarios #1 and #2 on p.312)

pp.76-7. See Tabarrok 2000 for exploration of the parallels between immigration and fertility.

p.78, panel 2. I was once accused of "suicidal compassion" for immigrants; see Caplan 2013c for my response.

p.79, panels 1–2. See Caplan 2007, pp.36–9 on "antiforeign bias," humans' tendency to underestimate the economic benefits of interacting with foreigners.

CHAPTER 4:
CRIMES AGAINST CULTURE

p.84, panel 2. Voltaire 1980, p.41.

p.85, panels 1–4. This section is partly inspired by my debate with Stephen Balch. (Institute for the Study of Western Civilization 2014) For follow-up discussion, see Caplan 2014d, 2014e.

p.86, panel 1. For a general history of probability and risk analysis, with extensive discussion of Gauss's contributions, see Bernstein 1998. Of course, most non-Western civilizations have used numbers to inform decision making. But the idea of *quantifying uncertainty* remained in its infancy until mathematicians Fermat and Pascal launched probability theory during the European Renaissance. (Bernstein 1998, pp.2-6)

p.86, panel 2. For the probability of being struck by lightning, see National Weather Service 2018.

p.87, panel 4. Nowrasteh 2016, p.6 reports 3,432 total U.S. deaths from terrorism during this period, 3,024 of whom were killed by foreign-born terrorists.

p.88, panel 4. FBI statistics exclude the 2,983 deaths from the 9/11 attacks. When you add these deaths to official FBI statistics (Disaster Center 2017), the sum is approximately 772,000 total murders.

p.88, panel 5. The total U.S. death rate during this period peaked at 8.9 per 1,000. (Knoema 2018) The murder rate during this period peaked in 1980 at 1 in 9,781. (Disaster Center 2017)

p.88, panel 6. Nowrasteh 2016, pp.4–5 reports a 1-in-3.6 million risk of death from foreign-born domestic terrorism. Dividing by .88 yields a 1-in-3.2 million risk of death from all terrorism.

p.89, panel 1. This meme was first posted by Donald Trump Jr. on his Twitter account. (Hauser 2016)

p.89, panel 5. In Plato's account of Socrates's deathbed oration, the philosopher famously counsels, "[T]he unexamined life is not worth living..." (Plato 2002, p.41)

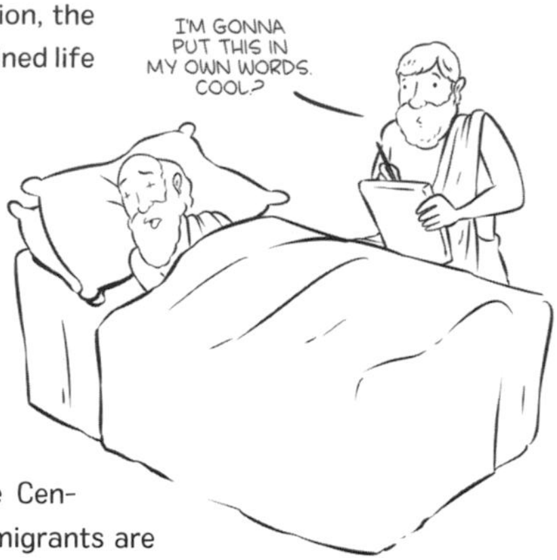
I'M GONNA PUT THIS IN MY OWN WORDS. COOL?

p.90, panel 3. Nowrasteh 2016, p.8 calculates that "one foreign-born terrorist entered the United States for every 7.38 million non-terrorist foreigners," implying that 99.999986% were *not* terrorists.

p.91, panel 2. See especially the National Academy of Sciences review (Waters and Pineau 2015, pp.326–330) as well as Lee and Martinez 2009 and Nowrasteh 2015. Even researchers at the Center for Immigration Studies claim not that immigrants are crime-prone, but that the evidence is "confused due to a lack of good data and contrary information." (Camarota and Vaughan 2009, p.1)

p.91, panel 3. United States Census Bureau 2018b. To reproduce my figures for the native population, divide each year's number of natives in Adult Correctional Facilities by the native population. Similarly, the foreign-born rate equals the number of foreign-born in these facilities divided by the foreign-born population.

p.92, panel 1. United States Census Bureau 2018b. To reproduce my figures for naturalized citizens, divide each year's number of incarcerated naturalized citizens by the number of naturalized citizens.

p.92, panel 2. United States Census Bureau 2018b. To reproduce my figures for non-citizens, divide each year's number of incarcerated non-citizens by the number of non-citizens. Note: If illegal immigration exceeds conventional estimates, then as a matter of arithmetic, conventional estimates *overstate* the criminality of non-citizens.

p.92, panel 3. Carson 2018, p.13 reports that over 21% of federal inmates were noncitizens, roughly triple their share of the U.S. population. In 2016, 13,300 federal inmates were serving time for immigration offenses. (Carson, p.19) Roughly 80% of immigration offenses are for illegal reentry. (United States Sentencing Commission 2017)

p.93, panel 3. Waters and Pineau 2015, p.327. For further discussion, see Waters and Pineau 2015, pp.330–2 as well as Lee and Martinez 2009 and Nowrasteh 2015.

p.93, panel 4. See Waters and Pineau 2015, p.329: "Although the second generation has higher crime rates than the first generation, their rates are generally lower than or very similar to the crime rate of the native-born in general."

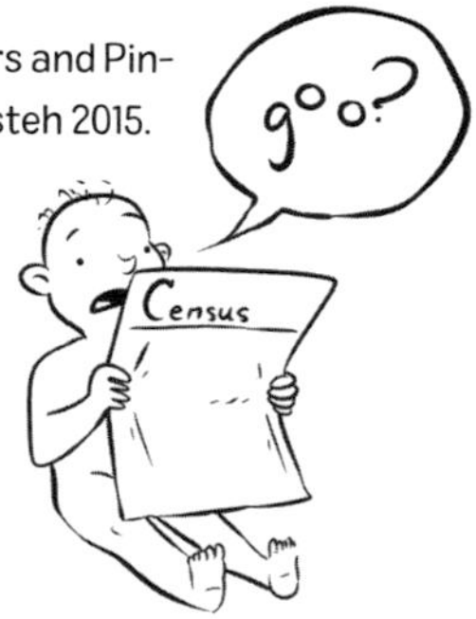
goo?
Census

p.95, panel 1. Psychologists have a name—"availability bias"—for humans' tendency to inflate the likelihood of vivid events. See Kahneman 2011, pp.129–145 for a review of the evidence, and

Kuran and Sunstein 1999 for analysis of the dysfunctional political effects of this bias.

p.96, panel 1. Ryan 2013, p.7. Language data are only available for persons five years and older. For obvious reasons, the Census does not ask about the speaking ability of infants or toddlers.

p.96, panel 2. Ryan 2013, p.11.

p.96, panel 3. I count speakers as "fluent" if they (a) speak only English at home, or (b) claim to speak English "very well." In 2010, 91% of the population so qualified. (Ryan 2013, p.3) In 1980, 95% so qualified. (Bureau of the Census 1984, p.1–12)

p.97, panel 3. Census-takers classified a majority of late 19th-century arrivals as simply unable to speak English. Their English improved over time, but since the Census used a binary measure ("Speaks English" or "Does Not Speak English") we can safely assume that most never became fluent. (Vigdor 2015, pp.81–84) Stevens 1999, p.555 confirms the common-sense conclusion that, "[P]roficiency in a second language among adults is strongly related to age at immigration."

p.97, panel 4. Chua 2011, p.86.

p.97, panel 5. Stevens 1999, pp.569–71, for example, estimates that nearly 100% of immigrants who arrive in infancy and remain in the country attain full fluency. Adult arrivals are far less likely to do so, even after decades of residence. See also Stevens 2015.

p.98, panels 2–3. Alba 2004, p.7.

p.99, panels 3–5. Rumbaut et al. 2006, pp.456–8.

p.100, panel 3. This point is heavily inspired by Smith 2012:

> [G]lobalization has half-Americanized half the world already. 19th-Century immigrants may have been *racially* more similar to America's white native majority, but they were less familiar with democracy, with the English language, with America via movies and music and TV, with American-style market capitalism, with Coke and McDonald's and Microsoft and Google and many other American firms, with blue jeans and free speech and religious tolerance, than a 19th-century immigrant from the Habsburg Empire or tsarist Russia.

p.100, panel 4. Wikipedia 2018c.

p.100, panel 5. Wikipedia 2018d.

p.101, panel 1. For overviews on the social benefits of trust, see Algan and Cahuc 2014 and Nannestad 2008.

p.101, panel 2. Map from Ortiz-Ospina and Roser 2017.

Putnam 2007 famously argues that immigration undermines trust by increasing ethnic diversity. But even in Putnam's own analysis (pp.151–3), this is a relatively minor effect; diverse American communities have low trust almost entirely because blacks and Hispanics have low trust, not because they are ethnically mixed. (Caplan 2017a) The far stronger reason to expect low-skilled immigration to reduce trust is the well-documented fact that trust in the third world is low. (Algan and Cahuc 2014, pp.62–4; Ortiz-Ospina and Roser 2017)

p.102, panel 1. Pieces arguing that trust assimilation is low include Algan and Cahuc 2010 and Uslaner 2008.

p.102, panels 2–3. Studies finding high assimilation include Dinesen 2012, and Dinesen and Hooghe 2010. Caplan 2017a notes that Uslaner 2008 finds only small effects and relies almost entirely on descendants of European immigrants. Algan and Cahuc 2010's modestly broader sample finds just 45% trust persistence.

p.102, panel 4. Caplan 2017a. Throughout this book, I try to rely on an overall topic-by-topic review of the research rather than presenting original results. But to the best of my knowledge, no trust specialist has taken full advantage of U.S. data to estimate trust persistence, so I had to fill this role myself.

Disclosure: The qualification "descendants of willing immigrants" is crucial. "Descendants" is crucial because first-generation trust *is* highly persistent. I estimate 70% persistence for immigrants, versus just 28% for their descendants. "Willing immigrants" is crucial because (a) almost all African Americans are descended from slaves, (b) African Americans are a numerous group, and (c) both African Americans and Africans generally have very low trust. If you count Africans like other immigrants, estimated trust persistence for immigrants' descendants doubles to 56%. Why distinguish between the descendants of free versus forced migrants? Because slavery persistently damaged trust in Africa (Nunn and Wantchekon 2011), and it seems plausible to think it had a similar effect in the United States.

p.103, panel 1. For skeptical analyses of the social benefits of trust, see Berggren et al. 2008 and Roth 2009. Bjørnskov 2007 finds that few alleged cross-country predictors of trust are genuinely significant; even the much-studied effect of ethnic diversity is marginal. Nannestad 2008 also presents detailed evidence that, popularizers notwithstanding, the social benefits of trust remain questionable.

p.103, panel 2. Putnam 2007, pp.144–50.

p.103, panel 3. Roth 2009, p.117.

p.103, panel 4. Butler et al. 2016, p.1165–7.

p.103, panel 5. On the distinction between trust and trustworthiness, see Glaeser et al. 2000.

p.104, panel 3. Schoenberg 1950, p.39.

pp.106–7. See generally Caplan 2014d, 2014e.

p.107, panel 3. The true author of this quote is unknown. (Quote Investigator 2015)

CHAPTER 5:
THE GOLDEN GOOSE ON TRIAL

p.112. Economists call this the problem of "political externalities of immigration." See Naik 2018a for an overview of the argument, including numerous links to defenders and critics.

p.113, panel 4. Caplan 2007.

p.114, panels 3–5.	All figures are from my analysis of the General Social Survey, 1980–2012, using two-party vote shares. Variable identifiers: pres80–pres12, if80who–if2012who. By "white" I mean "non-Hispanic white."
p.115, panel 1.	Contrary to popular opinion, the effect of material self-interest on voting and public opinion is slight. The primary drivers of political behavior are ideology and identity, not dollars and cents. See e.g. Mansbridge 1990 and Caplan 2007, pp.148–51.
p.115, panel 2.	Wikipedia 2018e.
p.115, panel 3.	In 2015, 90% of Indian households with children contained two married adults, versus 73% for the U.S. as a whole. (Pew Research Center 2017; Bureau of the Census 2018)
p.115, panel 4.	Junn et al. 2011, p.527.
p.115, panel 6.	While political scientists have long debated government responsiveness to public opinion, almost all acknowledge a major connection. The best single work on this title probably remains Gilens 2012, especially pp.50–123, which analyzes a large data set of policy-relevant surveys and actual political results. This approach likely understates the power of public opinion, because pollsters rarely bother to ask about extremely popular or unpopular proposals.
p.116, panel 1.	Nowrasteh and Wilson 2017 provides a detailed comparison of the political views of immigrants versus natives. I have reanalyzed the same data set (the General Social Survey, 2000–16) to simplify the presentation, but our overall results are quite consistent.
p.116, panel 2.	GSS variable identifier POLVIEWS.
p.116, panel 3.	GSS variable identifier HELPNOT.
p.116, panel 4.	GSS variable identifiers TAXPOOR, TAXMID, and TAXRICH.
p.117, panel 1.	GSS variable identifier NATFARE. All results on this page analyze opinion for 2000–16.
p.117, panel 2.	GSS variable identifiers NATSOC, NATHEAL, NATEDUC, NATENVIR, and NATARMS.
p.117, panels 4–7.	GSS variables identifiers ABANY, MARHOMO, GRASS, and SPKMSLM. Since social attitudes have rapidly liberalized as the foreign-born population share has risen, some of these patterns are not instantly visible in the data; to detect them, you must look year-by-year. In technical terms, a multiple regression of these social attitudes on nativity and year consistently confirms that the foreign-born are more socially conservative on all four questions.
p.117, panels 8–9.	GSS variable identifier LETIN1. Remember that this averages attitudes from 2000 to 2016, so there is no real conflict with recent Gallup data showing markedly higher support for liberalization. (Brenan 2018)
p.118, panels 3–4.	See Caplan and Naik 2015, pp.193–5 for the construction of these measures. The "U.S. Mean" is the average answer for *all* respondents in the U.S.-based General Social Survey, which includes natives, immigrants, and foreign citizens. The normal distributions are a simplification; the critical facts are (a) the mean and (b) subgroups' deviation from the mean (measured in standard deviations).
p.119, panel 2.	GSS variable identifier VOTE12.
p.119, panel 3.	GSS variable identifier VOTE12, sub-sample with DEGREE=0.
p.119, panels 4–5.	On low influence of poor voters, see Gilens 2012. Critics accuse Gilens of under-

stating government responsiveness to *middle*-class voters. (Bashir 2015, Matthews 2016) But even the authors of the two main critical pieces do not dispute Gilens's conclusion that poor voters lack political influence. (Private email correspondence with both Bashir and Matthews)

p.119, panel 6.   See e.g. Nowrasteh and Wilson 2017.

p.120, panel 2.   Gochenour and Nowrasteh 2014, pp.5–8, surveys this literature; leading papers include Alesina et al. 2001, Alesina et al. 2018, and Soroka et al. 2006.

p.120, panel 3.   Bay and Pedersen 2006, pps.424–8. The table on p.428 seems to indicate 68% initial support, but only because it excludes the undecided respondents shown on p.425. Since "Change Position" includes a change to "undecided" (p.434, fn 9), I base the treatment effect on the authors' statement (p.428) that, "Only 45 percent of the entire sample are ready to support a basic income scheme that they have been reminded will include non-citizens."

p.121, panels 1–2.   See e.g. Derbyshire 2015.

p.123.   Top papers on the long-run effects of national ancestry include Putterman and Weil 2010, Comin et al. 2010, and Spolaore and Wacziarg 2013. "Advanced" by what standard? The researchers' three main measures are: (a) when your ancestors adopted agriculture, (b) when your ancestors developed centralized governments (usually called "state history"), and (c) when your ancestors adopted specific critical technologies. For detailed critiques of all three papers, see Caplan 2016a, 2016b, and 2016c.

p.124.   The original researchers barely hint at the implications for immigration, but my colleague Garett Jones explicitly bases his case for immigration restrictions on their work. (Jones 2015) The "SAT Score" in the title of his talk refers to ancestral "state history" (S), "agriculture" (A), and "technology" (T), not the familiar college admissions test.

p.125, panels 1–4.   Caplan 2016d highlights that China, India, and the U.S. are all serious outliers for Putterman and Weil 2010.

p.125, panel 5.   Caplan 2016e shows that population-weighting vitiates Putterman and Weil's 2010 results for both agriculture and state history. To the best of my knowledge, no one has reestimated Comin et al. 2010's results for ancestral technologies using population weighting.

p.126, panels 1–3.   See Caplan 2016a, 2016b, 2016c, and 2017b. Unlike ancestry results, the geographic results are robust to population weighting. (Caplan 2016e)

p.126, panel 4.   In fact, Putterman and Weil's 2010 results imply that moving the world's population to the United States would increase world GDP to almost four times its current level! (Caplan 2016d)

p.127, panels 2–4.   The research literature on cognitive ability is vast. For an overview, see Jensen 1998, esp. pp.270–305. Despite public controversy, there is a strong research consensus on the basic science of intelligence. (Gottfredsen 1994)

p.128, panel 1.   This map (IQ Research 2018) is derived from Lynn and Vanhanen 2002; Rindermann et al. 2009 and Lynn and Meisenberg 2010 present quite similar estimates. Wicherts et al. 2010 argues that earlier researchers seriously underestimate

	sub-Saharan African IQ, but still concludes that the region is well below the world average.
p.128, panel 2.	IQ is not only strongly correlated with national income (Jones 2016; Lynn and Vanhanen 2002); when "raced" against other explanatory variables, it outperforms almost all of them. (Jones and Schneider 2006)
p.128, panels 3–4.	Rich countries have less serious crime and more democracy than poor countries. (van Zanden et al. 2014, pps.154–5, 173–4) Given the positive correlation between GDP and IQ, we can infer that high-IQ countries have less serious crime and more democracy than low-IQ countries. Rindermann et al. 2009 documents the correlation between national IQ and both crime and democracy. Note: Even if income, not IQ, statistically accounted for these patterns, IQ would still ultimately deserve some credit as long as IQ genuinely caused higher income.
p.129, panels 1–2.	Jones 2016.
p.129, panel 3.	See Jones 2016, pp.85–102.
p.129, panels 4–5.	Jones 2016, pp.1–14; Jones and Schneider 2008.
p.130, panel 1.	Jones 2016, pp.103–37; Caplan 2007.
p.130, panel 2.	Caplan and Miller 2010.
p.130, panel 3.	Jones 2016, pp.161–3; Coulter 2015a. To the best of my knowledge, Jones never publicly praised Coulter, but Coulter has strongly praised Jones. Her Facebook page links to the book, stating, "Which reminds me: Low IQ immigrants are lowering your income, your freedom, your way of life. Read this book." (Coulter 2015b) While *Hive Mind*'s actual discussion of immigration is rather positive (Jones 2016, pp.153–63), he has subsequently drawn far more negative implications. (Jones 2017)
p.131, panel 1.	Both of *Hive Mind*'s measures of U.S. IQ put it at 98. (Jones 2016, p.170) Estimates of *humanity's* average IQ (as opposed to *nations'* average IQs) are scarce, but Rindermann 2018, p.448 estimates population-weighted global IQ at 87.
p.131, panels 2–3.	All GDP figures are adjusted for Purchasing Power Parity (PPP). (World Bank 2018e) I use 2016 data because this is the most recent year where World GDP is available.
	To follow the calculations, note that in *Hive Mind*, Jones builds upon his earlier work with Schneider, which estimates that raising national IQ by 1 point raises the natural logarithm of per-capita GDP by .061—approximately 6.1%. (Jones 2016, p.11; Jones and Schneider 2006, p.90) This implies that an 11-point fall in IQ multiplies initial GDP by $\exp(-.061\cdot11)=0.51$. If we drop the PPP adjustment, World GDP is only $10,201, implying that open borders would raise World GDP by 188%! (World Bank 2018e)
p.132.	Jones 2016, pp.49–64.
p.133, panel 1.	For overviews of the developmental effects of international adoption, see Juffer and van IJzendoorn 2009, and van IJzendoorn et al. 2005.
p.133, panel 2.	The key Swedish studies are Dalen et al. 2008 and Odenstad et al. 2008.
p.133, panels 3–4.	For a survey of the physical benefits of international adoption, see van IJzendoorn et al. 2007 and Juffer et al. 2009, pp.175–7.

p.133, panels 5–6. For a survey of the cognitive benefits of international adoption, see van IJzendoorn 2005 and Juffer et al. 2009, pp.178–180.

p.134, panels 1–2. For overviews of the relevant research on the weak effect of family environment on intelligence and the fade-out of early nurture effects, see Caplan 2011, pps.49–51, 76–80. See also Caplan 2016e.

p.134, panel 3. Dalen et al. 2008 and Odenstad et al. 2008 confirm large effects of international adoption on adult IQ; Vinnerljung et al. 2010 finds comparable effects of international adoption on high school performance. This research has a slightly pessimistic tone because it focuses on the fact that international adoptees score worse than native-born Swedes. They do, but international adoptees also do better than they would have done *if they had remained in their countries of birth.* (Caplan 2017c, 2017d) Note: The latter comparisons make the conservative assumption that adoptees would have grown up to have average IQ and educational performance for their home countries. Since adoptees tend to come from disadvantaged backgrounds (including third-world orphanages), they probably would have been well *below* average if they had stayed behind, implying even larger cognitive gains of adoption.

p.135, panel 2. For general discussions of nurture effects, see Caplan 2011, pp.37–91, Segal 2000, and Harris 2009.

p.137. For a history of the Berlin Wall, see Taylor 2008.

CHAPTER 6: KEYHOLE SOLUTIONS

p.140, panel 3. See Johns Hopkins Medicine 2018 for an introduction.

p.141, panel 1. To the best of my (and his) knowledge, Tim Harford originated the phrase "keyhole solution" in *The Undercover Economist.* (Harford 2012, pp.138–143) He has also done much to popularize the concept.

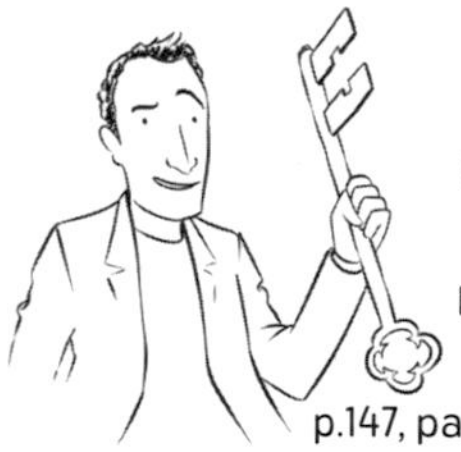

p.143. See Naik 2018b for overview and references, and Caplan 2012b for discussion of economic, fiscal, cultural, and political keyhole solutions.

p.144. Nathaniel Smith labels this the DRITI approach (short for "Don't Restrict Immigration; Tax It"). See Smith 2010, pp.109–124 for a policy blueprint.

p.147, panel 5. Nowrasteh and Cole 2013.

p.148. See Nowrasteh and Cole 2013 for further discussion.

p.151, panel 1. Though Trump has not strictly fulfilled his campaign promise "for a total and complete shutdown of Muslims entering the United States until our country's representatives can figure out what the hell is going on" (Johnson 2015), legal immigration from Muslim-majority countries has dramatically fallen during his administration. (Bier 2018)

p.151, panels 2–4. Comparative politics specialists continue to debate *why* the Muslim world has such a grim human rights record, but the fact is well established. See e.g. Fish 2002, Stepan and Robertson 2003, and Donno and Russett 2004.

p.151, panel 2.	In 2014, 276 Nigerian schoolgirls in the town of Chibok were kidnapped and forced into sexual slavery by the Islamist terrorist organization Boko Haram. Some were murdered, and over 100 are still missing. (Habila 2016)
p.152.	See generally Caplan 2015a.
p.152, panel 3.	Wikipedia 2018f.
p.154, panel 4.	Political scientists have long known that average citizens are politically apathetic (see e.g. Schubert, Dye, and Zeigler 2015) and participation among the eligible foreign-born is especially low in a wide range of countries. (Diehl and Wüst 2010) Globally, heavy migration to *both* Western democracies and oil-rich Gulf monarchies makes it clear that prosperity, not democracy, is the primary draw.
p.155, panel 3.	Some colleges even charge out-of-state tuition plus an extra foreign student surcharge! (Redden 2015)
p.156, panel 2.	See Office of the Assistant Secretary for Planning and Evaluation 2009 for the gory details.
p.156, panel 3.	USA.gov 2018 provides full instructions.
p.157, panel 1.	For the Bracero quotes, see National Museum of American History 2018a.
p.157, panels 2–3.	For details on the H1-B, H2-A, and H2-B temporary work programs, see USCIS 2017, USCIS 2018a, and USCIS 2018b.
p.160.	All Bible quotes from Genesis 18:20–32 of the New International Version. (Bible Gateway 2011a) In the original Bible story, Sodom lacks even ten righteous men, so God destroys the city anyway.

CHAPTER 7:
ALL ROADS LEAD TO OPEN BORDERS

p.166.	For a more detailed discussion, see Caplan and Naik 2015, pp.195–200.
pp.167–170.	Carens 1987 famously defends open borders from utilitarian, Rawlsian, and Nozickian premises.
p.170.	See Caplan 2013d for elaboration.
p.171.	Posner prefers the label "wealth maximization," but the substance is identical. See especially Posner 1979, 1980. In his later writings, Posner seems to largely abandon cost-benefit analysis in favor of a "pragmatism" that eschews almost any radical reform; see for example Posner 2003.
p.172.	Though Lee is primarily known as a politician, his writings are unusually philosophical for a man of action. The closing words of his history of modern Singapore: "[W]e stand a better chance of not failing if we abide by the basic principles that have helped us progress: social cohesion through sharing the benefits of progress, equal opportunities for all, and meritocracy, with the best man or woman for the job, especially as leaders in government." (Lee 2000)
p.174.	All Bible quotes from Luke 10:30-37 of the New International Version. (Bible Gateway 2011b)

pp.175–176. Kant's classic statement:

> Juridical punishment can never be administered merely as a means for promoting another good, either with regard to the criminal himself or to civil society, but must in all cases be imposed only because the individual on whom it is inflicted has committed a crime. For one man ought never to be dealt with merely as a means subservient to the purpose of another, nor be mixed up with the subjects of real right... He must first be found guilty and punishable, before there can be any thought of drawing from his punishment any benefit for himself or his fellow-citizens. (Kant 1887, p.195)

pp.177–180. Besides Huemer 2010, see also his critiques of social contract theory and democratic legitimacy in Huemer 2013, pp.20–80. Caplan 2012c analyzes the "trespassing" objection to open borders.

p.181, panel 2. High-quality surveys actually find that even Republicans are *slowly* becoming less hostile to immigration. (Brenan 2018) But 35% of Republicans now name immigration as "the nation's top problem," an all-time high (Newport 2018b), and Republican politicians and pundits are plainly more opposed.

p.183, panel 1. Reagan 1987. Reagan's Farewell Address almost explicitly calls for open borders:

> I've spoken of the shining city all my political life, but I don't know if I ever quite communicated what I saw when I said it. But in my mind it was a tall, proud city built on rocks stronger than oceans, windswept, God-blessed, and teeming with people of all kinds living in harmony and peace; a city with free ports that hummed with commerce and creativity. And if there had to be city walls, the walls had doors and the doors were open to anyone with the will and the heart to get here. (Reagan 1989; see also Caplan 2017e)

p.184, panel 4. This sign is not an expression of post–Pearl Harbor hysteria. It dates from soon after World War I, where the U.S. and Japan both fought for the Allies. (National Museum of American History 2018b)

pp.185–6. Trump 2016.

p.187. This is the classic economic case for free trade that runs from Smith to Bastiat to Krugman. (Smith 1982; Bastiat 1996; Krugman 1998)

p.189, panel 3. For an exploration of the Precautionary Principle, see Steel 2015. For a psychologically-minded critique of the Principle, see Sunstein 2005.

p.189, panel 4. Carlyle 1855, p.448.

CHAPTER 8:
FANTASTIC JOURNEYS . . . AND HOW TO FINISH THEM

p.196, panels 3–4. Cochrane 2011.

p.201. For a brief history of the evolution of the European Union, see Cini and Borragán. 2016, pp.11–50.

p.203, panel 2. Office for National Statistics 2012, Map 1.

p.203, panel 3. Aisch et al. 2016.

p.206. McCarthy 2017 provides data for 1966–2017; Brenan 2018 provides the latest update.

p.207, panel 2. See ReasonTV 2014 for video of a panel featuring me, Mark Krikorian, and Alex Nowrasteh. For my reaction to this debate, see Caplan 2014f. In 2015, I debated Krikorian before the Social Contract Writers Workshop, an annual summit of anti-immigration organizations; see Caplan 2015b for my reaction.

p.208. For background on the Overton Window, see Russell 2006.

p.209, panel 2. The quote is from Allen 1971.

REFERENCES

Abramitzky, Ran, Leah Boustan, and Katherine Eriksson. 2012. "Europe's Tired, Poor, Huddled Masses: Self-Selection and Economic Outcomes in the Age of Mass Migration." *American Economic Review* 102(5), pp. 1832–1856.

Aisch, Gregor, Adam Pearce, and Karl Russell. 2016. "How Britain Voted in the EU Referendum." *New York Times*, June 24. URL https://www.nytimes.com/interactive/2016/06/24/world/europe/how-britain-voted-brexit-referendum.html.

Alba, Richard. 2004. "Language Assimilation Today: Bilingualism Persists More Than in the Past, but English Still Dominates." *Center for Comparative Immigration Studies Working Paper* #111. URL http://ccis. ucsd. edu/_files/wp111.pdf.

Alesina, Alberto, Edward Glaeser, and Bruce Sacerdote. 2001. "Why Doesn't the United States Have a European-Style Welfare State?" *Brookings Papers on Economic Activity* 2, pp. 187–277.

Alesina, Alberto, Armando Miano, and Stefanie Stantcheva. 2018. "Immigration and Redistribution." *NBER Working Paper* No. 24733. URL http://www.nber.org/papers/w24733.

Algan, Yann, and Pierre Cahuc. 2010. "Inherited Trust and Growth." *American Economic Review* 100(5), pp. 2060–92.

Algan, Yann, and Pierre Cahuc. 2014. "Trust, Growth, and Well-Being: New Evidence and Policy Implications." In Aghion, Philippe, and Steven Durlauf, eds. *Handbook of Economic Growth*, vol. 2. Oxford: North-Holland, pp. 49–120.

Allen, Woody. 1971. *Bananas*. URL http://www.script-o-rama.com/movie_scripts/b/bananas-script-transcript-woody-allen.html.

Bashir, Omar. 2015. "Testing Inferences about American Politics: A Review of the 'Oligarchy' Result." *Research and Politics* 2(4), pp. 1–7.

Bastiat, Frédéric. 1996. *Economic Sophisms*. Irvington-on-Hudson, NY: Foundation for Economic Education.

Bay, Ann-Helén, and Axel West Pedersen. 2006. "The Limits of Social Solidarity: Basic Income, Immigration and the Legitimacy of the Universal Welfare State." *Acta Sociologica* 49(4), pp. 419–436.

Berggren, Niclas, Mikael Elinder, and Henrik Jordahl. 2008. "Trust and Growth: A Shaky Relationship." *Empirical Economics* 35(2), pp. 251–274.

Bernstein, Peter. 1998. *Against the Gods: The Remarkable Story of Risk*. NY: John Wiley and Sons.

Bertoli, Simone, J. Fernández-Huertas Moraga, and Francesc Ortega. 2013. "Crossing the Border: Self-Selection, Earnings, and Individual Migration Decisions." *Journal of Development Economics* 101, pp. 75–91.

Bible Gateway. 2011a. "New International Version: Genesis 18: 20-32." URL https://www.biblegateway.com/passage/?search=Genesis+18%3A20-32&version=NIV.

Bible Gateway. 2011b. "New International Version: Luke 10: 30-37." URL https://www.biblegateway.com/passage/ ?search=Luke+10%3A30-10%3A37&version=NIV.

Bier, David. 2018. "U. S. Approves Far Fewer Muslim Refugees, Immigrants, & Travelers." *Cato at Liberty*, April 23. URL https://www.cato.org/blog/us-approves-far-fewer-muslim-refugees-immigrants-travelers.

Bjørnskov, Christian. 2007. "Determinants of Generalized Trust: A Cross-Country Comparison." *Public Choice* 130(1/2), pp. 1–21.

Blattman, Christopher, and Edward Miguel. 2010. "Civil War." *Journal of Economic Literature* 48(1), pp. 3–57.

Blau, Francine, and Christopher Mackie, eds. 2016. *The Economic and Fiscal Consequences of Immigration*. Washington, DC: National Academies Press. URL https://www.nap.edu/catalog/23550/the-economic-and -fiscal-consequences-of-immigration.

Bloom, Nicholas, and John van Reenen. 2010. "Why Do Management Practices Differ across Firms and Countries?" *Journal of Economic Perspectives* 24(1), pp. 203–224.

Booker, Salih, and William Minter. 2001. "Global Apartheid." *The Nation*, June 21. URL https://www.thenation.com/ article/global-apartheid.

Borjas, George. 2001. *Heaven's Door: Immigration Policy and the American Economy*. Princeton, NJ: Princeton University Press.

Borjas, George. 2014. *Immigration Economics*. Cambridge, MA: Harvard University Press.

Borjas, George. 2015. "Immigration and Globalization: A Review Essay." *Journal of Economic Literature* 53(4), pp. 961–74.

Borjas, George. 2016. *We Wanted Workers: Unraveling the Immigration Narrative*. NY: W. W. Norton.

Borjas, George, and Lawrence Katz. 2007. "The Evolution of the Mexican-Born Workforce in the United States." In Borjas, George, ed. *Mexican Immigration to the United States*. Chicago: University of Chicago Press, pp. 13–55.

Brenan, Megan. 2018. "Record-High 75% of Americans Say Immigration Is Good Thing." *Gallup*, June 21. URL https:// news. gallup.com/poll/235793/record-high-americans-say-immigration-good-thing.aspx.

Brimelow, Peter. 1995. *Alien Nation: Common Sense About America's Immigration Disaster*. NY: Random House.

Bureau of the Census. 1984. *1980 Census of Population*. Washington, DC: U.S. Government Printing Office. URL https://www2.census. gov/prod2/decennial/documents/1980/1980censusofpopu8011un_bw.pdf.

Bureau of the Census. 2018. "Household Type: 2015." *American FactFinder.*

Butler, Jeffrey, Paola Giuliano, and Luigi Guiso. 2016. "The Right Amount of Trust." *Journal of the European Economic Association* 14(5), pp. 1155–80.

Camarota, Steven, and Jessica Vaughan. 2009. "Immigration and Crime: Assessing a Conflicted Issue." *Center for Immigration Studies Backgrounder*, November. URL https://www.cis.org/sites/cis.org/files/articles/2009/ crime.pdf.

Caplan, Bryan. 2005. "How Everyone Can Get Richer as Per-Capita Income Falls." *EconLog*, March 27. URL https://www .econlib.org/archives/2005/03/how_everyone_ca.html.

Caplan, Bryan. 2007. *The Myth of the Rational Voter: Why Democracies Choose Bad Policies*. Princeton, NJ: Princeton University Press.

Caplan, Bryan. 2008. "Milton Friedman Opposed a Pareto Improvement." *EconLog*, June 7. URL https://www.econlib .org/archives/2008/06/milton_friedman_10.html.

Caplan, Bryan. 2010. "You Don't Have to Raise the Average to Pull Your Weight." *EconLog*, September 17. URL https:// www.econlib.org/archives/2010/09/you_dont_have_t.html.

Caplan, Bryan. 2011. *Selfish Reasons to Have More Kids: Why Being a Great Parent Is Less Work and More Fun Than You Think*. NY: Basic Books.

Caplan, Bryan. 2012a. "Some Unpleasant Immigration Arithmetic." *EconLog*, November 19. https://www.econlib.org/ archives/2012/11/some_unpleasant.html.

Caplan, Bryan. 2012b. "Why Should We Restrict Immigration?" *Cato Journal* 32(1), pp. 5–24.

Caplan, Bryan. 2012c. "Immigration, Trespassing, and Socialism." *EconLog*, November 12. URL https://www.econlib .org/archives/2012/11/immigration_tre.html.

Caplan, Bryan. 2013a. "The Rights of the World's Poor: A Reply to Hassoun." *Cato Unbound*, March 19. URL https://www.cato-unbound.org/2013/03/19/bryan-caplan/rights-worlds-poor-reply-hassoun.

Caplan, Bryan. 2013b. "Let Anyone Take a Job Anywhere: My Opening Statement for IQ2." *EconLog*, November 1. URL http://www.econlib.org/archives/2013/11/let_anyone_take.html.

Caplan, Bryan. 2013c. "The Fine Line Between Social Darwinism and Suicidal Compassion." *EconLog*, June 6. URL https://www.econlib.org/archives/2013/06/my_hoover_immig.html.

Caplan, Bryan. 2013d. "Open Borders Is a Moderate Position." *EconLog*, September 3. URL https://www.econlib.org/archives/2013/09/the_golden_mean.html.

Caplan, Bryan. 2014a. "Trillion-Dollar Bills on the Sidewalk: The Borjas Critique." *EconLog*, July 16. URL https://www.econlib.org/archives/2014/07/open_borders_an_3.html.

Caplan, Bryan. 2014b. "Diasporas, Swamping, and Open Borders Abolitionism." *EconLog*, February 5. URL https://www.econlib.org/archives/2014/02/diasporas_swamp.html.

Caplan, Bryan. 2014c. "The Swamping that Wasn't: The Diaspora Dynamics of the Puerto Rican Open Borders Experiment." *EconLog*, March 27. URL https://www.econlib.org/archives/2014/03/the_swamping_th.html.

Caplan, Bryan. 2014d. "Meant for Each Other: Open Borders and Western Civilization." *EconLog*, May 7. URL https://www.econlib.org/archives/2014/05/meant_for_each.html.

Caplan, Bryan. 2014e. "A Hardy Weed: How Traditionalists Underestimate Western Civ." *Econlog,* June 23. URL https://www.econlib.org/archives/2014/06/a_hardy_week_ho.html.

Caplan, Bryan. 2014f. "Talking to Mark Krikorian." *EconLog*, April 24. URL https://www.econlib.org/archives/2014/04/talking_to_mark.html.

Caplan, Bryan. 2015a. "Demography and Decency." *EconLog*, December 15. URL https://www.econlib.org/archives/2015/12/demography_and.html.

Caplan, Bryan. 2015b. "What I Didn't Get to Say to Mark Krikorian." *EconLog*, October 26. URL https://www.econlib.org/archives/2015/10/what_i_didnt_ge.html.

Caplan, Bryan. 2016a. "Ancestry and Long-Run Growth Reading Club: Putterman and Weil." *EconLog*, January 27. URL https://www.econlib.org/archives/2016/01/ancestry_and_lo.html.

Caplan, Bryan. 2016b. "Ancestry and Long-Run Growth Reading Club: Comin, Easterly, and Gong." *EconLog*, February 3. URL https://www.econlib.org/archives/2016/02/ancestry_and_lo_1.html.

Caplan, Bryan. 2016c. "Ancestry and Long-Run Growth Reading Club: Spolaore and Wacziarg." *EconLog*, February 10. URL https://www.econlib.org/archives/2016/02/ancestry_and_lo_2.html.

Caplan, Bryan. 2016d. "Two Fun Facts from Putterman-Weil." *EconLog*, February 12. URL https://www.econlib.org/archives/2016/02/two_fun_facts_f.html.

Caplan, Bryan. 2016e. "National Origin as a Nurture Effect." *EconLog*, December 15. URL https://www.econlib.org/archives/2016/12/nationality_and.html.

Caplan, Bryan. 2017a. "Trust and Diversity: Not a Bang but a Whimper." *EconLog*, June 15. URL https://www.econlib.org/archives/2017/06/trust_and_diver.html.

Caplan, Bryan. 2017b. "Geography Is Policy." *EconLog*, May 15. URL https://www.econlib.org/archives/2017/05/geography_is_po.html.

Caplan, Bryan. 2017c. "The Wonder of International Adoption: Adult IQ in Sweden." *EconLog*, September 18. URL https://www.econlib.org/archives/2017/09/the_wonder_of_i.html.

Caplan, Bryan. 2017d. "The Wonder of International Adoption: High School Grades in Sweden." *EconLog*, September 20. URL https://www.econlib.org/archives/2017/09/the_wonder_of_i_1.html.

Caplan, Bryan. 2017e. "The Shining City on a Hill: Commentary on Reagan." *EconLog*, December 7. URL https://www.econlib.org/archives/2017/12/the_city_on_a_h.html.

Caplan, Bryan, and Stephen Miller. 2010. "Intelligence Makes People Think Like Economists: Evidence from the General Social Survey." *Intelligence* 38(6), pp. 636–647.

Caplan, Bryan, and Vipul Naik. 2015. "A Radical Case for Open Borders." In Powell, Benjamin, ed. *The Economics of Immigration: Market-Based Approaches, Social Science, and Public Policy*. Oxford: Oxford University Press, pp. 180–209.

Carens, Joseph. 1987. "Aliens and Citizens: The Case for Open Borders." *Review of Politics* 49(2), pp. 251–73.

Carlyle, Thomas, ed. 1855. *Oliver Cromwell's Letters and Speeches*, vol. 1. New York: Harper.

Carson, E. 2018. "Prisoners in 2016." *Bureau of Justice Statistics*, August 7. URL https://www.bjs. gov/content/pub/ pdf/p16.pdf.

Chang, Howard. 2003. "Immigration and the Workplace: Immigration Restrictions as Employment Discrimination." *Chicago-Kent Law Review* 78, pp. 291–328.

Chua, Amy. 2011. *Battle Hymn of the Tiger Mother*. NY: Penguin Books.

Cini, Michelle, and Nieves Borragán, eds. 2016. *European Union Politics*. Oxford: Oxford University Press.

Clemens, Michael. 2011. "Economics and Emigration: Trillion-Dollar Bills on the Sidewalk?" *Journal of Economic Perspectives* 25(3), pp. 83–106.

Clemens, Michael, and Lant Pritchett. 2008. "Income per Natural: Measuring Development for People Rather Than Places." *Population and Development Review* 34(3), pp. 395–434.

Clemens, Michael, and Lant Pritchett. 2016. "The New Economic Case for Migration Restrictions: An Assessment." *Center for Global Development Working Paper #423*. URL https://papers. ssrn.com/sol3/papers. cfm?abstract _id=2630295.

Clemens, Michael, Claudio Montenegro, and Lant Pritchett. forthcoming. "The Place Premium: Bounding the Price Equivalent of Migration Barriers." *Review of Economics and Statistics*.

Clifton, Jon. 2013. "More Than 100 Million Worldwide Dream of Life in the U.S." *Gallup World*, March 21. URL https:// news. gallup.com/poll/161435/100-million-worldwide-dream-life.aspx.

Cochrane, Kira. 2011. "Jose Antonio Vargas: My Secret Life as an Undocumented US Immigrant." *The Guardian*, July 26. URL https://www.theguardian.com/world/2011/jul/26/jose-antonio-vargas-undocumented-immigrant.

Collier, Paul. 1999. "On the Economic Consequences of Civil War." *Oxford Economic Papers* 51(1), pp. 168-83.

Collier, Paul. 2013. *Exodus: How Migration Is Changing Our World*. NY: Oxford University Press.

Comin, Diego, William Easterly, and Erick Gong. 2010. "Was the Wealth of Nations Determined in 1000 BC?" *American Economic Journal: Macroeconomics* 2(3): 65-97.

Congressional Budget Office. 2018. "The 2018 Long-Term Budget Outlook." URL https://www.cbo.gov/system/ files?file=2018-06/53919-2018ltbo.pdf.

Connor, Phillip, D'Vera Cohn, and Ana Gonzalez-Barrera. 2013. "Changing Patterns of Global Migration and Remittances." *Pew Research Center*, December 17. URL http://www.pewsocialtrends.org/2013/12/17/ changing-patterns-of-global-migration-and-remittances.

Cortés, Patricia, and José Tessada. 2011. "Low-Skilled Immigration and the Labor Supply of Highly Skilled Women." *American Economic Journal: Applied Economics* 3(3), pp. 88-123.

Coulter, Ann. 2015a. *¡Adios, America!: The Left's Plan to Turn Our Country Into a Third World Hellhole*. Washington, DC: Regnery.

Coulter, Ann. 2015b. December 22. URL https://www.facebook.com/OfficialAnnCoulter/posts/which-reminds-me-low-iq-immigrants-are-lowering-your-income-your-freedom-your-wa/802900983153051.

Cowen, Tyler, and Alex Tabarrok. 2018. *Modern Principles of Economics*, 4th edition. NY: Macmillan Learning.

D'Amuri, Francesco, and Giovanni Peri. 2014. "Immigration, Jobs, and Employment Protection: Evidence from Europe Before and During the Great Recession." *Journal of the European Economic Association* 12(2), pp. 432–464.

Dalen, Monica, Anders Hyern, Frank Lindblad, Anna Odenstad, Finn Rasmussen, and Bo Vinnerljung. 2008. "Educational Attainment and Cognitive Competence in Adopted Men: A Study of International and National Adoptees, Siblings and a General Swedish Population." *Children and Youth Services Review* 30(10), pp. 1211–9.

Delogu, Marco, Frédéric Docquier, and Joël Machado. 2018. "Globalizing Labor and the World Economy: The Role of Human Capital." *Journal of Economic Growth* 23(2), pp. 223–258.

Derbyshire, John. 2015. "John Derbyshire On Why Race Realism Makes More Sense Than 'Magic Dirt' Theory." *VDARE .com*, November 1. URL https://vdare.com/articles/john-derbyshire-on-why-race-realism-makes-more-sense -than-magic-dirt-theory.

Diehl, Claudia, and Andreas Wüst. 2010. "Voter Turnout Amongst Immigrants and Visible Minorities in Comparative Perspective." In Bird, Karen, Thomas Saalfeld, and Andreas Wüst, eds. *The Political Representation of Immigrants and Minorities: Voters, Parties and Parliaments in Liberal Democracies*. London: Routledge, pp. 25–65.

Dinesen, Peter. 2012. "Does Generalized (Dis)Trust Travel? Examining the Impact of Cultural Heritage and Destination-Country Environment on Trust of Immigrants." *Political Psychology* 33(4), pp. 495–511.

Dinesen, Peter, and Marc Hooghe. 2010. "When in Rome, Do as the Romans Do: The Acculturation of Generalized Trust among Immigrants in Western Europe." *International Migration Review* 44(3), pp. 697–727.

Disaster Center. 2017. "United States Crime Rates 1960-2016." URL http://www.disastercenter.com/crime/uscrime.htm.

Donno, Daniela, and Bruce Russett. 2004. "Islam, Authoritarianism, and Female Empowerment: What Are the Linkages?" *World Politics* 56(4), pp. 582–607.

Drury, A. Cooper, Jonathan Krieckhaus, and Michael Lusztig. 2006. "Corruption, Democracy, and Economic Growth." *International Political Science Review* 27(2), pp. 121–136.

Esipova, Neli, Anita Pugliese, and Julie Ray. 2017. "Potential Net Migration Index Falls in Middle East, Latin America." *Gallup World*, June 20. URL https://news.gallup.com/poll/212141/potential-net-migration-falls-middle-east -latin-america.aspx.

Esipova, Neli, and Julie Ray. 2012. "More Adults Would Move for Temporary Work Than Permanently." *Gallup World*, March 9. URL http://www.gallup.com/poll/153182/Adults-Move-Temporary-Work-Permanently.aspx.

Esipova, Neli, Rajesh Srinivasan, and Julie Ray. 2009. "Potential Net Migration Could Change Nations." *Gallup World*, November 6. URL http://www.gallup.com/poll/124193/potential-net-migration-change-developed-nations.aspx.

Esipova, Neli, Rajesh Srinivasan, and Julie Ray. 2014. "Potential Net Migration Index Declines in Many Countries." *Gallup World*, January 17. URL http://www.gallup.com/poll/166796/potential-net-migration-index-declines -countries.aspx.

Espinoza, Robert. 2017. "Immigrants and the Direct Care Workforce." *PHI*, June. URL https://phinational.org/wp -content/uploads/2017/06/immigrants_and_the_direct_care_workforce_-_phi_-_june_2017.pdf.

FindLaw. 2018. "Gonzales v. Williams." URL https://caselaw. findlaw.com/us-supreme-court/192/1.html.

Fish, M. 2002. "Islam and Authoritarianism." *World Politics* 55(1), pp. 4–37.

Friedman, Milton. 1999. "Q&A With Milton Friedman." ISIL Interview.

Gallup, John, Jeffrey Sachs, and Andrew Mellinger. 1999. "Geography and Economic Development." *International Regional Science Review* 22(2): 179–232.

Gerber, David. 2011. *American Immigration: A Very Short Introduction*. NY: Oxford University Press.

Gibson, John, and David McKenzie. 2011. "Eight Questions about Brain Drain." *Journal of Economic Perspectives* 25(3), pp. 107–28.

Gilens, Martin. 2012. *Affluence and Influence: Economic Inequality and Political Power in America*. Princeton, NJ: Princeton University Press and Russell Sage Foundation.

Gjelten, Tom. 2015. *A Nation of Nations: A Great American Immigration Story*. NY: Simon and Schuster.

Glaeser, Edward. 2017. "Reforming Land Use Regulations." *Brookings Center on Regulation and Markets Report*, April 24. URL https://www.brookings. edu/research/reforming-land-use-regulations.

Glaeser, Edward, David Laibson, Jose Scheinkman, and Christine Soutter. 2000. "Measured Trust." *Quarterly Journal of Economics* 115(3), pp. 811–46.

Gochenour, Zachary, and Alex Nowrasteh. 2014. "The Political Externalities of Immigration: Evidence from the United States." *Cato Working Paper*, January 15. URL https://object.cato.org/sites/cato.org/files/pubs/pdf/working -paper-14-3.pdf.

Gonzalez, Libertad, and Ortega, Francesc. 2013. "Immigration and Housing Booms: Evidence from Spain." *Journal of Regional Science* 53(1), pp. 37–59.

Gottfredsen, Linda. 1994. "Mainstream Science on Intelligence: An Editorial With 52 Signatories, History, and Bibliography." *Intelligence* 24(1), pp. 13–23.

Gwartney, James, Robert Lawson, and Joshua Hall. 2017. *Economic Freedom of the World: 2017 Annual Report*. Fraser Institute. URL https://www.fraserinstitute.org/sites/default/files/economic-freedom-of-the-world-2017.pdf.

Habila, Helon. 2016. *The Chibok Girls: The Boko Haram Kidnappings and Islamist Militancy in Nigeria*. NY: Columbia Global Reports.

Hamilton, Bob, and John Whalley. 1984. "Efficiency and Distributional Implications of Global Restrictions on Labour Mobility: Calculations and Policy Implications." *Journal of Development Economics* 14(1), pp. 61–75.

Harford, Tim. 2012. *The Undercover Economist: Exposing Why the Rich Are Rich, the Poor Are Poor—and Why You Can Never Buy a Decent Used Car!* Oxford: Oxford University Press.

Harris, Judith. 2009. *The Nurture Assumption: Why Children Turn Out the Way They Do*. NY: Free Press.

Hauser, Christine. 2016. "Donald Trump Jr. Compares Syrian Refugees to Skittles That 'Would Kill You.'" *New York Times*, September 20. URL https://www.nytimes.com/2016/09/21/us/politics/donald-trump-jr-faces-backlash-after-comparing-syrian-refugees-to-skittles-that-can-kill.html.

Havocscope. 2018. "Prices Charged by Human Smugglers." URL https://www.havocscope.com/black-market-prices/human-smuggling-fees.

Hendricks, Lutz. 2002. "How Important Is Human Capital for Development? Evidence from Immigrant Earnings." *American Economic Review* 92(1), pp. 198–219.

Herrnstein, Richard, and Mark Snyderman. 1983. "Intelligence Tests and the Immigration Act of 1924." *American Psychologist* 38(9), pp. 986–995.

Howley, Kerry. 2008. "Ending Global Apartheid." *Reason*, February. URL http://reason.com/archives/2008/01/24/ending-global-apartheid/singlepage.

Huemer, Michael. 2010. "Is There a Right to Immigrate?" *Social Theory and Practice* 36(3), pp. 429–61.

Huemer, Michael. 2013. *The Problem of Political Authority: An Examination of the Right to Coerce and the Duty to Obey*. NY: Palgrave Macmillan.

Institute for the Study of Western Civilization. 2014. "Debate on Immigration: Should the United States Significantly Liberalize Immigration?" URL http://www.depts.ttu.edu/westernciv/videos_others/debate_immigration.php.

International Organization for Migration. 2017. *World Migration Report 2018*. Geneva, Switzerland: International Organization for Migration. URL https://publications.iom.int/system/files/pdf/wmr_2018_en.pdf.

IQ Research. 2018. "World Ranking of Countries by Their Average IQ." URL https://iq-research.info/en/average-iq-by-country.

Iregui, Ana Maria. 2005. "Efficiency Gains from the Elimination of Global Restrictions on Labour Mobility." In Borjas, George, and Jeff Crisp, eds. *Poverty, International Migration and Asylum*. NY: Palgrave Macmillan, pp. 211–38.

Jensen, Arthur. 1998. *The g Factor: The Science of Mental Ability*. Westport, CT: Praeger.

Johns Hopkins Medicine. 2018. "Minimally Invasive Surgery: Types of Minimally Invasive Surgery." *HopkinsMedicine*. URL https://www.hopkinsmedicine.org/minimally_invasive_robotic_surgery/types.html.

Johnson, Jenna. 2015. "Trump Calls for 'Total and Complete Shutdown of Muslims Entering the United States.'" *Washington Post*, December 7. URL https://www.washingtonpost.com/news/post-politics/wp/2015/12/07/donald-trump-calls-for-total-and-complete-shutdown-of-muslims-entering-the-united-states/?utm_term=.d64a2406d24c.

Jones, Garett. 2015. "Will Open Borders Change Your Nation's SAT Score?" URL http://mason.gmu.edu/~gjonesb/OpenBordersSacrifice.pptx.

Jones, Garett. 2016. *Hive Mind: How Your Nation's IQ Matters So Much More Than Your Own*. Stanford, CA: Stanford University Press.

Jones, Garett. 2017. "Are the Global Benefits of Open Borders a Fallacy of Composition? Three Examples." URL https://www.dropbox.com/s/sdtrfig2vu81b8y/FallacyOfCompositionBeamerNUSFinal.pdf?dl=0.

Jones, Garett, and W. Schneider. 2006. "Intelligence, Human Capital, and Economic Growth: A Bayesian Averaging of Classical Estimates (BACE) Approach." *Journal of Economic Growth* 11(1), pp. 71–93.

Juffer, Femmie, and Marinus van IJzendoorn. 2009. "International Adoption Comes of Age: Development of International Adoptees from a Longitudinal and Meta-Analytical Perspective." In Wrobel, Gretchen, and Elsbeth Neil, eds. *International Advances in Adoption Research for Practice*. Chichester, UK: Wiley-Blackwell, pp. 169–192.

Junn, Jane, Taeku Lee, S. Ramakrishnan, and Janelle Wong. 2011. "Asian American Public Opinion." In Edwards, George, Lawrence Jacobs, and Robert Shapiro, eds. *The Oxford Handbook of American Public Opinion and the Media*. Oxford: Oxford University Press, pp. 520–34.

Kahneman, Daniel. 2011. *Thinking, Fast and Slow*. NY: Farrar, Straus, and Giroux.

Kant, Immanuel. 1887. *The Philosophy of Law: An Exposition of the Fundamental Principles of Jurisprudence as the Science of Right*. Edinburgh, UK: T&T Clark.

Kennan, John. 2013. "Open Borders." *Review of Economic Dynamics* 16(2), pp. L1–L13.

Kievit, Rogier, Willem Frankenhuis, Lourens Waldorp, and Denny Borsboom. 2013. "Simpson's Paradox in Psychological Science: A Practical Guide." *Frontiers in Psychology* 4, pp. 1–14.

Kim, Dongbin, Susan Twombly, and Lisa Wolf-Wendel. 2012. "International Faculty in American Universities: Experiences of Academic Life, Productivity, and Career Mobility." *New Directions in Institutional Research* 155, pp. 27–46.

King, Martin Luther. 1963. "I Have a Dream…" *National Archives*. URL https://www.archives.gov/files/press/exhibits/dream-speech.pdf.

Klein, Paul, and Gustavo Ventura. 2009. "Productivity Differences and the Dynamic Effects of Labor Movements." *Journal of Monetary Economics* 56(8), pp. 1059–73.

Knoema. 2018. "United States of America: Crude Death Rate." URL https://knoema.com/atlas/United-States-of-America/Death-rate.

"Know-Nothing." c. 1850. URL https://public-media.smithsonianmag.com/filer/fc/2d/fc2d8316-33df-49ee-b171-3b9a52545564/cwbwma.jpg.

Kotwal, Ashok, Bharat Ramaswami, and Wilima Wadhwa. 2011. "Economic Liberalization and Indian Economic Growth: What's the Evidence?" *Journal of Economic Literature* 49(4), pp. 1152–99.

Krikorian, Mark. 2008. *The New Case Against Immigration: Both Legal and Illegal*. NY: Sentinel.

Krikorian, Mark. 2010. *How Obama Is Transforming America Through Immigration*. NY: Encounter Books.

Krugman, Paul. 1998. *The Accidental Theorist: And Other Dispatches from the Dismal Science*. NY: W. W. Norton.

Krugman, Paul, and Robin Wells. 2017. *Essentials of Economics*, 4th edition. NY: Macmillan Learning.

Kuran, Timur, and Cass Sunstein. 1999. "Availability Cascades and Risk Regulation." *Stanford Law Review* 51(4), pp. 683–768.

Lee, Kwan Yew. 2000. *From the Third World to the First: The Singapore Story 1965-2000*. NY: HarperCollins.

Lee, Matthew, and Ramiro Martinez. 2009. "Immigration Reduces Crime: An Emerging Scholarly Consensus." *Sociology of Crime, Law and Deviance* 13, pp. 3–16.

Legrain, Philippe. 2007. *Immigrants: Your Country Needs Them*. Princeton, NJ: Princeton University Press.

Ludmerer, Kenneth. 1972. "Genetics, Eugenics, and the Immigration Restriction Act of 1924." *Bulletin of the History of Medicine* 46(1), pp. 59–81.

Lynn, Richard, and Gerhard Meisenberg. 2010. "National IQs Calculated and Validated for 108 Nations." *Intelligence* 38(4), pp. 353–60.

Lynn, Richard, and Tatu Vanhanen. 2002. *IQ and the Wealth of Nations*. Westport, CT: Praeger.

Maddison Project Database. 2018. URL https://www.rug.nl/ggdc/historicaldevelopment/maddison/releases/maddison-project-database-2018.

"The Magic Washer." 1886. URL https://www.loc.gov/resource/pga.02758.

Mankiw, N. Gregory. 2015. *Principles of Economics*, 7th edition. Stamford, CT: Cengage Learning.

Mansbridge, Jane. 1990. *Beyond Self-Interest*. Chicago: University of Chicago Press.

Matthews, Dylan. 2016. "Remember that Study Saying America Is an Oligarchy? 3 Rebuttals Say It's Wrong." *Vox*, May 9. URL https://www.vox.com/2016/5/9/11502464/gilens-page-oligarchy-study.

McCarthy, Justin. 2017. "Overall U.S. Desire to Decrease Immigration Unchanged in 2017." *Gallup*, June 27. URL https://news.gallup.com/poll/212846/overall-desire-decrease-immigration-unchanged-2017.aspx.

McKenzie, David, Steven Stillman, and John Gibson. 2010. "How Important Is Selection? Experimental vs. Non-Experimental Measures of the Income Gains from Migration." *Journal of the European Economic Association* 8(4), pp. 913–45.

Migration Policy Institute. 2016. "Age-Sex Pyramids of U. S. Immigrants and Native-Born Populations, 1970–Present." URL https://www.migrationpolicy.org/programs/data-hub/charts/age-sex-pyramids-immigrant-and-native-born-population-over-time.

Mishkin, Frederic. 2016. *The Economics of Money, Banking, and Financial Markets.* Boston: Pearson.

Mo, Pak-Hung. 2001. "Corruption and Economic Growth." *Journal of Comparative Economics* 29(1), pp. 66–79.

Moses, Jonathon, and Bjorn Letnes. 2004. "The Economic Costs to International Labor Restrictions: Revisiting the Empirical Discussion." *World Development,* 32(10), pp. 1609–26.

Moses, Jonathon, and Bjorn Letnes. 2005. "If People Were Money: Estimating the Gains and Scope of Free Migration." In Borjas, George, and Jeff Crisp, eds. *Poverty, International Migration and Asylum.* NY: Palgrave Macmillan, pp. 188–210.

Naik, Vipul. 2018a. "Political Externalities." *Open Borders: The Case.* URL https://openborders.info/political-externalities.

Naik, Vipul. 2018b. "Keyhole Solutions." *Open Borders: The Case.* URL https://openborders.info/keyhole-solutions.

Nannestad, Peter. 2008. "What Have We Learned About Generalized Trust, If Anything?" *Annual Review of Political Science* 11, pp. 413–36.

Nast, Thomas. 1871. "The Usual Irish Way of Doing Things." URL https://library.osu.edu/dc/concern/generic_works/g732x041f.

National Museum of American History. 2018a. "Legacy of the Bracero Program." *Bittersweet Harvest: The Bracero Program 1942-1964.* URL http://americanhistory.si.edu/bracero/legacy.

National Museum of American History. 2018b. "Japs Keep Moving – This Is a White Man's Neighborhood." *A More Perfect Union: Japanese Americans and the U. S. Constitution.* URL https://amhistory. si. edu/perfectunion/collection/image.asp?ID=411.

National Weather Service. 2018. "How Dangerous Is Lightning?" URL https://www.weather.gov/safety/lightning-odds.

Newport, Frank. 2018. "Immigration Surges to Top of Most Important Problem List." *Gallup*, July 18. URL https://news. gallup.com/poll/237389/immigration-surges-top-important-problem-list.aspx.

Ngai, Mae. 1999. "The Architecture of Race in American Immigration Law: A Reexamination of the Immigration Act of 1924." *Journal of American History* 86(1), pp. 67-92.

Nowrasteh, Alex. 2015. "Immigrant Crime: What the Research Says." *Cato at Liberty*, July 14. URL https://www.cato.org/blog/immigration-crime-what-research-says.

Nowrasteh, Alex. 2016. "Terrorism and Immigration: A Risk Analysis." *Cato Institute Policy Analysis*, September 13. URL https://object.cato.org/sites/cato.org/files/pubs/pdf/pa798_2.pdf.

Nowrasteh, Alex, and Sophie Cole. 2013. "Building a Wall Around the Welfare State, Instead of the Country." *Policy Analysis* 732, July 25. URL https://object.cato.org/sites/cato.org/files/pubs/pdf/pa732_web_1.pdf.

Nowrasteh, Alex, and Sam Wilson. 2017. "Immigrants Assimilate Into the Political Mainstream." *Cato Institute Economic Development Bulletin* 27, January 19. URL https://object.cato.org/sites/cato.org/files/pubs/pdf/edb_27.pdf.

Nunn, Nathan, and Leonard Wantchekon. 2011. "The Slave Trade and the Origin of Mistrust in Africa." *American Economic Review* 101(7), pp. 3221–3252.

Odenstad, Anna, Anders Hyern, Frank Lindblad, Finn Rasmussen, Bo Vinnerljung, and Monica Dalen. 2008. "Does Age at Adoption and Geographic Origin Matter? A National Cohort Study of Cognitive Test Performance in Adult Inter-Country Adoptees." *Psychological Medicine* 38(12), pp. 1803–14.

Office for National Statistics. 2012. "International Migrants in England and Wales: 2011." December 11. URL https://www.ons. gov. uk/peoplepopulationandcommunity/populationandmigration/internationalmigration/articles/internationalmigrantsinenglandandwales/2012-12-11.

Office of Management and Budget. 2017. *Historical Tables: Budget of the U.S. Government.* Washington, DC: Government Publishing Office. URL https://www.govinfo.gov/content/pkg/BUDGET-2017-TAB/pdf/BUDGET-2017-TAB.pdf.

Office of the Assistant Secretary for Planning and Evaluation. 2009. "Summary of Immigrant Eligibility Restrictions Under Current Law." *APSE*, February 25. URL https://aspe.hhs.gov/basic-report/summary-immigrant-eligibility-restrictions-under-current-law.

Ortiz-Ospina, Esteban, and Max Roser. 2017. "Trust." *OurWorldInData.org*. URL https://ourworldindata.org/trust.

Ottaviano, Gianmarco, and Giovanni Peri. 2006. "The Economic Value of Cultural Diversity: Evidence from U. S. Cities." *Journal of Economic Geography* 6(1), pp. 9–44.

Ottaviano, Gianmarco, and Giovanni Peri. 2012. "Rethinking the Effect of Immigration on Wages." *Journal of the European Economic Association* 10(1), pp. 152–197.

Parker, A. Warner. 1924. "The Quota Provisions of the Immigration Act of 1924." *American Journal of International Law* 18(4), pp. 737–754.

Peri, Giovanni, and Chad Sparber. 2009. "Task Specialization, Immigration, and Wages." *American Economic Journal: Applied Economics* 1(3), pp. 135–169.

Pew Research Center. 2017. "Indians in the U.S. Fact Sheet." *Social and Demographic Trends*, September 8. URL http://www.pewsocialtrends.org/fact-sheet/asian-americans-indians-in-the-u-s.

Plato. 2002. *Five Dialogues: Euthyphro, Apology, Crito, Meno, Phaedo.* Indianapolis, IN: Hackett Publishing.

Posner, Richard. 1979. "Utilitarianism, Economics, and Legal Theory." *Journal of Legal Studies* 8(1), pp. 103–140.

Posner, Richard. 1980. "The Ethical and Political Basis of the Efficiency Norm in Common Law Adjudication." *Hofstra Law Review* 8(3), pp. 487–507.

Posner, Richard. 2003. *Law, Pragmatism, and Democracy.* Cambridge, MA: Harvard University Press.

Pritchett, Lant. 2006. *Let Their People Come: Breaking the Gridlock on International Labor Mobility.* Washington, DC: Center for Global Development.

Pritchett, Lant, Clifford Gaddy, and Simon Johnson. 2006. "Boom Towns and Ghost Countries: Geography, Agglomeration, and Population Mobility." *Brookings Trade Forum: Global Labor Markets?*, pp. 1–56.

Putnam, Robert. 2007. "E Pluribus Unum: Diversity and Community in the Twenty-first Century." *Scandinavian Political Studies* 30(2), pp. 137–74.

Putterman, Louis, and David Weil. 2010. "Post-1500 Population Flows and the Long-Run Determinants of Economic Growth and Inequality." *Quarterly Journal of Economics* 125(4): 1627–1682.

Quote Investigator. 2015. "People Who Say It Cannot Be Done Should Not Interrupt Those Who Are Doing It." URL http://quoteinvestigator.com/2015/01/26/doing.

Ratha, Dilip, Sonia Plaza, Hanspeter Wyss, Supriyo De, Kirsten Schuettler, and Soonhwa Yi. 2006. "Trends in Remittances, 2016: A New Normal of Slow Growth." *People Move*, October 6. URL http://blogs.worldbank.org/peoplemove/trends-remittances-2016-new-normal-slow-growth.

Ratiner, Susan, ed. 2015. *The Poems of Emma Lazarus, vol. 1.* NY: Dover Publications.

Reagan, Ronald. 1987. "Remarks on East-West Relations at the Brandenburg Gate in West Berlin." *American Presidency Project*, June 12. URL https://www.presidency.ucsb.edu/documents/remarks-east-west-relations-the-brandenburg-gate-west-berlin.

Reagan, Ronald. 1989. "Farewell Address to the Nation." *American Presidency Project*, January 11. URL http://www.presidency.ucsb.edu/ws/index.php?pid=29650.

ReasonTV. 2014. "Should America Open Its Borders?" May 11. URL https://www.youtube.com/watch?v=yUrJkweaw34.

Redden, Elizabeth. 2015. "Fee for Being Foreign." *Inside Higher Ed*, May 8. URL https://www.insidehighered.com/news/2015/05/08/some-public-universities-are-charging-differentiated-tuition-rates-or-raising-fees.

Rindermann, Heiner. 2018. *Cognitive Capitalism: Human Capital and the Well-Being of Nations.* Cambridge: Cambridge University Press.

Rindermann, Heiner, Michael Sailer, and James Thompson. 2009. "The Impact of Smart Fractions, Cognitive Ability of Politicians and Average Competence of Peoples on Social Development." *Talent Development & Excellence* 1(1), pp. 3–25.

Roberts, Bryan, Edward Alden, and John Whitley. 2013. "Managing Illegal Immigration to the United States: How Effective Is Enforcement?" *Council on Foreign Relations*, May. URL https://cfrd8-files.cfr.org/sites/default/files/book_pdf/Managing_Illegal_Immigration_report%20%282%29.pdf.

Roberts, Bryan, Gordon Hanson, Derekh Cornwell, and Scott Borger. 2010. "An Analysis of Migrant Smuggling Costs along the Southwest Border." *Office of Immigration Statistics Working Paper.* URL https://www.dhs.gov/xlibrary/assets/statistics/publications/ois-smuggling-wp.pdf.

Roth, Felix. 2009. "Does Too Much Trust Hamper Economic Growth?" *Kyklos* 62(1), pp. 103–28.

Rumbaut, Rubén, Douglas Massey, and Frank Bean. 2006. "Linguistic Life Expectancies: Immigration Language Retention in Southern California." *Population and Development Review* 32(3), pp. 447–60.

Russell, Nathan. 2006. "An Introduction to the Overton Window of Political Possibilities." *Mackinac Center for Public Policy*, January 4. URL https://www.mackinac.org/7504.

Ryan, Camille. 2013. "Language Use in the United States: 2011." *American Community Survey Reports*, August. URL https://www2.census.gov/library/publications/2013/acs/acs-22/acs-22.pdf.

Sá, Filipa. 2015. "Immigration and House Prices in the UK." *Economic Journal* 125(587), pp. 1393–1424.

Sachs, Jeffrey. 2003. "Institutions Matter, but Not for Everything." *Finance and Development*, June, pp. 38–41.

Sachs, Jeffrey, and Andrew Warner. 1995a. "Economic Convergence and Economic Policies." *NBER Working Paper* No. 5039. National Bureau of Economic Research, Cambridge, MA.

Sachs, Jeffrey, and Andrew Warner. 1995b. "Economic Reform and the Process of Global Integration." *Brookings Papers on Economic Activity* 1, 1–95.

Sachs, Jeffrey, and Wing Woo. 2001. "Understanding China's Economic Performance." *Journal of Policy Reform* 4(1), pp. 1–50.

Saiz, Albert. 2007. "Immigration and Housing Rents in American Cities." *Journal of Urban Economics* 61(2), pp. 345–371.

Saiz, Albert, and Susan Wachter. 2011. "Immigration and the Neighborhood." *American Economic Journal: Economic Policy* 3(2), pp. 169–188.

Salam, Reihan. 2018. *Melting Pot or Civil War? A Son of Immigrants Makes the Case Against Open Borders.* NY: Sentinel.

Sankhe, Shirish, Ireena Vittal, Richard Dobbs, Ajit Mohan, Ankur Gulati, Jonathan Ablett, Shishir Gupta, Alex Kim, Sudipto Paul, Aditya Sanghvi, and Gurpreet Sethy. 2010. *India's Urban Awakening: Building Inclusive Cities, Sustaining Economic Growth.* McKinsey Global Institute, April. URL https://www.mckinsey.com/~/media/McKinsey/Featured%20Insights/Urbanization/Urban%20awakening%20in%20India/MGI_Indias_urban_awakening_full_report. ashx.

Schoenberg, Arnold. 1950. *Style and Idea.* NY: Philosophical Library.

Schubert, Louis, Thomas Dye, and Harmon Zeigler. 2015. *The Irony of Democracy: An Uncommon Introduction to American Politics.* Boston, MA: Cengage Learning.

Schwarz, Anita, and Omar Arias. 2014. *The Inverting Pyramid: Pension Systems Facing Demographic Challenges in Europe and Central Asia.* Washington, DC: The World Bank. URL https://elibrary.worldbank.org/doi/pdf/10.1596/978-0-8213-9908-8.

Segal, Nancy. 2000. *Entwined Lives: Twins and What They Tell Us About Human Behavior.* NY: Penguin Group.

Smith, Adam. 1982. *An Inquiry Into the Nature and Causes of the Wealth of Nations.* Indianapolis, IN: Liberty Fund.

Smith, Nathanael. 2010. *Principles of a Free Society.* Fairfax, VA: John Locke Institute.

Smith, Nathanael. 2012. "Robots or Immigrants?" *Open Borders: The Case*, December 15. URL https://openborders.info/blog/robots-or-immigrants.

Snopes. 2018. "William Sutton—'That's Where the Money Is.'" URL https://www.snopes.com/fact-check/willie-sutton.

Snyder, Thomas, Cristobal de Brey, and Sally Dillow. 2018. *Digest of Education Statistics 2016.* Washington, DC: National Center for Education Statistics. URL https://nces.ed.gov/pubs2017/2017094.pdf.

Soroka, Stuart, Keith Banting, and Richard Johnston. 2006. "Immigration and Redistribution in a Global Era." In Bardhan, Pranab, Samuel Bowles, and Michael Wallerstein, eds. *Globalization and Egalitarian Redistribution*. Princeton, NJ: Princeton University Press.

Spolaore, Enrico, and Romain Wacziarg. 2013. "How Deep Are the Roots of Economic Development?" *Journal of Economic Literature* 51(2): 325–369.

Steel, Daniel. 2015. *Philosophy and the Precautionary Principle: Science, Evidence, and Environmental Policy.* Cambridge: Cambridge University Press.

Stepan, Alfred, and Graeme Robertson. 2003. "An 'Arab' More Than a 'Muslim' Democracy Gap." *Journal of Democracy* 14(3), pp. 30–34.

Stevens, Gillian. 1999. "Age at Immigration and Second Language Proficiency Among Foreign-Born Adults." *Language in Society* 28, pp. 555–578.

Stevens, Gillian. 2015. "Trajectories of English Acquisition Among Foreign-Born Spanish-Language Children in the United States." *International Migration Review* 49(4), pp. 981–1000.

Sunstein, Cass. 2005. *The Laws of Fear: Beyond the Precautionary Principle.* Cambridge: Cambridge University Press.

Tabarrok, Alexander. 2000. "Economic and Moral Factors in Favor of Open Immigration." *Independent Institute*, September 14. URL http://www.independent.org/issues/article. asp?id=486.

Taylor, Frederick. 2008. *The Berlin Wall: A World Divided, 1961–1989.* NY: HarperCollins.

Trump, Donald. 2016. "Remarks on Foreign Policy at the National Press Club in Washington, DC." *American Presidency Project*, April 27. URL http://www.presidency. ucsb. edu/ws/index. php?pid=117813.

USCIS 2017. "H-1B Specialty Occupations, DOD Cooperative Research and Development Project Workers, and Fashion Models." URL https: //www.uscis.gov/working-united-states/temporary-workers/h-1b-specialty-occupations -dod-cooperative-research-and-development-project-workers-and-fashion-models.

USCIS 2018a. "H-2A Temporary Agricultural Workers." URL https://www.uscis.gov/working-united-states/ temporary-workers/h-2a-temporary-agricultural-workers.

USCIS 2018b. "H-2B Temporary Non-Agricultural Workers." URL https://www.uscis.gov/working-united-states/ temporary-workers/h-2b-temporary-non-agricultural-workers.

United States Census Bureau 2018a. "QuickFacts: Los Angeles County, California." U.S. Department of Commerce. URL https://www.census.gov/quickfacts/fact/table/losangelescountycalifornia/PST045217.

United States Census Bureau 2018b. "Characteristics of the Group Quarters Population by Group Quarters Type." *American FactFinder.*

United States Sentencing Commission. 2017. "Quick Facts: Illegal Reentry Statistics." URL https://www.ussc.gov/sites/ default/files/pdf/research-and-publications/quick-facts/Illegal_Reentry_FY17.pdf.

USA.gov. 2018. "How to Apply for U.S. Citizenship." URL https://www.usa.gov/become-us-citizen.

USGovernmentSpending.com. 2018. "Government Spending Details." URL https://www.usgovernmentspending.com/ year_spending_2015USbn_19bs2n_101713401200#usgs302.

Uslaner, Eric. 2008. "Where You Stand Depends on Where Your Grandparents Sat: The Inheritability of Generalized Trust." *Public Opinion Quarterly* 72(4), pp. 725–40.

Van der Vossen, Bas, and Jason Brennan. 2018. *In Defense of Openness: Why Global Freedom Is the Humane Solution to Global Poverty.* Oxford: Oxford University Press.

Van IJzendoorn, Marinus, Femmie Juffer, and Caroline Poelhuis. 2005. "Adoption and Cognitive Development: A Meta-Analytic Comparison of Adopted and Nonadopted Children's IQ and School Performance." *Psychological Bulletin* 131(2), pp. 301–16.

Van IJzendoorn, Marinus, Marian Bakermans-Kranenburg, and Femmie Juffer. 2007. "Plasticity of Growth in Height, Weight, and Head Circumference: Meta-Analytic Evidence of Massive Catch-Up After International Adoption." *Journal of Developmental and Behavioral Pediatrics* 28(4), pp. 334–43.

Van Zanden, Jan, Joerg Baten, Marco d'Ercole, Auke Rijpma, Conal Smith, and Marcel Timmer, eds. 2014. *How Was Life?: Global Well-Being Since 1820.* OECD Publishing. URL https://www.oecd-ilibrary.org/how-was -life_5jz41pwdz5zn.pdf?itemId=%2Fcontent%2Fpublication%2F9789264214262-en&mimewType=pdf.

Vigdor, Jacob. 2015. "The Civic and Cultural Assimilation of Immigrants to the United States." In Powell, Benjamin, ed. *The Economics of Immigration: Market-Based Approaches, Social Science, and Public Policy.* Oxford: Oxford University Press, pp. 70–91.

Vinnerljung, Bo, Frank Linkblad, Anders Hyern, Finn Rasmussen, and Monica Dalen. 2010. "School Performance at Age 16 Among International Adoptees: A Swedish National Cohort Study." *International Social Work* 53(4), pp. 510–527.

Voltaire, Francois. 1980. *Letters on England.* London: Penguin Classics.

Wagner, Clifford. 1982. "Simpson's Paradox in Real Life." *American Statistician* 36(1), pp. 46–8.

Waters, Mary, and Marisa Pineau, eds. 2015. *The Integration of Immigrants Into American Society.* Washington, DC: National Academies Press.

Whalen, Carmen. 2005. "Colonialism, Citizenship, and the Making of the Puerto Rican Diaspora: An Introduction." In Whalen, Carmen, and Víctor Vázquez-Hernández, eds. *The Puerto Rican Diaspora: Historical Perspectives.* Philadelphia, PA: Temple University Press, pp. 1–42.

"What We Would Like to See." 1888. URL http://cdn.calisphere.org/data/13030/29/hb4t1nb029/files/hb4t1nb029FID4.jpg.

Wicherts, Jelte, Conor Dolan, and Han van der Maas. 2010. "A Systematic Literature Review of the Average IQ of Sub-Saharan Africans." *Intelligence* 38(1), pp. 1–20.

Wikipedia. 2018a. "Demographics of Puerto Rico." URL https://en.wikipedia.org/wiki/Demographics_of_Puerto_Rico.

Wikipedia. 2018b. "Economy of Puerto Rico." URL https://en.wikipedia.org/wiki/Economy_of_Puerto_Rico.

Wikipedia. 2018c. "List of Languages by Number of Native Speakers." URL https://en.wikipedia.org/wiki/List_of_languages_by_number_of_native_speakers.

Wikipedia 2018d. "List of Languages by Total Number of Speakers." URL https://en.wikipedia.org/wiki/List_of_languages_by_total_number_of_speakers.

Wikipedia 2018d. "List of Ethnic Groups in the United States by Household Income." URL https://en.wikipedia.org/wiki/List_of_ethnic_groups_in_the_United_States_by_household_income.

Wikipedia 2018f. "Islam by Country." URL https://en.wikipedia.org/wiki/Islam_by_country.

Woetzel, Jonathan, Lenny Mendonca, Janamitra Devan, Stefano Negri, Yangmei Hu, Luke Jordan, Xiujun Li, Alexander Maasry, Geoff Tsen, Flora Yu. 2009. *Preparing for China's Urban Billion.* McKinsey Global Institute, March. URL https://www.mckinsey.com/~/media/McKinsey/Featured%20Insights/Urbanization/Preparing%20for%20urban%20billion%20in%20China/MGI_Preparing_for_Chinas_Urban_Billion_full_report. ashx.

World Bank Group. 2016. *Poverty and Shared Prosperity 2016: Taking on Inequality.* Washington, DC: The World Bank. URL https://openknowledge.worldbank.org/bitstream/handle/10986/25078/9781464809583.pdf.

World Bank. 2018a. "China." *The World Bank.* URL https://data. worldbank.org/country/china?view=chart.

World Bank. 2018b. "GDP Deflator: United States." *The World Bank.* URL https://data.worldbank.org/indicator/NY . GDP. DEFL. ZS?locations=US.

World Bank. 2018c. "India." *The World Bank.* URL https://data.worldbank.org/country/india?view=chart.

World Bank. 2018d. "GDP per capita, PPP (current international $)." URL http: //api.worldbank.org/v2/en/indicator/NY . GDP. PCAP. PP. CD?downloadformat=excel.

World Bank. 2018e. "GDP per capita (current US$)." URL http://api.worldbank.org/v2/en/indicator/NY. GDP.PCAP . CD?downloadformat=excel.

ACKNOWLEDGMENTS

I am blessed with stellar colleagues—brilliant, cheerful, demanding, and candid. Tyler Cowen, Robin Hanson, Alex Tabarrok, and Garett Jones have enriched all my books—and *Open Borders* is no exception. Never before, however, has one of my books been blessed with a stellar coauthor. Working with Zach Weinersmith has been a daydream come true. Who would believe that a mere fanboy would get to team up with one of the world's greatest—and most thoughtful—graphic artists? Zach's ability to bring my imagination to life is nothing short of a superpower—and his soul is pure can-do sunshine. Working together has been one of my life's greatest highlights. Eternal gratitude, buddy.

I'd also like to thank the many helpful immigration researchers and activists I know, especially Michael Clemens, Shikha Dalmia, Tim Kane, Vipul Naik, Alex Nowrasteh, Lant Pritchett, Fabio Rojas, and everyone at openborders.info; GMU colleagues Nathaniel Bechhofer, Pete Boettke, Don Boudreaux, Dan Houser, Dan Klein, Steve Pearlstein, and Keller Scholl; EconLog co-bloggers David Henderson and Scott Sumner; Steven Blatt, for introducing me to graphic novels when we were students at UC Berkeley; comics guru Brian Doherty for urging me to broaden my reading; and my wife, Corina Caplan, and her parents, Corneliu and Maria Mateescu, for making me part of their family's immigration story. Our voraciously curious sons, Aidan and Tristan, have guided me every page of the way, and their younger siblings, Simon and Vali, have been hilarious sounding boards. Editors Calista Brill and Rachel Stark polished both words and pictures with great energy, Anthony Good provided above-and-beyond research assistance, and colorist Mary Cagle opened my eyes to a whole new world of hue. The Institute for Humane Studies and the Center for Study of Public Choice both provided generous financial support. Last, though we've never even talked, I owe a great intellectual debt to graphic novelists Scott McCloud and Larry Gonick. I have no idea what they think about immigration, but McCloud and Gonick showed me what graphic novels can do that mere words cannot.

—Bryan Caplan

Thank you to my wife, Kelly, who allowed me to take on this project when neither of us knew where we'd find the time, and who did well more than her fair share of housework during the sprint toward the final inks. Thanks to Bryan for roping me into this. It's rare enough in life you get to meet a favorite author, rarer that you get to work with him, and rarer still that he's as kind and intelligent as you imagined. His clear optimism even on such an uphill fight always helped me to relax as I worked. I wish to thank our editors, Calista and Rachel. Their guidance would've been welcome on any project, but with this book's sensitive topic, their suggestions were particularly valuable. I want to thank Mary Cagle, whose skill as a colorist made me look a whole lot better than I deserve to. Thanks to Lloyd James for doing some computer wizardry to make the maps look nice. I wish to thank my manager Mark Saffian for his usual guidance, and my literary agent Seth Fishman for getting us to the perfect place for this project. And I wish to thank my longtime assistant, Michael Johnson, for helping me with everything on this project from the pitch packet all the way to the website launch.

—Zach Weinersmith

First Second

Published by First Second
First Second is an imprint of Roaring Brook Press,
a division of Holtzbrinck Publishing Holdings Limited Partnership
120 Broadway, New York, NY 10271

Don't miss your next favorite book from First Second! For the latest updates go to
firstsecondnewsletter.com and sign up for our enewsletter.

Library of Congress Control Number: 2018953661
ISBN: 978-1-250-31696-7

Our books may be purchased in bulk for promotional, educational, or business use. Please contact your local
bookseller or the Macmillan Corporate and Premium Sales Department at (800) 221-7945 ext. 5442
or by email at MacmillanSpecialMarkets@macmillan.com.

FIRST EDITION

First edition, 2019
Edited by Calista Brill and Rachel Stark
Book design by Andrew Arnold and Rob Steen
Colors by Mary Cagle
Color assistance by Lindsey Little, Edriel Fimbres, and Polyna Kim
Printed in Canada

Created entirely on a Wacom Cintiq, using ClipStudio.

Paperback: 10 9 8 7 6 5 4 3 2 1
Hardcover: 10 9 8 7 6 5 4 3 2 1

BY ART WE LIVE